Dictionary of Literary Biography • Volume Forty-six

American Literary Publishing Houses, 1900-1980: Trade and Paperback

Dictionary of Literary Biography

1: *The American Renaissance in New England*, edited by Joel Myerson (1978)

2: *American Novelists Since World War II*, edited by Jeffrey Helterman and Richard Layman (1978)

3: *Antebellum Writers in New York and the South*, edited by Joel Myerson (1979)

4: *American Writers in Paris, 1920-1939*, edited by Karen Lane Rood (1980)

5: *American Poets Since World War II*, 2 parts, edited by Donald J. Greiner (1980)

6: *American Novelists Since World War II*, Second Series, edited by James E. Kibler, Jr. (1980)

7: *Twentieth-Century American Dramatists*, 2 parts, edited by John Mac-Nicholas (1981)

8: *Twentieth-Century American Science-Fiction Writers*, 2 parts, edited by David Cowart and Thomas L. Wymer (1981)

9: *American Novelists, 1910-1945*, 3 parts, edited by James J. Martine (1981)

10: *Modern British Dramatists, 1900-1945*, 2 parts, edited by Stanley Weintraub (1982)

11: *American Humorists, 1800-1950*, 2 parts, edited by Stanley Trachtenberg (1982)

12: *American Realists and Naturalists*, edited by Donald Pizer and Earl N. Harbert (1982)

13: *British Dramatists Since World War II*, 2 parts, edited by Stanley Weintraub (1982)

14: *British Novelists Since 1960*, 2 parts, edited by Jay L. Halio (1983)

15: *British Novelists, 1930-1959*, 2 parts, edited by Bernard Oldsey (1983)

16: *The Beats: Literary Bohemians in Postwar America*, 2 parts, edited by Ann Charters (1983)

17: *Twentieth-Century American Historians*, edited by Clyde N. Wilson (1983)

18: *Victorian Novelists After 1885*, edited by Ira B. Nadel and William E. Fredeman (1983)

19: *British Poets, 1880-1914*, edited by Donald E. Stanford (1983)

20: *British Poets, 1914-1945*, edited by Donald E. Stanford (1983)

21: *Victorian Novelists Before 1885*, edited by Ira B. Nadel and William E. Fredeman (1983)

22: *American Writers for Children, 1900-1960*, edited by John Cech (1983)

23: *American Newspaper Journalists, 1873-1900*, edited by Perry J. Ashley (1983)

24: *American Colonial Writers, 1606-1734*, edited by Emory Elliott (1984)

25: *American Newspaper Journalists, 1901-1925*, edited by Perry J. Ashley (1984)

26: *American Screenwriters*, edited by Robert E. Morsberger, Stephen O. Lesser, and Randall Clark (1984)

27: *Poets of Great Britain and Ireland, 1945-1960*, edited by Vincent B. Sherry, Jr. (1984)

28: *Twentieth-Century American-Jewish Fiction Writers*, edited by Daniel Walden (1984)

29: *American Newspaper Journalists, 1926-1950*, edited by Perry J. Ashley (1984)

30: *American Historians, 1607-1865*, edited by Clyde N. Wilson (1984)

31: *American Colonial Writers, 1735-1781*, edited by Emory Elliott (1984)

32: *Victorian Poets Before 1850*, edited by William E. Fredeman and Ira B. Nadel (1984)

33: *Afro-American Fiction Writers After 1955*, edited by Thadious M. Davis and Trudier Harris (1984)

34: *British Novelists, 1890-1929: Traditionalists*, edited by Thomas F. Staley (1985)

35: *Victorian Poets After 1850*, edited by William E. Fredeman and Ira B. Nadel (1985)

36: *British Novelists, 1890-1929: Modernists*, edited by Thomas F. Staley (1985)

37: *American Writers of the Early Republic*, edited by Emory Elliott (1985)

38: *Afro-American Writers After 1955: Dramatists and Prose Writers*, edited by Thadious M. Davis and Trudier Harris (1985)

39: *British Novelists, 1660-1800*, 2 parts, edited by Martin C. Battestin (1985)

40: *Poets of Great Britain and Ireland Since 1960*, 2 parts, edited by Vincent B. Sherry, Jr. (1985)

41: *Afro-American Poets Since 1955*, 2 parts, edited by Trudier Harris and Thadious M. Davis (1985)

42: *American Writers for Children Before 1900*, edited by Glenn E. Estes (1985)

43: *American Newspaper Journalists, 1690-1872*, edited by Perry J. Ashley (1986)

44: *American Screenwriters*, Second Series, edited by Randall Clark (1986)

45: *American Poets, 1880-1945*, First Series, edited by Peter Quartermain (1986)

46: *American Literary Publishing Houses, 1900-1980: Trade and Paperback*, edited by Peter Dzwonkoski (1986)

Documentary Series

1: *Sherwood Anderson, Willa Cather, John Dos Passos, Theodore Dreiser, F. Scott Fitzgerald, Ernest Hemingway, Sinclair Lewis*, edited by Margaret A. Van Antwerp (1982)

2: *James Gould Cozzens, James T. Farrell, William Faulkner, John O'Hara, John Steinbeck, Thomas Wolfe, Richard Wright*, edited by Margaret A. Van Antwerp (1982)

3: *Saul Bellow, Jack Kerouac, Norman Mailer, Vladimir Nabokov, John Updike, Kurt Vonnegut*, edited by Mary Bruccoli (1983)

4: *Tennessee Williams*, edited by Margaret A. Van Antwerp and Sally Johns (1984)

Yearbooks

1980, edited by Karen L. Rood, Jean W. Ross, and Richard Ziegfeld (1981)

1981, edited by Karen L. Rood, Jean W. Ross, and Richard Ziegfeld (1982)

1982, edited by Richard Ziegfeld; associate editors: Jean W. Ross and Lynne C. Zeigler (1983)

1983, edited by Mary Bruccoli and Jean W. Ross; associate editor: Richard Ziegfeld (1984)

1984, edited by Jean W. Ross (1985)

Dictionary of Literary Biography • Volume Forty-six

American Literary Publishing Houses, 1900-1980: Trade and Paperback

Edited by
Peter Dzwonkoski
University of Rochester

A Bruccoli Clark Book
Gale Research Company • Book Tower • Detroit, Michigan 48226

Manufactured by Edwards Brothers, Inc.
Ann Arbor, Michigan
Printed in the United States of America

Library of Congress Cataloging-in-Publication Data
Main entry under title:

American literary publishing houses, 1900- 1980.
    Trade and paperback.

    (Dictionary of literary biography; v. 46)
    "A Bruccoli Clark book."
    Includes index.
    1. Literature—Publishing—United States—
History—20th century—Dictionaries. 2. Pub-
lishers and publishing—United States—His-
tory—20th century—Dictionaries. 3. Paperbacks
—Publishing—United States—History—20th
century—Dictionaries. I. Dzwonkoski, Peter.
II. Series.
Z479.A45   1986   070.5'0973   86-2210
ISBN 0-8103-1724-9

Project Associates

Associate Editors: David Dzwonkoski

Martha A. Bartter
University of Rochester

Elizabeth Hoffman
University of Rochester

Graphics Editor: Mary M. Huth
University of Rochester

Research Assistants: Ruth Bennett
Theodora Mills

For my mother and father

Contents

Plan of the Series...xv

Foreword...xvii

Acknowledgments..xix

Abelard-Schuman 3
Theodora Mills

Academy Chicago Publishers............................5
Christopher T. Lee

Ace Books 5
David Dzwonkoski

Algonquin Books of Chapel Hill.....................8
Christopher Surr

Appleton-Century-Crofts...................................8
David Dzwonkoski

Apple-wood Books...12
Christopher T. Lee

Arbor House Publishing Company 13
Ada Fan

Arcadia House 15
Peter Dzwonkoski

Armed Services Editions...................................16
Carol Ann Wilkinson

Arno Press...18
Alma Burner Creek

Atheneum Publishers..18
Elizabeth A. Dzwonkoski

The Atlantic Monthly Press..............................22
Bill Oliver

Authors and Newspapers Association 23
Theodora Mills

Avalon Books 24
Martha A. Bartter

Avon Books 26
Martha A. Bartter

Ballantine Books 29
Martha A. Bartter

Robert O. Ballou 33
Ada Fan

Bantam Books...35
David Dzwonkoski and Philip Dematteis

Barnes and Noble Books 40
Carol Ann Wilkinson

Richard W. Baron Publishing Company............42
Peter Dzwonkoski

Barse and Hopkins 42
Sharon Ann Jaeger

Basic Books 44
David Dzwonkoski

Belmont Productions 46
Martha A. Bartter

The Berkley Publishing Corporation 47
David Dzwonkoski

Walter J. Black...49
Shirley Ricker

The Bobbs-Merrill Company..............................49
Timothy D. Murray

Albert and Charles Boni......................................54
Carmen R. Russell and David Dzwonkoski

Boni and Liveright...57
Carmen R. Russell

The Book League of America.............................63
Deborah G. Gorman

Branden Press..64
Timothy D. Murray

George Braziller...64
Timothy D. Murray

Brewer, Warren and Putnam 68
Carole B. Michaels-Katz and
Elizabeth Hoffman

B. J. Brimmer Company 71
David Dzwonkoski

Broadway Publishing Company 71
Peter Dzwonkoski

Bruce Humphries 73
David Dzwonkoski

Jonathan Cape and Harrison Smith 75
    Timothy D. Murray

Carroll and Graf Publishers 77
    Botham Stone

The Caxton Printers, Limited 78
    Timothy D. Murray

Chelsea House 82
    Timothy D. Murray

Chilton Book Company 83
    Gregory P. Ames

City Lights Books..84
    Kathleen R. Davis

C. M. Clark Publishing Company 86
    David Dzwonkoski

Edward J. Clode 88
    Carole B. Michaels-Katz

Cosmopolitan Book Corporation 91
    Timothy D. Murray and Theodora Mills

Covici-Friede..92
    Alan J. Filreis

Coward, McCann and Geoghegan 96
    Laura Masotti Humphrey

Creative Age Press..99
    Donna Nance

Crown Publishers..101
    Elizabeth Scott Pryor

Cupples and Leon..102
    Joan Gillen Conners

DAW Books 104
    Martha A. Bartter and Linda Quinlan

The John Day Company 104
    Elizabeth Scott Pryor

Dell Publishing Company 108
    Elizabeth Hoffman

The Derrydale Press....................................112
    Deborah G. Gorman

The Devin-Adair Company............................112
    Vincent Prestianni

The Dial Press..115
    Ernest Bevan, Jr.

B. W. Dodge and Company 119
    David Dzwonkoski

George H. Doran Company 119
    Sharon Ann Jaeger

Dover Publications 125
    Christine Garrison

Dramatists Play Service................................125
    Phyllis Andrews

Duell, Sloan and Pearce................................127
    Harry F. Thompson

Duffield and Green 131
    Laura Masotti Humphrey

Ecco Press..133
    Sharon Ann Jaeger

M. Evans and Company 133
    David Dzwonkoski

Fantasy Press Publishers 134
    Martha A. Bartter

Farrar and Rinehart 135
    Deborah G. Gorman

Farrar, Straus and Giroux..............................138
    Jon Griffin

Fawcett Books 143
    Martha A. Bartter

Federal Writers' Project................................147
    Jerre Mangione

Frederick Fell Publishers 152
    Anne Frascarelli

Follett Publishing Company 153
    Margaret Becket

Four Seas Company......................................154
    Lynne P. Shackelford

Four Winds Press..155
    Timothy D. Murray

Franklin Library 155
    Peter Dzwonkoski

Galaxy Science Fiction Novels 156
    Martha A. Bartter

Gambit..156
    Shirley Ricker

Bernard Geis Associates 158
    Kathleen R. Davis

David R. Godine, Publisher............................160
    Vincent Prestianni

Goldsmith Publishing Company......................162
    Peter Dzwonkoski

Laurence James Gomme 163
    Deborah G. Gorman

Greenberg: Publisher.......................164
    Joseph Heininger

Green Tiger Press............................164
    Timothy D. Murray

Greenwillow Books 166
    Theodora Mills

Gregg Press....................................167
    Martha A. Bartter

Grossman Publishers.......................167
    Richard Horvath

Grove Press 170
    David Dzwonkoski

Haldeman-Julius Company 176
    Judith Bushnell

Hallmark Editions...........................178
    Anuradha Mookerjee

Harcourt Brace Jovanovich 180
    Elizabeth A. Dzwonkoski

Heritage Press................................183
    Christy Brown

Lawrence Hill and Company Publishers..........184
    Botham Stone

Hill and Wang 186
    Arthur W. Wang

Holiday House 187
    Theodora Mills

Holloway House Publishing Company.............189
    Linda Quinlan

Holt, Rinehart and Winston 190
    David Dzwonkoski

John H. Hopkins and Son..................191
    Peter Dzwonkoski and Ruth Bennett

Horizon Press.................................193
    David Dzwonkoski

Howell, Soskin and Company 193
    Vincent L. Tollers

B. W. Huebsch................................194
    Daniel Borus

International Publishers Company...................196
    Judith Bushnell

Claude Kendall 199
    Mary M. Huth

Mitchell Kennerley...........................200
    Harry F. Thompson

Alfred A. Knopf 202
    Herbert H. Johnson and Margaret Becket

Lancer Books 209
    Martha A. Bartter

Limited Editions Club.......................210
    Margaret W. Fleming

Lion Books 211
    Martha A. Bartter

Loring and Mussey 213
    Peter Dzwonkoski

John W. Luce and Company...............214
    Theodora Mills

Macaulay Company..........................214
    Alison Tanner Stauffer

Macrae Smith Company 216
    Arlene Shaner

Macy-Masius...................................218
    David Dzwonkoski

Major Books...................................220
    Martha A. Bartter

Manor Books..................................220
    Martha A. Bartter

Richard Marek Books.......................222
    Theodora Mills

Robert M. McBride and Company...................224
    Chris M. Anson

McClure, Phillips and Company 227
    Nandita Batra and David Dzwonkoski

McDowell, Obolensky 229
    Vincent Prestianni

McGraw-Hill....................................231
    Carole B. Michaels-Katz and
    Martha A. Bartter

Julian Messner 235
    Susan K. Ahern

Minton, Balch and Company 237
  Edward J. Hall

Modern Age Books..239
  Jane I. Thesing

The Modern Library 242
  Timothy D. Murray

Moffat, Yard and Company 245
  Nancy Hill Evans

William Morrow and Company......................247
  Christopher Camuto

The New American Library 250
  Philip A. Metzger

New Directions Publishing Corporation 255
  D. W. Faulkner, John Harrison,
  and David Dzwonkoski

Noonday Press 261
  Carol Kuniholm

North Point Press..261
  Margaret Becket

W. W. Norton and Company 264
  Timothy D. Murray

Outing Publishing Company 267
  Gary R. Treadway

The Overlook Press 269
  Xinmin Liu

Padell Publishing Company............................270
  Timothy D. Murray

Pantheon Books 270
  Carol Kuniholm

Paperback Library.......................................272
  Martha A. Bartter

Parents' Magazine Press...............................273
  Deborah G. Gorman

Peter Pauper Press......................................275
  Ronelle K. H. Thompson

Payson and Clarke 277
  Joan Gillen Conners and Anne Ludlow

Peachtree Publishers, Limited 278
  Christopher T. Lee

Pellegrini and Cudahy 280
  Kathleen R. Davis

Penguin Books 281
  Gregory P. Ames

Permabooks..284
  Ronelle K. H. Thompson

Philosophical Library 286
  Edward J. Hall

Pinnacle Books...288
  Martha A. Bartter

Platt and Munk Company 289
  Kathleen McGowan

Playboy Press..291
  Edward J. Hall

Pocket Books..293
  Timothy D. Murray

Popular Library 297
  Martha A. Bartter

Praeger Publishers 298
  Jutta Willman

Prentice-Hall 299
  Stephen Elwell

Pyramid Books 300
  David Dzwonkoski

Harlin Quist Books......................................303
  Karin S. Mabe

Random House 305
  Margaret Becket

Reader's Digest Condensed Books 312
  Nandita Batra

Henry Regnery Company 313
  Stephen Elwell

Reilly and Lee Publishing Company 315
  Annie E. Stevens

Reynal and Hitchcock..................................318
  Philip A. Metzger

Rinehart and Company 321
  Annie E. Stevens

The Saalfield Publishing Company.................324
  Dean H. Keller

St. Martin's Press 326
  Stephen Elwell

Saturday Review Press.................................328
  Carole B. Michaels-Katz

Schocken Books 328
  Deborah G. Gorman

William R. Scott 329
  Theodora Mills

Sears Publishing Company 331
  David W. Raymond

Thomas Seltzer 333
  Neal L. Edgar

Sharon Publications 335
  Botham Stone

Frank Shay 337
  Neal L. Edgar

Sheed and Ward 337
  Annie E. Stevens

Simon and Schuster 340
  Jane I. Thesing

Upton Sinclair 346
  Earl G. Ingersoll

William Sloane Associates 347
  Annie E. Stevens

Harrison Smith and Robert Haas 349
  Arlene Shaner

Stein and Day Publishers 351
  Kathleen R. Davis

Stewart and Kidd Company 352
  David Dzwonkoski

Lyle Stuart 354
  Donna Nance

Swallow Press 354
  Phyllis Andrews

Ticknor and Fields 357
  Theodora Mills

Time-Life Books 357
  Neal L. Edgar

Times Books 358
  Christopher Surr

Tor Books 358
  Christopher Surr

Tower Publications 361
  Martha A. Bartter

Universal Publishing and Distributing
  Corporation 363
  Martha A. Bartter

Vanguard Press 364
  Timothy D. Murray

The Viking Press 365
  Elizabeth A. Dzwonkoski

P. F. Volland Company 371
  Elizabeth A. Dzwonkoski

Henry Z. Walck 372
  Peter Dzwonkoski

Walker and Company 372
  Stephen Elwell

Warner Books 374
  David Dzwonkoski

W. J. Watt and Company 375
  Theodora Mills

Franklin Watts 378
  Carol Kuniholm

A. Wessels and Company 379
  Theodora Mills

Western Publishing Company 379
  Karin S. Mabe

Whitman Publishing Company............383
  Gregory P. Ames

Albert Whitman and Company 383
  Gregory P. Ames

Whittlesey House 384
  Margaret Becket

World Publishing Company 386
  Kathleen McGowan

Thomas Yoseloff.............................390
  Stephen Elwell

Zebra Books 392
  Christopher Surr

Appendix

Trends in Twentieth-Century
  Mass Market Publishing..................397
  Kenneth C. Davis

Main Trends in Twentieth-
  Century Book Clubs 407
  John Tebbel

Books for Further Reading 417

Contributors 419

Cumulative Index 423

Plan of the Series

. . . Almost the most prodigious asset of a country, and perhaps its most precious possession, is its native literary product—when that product is fine and noble and enduring.

Mark Twain*

The advisory board, the editors, and the publisher of the *Dictionary of Literary Biography* are joined in endorsing Mark Twain's declaration. The literature of a nation provides an inexhaustible resource of permanent worth. It is our expectation that this endeavor will make literature and its creators better understood and more accessible to students and the literate public, while satisfying the standards of teachers and scholars.

To meet these requirements, *literary biography* has been construed in terms of the author's achievement. The most important thing about a writer is his writing. Accordingly, the entries in *DLB* are career biographies, tracing the development of the author's canon and the evolution of his reputation.

The publication plan for *DLB* resulted from two years of preparation. The project was proposed to Bruccoli Clark by Frederick G. Ruffner, president of the Gale Research Company, in November 1975. After specimen entries were prepared and typeset, an advisory board was formed to refine the entry format and develop the series rationale. In meetings held during 1976, the publisher, series editors, and advisory board approved the scheme for a comprehensive biographical dictionary of persons who contributed to North American literature. Editorial work on the first volume began in January 1977, and it was published in 1978.

In order to make *DLB* more than a reference tool and to compile volumes that individually have claim to status as literary history, it was decided to organize volumes by topic or period or genre. Each of these freestanding volumes provides a biographical-bibliographical guide and overview for a particular area of literature. We are convinced that this organization—as opposed to a single alphabet method—constitutes a valuable innovation in the

presentation of reference material. The volume plan necessarily requires many decisions for the placement and treatment of authors who might properly be included in two or three volumes. In some instances a major figure will be included in separate volumes, but with different entries emphasizing the aspect of his career appropriate to each volume. Ernest Hemingway, for example, is represented in *American Writers in Paris, 1920-1939* by an entry focusing on his expatriate apprenticeship; he is also in *American Novelists, 1910-1945* with an entry surveying his entire career. Each volume includes a cumulative index of subject authors. The final *DLB* volume will be a comprehensive index to the entire series.

With volume ten in 1982 it was decided to enlarge the scope of *DLB* beyond the literature of the United States. By the end of 1985 twenty-one volumes treating British literature had been published, and volumes for Commonwealth and Modern European literature were in progress. The series has been further augmented by the *DLB Yearbooks* (since 1981) which update published entries and add new entries to keep the *DLB* current with contemporary activity. There have also been occasional *DLB Documentary Series* volumes which provide biographical and critical background source materials for figures whose work is judged to have particular interest for students. One of these companion volumes is entirely devoted to Tennessee Williams.

The purpose of *DLB* is not only to provide reliable information in a convenient format but also to place the figures in the larger perspective of literary history and to offer appraisals of their accomplishments by qualified scholars.

We define literature as the *intellectual commerce of a nation:* not merely as belles lettres, but as that ample and complex process by which ideas are generated, shaped, and transmitted. *DLB* entries are not limited to "creative writers" but extend to other figures who in this time and in this way influenced the mind of a people. Thus the series encompasses historians, journalists, publishers, and screenwriters. By this means readers of *DLB* may be aided to perceive literature not as cult scripture in the keeping of cultural high priests, but as at the center of a nation's life.

*From an unpublished section of Mark Twain's autobiography, copyright © by the Mark Twain Company.

DLB includes the major writers appropriate to each volume and those standing in the ranks immediately behind them. Scholarly and critical counsel has been sought in deciding which minor figures to include and how full their entries should be. Wherever possible, useful references will be made to figures who do not warrant separate entries.

Each *DLB* volume has a volume editor responsible for planning the volume, selecting the figures for inclusion, and assigning the entries. Volume editors are also responsible for preparing, where appropriate, appendices surveying the major periodicals and literary and intellectual movements for their volumes, as well as lists of further readings. Work on the series as a whole is coordinated at the Bruccoli Clark editorial center in Columbia, South Carolina, where the editorial staff is responsible for the accuracy of the published volumes.

One feature that distinguishes *DLB* is the illustration policy—its concern with the iconography of literature. Just as an author is influenced by his surroundings, so is the reader's understanding of the author enhanced by a knowledge of his environment. Therefore *DLB* volumes include not only drawings, paintings, and photographs of authors, often depicting them at various stages in their careers, but also illustrations of their families and places where they lived. Title pages are regularly reproduced in facsimile along with dust jackets for modern authors. The dust jackets are a special feature of *DLB* because they often document better than anything else the way in which an author's work was launched in its own time. Specimens of the writers' manuscripts are included when feasible.

A supplement to *DLB*—tentatively titled *A Guide, Chronology, and Glossary for American Literature*—will outline the history of literature in North America and trace the influences that shaped it. This volume will provide a framework for the study of American literature by means of chronological tables, literary affiliation charts, glossarial entries, and concise surveys of the major movements. It has been planned to stand on its own as a vade mecum, providing a ready-reference guide to the study of American literature as well as a companion to the *DLB* volumes for American literature.

Samuel Johnson rightly decreed that "The chief glory of every people arises from its authors." The purpose of the *Dictionary of Literary Biography* is to compile literary history in the surest way available to us—by accurate and comprehensive treatment of the lives and work of those who contributed to it.

The *DLB* Advisory Board

Foreword

The three volumes of the *Dictionary of Literary Biography* on American book publishers contain entries on the history and character of American publishers of literature in book format. American publishers from the earliest times to the present are included. This, the first volume, includes entries on trade, mass market, and children's book publishers founded since 1900. The second volume will be devoted to twentieth-century small presses, university presses, and publishers of literary reference works, while the third volume will concentrate on firms founded prior to 1900.

Literary has been defined here in terms of form rather than quality. Publishers of novels, collections of short stories, poetry, drama, literary essays, and sketches—all of the forms in which literature occurs—have been included, even when the output of the firm merits no particular attention as "literature." Thus, entries on publishers of dime novels as well as classics of narrative art, of doggerel as well as serious verse, of melodrama as well as high drama will be found in these volumes. Fullest attention has been paid, however, to firms that have made a significant impact upon American literary book publishing. Because their literary output may have been limited, certain important firms (for example, Derrydale Press) have received less attention than they might in a more general guide to American book publishing. Some important publishers (for example, Schirmer and Scott, Foresman) have been omitted because their literary production has been scant or nonexistent. Religious publishers have been included only if a substantial proportion of their output included novels, poetry, or other literature. The more important publishers of children's literature have been included. Vanity or subsidy presses have been excluded.

Even within these guidelines, it has been impossible to include entries on all American trade, mass market, and children's book publishers in this volume. The selection of which publishers to include has inevitably involved difficult decisions. Obviously, major firms, such as Simon and Schuster, Random House, Harcourt Brace Jovanovich, Alfred A. Knopf, Pocket Books, and Ballantine Books, had to be included. Smaller, but significant, literary firms such as Mitchell Kennerley and B. W.

Huebsch were also easy choices. Beyond these, the judgment of the editors came more into play in deciding which firms made significant enough contributions to American literary publishing to warrant inclusion and which did not.

American literary book publishing is a complex of interrelationships: individuals move from one firm to another or start new firms, sometimes in partnership with individuals from other publishing houses; and firms merge, separate, and rechristen themselves. Generally, publishing houses are listed in this volume according to the company name that appears on the title pages of the books they have published. Firms that have undergone name changes have been listed according to the names by which they are best known, with the other names appearing below the main heading. Some imprints which have only existed as subsidiaries of other firms—such as McGraw-Hill's Whittlesey House and William Morrow's Greenwillow Books and The Modern Library, which was started by Boni and Liveright and sold to Random House—are so well known that they have been accorded separate entries. If a major firm was the result of a merger or a split-up of other important companies, a separate entry may be included on each of the component firms, possibly in different volumes. For example, the Holt, Rinehart and Winston and Rinehart and Company entries are in this volume; the Henry Holt and Company entry will be in the third volume.

Most entries supply such basic information as the dates of founding and closing of the firm, the name of founder or founders, the general nature of its literary publications, representative titles and authors, and significant changes in leadership and location, but even this basic information may not be available for every small or medium-sized firm.

References, when available, are listed at the conclusions of the entries. Standard sources for the study of publishing history are listed in the selected bibliography at the end of the volume.

The present volume deals with three categories of firms. Trade publishers are those which publish books for the "book trade"—that is, to be sold in bookstores. Such books include both hardcover volumes and higher priced ("quality") paperbacks. Mass market publishers produce inexpensive paperbacks to be sold in nontraditional outlets, such as newsstands, supermarkets, bus and train stations, and airports, as well as in bookstores. Starting with Pocket Books in 1939, the twentieth century has witnessed the phenomenon known as the Paperback Revolution. Paperbacks have made more books—from quality literature to salacious trash—available to more readers than ever before. The third kind of publishing firm dealt with in this volume overlaps with the other two: these are the publishers who specialize in children's literature.

It is probably a rare reader—other than a bibliophile, a bibliographer, or a reviewer—who ever notices who published the book he has just bought; probably few readers decide to read a book *because* it was published by a certain firm. Nevertheless, it is the judgment and taste of the editors at those publishing firms that decide which works will be made available to the public at all. It is the purpose of these volumes to shed some light on an industry which performs a vital function in society and yet is surprisingly unknown to the general public.

The judgments involved in deciding whether to publish a particular book are not just aesthetic; they are also commercial, since publishing is, after all, a business. A publishing house must make a profit—or, at least, not suffer too many losses—in order to survive. This is particularly true of the kinds of firms treated in this volume, who are at the mercy of the marketplace. Small presses, which are frequently run almost as a hobby, and university presses, which receive subsidies, are included in the second volume.

In the twentieth century, publishing has become *big* business. The small, personal trade houses that abounded in the United States in the early decades of the century have largely been replaced by or merged into giant publishing firms, which have themselves almost all been absorbed by still larger corporations and conglomerates from outside of the publishing industry. The personal, idiosyncratic, intuitive, somewhat disorganized character of publishing has largely been transformed into an efficient corporate enterprise, for better and for worse.

The volatile nature of the modern publishing industry almost guarantees that some of the information about some of the existing firms will be outdated by the time this volume appears in print. Mergers, acquisitions, divestitures, changes in key personnel, and even address changes are occurring constantly. We have made every effort to include such information.

—*Peter Dzwonkoski*

Acknowledgments

This book was produced by BC Research. Karen L. Rood is senior editor for the *Dictionary of Literary Biography* series. Philip B. Dematteis was the in-house editor.

Art supervisor is Patricia M. Flanagan. Copyediting supervisor is Patricia Coate. Production coordinator is Kimberly Casey. Typesetting supervisor is Laura Ingram. The production staff includes Rowena Betts, David R. Bowdler, Deborah Cavanaugh, Kathleen M. Flanagan, Joyce Fowler, Ellen Hassell, Pamela Haynes, Judith K. Ingle, Beatrice McClain, Judith E. McCray, Mary Scott Sims, Joycelyn R. Smith, and Lucia Tarbox. Jean W. Ross is permissions editor. Joseph Caldwell, photography editor, and James Adam Sutton did photographic copy work for the volume.

Walter W. Ross did the library research with the assistance of the staff at the Thomas Cooper Library of the University of South Carolina: Lynn Barron, Daniel Boice, Connie Crider, Kathy Eckman, Michael Freeman, Gary Geer, David L. Haggard, Jens Holley, Marcia Martin, Dana Rabon, Jean Rhyne, Jan Squire, Ellen Tillett, and Virginia Weathers.

Special acknowledgment is given to the editors of *Publishers Weekly* for their generous assistance in providing material for illustrations for this volume. Unless otherwise credited, all advertisements reproduced here were taken from the pages of that magazine; many photographs of individuals were also derived from that source.

The editor would also like to thank the project associates for the *DLB* volumes on American literary book publishing and the many others who have been involved in this work. One of the associate editors, David Dzwonkoski, should be singled out for special praise. He has written many entries, revised and sometimes rewritten others, edited hundreds, and coordinated many aspects of a complicated enterprise. A former member of the University of Rochester Library staff, Barbara Salvage, compiled the university press entries in the second volume and also helped with general editing. An indispensable mainstay of the research staff has been Theodora Mills. Formerly a reference librarian at the University of Rochester Library, Ms. Mills has written, rewritten, checked, fact-found, substantiated, and generally dug around in library caverns in aid of the project. A gifted researcher, she has helped and trained others in their work for these volumes. Another member of the research staff, Ruth Bennett, long an editor and researcher with the University of Rochester's Ralph Waldo Emerson project, brought solid experience, careful attention to detail, and a quick intelligence to the project.

Administrative Assistant Marguerite Barrett coordinated the day-to-day work of the project for five years. She typed, filed, kept track of contributors, and devised and maintained a flow chart for nearly 800 entries. She was indispensable in the maintenance of order and morale and in countless other ways.

This has been very much a Rochester project, more specifically a University of Rochester project, more specifically still a University of Rochester Library project. Two of the project editors and more than ten major contributors are full-time members of the University of Rochester Library staff. Faculty members in the Department of English as well as many graduate students in English have also contributed. Special recognition is due the late Professor Rowland L. Collins. Some entries are the work of helpful people in the Rochester community not connected with the university. Other contributors have come from many of the major Eastern universities, including the State Universities of New York at Albany, Binghamton, and Buffalo; the Universities of Pennsylvania, Pittsburgh, Virginia, North Carolina, South Carolina, and Florida; Duke University; Indiana University; Kent State University; Syracuse University; Cornell University; and Yale University.

Other individuals who have helped the project in various ways include Pauline Anderson, Tamara Knight-Anttonen, Thomas Berger, Albert Bergeron, John Bidwell, James Brunner, Dale Carrithers, Christie Chappelle, Peter Conn, Robert Creeley, Chris Drzyzga, Hoyt Duggan, Frances Dzwonkoski, William Ewert, Lois Frankforter, Donald Gallup, Philip Gerber, John Hench, Tom Hickman, Thomas Hill, Howard Horsford, Sidney Huttner, Desirée Johnson, William Joyce, Gail Junion, Dean Keller, Eugene Robert Kintgen, Jr., Anuradha Mookerjee, Jean Murphy, Linda Quinlan, Gail Reisman, Bernard Rosenthal, Justin G. Schiller, Rollo Silver, Alison Tanner Stauffer, Madeleine B. Stern, Paul Strohm, Ling Ling Sun,

John Tebbel, Paul F. Theiner, Robert A. Tibbetts, Robert Torry, and Anne Whelpley. Margaret Becket and Kathy McGowan of the University of Rochester Library reference staff were unfailingly ready to help, instruct, write, and advise.

In its final stages the project has relied heavily on the careful and steady work of several editorial assistants who performed the arduous and time-consuming task of checking for accuracy the thousands of bibliographical references included in the entries and of checking many other facts, as well. These volunteers are Dorothy Harper, Peggy Look, Anne Ludlow, Bob Rugg, Nancy Sleeth, and Lyndon Wells.

The editor owes special thanks to his supervisors at the University of Rochester Library. Past Director of University Libraries Alan Taylor permitted him to accept the general editorship in the knowledge that it would make demands upon his time and that of other library staff members. Mr. Taylor's successor, James Wyatt, has also supported the project, and, before she left Rochester for a new position, Assistant Director Margaret Perry did, too. Her successor, Janice Holladay, has been most patient and supportive. Grady Ballenger, Daniel H. Borus, Timothy Murray, Vincent Tollers, and Everett C. Wilkie, Jr., also merit special thanks.

Finally, no bibliographic project can hope to succeed without the support of an appropriate library or collection. The many bibliographical strengths and research facilities of the University of Rochester's Rush Rhees Library have made these volumes possible.

Dictionary of Literary Biography • Volume Forty-six

American Literary Publishing Houses, 1900-1980: Trade and Paperback

Dictionary of Literary Biography

Abelard-Schuman
(New York: 1953-)

Abelard-Schuman, Incorporated was formed in New York in 1953 by the merger of Abelard Press, founded in 1948 by Lew Schwartz, and Henry Schuman, Incorporated, founded in 1946. In 1960 the company—by then known as Abelard-Schuman, Limited—bought a controlling interest in Criterion Books, Incorporated, which had been founded in 1953; but both companies continued to use their own imprints. In 1969 both imprints became a division of the International Textbook Company, which later changed its name to Intext Educational Publishers. In 1974 Thomas Y. Crowell purchased the assets of Intext Publishers Group, of which Intext Educational Publishers was a subsidiary, and Abelard-Schuman and Criterion Books became parts of a division of Crowell; in 1977 Crowell was absorbed by Harper and Row. With each of these changes the smaller firm moved to the address of the larger, always within Manhattan.

Before their mergers, Abelard had published trade books and juveniles; Schuman had published nonfiction, with emphasis on medicine and the history of science; and Criterion had published fiction, reference books, social sciences, gardening, and juveniles. Abelard-Schuman publishes the Ram's Horn Books (Jewish interest), the Life of Science Library, and Raven Books (mysteries). The firm's relatively few literary titles have included *The Literature of Modern Israel* (1957) by Reuben Wallenrod; Marvin Magalaner's *Time of Apprenticeship: The Fiction of Young James Joyce* (1959); and Jerre Mangione's *Life Sentences for Everybody* (1965). It is only in the juvenile and nonfiction categories that Abelard-Schuman has published multiple titles by the same author, such as those by Isaac Asimov, Ashley Montagu, and Miriam Schlein. The number of titles offered each year peaked at well over 100 in the late 1950s and early 1960s, when books for children and teenagers became a larger portion of the firm's output.

Abelard-Schuman's address is the same as that of Harper and Row: 10 East Fifty-third Street, New York 10022.

—*Theodora Mills*

1954 advertisement

Academy Chicago Publishers

(Chicago: 1975-)

Academy Chicago Publishers was founded in 1975 by Jordan and Anita Miller. Anita Miller, the president of the company, has a Ph.D. in English literature from Northwestern University; she handles editorial duties. Jordan Miller, the vice-president, handles promotion. Neither had previous publishing experience, and they consciously set out to publish what they call "a personal list"—books they like, emphasizing neglected classics.

Academy's first book, published in 1976, was *A Guide to Non-sexist Children's Books* by Judith Adell and H. D. Klein; an introduction by actor Alan Alda attracted attention to the book, and its success encouraged the Millers to pursue a publishing program that reflected their predilection for English literature and books about art, history, and women's studies. They established the policy of reprinting the lesser works of nineteenth- and early twentieth-century Continental and British writers, such as George Sand and Arnold Bennett, and they cultivated a relationship with the British publishers Granada and Boydell and Brewer, importing British books for sale in America.

In 1980 Academy published its first mystery novels, five works by British writer Leo Bruce originally published in England between 1936 and 1952; all of them feature his bumbling yet emi-nently sensible detective, Sergeant Beef. Subsequently Academy began aggressively publishing mystery fiction, and by 1985 mysteries accounted for about one-third of its list. Academy's backlist includes six Inspector Ghote novels by H. R. F. Keating, two novels by Colin Wilson, and twelve novels by Bruce.

By 1985 Academy was publishing some fifty books a year, about half of them titles imported from Great Britain. Its backlist of 340 books was evenly divided between fiction and nonfiction. The nonfiction books are predominantly histories and biographies; the fiction backlist includes an impressive array of writers: Robert Graves, Angus Wilson, Fay Weldon, Elinor Wylie, E. M. Delafield, Philip K. Dick, John P. Marquand, and Samuel Pepys.

Academy Chicago Publishers is located at 425 North Michigan Avenue, Chicago 60611.

Reference:

Jane Stewart Spitzer, "The Millers of Academy Chicago," *Christian Science Monitor*, 4 January 1985, p. B7.

—*Christopher T. Lee*

Ace Books

(New York: 1952-)

Organized in 1952 as a division of the magazine publishing house A. A. Wyn, Incorporated, Ace Books began at 23 West Forty-seventh Street, New York, with A. A. Wyn as president and publisher and Donald A. Wollheim as editor. The firm's first publications were in the innovative format of two titles in one paperback volume: Samuel W. Taylor's *The Grinning Gismo* with Keith Vining's *Too Hot for Hell* (mysteries), and J. Edward Leit-head's *Bloody Hoofs* with William Colt MacDonald's *Bad Man's Return* (westerns). By the end of 1953 Ace was publishing eight titles a month in this format; among them were A. E. Van Vogt's *The Universe Maker* with his *The World of Null-A*—the firm's first science fiction titles—and Robert E. Howard's *Conan the Conqueror* with Leigh Brackett's *The Sword of Rhiannon*.

In 1954 Ace began publishing single-title pa-

ACE BOOKS   ACE CHARTER   ACE SCIENCE FICTION   ACE TEMPO BOOKS

perbacks. Within two years science fiction and fantasy in both single and double volumes comprised about half of Ace's ninety-nine titles. These included Isaac Asimov's *The Man Who Upset the Universe* (1955) as a single; Philip K. Dick's first novel, *Solar Lottery*, published jointly with Brackett's *The Big Jump* (1955); and Andre Norton's *Daybreak: 2250 A.D.*, published with *Beyond Earth's Gates* (1954) by C. L. Moore and Lewis Padgett (Henry Kuttner). Other double-volume titles were by Poul Anderson, Gordon R. Dickson, Clifford D. Simak, L. Sprague de Camp, and L. Ron Hubbard. General fiction constituted roughly three-quarters of Ace's titles, with nonfiction, cartoon, and joke books comprising the remaining one-fourth. Among the more significant literary titles was the first edition of William S. Burroughs's first novel, *Junkie,* in a 1953 double volume with Maurice Helbrant's *Narcotic Agent.* The autobiographical *Junkie* was recommended to Wyn by his nephew, Carl Solomon, who was then an editor at Ace. *Junkie* appeared under the pseudonym of William Lee, with prefaces, designed to minimize controversy, by Solomon and Burroughs.

Although Ace occasionally published such important works of general fiction as the first edition of John A. Williams's first book, *The Angry Ones* (1960), during the late 1950s and early 1960s the firm continued to emphasize high-quality science fiction novels. Several of these won Hugo awards, and Ace itself won a Hugo award as best science fiction publisher in 1964. By 1968 the firm had added John Brunner, Brian W. Aldiss, Harlan Ellison, Edgar Rice Burroughs, Philip José Farmer, Samuel R. Delany, Ursula K. Le Guin, and Fritz Lieber to its list of authors.

Incorporated in 1958, Ace books became a subsidiary of Ace Publishing Corporation ten years later. Robert M. Leopold was chairman of the corporation's board, while A. Barry Merkin served as president. Russell W. Barich was named president of Ace Books, with Wollheim as vice-president and editor, Terry Carr as editor, and Charles Volpe as art director. Carr established the Ace Science Fic-

tion Specials, which included award-winning works such as Alexei Panshin's *Rite of Passage* (1976), Le Guin's *The Left Hand of Darkness* (1976), and Wilson Tucker's *The Year of the Quiet Sun* (1977). Under Volpe, Ace presented cover art by Leo and Diane Dillon; earlier illustrators had included Kelly Freas, Jeff Jones, Frank Frazetta, and Ed Emshwiller.

In 1969 Ace Books became a division of Charter Communications, Incorporated, with E. P. Thomas as vice-president and Frederik Pohl and Evelyn Grippo as senior editors. During this period Ace offered mostly reprints from its backlist. In 1977 Grosset and Dunlap—a subsidiary of Filmways Incorporated—purchased Charter Communications. Harold Roth assumed the presidency of Ace. He was succeeded in 1979 by Jack Artenstein. The same year, the firm moved to 360 Park Avenue South, after sixteen years at 1120 Avenue of the Americas.

When Jim Baen, formerly of *Galaxy* magazine, became science fiction editor in 1977, he helped to settle a five-year-long series of royalty disputes and boycotts by the Science Fiction Writers of America. The firm then returned to publishing new titles including Bob Shaw's *Orbitsville* (1977), Jerry Pournelle's *Janissaries* (1980), Dickson's *Soldier, Ask Not* (1980), Anderson's Flandry series, and *The Demon of Scattery* (1980) by Anderson and Mildred D. Broxon. Ace also began a series of large-format paperbacks with titles including Dickson's *Masters of Everon* (1980), Roger Zelazny's *Changeling* (1980), and Lynn Abbey's *The Black Flame* (1980).

In 1980 Michael Cohn was named president and chief operating officer at the firm's new address, 51 Madison Avenue. Susanne Jaffe served as vice-president and editor in chief of Ace Books, while Baen became executive editor of the new imprint Ace Science Fiction. Other imprints of Charter Communications, Incorporated include Charter Books, Cinnamon House, and Tempo Books. In July 1982 Grosset and Dunlap was absorbed into the Putnam Group, a subsidiary of MCA, Incorporated. The address of Ace Books is now the same as that of the Putnam Group: 200 Madison Avenue, New York 10016.

Cover for first edition of William S. Burroughs's first novel, published under a pseudonym

Cover for one volume of Ace's unauthorized edition of the Lord of the Rings *trilogy. Ballantine Books published the authorized edition.*

References:

Billy C. Lee, "Interview with Donald A. Wollheim," *Paperback Quarterly*, 1 (Fall 1978): 23-27;

J. Grant Thiessen, "Ace Books Checklist," *Science Fiction Collector No. 1* (Fall 1976): 5-47.

—*David Dzwonkoski*

Algonquin Books of Chapel Hill

(Chapel Hill, North Carolina: 1982-   )

Algonquin Books of Chapel Hill was organized in 1982 by Louis D. Rubin, Jr., professor of English at the University of North Carolina and an authority on Southern literature. Dr. Rubin is president of the firm; Charles S. Pitcher is publisher; and Shannon Ravenel is senior editor.

The first Algonquin announcement set forth the firm's publishing rationale: "We wanted to publish books for a national, not just a regional, audience. We believed that the time had come when it was possible for a small but full-fledged commercial publishing house with high editorial standards, located outside the metropolitan Northeast, not only to survive in the literary marketplace, but to flourish. . . . Good books of fiction and non-fic-

tion were going unpublished because they might not appeal to metropolitan literary tastes."

The initial list of five books included Vermont Royster's *My Own, My Country's Time;* Leon V. Driskell's *Passing Through,* a volume of fiction; Bob Simpson's *When the Water Smokes: A Peltier Creek Chronicle;* Katie Letcher Lyle's *Scalded to Death by the Steam,* a chronicle of railroad wrecks; and Sylvia Wilkenson's *Dirt Tracks to Glory,* a history of stock car racing. Fourteen titles were published in 1985.

The address of Algonquin Books of Chapel Hill is Box 2225, Chapel Hill, North Carolina 27515.

—*Christopher Surr*

Appleton-Century-Crofts
(New York: 1948-   )
The D. Appleton-Century Company
(New York: 1933-1948)

In March 1933 D. Appleton and Company merged with The Century Company. Though both firms had long literary histories, the new D. Appleton-Century Company gradually began to move away from publishing current fiction. Located at 35 West Thirty-second Street, New York, with Ap-

pleton president John W. Hiltman as chairman and Century president W. Morgan Shuster as president, The D. Appleton-Century Company continued to publish the literary works mainly of authors already connected with the original firms. Since Century's list at the time of the merger was largely

John W. Hiltman, first chairman of the D. Appleton-Century Company

Cover for tenth anniversary catalogue

1933   *1940s*   *1948*   *1950s*   *1970s*

nonfiction, most of the new firm's literary authors were retained through their association with Appleton.

Several of these writers were nearing the end of their careers while others had only a few titles published by the firm before moving on to other houses. Works by these authors include Zona Gale's *Old-fashioned Tales* (1933) and *Magna* (1939), Alice Brown's *Jeremy Hamlin* (1934), Donn Byrne's *A Daughter of the Medici, and Other Stories* (1935), Ernest Thompson Seton's *The Biography of an Arctic Fox* (1937) and *Trail and Camp-fire Stories* (1940), Edgar Lee Masters's *The New World* (1937) and *More People* (1939), Clements Ripley's *Clear for Action* (1940) and *Mississippi Belle* (1942), Gertrude Atherton's *The House of Lee* (1940) and *The Horn of Life* (1942), and André Maurois's *A Time for Silence* (1942).

Before her death in 1937, Edith Wharton had three books published by the firm: *A Backward Glance* (1934), *The World Over* (1936), and *Ghosts* (1937); *The Buccaneers* (1938) was published posthumously. Three other Appleton veterans, Hector Bolitho, Joseph C. Lincoln, and E. F. Benson, remained steady contributors for some years. Bolitho's titles include *Older People* (1935) and *The House in Half Moon Street and Other Stories* (1936); Lincoln's *Storm Signals* (1935) was followed by *Out of the Fog* (1940) and a book of poems, *Rhymes of the Old Cape* (1939). One of Appleton's most popular authors, Benson finished his career at the firm with *Old London* (four volumes, 1937) and *Queen Victoria's Daughters* (1938).

D. Appleton-Century's one major discovery during the 1930s was Andre Norton. Though she is now noted for her science fiction, her first two books, published by D. Appleton-Century, were *The Prince Commands* (1934) and *Ralestone Luck* (1938). Other additions to the firm included Jean Plaidy (pseudonym of Eleanor Hibbert) with *Beyond the Blue Mountains* (1947) and *Queen Jezebel* (1953).

With the purchase in 1948 of the twenty-four-year-old F. S. Crofts, Incorporated, which was noted for its line of college textbooks, Appleton-Century-Crofts became a formidable academic publisher. To Century's distinguished series in chemistry, earth science, history, modern languages, philosophy, political science, sociology, psychology, and economics were added the Crofts American History series, the Crofts Classics, the Eastman School of Music series, and books on social science, English, theater arts, and foreign languages—400 titles in all, for a combined total of over 1,000 textbooks. The firm also continued to publish its famous *Century Dictionary;* the *Century Cyclopedia of Names,* which was revised in 1954; and the *Century Atlas of the World.*

In March 1952 Shuster was elected chairman and Dana H. Ferrin was named president of Appleton-Century-Crofts. Shuster replaced Howard C. Smith, who had assumed the chairmanship after Hiltman's death in 1941. The fact that Ferrin had been head of the educational department is a further indication of the firm's shift away from trade books. From the late 1940s to the early 1960s the trade department was headed by Samuel Rapport. Under his direction, the firm published Horace McCoy's *Scalpel* (1952), mystery writer John D. MacDonald's *Cancel All Our Vows* (1953) and *Contrary Pleasure* (1954), and two first novels: John Barth's *The Floating Opera* (1956) and Richard Condon's *The Oldest Confession* (1958).

Appleton-Century-Crofts was acquired by the Meredith Publishing Company in 1960, with Allan W. Ferrin, Dana Ferrin's son, as president. Within a few years Appleton-Century-Crofts was split: educational books carried the Appleton-Century-Crofts imprint; the Appleton-Century imprint was revived for trade books, which by then were under the direction of another Meredith subsidiary, Duell, Sloan, and Pearce. C. Halliwell Duell served as managing director and C. A. Pearce as executive

Louis D. Rubin, Jr., founder and president of Algonquin Books of Chapel Hill

Catalogue cover

editor. By 1971 the Appleton-Century line had been dropped entirely, and Appleton-Century-Crofts was listed as the educational division of the Meredith Corporation.

In 1974 Appleton-Century-Crofts was purchased by Prentice-Hall. As a division of that firm, it specializes in books and journals about medicine, nursing, dentistry, pharmacy, and veterinary science. In 1982, the firm moved to 25 Van Zant Street, East Norwalk, Connecticut 06855. With the purchase of Prentice-Hall by Gulf + Western in 1984, Appleton became the health sciences publisher for the corporation.

References:

"Appleton-Century-Crofts Observes Its 125th Anniversary," *Publishers' Weekly,* 158 (8 July 1950): 120-127;

Samuel C. Chew, "The History," in Chew, ed., *Fruit among the Leaves: An Anniversary Anthology* (New York: Appleton-Century-Crofts, 1950), pp. 3-157;

The House of Appleton-Century (New York: Appleton-Century, 1936);

"John W. Hiltman [obituary]," *New York Times,* 16 April 1941, p. 23.

—*David Dzwonkoski*

Apple-wood Books
(Cambridge, Massachusetts: 1980-)

Apple-wood Books, Incorporated was founded in Cambridge, Massachusetts, in 1980 by Phil Zuckerman and Ned Perkins; it was capitalized with $30,000 borrowed from their parents and another $30,000 in loans. Apple-wood Books incorporated Apple-wood Press, which had been a part-time endeavor for Zuckerman since he published his first book, a hardbound hand-printed volume of four anonymous poems from the Middle Ages, in 1976. By 1980 Apple-wood Press had published fourteen books and was ready to grow into a full-time endeavor.

Sales of Apple-wood Books in 1981 were $79,000, with a list composed predominantly of literary works by young writers. Among the nine books on Apple-wood's list were *The Bohemians,* a fictional autobiography of John Reed by Alan Cheuse; Richard Elman's sketchbook of events in revolutionary Nicaragua, *Cocktails at Somoza's;* and William Zaranka's *The Brand-X Anthology of Poetry,* a parody of survey-course literary anthologies such as those published by Norton. A companion volume, *The Brand-X Anthology of Fiction,* also edited by Zaranka, was published in 1983.

In fall 1982 Apple-wood introduced *The Personal History, Adventures, Experiences & Observations of Peter Leroy* by Eric Kraft, a "serial novel." Installments in Kraft's serial have been published at the rate of three or four books per year and promoted in an advertising campaign built around the phrase "because life doesn't happen all at once."

By Fall 1984 Apple-wood had published some forty books, of which about one-third were poetry collections, one-third fiction, and the remainder specialty books and nonfiction. Beginning in 1985, distribution for Apple-wood Books, which had been handled since 1982 by Independent Publishers Group, was taken over by Arbor House.

The address of Apple-wood Books is Box 2870, Cambridge 02139. Zuckerman is president; Perkins is vice-president.

References:

Gayle Turim, "Getting Serial: Apple-wood Rethinks its Peter Leroy Strategy for Success," *Publishers Weekly,* 226 (5 October 1984): 47, 50, 52;

Phil Zuckerman, "A Notable Change of Name," *Publishers Weekly,* 222 (10 September 1982): 28.

—*Christopher T. Lee*

Arbor House Publishing Company
(New York: 1969-   )

ARBOR HOUSE

Arbor House Publishing Company was founded in July 1969 by Donald I. Fine, who served as president, publisher, and chief executive officer until 1983. Fine began his publishing career as a clerk at Doubleday and soon became an assistant editor for Doubleday's paperback branch, Permabooks. After moving to the Western Printing and Lithographing Company in 1951 and rising to managing editor, he was hired as editor in chief by Popular Library in 1958. Fine raised Popular Library out of heavy debts and acquired paperback rights to Eliot Ness and Oscar Fraley's *The Untouchables* (1957) and Harper Lee's *To Kill a Mockingbird* (1960). In 1960 he became vice-president at the Dell Publishing Company and editor in chief of Dell Books; he brought Dell to the forefront of paperback publishers and established the Delacorte Press. Fine lured James Jones, Irwin Shaw, and Norman Mailer to Delacorte; Mailer was also published by the new Dell subsidiary, Dial Press, the acquisition of which Fine had effected. In 1967 Fine moved to Putnam/Coward-McCann, where he served as executive vice-president and editor in chief. Fine left his position there to found Arbor House.

Described by the *New York Times* as "the paragon of the dictatorial publishing house," the firm was driven to success by Fine's acquisition and editing of Gerald A. Browne's *Eleven Harrowhouse* (1972) and *Nineteen Purchase Street* (1982), Ken Follett's *Eye of the Needle* (1978) and *Triple* (1979), Cynthia Freeman's novels, Margaret Truman's Washington-based murder mysteries, and works by Elmore Leonard, Dan Sherman, Ed McBain (Evan Hunter), Fred Mustard Stewart, Ernest K. Gann, Joanna Barnes, Cleveland Amory, Robert Silverberg, Robin Moore, and Herbert Mitgang. Fine's success in placing paperback and book club rights for Arbor House titles was of great importance to

the firm and its authors. Fine maintained control even after selling the company to the Hearst Corporation in December 1978; the house continued to prosper, reaching revenues of some $6 million in a single year.

Arbor House made a significant contribution to literature with Fine's acquisition of James Purdy's *In a Shallow Grave* (1975), followed by *Narrow Rooms* (1978). In 1976 Jerome Charyn had two books published by Arbor House, *Marilyn the Wild* and *The Education of Patrick Silver*. In 1971, with the acquisition of *Queenie*, Arbor House became the main publisher of Hortense Calisher. *Queenie* was followed by *Herself* (1972), *Standard Dreaming* (1972), *Eagle Eye* (1973), and *The Collected Stories of Hortense Calisher* (1975). Other literary publications include, all acquired and edited by Fine, Nelson Algren's posthumous novel *The Devil's Stocking* (1983), Irvin Faust's *Willy Remembers* (1971) and *Foreign Devils* (1973), and Herbert Gold's *Slave Trade* (1979).

From 1972 until 1981 Arbor House books were distributed by, successively, World Publishing Company, David McKay Company, and E. P. Dutton, but in 1981 the firm began distributing its own books. The firm moved several times from its original office at 15-17 West Forty-fourth Street in New York—first to 757 Third Avenue, then to 641 Lexington Avenue, and finally to 235 East Forty-fifth Street, New York 10017.

In October 1983 Fine left Arbor House after the Hearst Corporation refused to sell the company back to him. Eden Collinsworth, whom Fine had originally hired as a publicist, was named publisher. In November 1984 Fine organized a new firm, Donald I. Fine, Incorporated, at 128 East Thirty-sixth Street, New York 10016. Fine's first list included the Robert Silverberg Science Fiction line, the paperback Primus Library of Contemporary

Donald I. Fine

Advertisement

Advertisement from Arcadia House's first year, 1934

Americana, and a new line of juveniles. In its first two years the firm's output grew to about thirty titles per list.

Reference:

"Saga at Arbor House: Sale of Concern to Hearst," *New York Times,* 29 September 1979, pp. 25, 28.

—Ada Fan

Arcadia House

(New York: 1934-1964)

Organized in the fall of 1934 by Alex Hillman at 66 Fifth Avenue, New York, Arcadia House published what it called "romances reflecting the idealism and optimism of modern American youth." The firm experienced marked success with readers and libraries. Bellamy Partridge was editor until 1936; he was succeeded by Bennie Hall. Typical titles in the Arcadia House list were *This Side of Heaven* (1943) and *Undertow* (1943) by Anne Tedlock Brooks, *Frontier Nurse* (1943) by Watkins E. Wright, and *Stormy Hearts* (1944) by Dorothy Clewes.

By 1946 Arcadia House had been acquired by Samuel Curl, Incorporated. Curl had served as president of Arcadia House since at least 1942. The firm moved from 70 Fifth Avenue to 123 East Eighteenth Street in 1946.

In 1948 the assets of the firm were sold to Crown Publishers, and the Arcadia House imprint ceased for several years. From 1953 to 1963 Arcadia House was listed as a separate company sharing offices with Crown at 419 Park Avenue South. During this period fifty to sixty books a year—chiefly light fiction, mysteries, and westerns—were published under the Arcadia House imprint. The imprint terminated in 1964.

—Peter Dzwonkoski

Armed Services Editions
(New York: 1943-1944)
Editions for the Armed Services
(New York: 1944-1947)

In 1943 the Council on Books in Wartime began a government-run publishing operation for servicemen, Armed Services Editions, Incorporated. On the company's planning committee were Malcolm Johnson of D. Van Nostrand; William Sloane of Henry Holt; and John Farrar of Farrar and Rinehart. The committee proposed that several categories of books be printed and distributed free to servicemen: books about the war; popular fiction; humor; literary classics; nonfiction suggested by the army and navy; and original anthologies or "made" books, compiled specifically for the troops and unavailable elsewhere. Philip Van Doren Stern of Pocket Books was selected to manage the operation.

Trade publishers selected appropriate titles from their own lists, and from these an editorial advisory committee and army and navy representatives chose books to be printed as Armed Services Editions. The first, or "A" series, list included *The Education of H*Y*M*A*N K*A*P*L*A*N* by Leonard Q. Ross (Leo Rosten), *Report from Tokyo* by Joseph C. Grew, *Oliver Twist* (abridged) by Charles Dickens, *Mama's Bank Account* by Kathryn Forbes, and *The Fireside Book of Dog Stories,* edited by Jack Goodman. "Made" books in later series included Katherine Anne Porter's *Selected Short Stories; Great Poems from Chaucer to Whitman* and *Selected Poems of Percy Bysshe Shelley,* both edited by Louis Untermeyer; and F. Scott Fitzgerald's *The Diamond as Big as the Ritz and Other Stories.*

Designed to fit into uniform pockets, most of the paperbound books were set two columns to a page, were printed in two sizes—5 1/2 by 3 7/8 inches for books up to 320 pages long and 6 1/2 by 4 1/2 inches for books up to 512 pages long—

and were bound with staples along one of the short sides. From October 1946 until the series ended the following year, the books were published in standard paperback format. The Armed Services Editions were not available to civilians and were deliberately flimsily made so that they would not flood the market when the soldiers returned home after the war. At the height of its production, the company—which changed its name to Editions for the Armed Services, Incorporated in May 1944—printed 155,000 copies each of forty titles per month. When the operation ended in September 1947, nearly 123 million copies of 1,322 titles had been put in circulation.

In quality, quantity, and popularity among the members of the armed forces, the enterprise was a success. W. W. Norton, chairman of the Council on Books in Wartime, wrote in 1942: "The very fact that millions of men will have an opportunity to learn what a book is and what it can mean is likely now and in post-war years to exert a tremendous influence on the post-war course of the industry."

References:

John Y. Cole, ed., *Books in Action: The Armed Services Editions* (Washington, D.C.: Library of Congress, 1984);

Editions for the Armed Services, Inc., A History Together with the Complete List of 1324 [sic] Books Published for American Armed Forces Overseas (New York, 1948);

A List of the First 774 Books Published for American Armed Forces Overseas, Listed by Number and Alphabetically by Author (New York, 1945).

—*Carol Ann Wilkinson*

Cover for the first book on the first Armed Services Editions list

Philip Van Doren Stern

*Cover for Armed Services Editions book published in standard
paperback format (1946)*

Arno Press

(New York: 1962-   )

ARNO PRESS
A New York Times Company
Three Park Avenue, New York, N.Y. 10016

Arno Press was founded in 1962 by Arnold Zohn. In 1968 the New York Times Company acquired a controlling interest in Arno and organized it to reprint, according to the *Annual Report* of 1970, collections of books "of importance to understanding America and Americans." The books were sold primarily to libraries and other institutions as collections or as individual volumes. The initial offering of six collections included the series The American Negro, Eyewitness Accounts of the American Revolution, the German Air Force in World War II, Museum of Modern Art Reprints, and Tate Gallery Publications. During the next decade the list expanded steadily, adding eighteen to twenty series each year, including The Romantic Tradition in American Literature, Gothic Novels (three series), and Utopian Literature, as well as series of mystery and detection, science fiction, and supernatural and the occult. Also of note were *New York Times Book Reviews, 1896-1968, New York Times Theatre Reviews 1920-1970,* and *New York Times Film Reviews 1913-1968.*

In 1975 the company acquired Benjamin Blom, Incorporated, with an inventory of 1,100 art, architecture, and theater titles. In 1976 Arno branched out into general retail publishing with volumes compiled from historic front pages of the *Times.* Although the firm has reduced its output due to a shrinking institutional market, Arno Press reported 186 series in print in the primary collections in 1981. The firm's address is 3 Park Avenue, New York 10016.

—Alma Burner Creek

Atheneum Publishers

(New York: 1959-   )

Atheneum was founded by three men who were already near the top of their respective companies: Alfred A. Knopf, Jr., vice-president of his father's firm; Hiram Haydn, editor in chief at Random House; and Simon Michael Bessie, senior editor at Harper and Brothers. The *New York Times* commented, "It is as if the presidents of General Motors, Chrysler, and Ford left their jobs to start a new automobile company." When the announcement of the firm was made in March 1959, Bessie elaborated on the reasons for the venture: "It is a matter of leaving good places to set up our own

1970 advertisement

shop. . . . No one can be seriously in publishing for any length of time and not want the full challenge, in partnership with others, of directing his own publishing house." Offices were set up in a townhouse at 162 East Thirty-eighth Street in New York, and an organizational plan, under which the three founding partners would constitute an executive committee with a yearly rotating presidency, was established. The company's first list appeared in late spring 1960 and contained about twenty books, including Jan de Hartog's *The Inspector,* Loren Eiseley's *The Firmament of Time,* and André Schwarz-Bart's *The Last of the Just;* other titles were by Ignazio Silone, Prudencio de Pereda, Wright Morris, and William Goldman.

Atheneum's literary output was diverse, but was especially strong in poetry, under the aegis of Harry Ford, with several winners of the Pulitzer Prize and the National Book Award. The former went to Anthony Hecht for *The Hard Hours* (1967), Richard Howard for *Untitled Subjects* (1969), W. S. Merwin for *The Carrier of Ladders* (1970), and James Merrill for *Divine Comedies* (1976); recipients of National Book Awards included Merrill for *Nights and Days* (1966) and Howard Moss for *Selected Poems* (1971). Conrad Aiken's *Cats and Bats and Things with Wings* (1965) was followed by his posthumous *Who's Zoo* (1977). Also published were three works by Randall Jarrell: *The Woman at the Washington Zoo: Poems and Translations* (1960), *A Sad Heart at the Supermarket: Essays and Fables* (1962), and *Selected Poems* (1964).

Novelists whose work was published by Atheneum included Reynolds Price, Frederick Buechner, Eudora Welty, James Clavell, Donald Barthelme, and Eric Ambler.

Edward Albee won Pulitzer Prizes for drama for *A Delicate Balance* (1966) and *Seascape* (1975); Albee's other plays published by Atheneum include *Who's Afraid of Virginia Woolf?* (1962), *Tiny Alice* (1965), *Box* [and] *Quotations from Chairman Mao Tse-Tung* (1969), and *Counting the Ways and Listening: Two Plays* (1977). Atheneum also published the imaginative dramas of Peter Weiss, including *The Investigation* (1966) and *The Persecution and Assassination of Jean Paul Marat as Performed by the Inmates of the Asylum of Charenton under the Direction of the Marquis de Sade* (1966). Drama critics whose works were published by the firm included Kenneth Tynan and Eric Bentley; among other critics and historians of literature whose books were published by Atheneum was Nigel Nicholson.

Successful nonfiction titles of the 1960s were

Theodore H. White's *The Making of the President, 1960* (1961), the first in a series and a Pulitzer Prize winner for general nonfiction; Frederic Morton's *The Rothschilds* (1962); Luigi Barzini's *The Italians* (1964); Robert Ardrey's *The Territorial Imperative* (1966); and Robert K. Massie's *Nicholas and Alexandra* (1967). Atheneum's nonfiction list also included books by Dean Acheson, Harrison Salisbury, Arthur Schlesinger, Sr., Daniel J. Boorstin, George F. Kennan, Oscar Handlin, Jerome S. Bruner, W. E. B. Du Bois, William Sloan Coffin, Jr., Felix Frankfurter, and Martin Buber. Also popular were books on cuisine by James Beard and Craig Claiborne, on sports by Arthur Ashe and Sam Snead, on the occult by Jeanne Dixon, and on show business by Garson Kanin.

In 1961 Atheneum established a juvenile department headed by Jean Karl, who had previously been juvenile editor at Abingdon Press. This department became known for the high quality of its books, putting out approximately fifty titles a year by leading children's authors including Judith Viorst, Barbara Cocoran, Ellen Raskin, and Eve Merriam. Maia Wojciechowska won the Newbery Medal for *Shadow of a Bull* (1964) in 1965; the same year, the Caldecott Medal was awarded to Beni Montresor for his illustrations for *May I Bring a Friend?* (1964) by Beatrice S. de Regniers. Three years later, another Newbery prize went to Elaine Konigsburg for *From the Mixed-up Files of Mrs. Basil E. Frankweiler* (1967).

Financial pressures and personality conflicts led to serious differences among the partners, resulting in the departure of Haydn for Harcourt, Brace and World in 1964. The rotating presidency was dropped; Bessie became president, Knopf became chairman of the board, and Karl was made vice-president. Haydn died in 1973.

Further expansion came with the 1965 acquisition of Russell and Russell, reprinters of scholarly books; the development of Atheneum Paperbacks; and the firm's agreement with several university presses, among them Harvard, Princeton, and Stanford, to issue a selection of the hardbound titles of these presses in paperback editions. The latter two moves reinforced Bessie's early policy statement that "we hope to publish as naturally in paper as in cloth, depending on the individual book." To meet the expansion, the firm moved to 122 East Forty-second Street in May 1967.

In 1975, after continued financial difficulties, there was a second split between the remaining founders; Bessie rejoined his old firm, which had become Harper and Row, and Marvin Brown was

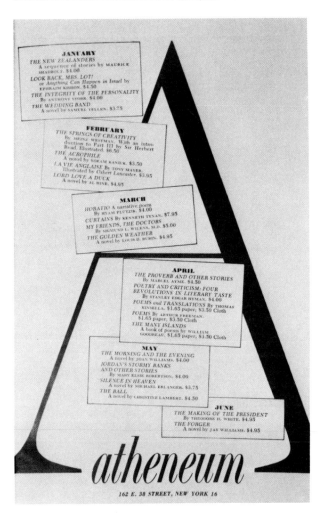

1961 advertisement

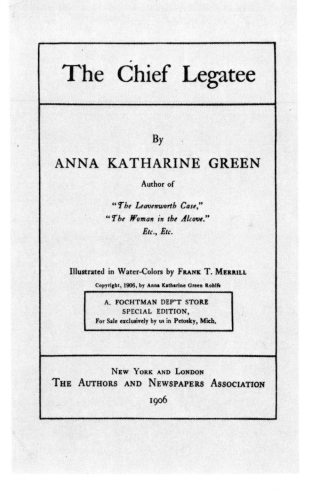

*Title page for an Authors and Newspapers Association edition.
Only one store in a given city had the right to sell the book; the
store's name was printed on the title page.*

elected president. The basis for the disagreement was Harper and Row's efforts to acquire Atheneum, a move which Bessie favored and Knopf opposed. Bessie felt that it was hard for a small firm to remain independent and maintain its quality. Indeed, Atheneum did not long remain independent: in 1979, it merged with Scribner to form the Scribner Book Companies, in which Atheneum would operate as a wholly owned subsidiary and Scribner would operate as a separate division. Charles Scribner, Jr., stated, "We are both medium sized publishers. This will make us larger medium sized publishers and still allow us to keep our identities." Scribner was made chairman of the board and chief executive officer and Knopf became vice-chairman. One way they hoped to save money was by combining warehouse and shipping facilities. Atheneum moved to the Scribner Building at 597 Fifth Avenue in 1980.

Another development of 1979 was the introduction of the Argo line of science fiction and fantasy titles. Atheneum's science fiction authors include Ursula K. Le Guin and Andre Norton.

Atheneum published 122 titles in 1979 and distributed books for Gordon Cremonesi Books, Chelsea House Publishers, Heritage Press, and Rawson, Wade. In the summer of 1984 the Scribner Book Companies were purchased by Macmillan. Atheneum's address is the Macmillan Building at 115 Fifth Avenue, New York 10003.

References:

"Atheneum Publishers: Officers, Directors, Plans," *Publishers' Weekly*, 175 (25 May 1959): 73-74;

"Bessie Leaves Atheneum; Rejoins Harper & Row," *Publishers Weekly*, 208 (18 August 1975): 20;

"Hiram Haydn [obituary]," *New York Times*, 3 December 1973, p. 42;

John Mutter, "Macmillan Buys Scribner for $15 Million in Stock," *Publishers Weekly*, 225 (11 May 1984): 152, 154;

"Scribner's and Atheneum to Merge in the Fall," *Publishers Weekly*, 214 (7 August 1978): 16.

—Elizabeth A. Dzwonkoski

The Atlantic Monthly Press
(Boston: 1917-)

An Atlantic Monthly Press Book

THE ATLANTIC MONTHLY PRESS
BOSTON

The Atlantic Monthly Press, founded in 1917 in Boston, is the book publishing division of the Atlantic Monthly Company, which publishes *Atlantic Monthly* magazine. The firm resulted from *Atlantic Monthly* editor Ellery Sedgwick's recognition that books are often spawned by magazine articles and stories. It is one of the few houses carrying on the nineteenth-century tradition of a symbiotic relationship between magazine and book publishing. Sedgwick was the firm's first director.

The Atlantic Monthly Press's first publication, Vernon Kellogg's *Headquarters Nights* (1917), was followed by two nonfiction Pulitzer Prize winners, James Truslow Adams's *The Founding of New England* (1921) and M. A. De Wolfe Howe's *Barrett Wendell and His Letters* (1924), as well as a Newbery Medal winner, Charles Boardman Hawes's *The Dark Frigate* (1923). These critical triumphs did not bring the firm commercial success, however, and in 1925 Sedgwick arranged a merger with Little, Brown and Company. The latter took over the distribution of the Atlantic list and agreed to publish future titles produced by the editors of The Atlantic Monthly Press. These books bear the imprint

"The Atlantic Monthly Press/Little, Brown and Company."

In 1927 the company began its Atlantic Novel Contest. The first winner, Mazo de la Roche's *Jalna*, initiated a series of Jalna books, some of which have remained in print into the 1980s. Successful books for the firm during the 1930s included Charles Nordhoff and James Norman Hall's *Bounty* trilogy (1932-1934); James Hilton's *Good-bye Mr. Chips* (1934); Walter D. Edmonds's *Drums Along the Mohawk* (1936); and Mari Sandoz's first novel, *Slogum House* (1937), as well as her *Capital City* (1939).

The 1950s and especially the 1960s brought novels that were both critical and financial successes by both newcomers and established authors: Kathryn Hulme's *The Nun's Story* (1956); Edwin O'Connor's *The Last Hurrah* (1956), *The Edge of Sadness* (1961), and *All in the Family* (1966); Katherine Anne Porter's *Ship of Fools* (1962); and J. B. Priestley's *Lost Empires* (1965). James Alan McPherson, whose short stories in the *Atlantic Monthly* and in his collection *Hue and Cry* (1969) received national attention, was awarded the Pulitzer Prize for *Elbow Room* (1977), his second collection.

Poetry volumes published by the firm include Jorge Guillén's *Cántico: A Selection* (1965), David Ignatow's *Facing the Tree* (1975), L. E. Sissman's *Hello Darkness* (1978), May Swenson's *New and Selected Things Taking Place: Poems* (1978), and Stanley Kunitz's *The Poems of Stanley Kunitz: NineteenTwenty-Eight to Nineteen Seventy-Eight* (1979).

The company has published juvenile titles by Eleanor Cameron, Sheila Burnford, Sid Fleisch-man, and Miska Miles. The nonfiction list has included works by Robert Coles, Carleton S. Coon, Frances FitzGerald, Oscar Handlin, Carl G. Jung, Louis Kronenberger, George F. Kennan, Walter Lippmann, Bertrand Russell, Francis Steegmuller, George Seferis, and Tracy Kidder. Among the writers whose work was first published by The Atlantic Monthly Press are Geoffrey Household, Agnes Newton Keith, Richard Bissell, A. E. Ellis, Jesse Hill Ford, and Joseph Wambaugh.

In 1979 Peter Davison stepped down as director, a post he had held since 1964, but remained a senior editor as well as a poetry editor of the *Atlantic Monthly*. He was replaced as director by Upton Birnie Brady. Natalie Greenberg serves as managing director, and Melanie Kroupa edits children's books. Sedgwick died in 1960. The firm has been located since its founding at 8 Arlington Street, Boston 02116.

References:

Peter Davison, "After 50 Years, People Still Ask: What Is the Atlantic Monthly Press?," *Publishers' Weekly*, 192 (16 October 1967): 32-34;

"Ellery Sedgwick [obituary]," *New York Times*, 22 April 1960, p. 31;

Ellery Sedgwick, *The Happy Profession* (Boston: Little, Brown, 1946);

Edward Weeks, *The Open Heart* (Boston: Little, Brown, 1955);

Weeks and Emily Flint, eds., *Jubilee: One Hundred Years of the Atlantic* (Boston: Little, Brown, 1957).

—*Bill Oliver*

Authors and Newspapers Association
(New York: 1906-1908)

The Authors and Newspapers Association, an independent publisher from 1906 to 1908, briefly succeeded in an innovative effort to sell popular British and American fiction at half price without diminishing the physical quality of the books.

On 28 April 1906 *Publishers' Weekly* announced the first publishing efforts of the new firm, located at 11 Pine Street in New York and headed by Frank F. Lovell. In spite of the firm's name, it was not an authors' cooperative but a new publisher with an original idea. (It should not be confused with the International Association of Newspapers and Authors of New York, a firm which in 1901 published twenty-five-cent reprints of works by popular authors.) Arrangements had been made by the Authors and Newspapers Association to publish new works by six English and six American writers of fiction. The British writers were Robert Barr, Amelia E. Barr, E. F. Benson, C. J. Cutcliffe Hyne, Max Pemberton, and Eden Phillpotts; the Americans were Gertrude Atherton, Mary E. Wilkins Freeman, Anna Katharine Green,

Mrs. Burton Harrison, Albert Payson Terhune, and the husband-and-wife team of C. N. and A. M. Williamson. Each work was first serialized in the Sunday issues of seventy-five selected newspapers and then was published in a clothbound, illustrated edition selling for fifty cents. These books were sold only in certain bookstores, one store per city. Each store had exclusive rights to sell the book at this price for eighteen months, and the name of the bookstore was printed on the title page. These unique arrangements were protected by contracts printed in each volume, and were upheld in court when The O'Gorman Company, a Providence bookstore, brought suit in 1906.

After publishing the first dozen books, in 1907 the association announced contracts with more than twenty eminent authors for future publication. Because of the rapid growth of the newspaper branch of the association, book publishing was to be handled by Lovell's Empire Publishing Company at 11 Pine Street and marketing by the American News Company. The latter would observe conventional practice in distribution and pricing. But shortly after moving in December 1908 to 68 Murray Street, the Authors and Newspapers Association seems to have discontinued its publishing activities.

Reference:

"A New Publishing Scheme," *Publishers' Weekly*, 69 (28 April 1906): 1261-1262.

—Theodora Mills

Avalon Books
(New York: 1950-   )

In January 1950 Thomas Bouregy and Samuel Curl announced the formation of Bouregy and Curl at 22 East Sixtieth Street in New York. Bouregy worked for the Collier Photo Engraving Company; Curl was vice-president of Hillman-Curl and owner of Arcadia House and Samuel Curl, Incorporated. Bouregy, Curl, and editor Lucy Mabry formed the staff of the new firm, which published under the Avalon Books imprint.

Avalon's publication schedule began with three novels, each priced at two dollars in full cloth binding. Released in February 1950, these were *Once upon a Summer* by Natalie Shipman, *Hold Me Fast* by Cecile Gilmore, and *Fair Is My Love* by Frances Sarah Moore (pseudonym of Elsie Frances Mack). The bulk of the Avalon list is made up of romances, gothics, nurse novels, and adventures. Until 1968, Avalon published an impressive list of science fiction. *Police Your Planet* (1956) by Erik van Lhin (a pseudonym of Lester del Rey), *The Infinite Brain* (1957) by Charles R. Long, *The Blue Barbarian* (1958) by Stanton A. Coblentz, *The Glory That Was* (1960) by L. Sprague de Camp, and *Destiny's Orbit* (1961) by Donald A. Wollheim under his pseudonym David Grinnell are representative of the science-fiction list.

The number of titles published under the Avalon imprint remains at sixty per year. A separate paperback imprint, Airmont, was begun in January 1962, with Bouregy as president and Curl as manager of the southern district. Airmont publishes a series of reprints of classics, including *Pride and Prejudice, Treasure Island,* and *The Adventures of Huckleberry Finn.* There are presently 238 Airmont Classics, including 24 Shakespeare titles. Though Bouregy died in 1978 and Curl predeceased him, the firm is still family owned. The firm moved in 1985 to 401 Lafayette Street, New York 10003.

Reference:

"Airmont Books: New Mass Market Paperbacks," *Publishers' Weekly*, 180 (2 October 1961): 34.

—Martha A. Bartter

MYSTERIES • CRIME & DETECTIVE STORIES
ANTHOLOGIES • NOVELS • CLASSICS

The NEW *Avon* pocket-size *Books*
GOOD BOOKS complete IN EVERY WAY

The New Avon Books are well-printed on good paper, with large, clear type; strongly bound in colorful, glossy covers treated to resist wear and tear! In many instances the books are printed from the publishers' original $2 and $2.50 plates.

Some are illustrated throughout by renowned artists. The text of all Avon Books is exactly as published in the original higher-priced editions, and is not expurgated, cut, or condensed.

ONLY
25¢
EACH

IN U. S. A.

Because the New Avon Books are easy to open, light to hold, thrilling to read and compact to carry or store in clothing or bags, they are ideal as gifts to the boys in the Armed Forces.

1941 advertisement

Avon Books

(New York: 1941-   )

Joseph (Jo) Meyers had long experience in publishing when he began Avon Publications, Incorporated in 1941. He had founded the Illustrated Editions Company in 1929, and in 1936 he had entered the popular reprint field by buying J. S. Ogilvie Publications Company. The first advertisements for "Avon Pocket-Size Books" appeared in November 1941, promising complete, unabridged editions of books by the "world's leading writers of fiction, nonfiction, biography, poetry, plays and the best of the world's classics," some of which would be "illustrated throughout," for twenty-five cents a copy. The first twelve titles, published in runs of 500,000 copies with four-color varnished covers and red-stained edges, included James Hilton's *Ill Wind*, Sinclair Lewis's *Elmer Gantry*, William Faulkner's *Mosquitoes*, Agatha Christie's *The Big Four*, and the *Rubáiyát of Omar Khayyám*.

Almost at once, Robert de Graff of Pocket Books asked the New York Supreme Court for an injunction against Avon, claiming that the two lines were identical in format and that the new company was engaged in unfair competition. Although the first decision favored Avon, an appeal resulted in an injunction in October 1942 against its continuing to imitate the Pocket Books format. Avon dropped the word "Pocket-Size" from its covers and began using various colors of stain on the page edges; in January 1944 the court deemed these changes sufficient to distinguish between the products of the two firms.

By the end of 1943 Avon's list included forty titles; it was dominated by mysteries, although works by Thomas Wolfe, Booth Tarkington, John Steinbeck, and D. H. Lawrence were also reprinted. In 1946 several series of digest-sized magazines were added to the line. The *Avon Modern Short Story Monthly, Avon Monthly Novel, Avon Mystery Monthly,* and *Rex Stout Mystery Monthly* were followed in 1947 by the *Avon Fantasy Reader,* edited by Donald A. Wollheim. Some of these publications continued until 1952.

In the 1940s Avon was located at 119 West Fifty-seventh Street, with Meyers as president, Edna B. Williams as vice-president, and Maurice Diamond as vice-president and general manager. By 1949 Wollheim was an editor and Williams had left; Charles R. Byrne became assistant to the president in 1950 and editor in chief and publisher in 1951. By 1952 the firm had moved to 575 Madison Avenue.

Avon Double-Size Books were added in 1951 to handle longer reprints and anthologies; they sold for fifty cents. The first titles in this format were *Jew Süss* by Lion Feuchtwanger and *The Avon All-American Fiction Reader.* In 1952 Avon developed a thirty-five-cent line for works of intermediate length and began a popular series of books for children, the Avon Jolly Books, which sold for twenty-five cents.

The company began to publish original fiction in the 1950s. Many Avon books featured provocative covers, with titles such as *Desire in the Deep South* (1955) by Ward Greene and *Dishonor* by Gerald Kersh (1955). R. V. Cassill's *The Hungering Shame* (1956), *The Wound of Love* (1956), *Lustful Summer* (1958), and *My Sister's Keeper* (1960) were first published by Avon. In May 1955 Avon an-

Cover for a 1949 Avon paperback

Ian and Betty Ballantine in the 1940s (photo: Phillip Album)

nounced the introduction of Bard Books, a quality line that had been in preparation for a year. Bard Books were to be sold only in bookstores; the first titles, appearing in July, were *The Rubáiyát of Omar Khayyám* for thirty-five cents and *The Meaning and Psychology of Dreams* by Wilhelm Stekel for fifty cents. These books were "tastefully bound and with intelligent jacket copy."

Meyers died on 2 November 1957. Business was carried on under executive vice-president Joseph M. Mann, and the office of president was not immediately filled. In June 1959 the Hearst Corporation purchased a controlling interest in Avon, and in 1960 the Avon Book Division of the Hearst Corporation moved to 959 Eighth Avenue, with Mann as publisher.

The biggest sellers on the Avon list in 1960 were biographies: Earl Mazo's *Richard Nixon,* a reprint, and John Donovan's *Eichmann—Man of Slaughter,* a paperback original. In the same year Avon published Jack Kerouac's *Tristessa,* a paperback original. Frank E. Taylor became publisher in 1963. The Avon reprint of Henry Roth's 1934 novel *Call It Sleep* made the best-seller lists in both 1964 and 1965. Peter M. Mayer, the education editor who had discovered Roth's book, was made editor in chief in 1964 and publisher in 1965.

In 1967 Avon expanded the Camelot juvenile line, including titles such as *The Wind in the Willows* by Kenneth Grahame and *Lions in the Way* by Bella Rodman. It also introduced the Discus imprint for nonfiction. The Avon Library, a paperback imprint for quality fiction, was announced in mid-1968 with the reprinting of *I Thought of Daisy* by Edmund Wilson and *In This Our Life* by Ellen Glasgow. Bel Kaufman's *Up the Down Staircase* (1966), Catherine Marshall's *Christy* (1968), Haim Ginott's *Between Parent and Child* (1969), and Fletcher Knebel's *Van-*

ished (1969) helped create Avon's strong list.

In 1971 two new imprints were introduced: Flare, a large-format trade paperback line emphasizing visual interest; and Equinox, another large-format line for quality publications. The first Equinox titles included Kate Millett's *Sexual Politics* and Leslie Halliwell's *The Filmgoer's Companion.* Avon published an original novel by Kathleen Woodiwiss, *The Flame and the Flower,* in 1972, and by 1977 it had sold over two-and-a-half million copies. Other popular authors of romantic historical novels were Rosemary Rogers, Laurie McBain, and Patricia Gallagher. *Jonathan Livingston Seagull* (1973) by Richard Bach and *I'm O.K.—You're O.K.* (1973) by Thomas Harris each cost Avon over $1 million to acquire; *The Final Days* (1977) by Bob Woodward and Carl Bernstein cost $1.5 million; and Avon paid $1.9 million for Colleen McCullough's *The Thorn Birds* (1978). In 1975 Avon reprinted some of the novels of Nobel Prize winner Patrick White. Walter Meade, who succeeded Mayer as editor in chief in 1977, continued Mayer's emphasis on original novels, especially from new authors, to avoid the high cost of reprint rights. Meade became executive vice-president and publisher, as well as editor in chief, in 1979. Avon's current address is 1790 Broadway, New York 10019.

References:

Kenneth C. Davis, "The Cinderella Story of Paperback Originals," *Publishers Weekly,* 217 (11 January 1980): 43-50;

"Joseph Meyers [obituary]," *Publishers' Weekly,* 172 (18 November 1957): 32;

"The Seventies: A Paperback Montage," *Publishers Weekly,* 217 (22 February 1980): 46-47.

—Martha A. Bartter

Ballantine Books

(New York: 1952-   )

In 1939 Ian Ballantine had persuaded Sir Allan Lane to set up a branch of Penguin Books, Limited in the United States, with himself as manager. In June 1945, after The New American Library absorbed that operation, he left to organize and serve as president and publisher of Bantam Books for Grosset and Dunlap. Ballantine was particularly interested in original publishing, which Penguin Books had done but Bantam did not do. He left Bantam in February 1952 to found Ballantine Books, Incorporated with his wife, Betty.

Almost immediately he proposed the Ballantine Plan, offering to publish original titles in paperback simultaneously with their publication in hardcover by a trade house, with a joint imprint on the paperbacks and joint financing. The trade publisher would advance the manufacturing costs of the paperback edition and a fee for supervising distribution; Ballantine would provide the sheets for binding in hardcover. Authors would get royalties of eight percent for the paperback edition instead of the usual two-and-a-half percent. The paperbacks would sell for thirty-five or fifty cents, rather than the twenty-five cents that was standard at that time. While the idea of original paperback publishing was not new—Fawcett's Gold Medal line had been doing it since 1950—the Ballantine Plan allowed a small, undercapitalized firm to handle important titles on a large scale. Farrar, Straus and Young and Houghton Mifflin were the first trade houses to participate in the plan.

For the first six months, the Ballantines and their editorial assistants, Stanley Kaufman and Bernard Shir-Cliff, worked out of the Ballantines' apartment at 440 West Twenty-fourth Street. Ian Ballantine was president, Betty Ballantine secretary, and Robert Arnold vice-president and sales manager; like Ballantine, Kaufman and Arnold had both worked at Bantam.

The first book from Ballantine/Houghton Mifflin was Cameron Hawley's *Executive Suite,* published on 10 November 1952; in eight months it sold 22,000 hardcover copies at three dollars and 475,000 copies in the thirty-five-cent paperbound edition. In 1954, when the movie was released, Ballantine did a "second shot"; sales of the paperback rose to 800,000 copies, an enormous figure for the time. Houghton Mifflin, impressed, bought a twenty-five percent share of the new company.

Betty Ballantine was science fiction editor; she published Arthur C. Clarke's *Childhood's End,* Ward Moore's *Bring the Jubilee,* and Frederik Pohl and C. M. Kornbluth's *Space Merchants* in 1953. Pohl was hired that year to edit the *Star Science Fiction Stories* series. In 1954 the Hearst Corporation canceled Ballantine's distribution contract, costing Ballantine $600,000 and pushing the firm close to bankruptcy. Forced to cut its publication schedule, Ballantine brought out just one title in May: 10,000 copies, in hardcover only, of Howard Swiggett's *The Power and the Prize,* a Reader's Digest Book Club Selection. By October Ballantine was able to increase its publication schedule to three titles a month, including *Star Short Novels,* edited by Pohl and published in both hard and soft covers.

Ballantine did some reprints, mostly of short stories by noted science fiction writers whose work had previously appeared only in magazines. By 1955 Ballantine had published Robert Sheckley's *Untouched by Human Hands* (1954), Clarke's *Earthlight* (1955), and William Tenn's *Of All Possible Worlds* (1955). John Wyndham's *Out of the Deeps* (1953) and *Re-birth* (1955) and Ray Bradbury's *Fahrenheit 451* (1953) and *October Country* (1956) sold very well. *The Mad Reader* (1954)—reprints from *Mad* magazine—sold a million copies at thirty-five cents. In 1957 Ballantine published Harold Flender's *Paris Blues* and the second volume of the original poetry anthology *New Poems by American Poets,* edited by Rolfe Humphries (the first volume had been published in 1953). The company's switchboard operator introduced Betty Ballantine to J. R. R. Tolkien's *Lord of the Rings* trilogy, which she, in turn, encouraged Bernard Shir-Cliff to read. In 1965 Ballantine published the only paperback edition authorized by Tolkien. Each copy of the three-volume set displayed a letter from Tolkien on the cover urging that "those who approve of courtesy (at least) to living authors will purchase it and no other." This move garnered much publicity, large sales, and eventually a concession from Ace Books, which had earlier published an unauthorized edition. Tolkien's *The Hobbit* (1966)—the firm's all-time best-seller—has sold more than eight million copies.

Ballantine had already published art books by Norman Rockwell and M. C. Escher; in 1967 it produced a paperbound gift book, the Sierra Club's

1986 advertisement. Ballantine helped organize Bantam in 1945.

In Wilderness is the Preservation of the World. Paul Ehrlich's *The Population Bomb* (1968) was a big seller and was often reprinted. Ballantine reprinted Anthony Burgess's *The Wanting Seed* (1964), *A Clockwork Orange* (1965), and *ReJoyce* (1965); Christopher Isherwood's *Prater Violet* (1967) and *The World in the Evening* (1967); sixteen books by Nevil Shute, including *The Legacy* (1963) and *In the Wet* (1964); and Doris Lessing's *African Stories* (1966) and *The Golden Notebook* (1968).

In 1969 Ballantine Books was sold to Intext of Scranton, Pennsylvania. Ian Ballantine remained as chief executive officer; distribution changed from Pocket Books, which had handled it since 1963, to Curtis Distribution Company. In January 1973, Ian Ballantine helped arrange the sale of the firm to Random House, and in December of that year he became chairman. Ron Busch joined the company as president in January 1974 when Ian and Betty Ballantine left to form a short-lived packaging company, Rufus Publications; they then went to Bantam to start a trade paperback division, the Peacock Press. Under Busch's direction, Ballantine Books moved carefully into the big-money auction market. William Safire's *Full Disclosure* (1977) was bought for over $1 million. Busch also bought Joseph Heller's *Something Happened* (1975) and several titles by Paul Theroux. In 1976 Ballantine published George Lucas's *Star Wars.* Editor Judy-Lynn del Rey's original science fiction line soon had its own imprint, Del Rey Books; the Del Rey line added hardcover publications with *Gloryhits* (1978) by Bob Stickgold and Mark Noble, *The White Dragon* (1979) by Anne McCaffrey, and *Splinter of the Mind's Eye* (1981) by Alan D. Foster. In November 1979 Ballantine and Warner Books combined their sales and distribution functions.

In March 1980 Random House—including Ballantine, which was then publishing 200 books a year—was sold to Newhouse Publications. In March 1981 Ian Ballantine, while continuing to work with the Peacock Press, returned as a consultant to Ballantine Books.

Early in 1982 CBS sold Fawcett Books, which it had purchased in 1977, to Random House. Fawcett's imprints—Crest, Gold Medal, Columbine, Premier, Coventry, and Juniper—became a part of Ballantine/Del Rey. Susan J. Petersen was named president of Ballantine/Del Rey/Fawcett in July 1982; Robert B. Wyatt is editor in chief of the Ballantine mass market list, while Joelle Delbourgo is editor in chief of the Ballantine trade paperback line.

One of the greatest commercial successes in the history of Ballantine—or of any publisher—came in the fall of 1982, when Jim Davis, creator of Garfield, the cartoon cat, became the first author to have seven titles on the *New York Times Book Review* paperback best-seller list at the same time, with a total of 6.5 million Garfield books in print. In the same year Ballantine published Clarke's best-selling *2010: Odyssey Two* in hardcover. The firm is located at 201 East Fiftieth Street, New York 10022.

References:
"Ballantine Unveils Multimedia Marketing Plan to Aid All Titles," *Publishers Weekly,* 218 (21 November 1980): 44-45;

Kenneth C. Davis, "The Building of Ballantine," *Publishers Weekly,* 225 (27 April 1984): 25-29;

Thomas Weyr, "Ballantine Books at Quarter Century, Part 1: The Founders," *Publishers Weekly,* 212 (12 December 1977): 30-33;

Weyr, "Ballantine Books at Quarter Century, Part 2: The New Regime," *Publishers Weekly,* 212 (26 December 1977): 44-46.

—Martha A. Bartter

The first Ballantine book (1952)

Cover for a 1953 Ballantine book

Robert O. Ballou
(New York: 1932-1935)

Robert O. Ballou was born in the Chicago area in 1892. After graduating from Oberlin College, he worked as a traveling salesman and as a reporter. During World War I he served in the army ambulance corps; after the war he became a cost accountant in Allentown, Pennsylvania. Finally, he returned to Chicago and was appointed editor of the *Typothetae Bulletin of the United Typothetae of America.*

He began writing editorials for the *Chicago Evening Post;* he also edited *Ben Franklin's Monthly,* a printer's trade publication. His growing fascination with print manifested itself in several articles on typography in that journal. He became head of the proofroom, then assistant editor and book designer at the University of Chicago Press; he continued in a consulting position with the press when he became an editor at *Publishers' Weekly.* He also served as assistant literary editor and then literary editor on the *Chicago Daily News.*

Ballou joined Jonathan Cape and Harrison Smith when it was established in New York in January 1929. He was head of manufacturing and treasurer, and later business manager. For a few months in 1932 he was vice-president of the short-lived firm of Jonathan Cape and Robert Ballou, Incorporated. From there he moved on to Brewer, Warren and Putnam, taking some of the Cape and Ballou books with him. He also took a contract for three books by John Steinbeck, who was then virtually unknown, having only *Cup of Gold* (1929) to his credit.

Brewer, Warren and Putnam published Steinbeck's *The Pastures of Heaven* (1932) during the firm's last year of existence; Ballou retained the book in his stock and inserted a new title page when he established his own imprint at 347 Fifth Avenue in 1932. Ballou also published the first edition of Steinbeck's *To a God Unknown* in 1933. Julia Peter-kin's *Roll, Jordan, Roll* with photographs by Doris Ulmann was also published in a limited edition in 1933; it was followed a year later by Henry Roth's only book, *Call It Sleep.*

In 1935 Ballou joined Robert M. McBride and Company but stayed less than a year. By 1938 he was an editorial representative for Jonathan Cape, Limited of London. In 1942 he joined the British Information Services; in 1943 he returned to the United States to work for the Viking Press. Ballou was the author of *The Glory of God,* which was also published as *This I Believe* (1938). He died in 1977.

Ballou was widely respected as a book designer; he was known for his careful selection of illustrations and for his simple but elegant title pages. He was also a good editor; his lack of success as a businessman may have been partly due to the Depression. Steinbeck characterized him in a 1935 letter as "a fine man and a sensitive man but I do not think he is fitted to fight the battle of New York. He is a gentleman. He can't bring himself to do the things required for success."

References:

Robert O. Ballou, "How Poetry Is Set in America," *Publishers' Weekly,* 109 (17 April 1926): 1319-1322;

"Ballou Joins Robert M. McBride," *Publishers' Weekly,* 128 (20 July 1935): 156;

Paul A. Bennett, "Robert O. Ballou of Cape & Smith," *Linotype News,* 9 (June 1931): 5;

"Brewer, Warren & Putnam Acquired by Harcourt, Brace & Co.," *Publishers' Weekly,* 122 (5 November 1932): 1789;

"Robert O. Ballou [obituary]," *New York Times,* 14 October 1977, II: 6;

Elaine Steinbeck and Robert Wallsten, eds., *Steinbeck: A Life in Letters* (New York: Viking, 1975).

—Ada Fan

Robert O. Ballou

Cover for the first title published by Bantam Books

Bantam Books

(New York: 1945-   )

After resigning as manager of the American branch of Penguin Books in June 1945, Ian Ballantine started a new paperback firm, Ballantine and Company. Ballantine took with him from Penguin Sidney Kramer and Walter B. Pitkin, Jr.

The firm published a few original titles under the Ballantine imprint and some reprints as Superior Reprints, but it needed more capital. Ballantine obtained half of the financing from Grosset and Dunlap—which since the previous year had been owned jointly by Random House; Harper and Brothers; Scribner; Little, Brown; and the Book-of-the-Month Club—and half from Curtis Publishing Company. In addition to funds, this arrangement gave Ballantine access to the titles published by Grosset and Dunlap and the firms which owned it, as well as access to the Curtis Magazine distribution network.

In August 1945 Ballantine and Company became Bantam Books—a name suggested by Bernard Geis, then an editor at Grosset and Dunlap—with Ballantine as president, Pitkin as vice-president and editor, and Kramer as treasurer. The board of directors included Cass Canfield of Harper, Bennett Cerf of Random House, John O'Connor of Grosset and Dunlap, and Meredith Wood of the Book-of-the-Month Club. The firm's first office was located at Grosset and Dunlap's headquarters at 1107 Broadway in New York.

Released on 3 January 1946, Bantam's first twenty titles included Mark Twain's *Life on the Mississippi*, John Steinbeck's *The Grapes of Wrath*, F. Scott Fitzgerald's *The Great Gatsby*, and Budd Schulberg's *What Makes Sammy Run?* After the initial list, Bantam published four titles a month. In 1947 the monthly output was increased to six titles. The following year Bantam initiated a book-and-film tie-in program: Frances Winwar's *Joan of Arc* (1948)

was intended to capitalize on Victor Fleming's film version, which had been released earlier that year. Later book-movie tie-ins included Leon Uris's *Battle Cry* (1954), Steinbeck's *East of Eden* (1955), and Pierre Boulle's *The Bridge over the River Kwai* (1957).

In 1949 Bantam began issuing a monthly list of its best-sellers, the first such list in the twenty-five-cent-book field. At the top of the first list were Lillian Ross's *The Stranger* and Worth Hedden's *The Other Room*. The following year Ballantine established a London subsidiary, Transworld Publishers, Limited for the publication, under the Corgi imprint, of Bantam Books. This move coincided with Pocket Books's establishment of a British subsidiary, Pocket Books, Limited. Transworld now operates independently of Bantam, and non-Bantam books also appear in Britain as Corgis. Also in 1950, Bantam moved to 25 West Forty-fifth Street.

Bantam was the first to raise the price of paperback books from twenty-five cents to thirty-five cents with its Bantam Giants in 1950, and then to fifty cents in 1951. Other paperback houses quickly followed suit.

After a series of disputes with the board of directors, Ballantine was forced out of Bantam in February 1952; he went on to establish Ballantine Books. Pitkin served as acting president of Bantam until January 1954, when he also left the firm. Oscar Dystel was hired as president in July 1954. At that time Bantam, along with the rest of the paperback industry, was losing money due to rising costs and overproduction. Dystel recalled millions of copies of books from the wholesalers' warehouses and cut back on initial printings of new titles. He also reduced the proportion of western novels in Bantam's list. By 1955 the firm was again showing a profit. It moved in 1959 to 271 Madison Avenue.

An early Bantam Books advertisement (continued overleaves)

CONTINUED FROM PRECEDING PAGE

5.

SCARAMOUCHE

By RAFAEL SABATINI. Love and adventure during the Reign of Terror in France. Sabatini's first and biggest best seller. (Novel)

6.

A MURDER BY MARRIAGE

By ROBERT G. DEAN. In which tough-minded Tony Hunter finds himself lured into a meaty murder case. (Mystery)

7.

THE GRAPES OF WRATH

By JOHN STEINBECK. Steinbeck's ninth book and biggest best seller. It won him the Pulitzer Prize. (Novel)

8.

THE GREAT GATSBY

By F. SCOTT FITZGERALD. The most talked-about novel of this great writer. Love and adventure on Long Island. (Novel)

9.

ROGUE MALE

By GEOFFREY HOUSEHOLD. The movie *Man Hunt* was made from this spy story about a big game hunter who stalked a Dictator. (Spy)

10.

SOUTH MOON UNDER

By MARJORIE KINNAN RAWLINGS. A great and beautiful novel about the Florida backwoods by the best selling author of *The Yearling.* (Novel)

11.

MR. & MRS. CUGAT

By ISABEL SCOTT RORICK. A surprise best seller. The loves and laughter of a married couple. (Humor)

12.

THEN THERE WERE THREE

By GEOFFREY HOMES. A carefully plotted story of murder in a small California town. (Mystery)

In 1964 Curtis Publishing Company sold its stock in Bantam to Grosset and Dunlap, and Bantam signed a distribution agreement with Select Magazines. Kramer, the last of the three founders of the firm, left in 1967.

Bantam Books was sold in 1968, along with the parent firm of Grosset and Dunlap, to a conglomerate, National General Corporation. In 1973 National General Corporation was acquired by the American Financial Corporation; the following year Bantam was sold to an Italian conglomerate, IFI International. In 1977 IFI sold a controlling interest in Bantam to the Bertelsmann Publishing Group of West Germany. Dystel was made a consultant in 1980; he was replaced as chief executive officer by Louis Wolfe, who was brought in from Avon Books. Marc Jaffe was promoted from editor in chief to president and publisher, but he left in April 1980 to head Ballantine Books (which by then had been acquired by Random House). Jack Romanos succeeded Jaffe as publisher at Bantam, which by then was the leading paperback house in the United States with twenty-two percent of the market and $85 million in annual sales. Bertelsmann became sole owner of Bantam Books in May 1981.

Although most of Bantam's roughly 400 titles per year are reprints, the firm has published an increasing number of original titles, especially westerns, romances, mysteries, thrillers, and science fiction. Among westerns, Bantam has issued more than forty originals by Louis L'Amour. On a subscription basis, the firm has inaugurated The Louis L'Amour Collection, with a choice of cloth or leather bindings. The firm also published the western novels of Frederick D. Glidden, who wrote under the pseudonym Luke Short until his death in 1975.

In addition to publishing over 100 original romance novels by Barbara Cartland, Bantam has reprinted romances by Emilie Loring, Eugenia Price, and Grace Livingston Hill. Occasional original mysteries, such as *The Name Is Archer* (1955) by Kenneth Millar under the pseudonym Ross Macdonald, have supplemented reprints by Macdonald, Agatha Christie, Rex Stout, and Patricia Wentworth. Some of the firm's best-selling books have been thrillers by Robert Ludlum, Frederick Forsyth, and Jack Higgins.

Science fiction originals include Ray Bradbury's *Timeless Stories for Today and Tomorrow* (1952); Samuel Delany's *Dhalgren* (1975), *Triton* (1976), *Tale of Nevèrÿon* (1979), and *The Heavenly Breakfast* (1979); and Philip K. Dick's *Valis* (1981). Bantam

has also reprinted works by Harry Harrison, L. Sprague de Camp, Lin Carter, Ursula K. Le Guin, and Frederik Pohl.

Original titles in Bantam's general fiction list include William Inge's *Splendor in the Grass* (1961), MacKinlay Kantor's *If the South Had Won the Civil War* (1961), Robert Gover's *Going for Mr. Big* (1973), and Jacqueline Susann's *Yargo* (1979). In 1979 Bantam and William Morrow and Company established Perigord Press, a joint imprint for "the simultaneous acquisition of hardcover and paperback rights to works of fiction and nonfiction." The following year Bantam published Tom Robbins's *Still Life with Woodpecker* under its own imprint in both hardcover and paperback. In 1982 Bantam published as hardcover originals Jerzy Kosinski's *Pinball* and John M. Del Vecchio's first novel, *The Thirteenth Valley*.

While some of its original titles have been best-sellers, Bantam's most successful books have been reprints. Topping the list is William Peter Blatty's *The Exorcist* (1973), with sales of twelve million copies. (*The Exorcist* was originally sold to Bantam for a $26,000 advance; Bantam then leased the book to Harper and Row to take advantage of the prestige and promotion that came with an initial publication in hardcover.) John Steinbeck's *The Pearl* (1948, 1956), Jacqueline Susann's *Valley of the Dolls* (1966), David Rubin's *Everything You Always Wanted to Know about Sex but Were Afraid to Ask* (1971), and Peter Benchley's *Jaws* (1975) each have sold eight million copies. The Steinbeck title was also published under Bantam's Pathfinder imprint, a line of contemporary works aimed at junior and senior high school readers. Other Bantam imprints have been the Minibooks, Peacock Press (an art books division created by Ian Ballantine, who returned to Bantam in 1974), New Age Books, and Skylark Books for Young Readers.

Although it did not originate the concept (it was preceded in the field by Penguin, New American Library, and Pocket Books), Bantam has become identified with the production of "instant" books of nonfiction on topical subjects—the Bantam Extras. The first of these was *The Warren Commission Report on the Assassination of President Kennedy* (1964), which went on sale eighty hours after the 385,000-word report was released to the public. More than seventy Bantam Extras have been published, including *The Report of the Commission on Obscenity and Pornography* (1970), *The Pentagon Papers* (1971), *The Watergate Hearings* (1973), and *The White House Transcripts* (1974). Bantam has been located since 1970 at 666 Fifth Avenue, New York 10019.

References:

"For Marc Jaffe of Bantam Books, All of Publishing, Hardcover and Paperback, Is a Continuum—and Flexibility Is the Thing," *Publishers Weekly*, 209 (22 March 1976): 24-27;

Clarence Petersen, *The Bantam Story: Thirty Years of*

Paperback Publishing (New York: Bantam, 1975).

"Something to Crow About: Bantam's 25th Year," *Publishers' Weekly*, 197 (22 June 1970): 30-35;

—David Dzwonkoski
Philip Dematteis

Barnes and Noble Books
(New York: 1971-)
Barnes and Noble
(New York: 1931-1971)

NEW YORK
BARNES & NOBLE, INC.
1960s

1950s

Although the imprint of Barnes and Noble, Incorporated began in 1931, its origin lies in the establishment of the Barnes and Noble bookstore in 1917, with William R. Barnes as president and G. Clifford Noble as secretary-treasurer. In 1929 Noble sold his interest in the business to Barnes's son, John W. Barnes, leaving William R. Barnes as the company's sole director.

Barnes and Noble entered the publishing field in 1931 with a line of books summarizing the material in various college courses; the publishing division was headed by A. W. Littlefield. The College Outline Series became the most famous of the firm's educational lines. By 1949, when Littlefield left to start his own educational publishing house, Barnes and Noble had published sixty-five of these titles; among them was *Outlines of Shakespeare's Plays* (1934), a book of synopses and background material by Homer A. Watt, Karl J. Holzknecht, and Raymond Ross. The firm also reprints classics by Dickens, Austen, Thackeray, and Cooper, as well

as literary criticism such as T. S. Eliot's *The Sacred Wood* (1960) and Northrop Frye's *T. S. Eliot* (1966); but its emphasis remains more technical than literary.

John W. Barnes became president of the firm in 1942; his father, who was then made chairman of the board, died in 1945. John W. Barnes died in 1964. In 1969, the company was bought by Ampel, Incorporated, which sold the publishing division to Harper and Row two years later. Reorganized as Barnes and Noble Books at 10 East Fifty-third Street, New York 10022, the firm has a current list of more than 500 titles.

References:

"Obituary Notes: John W. Barnes," *Publishers' Weekly*, 186 (28 December 1964): 52;

"William R. Barnes [obituary]," *New York Times*, 10 February 1945, p. 11.

—Carol Wilkinson

William R. Barnes   *G. Clifford Noble*

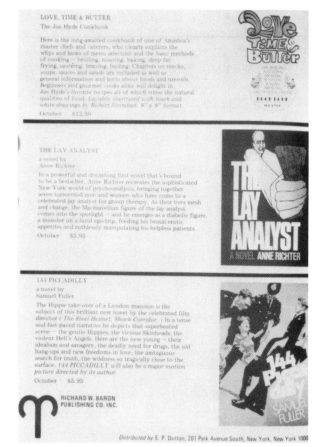

1971 advertisement

Richard W. Baron Publishing Company
(New York: 1969-   )

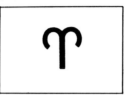

Located first at 243A East Forty-ninth Street and later at 210 Park Avenue South in New York, the Richard W. Baron Publishing Company, Incorporated was founded in 1969 as a publisher of general trade books and works on civil rights, social activism, and similar topics. Richard Baron was formerly the owner and publisher of the Dial Press. The firm's books are distributed by E. P. Dutton. Baron titles have included Nat Hentoff's *Black Anti-Semitism and Jewish Racism* (1969), R. Alfred Hassler's *Saigon, U.S.A.* (1970), and Chandler Brossard's *Wake Up, We're Almost There* (1971). The firm's chief literary author—before he moved to Delacorte—was Thomas Berger, whose *Vital Parts* was first published by Baron in 1970. Baron has also republished Berger's first two books, *Crazy in Berlin* (1970) and *Reinhart in Love* (1970). Baron published three titles in 1984. The firm is presently located at 20 Fifth Avenue, New York 10011.

Reference:

"Baron Announces First Trade List," *Publishers' Weekly*, 195 (7 April 1969): 33.

—*Peter Dzwonkoski*

Barse and Hopkins
(New York; Newark, New Jersey: 1909-1928)
Barse and Company
(New York: 1928-1932)

Barse and Hopkins, the publisher of Robert W. Service, was formed in 1909 when William J. Barse, who had operated in Chicago as Brewer, Barse and Company, moved to New York and went into partnership with John H. Hopkins. In 1922 Barse and Hopkins was located at 23 East Twenty-sixth Street, New York; by 1925 it had moved to 21 Division Street, Newark, New Jersey.

Service, the bard of the Yukon, was a blue-chip discovery for Barse and Hopkins. The first Barse and Hopkins catalogue included Service's *Ballads of a Cheechako* (1909). The firm later issued his *The Spell of the Yukon* (1913); *Rhymes of a Red Cross Man* (1916), which topped the general nonfiction best-seller list in 1917 and 1918; *Ballads of a Bohemian* (1921); and *The Master of the Microbe* (1926).

Barse and Hopkins's standbys were reprints of classics. In 1910 the firm had almost three dozen reprint series in bindings ranging from paper wrappers to Persian ooze. Authors reprinted included Coleridge, Kipling, Stevenson, Dickens, the Brownings, Goldsmith, Tennyson, Longfellow, Thoreau, Hawthorne, Irving, Poe, Bryant, Lowell, Wilde, and Omar Khayyám. The firm also relied on sales of manuals on etiquette, car repair, civil service examinations, and games, as well as albums for family memorabilia. Perennially popular and highlighted in every catalogue was Dr. J.R. Phelps's *Birthday Horoscopes,* which had originally been published by Brewer, Barse and Company in 1908.

Barse and Hopkins's offerings in children's fiction reflected shifts in popular taste over the years. In the 1920s, the patriotism of the post-World War I era was manifested in the Famous Americans for Young Readers, Boy Scout Life, and Camp Fire Boy series. The Yank Brown and Big League series were geared to sports, while the College Life series—including Gilbert Patten's *Boltwood of Yale* (1914) and *Sons of Old Eli* (1923)—and

1928 advertisement

Everett T. Tomlinson's tales of Tait School had student heroes. A few flapper novels for adolescent girls also appeared under the firm's imprint.

When Hopkins withdrew in 1928 to become a literary agent—he later formed another publishing company, John H. Hopkins and Son—Barse continued in business as Barse and Company. Located at 200 Fifth Avenue in New York, with the warehouse in New Jersey, Barse and Company went bankrupt in 1932. Its stock was acquired by Grosset and Dunlap. Barse died in 1951.

Reference:

"Obituary Notes [William J. Barse]," *Publishers' Weekly*, 160 (18 August 1951): 629.

—Sharon Ann Jaeger

Basic Books
(New York: 1952-   )

Basic Books, Incorporated was the outgrowth of a book club started in 1945 for the distribution of books on psychoanalysis and psychiatry. By 1952 the club had moved from 357 Bleecker Street to 59 Fourth Avenue, New York, and had begun to publish books. Arthur J. Rosenthal was president of the firm; its first chairman was Nicholas Freydberg. Some of the firm's most important works have been in its original specializations, psychoanalysis and psychiatry, although Basic Books has expanded into other areas of science and social science. The firm has published more than ten titles by Jean Piaget, as well as Ernest Jones's three-volume *The Life and Work of Sigmund Freud* (1953-1957) and a five-volume collection of Freud's papers (1959). Other noteworthy scientists and social scientists on the firm's list include Claude Levi-Strauss, Daniel Bell, Oscar Lewis, Rollo May, Lucien Pye, Thomas Szasz, Christopher Lasch, Isaac Asimov, and Kurt Gödel. Philosopher Robert Nozick's *Anarchy, State and Utopia* (1974) won the National Book Award, and Douglas Hofstadter's *Gödel, Escher, Bach: An Eternal Golden Braid* (1979) and Paul Starr's *The Social Transformation of American Medicine* (1983) were awarded the Pulitzer Prize.

The few literary titles published by the firm include *Poets on Poetry* (1966), edited by Howard Nemerov; *Antiworlds: Poetry* (1966) by Andrei Voznesensky; *The Desert* (1970), a novel by psychiatrist Allen Wheelis; *The Way of the Samurai* (1977), a nonfiction work by Jocho Yamamoto on the novelist Yukio Mishima; and *On Moral Fiction* (1978) by John Gardner. Rosenthal organized several book clubs during the late 1950s: the Library of Science, the Natural History Book Club, and the Readers' Subscription. He sold all but the last to Crowell-Collier Macmillan in 1962. Basic Books has been a subsidiary of Harper and Row since 1969 and has been relocated at the parent firm's New York headquarters, 10 East Fifty-third Street, New York 10022. Rosenthal left in 1972 to become director of Harvard University Press. Irving Kristol was senior editor from 1969 until 1979; he was succeeded by Midge Decter, who left in 1981. Martin Kessler is president, copublisher, and editorial director.

Reference:

"Basic Books' First Ten Years of Publishing," *Publishers' Weekly*, 184 (30 December 1963): 39.

—David Dzwonkoski

important
new
basic books
in
psychiatry
and child
guidance

SPECIALIZED TECHNIQUES IN PSYCHOTHERAPY

Edited by Gustav Bychowski, M.D.
and J. Louise Despert, M.D.

The first-hand experience of nineteen of the country's leading psychiatrists in the treatment of special situations in mental disorders. "An excellent book that will bring all of us up to date in psychotherapeutic theories and proceedings."—Nolan D. C. Lewis, M.D., Director, New York State Psychiatric Institute. $5.00

EGO PSYCHOLOGY AND THE PSYCHOSES

By Paul Federn, M.D.

A rich sourcebook containing many heretofore unpublished papers by one of Freud's most gifted collaborators who discovered the way to successfully treat and cure the psychotic.

To be published in November, $6.00

Further Contributions to

THE THEORY AND TECHNIQUE OF PSYCHOANALYSIS

By Sandor Ferenczi, M.D.

The first American edition of a major work which has just had its third printing in England. Recommended as "of outstanding significance" in Dr. Karl Menninger's A Guide to Psychiatric Books. $5.00

LIFE AND WAYS OF THE TWO-YEAR-OLD

By Louise P. Woodcock

The most comprehensive guide available for the handling and understanding of the two-year-old, based on studies made at the Harriet Johnson Nursery School. For parents and teachers. $3.00

LIFE AND WAYS OF THE SEVEN-TO EIGHT YEAR OLD

By Barbara Biber, Lois B. Murphy, Louise P. Woodcock and Irma S. Black

A study of ten children using psychological and sociological methods to determine better ways to understand and educate them. For teachers, psychologists and parents. $4.50

Distributed in the United States and its Possessions by the sales representatives of Rinehart & Company.

BASIC BOOKS, INC. 59 Fourth Avenue, New York 3, New York

1952 advertisement

Belmont Productions
(New York: 1960-1973)
Belmont-Tower Books
(New York: 1973-1975)
Tower Publications
(New York: 1975-1982)

In May 1960 Archie Comic Publications formed Belmont Productions, Incorporated to publish Merit paperback books. John L. Goldwater of Archie Comics was president; Louis H. Silberkleit, also of Archie Comics, was first vice-president; and Samuel H. Post, formerly of Hillman Books, was vice-president of Belmont and editor in chief of Merit Books. The address of the new firm was 66 Leonard Street in New York. Before any books were published, Belmont Productions, having discovered that Merit Books had already been used as an imprint for a paperback house, changed the name of its line to Belmont Books.

Distributed by the Publishers Distributing Corporation, Belmont Books published both reprints and original works, with an emphasis on fiction. Four books per month were released starting in August 1960. Post planned to emphasize "both quality titles and those with a strong mass market appeal." Reprints in 1960 included *Temptress* by André Maurois, *The Question* by Henri Alleg, *Payola Woman* by Carson Bingham, *Johnny Havoc* by John Jakes, *The Slave* by Micheline Maurel, *Cage of Passion* by Isa Mari, and *Hong Kong Kill* by Bryan Peters. All were priced at thirty-five cents. *Varieties of Love* by Herbert Kubly was Belmont's first fifty-cent book.

From the start, Belmont planned to exploit media tie-ins. Alex Karmel's *Mary Ann*, published in hardcover by Viking in 1958, was retitled *Something Wild* when released as a film in 1962; Belmont published the paperback as *Something Wild*, with the subtitle *Mary Ann*. Belmont published novels based on television shows such as the "M-Squad" and "City Detective" series. The firm also developed series not related to other media, such as Gardner F. Fox's Kothar novels.

Bartell Media Corporation began distributing Belmont Books in 1965. Belmont moved to 1116 First Avenue; Gail Wendroff became managing editor, and editor in chief the following year. In 1969 Belmont Productions was merged with Tower Publications, and Belmont moved to the Tower offices at 185 Madison Avenue. Peter McCurtin was made editor in chief of Belmont Books; under his leadership the firm developed an emphasis on sexual themes. Belmont published several original science fiction novels in double volumes, among them *The Flame of Tridar* by Lin Carter with *The Peril of the Starmen* by Kris Neville (1967).

Although Belmont and Tower were under the same ownership, the imprints remained separate until 1973, when they became Belmont-Tower Books, Incorporated. Belmont-Tower Books were distributed by the Capitol Distributing Company. In 1975 Belmont-Tower Books, Incorporated became Tower Publications, Incorporated, with Belmont-Tower as an imprint. In 1977 Belmont-Tower Books moved to 2 Park Avenue. On 18 August 1982, Offset Paperback Manufacturers of Dallas, Pennsylvania, the major secured creditor of Tower Publications, bought most of Tower's assets at a bankruptcy auction. Offset said that it would sell the assets, which included Tower Books, Leisure Books, and Midwood Books, as it did not intend to become a publishing house. All of the imprints have ceased to exist.

References:
"Belmont Denies FTC Charges on Reprints," *Publishers' Weekly*, 185 (23 March 1964): 34;
"Court Approves Auction of Tower Books Assets," *Publishers Weekly*, 222 (17 September 1982): 61.

—Martha A. Bartter

The Berkley Publishing Corporation

(New York: 1954-   )

A BERKLEY MEDALLION BOOK
published by
BERKLEY PUBLISHING CORP.

With former Avon Books executives Frederick Klein and Charles R. Byrne as president and executive vice-president/editor in chief, respectively, Berkley began publishing in 1954 at 145 West Fifty-seventh Street, New York, with two magazines—*Chic,* a women's periodical, and *News.* A year later, these were discontinued in favor of paperback reprints; among the first of these was James Gould Cozzens's *S. S. San Pedro.* In 1956 Klein quit the firm, leaving Byrne as president and editor in chief. Under Byrne, Berkley published primarily westerns and mysteries, but also reprints of Flaubert's *Salambo* (1955) and Robert Penn Warren's *Night Rider* (1956). After Stephen Conland became president in 1960, Berkley emphasized prominent science fiction writers Philip José Farmer, Philip K. Dick, Roger Zelazny, Clifford D. Simak, and Robert E. Howard.

Berkley moved twice in the early 1960s—first to 101 Fifth Avenue, then to East Twenty-sixth Street. In 1965 Berkley became the paperback arm of G. P. Putnam's Sons and moved to 200 Madison Avenue. In 1975 Putnam was bought by MCA, Incorporated. The firm continued to publish high-quality science fiction: among its important reprints were Robert A. Heinlein's *Stranger in a Strange Land* (1968)—Berkley's best-selling title in 1969—and Frank Herbert's *Dune Messiah* (1975) and *Children of Dune* (1976). Berkley's more recent best-sellers,

including books by Lawrence Sanders and Anton Myrer, exemplify the firm's successful expansion into general fiction since its takeover by Putnam.

In the spring of 1979 Berkley acquired Jove Publications, Incorporated—formerly Pyramid Books—from Harcourt Brace Jovanovich. Berkley's and Jove's publishing activities remain separate, but the two companies share sales operations. In 1982 Berkley achieved a major success with its paperback version of the movie *E. T.,* William Kotzwinkle's *E. T. the Extra-Terrestrial,* which sold over three million copies.

In July 1982, the Putnam Group absorbed Grosset & Dunlap, and their paperback imprints, Charter and Ace, became divisions of the Berkeley Publishing Corporation, along with Jove and Berkeley Books. Peter Israel, president of the Putnam Publishing Group, also became president of The Berkeley Publishing Corporation in 1983; subsequently David Shanks became president. The four divisions of Berkeley published over 800 books in 1985. Berkley's address is 200 Madison Avenue, New York 10016.

Reference:
Madalynne Porter, "Berkley and Jove Set Up to Share Sales Operation," *Publishers Weekly,* 215 (26 March 1979): 20-21.

—David Dzwonkoski

Cover for 1965 double science fiction volume

Cover for 1955 reprint of a classic novel

Walter J. Black
(New York; Roslyn, New York: 1928-   )
Plymouth Publishing Company
(New York: 1923-1928)

Reg. U. S. Pat. Off.

WALTER J. BLACK, Inc.

FLOWER HILL

ROSLYN, N. Y. 11576

Subscription reprints are the specialty of Walter J. Black, Incorporated, which Black founded in New York in 1923 as the Plymouth Publishing Company. The company was incorporated in 1928 under its founder's name. The firm distributed a one-volume mail-order edition of Shakespeare and reprinted works by Ibsen, Kipling, Stevenson, and Tolstoy.

In 1941 Black organized the Classics Club, a subscription service offering low-priced editions. A committee consisting of Pearl S. Buck, John Kieran, William Lyon Phelps, and Hendrik Willem van Loon picked the first of the club selections, an edition of *The Autobiography of Benjamin Franklin* (1941). In March 1942 Black started the Detective Book Club, another subscription service, which features an omnibus volume of three mystery novels each month.

In subsequent years the house created four more book clubs and subscription series: the Golden Giants of Literature series in 1948, the Zane Grey Library in 1950, the Erle Stanley Gardner Mystery Library in 1963, and Ellery Queen's Mystery Club in 1978. The firm moved to Flower Hill, Roslyn, New York 11576 in 1954. Black's son, Theodore, has been president since his father's death in 1958.

References:

"Classics as Merchandise," *Publishers' Weekly*, 127 (30 March 1935): 1338;

"Walter J. Black [obituary]," *Publishers' Weekly*, 173 (28 April 1958): 28.

—Shirley Ricker

The Bobbs-Merrill Company
(Indianapolis: 1903-1985)

The Bobbs-Merrill Company was formed in 1903 when the Bowen-Merrill Company of Indianapolis underwent a reorganization. William C. Bobbs, president of Bowen-Merrill since 1895, replaced Silas Bowen in the partnership. The reorganization did not alter the firm's publishing policy, since Bobbs and John Jay Curtis, head of the trade department and the firm's New York office, had dominated Bowen-Merrill's operation for the previous two decades. Bobbs-Merrill inherited strong law and textbook divisions, but it was the firm's list

of popular fiction that had brought it into the forefront of American trade publishing. In the 1890s Curtis had developed the innovative promotional and advertising techniques—single-title advertising, colored book jackets, full-page newspaper ads, and blurbs—that did much to stimulate sales and helped Bowen-Merrill become one of the leading publishers of best-selling fiction.

At the time of the reorganization Bobbs-Merrill possessed a strong backlist of fiction, including L. Frank Baum's *The Wonderful Wizard of Oz*, orig-

Walter J. Black

Theodore M. Black, Sr., president of Walter J. Black since 1958

John Jay Curtis, who became president of Bobbs-Merrill in 1926

D. Laurance Chambers, president of Bobbs-Merrill from 1935 to 1958

THE **BOBBS-MERRILL** COMPANY, INC.
A SUBSIDIARY OF HOWARD W. SAMS & CO., INC.
Publishers • INDIANAPOLIS • NEW YORK

inally published in 1900 by George M. Hill, which—before it went out of copyright in 1950—sold more than three million copies for the firm. Between 1903 and 1915 Bobbs-Merrill published a phenomenal number of commercially successful novels, including Miriam Michelson's *In the Bishop's Carriage* (1904), Meredith Nicholson's *The House of a Thousand Candles* (1905), Herbert Quick's *Double Trouble* (1906), Brand Whitlock's *The Turn of the Balance* (1907), Louis Joseph Vance's *The Brass Bowl* (1907) and *The Black Bag* (1908), Emerson Hough's *54-40 or Fight* (1909), Gaston Leroux's *The Phantom of the Opera* (1911), Vaughn Kester's *The Prodigal Judge* (1911) and *The Just and the Unjust* (1912), William B. Maxwell's *The Devil's Garden* (1914), and Owen Johnson's *The Salamander* (1914).

Most of the firm's top-selling books and their authors are no longer read or remembered. One tremendously popular novelist whose work Bobbs-Merrill started publishing in the first decade of the twentieth century, however, is still popular: mystery writer Mary Roberts Rinehart. Beginning in 1908 with *The Circular Staircase*, Rinehart's first novel, Bobbs-Merrill had published eight of her novels by 1913; most of them were highly successful. Her second, *The Man in Lower Ten* (1909), became the first mystery novel to reach the top ten on the annual best-seller list. Other popular Bobbs-Merrill authors of the period included David Graham Phillips, Zona Gale, Gene Stratton-Porter, and humorist Gelett Burgess.

Bobbs-Merrill also became involved in magazine publishing. Besides being profitable in themselves, magazines offered the incentive to authors of built-in advertising for their books, which Bobbs-Merrill would publish after serialization in the magazine. Bobbs-Merrill purchased the *Reader*, a literary journal, from Mitchell Kennerley in 1904, and the popular *Home Magazine* in 1906. Although Bobbs-Merrill was able to lure authors into its fold through the magazines, both publications incurred financial losses and were sold in 1908.

Partly due to its unsuccessful venture in mag-

azine publishing, the firm found itself more than three-quarters of a million dollars in debt. Bobbs, Curtis, and Charles W. Merrill sold 2,250 shares of common stock to other members of the firm, bringing in the capital necessary to enable Bobbs-Merrill to continue publishing under the same management. In 1909 the company sold its bookstore operation to W. K. Stewart, an Indianapolis bookseller.

Even with its influx of new capital, by 1915 Bobbs-Merrill was having problems; the firm's string of best-sellers had come to a temporary halt. The law and textbook divisions continued to be successful, but the trade division was showing less and less profit. The board of directors eliminated single-title advertising—a serious blow to Curtis's promotional strategy. In 1916 the board considered doing away with the trade division entirely and concentrating exclusively on law and educational books. Around this time also Bobbs-Merrill moved its offices to 18 University Square in Indianapolis.

Although the trade division did not become prominent again until the mid-1920s, the firm did publish popular and critical successes during this period. These included Quick's *The Brown Mouse* (1915) and *The Fairview Idea* (1919); Harold R. Peat's wartime memoir *Private Peat* (1917); two popular novels by Irving Bacheller, *The Light in the Clearing* (1917) and *A Man for the Ages* (1919); and Talbot Mundy's *The Ivory Trail* (1919). Between 1917 and 1921 Bobbs-Merrill published eight books by Ring Lardner. Bowen-Merrill and Bobbs-Merrill also published more than sixty books by the Indiana poet James Whitcomb Riley between the late 1880s and the early 1920s.

Hewitt Howland, Curtis's chief collaborator in developing the list of popular novels that had brought the firm so much success, left in 1925 to become editor of *Century* magazine. But at about this time the firm had the good fortune to discover three unknown authors whose first books—as well as most of their subsequent efforts—were highly successful. Bruce Barton, son of the distinguished

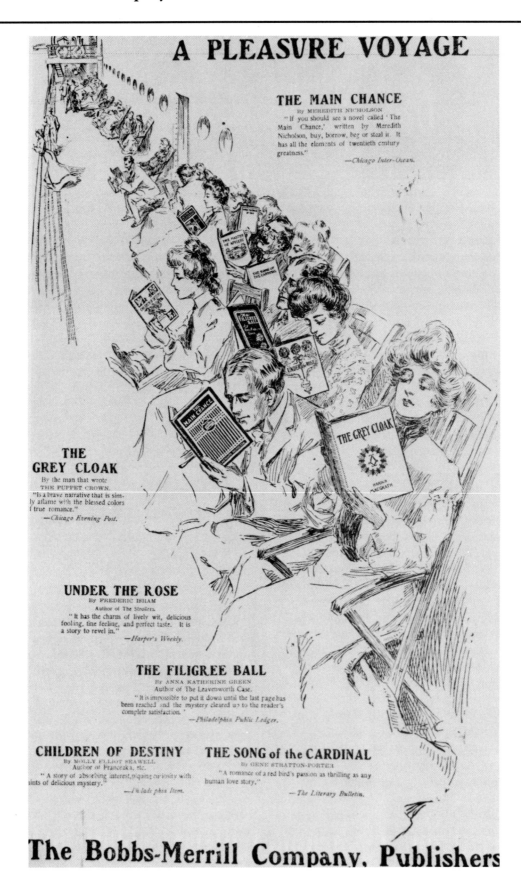

1903 advertisement (New York Times)

clergyman (and Bobbs-Merrill author) W. E. Barton, wrote *The Man Nobody Knows* (1925), which characterizes Christ as the father of modern business and depicts the events of his life as masterpieces of corporate strategy. The work was an instant best-seller. Barton wrote more books for Bobbs-Merrill, including *The Book Nobody Knows* (1926), a successful follow-up to his first work. Richard Halliburton's first book, the travel memoir *The Royal Road to Romance* (1925), was a spectacular best-seller. Bobbs-Merrill published nine more Halliburton titles before he was lost in the South Pacific in 1939 while involved in yet another adventure. John Erskine's first novel, *The Private Life of Helen of Troy* (1925), was one of the top selling books of 1926. Erskine wrote thirteen more books for Bobbs-Merrill between 1925 and 1937, though none equaled the success of his first.

Bobbs died in February 1926, and Curtis became president. In the same year Bobbs-Merrill moved to 724 North Meridian Street in Indianapolis. Titles published by the firm in the late 1920s included Janet Fairbank's *The Smiths* (1925), W. E. Barton's *The Life of Abraham Lincoln* (1925), Julia Peterkin's *Scarlet Sister Mary* (1928), and Marquis James's *The Raven: A Biography of Sam Houston* (1929). It was during this period also that Bobbs-Merrill published Earl Derr Biggers's first three novels about his detective Charlie Chan: *The House without a Key* (1925), *The Chinese Parrot* (1926), and *Behind That Curtain* (1928). Biggers wrote a total of six Chan novels, as well as several other books, for Bobbs-Merrill. Bobbs-Merrill also published five of Robert Nathan's novels between 1927 and 1931.

In June 1929 Bobbs's widow and his son Julian, then treasurer of Bobbs-Merrill, sold their interest in the firm to several other stockholders. Bobbs-Merrill went public at this time, offering more than 30,000 shares of common stock for sale. Curtis retained his position as president, but D. Laurance Chambers, vice-president and manager of the trade department, emerged as the dominant figure.

In 1931 Curtis died and Chambers assumed control of Bobbs-Merrill, although he was not elected president until 1935. Chambers moved up to chairman of the board in 1953 when Lowe Berger assumed the presidency, but Chambers remained in control of the firm. Though Chambers had served as editor during Curtis's best-seller years, as president he adopted a much more conservative approach to the trade division.

Bobbs-Merrill lists of the 1930s, 1940s, and 1950s featured works by Biggers; Inglis Fletcher;

Pietro de Donato; Alice Tisdale Hobart; and Irvin S. Cobb, whose memoir *Exit Laughing* was one of the most popular books of 1941. Fiction published during Chambers's tenure included Emily Hahn's *With Naked Foot* (1934) and *Affair* (1935); Andrew Lytle's *The Long Night* (1936), *At the Moon's Inn* (1941), and *A Name for Evil* (1947); Ayn Rand's *The Fountainhead* (1943); William Styron's first novel, *Lie Down in Darkness* (1951); and early works by Mark Harris.

In 1958 Bobbs-Merrill moved again, this time to 1720 East Thirty-eighth Street in Indianapolis. In November of that year, amid rumors that the firm was in difficulty, Howard W. Sams, owner of the Waldemer Press, purchased a controlling interest in Bobbs-Merrill for one million dollars. Sams reorganized the firm quickly, bringing in M. Hughes Miller as president. Sams was elected chairman of the board in 1958; Chambers became chairman emeritus.

In trying to restore Bobbs-Merrill to its former eminence, one of Sams's first moves was to strengthen the educational division. In 1959 the Public School Publishing Company and the Gregory Publishing Company, two established educational publishing firms, were acquired. In 1960 Bobbs-Merrill purchased Scribner's elementary textbooks lists for science and social science. The following year the firm's newly created college division took over the Liberal Arts Press, through which it acquired a quality paperback list of more than 180 titles. Former Bobbs-Merrill treasurer Leo C. Gobin became president of the firm in 1965.

Sams was also determined to revitalize the languishing trade department. He reinstated some of Curtis's promotional strategies; for example, he spent more than $100,000 to promote the latest edition of Irma Rombauer's *The Joy of Cooking*, which Bobbs-Merrill had first published in 1936. But the trade department never regained its former stature, and Bobbs-Merrill's main emphasis would be on educational, juvenile, and specialized publishing. These tendencies became even clearer after ITT Corporation acquired Howard W. Sams and Company, and thus a controlling interest in Bobbs-Merrill, in 1966. By 1978 Stanley Sills, general manager of ITT Publishing and chairman of Bobbs-Merrill, was officially moving to de-emphasize trade publishing. Sills fired seven top people in the New York headquarters of the trade department and announced that the company was reducing its annual trade list by half.

During the 1960s and 1970s Bobbs-Merrill published six books by Colette; science fiction novels by Robert Silverberg, Jack Vance, and Jack Williamson; and books by Fielding Dawson, Robert Joe Stout, and Edward Gorey. In the late 1960s—for the first time since James Whitcomb Riley's heyday—Bobbs-Merrill began publishing contemporary poetry. Titles by Carol Bergé, Michael Brownstein, LeRoi Jones, Joel Oppenheimer, Barbara Howes, Robert Vas Dias, and Anne Waldman appeared on the Bobbs-Merrill lists of the 1960s and 1970s. The firm also brought out several poetry anthologies, including Waldman's *The World Anthology* (1969) and *Another World* (1971); Edward Lucie-Smith's *Primer of Experimental Poetry* (1971); and William Heyen's *American Poets in 1976* (1976). Bobbs-Merrill also published four collections of Sam Shepard's plays, as well as collections of plays by Jones and by Ed Bullins. The firm's nonfiction list featured Oppenheimer, Nikki Giovanni, Robin Skelton, Paul Goodman, and Peter Levi.

By the end of the 1970s Bobbs-Merrill was no longer an active publisher of contemporary literature. By 1980, with its Indianapolis offices at 4300 West Sixty-second Street, the firm had limited its commitment to trade publishing almost entirely to its cookbook line. In April 1985 Bobbs-Merrill was acquired by Macmillan. Macmillan deemed the Bobbs-Merrill operation uneconomical and dissolved the firm in May.

References:

"Bobbs-Merrill Reorganizes New York Trade Office," *Publishers Weekly*, 215 (14 May 1979): 126;

Edwin H. Cady, ed., "Studies in the Bobbs-Merrill Papers," *Indiana University Bookman*, 8 (March 1967);

John J. Curtis, "Reminiscences of a Publisher," *Publishers' Weekly*, 117 (10 May 1930): 2419-2420;

The Hoosier House (Indianapolis: Bobbs-Merrill, 1927);

Jack O'Bar, "A History of the Bobbs-Merrill Company, 1850-1940: With a Postlude through the early 1960s," Ph.D. dissertation, Indiana University, 1975;

"William C. Bobbs [obituary]," *Publishers' Weekly*, 109 (20 February 1926): 604-606.

—*Timothy D. Murray*

Albert and Charles Boni
(New York: 1923-1939)

Albert & Charles Boni · New York

The firm of Albert and Charles Boni was modest in size and struggled at times to survive; yet it had connections in the literary world that led to the publication of now-classic twentieth-century literature.

The Boni brothers were the sons of Charles Boni, an insurance executive, and Bertha Saslavsky Boni. Albert was born in New York City in 1892 and attended Cornell and Harvard Universities; Charles was born in Newark, New Jersey, in 1894. While Charles was still at Harvard, from which he graduated in 1915, the brothers opened the Washington Square Book Shop at 137 MacDougal Street in New York in 1913. The shop became a gathering place for the bohemian writers of Greenwich Village. From this location the Bonis published their first book, Robert Blatchford's *Not Guilty* (1914), and the *Glebe*, a short-lived (ten issues) magazine noted for its first printings of the Imagist poets. In 1915 they founded, with Harry Scherman, the Little Leather Library, a set of thirty pocket-sized reprints of classics, sold both over-the-counter and by mail for $2.98 per set. Sales reached nearly a million copies the first year. Although the Little Leather Library and the bookshop were both successful, other financial obligations forced the Bonis to sell their interest in the Little Leather Library to Scherman and Maxwell Sackheim, while the bookshop went to Frank Shay. Albert Boni established the firm of Boni and Liveright with Horace Liveright in 1917. Although Boni left the partnership in 1918, the firm retained his name until 1928, throughout the years of its greatest success.

The Boni brothers purchased the small firm of Lieber and Lewis in 1923 and founded Albert and Charles Boni in the basement of a house at 19 Barrow Street. Within months, they moved to larger quarters at 39 West Eighth Street.

Issued in 1924, the firm's first list was a mixture of the popular, such as Jim Tully's *Beggars of Life* and Will Rogers's *The Illiterate Digest,* and the more literary, such as Hugh de Selincourt's *One Little Boy.* Also in 1924, Boni published the French novelist Joris Karl Huysmans's posthumous *Down There* and reprinted his *Against the Grain,* which Lieber and Lewis had published in 1922. Among Boni's first innovations were the Cosmos Library of popular science books and the American Library, which it inaugurated with Christopher Columbus's *Journal of First Voyage to America* (1924). Edited by Van Wyck Brooks and others, the low-priced American Library series included by 1926 reprints of works by Herman Melville, Ambrose Bierce, Henry James, and Artemus Ward. Boni also began to develop an impressive list of biographies, histories, and general nonfiction. By the end of 1924 the firm had doubled its capitalization and hired Lewis S. Baer as secretary and treasurer. Boni published a few noteworthy titles in 1925—Donald Ogden Stewart's *The Crazy Fool,* de Selincourt's *Young Mischief and the Perfect Pair,* and William Carlos Williams's *In the American Grain.* One of the firm's best-sellers that year was Ford Madox Ford's *No More Parades,* which went through two printings in the first two weeks.

By far the most important year for the brothers was 1926, when they purchased the firm of their uncle, Thomas Seltzer, Incorporated, and moved to larger offices at 66 Fifth Avenue; within the year they had to move to still larger quarters at 39 West Eighth Street. Ford's *No More Parades* was followed in 1926 by its sequel, *A Man Could Stand Up,* and his nonfiction work *A Mirror to France.* Another important publication that year was Gertrude Stein's *The Making of Americans,* a year after its first edition in Paris. In response to the current interest in the French Symbolists, Boni published Charles Baudelaire's *Prose and Poetry* (1926), translated by Arthur Symons. Other 1926 titles were Edmund

Wilson's *Discordant Encounters: Plays and Dialogues;* E. R. Eddison's fantasy *The Worm Ouroboros;* the Danish writer Georg M. C. Brandes's *Jesus: A Myth;* Wilhem Bolsche's *Love-Life in Nature;* and Thornton Wilder's first book, *The Cabala.*

The firm's 1927 list revealed the Bonis' political leanings. With the publication of Upton Sinclair's novel *Oil!,* Boni became the first trade house to publish a work by Sinclair since Boni and Liveright brought out *They Call Me Carpenter* in 1922. As Boni published his *Money Writes!* (1927), *Boston* (1928), *Mental Radio* (1930), and *Mountain City* (1930), Sinclair simultaneously published the books at his own press in Pasadena, California. Boni also published in 1927 *Breaking Through* and *Marx and Lenin: The Science of Revolution* by another radical writer, Max Eastman, who later translated Leon Trotsky's *The History of the Russian Revolution* (1931) for Boni. Also in 1927 Boni began publishing *Creative Art,* which the firm billed as "the leading journal of the arts in America."

The major event of 1927 was the addition of Marcel Proust to the firm's list. Boni had obtained the rights to Proust's works when it acquired Thomas Seltzer, Incorporated, which had published translations of the second and third volumes of Proust's seven-volume *Remembrance of Things Past.* Boni published the remainder of the work, beginning with *Cities of the Plain* (1927) and continuing with *The Captive* (1929) and *The Sweet Cheat Gone* (1930), all translated by C. K. Scott Moncrieff. In 1930 Boni published a uniform edition of the complete translation to that time; two years later, the final volume, *The Past Recaptured,* appeared under the Boni imprint in a translation by Frederick A. Blossom. Thornton Wilder's *The Bridge of San Luis Rey* (1927), which had sold 240,000 copies in its first year, was awarded the Pulitzer Prize in 1928. One more Wilder novel, *The Woman of Andros* (1930), was published by the firm.

In early 1929 the Boni Books series of hardcover reprints was followed by a more ambitious plan. A major conflict had been brewing among publishers and booksellers ever since Scherman founded the Book-of-the-Month Club in 1926. Influenced by their former partner's success, the Bonis formed the Charles Boni Paper Books Club, which offered twelve paperbound volumes a year—each book attractively designed by Rockwell Kent—for a five-dollar subscription. As a further inducement, free copies of *The Bridge of San Luis Rey* (1927) were offered to all subscribers. In response, on 27 May 1929 Louis Brentano, the vice-president of Brentano's, which ran both booksell-

1929 subscription form

Cover for paperback edition of Pulitzer Prize-winning 1927
novel. Free copies of the book were offered to subscribers to the
Charles Boni Paper Books Club in 1929.

*Drawing of the Albert and Charles Boni office at 26 West Fifty-
sixth Street. The firm moved to this location in 1935.*

ing and publishing operations, announced that his firm would no longer carry Boni books. Boni's plans were further dampened by the stock market crash in October. The firm reacted by doubling prices, but the club was a liability which was sold to Doubleday, Doran in 1931; the firm itself was in major trouble by that time. Charles Boni left in 1930 to found the Living American Art Company, reproducers of modern art.

Albert Boni published *Claudine at School* (1930) by Colette and "Willy" (Henri Gauthier-Villars); John Huston's proletarian drama *Frankie and Johnny* (1930); Tiffany Thayer's *The Greek* (1931); and Mark Van Doren's *Jonathan Gentry* (1931). Proust's *The Past Recaptured* (1932) was one of the last major works published by the firm. Nevertheless, Boni kept the business going and revived it once more in 1935, when the firm expanded and moved to 26 West Fifty-sixth Street. By this time the firm was concentrating on nonfiction and reprints, and few new titles of literary significance appeared. Albert and Charles Boni went out of business in 1939.

Albert Boni's interests had been turning increasingly to microfilm, and in 1939, having per-

fected the Readex Machine, which used microfiche instead of film, he founded the Readex Microprint Corporation. The company issued more than a half million titles—mostly out-of-print books—in its first fifteen years. Upon Albert's retirement in 1974, his son William took over. Albert Boni died in 1981.

Charles Boni had returned to publishing in 1946 in partnership with Joseph Gaer, with whom he formed Boni and Gaer at 133 West Forty-fourth Street. The short-lived firm published Carl Van Doren and Carl Carmer's *American Scriptures;* Maxim Gorky's previously unpublished first novel, *Orphan Paul;* and I. F. Stone's *Underground to Palestine,* all in 1946. Charles Boni left the firm in 1948; he died in 1969.

References:

"A. & C. Boni in New Quarters," *Publishers' Weekly,* 109 (20 February 1926): 607;

"Obituary Notes [Albert Boni]," *Publishers Weekly,* 220 (14 August 1981): 13, 16;

"Obituary Notes [Charles Boni]," *Publishers' Weekly,* 195 (3 March 1969): 36.

—*Carmen R. Russell*
David Dzwonkoski

Boni and Liveright
(New York: 1917-1928)
Horace Liveright
(New York: 1928-1933)
Liveright
(New York: 1933)
Liveright Publishing Corporation
(New York: 1933-   )

Boni and Liveright began publishing in 1917 with its highly popular series of reprints, The Modern Library; the company soon expanded into one of the most progressive publishing houses of the 1920s, taking chances with young, unknown, or controversial writers, seven of whom eventually won Nobel Prizes. Almost 80 titles appeared yearly under the Boni and Liveright imprint; in addition, the firm published a total of more than 100 Modern Library titles in literature, economics, psychology, and history.

Albert Boni was born in 1892. He dropped out of Harvard University in 1912, and a year later he and his brother Charles established the Wash-

ington Square Book Shop on MacDougal Street in New York's Greenwich Village. In 1915 they and Harry Scherman began publishing the Little Leather Library, a set of pocket-size reprints of the classics. Although both the bookshop and the Little Leather Library were successful, the Bonis had overextended themselves financially; they sold both ventures in 1916.

Horace Brisbin Liveright was born in 1886 and raised in Philadelphia. He was a clerk at a brokerage firm when, at the age of seventeen, he wrote a comic opera that would have been produced on Broadway had the backer not run out of money. At twenty-two Liveright moved to New

NEW YORK
BONI AND LIVERIGHT
1919

BONI AND LIVERIGHT
Publishers   :   New York

York City and found a job on Wall Street. Later, after failing in an attempt to market a new line of toilet paper, he convinced his father-in-law to back him one more time. He was looking for a project when he met Albert Boni, who proposed that they publish a series of reprints of modern classics and popular fiction which would be sold at a much lower price than any publisher was then charging. The Modern Library of the World's Best Books would contain works more current than those of the Little Leather Library in a larger, though somewhat similar, format. Because the venture was Boni's idea they became equal partners, even though Boni invested only $4,000 to Liveright's $12,500.

In May 1917 the firm of Boni and Liveright, located in three small rooms at 105 West Forty-eighth Street, published its first twelve Modern Library titles. The inexpensive reprints, bound in limp Leatherette, were an instant success, not only because of the low price of sixty cents each but also because the texts could not be found elsewhere in such a convenient, attractive form. The list, which included titles that either were out of print or had never before been available in the United States, reflected Boni's taste and that of his Greenwich Village friends: Wilde's *The Picture of Dorian Gray*, Strindberg's *Married*, Anatole France's *The Red Lily*, and works of Maupassant, Gorky, Nietzsche, Dostoevski, Maeterlinck, and Schopenhauer.

Income from The Modern Library enabled Boni and Liveright to bring out works that the more established houses avoided. Among the firm's publications were reprints or translations of G. K. Chesterton's *Utopia of Usurers, and Other Essays* (1917), Gustavus Myers's *The History of Tammany Hall* (1917), Leon Trotsky's *The Bolsheviki and World Peace* (1918), Adolf Andreas Latzko's *Men in War* (1918), Henri Barbusse's *The Inferno* (1918), and George Bernard Shaw's *The Sanity of Art* (1919).

Perhaps the firm's biggest gamble was on Theodore Dreiser, whose works were frequently rejected by publishers or banned as obscene. Having passed through several other publishers, Dreiser had arranged to have *Sister Carrie* (1900) reprinted by Frank Shay, the new owner of the Bonis' Washington Square Book Shop. When Shay was drafted into the army, he introduced Dreiser to Liveright. The sales record of Dreiser's books was unimpressive and Dreiser himself was difficult to get along with, but Liveright was excited about his writing. The firm quickly reprinted *Sister Carrie* (1917) and published Dreiser's *The Hand of the Potter* (1918), *Free, and Other Stories* (1918), *Twelve Men* (1919), and *Hey Rub-a-Dub-Dub* (1920). Liveright then negotiated for six years with the novelist before publishing Dreiser's masterpiece and first real best-seller, *An American Tragedy* (1925).

By then, Boni and Liveright had established itself as a respected firm. In August 1918 *Publishers' Weekly* stated: "Publishers are judged by the books they publish; and certainly Boni and Liveright should rank high among publishers who try for the worthwhile in literature. The titles of the Modern Library are an encouragement to good literature. Their publication of Dreiser's book [*Free, and Other Stories*] is equally an encouraging sign of the times."

The federal government did not always share this opinion. While the country was in the worst stages of World War I hysteria, Boni and Liveright was publishing pacifist and socialist books. Although *Men in War* and *The Bolsheviki and World Peace* were both suppressed, the house continued to publish works of this kind. But whereas Boni and his uncle, Thomas Seltzer, who had become a vice-president and editor of The Modern Library, favored the sociopolitical works of Continental writers, Liveright was eager to publish works by unknown Americans. Finally, in July 1918, the differences between Liveright and Boni led to a split. Since neither would sell out, they flipped a coin to see who would control the firm; Liveright won.

Horace Liveright

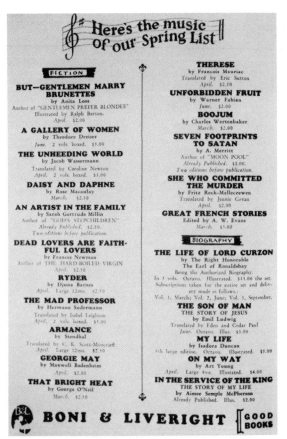

1928 advertisement. The firm became Horace Liveright, Incorporated later that year.

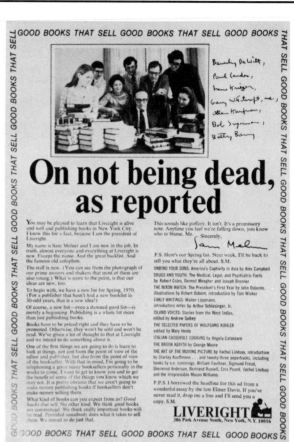

1970 advertisement

Catalogue cover

Seltzer left in November to establish Scott and Seltzer with Temple Scott; Boni traveled to Europe and later joined his brother Charles in another publishing venture. Retaining the firm's original name, Liveright then turned to publishing the work of native-born political and literary radicals. His outstanding 1919 list included John Reed's sensational *Ten Days That Shook the World,* the first edition of Mark Twain's *The Curious Republic of Gondour, and Other Whimsical Sketches,* Upton Sinclair's *Jimmie Higgins,* Eugene O'Neill's *The Moon of the Caribbees, and Six Other Plays of the Sea,* and George Moore's *Avowals,* as well as works by Mary Austin, Konrad Bercovici, and Waldo Frank.

The Bonis had published Ezra Pound's poetry in their magazine the *Glebe* as early as February 1914. In that issue, subtitled *Des Imagistes: An Anthology,* works by Hilda Doolittle, James Joyce, and John Cournos also appeared. Doolittle's and Cournos's works were eventually published by Boni and Liveright in book form, upon Pound's recommendation. Pound also urged Liveright to publish Joyce's *Ulysses,* but Liveright, fearing censorship, decided against doing so. While neither Pound's *Instigations* (1920) nor his *Poems: 1918-21* (1921) sold well, the poet proved to be a valuable literary connection. Liveright signed him to a contract as a translator for a minimum of $500 yearly; the contract was beneficial to both parties, since Pound's translations were often good sellers. Pound also persuaded Liveright to publish T. S. Eliot's *The Waste Land* (1922).

O'Neill's *The Moon of the Caribbees,* his third book, had been a gamble for Liveright, who had made an exception in this case to his policy of publishing only plays that had run successfully on Broadway. O'Neill's next play, *Beyond the Horizon* (1920), won the Pulitzer Prize. Other O'Neill books published by the firm included *The Emperor Jones/Diff'rent/The Straw* (1921), *The Hairy Ape/Anna Christie/The First Man* (1922), *Desire under the Elms* (1925), *The Great God Brown/The Fountain/The Moon of the Caribbees, and Other Plays* (1926), *Strange Interlude* (1928), and *Mourning Becomes Electra* (1931).

In 1920 Sigmund Freud accepted Liveright's offer to publish his introductory lectures on psychoanalysis. *A General Introduction to Psychoanalysis* remained a steady seller throughout the 1920s. The firm also published James Huneker's scandalous novel *Painted Veils* in 1920.

Liveright was editor as well as chief executive until he hired Thomas R. Smith in 1921. An experienced editor with useful literary contacts, Smith was the first of many able associates who worked with Boni and Liveright; Julian Messner, Manuel Komroff, Louis Kronenberger, Isidor Schneider, Richard Simon, Edward A. Weeks, Donald Friede, and Bennett Cerf were others, but it was Smith upon whom Liveright most relied. Smith persuaded Hendrik Willem Van Loon to condense a proposed twelve-volume historical series for children into one volume that would appeal to adults. The first edition of *The Story of Mankind* (1921) sold 150,000 copies at five dollars each; the book went through thirty American printings and was translated into at least a dozen languages. Smith was also responsible for the monumental cutting and editing of Dreiser's *An American Tragedy.*

During the next six years, the profits from Van Loon's book, an occasional best-selling novel, and The Modern Library enabled the firm to add works—often early ones—by major writers. In 1922 Boni and Liveright published E. E. Cummings's autobiographical novel *The Enormous Room;* Upton Sinclair's *They Call Me Carpenter: A Tale of the Second Coming;* and *Gargoyles,* the first of four works by Ben Hecht. In 1923 the firm moved to a spacious brownstone at 61 West Forty-eighth Street. Djuna Barnes's 1923 collection of stories, poems, plays, and drawings, *A Book,* was followed in 1928 by her novel *Ryder.* Gertrude Atherton's *Black Oxen* (1923) sold well, as did her *The Crystal Cup* (1925). The firm published Edgar Lee Masters's *The Nuptial Flight* (1923), *The New Spoon River* (1924), *Mirage* (1924), *Gettysburg, Manila, Acoma* (1930), and *Lichee Nuts* (1930). In 1924 Boni and Liveright published the first American edition of Liam O'Flaherty's first book, *Thy Neighbour's Wife.*

Boni and Liveright had had obscenity cases dismissed for Hutchins Hapgood's *The Story of a Lover* (1919) and for a translation of the Latin classic *The Satyricon of Petronius Arbiter* (1922). In June 1925 Liveright, Smith, and Maxwell Bodenheim were indicted for obscenity by a New York grand jury. The charges against Bodenheim's novel *Replenishing Jessica* (1925) were brought by the New York Society for the Suppression of Vice, headed by John Sumner. In the 1928 trial, the novel was read to jurors in a monotone by the prosecutor, James G. Wallace. After this put some of the jurors to sleep, a verdict of not guilty was declared. Liveright later published Bodenheim's *Duke Herring* (1931) and *Naked on Roller Skates* (1931).

In 1925 Liveright sold The Modern Library to Cerf and Donald Klopfer, thus paving the way for the founding of Random House. Cerf had come to Boni and Liveright in 1923 from Wall Street, with no publishing experience. Hired as a salesman, Cerf became a vice-president after investing $25,000 in the firm and lending an equal sum to Liveright. Although his staff strongly objected to selling The Modern Library, Liveright accepted $150,000 plus cancellation of Cerf's loans and investments, largely because he needed the money for his theatrical and stock market ventures.

In spite of its legal and financial difficulties, 1925 was a high point for Boni and Liveright from a literary perspective. In addition to *An American Tragedy* and *Desire under the Elms*, the firm published Conrad Aiken's *Bring! Bring! and Other Stories*, as well as Robinson Jeffers's *Roan Stallion, Tamar, and Other Poems*. Also in 1925 Liveright lured Sherwood Anderson away from B. W. Huebsch and published his *Dark Laughter*. Liveright published six more titles by Anderson, including *A New Testament* (1927), *Perhaps Women* (1931), and *Beyond Desire* (1932).

Ernest Hemingway's first American book publication was *In Our Time* (1925), under the Boni and Liveright imprint. Liveright eagerly anticipated Hemingway's *The Sun Also Rises* (1926), but the author sent him, instead, a parody of Anderson, *The Torrents of Spring* (1926). Liveright rejected the pastiche; Hemingway, released from his contract, moved to Scribner.

Another important first appearance came the following year with William Faulkner's first novel, *Soldiers' Pay* (1926). Anderson had recommended Faulkner to Liveright. Neither *Soldiers' Pay* nor Faulkner's second Boni and Liveright novel, *Mosquitoes* (1927), sold well. When Faulkner submitted "Flags in the Dust," Liveright rejected it as overly long and rambling, but he offered Faulkner an advance on another novel. Instead of accepting the offer Faulkner took the work to Harcourt, Brace, where it was edited and published as *Sartoris* (1929).

Liveright published Hart Crane's first book of poetry, *White Buildings* (1926), and his long poem *The Bridge* (1930); Liveright's advances to Crane exceeded the income from his books. Anita Loos's *"Gentlemen Prefer Blondes"* (1925), however, was a best-seller in 1926; and two volumes of poetry by Dorothy Parker, *Enough Rope* (1926) and *Sunset Gun* (1928), also sold well. Liveright published the first American edition of Elizabeth Bowen's first book, a collection of stories entitled *Encounters* (1925), as well as the first edition of her third book, *Ann Lee's: & Other Stories* (1926).

In 1927 *An American Tragedy* was banned in Boston. Under Boston's unusually strict law, one of Liveright's editors, Donald Friede, was found guilty of selling obscene material and fined $300.

Friede had made the sale to a police officer in order to test the law. Liveright won praise from other publishers for fighting the case, and eventually the law was modified.

When Liveright changed the name of the firm to Horace Liveright, Incorporated in 1928, the company was in financial trouble due to his unsuccessful theatrical productions and stock market investments. Several recent Liveright titles had been well received and sales of the Boni and Liveright backlist were good, but the firm was too far in debt to recover. Harold Loeb's *Tumbling Mustard* appeared in 1929, as did MacKnight Black's first book, *Machinery*, and S. J. Perelman's first book, *Dawn Ginsbergh's Revenge*. The Wall Street crash of 1929 accelerated Liveright's insolvency. The firm moved from the legendary brownstone to an office building at 31 West Forty-seventh Street.

Arthur Pell, Liveright's bookkeeper, had been supplying cash to Liveright in exchange for company stock. After the crash, Pell gained control of the business. Liveright moved to Hollywood, where he worked as a novel and play adviser for Paramount Studios; in 1931 he returned to New York, jobless but planning new publishing projects for which he never gained the necessary financial backing. He died in 1933.

The removal of Liveright did not help Pell improve the company's fortunes, although the firm continued to publish works by its established authors as well as publishing works by new ones. In 1930 the firm published Frances Parkinson Keyes's *Queen Anne's Lace*, followed a year later by *Lady Blanche Farm: A Romance of the Commonplace*. Pell changed the house's name to Liveright, Incorporated and, in 1933, published *The Collected Poems of Hart Crane* and Nathanael West's *Miss Lonelyhearts*, but the company foundered. In May 1933 Pell filed for bankruptcy. Victor Gold bought the firm for $18,000. Pell retained his stock, however, and soon regained control. The company, renamed the Liveright Publishing Corporation, subsisted largely on reprint rights until it was acquired in 1969 by Gilbert Harrison of the *New Republic*. Samuel B. Melner, formerly of Pitman Publishing, became president.

The Liveright Publishing Corporation became a subsidiary of W. W. Norton and Company in 1974. It earns most of its income from the backlist established under the firm's original name, Boni and Liveright, although in 1983 it published *Etcetera: The Unpublished Poems of E. E. Cummings*, edited by George J. Firmage and Richard S. Kennedy, and

Cummings's *Hist Whist and Other Poems for Children,* edited by Firmage. Its address is 500 Fifth Avenue, New York 10110.

References:

"Among the Publishers," *Publishers' Weekly,* 94 (31 August 1918): 634;

Bennett Cerf, *At Random* (New York: Random House, 1977);

Walker Gilmer, *Horace Liveright: Publisher of the Twenties* (New York: Lewis, 1970);

"Horace Liveright [obituary]," *New York Times,* 25 September 1933, p. 15;

"The House of Boni and Liveright," *Literary Digest International Book Review,* 2 (1923-1924): 686-687;

Louis Kronenberger, "Gambler in Publishing: Horace Liveright," *Atlantic,* 215 (January 1965): 94-104;

Edith M. Stern, "A Man Who Was Unafraid," *Saturday Review of Literature,* 24 (28 June 1941): 10, 14.

—Carmen R. Russell

The Book League of America

(New York: 1928-1932)

The Book League of America was established in September 1928 by Samuel Craig, a founder and former owner of the Literary Guild. At a time when book clubs were competing with book publishers in price-cutting wars, the Book League of America tried a different approach. For eighteen dollars a year, subscribers were to receive a new, complete book in magazine format each month. Each magazine was also to include letters, book reviews, and essays on contemporary literature. Along with the magazines, the subscriber would receive a monthly reprint of such standard works as *Adventures of Huckleberry Finn,* Butler's *The Way of All Flesh,* and Wells's *The Outline of History;* these were in book format, with cloth bindings.

Prospective subscribers elected, from a list of thirty names, a committee responsible for the selection of both new titles and classics. Among those elected to the committee were Edwin Arlington Robinson and Van Wyck Brooks.

The first number of the *Book League Monthly* appeared in November 1928, featuring Matthew Josephson's *Zola and His Times,* originally published in October by the Macaulay Company. The February 1929 issue contained *Prima Donna* by Pits Sanborn, originally published by Longmans, Green the previous month. In September 1932 the Book League of America was bought by the Literary Guild. It functioned briefly, along with the Literary Guild and the Dollar Book Club, as one of the Doubleday group of clubs.

References:

"Guild Takes Over Book League," *Publishers' Weekly,* 122 (3 September 1932): 780;

"A New Book Club—The Book League of America," *Publishers' Weekly,* 114 (8 September 1928): 781.

—Deborah G. Gorman

Branden Press

(Boston; Brookline Village, Massachusetts: 1965-   )

Branden Press, Incorporated was founded in 1965 by Edmund R. Brown, a longtime publisher with the Four Seas Company and its successor, Bruce Humphries; John William Andrews, a poet and editor of the literary magazine *Poet Lore;* and Hugo Norden, a composer. These three, from whose names the firm's name derives, started Branden with capital of $3,000. The first offices of the firm were at 36 Melrose Street in Boston.

Branden Press published six titles in its first year of operation and also published a book review magazine, *The World in Books.* Branden benefited from its connection with *Poet Lore:* in addition to receiving a generous amount of advertising in the magazine, Branden was the sole distributor of back issues of *Poet Lore*'s drama, poetry, and criticism titles, including the Poet Lore Play Series, which Brown brought from Bruce Humphries. Branden published *A Comprehensive Index of Poet Lore, V. 1-58: 1889-1963* in 1966.

Branden publishes chiefly poetry, music, art, general nonfiction, and reprints of literary classics. Poets whose work Branden has published include Andrews, Horatio Colony, Gary Fincke, John Kolyer, Ruth Lechleitner, and Paul Scott Mowrer.

In 1969 the firm moved to 221 Columbus Avenue. In the same year Branden Press purchased the Brashear Music Company; in 1971 it acquired Bruce Humphries, including the International Pocket Reprints series. In 1979 Branden Press moved to 21 Station Street, Brookline Village, Massachusetts 02147; in March 1985 its address changed to 17 Station Street. It published sixteen new titles in 1980, down from its peak rate of approximately seventy titles per year in the early 1970s. Branden serves as distributor for several other publishers, including Dante University of America Press, Claude Stark and Company, and Popular Technology.

—Timothy D. Murray

George Braziller

(New York: 1955-   )

George Braziller founded the publishing firm that bears his name in 1955 with offices at 215 Fourth Avenue in New York. Although this was Braziller's initial venture into book publishing, he had been active in the book world since the early 1940s as the director of two successful book clubs: in 1942 he founded the Book Find Club, a national book club specializing in quality nonfiction, which by the end of the decade numbered 100,000 members; in the early 1950s he started the Seven Arts Book Society. He sold his interest in the clubs to Time, Incorporated in 1969 for $350,000. In 1955

Braziller published its first original title, Jacob Bronowski's *The Face of Violence,* and the first of a series of hardcover reprints, *The Notebooks of Leonardo da Vinci.*

As a small independent, Braziller could not compete with larger publishers for the work of established American novelists; therefore, he looked to other countries. In France, Braziller found an emerging group of avant-garde novelists—or "anti-novelists," as many of them have come to be called—whose work interested him, and he published English translations of novels by Claude

Edmund R. Brown, founder of the Branden Press (photo by A. Caso)

George Braziller

1955 advertisement

Mauriac, Julien Gracq, Claude Simon, Edouard Glissant, Nathalie Sarraute, Pierre Gascar, and Geneviève Dormann. Braziller extended his publishing of French fiction to France's former colonies with French Canadian author Robert Goulet's *The Violent Season* (1961) and several books by Algerian author Kateb Yacine. Jean-Paul Sartre's autobiography *The Words* (1964) was one of the firm's most successful titles.

Braziller has published fiction by Rudolfo Celletti, Sylvano Ceccherini, Giovanni Arpino, and Carlo Gadda of Italy; Jan Wolkers of The Netherlands; Sara Lidman of Sweden; and Xavier Dominga of Spain. British novelist Beryl Bainbridge has become one of the firm's most successful authors and since the early 1970s has brought out more than a dozen of her books under the Braziller imprint. Braziller has also published work by British novelists A. L. Barker and Caroline Blackwood, as well as London-based Nigerian author Buchi Emecheta.

One of the firm's notable fiction successes was Korean author Richard Kim's first novel, *The Martyred* (1964). New Zealand novelist Janet Frame had nearly twenty books published by Braziller between 1960 and 1985. Braziller has begun publishing work by a new generation of novelists, including David Malouf and David Ireland of Australia, and Desmond Hogan, Niall Quinn, Kate Cruise O'Brien, Neil Jordan, Michael Curtin, and Bernard MacLaverty of Ireland.

Braziller's American novelists, including Lilian Hale, James Fritzhand, Joseph Bennett, Alfred Grossman, Alan Kapelener, and Josiah Bunting, have not achieved the critical and commercial success that their foreign counterparts have; but the firm's commitment to quality American fiction is evident through its support of the Fiction Collective, Incorporated, founded in 1974 by a group of authors as a publishing outlet for noncommercial American fiction. Braziller served as the principal distributor for Fiction Collective titles for several years after the group's inception.

While Braziller had published Wendell Berry's *November Twenty Six Nineteen Hundred Sixty Three* (1964), Frame's *The Pocket Mirror* (1967), and Conrad Aiken's *Thee* (1967), the firm was not particularly active in publishing poetry until 1971, when it started the Braziller Series of Poetry under the editorship of Pulitzer Prize-winning poet Richard Howard. The series has brought out work by Charles Simic, Chester Kallman, Carl Dennis, Constance Urdang, Cynthia MacDonald, Turner Cassity, Madeline de Frees, and Norman Dubie. Apart from the series, Braziller has also published the poetry of Stanley Burnshaw, Andrei Codrescu, George Keithley, Norman Rosten, Ettore Rella, and Charles Morris.

The area in which George Braziller, Incorporated is perhaps best known and most successful is art and architecture publishing. The American Artist Series, begun in 1965, offered early critical treatments of the work of Jackson Pollock, William de Kooning, and Stuart Davis. The Library of Illuminated Manuscripts, a series of high quality yet inexpensive facsimile reprints, was launched in 1966 with *The Hours of Catherine of Cleves,* for which the firm won the Carey-Thomas award for creative publishing. The Library of Illuminated Manuscripts includes more than twenty-five titles. This rather specialized series has been commercially successful, with *The Hours of Catherine of Cleves* and *The Tres Riches Heures of Jean, Duke of Berry* (1969) each having sold over 100,000 copies. The Masters of World Architecture, Makers of Contemporary Architecture, Arts of Mankind, New Directions in Architecture, and Vision and Value series were also sponsored by the firm.

George Braziller, Incorporated has always maintained an eclectic list, with particular strengths in literature, history, philosophy, and music. The firm has a strong program in the social sciences and since the mid-1960s has published books dealing with urban affairs, ecology, environmental problems, and American culture. With offices since 1965 at 1 Park Avenue, New York 10016, Braziller publishes between twenty and thirty new titles per year.

References:

Cleveland Amory, "Trade Winds," *Saturday Review,* 55 (15 April 1972): 5;

"George Braziller [of George Braziller] Talks About . . . ," *Publishers Weekly,* 221 (15 January 1982): 58-64.

—Timothy D. Murray

Brewer, Warren and Putnam
(New York: 1931-1932)
Brewer and Warren
(New York: 1930-1931)

On 1 January 1930 Joseph Brewer and Edward Kunhardt Warren changed the name of the publishing firm of Payson and Clarke, Limited to Brewer and Warren, Incorporated. Brewer had been president of Payson and Clarke since 1928; Warren had been vice-president and treasurer since 1927. The new firm remained in the offices of the old one at 8 East Fifty-third Street in New York.

Under editor William Rose Benét, the firm had a wide-ranging list of publications. It published facsimiles of the 1609 edition of Shakespeare's *Sonnets*, the 1612 edition of Jonson's *The Alchemist*, the 1645 edition of Milton's *Minor Poems*, and the 1783 edition of Blake's *Poetical Sketches*.

The firm's 1930 titles included Dorothy L. Sayers's *Lord Peter Views the Body* and *Strong Poison;* Gertrude Stein's *Useful Knowledge;* Madame Tolstoy's *Diary of Tolstoy's Wife;* Robert Penn Warren's first book, *John Brown: The Making of a Martyr;* W. E. Süskind's *The Web of Youth;* Clements Ripley's *Devil Drums;* and Nathan Asch's *Pay Day.*

In April 1930 the New York Society for the Suppression of Vice brought obscenity charges against Brewer and Warren. The judge in the magistrate's court, while acknowledging the explicit sexual passages in *Pay Day*, dismissed the case on the grounds that the character, Jim, was made to pay for his transgressions. In June the society's president, John S. Sumner, reinstigated the charges with the grand jury of New York County. Although the grand jury indicted Brewer and Warren, the firm was eventually exonerated.

In March 1931 the company's name was changed to Brewer, Warren and Putnam when George Palmer Putnam became a vice-president after selling his interest in G. P. Putnam's Sons. In that year the list of titles included *A Letter from Greenland* by Rockwell Kent.

Putnam left the firm in June 1932 to become chairman of the editorial board at Paramount Studios; Robert O. Ballou replaced him as director of the editorial department.

On Brewer, Warren and Putnam's list for 1932 were John Steinbeck's *The Pastures of Heaven* and Amelia Earhart's *The Fun of It.* In November Harcourt, Brace took over the firm. Ballou retained some of the titles and began a publishing house under his own name at 347 Fifth Avenue, New York. Other authors whose books appeared on Brewer, Warren and Putnam's list at the time of its dissolution included William Beebe, George Seldes, and David Garnett.

Reference:

"George Palmer Putnam [obituary]," *New York Times*, 5 January 1950, p. 25.

—Carole Michaels-Katz
Elizabeth Hoffman

Joseph Brewer (left) and Ford Madox Ford

*William Stanley Braithwaite, editor in chief of B. J. Brimmer (photo by Carl Van Vechten; by permission of Joseph Solomon,
the Estate of Carl Van Vechten)*

1931 advertisement

B. J. Brimmer Company

(Boston: 1921-1927)

Founded in 1921, with the black poet and anthologist William Stanley Braithwaite as editor in chief, the B. J. Brimmer Company published nonfiction, drama, and poetry. From its office at the Allen Building, 384 Boylston Street, Boston, the firm sought out new poetry and was especially responsive to new black writers. Georgia Douglas Johnson's *Bronze: A Book of Verse* appeared in 1922, followed the next year by James Starkey's pseudonymous *The Poems of Seumas O'Sullivan*, Robert Silliman Hillyer's *The Hills Give Promise, a Volume of Lyrics, Together with Carmus: A Symphonic Poem*, and first books of poems by Benjamin Rosenbaum and Cecilia MacKinnon. Braithwaite also edited the annual *Anthology of Magazine Verse*. In addition to its trade printings, the firm published titles in all genres in limited, signed editions printed on handmade paper.

Although the firm published few novels, James Gould Cozzens's first novel, *Confusion*, appeared with the Brimmer imprint in 1924. The book failed to boost Brimmer's sales, and the firm went bankrupt in 1927.

Reference:

"William Stanley Braithwaite [obituary]," *New York Times*, 9 June 1962, p. 25.

—*David Dzwonkoski*

Broadway Publishing Company

(New York: circa 1901-circa 1912)

Located at 835 Broadway, New York, the Broadway Publishing Company produced novels and books of verse by minor authors. Some of the firm's books were well bound and printed on high quality paper with gilt edges. Limited editions sometimes accompanied the trade editions. Titles published by the firm included *Llewellyn: A Novel* (1904) by Hadley S. Kimberling, *Evelyn: A Story of the West and Far East* (1904) by Mrs. Ansel Oppenheim, *Marcelle: A Tale of the Revolution* (1904) by Willibert Davis and Claudia Brannon, and *Lost in the Mammoth Cave* (1905) by D. Riley Guernsey. Broadway also published nonfiction, including Rosa B. Hitts's *The Instrument Tuned* (1904), a self-

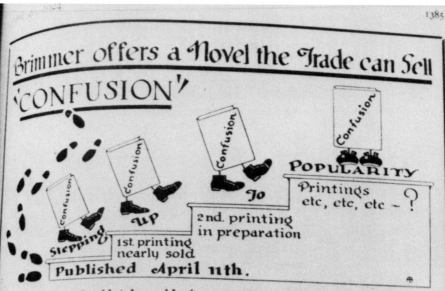

1924 advertisement for James Gould Cozzens's first novel

help book on relaxation and harmony with natural laws; and *The New Womanhood* (1904) by Winnifred Harper Cooley, which the firm described as "in the vanguard of the [womanhood] movement."

—*Peter Dzwonkoski*

Bruce Humphries
(Boston: 1930-1971)

John W. Luce and Company, Chapman and Grimes, the Poet Lore Company, and the Four Seas Company merged in 1930 to form Bruce Humphries, Incorporated at 470 Stuart Street, Boston, with Edmund R. Brown as president. Although the Luce, Poet Lore, and Four Seas backlists were of literary importance, the new firm ventured into other areas, quadrupling its output in six years with series such as Individual Psychology Publications, the Life and Color series of books on the arts, the Psychic Research series, the Tourist Library, and Music Publications. Fiction series included the Poet Lore Plays priced at two dollars each, the Friendly Books series at one dollar, the Silver Seal Fiction series at seventy-five cents, and the Players series at twenty-five cents. After 1936 Bruce Humphries's output leveled off, and the firm relied largely on its backlist. Around this time Brown created a subsidiary, the International Pocket Library Corporation, publishing classics in twenty-five-cent paperbacks.

Among the few noteworthy literary titles published by Bruce Humphries were John Wheelwright's *Rock and Shell* (1933) in a limited, signed edition; Amanda B. Hall's *The Cinnamon Saint: A Narrative Poem* (1937); *The Bomb That Wouldn't Go Off* (1941) by John Phillips, with pictographs by W. A. Dwiggins; and *The Poems of Max Ehrmann* (1948) and *The Journal of Max Ehrmann* (1952). Nonfiction authors included Alfred Adler, William Stekel, and J. B. Rhine, whose landmark *Extra-Sensory Perception* appeared in its first trade edition in 1935 under the Bruce Humphries imprint. Eventually, the firm became largely a vanity press.

For a time, Bruce Humphries published *Poet Lore* magazine. Founded in 1889 by Charlotte Porter and Helen A. Clarke, this journal was originally published by the Poet Lore Company, part of the

Richard G. Badger firm. When the Poet Lore Company merged into Bruce Humphries in 1930, Brown became managing editor of the magazine; Badger was acquired by Bruce Humphries in 1932. Publication of *Poet Lore* was suspended in 1953. Bruce Humphries became a subsidiary of the Reliance Corporation in 1960; Robert L. Bell became president and Brown vice-president of Bruce Humphries. In 1962 Bell abandoned subsidy publishing, revived *Poet Lore*, and announced a small list of books on music, such as Sergei I. Taneev's *Convertible Counterpoint in the Strict Style* and trade titles such as F. James Hope's *Mother Had Hopes*, a book about Bob Hope's family.

Brown left Bruce Humphries in 1964 to found the Branden Press, taking the Poet Lore titles and much of the Four Seas backlist with him. Brown was succeeded as president of Bruce Humphries by Robert R. Larsen. *Poet Lore* was then published by Literary Publications, Incorporated, of which Larsen was president and Bell vice-president.

Bruce Humphries moved to 306 Stuart Street in 1934, to 30 Winchester Street in 1939, to 48-50 Melrose Street in 1956, and finally to 66-68 Beacon Street in 1968. By the time of this final move, the firm was disintegrating. Brown had left; Bell had formed Crescendo Publishers in 1967 to publish books on music from the Bruce Humphries address. When Bell and Larsen dissolved Reliance in 1968, the current Bruce Humphries list went to R.R. Larsen and Company, Incorporated, while the backlist went to Bell. In 1971 what remained of Bruce Humphries was purchased by the Branden Press.

References:
"Bruce Humphries, Boston, Enters General Trade

1937 advertisement

Field," *Publishers' Weekly,* 181 (8 January 1962): 58;

"Bruce Humphries, Crescendo Reach Rights

Agreement," *Publishers' Weekly,* 194 (2 December 1968): 18.

—*David Dzwonkoski*

Jonathan Cape and
Harrison Smith
(New York: 1929-1932)
Jonathan Cape and
Robert Ballou
(New York: 1932)

Jonathan Cape, who had started the British publishing house Jonathan Cape, Limited in 1921, had decided by 1928 to tap the American book market. Not content simply to open an American branch office for his firm, Cape wanted to establish a new publishing house in the United States. By doing so he could retain the American rights to the publications of Jonathan Cape, and, he hoped, publish American titles as well, and thus compete with American publishers on their own home ground.

Cape proposed that the New York publisher Harcourt, Brace become his partner in the new firm. Harcourt, Brace, a shareholder in Jonathan Cape, Limited, was amenable to the plan; but the firm's chief editor, Harrison Smith, had long wanted to go into publishing on his own. With the blessing of Harcourt, Brace, which then withdrew from the project, Smith invested his own money and joined Cape in forming Jonathan Cape and Harrison Smith in January 1929 at 139 East Forty-sixth Street in New York.

Cape had contacts with the British literary and publishing community, while Smith could provide the same sort of contacts in America. Smith soon brought in Robert O. Ballou, literary editor of the *Chicago Daily News,* as treasurer and head of the manufacturing department. Ballou was responsible for the high design standards that brought the firm acclaim for its early books.

From the outset, Cape and Smith was able to attract promising American authors. The firm published Kay Boyle's *Wedding Day and Other Stories* (1930) and *Plagued by the Nightingale* (1931), Babette Deutsch's *Fire for the Night* (1930) and *Epistle to Prometheus* (1931), and works by the popular novelists Ursula Parrott and Evelyn Scott. Cape and Smith published Malcolm Cowley's first book of poetry, *Blue Juniata* (1929), as well as William Faulkner's *The Sound and the Fury* (1929), *As I Lay Dying* (1930), *Sanctuary* (1931), and *These 13.* Other American authors on the Cape and Smith lists included Maurice Hindus, Joseph Wood Krutch, Floyd Gibbons, Louis Fischer, and Morris L. Ernst. In 1929 the firm published Lynd Ward's *God's Man,* a novel told entirely in woodcuts.

About half of the Cape and Smith list was made up of British titles, including *The Collected Poems of D. H. Lawrence* (1929), Robert Graves's *Goodbye to All That* (1930), Evelyn Waugh's *Vile Bodies* (1930) and *A Bachelor Abroad* (1930), and Hickman Powell's *The Last Paradise* (1930). Radclyffe Hall had four books published by the firm. Cape and Smith also published works by Norman Douglas, Eric Linklater, Laurence Housman, John Middleton Murry, Arthur Symons, Julian Huxley, and Edgar Wallace. Almost all of the books were published first in England, usually by Jonathan Cape, Limited. Cape and Smith also published Maxim Gorki's *The Bystander* (1930) and *The Magnet* (1931) and the first English-language edition of Sigmund Freud's *Civilization and Its Discontents* (1930).

Though its impressive list of authors brought Cape and Smith critical acclaim, the firm was un-

Jonathan Cape in the 1920s (Michael S. Howard, Jonathan Cape, Publisher, *1971)*

Title page for 1926 "novel" told entirely in woodcuts

able to achieve comparable financial success. Soon after Cape and Smith opened for business the American economy collapsed in the stock market crash of October 1929. Equally devastating to the firm was the inability of its two partners to work well together. Smith, though he had had seven years of editorial experience at Harcourt, Brace, was inexperienced in the business end of publishing and lacking in organizational skills. He was prone to overestimate the sales potential of books, and while Cape and Smith's list grew—reaching more than 200 titles within two years—so did its backlog of stock, a situation which other book publishers also faced during the Depression. Finally, Smith had never really regarded the firm as anything more than a stepping stone toward his goal of founding his own publishing house. In the fall of 1931 he left to start Harrison Smith, Incorporated; early the next year he joined Robert K. Haas, a founder of the Book-of-the-Month Club, to form Smith and Haas.

Cape shared the blame for the downfall of Cape and Smith. He tended to regard the firm as simply an American market for English titles, particularly those of Jonathan Cape, Limited; on several occasions Cape used Cape and Smith to fulfill commitments he had incurred at his London firm. He also tended to overestimate the market for British books in America. Following Smith's exit, Ballou offered to enter into a partnership with Cape to keep the firm going. Cape initially agreed to Ballou's plan; but early in 1932 he suddenly went back on his commitment and decided to abandon any attempt to save the firm, even after Ballou offered to buy his shares. Although some books were issued under a Cape and Ballou imprint, the firm was out of business by the summer of 1932. Its assets were put into receivership and were liquidated within a year.

References:

Paul A. Bennett, "Robert O. Ballou of Cape & Smith," *Linotype News*, 9 (June 1931): 5;

Michael S. Howard, *Jonathan Cape, Publisher* (London: Cape, 1971).

—*Timothy D. Murray*

Carroll and Graf Publishers
(New York: 1982-   )

Carroll and Graf Publishers, Incorporated was founded late in 1982 by Kent Carroll and Herman Graf, who combined some thirty-five years of publishing experience to form a new house devoted to the publication of quality books, including fiction, history, and biography. Before they started their own company, both men were vice-presidents at Grove Press, where Carroll was editor in chief and Graf was marketing and sales director. While acquisitions responsibilities are shared between them at Carroll and Graf, editorial duties are under Carroll's authority and Graf handles marketing and promotion.

Relying heavily on quality reprints of literary interest, Carroll and Graf published its first list in spring 1983. The list consisted of ten books, including *Summer in Williamsburg* by Daniel Fuchs; *East River* and *Three Cities* by Sholem Asch; and two collections of public domain stories by Louis L'A-mour, *The Hills of Homicide* and *The Law of the Desert Born*. L'Amour sued the firm, contending that the books were advertised in a way that made it seem that he had authorized publication; the suit was settled out of court. At the end of the year, Carroll and Graf had published some thirty-five titles.

By 1985 Carroll and Graf was publishing some 100 books a year, about ninety percent of which were paperbacks; of the paperbacks about half were republications of quality books that had gone out of print and half were first paperback publications of current hardbound books. The firm publishes in three formats to provide bookstores with what Graf calls a "receptive" list in which each book is worthy of a place on the shelf. Mass market paperbacks include *Bodies and Souls* (1983) by John Rechy; *The Rasp* (1984) by Philip MacDonald; *City on a Hill* (1985), *Cogan's Trade* (1985), and *A Choice of Enemies* (1985), all by George V. Higgins; *Hope of Heaven* (1985) and *Ten North Frederick* (1985) by John O'Hara; *Lost Gallows* (1986) by John Dickson Carr; and *Cabot Wright Begins* (1986) by James Purdy. Trade paperbacks include *The Last Adam* (1985) by James Gould Cozzens, *Proust: Portrait of a Genius* (1984) by André Maurois, and *The Lonely Hunter: A Biography of Carson McCullers* (1985) by Virginia Spencer Carr. The hardbound books, of which Carroll and Graf publishes about ten a year, include general interest fiction, such as *The Good Father* (1985) by Peter Prince and *Folie D'Amour*

(1985) by Anne-Marie Villefranche; nonfiction, such as *The Painted Witch* (1985), an art history book by Edwin Mullins; and biographies, such as *Una Troubridge: The Friend of Radclyffe Hall* (1985) by Richard Ormrod.

Distribution for Carroll and Graf is handled by Publishers Group West, though Graf insists on calling personally on all major accounts. Carroll and Graf is located at 260 Fifth Avenue, New York 10010.

—*Botham Stone*

The Caxton Printers, Limited
(Caldwell, Idaho: 1903-   )

THE CAXTON PRINTERS, LTD.
CALDWELL, IDAHO

In 1895 Albert E. Gipson founded the *Gem State Rural,* a small farm newspaper in Caldwell, Idaho. He was forced to suspend operations shortly thereafter, but in 1902—after purchasing the equipment of another failed newspaper—he revived the *Gem State Rural,* adding a printer, William Earle Norton, to the staff. The firm, then called Gem State Publishing Company, began taking on job printing. In 1903, when Gipson's son, James Herrick Gipson, joined the firm, its name was changed to The Caxton Printers, Limited after the fifteenth-century English printer William Caxton. The firm adopted Caxton's logo to symbolize its desire to meet the earlier printer's high standards. The Caxton Printers, Limited was incorporated in 1907 with $10,000 in capital. The first stockholders were Albert E. Gipson, president; A. W. Gipson, secretary and treasurer; W. E. Norton, vice-president; James H. Gipson, general manager; and Mrs. Albert E. Gipson.

The Caxton Printers, Limited purchased the *Idaho Odd Fellow* in 1907 and the *Caldwell News* in 1913. Caxton also began selling office supplies and stationery supplies, primarily to Idaho state government agencies. The firm published its first book in 1920: *Behind Gray Walls* by Patrick Charles Mur-

phy, an inmate in the Idaho State Penitentiary. In 1925 the firm obtained the exclusive right to print textbooks for Idaho schools. One of the texts, Fred E. Lucker's *The Idaho Citizen* (1925), achieved such good sales that Caxton obtained the publishing rights. Caxton next published Murphy's *Shadows of the Gallows* (1928). In 1928-1929 the firm published ten books, and by the early 1930s it was publishing over twenty new titles per year.

In 1932 Caxton published Vardis Fisher's autobiographical novel *In Tragic Life;* Fisher had tried unsuccessfully to sell the book to Eastern publishers before James Gipson accepted it. *In Tragic Life, Passions Spin the Plot* (1934), *We Are Betrayed* (1935), and *No Villain Need Be* (1936) formed the Vridar Hunter Tetralogy, which launched Fisher—and The Caxton Printers—into literary prominence. The success of *In Tragic Life* prompted Doubleday, Doran to republish it, and to publish the remaining three books in the tetralogy, jointly with Caxton.

Caxton's offices and printing plant were destroyed by a fire in March 1937. Within two months, using borrowed equipment and operating out of temporary quarters, the firm was functioning again.

When Caxton published Fisher's novels *April:*

*James H. Gipson, Sr., president of The Caxton Printers,
Limited, in 1939*

Second printing plant of The Caxton Printers in Caldwell, Idaho, in 1939. The firm's first plant was destroyed by fire in 1937.

A Fable of Love (1937) and *Forgive Us Our Virtues: A Comedy of Evasions* (1938), Fisher was the director of the Idaho Writers' Project of the Federal Works Progress Administration. The agency produced *Idaho: A Guide in Word and Picture* (1937), *The Idaho Encyclopedia* (1938), and *Idaho Lore* (1939), all published by The Caxton Printers, Limited. Caxton also published Fisher's *City of Illusion* (1941) and his textbook *God or Caesar? The Writing of Fiction for Beginners* (1953).

Fisher was the most significant literary figure whose works were originally published by The Caxton Printers. The firm has reprinted works by classical and prominent contemporary authors—for instance, *An Ozark Anthology* (1941) featured Thomas Hart Benton and Mackinlay Kantor—but most of Caxton's original literary productions have been the work of regional authors. Dorothy Bennett, Frank B. Camp, Laurence Pratt, George Dixon Snell, and Grace Stone Coates, for example, have never had a substantial audience outside the Rocky Mountain area. The largest part of the Caxton list has been made up of works on the American West, particularly the Northwest, the Rocky Mountains, and Idaho. *Steens Mountain* (1967) by Russell Jackman, Charles Conkling, and John Scharf; *High on the Wild with Hemingway* (1968) by Lloyd Arnold; and *Snake River Country* (1971) by Bill Gulick have received national attention and are sought by collectors.

Active in regional and national politics, James Gipson was the western manager of Theodore Roosevelt's 1916 Bull Moose campaign. In 1938 he started the Libertarian Library to publish works that reflected his individualistic philosophy of opposition to government interference in business and private life. The Libertarian Library consists of reprints of classic texts as well as work by contemporary authors. The first volume in the series was Herbert Spencer's *The Man versus the State* (1940). Other authors in the series include Albert Jay Nock, Garet Garrett, Oscar W. Cooley, and Wheeler McMillen. In 1946 Caxton published the first trade edition of Ayn Rand's *Anthem*, which had been available only in pamphlet form.

Caxton's profits are derived entirely from its textbook printing, job printing, newspapers, and other commercial activities, while its book publishing program operates at a loss. Under the management of President James H. Gipson, Jr.—James H. Gipson, Sr., died in 1965—the firm brings out five or six titles per year and maintains a strong backlist; it remains one of the most prominent regional publishers in the United States. The firm's address is P.O. Box 700, Caldwell, Idaho 83605.

References:

Vardis Fisher, *The Caxton Printers in Idaho: A Short History* (Cincinnati: Society of Bibliographers, 1944);

Paul E. Johnston, "Caxton Printers, Ltd. Regional Publishers," *Pacific Northwest Quarterly*, 48 (July 1957): 100-105;

Johnston, "History of Caxton Printers, Ltd. of Caldwell, Idaho," M.A. thesis, University of California at Berkeley, 1956;

Wallace Stegner, "A Decade of Regional Publishing," *Publishers' Weekly*, 135 (11 March 1939): 1060-1064;

Felix Wittmer, "Caxton of the Rockies," *American Mercury*, 78 (June 1954): 91-93.

—Timothy D. Murray

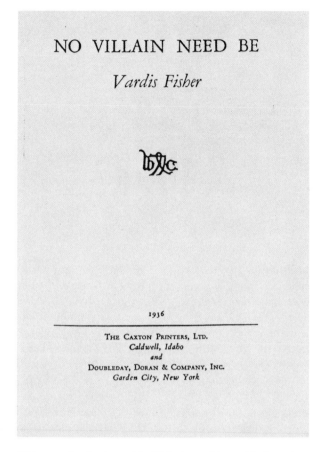

Title page for final novel in Fisher's autobiographical tetralogy

Vardis Fisher, Caxton's most important literary author

Chelsea House
(New York: 1921-circa 1933)

Chelsea House was established in 1921 by Ormond Smith, co-owner with Francis Smith of Street and Smith, one of the largest magazine and paperback publishers in America. Through Chelsea House, Smith hoped to compete with the established trade publishers. Under the direction of Henry William Ralston, senior vice-president at Street and Smith, Chelsea House—operating out of Street and Smith's offices at 79 Seventh Avenue in New York—began publishing clothbound books priced at $1.75 per copy. The first title published was Frederick Faust's *Free Range Lanning* (1921), a western novel written under the pseudonym George Owen Baxter. Faust wrote more than twenty novels for Chelsea House under the pseudonyms Baxter, David Manning, and Max Brand.

Other popular Chelsea House authors were Christopher Booth; Arthur Preston Hankins; Joseph Montague; and Reginald Wright Kauffman, whose *Share and Share Alike; An Adventure Story* appeared in 1925. Chelsea House writers produced westerns, thrillers, detective novels, and adventure stories at a rapid pace. By 1924 Chelsea House had published more than fifty-two titles, with sales for each title averaging almost 20,000 copies.

In addition to its clothbound originals, Chelsea House published paperback reprints of novels which had appeared as serials in magazines. These paperbacks sold for seventy-five cents apiece; between 1921 and 1933 more than 362 titles appeared.

Chelsea House achieved much success in the 1920s, but sales dropped dramatically with the onset of the Depression. By 1933 Chelsea House was no longer in existence.

—*Timothy D. Murray*

Chilton Book Company
(Philadelphia; Radnor, Pennsylvania: 1967-   )
Chilton Book Division
(Philadelphia: 1955-1967)

The Chilton Company, located at Fifty-sixth and Chestnut Streets in Philadelphia, in 1955 had long been recognized as the publisher of the respected business and trade journals *Iron Age, Distribution Age, Hardware Age,* and *Automotive Marketing.* Though Chilton's first book, *Rapid Flat Rate and Repair Data,* dated back to 1926, regular book publishing had not begun until 1950, and then titles were available only through direct mail. In early 1955 the company established the Chilton Book Division to offer its titles to the retail book trade through a franchising program in which all orders to the publisher were referred to booksellers. By mid-1956 over 3 million copies of Chilton's staple, the *Automotive Repair Manual,* were in print, and Chilton had become a byword for automotive repair guides.

In 1955 Chilton acquired 31 Conover-Mast technical titles; Greenberg: Publisher was purchased three years later, bringing nearly 1,000 titles to Chilton's list. Jae Greenberg stayed on as a consultant to Chilton. In 1964 the Book Division was divided into the Trade Book Division, with Nic. Groenevelt as general manager, and the Educational Book Division, headed by Charles Heinle. Heinle had been the Book Division's manager since its inception. Groenevelt remained until 1971 as general manager and vice-president. In 1967 the Chilton Book Division was renamed the Chilton Book Company. Educational Book Division titles had by then been transferred to the Trade Book Division.

In 1965 Chilton ventured into science fiction with the publication of Frank Herbert's *Dune,* which was an immediate popular and critical success and received the prestigious Hugo and Nebula awards; Robert Silverberg's *To Worlds Beyond;* Poul Anderson's *Agent of the Terran Empire;* and James Schmitz's *A Nice Day for Screaming and Other Tales of the Hub.* Strong *Dune* sales prompted the publication of other science fiction titles, including Sterling E. Lanier's *Hiero's Journey* (1973), Anderson's *Inheritors of Earth* (1974), Philip José Farmer's *Mother Was a Lovely Beast* (1974), and Ben Bova's *The Starcrossed* (1975), as well as *The Many Worlds of Poul Anderson* (1974) and other anthologies edited by Roger Elwood. A decision to concentrate on car repair, technical, and crafts books led Chilton to cancel its science fiction program, and by 1981 only *Dune* remained on its active list. Chilton also published biographies, including Barbara Bonham's *Willa Cather* (1970) and Edwin P. Hoyt's *Horatio Boys: The Life and Works of Horatio Alger, Jr.* (1974). Included in the Young Adult series was Kin Platt's popular *Mystery of the Witch Who Wouldn't* (1969). Since 1968 Chilton has published *The Best Short Plays,* an annual anthology established by Margaret Mayorga in 1919. The series was edited by Stanley Richards from 1968 until his death in 1980.

In 1978 book publishing accounted for sixteen percent of the company's total sales. In early August 1979 the American Broadcasting Corporation purchased Chilton for $52 million. William A. Barbour, who had been president since 1971, stayed on in that capacity until 1982, when he took a newly created post as chairman. Citing a conflict in management styles, he retired the next year.

Gary Ingersoll, formerly of ITT's and IBM's publishing divisions, was brought in as president in 1982, but remained only nine months before being named president of Compute! Publications, a recently acquired ABC division. He was succeeded by Lawrence A. Fornasieri, who had been vice-president of CBS's Educational and Professional Publishing Division. John P. Kushnerick is vice-president and general manager.

In addition to auto repair and arts and crafts, Chilton publishes cooking, self-improvement, and technical titles. Recent additions to its list include a wide variety of computer-related titles. The firm is also active in marketing and opinion research services. Since 1973 its address has been Chilton Way, Radnor, Pennsylvania 19089.

References:
"ABC Plans to Acquire Chilton for $86 a Share," *Publishers Weekly,* 215 (26 February 1979): 97-98;

"Chilton Discloses Plans to Broaden Its Publishing Base," *Publishers Weekly,* 203 (25 June 1973): 65.

—*Gregory P. Ames*

City Lights Books
(San Francisco: 1953-   )

See also the Lawrence Ferlinghetti entry in *DLB 16, The Beats: Literary Bohemians in Postwar America.*

City Lights Books was founded in 1953 as a paperback bookstore by the poet Lawrence Ferlinghetti and Peter Dean Martin, a sociology professor at San Francisco State University, to support Martin's cinema magazine *City Lights,* named in honor of the 1931 Chaplin film. The store became the headquarters for poets and writers of the Beat Generation, and poetry readings were hosted in the store's basement. Martin sold his share of City Lights and moved to New York, where he opened the New Yorker Bookshop. Shigeyoshi Murao became Ferlinghetti's new partner and remained associated with the firm until ill health forced him to retire in 1977. He was replaced by Nancy J. Peters.

The first book published by City Lights Books was Ferlinghetti's *Pictures of the Gone World* (1955), in hardcover (25 signed copies) and in wrappers (500 copies). This was also Ferlinghetti's first book and the first in City Lights' Pocket Poets series. In their two-color (usually black and white) wrappers and duodecimo format, the Pocket Poets books have offered the work of some of the leading contemporary avant garde poets. The most important of the more than seventy titles published in the series was Allen Ginsberg's *Howl and Other Poems* (1956). This outcry against the corruption and emptiness of modern life was alleged to be obscene, and the subsequent trial and acquittal brought national attention to the poem, to Ginsberg, and to City Lights. Perhaps the firm's all-time best-seller, *Howl* has been reprinted many times. Other Ginsberg titles published by City Lights include *Kaddish and Other Poems, 1958-1960* (1961); *Reality Sandwiches, 1953-60* (1963); and *The Fall of America: Poems of These States 1965-1971* (1972), which won the National Book Award for poetry.

Other works in the Pocket Poets series include Kenneth Patchen's *Poems of Humor & Protest* (1955) and *The Love Poems of Kenneth Patchen* (1960); Denise Levertov's *Here and Now* (1957); *Kora in Hell: Improvisations* (1957) by William Carlos Williams, a new edition of the 1920 work; and Gregory Corso's *Gasoline* (1958). Volumes of selections from Robert Duncan, Malcolm Lowry, and Philip Lamantia also appeared in the Pocket Poets series, as did translations by Ferlinghetti, Jerome Rothenberg, and Anselm Hollo.

Charles Bukowski's City Lights titles have included *Erections, Ejaculations, Exhibitions and General*

Lawrence Ferlinghetti (left), founder of City Lights Books, with poet Gregory Corso

Cover of the book that brought national attention to City Lights

Tales of Ordinary Madness (1972) and *Shakespeare Never Did This* (1979). Other publications have been Mikhail Horowitz's *Big League Poets* (1978), *Edgar Allan Poe: The Unknown Poe*, edited by Raymond Foye (1980), and Ferlinghetti and Peters's photographic history *Literary San Francisco* (1980). City Lights has also ventured into the publication of social and political works, including Norman Mailer's *The White Negro* (1957), Mary Low and Juan Bréa's *Red Spanish Notebook* (1979), and William Burroughs's *Roosevelt after Inauguration and Other Atrocities* (1979). Other comtemporary writers whose work has been published by City Lights include Jack Kerouac, Neal Cassady, Diane DiPrima, John Reed, Frank O'Hara, Michael McClure, Stefan Brecht, Gary Snyder, Alan Watts, Paul Bowles, and Charles Olson. City Lights Books is located at 261 Columbus Avenue, San Francisco 94133.

—*Kathleen R. Davis*

C. M. Clark Publishing Company
(Boston: 1900-1912)

Founded by Carro Morrell Clark in 1900 at 211 Tremont Street, the C. M. Clark Publishing Company was the only publishing house in turn-of-the-century Boston owned by a woman. Clark was also the first book publisher to advertise on billboards and walls. She began her career as a bookseller and stationer. In 1900, after listening to Charles Felton Pidgin read from the manuscript of his novel *Quincy Adams Sawyer and Mason's Corner Folks*, Clark decided to publish the work, and quickly signed Pidgin to a contract. She then began a massive advertising campaign using billboards, large spreads in magazines and newspapers, and a national tour to promote the book. Her enthusiasm was rewarded by sales of almost 250,000 copies. Advertising for the books that followed, combined with her shrewd judgment, resulted in a string of best-sellers.

In an interview with the *International Printer* in 1906, she summarized her philosophy: "A book is often very much like a play, you want to make it and put it before the public in its best dress. If there are enough of them sold at the start to secure a hearing the public will do the rest, if there is something in the book to back it; if there is not it will fall flat." (Clark may have been inclined to use a play as a simile for a book because she had recently married Charles F. Atkinson, who helped to shape *Quincy Adams Sawyer* into a successful play.)

Clark published four more historical romances by Pidgin: *Blennerhassett; or, The Decrees of Fate* (1901), *The Climax; or, What Might Have Been. A Romance of the Great Republic* (1902), *The Toymakers* (1907), and *Theodosia, the First Gentlewoman of Her Time* (1907). In 1902 the firm published William Henry Carson's *Hester Blair: The Romance of a Country Girl*, which was followed by his *Tito* in 1903. The first of four novels by Dwight Tilton published by Clark, *Miss Petticoats* (1902), was later dramatized by Kathryn Osterman. In 1903 Clark published the first of three western romances by Frances Parker, *Marjie of the Lower Ranch*, and Mildred Champagne's *Love Stories from Real Life*. The latter title was promoted with the offer of a free poster of one of the stories, "Beatrice, the College Girl Heroine," drawn by Fred Kulz. Other titles were illustrated by Charles H. Stephens.

Many of the firm's titles were also the first books by their authors: Clark often worked with unknown writers who soon became well known through the firm's publicity. None of Clark's publications had great literary merit, however, and their authors generally returned to obscurity after three or four books. Clark's most noteworthy dis-

Page from 1903 catalogue

covery may have been Charles M. Russell, whose illustrations first appeared in a portfolio assembled to promote *Marjie of the Lower Ranch*.

In 1910 Clark began an expansion into educational materials. For reasons that remain unclear, the firm fell deeply into debt, and in April 1912 an assignment was made to pay off its creditors.

References:

William E. Harris, "Women in Publishing," *Publishers' Weekly*, 113 (24 March 1928): 1353-1355.

—*David Dzwonkoski*

Edward J. Clode
(New York: circa 1900-circa 1938)

Edward J. Clode was born in Paris, Ontario, Canada, about 1868. He came to the United States early in his life and worked for Brentano's bookstore and as a printer before starting his own publishing company at 156 Fifth Avenue in New York. An ambitious, independent publisher, Clode launched his effort with a contest for ideas on how best to sell books. An important part of the Clode operation was keeping books alive by regularly advertising them.

The main Clode author was Louis Tracy, more than forty of whose works were published by the firm in decorated or illustrated cloth covers. Clode's relationship with Tracy included the publication of *The Wings of the Morning* (1903), a story of adventure and romance and perhaps Tracy's best-known work; *A Mysterious Disappearance* (1905) and *The Arncliffe Puzzle* (1906), detective novels written under the pseudonym Gordon Holmes; *The Sandling Case* (1931); and *A Dangerous Situation*

(1932). Many of Tracy's novels were reprinted by Grosset and Dunlap, and some are still read by mystery fans.

Other novels published by Clode include M. P. Shiel's *The Lost Viol* (1905); John R. Carlings's *The Doomed City* (1910), about the siege and fall of Jerusalem and the burning of the Temple in A.D. 70; and Faith Baldwin Cuthrell's *Betty* and *Rosalie's Career*, both published in 1928. Clode summarized his philosophy of publishing: "My imprint on a book usually means it has adventure, romance, lots of action and human interest." The firm apparently closed about 1938 when Clode retired at seventy. He died on 11 April 1941 in Buffalo, New York.

Reference:

"Edward J. Clode [obituary]," *Publishers' Weekly*, 139 (10 May 1941): 1939.

—*Carole Michaels-Katz*

1903 advertisement (New York Times)

1928 advertisement

Cosmopolitan Book
Corporation
(New York: 1919-1931)
Hearst's International Library
Company
(New York: 1913-1919)

See also the William Randolph Hearst entry in *DLB 25, American Newspaper Journalists, 1901-1925.*

William Randolph Hearst entered book publishing in the fall of 1913 with Hearst's International Library Company at 119 West Fortieth Street in New York. The first publication of the company was Henry Thomas Buckle's *History of Civilization in England* (1913), followed in 1914 by the first volumes of the National Dickens series, a cheap reprint of the forty-volume Chapman and Hall English National Edition. Chiefly a reprint house, with editions of Emerson, Poe, Shakespeare, and Plato, Hearst's International Library did publish some original fiction and nonfiction, usually by authors who were writing for Hearst magazines. In 1915 the firm published first editions of Margaret Widdemer's *Why Not?* and Corra Harris's *Justice.* The work of Arthur Benjamin Reene, the creator of the Craig Kennedy detective stories in *Cosmopolitan* magazine, was published in book form with *The Exploits of Elaine* and *The Social Gangster,* both in 1915. The following year the company published American editions of two of Mrs. Humphry Ward's novels, *A Great Success* and *Lady Connie,* and an illustrated gift edition of poems by Ella Wheeler Wilcox, *World Voices.*

In April 1919 Harold J. Kinsey, formerly sales manager for Doubleday, Page and Company, became manager of Hearst's International Library Company. Later that year the name of the firm was changed to Cosmopolitan Book Corporation. Peter B. Kyne, a well-known author of adventure stories, and James Oliver Curwood, a popular author of

wilderness tales, had many works published by Cosmopolitan, including Kyne's *Kindred of the Dust* (1920), *Cappy Ricks Retires* (1922), and *Tide of Empire* (1928) and Curwood's *The River's End* (1919) and *The Valley of Silent Men* (1920).

In 1927 Joseph Anthony took charge of Cosmopolitan; under his leadership the firm became competitive with the established publishing houses. Anthony added Irvin S. Cobb to the Cosmopolitan list, and the popular humorist produced six books for Cosmopolitan between 1927 and 1930. Other Cosmopolitan publications included Harry Leon Wilson's *Lone Tree* (1929) and *Two Black Sheep* (1931); Stanton Coblentz's *The Wonder Stick* (1929), a juvenile fantasy; and Ross Santee's *The Pooch* (1931). The firm moved to Fifty-seventh Street and Eighth Avenue in 1928 and to 572 Madison Avenue in 1931.

In 1929 Saul Flaum succeeded Anthony, and Cosmopolitan surged into prominence with Louis Golding's *Give Up Your Lovers* (1930), Faith Baldwin's *Skyscraper* (1931), Rex Beach's *Money Mad* (1931), and Fanny Hurst's *Back Street* (1931). Flaum went on to sign Louis Bromfield, Ruth Suckow, Anita Loos, Erich Maria Remarque, and Colette; but before Cosmopolitan was able to publish any of their works, Hearst sold the business to Farrar and Rinehart in 1931. The Cosmopolitan list developed by Flaum helped launch Farrar and Rinehart into the forefront of American publishing.

References:

"Cosmopolitan Book Corporation Sold to Farrar &

Rinehart," *Publishers' Weekly*, 120 (26 September 1931): 1489-1490;

George Murray, *The Madhouse on Madison Street* (Chicago: Follett, 1965);

John Tebbel, *The Life and Good Times of William Randolph Hearst* (New York: Dutton, 1952).

—Timothy D. Murray
Theodora Mills

Covici-Friede
(New York: 1928-1938)

Born in Rumania, Pascal (Pat) Covici opened a bookstore with William McGee on Washington Street between Clark and LaSalle in Chicago in 1922. Covici started publishing books that year under the imprint of Covici-McGee with Ben Hecht's *1001 Afternoons in Chicago*. Covici-McGee also published two books of poems by Maxwell Bodenheim: *Blackguard* (1923) with illustrations by Wallace Smith and *The Sardonic Arm* (1923) in a limited edition of 575 copies. In 1925 Covici published an illustrated edition of Erasmus's *In Praise of Folly* under the imprint of Pascal Covici. He also published poetry, prose, and translations by Richard Aldington, including a book of prose poems, *The Love of Myrrhine and Konallis* (1926), designed by Frank Mechau. Later, Covici published Aldington's extensive selections and translations from the works of Remy de Gourmont (1928), illustrated by André Rouveyre. In 1927 Covici published Samuel Putnam's translations of a previously unpublished manuscript by the Marquis de Sade, *Dialogue between a Priest and a Dying Man,* and of Joris Karl Huysmans's *Down Stream and Other Works*.

On a trip to New York in January 1928, Covici had dinner at Alexander King's house. Also present was Donald Friede, who had just left Boni and Liveright to go into business for himself. After a conversation which is said to have lasted for three days, Covici-Friede was born. Covici's business was valued at $30,000; Friede matched Covici's contribution with money left from an inheritance. The business officially opened on 4 July 1928 in a small office at 79 West Forty-fifth Street. Friede's wife

read the manuscripts, and Covici's wife headed the business department.

Covici-Friede capitalized on the 1920s vogue for collecting limited editions. The firm's first publication was a set of the complete works of François Villon; the second was a collection of thirty lithographs by King under the title *The Gospel of the Goat*. The firm's first trade book was Walter Blair's edition of Mrs. Julia Moore's *The Sweet Singer of Michigan* (1928), which Friede called "the worst volume of poetry ever written by anybody, anywhere." Also on Covici-Friede's first list were Hecht and Charles MacArthur's *The Front Page*, which became the first published American play to achieve significant sales; Aldington's *Collected Poems;* and a narrative poem by Joseph March, *The Set-Up*. Along with the successful titles came such failures as Wyndham Lewis's immense novel *The Childermas*, which Covici-Friede planned to publish in three volumes. The first volume did not sell, and the firm never published the other two; nor did it have any further contact with Lewis.

One financial success led to troubles of another sort. In 1928 the firm published Radclyffe Hall's *The Well of Loneliness,* a sensitive portrayal of lesbianism. The book had already been banned in England, where it had been published by Jonathan Cape, Limited. After John S. Sumner, the superintendent of the New York Society for the Suppression of Vice, took Covici-Friede to magistrate's court, sales of the book doubled. Sumner seized 865 copies of the book from Covici-Friede's offices, but the publishers had already moved the printing

1928 advertisement

Pascal Covici (left) and Donald Friede in 1928, the year they
founded their publishing house

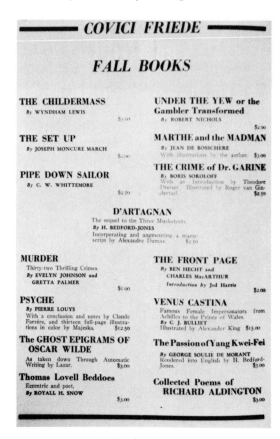

1928 advertisement

plates to a plant in New Jersey. Friede was arrested and convicted, but the conviction was overturned on appeal.

In the middle of 1929 Friede took a trip to Europe, during which he secured Aldington's new novel, *Death of a Hero* (1929). When Friede returned he found that Covici had expanded: Joseph Margolies, formerly a book buyer at Brentano's, was the new sales manager; George Joel, also from Brentano's, was the new publicity director. With the money from *The Well of Loneliness*, Covici-Friede took greater risks. The 1929 fall list included a novel by the young Russian refugee Ilya Ehrenbourg; the Theatre Guild play *Wings over Europe* by Robert Nichols; and three books by Putnam—translations of Joseph Delteil's *On the River Amour* and François Mauriac's *The Desertion of Love*, and an original work of art criticism, *The Glistening Bridge: Leopold Survage and the Spatial Problem in Painting*. A few months before the stock market crash, Covici-Friede moved to Fourth Avenue, then the center of the publishing district. In 1930 Covici-Friede continued to publish limited editions but depended more and more heavily on its "regular list." The firm published new novels by Aldington; Mauriac's *The Family*, translated by Lewis Galantière; two books by E. E. Cummings; Horace Gregory's first book, *Chelsea Rooming House;* and *My Thirty Years' War*, Margaret Anderson's account of the *Little Review* magazine.

Covici and Hecht were close friends, and Covici-Friede took over what Friede later called Covici's "pleasant pastime" of publishing most of Hecht's novels, short stories, and plays, both good and bad. In 1931 the firm published *The Champion from Far Away* and used the Covici-McGee plates of *1001 Afternoons* to reissue the book for the first of several times.

The Depression finally forced Covici-Friede to stop printing expensive books in limited editions. One of the last was a two-volume folio edition of *The Canterbury Tales* (1930) in modern English verse. Of the 999 copies, 75 were bound in pigskin and contained extra two-color Rockwell Kent illustrations; Covici-Friede received orders for 126 copies of this deluxe edition at $250 each. Another of these "well-done" books of classic literature in limited editions was Putnam's translation of *The Works of Pietro Aretino* (1933) in a set illustrated by Marquis de Bayros.

In 1932 Covici and Friede decided to publish what Friede called "machine-made fiction," novels "in which we did not believe." The first, *Speakeasy Girl*, started out as a title only. Then the firm came

up with its jacket blurb: "There is a new kind of girl in America. She arrived on the scene with Prohibition and she has now come of age. She is as immoral as she is wise, as pretty as she is young. The speakeasy is her office. . . ." An eye-catching book jacket was then run as a double-page advertisement in *Publishers' Weekly*. Booksellers expressed immediate interest and motion picture companies sent messages requesting a copy of the manuscript, which did not as yet exist. Covici and Friede commissioned Bobbie Meredith to write it, and in six weeks they had a novel. Covici and Friede realized how easily they had tapped a new market and soon added to the firm's list such titles as *Bachelor's Wife* (1932) by George A. Bagby and *Boy Crazy* (1932) by Grace Perkins (Mrs. Fulton Oursler).

Soon, however, Covici said, "If we must lose money in publishing, let us at least lose it on good books." In 1931 the firm had published Horace Gregory's translation of *The Poems of Catullus* and Gene Fowler's *The Great Mouthpiece* (1931); in 1932 it added Putnam's translation of Jacques Roberti's *Without Sin*, George Priest's translation of Goethe's *Faust*, and a collection of speeches by Franklin D. Roosevelt. This last publication—and the surprise success of John Strachey's *The Coming Struggle for Power* (1933), which went through eight printings and a revised edition in one year—brought the firm into what Friede called "the deadly serious, if-it-isn't-proletarian-it-can't-be-good phase." In 1935 it published Robert Forsythe's *Redder than the Rose*, James A. Wechsler's *Revolt on the Campus*, more books by Strachey, and *Three Plays* (1935) by Clifford Odets.

In 1935 Covici got the manuscript of *Tortilla Flat* from John Steinbeck's agent. In order to call attention to the novel, Covici and Friede had it illustrated (an unusual move for a failing house during the Depression) by Ruth Gannett, the wife of the important *New York Herald Tribune* critic Lewis Gannett. By the time *Tortilla Flat* was published in 1935, Steinbeck had completed his next Covici-Friede novel, *In Dubious Battle* (1936).

By 1935 the firm had accumulated huge debts to its printers, J. J. Little and Ives. Friede resigned because "I did not enjoy evaluating manuscripts for their value as possible remainders" and went to Hollywood as a literary agent. Steinbeck's *Of Mice and Men* (1937) became the firm's first book club selection, and his *The Red Pony* (1937) was issued in a beautifully designed edition of 699 copies. The firm published Hecht's *Actor's Blood* (1936) and his play *To Quito and Back* (1937).

By the beginning of 1938 Little and Ives was

in complete financial control of Covici-Friede. That summer Col. Arthur Ives called a meeting of creditors and announced that Covici-Friede was being dissolved. All creditors were paid in full and all royalties were paid to the authors, but Covici and Friede lost their entire investment.

After the failure of the firm, Margolies returned to Brentano's; Joel became head of Dial Press. Covici took Steinbeck with him to Viking Press, where they continued their close relationship for the next twenty-five years. At Viking Covici also worked with Marianne Moore, Arthur Miller, Saul Bellow, Lionel Trilling, Willy Ley, and Gene Fowler. In late June 1943 Crown Publishers of New York purchased the assets of Covici-Friede and announced that some of the 200 titles would be republished under the Crown imprint. Friede remained in Hollywood until he returned to the

book business in 1953 as trade editor with World Publishing Company; he moved to Doubleday as a senior editor in 1964. Covici died in 1964; Friede died in 1965.

References:
"Covici and Steinbeck to Viking," *Publishers' Weekly,* 134 (20 August 1938): 499;
"Donald Friede [obituary]," *New York Times,* 31 May 1965, p. 17;
Donald Friede, *The Mechanical Angel* (New York: Knopf, 1938);
"Obituary Notes [Pascal Covici]," *Publishers' Weekly,* 186 (24 October 1964): 26-27;
"Plans Go Forward for Liquidation of Covici, Friede," *Publishers' Weekly,* 134 (20 August 1938): 500.

—Alan J. Filreis

Coward, McCann and Geoghegan
(New York: 1971-)
Coward-McCann Publishing Company
(New York: 1928-1971)

Thomas R. Coward and James A. McCann, who had both worked for Bobbs-Merrill, began their own publishing business in 1928. Coward, president of the new company, had also acquired publishing experience at the Yale University Press.

McCann, vice-president and treasurer, had begun with Doubleday, Page and had headed his own publishing house for two years before joining Bobbs-Merrill.

The Coward-McCann Publishing Company

Thomas R. Coward (left) and James A. McCann in 1938

1929 advertisement

was originally located at 522 Fifth Avenue, New York, but soon moved to 55 Fifth Avenue. Totaling thirty titles in fiction, biography, history, current events, and children's books, the firm's first list promised success for the fledgling house. Its first book, published on 30 July 1928, was *Diversey*, Mackinlay Kantor's first novel. An additional seventeen books by Kantor were published by Coward-McCann during the next twenty-five years. Other titles on the first list were Thornton Wilder's *The Angel That Troubled the Waters*, Alexander Woollcott's *Two Gentlemen and a Lady*, and Josephine Herbst's first book, *Nothing Is Sacred*. Books by Nathalia Crane and Alfred Kreymborg also appeared on the 1928 list.

Children's books were one of Coward-McCann's early strengths. The firm's first children's book editor, Katherine Ulrich, was succeeded by Ernestine Evans, Rose Dobbs, Alice Torrey, and Ferdinand N. Monjo. The first children's book published by Coward-McCann was *Millions of Cats* (1928) by Wanda Gág. It was followed by other Gág picture books, including *The Funny Thing* (1929), *Snippy and Snappy* (1931), and *The ABC Bunny* (1933). Other children's books included William Nicholson's *Pirate Twins* and Kurt Wiese's *Karoo, the Kangaroo*, both published in 1929.

In 1931 Coward-McCann arranged for Dodd, Mead to distribute its books. Two years later, the firm broadened its list by acquiring Brentano's publishing department. In the same year, Coward-McCann switched distribution functions to Putnam. In 1936, when Coward-McCann became an autonomous division of Putnam, it moved to that firm's address at 2 West Forty-fifth Street.

In the 1930s Coward-McCann flourished with the continued publication of children's books, including Claire Huchet Bishop's *The Five Chinese Brothers* (1938), illustrated by Wiese. Titles for an older audience included Joseph C. Lincoln's . . . *All Alongshore* (1931) which became the firm's best-selling collection of short stories; *Two Thieves* (1931) and *Waterloo* (1936) by Manuel Komroff; and *Long Remember* (1934) and *The Voice of Bugle Ann* (1935) by Kantor. Other Coward-McCann fiction of the 1930s included Helen Hull's *Heat Lightning* (1932), a Book-of-the-Month Club selection, and Elmer Rice's best-selling novel *Imperial City* (1937). Coward-McCann also published several plays by Rice, as well as Wilder's *Our Town* (1938). Coward-McCann's nonfiction of the 1930s included *The Age of Hate* (1930), a biography of Andrew Johnson by George Fort Milton; Sir William Rothenstein's

three-volume *Men and Memories* (1931-1940); and Kreymborg's studies of American poetry. McCann left the firm in 1946.

Before Coward's death in 1957, Coward-McCann published the first American edition of William Golding's first novel, *Lord of the Flies* (1955), and the novels of Elizabeth Goudge.

In 1956 Putnam president Walter J. Minton named John J. Geoghegan, sales manager for the World Publishing Company, vice-president and trade director of Coward-McCann. It was understood that Geoghegan would be offered the presidency if he were able to strengthen the firm. While developing Coward-McCann's American line, Geoghegan also courted British publishing houses. Through aggressive promotion and publicity, he began to sell the works of the English novelist Dorothy Eden, and a new hardcover edition of *Lord of the Flies* sold 75,000 copies. The firm thus began to publish one of the best British lists in New York. Geoghegan became president of Coward-McCann in 1958.

In many cases Geoghegan's British authors were better known in the United States than in Britain. For example, John Le Carré's *The Spy Who Came in from the Cold*, which had achieved only modest sales in Britain, had great success in America: after publication by Coward-McCann in January 1964, the novel sold 45,000 copies in a month. This success helped to establish Geoghegan's reputation with British publishers. In the 1960s Coward-McCann began to strengthen its nonfiction list and to publish more American writers, including a volume of plays by Edward Albee in 1960. On 1 January 1971 the firm's name was changed to Coward, McCann and Geoghegan.

Realizing that in order to compete with the paperback houses it had to emphasize quality and continue to work with its established authors, the firm cut back to about eighty books a year in the 1970s, including *Ghost Story* by Peter Straub (1979); *The Rise of Theodore Roosevelt* (1979) by Edmund Morris, winner of the 1979 Pulitzer Prize; *King of the Jews* (1979) by Leslie Epstein; and the works of Muriel Spark, Ruth Montgomery, Norah Lofts, Rod McKuen, and Evelyn Anthony. Sarah Harrison's first novel, *Flowers of the Field* (1980), was sold to the Book-of-the-Month Club and to Dell.

In January 1980 Patricia Soliman became president of Coward, McCann and Geoghegan. Geoghegan was named chairman of the board and Joseph Kanon editor in chief. At the time the firm was publishing approximately sixty titles a year and maintaining emphasis on editorial quality. In 1981, criticizing "the corporate business school mentality" of publishing, Geoghegan resigned from Coward, McCann and Geoghegan after twenty-five years. His resignation was followed by that of Soliman. Donald Braunstein, formerly vice-president of administration at Doubleday and vice-president of the Putnam Publishing Group since October 1980, was named president of Coward, McCann and Geoghegan. The firm's address is 200 Madison Avenue, New York 10016.

References:

A Brief History of Coward McCann, Inc., Publishers,

1928-1953 (New York, 1953?);

"Coward-McCann's 10th Anniversary," *Publishers' Weekly*, 134 (23 July 1938): 230-232;

Muriel Fuller, "Rose Dobbs of Coward-McCann," *Publishers' Weekly*, 134 (22 October 1938): 1522-1524;

"Thomas R. Coward [obituary]," *New York Times*, 13 January 1957, p. 84;

Thomas Weyr, "Coward, McCann & Geoghegan: 50 Years in the Business of Books," *Publishers Weekly*, 213 (3 April 1978): 33-36.

—*Laura Masotti Humphrey*

Creative Age Press
(New York: 1941-1951)

The Creative Age Press was established by Eileen Garrett at 11 West Forty-fourth Street, New York, in March 1941. The publisher of the futurist magazine *Tomorrow* and a self-proclaimed mystic, Garrett planned to publish books on metaphysics, religion, psychology, philosophy, and the arts. The firm's managing editor was Florence Brobeck. Creative Age scored some early successes, notably Lee McCann's *Nostradamus* (1941), the first English-language biography of the sixteenth-century French prophet, and *Against This Rock* (1943), a novel by Louis Zara.

During the ten years that the Creative Age Press existed, it published titles by a variety of literary figures. Among them were Claude Bragdon's *Arch Lectures* (1942); *Small Town Tyrant* (1944), a translation of Heinrich Mann's best-known work, *Professor Unrat*, from which the film *The Blue Angel* was made; historian Salvador de Madariaga's romance of Aztec Mexico, *The Heart of Jade* (1944); *Mr. Petunia* (1945) and *Mourning Becomes Mrs. Spendlove* (1948) by Oliver St. John Gogarty; and *Tender Mercy* (1949) by Lenard Kaufman. Creative Age also published Frances Frost's *Mid-Century Poems* and Damon Runyon's *In Our Town*, both in 1946. August Derleth's *The Milwaukee Road* (1948) was a

nonfiction account of that railroad. Garrett published three of her own novels under the pseudonym Jean Lytle.

By far the most important works the firm published were those of Robert Graves. In addition to several historical novels, such as *Wife to Mr. Milton* (1944), *Hercules, My Shipmate* (1945), and *King Jesus* (1946), Creative Age published a volume of his poetry and one of his best-known works of criticism, *The White Goddess* (1948).

Creative Age Press was taken over by Farrar, Straus and Young in 1951. The imprint was used for a few years for titles in production or under contract at the time of the merger.

References:

"Creative Age Starts 3rd Year with Potential Seller," *Publishers' Weekly*, 144 (4 September 1943): 818-819;

"Eileen J. Garrett [obituary]," *New York Times*, 17 September 1970, p. 47;

"Farrar, Straus & Young Takes Creative Age Titles," *Publishers' Weekly*, 159 (31 March 1951): 1479-1480.

—*Donna Nance*

Advertisement from the firm's second year

Crown Publishers

(New York: 1936-   )

In 1934 Nat Wartels and Robert Simon bought the name and stock of the Outlet Book Company, a remainder house that was a subsidiary of Greenberg: Publisher. Wartels, who had been managing Outlet, and Simon, a Greenberg salesman, set themselves up as an independent firm and continued selling remainders. Crown Publishers was officially founded in 1936 to publish original works. The firm's first big seller was Joseph Aronson's *The Book of Furniture and Decoration* (1936), with sales of more than 100,000 copies. Crown was located for many years at 449 Fifth Avenue, New York. Hiram Haydn started his publishing career as an editor with the firm, leaving in 1950 to join Bobbs-Merrill.

The growth of Crown was based on the acquisition of small or floundering firms. When Long and Smith went bankrupt in 1933, Wartels and Simon bought the rights to Ray Long's extremely popular anthology *Twenty Best Stories*. In 1943 Crown purchased Lothrop, Lee and Shepard and continued the imprint, which was known for its juvenile literature, including the Five Little Peppers series; Lothrop, Lee and Shepard was sold to Scott, Foresman in 1965. In its first decade Crown also acquired the failing Covici-Friede and Henkle-Yewdale publishing companies; it purchased Robert M. McBride and Company in 1949.

In the 1940s Crown began to publish annuals which became extremely successful, among them *Best Film Plays of the Year* and *Best Cartoons of the Year*. This emphasis on media-oriented anthologies and books continues. The firm also published *Men at War* (1942), edited by Ernest Hemingway. Later Crown titles include Donald Barr Chidsey's *Captain Adam* (1953), Langston Hughes and Milton Meltzer's *A Pictorial History of the Negro in America* (1956), Jerre Mangione's *Night Search* (1965), Reed Whittemore's *From Zero to the Absolute* (1967), Madison Jones's *A Cry of Absence* (1971), Andrew Lytle's *A Wake for the Living: A Family Chronicle* (1975), James Dickey's children's book *Tucky the Hunter* (1978), and Alan Ebert and Janice Rotchstein's *Traditions* (1981).

During Crown's first decade, it issued about ten titles annually; in 1977 it published 546 titles. This expansion led the firm to move in 1976 to 1 Park Avenue. In the same year Crown acquired the Julian Press, publishers of psychology and occult books by Fritz Perls, John Lilly, and Ira Progroff. Crown's Harmony Books division, founded in 1972, publishes forty-five to fifty books a year—mainly nonfiction but also novels, such as Douglas Adams's satirical science fiction work *The Hitchhiker's Guide to the Galaxy* (1979) and its sequels. Harmony's publisher is Bruce Harris.

Crown's philosophy, as stated by Wartels, is mass market oriented: to "perceive what people in the market place want and find the right author, art director, and whoever else is needed to shape the book for the audience." To this end Crown paid a record sum in 1979 to one of its more successful novelists: more than $3 million for *Princess Daisy* (1980) by Judith Krantz, author of the Crown best-seller *Scruples* (1978). Crown also paid perhaps the largest advance up to that time for a first novel—more than $100,000 for Jean Auel's *The Clan of the Cave Bear* (1980). Other Crown best-sellers include Alex Comfort's *The Joy of Sex* (1972), Sparky Lyle's *The Bronx Zoo* (1979), Neal Travis's *Manhattan* (1979), Trevanian's *Shibumi* (1979), and Robert Moss and Arnaud de Borchgrave's *The Spike* (1980).

Crown and its subsidiary Clarkson N. Potter, Incorporated handle original trade publishing, while the Outlet Book Company handles sales merchandising, which includes remainders, reprints, and special imports. The Publishers Central Bureau, Crown's direct mail company, sends out book catalogues to consumers; popular response to these catalogues is used as a gauge of the market. Wartels is chairman and Alan Mirken is president of Crown; Betty A. Prashke serves as editor in chief. Simon died in 1966. In December 1985 the firm moved to 225 Park Avenue South, New York 10003.

References:

"Crown Publishers: The First Ten Years," *Publishers' Weekly*, 150 (16 November 1946): 2806-2810;

"Nat Wartels of Crown," *Publishers Weekly*, 213 (15 May 1978): 68-71.

—*Elizabeth Scott Pryor*

Cupples and Leon
(New York: 1902-1956)

Victor Cupples was introduced to the publishing world through his uncle, Joseph G. Cupples, who had established Cupples, Upham and Company in Boston in 1883. Victor Cupples worked briefly for the Riverside Press and D. Lothrop Company before going into partnership in March 1902 with Arthur T. Leon, who had been associated with Laird and Lee. In offices at 156 Fifth Avenue, New York, Cupples and Leon started by selling on commission the books of other companies, including Saalfield and F. J. Drake.

Cupples and Leon became a successful specialty house by tapping the market for comic books, series books, children's books, and dictionaries. In 1906 the company published *Buster Brown, His Dog Tige, and Their Jolly Times*, followed by other collections of comic strips including *Happy Hooligan, The Katzenjammer Kids, Alphonse and Gaston, Bringing Up Father*, and *Mutt and Jeff*. Among its series books were The White and Gold Series of Popular Titles and the Motor Boys and Ruth Fielding series for children. Cupples and Leon's edition of *Webster's New Century Dictionary* was also a strong seller.

In 1921, in one of the largest contracts ever negotiated to that time, the firm agreed to sell over $400,000 worth of comic books to the American News Company. By its twenty-fifth anniversary in 1927, Cupples and Leon was well established and was located in the Dodd, Mead Building at 449 Fourth Avenue, where it had moved in 1911. The firm continued to sell millions of copies of its twenty-five- and fifty-cent serial books into the 1930s, when they were unable to compete with the ten-cent comic magazines which had begun to appear on the newsstands.

Cupples retired in 1932; he died in 1941. The business was carried on by Leon until his death in 1943. His son, Walter T. Leon, continued until 1956, when the firm was sold to the Platt and Munk Company.

References:

"Arthur T. Leon [obituary]," *New York Times*, 17 December 1943, p. 28;

"Cupples & Leon Anniversary," *Publishers' Weekly*, 111 (2 April 1927): 1410;

"Platt & Munk Take Over Cupples and Leon," *Publishers' Weekly*, 169 (11 June 1956): 2523;

"Victor W. Cupples [obituary]," *New York Times*, 30 July 1941, p. 17.

—*Joan Gillen Conners*

Donald A. Wollheim, copublisher of DAW Books

DAW Books

(New York: 1971-   )

DAW≡sf
BOOKS

Donald A. Wollheim has been involved with science fiction since the 1930s, when he wrote science fiction stories and was a member of the Futurians. He became an editor with the magazine publisher A. A. Wyn, Incorporated in 1942 and editor in chief of Avon Books in 1947. At Wyn's invitation, he moved to Ace Books as editor in chief in 1952. Under Wollheim's editorship, Ace soon became famous for its high quality science fiction. Early works of then-unknown writers Samuel R. Delany, Philip K. Dick, Harlan Ellison, Ursula K. Le Guin, and Robert Silverberg were published in the Ace double-novel format.

In November 1971, after Wyn's death resulted in a change of management at Ace, Wollheim accepted an offer from New American Library to copublish a line of science fiction books under the DAW imprint. DAW offered its first titles in 1972: Brian N. Ball's *The Probability Man,* Joseph Green's *The Man behind the Eye,* Andre Norton's *Spell of the Witch World,* and A. E. Van Vogt's *The Book of Van Vogt.* As editor and publisher of DAW Books, Wollheim has continued to develop new writers, though he does not favor "experimental writing." Tanith Lee's *The Birthgrave* (1975) and *Don't Bite the Sun* (1976); C. J. Cherryh's *Gate of Ivrel* (1976), *Brothers of Earth* (1976), and Faded Sun series; and M. A. Foster's *The Warriors of Dawn* (1975) and *The Gameplayers of Zan* (1977) are among his discoveries. Important works by established writers published first by DAW include Lin Carter's *Under the Green Star* (1972), Dick's *We Can Build You*

(1972) and *The Book of Philip K. Dick* (1973), and Gordon R. Dickson's *Dorsai!* (1976). Wollheim edits and publishes an annual anthology of short science fiction, *The Annual World's Best S. F.*

DAW is also noted for publishing translations of works of leading European science fiction writers, including Egon Friedell's *The Return of the Time Machine;* Gerard Klein's *The Day before Tomorrow* (1972) and *The Overlords of War* (1974); Pierre Barbet's *Baphomet's Meteor* (1972), *Games Psyborgs Play* (1973), and *The Enchanted Planet* (1975); and Paul van Herck's *Where Were You Last Pluterday?* (1973). The firm publishes the fiction of Alan Burt Akers, Marion Zimmer Bradley, John Brunner, Philip José Farmer, Michael Moorcock, and John Norman. Elsie B. Wollheim, Wollheim's wife and executive vice-president of DAW Books, maintains a complete publication list for collectors; Betsy Wollheim, the Wollheim's daughter, is editor in chief. The address of DAW Books is 1633 Broadway, New York 10019.

References:

Robert Dahlin, "Trade News: Science Fiction Proves to Be No Fantasy for DAW Books, Five Years Old This Month," *Publishers Weekly,* 211 (11 April 1977): 52;

"DAW Books: New Sci-Fi Paperback Line from NAL," *Publishers' Weekly,* 200 (13 December 1971): 26.

—Martha A. Bartter and Linda Quinlan

The John Day Company

(New York: 1926-   )

Named after an Elizabethan printer, The John Day Company was founded in 1926 by Richard J. Walsh, Cleland Austin, Trell Yocum, and Guy Holt at 25 West Forty-fifth Street, New York. Day's first list that year consisted of James Branch Cabell's *The Music from behind the Moon,* Charles

Caldwell Dobie's *Less than Kin,* and Charles Brackett's *That Last Infirmity.* Holt left in 1930 to help start Whittlesey House for McGraw-Hill. In 1931 Day published Pearl Buck's *The Good Earth,* which stayed on the best-seller list for nearly two years. John Day became the main publisher for Buck, who

1981 advertisement

married the firm's president, Walsh, in 1935. After publishing several of Buck's works, Day began specializing in books on the Orient, publishing Dagny Carter's *China Magnificent* (1935) and Lin Yutang's *My Country and My People* (1937).

John Day was a leader in publishing books on progressive education by George S. Counts, A. Gordon Melvin, Carleton Washburne, and Satis N. Coleman. Day published two books by Franklin D. Roosevelt, *Looking Forward* (1933) and *On Our Way* (1934). The firm also published books on politics and economics by Sidney Hook, Frances Perkins, John Chamberlain, and Harvey O'Connor. The 1935 Pulitzer Prize winner in poetry, Audrey Wurdemann's *Bright Ambush* (1934), was a John Day book.

Except for Buck, many of whose novels of oriental life were published by the firm in uniform brown covers, John Day had no best-selling authors on its lists in the 1920s and 1930s; but the firm did publish works by some well-known contemporary American writers. Leonie Adams's *High Falcon and Other Poems* appeared in 1929, along with Meyer Levin's first book, *Reporter*. In 1930 the firm published Christopher Morley's *Rudolph and Amina* and *A Book of Days*.

Because of financial problems in the 1930s, Day arranged for Reynal and Hitchcock to handle its manufacturing and distribution while Day's editorial and promotional departments remained separate. Beginning in 1935, only Day's editorial department remained independent from Reynal and Hitchcock; books developed by Day's editors were called John Day Books but were published under the Reynal and Hitchcock imprint. In 1939

Day transferred its distribution functions from Reynal and Hitchcock to Putnam and resumed publishing under its own imprint.

The firm continued its emphasis on books with oriental themes and had a best-seller in 1944 with Margaret Landon's *Anna and the King of Siam.* Two years later Walsh started a subsidiary imprint, Asia Press, for the publication of books on Eastern subjects.

Walsh became chairman of the board in 1959 and his son, Richard Jr., became president. The elder Walsh died the following year.

In 1968 Day became a wholly-owned subsidiary of the International Textbook Company (Intext), with Walsh continuing as president and Day's offices remaining at 62 West Forty-fifth Street. In 1974 the New York division of Intext Publishing Group was purchased by Thomas Y. Crowell, which was acquired in 1977 by Harper and Row. As a division of Harper and Row, John Day publishes trade books, children's books, fiction, nonfiction, and special education works for the retarded and the handicapped. John Day's address is now the same as that of Harper and Row: 10 East Fifty-third Street, New York 10022.

References:

"Intext Purchases the John Day Company," *Publishers' Weekly*, 194 (30 December 1968): 46;

"John Day Celebrates Its Tenth Anniversary," *Publishers' Weekly*, 130 (25 July 1936): 255-256;

"The John Day Company," *Publishers' Weekly*, 109 (17 April 1926): 1330-1332.

—Elizabeth Pryor

Richard J. Walsh, founder of The John Day Company, in 1936

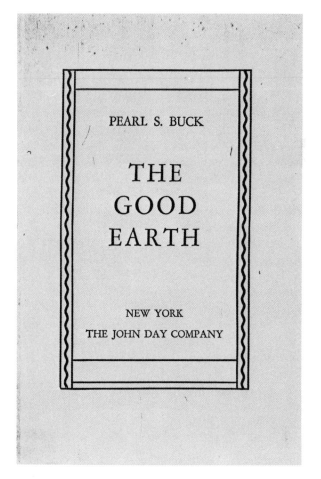

Title page for Day's most successful book, which stayed on the best-seller list for two years and earned a Nobel Prize for Buck

Dell Publishing Company

(New York: 1921-   )

 Delta **Books**

 LAUREL EDITIONS Of interest to both the discerning reader and the student.

 LAUREL-LEAF LIBRARY Reprints and originals selected especially for junior and senior high school students.

YEARLING BOOKS Reprints of outstanding literature for children grades 2-8, in paperback format, 5⅛" x 7⅝", featuring original illustrations and large type.

George T. Delacorte, Jr., founded the Dell Publishing Company in New York City in 1921. Dell's success lay in its ability to diversify. Originally a publisher of popular magazines, the company increasingly developed new lines; its output now includes fiction and nonfiction in hardcover and paperback editions. Dealing mainly in reprints of both popular and classical literature, Dell has also been the first publisher of some well-known contemporary authors.

For its first twenty-two years Dell's business consisted solely of mass-audience magazines such as *I Confess, Ballyhoo, Modern Screen, Modern Romances,* and *Inside Detective.* In the 1930s, with its *New Funnies, Looney Tunes,* and *Walt Disney's Comics,* the firm became the world's leading publisher of comic books. Starting in 1936, Dell comics were edited and printed by Western Printing and Lithographing Company of Racine, Wisconsin, and Poughkeepsie, New York. Over a span of fifty years, Dell published around 700 magazines, most of which lasted only a short time.

Delacorte's keen sense of the tastes of mass audiences led him into publishing paperback reprints in 1943 with the Dell Mystery Books; the first title in the series was *Death in the Library* by Philip Ketchum. The novels of Ellery Queen, Dashiell Hammett, Dorothy Hughes, Rex Stout, and Agatha Christie with their "mapbacks"—back covers with colorful illustrations of the scenes of the crimes—attracted millions of buyers. As in the case of the comics, all Dell books were edited and manufactured by Western Printing and Lithographing Company through its Dell Book Division; Dell Publishing Company handled promotion and distribution. This arrangement continued until 1962. In 1951 Dell started a series of reprints of long short stories or novelettes by leading authors: these were the Dell Ten-Cent Books. The Ten-Cent Books were each a maximum of sixty-four pages in length and, as the name implied, sold for a dime. The first twelve books in the series, published on 26 January, included W. Somerset Maugham's *Rain* and John O'Hara's *Pal Joey.* The series was discontinued after thirty-six titles had been published.

In September 1953 Dell began publishing original paperbacks in the Dell First Editions line. The books displayed the words "Not a Reprint" prominently on the cover. Among the early Dell First Editions was *The Body Snatchers* (1955) by Jack Finney.

Dell published its biggest best-seller in 1957: Grace Metalious's *Peyton Place,* which sold over ten million copies. Also in 1957 Dell introduced Laurel Editions, paperback reprints of superior American and British literature. Edited by such critics as David Levin and Richard Wilbur, these volumes served a new market of college students. Later, the Laurel Language Library published—in the original languages—the works of French and Spanish writers.

In 1962 Dell took over the editorial and production functions for its books from Western, which by then had changed its name to Western Publishing Company. That year Dell began publishing Delta Books, large trade paperbacks—both reprints and originals—aimed at "discriminating readers who desire superior works of fiction and nonfiction." Social and educational commentary, biographies, and literary criticism appeared on Delta's nonfiction lists. Fiction included *Drive, He Said* in 1964 by Jeremy Larner, who won the Delta Prize that year.

The Delacorte Press, Dell's hardcover line, was launched in February 1964 with Burton Wohl's *The Jet Set*. During its first decade Delacorte advertised its titles in conjunction with the Dial Press, which Dell acquired in 1964; the next year Noble and Noble also became a subsidiary of Dell. In 1965 Dell followed the lead of Harcourt Brace Jovanovich in joining a personal imprint with that of a publishing house: Delacorte Press/Seymour Lawrence. Lawrence selected authors and manuscripts, while Delacorte handled the rest of the publishing process. The first Delacorte/Lawrence publication was an unexpurgated version of J. P. Donleavy's *The Ginger Man* (1965), followed by his *The Saddest Summer of Samuel S.* (1966) and *The Beastly Beatitudes of Balthazar B.* (1968). Kurt Vonnegut's *Welcome to the Monkey House* (1968), *Slaughterhouse-Five* (1969), *Happy Birthday, Wanda June* (1971), *Breakfast of Champions* (1973), *Slapstick* (1976), *Jailbird* (1979), and *Deadeye Dick* (1982) were all published under the Delacorte/Lawrence imprint.

Other Delacorte titles include William Bradford Huie's *The Klansman* (1967); Katherine Anne Porter's *Collected Essays and Occasional Writings* (1970); James Jones's *Go to the Widow-maker* (1967), *The Merry Month of May* (1971), and *Viet Journal* (1974); William Goldman's *Marathon Man* (1974) and *Tinsel* (1979); Richard Yates's *Easter Parade* (1976) and *Liars in Love* (1981); Thomas Berger's *Who Is Teddy Villanova?* (1977), *Arthur Rex* (1978), and *Reinhart's Women* (1981); and Jim Harrison's *Revenge* (1979), *Legends of the Fall* (1979), and *Warlock* (1981).

Dell established the Laurel Leaf Library for junior and senior high school students in 1957; Yearling Books are for children in grades two through seven. Delacorte Press published other children's books, including Kenneth Townsend's *Felix the Bald-Headed Lion* (1967), Auro Roselli's *Cats of the Eiffel Tower* (1967), and Jan Balet's *The Gift* (1967).

Although much of the credit for Dell's tremendous expansion goes to George Delacorte, other persons in the company played significant roles. Helen Meyer, who joined the firm in 1924 and became president in 1957, directed the company's activities during a time when Dell underwent its greatest diversification. Donald Fine, editor in chief of Dell Books and editor of Delacorte Press, was influential in publishing some of Dell's best-selling paperback reprints, including Joseph Heller's *Catch-22* (1962), James Baldwin's *The Fire Next Time* (1963), and Morris West's *The Shoes of the Fisherman* (1964).

In 1976 Doubleday acquired Dell Publishing Company for a reported $35 million. Meyer retained the presidency until her retirement in 1979, when Carl W. Tobey took the position. Currently William A. Lindsay is president, and Carole Baron is vice-president and publisher. Dell's address is One Dag Hammarskjold Plaza, New York 10017.

References:

"Dell, Publishers of Magazines and Reprints," *Publishers' Weekly*, 147 (19 May 1945): 1990-1993;

"The Story of Dell Publishing Company, Inc.," *Book Production Magazine*, 80 (November 1964): 32-35.

—Elizabeth Hoffman

(photo by Piet Schreuders)
George T. Delacorte, Jr., founder of Dell Publishing Company

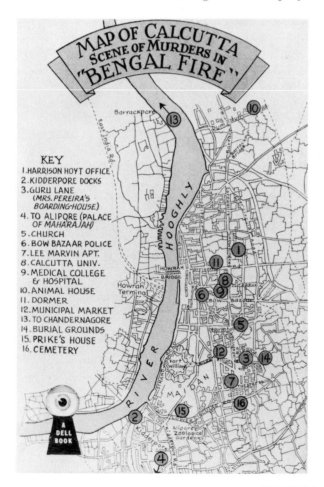 

1949 Dell "mapback" cover

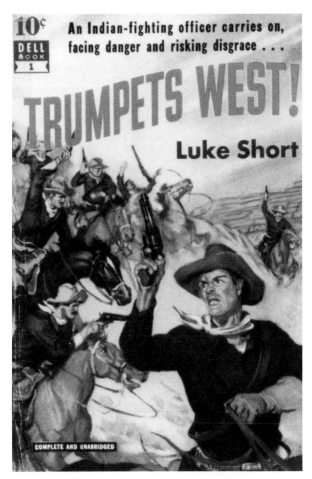

First Dell ten-cent paperback, published in 1951

1954 advertisement

The Derrydale Press
(New York: 1927-1942)

Eugene V. Connett III established The Derrydale Press in 1927 to reprint rare early British and American books on sport, to publish on rag paper handcolored prints that depicted contemporary sport in America, and to produce high-quality books on American sport, chiefly hunting and fishing. After short stays in two other locations in New York, Connett set up his press in a brownstone house on East Thirty-fourth Street between Park and Lexington Avenues.

The 128 Derrydale titles, much prized by collectors, were often published in editions limited to fewer than 1,000 copies, handsomely printed and bound, and illustrated with original drawings and photographs. The Derrydale line began in 1927 with Connett's *Magic Hours*, a reprint of Frank Forester's *Trouting along the Catasaque*, the *Memoirs of the Gloucester Foxhunting Club*, and a reprint of the Hitchcock edition of the sporting works of Edith Somerville and Martin Ross.

Derrydale also published "sporting fiction," including Philip H. Babcock's *Falling Leaves* (1937), a collection of shooting stories set in New England; three collections of stories by Burton L. Spiller; and two by Nash Buckingham. *American Big Game Fishing,* with a contribution by Ernest Hemingway, appeared in 1935. Starting in 1933, Derrydale produced inexpensive trade editions of its books under the Windward House imprint. Windward House was sold to Doubleday in 1936.

Connett sold Derrydale in 1942 to his vice-president and salesman, Frank J. Lowe. Lowe changed the name of the company to Frank J. Lowe, Publisher of Fine Sporting Prints and Sporting Books and Derrydale Sporting Prints. After a period of government service, Connett joined D. Van Nostrand and Company in 1947 as editor of its Sporting Books series. Lowe became a salesman for Van Nostrand in 1948. Connett retired in 1964 and died at seventy-eight in 1969.

References:

Hannah Hastings Catlin, *The Derrydale Press . . . with a Checklist of the Derrydale Books Printed after the Summer of 1937* (Charlottesville: Bibliographical Society of University of Virginia, 1951);

Eugene V. Connett III, *A Decade of American Sporting Books & Prints by The Derrydale Press, 1927-1937* (New York: The Derrydale Press, 1937);

"Derrydale Press Books and Prints Sold," *Publishers' Weekly,* 142 (19 December 1942): 2425;

"Eugene V. Connett III [obituary]," *New York Times,* 21 September 1969, p. 81;

"Ten Years of Sporting Books," *Publishers' Weekly,* 131 (6 March 1937): 1114-1116.

—Deborah G. Gorman

The Devin-Adair Company
(New York and Old Greenwich, Connecticut: 1911-   )

Named for the founder's mother and mother-in-law, The Devin-Adair Company was established in New York in 1911 by Henry Garrity, an Irishman from Indiana. Irish literature and books on Ireland became specialties of the firm. The company was first located at Fifth Avenue and Thirty-ninth Street and later at 23 East Twenty-sixth Street. Devin Adair Garrity, the founder's son, assumed the presidency upon his father's death in 1939.

Devin-Adair's first book was *My Unknown Chum: "Aguecheek"* (1912), a nostalgic travelogue by Garrity. It became a steady seller and long remained in print. Devin-Adair pioneered the subject of organic farming, publishing J. I. Rodale's first book, *Pay Dirt,* in 1945. It was also among the first to publish books on ecology with John H. Storer's *The Web of Life* (1953). Conservative politics was another specialty: George Morgenstern's *Pearl Harbor: The Story of the Secret War* (1947) was followed by John T. Flynn's *The Roosevelt Myth* (1948). In 1968 appeared *The Creative Society,* a collection of comments by Governor Ronald Reagan of California. Other subjects include Americana, natural history, and health and nutrition. In 1974 Devin-Adair acquired the Chatham Press, which specialized in books on Cape Cod and New England, natural history, and photography.

Devin-Adair sells some forty Irish titles from its active list of approximately 300 books. The cornerstone author of the house's Irish line is Seumas MacManus, whose *The Story of the Irish Race* (1921) has sold 300,000 copies. Other MacManus titles include *Yourself and the Neighbours* (1914), *The Rocky Road to Dublin* (1947), and *The Well o' the World's End* (1949). Liam O'Flaherty and Sean O'Faoláin are also Devin-Adair authors. O'Flaherty's *Two Lovely Beasts and Other Stories* came out in 1950, *The Stories of Liam O'Flaherty* in 1956. O'Faoláin is represented by *The Man Who Invented Sin* (1948), a short story collection; the twin travel books *A Summer in Italy* (1950) and *An Autumn in Italy* (1953); *The Short Story* (1951); and *Newman's Way: The Odyssey of John Henry Newman* (1952). Other Devin-

Adair story collections are Daniel Corkery's *The Wager* (1950), Lord Dunsany's *The Sword of Welleran* (1954), and James Plunkett's *The Trusting and the Maimed* (1955). Other books by Irish authors include the collected poems of Padraic Colum (1953), Oliver St. John Gogarty (1954), and Patrick Kavanagh (1964), and Paul Vincent Carroll's *Irish Stories and Plays* (1958). Devin Adair Garrity edited several anthologies of Irish literature, among them *New Irish Poets* (1948) and *44 Irish Short Stories* (1955).

Book clubs have been favorite projects of Devin-Adair. In 1958 Garrity inaugurated the Irish Book Club, which distributed about six titles a year. The firm organized the Gardener's Book Club in 1946 and the Farmer's Book Club in 1950. Currently operating are the Ecological Book Club, established in 1970, and the Veritas Book Club, begun in 1971 to distribute libertarian books of revisionist modern history. Since 1970 the firm has been located in Old Greenwich, Connecticut. Its address is 143 Sound Beach Avenue, Old Greenwich 06870. Claudine De La Belle Issue is the publisher of Devin-Adair books. Devin Adair Garrity died in January 1981.

References:

"The Devin-Adair Company, Inc.; The Chatham Press, Inc.," *Publishers Weekly,* 208 (17 November 1975): 52, 57;

"Obituary Notes. Devin Adair Garrity," *Publishers Weekly,* 219 (30 January 1981): 26.

—Vincent Prestianni

Eugene V. Connett III, founder of The Derrydale Press, in 1937 (photo by Disraeli)

Helen Meyer, president of Dell from 1957 until 1979 (photo by Piet Schreuders)

The Dial Press

(New York: 1923-   )

After rising to the rank of major during World War I, Lincoln MacVeagh returned to his editorial position at Henry Holt and Company, where he rose to a directorship. He left Holt in December 1923 when an old friend from his Harvard days, Scofield Thayer, editor and part owner of the influential literary magazine the *Dial*, invited him to join in forming The Dial Press. Although MacVeagh replaced Samuel Craig as secretary-treasurer of the Dial Publishing Company, the publisher of the magazine, he devoted most of his energies to The Dial Press, of which he was manager and director. The Dial Press occupied the same brownstone as the magazine at 152 West Thirteenth Street, New York, and the two firms shared officers and stockholders; but The Dial Press was established separately from the magazine to publish in a wider range of areas than did the *Dial*. MacVeagh supplied The Dial Press's logo—Cupid astride a lion—from the design on his signet ring.

While there were crossover authors, such as D. H. Lawrence and Marianne Moore, The Dial Press's first list in 1924 showed its independence from the *Dial*'s literary concerns: the twenty-seven volumes included fiction, poetry, biographies, collections of essays, and works in science, history, and philosophy. Perhaps the closest connection in The Dial Press's first year was the publication of *Stories from the Dial* (1924), which included Lawrence's "Rex."

Under MacVeagh's direction, The Dial Press developed a strong list of quality literature. Its first important volumes of poetry were Moore's *Observations* (1924) and E. E. Cummings's *XLI Poems* (1925). Paul Rosenfeld's *Men Seen: Twenty-four Modern Authors* (1925) included essays on Joyce, Lawrence, Proust, Stevens, and Moore. The firm's first fiction best-seller was Elizabeth Bowen's *The Hotel* (1928), which became a Book-of-the-Month Club selection. Works of the 1920s which received critical attention were Glenway Wescott's *The Apple of the Eye* (1924); R. H. Mottram's *The Spanish Farm*

(1927); W. R. Burnett's *Little Caesar* (1929), a Literary Guild selection; and Valentine Kataev's *The Embezzlers* (1929). Dial also published Charles Bugnet's conversations with Marshal Foch, *Foch Speaks* (1929). MacVeagh was aggressive in bringing in foreign authors, especially British, while keeping a keen eye on American writing. A major project of the early years was the Library of Living Classics, edited by Manuel Komroff.

When MacVeagh was appointed American minister to Greece in 1933, The Dial Press was sold to Max Salop; MacVeagh continued to hold stock in the firm. Under Salop's guidance, Dial generally maintained the policies and tastes inherited from MacVeagh. In 1938 Burton Hoffman, the head of Knight Publishers, bought the firm from Salop. Hoffman brought with him manuscripts originally to have been published by Knight. He kept Grenville Vernon as editor, a position he had occupied since 1927.

Under Hoffman, Dial adhered to its traditional policies but also began to increase its offerings of popular works. Its books ranged from Ford Madox Ford's *The March of Literature* (1938) and Giovanni Bach's *The History of the Scandinavian Literatures* (1938) to works dealing with war themes, such as André Simone's *J'Accuse* (1940) and Pierre van Paasen's *That Day Alone* (1941). In 1944, 400 copies of Lawrence's *The First Lady Chatterley*, the original version of *Lady Chatterley's Lover*, were seized at the Dial offices by John S. Sumner, executive secretary of the New York Society for the Suppression of Vice. The case was ultimately dismissed.

Hoffman's move toward popular fiction was rewarded with Gladys Schmitt's *David the King* (1946), a Literary Guild selection which went on to sell almost a million copies. Frank Yerby's first novel, *The Foxes of Harrow* (1946), established him as a major money-maker for Dial. Van Paasen's *Days of Our Years* (1946) surpassed 800,000 in sales, and Peggy Guggenheim's *Out of This Century* (1946) also did well. Hoffman oversaw the publication of Salvador Dali's autobiography *The Secret Life of Salvador Dali* (1942) and Dali's novel *Hidden Faces* (1944). In addition, Dial introduced a series of popular anthologies, The Permanent Library.

In 1951 Dial was purchased by George Joel, who had come to the house from Covici-Friede in 1938. Under his direction, and with Clarkson N. Potter as managing editor in the late 1950s, the firm continued its mixed list of popular fiction and quality literature. The most significant writer published by Dial in the 1950s was James Baldwin, who began a long association with the house when his novel *Giovanni's Room* was published in 1956.

Richard W. Baron purchased Dial in 1959; Potter left to start his own publishing firm. In 1961 Dial, in a joint venture with William Morrow, Dodd, Mead and Company, and Crowell, launched Apollo Editions, a line of quality paperbacks aimed at the college market. Two years later Dell Publishing Company acquired sixty percent of Dial's stock; in 1968 it took over complete ownership. Baron left to start the Richard W. Baron Publishing Company.

Under editor in chief E. L. Doctorow, Dial established a longer and more varied list of fiction and nonfiction—especially works on social and political themes—in the 1960s. Probably the most significant publication of the period was Aleksandr Solzhenitsyn's *The Cancer Ward* (1968). Baldwin's *Nobody Knows My Name* came out in 1961, followed by his *Another Country* in 1962 and *The Fire Next Time* in 1963. Dial also published Herbert Gold's *Salt* (1963), Thomas Berger's *Little Big Man* (1964), Norman Mailer's *An American Dream* (1965), and Larry McMurtry's *The Last Picture Show* (1966). Popular fiction included Earl Hamner's *Spencer's Mountain* (1961) and Richard Condon's *The Ecstasy Business* (1967). In nonfiction, the greatest success was George Waller's *Kidnap* (1961), the story of the Lindbergh case, with a first printing of 210,000 copies. Books on the civil rights movement in-

cluded Julius Lester's *Look Out, Whitey!* (1968) and *Search for the New Land* (1969) and H. Rap Brown's *Die, Nigger, Die!* (1969). Other nonfiction works were *Frederic Remington's Own West* (1960) and Leonard Lewin's *Report from Iron Mountain* (1967).

The 1970s were profitable years for The Dial Press, especially in sales of popular fiction: Ernest J. Gaines's *The Autobiography of Miss Jane Pittman* (1971), Condon's *Arigato* (1972) and *Winter Kills* (1974), and Baldwin's *If Beale Street Could Talk* (1974) were all successful. Robert Ludlum began a series of best-sellers with *The Matlock Paper* (1973). The house also had success with nonfiction books, including Adam Clayton Powell's autobiography *Adam by Adam* (1971), Manuel Smith's self-help best-seller *When I Say No, I Feel Guilty* (1975), Victor Lasky's *It Didn't Start with Watergate* (1977), and Michelle Wallace's *Black Macho and the Myth of the Superwoman* (1978).

The Dial Press is now an imprint of Doubleday and Company, which acquired Dial when it purchased Dell in 1976. Dial's address is the same as Doubleday's: 245 Park Avenue, New York 10017. MacVeagh died in 1972.

References:

"Dell Drops Baron as Head of Dial Press," *Publishers' Weekly*, 194 (19 August 1968): 39-40;

"Dial Press Acquired by Hoffman," *Publishers' Weekly*, 133 (14 May 1938): 1936-1937;

"Expansion Plans Mark Dial Press's 20th Anniversary," *Publishers' Weekly*, 173 (28 April 1958): 18-20;

"Lincoln MacVeagh and the Dial Press: Another New Publishing Firm Is Founded," *Publishers' Weekly*, 105 (14 June 1924): 1901-1902;

"Lincoln MacVeagh [obituary]," *New York Times*, 17 January 1972, p. 34.

—*Ernest Bevan, Jr.*

Title page for book by one of Devin-Adair's Irish authors

Lincoln MacVeagh, cofounder, manager, and director of The Dial Press

1928 advertisement

B. W. Dodge and Company

(New York: circa 1903-1911)

NEW YORK

DODGE PUBLISHING COMPANY

B. W. Dodge and Company was founded at 43-45 East Nineteenth Street, New York, around 1903. Among its earliest titles were Fergus Hume's *The Mystery of the Shadow* and Henry A. Hering's *The Burglar's Club*, both in 1906. In the following year it published the second edition of Theodore Dreiser's first book, *Sister Carrie*, from a new address, 24 East Twenty-first Street. The firm is perhaps best remembered for its publication of two novels by Upton Sinclair: *The Moneychangers* (1908) and *Samuel the Seeker* (1910). After moving in 1908 to 43 West Twenty-ninth Street, it published

Charles Fort's *The Outcast Manufacturers* and Arthur Stringer's *The Gun-runner*, both in 1909.

In 1911 Dodge was purchased by William Rickey and Company of New York, a small firm that published some fiction. Rickey's most notable publication was *An American Suffragette* (1911) by Isaac N. Stevens, "one of the foremost American champions of women suffrage," whose *The Liberators* had been published by Dodge in 1908. Rickey went out of business around 1913.

—David Dzwonkoski

George H. Doran Company
(New York and Toronto: 1908-1927)
Doubleday, Doran and Company
(New York: 1927-1945)

The George H. Doran Company was notable for its distinguished fiction, including works by Arnold Bennett, W. Somerset Maugham, Hugh Walpole, Frank Swinnerton, Aldous Huxley, John Dos Passos, and Charles Norris; for its extensive religious and theological offerings; and for its prominent participation in the Anglo-American propaganda effort during the First World War. The Doran firm averaged over 250 new titles a year, second only to Macmillan, in the almost two decades of its independent existence; in the *Publishers' Trade List Annual* for 1927, the year of the firm's merger with Doubleday, Page and Company, Doran featured 3,346 titles.

George H. Doran was born into a staunch Presbyterian family in Toronto in 1869. He fin-

ished school at fourteen and responded to a sign in the window of the Toronto Willard Tract Depository that said "Smart Boy Wanted." For a weekly salary of two dollars Doran worked six days a week, learning all phases of evangelical publishing. In January 1892, at twenty-one, he left for Chicago to join the interdenominational house of Fleming H. Revell, which purchased the Toronto Willard Tract Depository in 1893. He became Revell's traveling representative west of the Alleghenies and eventually vice-president of the firm. But when Revell's branches were consolidated and the headquarters shifted to New York in 1907, Doran's new position of "coordinate managing director" proved in less than a year to be unsatisfactory. Doran went into business for himself for a while, then back into

publishing, this time breaking free of the narrow world of religious publishing.

Doran started his own publishing house as George H. Doran, Limited at 215 Victoria Street in Toronto, representing the English publishers Hodder and Stoughton in the United States and Canada. Retaining the Canadian operation as a subsidiary, he moved his offices on 22 February 1908 to the Builders' Exchange building at 35 West Thirty-second Street in New York. A fire at the end of April 1912 wiped out the firm's book stock of about half a million volumes but left business records—including a crucial fire insurance receipt—intact. Doran relocated in larger quarters at 38 West Thirty-second Street. On 19 January 1918 the firm moved to 244 Madison Avenue; in May 1923, Doran acquired a floor at Tenth Avenue and Thirty-sixth Street for expanded shipping and mailing operations.

Initially, Hodder and Stoughton owned a twenty-five percent share in the business, a friend of Doran's owned twenty percent, and Doran held fifty-five percent. Doran acquired fiction, art books, children's books, and general titles from Hodder and Stoughton. When Doran's slender personal capital of $10,000 needed augmenting, John Duffy, president and principal owner of the paper dealers Perkins, Goodwin and Company, extended credit to Doran on his word. Duffy asked, "Do you expect to pay for this paper?" Doran replied, "Yes, if it is the last thing I do on earth." Doran always considered his first year in business a "miracle of publishing operation": the firm grossed $200,000, for a net profit of about $40,000.

In 1909 Doran was recapitalized as an American corporation. Hodder and Stoughton, whose investment had yielded a fourfold profit, now held a third of the stock. Messmore Kendall became director and secretary with five percent of the stock; Doran held fifty-six percent. By acquiring A. C. Armstrong and Son in 1910, Doran rounded out its list with a substantial stock of religious titles. In

1918 Doran purchased the respected literary periodical the *Bookman* from Dodd, Mead and Company. Under the editorship of John Farrar, the publication achieved a wider appeal and the largest circulation it had ever had. For Doran, it was a source of great pride, if not profits.

One of the first titles published by Doran's new corporation was a novel, *The Foreigner* (1909), by Ralph Connor (Rev. Charles William Gordon), which sold 125,000 copies. Doran made its mark nationally with an American edition of Bennett's *The Old Wives Tale* (1911), which Scribner had turned down. The book sold 100,000 copies in three years. Doran acquired the rights to several of Bennett's previously published works and formed a lifelong friendship with the author which yielded contacts with other major British writers, such as Swinnerton and Walpole. Other novels by Bennett appeared under Doran's imprint, including *Anna of the Five Towns* (1910), *Clayhanger* (1910), *Helen with the High Hand* (1911), and *Hilda Lessways* (1911), together with the play *The Love Match* (1922) and volumes of essays.

Doran introduced Swinnerton to America with *Nocturne* (1917); fifteen other novels and critical studies followed. Walpole's work had appeared under other American imprints before Doran published *Fortitude* (1913), the first of the firm's twenty Walpole titles, including *Maradick at Forty* (1914), *The Duchess of Wrexe* (1914), and *Jeremy* (1919). H. G. Wells also had work published in America by other firms, but Doran was able to get the rights to seven of his works, including *The World of William Clissold* (1926). Doran published Rebecca West's *The Return of the Soldier* (1918) and *The Judge* (1922).

Another major acquisition of Doran's was Maugham. Doran considered *Of Human Bondage* (1915) to be the novel he would like most to have written himself. *The Moon and Sixpence* (1919) followed. Doran published fifteen works of fiction and drama by Maugham, including *On a Chinese Screen* (1922), *The Painted Veil* (1925), and *The Constant Wife* (1926).

One of the ten novels Doran published by Ralph Connor, *The Sky Pilot in No Man's Land* (1919) made the best-seller list; so did *Sonia: Between Two Worlds* (1917) by Stephen McKenna, *In Secret* (1919) by Robert W. Chambers, and *The Heirs Apparent* (1924) by Sir Philip H. Gibbs. Mary Roberts Rinehart appeared on best-seller lists with *The Amazing Interlude* (1918), *Dangerous Days* (1919), *A Poor Wise Man* (1920), *The Breaking Point* (1922)—a best-seller for two years—and *Lost Ecstasy* (1927). Some of Doran's nonfiction made the best-seller lists: Sir Oliver J. Lodge's *Raymond, or Life and Death* (1916); *The Autobiography of Margot Asquith* (1920-1922); and *Revolt in the Desert* (1927) by T. E. Lawrence.

Huxley's novels, plays, and essays published by Doran included *Limbo* (1920), *Crome Yellow* (1922), and *Antic Hay* (1923); V. Sackville-West's varied output included *The Heir* (1922), *Grey Wethers* (1923), *Seducers in Ecuador* (1925), and *Passenger to Teheran* (1927). *The Green Hat* (1924), one of the seven books by Michael Arlen that Doran published, became a best-seller. Hodder and Stoughton objected to the publication of *The Green Hat* and some other books; as a result, Doran bought out the British firm's share in his company in 1924.

Other Doran authors included P. G. Wodehouse, with *Three Men and a Maid* (1922), *Golf Without Tears* (1924), and *Carry On, Jeeves!* (1927); Irvin S. Cobb, with *Back Home* (1912), *"Speaking of Operations!"* (1915), *Paths of Glory* (1915), *Old Judge Priest* (1916), *J. Poindexter, Colored* (1922), and *Prose and Cons* (1926); and nine-year-old Daisy Ashford with *The Young Visiters* (1919), which sold 200,000 copies. The Doran list also included works by Compton Mackenzie, Robert Hichens, Cyril Hume, Heywood Broun, Robert Cortes Holliday, John Buchan, Philip Gibbs, Albert Payson Terhune, Donald Ogden Stewart, Stewart Edward White, Frank L. Packard, and John Thomas. Some Doran authors forgotten today were immensely popular and profitable in their time, such as Mrs. Oliver Onions (Berta Ruck), G. A. Birmingham (James Owen Hannay), and Marie Corelli.

Authors who were not retained by Doran included Frank Harris, whose *The Veils of Isis, and Other Stories* appeared in 1915, and Charles Norris, whose *The Amateur* was published in 1916. Doran published John Dos Passos's *Three Soldiers* (1921) and *Rosinante to the Road Again* (1922) but declined further work from Dos Passos because of the author's language, which had been edited to eliminate "obscenities" in *Three Soldiers*. Doran was proud of having rejected everything by "that ruffian" Theo-

dore Dreiser and turned down D. H. Lawrence's *Women in Love* because of its "immoral" elements. When an author asked him about his publishing credo, Doran declared: "I would publish no book which would destroy a man's simple faith in God without providing an adequate substitute. I would publish no book which would destroy the institution of marriage without providing a substitute order of society which would be protective of the younger generation. All else I would cheerfully publish."

Doran had, however, a strong sense of his public as well as of his own principles. He once said, "To be purely professional and aesthetic, to publish only for the gratification of personal taste or desire, is to invite failure in a commercial sense, and I am not sure that in the ultimate it would not mean artistic failure, for only an endowed protagonist may at all times seek to impose his own ideals and ideas and prejudices upon a public." Doran was open to intellectual currents not reflecting his own beliefs, notwithstanding his moral conservatism. His firm published books by Lodge and by Sir Arthur Conan Doyle which advocated spiritualism, in which Doran took no stock, and leftist social commentary, such as Charles Edward Russell's *Why I Am a Socialist* (1910) and Wells's *Russia in the Shadows* (1921) and *Democracy Under Revision* (1927).

Doran's poetry selection was not extensive. As he said in his memoirs, *Chronicles of Barabbas* (1952), "The simple ballad always pleased my sensibilities, but the verse that pleased the real poetry-lover fell unresponsively on my all too practical soul." Doran published Elinor Wylie's second book of poems, *Black Armour* (1923); William Rose Benét's *Man Possessed* (1927) and *Moons of Grandeur* (1920); Joyce Kilmer's *Trees and Other Poems* (1917); and Christopher Morley's books of whimsical verse *Songs for a Little House* (1917), *The Rocking Horse* (1919), *Chimneysmoke* (1921), and *Parsons' Pleasure* (1923).

During World War I Doran specialized in war books, publishing Allied propaganda from Wellington House—the publicity organization of the British Foreign Office—and other patriotic works, including Rinehart's essays from the front, *Kings, Queens and Pawns* (1915), and Theodore Roosevelt's *Fear God and Take Your Own Part* (1916) and *The Foes of Our Own Household* (1917). Several Doran titles were best-sellers in the war books category: *My Home in the Field of Honor* (1916) by Frances W. Huard; *The Land of Deepening Shadow: Germany-at-War* (1917) by D. Thomas Curtin; and the phenomenally successful *My Four Years in Germany* (1917) by Ambassador James W. Gerard, as well as Gerard's *Face to Face with Kaiserism* (1918). Doran also published Woodrow Wilson's *State Papers and Addresses* (1918), Father Francis P. Duffy's story of the Sixty-ninth Regiment (1919), and works by Lloyd George, Lord Northcliffe, and General Sir Ian Hamilton.

Well-known illustrators enhanced the appeal of Doran books. These included Arthur Rackham, who illustrated Nathaniel Hawthorne's *A Wonder Book* (1922), as well as Edmund Dulac, Kay Nielson, Jean de Bosschere, C. A. Federer, Noel Pocock, William Nicholson, Thomas Fogarty, Elizabeth MacKinstry, and May Wilson Preston.

Doran believed in good publicity. Grant Overton, a young editor, wrote an entire volume, *When Winter Comes to Main Street* (1922), suggesting good Doran reading to while away long, dark winter nights. Overton's book—"the high-water mark of publishing promotion," wrote Doran in his memoirs—sold 48,500 copies. Doran went along on Bennett's triumphal tour of the United States in 1911 and presented Walpole at the 1919 Marshall Field Book Fair in Chicago. On 19 October 1925 Doran and Farrar started the *Doran Free Press*, a postcard-size house organ sent daily to the book trade with messages about publishing, bookselling, and books; the publication's two-month life span coincided with the pre-Christmas selling season. A strong sales network across the United States and in Canada supported such publicity. Doran's executive staff included Doran's son-in-law Stanley M. Rinehart, Jr., general manager; Alan Rinehart, director of publicity; and Frederick K. Rinehart in manufacturing. Besides Farrar and Overton, editors included—at different times—Eugene F. Saxton, Sinclair Lewis, Robert Cortes Holliday, Coningsby Dawson, Richard Hillis, and Paul Dwight Moody.

As Doran neared retirement, he wanted to provide for the continued financial stability of his company and the career prospects of his younger staff. Thus Doran accepted a merger offer from Doubleday, Page and Company. On 23 September 1927 there was an exchange of stock and on 31 December the names of the firms were officially blended as Doubleday, Doran and Company, Incorporated.

Doubleday had more to gain from Doran's outstanding and considerably larger lists; Doran hoped only to see all that he had worked for carried on. But the merger quickly vindicated the misgivings Doran had about it. Doran was the ninth partner or major associate of F. N. Doubleday. With the ailing Doubleday, chairman of the board, more active in the firm's affairs than Doran had expected, with Nelson Doubleday as president, and with all three men being strong-minded leaders, a parting of the ways was inevitable.

Within two years Farrar and Stanley and Frederick Rinehart left to found Farrar and Rinehart. Referring to differences resulting from the "human equation," Doran resigned on 1 August 1930 to take an executive position representing the book and magazine publishing interests of Hearst's International Magazine Company in the United States and England. Doran retained his stock, however, and it was not until 31 December 1945 that Nelson Doubleday deleted *Doran* from the company's name. "So ended a great plan," wrote Doran in his memoirs. Doran died in 1956.

References:

George H. Doran, *Chronicles of Barabbas, 1884-1934* (New York: Harcourt, Brace, 1935); revised as *Chronicles of Barabbas, 1884-1934; Further Chronicles and Comments, 1952* (New York: Rinehart, 1952);

"Doubleday and Doran Firms Combine," *Publishers' Weekly*, 112 (24 September 1927): 1079-1083;

"Doubleday, Doran & Co.," *Fortune*, 13 (February 1936): 73-77, 161-162, 164, 166, 168, 170, 172, 178-181;

"The House of Doran," *Literary Digest International Book Review*, 2 (1923-1924): 550-551;

"Obituary Notes [George H. Doran]," *Publishers' Weekly*, 169 (14 January 1956): 121-123.

—Sharon Ann Jaeger

1908 advertisement (New York Times)

George H. Doran in 1935 (photo by Blank & Stoller)

May 15, 1920

THE PUBLISHERS' WEEKLY

1491

Summer Reading of
Unusual Selling Quality

DORAN BOOKS

Frank L. PACKARD

THE WHITE MOLL
The story of a girl who is a worthy successor to the famous JIMMIE DALE. Her thrilling escapades in the underworld make one of Packard's best. Net, $1.90

W. Somerset MAUGHAM

THE EXPLORER
By the author of THE MOON AND SIXPENCE, combines the uncanny character-analysis of his Strickland portrait with the sparkling brilliancy of his plays. Net, $1.90

Sophie KERR

PAINTED MEADOWS
By the author of "The See-Saw," an engrossing drama of passion, tragedy and a unique happiness in a lovely Southern town. Net, $1.90

Wallace IRWIN

TRIMMED WITH RED
A hilarious story of Parlor Bolshevics, by the creator of "Hashimura Togo" and "Venus in the East." Net, $1.75

H. G. WELLS

LOVE AND MR. LEWISHAM
Wells' favorite book, a new edition of one of his early and most popular novels. Net, $1.90

James E. AGATE

RESPONSIBILITY
A first novel destined for the enduring success of "The Way of All Flesh." Net, $1.90

Alec WAUGH

THE LOOM OF YOUTH
A memorable first book by a seventeen-year-old author. Net, $1.90

Henry OYEN

THE PLUNDERERS
"A thousand thrills, the Florida Swamps, land swindlers, love and a dash of magic," by the author of "The Man Trail." Net, $1.75

Baroness ORCZY

HIS MAJESTY'S WELL-BELOVED
"A new hero as fascinating as 'The Scarlet Pimpernel.'"—*New York Times*. Net, $1.75

Virginia WOOLF

THE VOYAGE OUT
A first novel of serious artistic value, brilliance, emotion, humor, absolutely unafraid. Net, $2.25

Mrs. Victor RICKARD

CATHY ROSSITER
"An unusually sensational story," by the author of "The Light Above the Cross Roads." Net, $1.75

1920 advertisement

Dover Publications

(New York: 1942-   )

Dover Publications, Incorporated was founded in 1942 at 31 East Twenty-seventh Street, New York, by Hayward Cirker to sell inexpensive but high quality reprints of scientific and technical reference works. It soon branched out into other areas, publishing its first literary book, a reprint of John Gassner's *Masters of the Drama,* in 1945. It was one of the earliest publishers of quality paperbacks. Although Dover now originates more than half of its material, it is still recognized primarily for its reprint editions of works from a wide variety of fields.

Dover's literary production grew under the editorial direction of Everett Bleiler, now retired, and John Grafton. Especially notable are its reprints of children's classics, detective novels, fantasies, ghost stories, science fiction, and Victorian novels by L. Frank Baum, Lewis Carroll, Beatrix Potter, H. G. Wells, Wilkie Collins, H. Rider Haggard, Anthony Trollope, and George Gissing. It has reprinted Shakespeare's plays, as well as works by Blake, Twain, and Thoreau.

The firm publishes a large line of art books, including *The Notebooks of Leonardo da Vinci* (1970); *The Doré Illustrations for Dante's Divine Comedy* (1976); and *The Art Nouveau Style . . .* (1977), edited by Roberta Waddell, as well as books on art instruction. Other popular lines include full-color paper dolls and toy and novelty books such as Edmund V. Gillon's *Cut and Assemble an Early New England Village* (1977) and Frank J. Moore's *The Magic Moving Alphabet Book* (1978).

Dover is a family-held enterprise. Cirker is president of the company; his wife, Blanche, is a vice-president. Having steadily expanded since the 1940s, the firm publishes 200 to 235 titles annually and lists more than 2,900 titles in its catalogue.

The company has moved several times since its founding: first to 1780 Broadway, then to 920 Broadway, and then, in 1960, to 180 Varick Street, New York 10014. In 1983 the entire company, except for the editorial staff, moved to 31 East 2nd St., Mineola, N.Y., 11501.

References:

John F. Baker, "What's Doing at Dover," *Publishers Weekly,* 220 (14 August 1981): 21-26;

"The White Clips of Dover," *Time,* 111 (27 March 1978): 97-98.

—Christine Garrison

Dramatists Play Service

(New York: 1936-   )

Dramatists Play Service was established in New York in 1936 by members of the Dramatists Guild. Barrett H. Clark, a writer and lecturer on the theater, became the first head of the firm. It is the largest agency in America devoted to publishing and distributing plays for amateur productions and to handling production rights to those plays.

Before the Dramatists Play Service was formed, performance fees paid to playwrights var-

ied widely; some inexperienced dramatists sold all amateur rights outright, thereby foregoing the benefits of having their plays handled on commission. For five years after its founding, almost all established dramatists turned their plays over to Dramatists Play Service without any advance or guarantee. By the end of that period, the company's catalogue offered plays by Maxwell Anderson, Edna Ferber, Moss Hart, Ben Hecht, Lillian Hell-

Hayward Cirker, founder and president, and Blanche Cirker, executive vice-president of Dover Publications

man, DuBose Heyward, Sidney Howard, George S. Kaufman, Clifford Odets, Eugene O'Neill, Elmer Rice, and Robert E. Sherwood.

Eventually Dramatists Play Service had to respond to the competition it had helped to stimulate among play agencies. The firm began offering variable cash advances to playwrights; another option was a guarantee that royalties would reach an agreed amount within a certain number of years. The company currently publishes thirty to fifty new plays each year, while keeping most of its previously published plays in print indefinitely. The firm

offers over 1,500 plays by 600 writers, including selected English and European playwrights and many minor American dramatists. The plays are appropriate for productions in schools, colleges, and community theaters and include short plays, monologues, musicals, and plays of special interest to religious groups; the largest selection are full-length plays for college and community groups. F. Andrew Leslie is president of the firm. Dramatists Play Service's address is 440 Park Avenue South, New York 10016.

—*Phyllis Andrews*

Duell, Sloan and Pearce
(New York: 1939-1966)

Duell, Sloan and Pearce's contribution to literature and the book trade included the publication of the works of Archibald MacLeish, John O'Hara, Erskine Caldwell, Anaïs Nin, Conrad Aiken, and Wallace Stegner. The firm was also influential in the popularization of photographic essays, most notably through the *U.S. Camera* annuals; the rapid dissemination of information on current events; the explanation of complex mechanical operations in simplified format; and innovations in advertising.

The founder and president of Duell, Sloan and Pearce was C. Halliwell Duell, known to the trade as "Charlie." A 1927 graduate of Yale, Duell had worked in advertising research at Crowell and as advertising manager at Doubleday, Doran and was vice-president of William Morrow until June 1939. Samuel Sloan, vice-president and treasurer, had graduated from Princeton in 1927 and had received an M.A. from Harvard in 1929, had worked with a literary agency, and had served as an editor at Harcourt, Brace from 1932 to 1939. Charles A. ("Cap") Pearce, secretary, had graduated from Hobart in 1927 and had worked in the editorial departments at D. Appleton and Company and later at Harcourt, Brace, where he was editor in chief until he resigned in May 1939. The

new publishing house began at 270 Madison Avenue, New York, with a complete sales force and with experienced managers in its advertising and manufacturing departments. General editorial work was handled by Frederica P. Barach, former editor of *Golden Book;* Marie Fried Rodell was editor of mystery fiction.

Duell, Sloan and Pearce announced in October 1939 that it would publish general fiction and nonfiction, but no westerns, light romances, or children's books. The firm's first book, MacLeish's new poem *America Was Promises*, was published on 1 December 1939. The firm issued its first catalogue on 1 January 1940; it included Aiken's collection of poems *And in the Human Heart;* Caldwell's novel *Trouble in July* and his collection of short stories, *Jackpot;* E.E. Cummings's *Fifty Poems;* O'Hara's short-story collection *Pal Joey;* Merle Colby's *Alaska: A Profile, with Pictures,* from the Federal Writers' Project; Rockwell Kent's *This Is My Own;* and Ruby Black's *Eleanor Roosevelt,* the first of several books on the Roosevelt family to be published by Duell, Sloan and Pearce.

In August 1940 the company became sales agent for Musette Publishers, whose children's books were based on Madge Tucker's "Lady Next Door" radio program. Each Musette book contained the complete radio script, the music for the songs, and a ten-inch phonograph record. The first two Musette titles, *Gingerbread Boy* and *Cinderella*, were released in September 1941; they inaugurated Duell, Sloan and Pearce's commitment to children's literature, which resulted in the publication of the Colonel Red Reeder series, the colorful Splendor Books, and August Derleth's *The Captive Island* (1952) and *The Mill Creek Irregulars: Special Detectives* (1959).

In the same year that Duell, Sloan and Pearce introduced its books for children, *U.S. Camera 1941* was banned in Boston for its nude photography. Also in 1941 the firm published Stegner's novel *Fire and Ice;* Caldwell's *Say! Is This the U.S.A.* with Margaret Bourke-White's photographs; Frederick Gutheim's *Frank Lloyd Wright on Architecture;* and the first volumes in the celebrated American Folkways series, edited by Caldwell with individual volumes written by eminent authors. *The Last Frontier* (1941) was the first of several of Howard Fast's socialist historical novels published by Duell, Sloan and Pearce. Before abandoning Fast following his indictment in 1947 for contempt of Congress, the firm published *The Unvanquished* (1942), *Citizen Tom Paine* (1943), *Freedom Road* (1944), *The American* (1946), *The Children* (1947), and *Clarkton* (1947).

Caldwell's novel *All Night Long;* the two-volume *Latin American Guides;* and *The Great O'Neill,* Sean O'Faolain's biography of Hugh O'Neill, Earl of Tyrone, were published in 1942. Also in 1942 Duell, Sloan and Pearce agreed to handle all advertising, promotion, selling, and distribution of Eagle Books titles. To inaugurate the Eagle list, Kathrine Kressman Taylor's novel *Until That Day* (1942) and the five-color *United States Service Symbols* (1942) by Cleveland H. Smith and Gertrude R. Taylor were published. Eagle announced that it would publish fiction, nonfiction, and juveniles and concentrate on a small, selective list, giving the books intensive promotion. New titles in the 1943 catalogue included Stegner's novel *The Big Rock Candy Mountain;* Elswyth Thane's *Dawn's Early Light;* Caldwell's collection of short stories *Georgia Boy;* and *Aircraft Engines* and *Aircraft Instruments,* both by Emanuele Stierl, in the illustrated Essential Books series.

The firm was deeply and profitably involved in current affairs, most notably during the Second World War. The house published the sensational *The Black Book* (1946), an account of Nazi atrocities against the Jews written by representatives of leading Jewish organizations around the world. Duell,

Sloan and Pearce handled promotion and publicity for a rally in Madison Square Garden on the day of the book's publication. Throughout the three-hour rally a spotlight illuminated a copy of *The Black Book* on a platform in front of the podium.

Duell, Sloan and Pearce expanded rapidly after the war. The firm's staff, which had been reduced during the war, was again complete; its offices were greatly enlarged; and its list of publications was longer than ever. Duell continued as president; since Sloan's death in March 1945, Pearce had moved up to vice-president. Sloan's widow, Marjorie Howe Sloan, became a member of the board of directors. Frank Henry was publisher of Essential Books; Rodell continued as editor of mystery fiction, now known as Bloodhound Mysteries.

In 1946 Duell, Sloan and Pearce published Caldwell's *A House in the Uplands,* Malcolm Cowley and Hannah Josephson's *Aragon: Poet of the French Resistance,* Carey McWilliams's *Southern California Country,* O'Hara's collection *Here's O'Hara,* Richard Aldington's *The Romance of Casanova,* and Dr. Benjamin Spock's *The Common Sense Book of Baby and Child Care.* In January 1947 the Carey-Thomas Award for the best example of creative publishing was presented to Duell, Sloan and Pearce for its handling of Stefan Lorant's *New World* (1946). The New American Naturalist series, edited by a staff headed by Dr. Clyde Fisher of the American Museum of Natural History and Julian Huxley, was introduced in 1947. Each volume contained twenty-four to forty-eight color plates printed in England and numerous black-and-white illustrations. The series was to provide a comprehensive survey of American flora and fauna for the general reader.

In 1948 the firm published the first two volumes of its Uniform Library Edition of Caldwell's works, *Tobacco Road* and *Tragic Ground.* Duell, Sloan and Pearce won a censorship battle in 1949 over Caldwell's *God's Little Acre,* which it was publishing as part of the Uniform Library Edition. Before Caldwell turned to Little, Brown in the mid-1950s, Duell, Sloan and Pearce published *Place Called Estherville* (1949) and *Episode in Palmetto* (1950).

In 1950 the firm published Nin's novel *The Four-Chambered Heart* and reprinted two former Dutton titles by Nin, the collection of short stories *Under a Glass Bell* and the novel *Children of the Albatross.* The four-volume *F. D. R.: His Personal Letters,* edited by Elliott Roosevelt, was completed in 1950; the first volume had appeared in 1947.

Duell, Sloan and Pearce was the first American publisher to print the Library of Congress catalog card number on the copyright page of all its books, beginning with those published in April 1951. In 1951 the firm had over 600 titles in twenty-eight subject categories in print. To cut costs, Duell, Sloan and Pearce entered into a thirty-year contract in July under which Little, Brown assumed responsibility for the manufacturing, warehousing, promotion, and selling of all Duell, Sloan and Pearce titles. Duell, Sloan and Pearce's inventory was transferred to Little, Brown's warehouse in Cambridge, Massachusetts. Little, Brown and Duell, Sloan and Pearce books carried a joint imprint after 1 January 1952, though there was no change in the ownership of either firm. Later in 1952 Duell, Sloan and Pearce moved to 124 East Thirtieth Street.

Duell, Sloan and Pearce inaugurated its independent subsidiary Arrowhead Books with the publication of Paul Campbell and Peter Howard's *Remaking Men* (1954). Other Arrowhead Books were Katharine O. Wright's *Christmas at Thunder Gap* (1954), John Hadfield's *A Book of Delights* (1954), and Lee Vrooman's *The Faith That Built America* (1955). The firm continued its emphasis on popular medical works with the publication of Spock and Miriam E. Lowenberg's *Feeding Your Baby and Child* (1955) and Spock and Dr. John Reinhart's *A Baby's First Year* (1955).

On 30 June 1956 the alliance between Duell, Sloan and Pearce and Little, Brown was terminated. Duell, Sloan and Pearce joined the McKay Group, a cooperative selling and manufacturing association in New York, with shipping handled from the Long Island City warehouse of McKay-Longmans. Manufacturing and sales were handled through the David McKay Company while advertising and promotion were carried out by Duell, Sloan and Pearce. The company had approximately 250 titles in print, and it intended to publish 30 to 35 titles a year thereafter.

Publications for 1958 included Earl Browder's *Marx and America*, Merle Armitage's *George Gershwin: Man and Legend*, and Richard Harrity and Ralph G. Martin's *Eleanor Roosevelt: Her Life in Pictures*. In 1960 the firm published Ray M. Lawless's *Folksingers and Folksongs in America* and a new edition of MacLeish's *The American Story*. The publication of Robert Frank Futrell's official history *The United States Air Force in Korea 1950-1953* (1961), Lowell Thomas, Jr.'s *The Dalai Lama* (1961) for young readers, and Burl Ives's *Song in America*

(1962), demonstrates the firm's continued diversity in its final months as an autonomous publishing house.

In March 1961 Meredith Publishing Company made an attractive offer, and in June Duell, Sloan and Pearce became an affiliate of the Meredith publishing conglomerate and relocated to 60 East Forty-second Street. At the time, Duell, Sloan and Pearce was publishing between 45 and 50 titles a year, with an active backlist of over 500 titles. Aviation, biography, folklore and folksongs, household reference works, nature, photography, and travel were the firm's areas of concentration. Duell and Pearce continued in executive capacities, but the firm had relinquished its position as a creative force in the publishing world.

In its first years as an affiliate of Meredith Press, Duell, Sloan and Pearce continued to publish new titles, particularly in juvenile literature. Eric Protter's Folk and Fairy Tales series began with *A Children's Treasury of Folk and Fairy Tales* in 1961. From 1961 to 1967 eleven volumes were added to Charles R. Joy's Young People of the World Books series. C. B. Colby's *Fur and Fury* (1963) inaugurated a new series on the families of the animal kingdom. Several volumes of John Upton Terrel's U. S. Government Department Books, designed for young readers, were published from 1964 to 1966. Edward Miller's Halls of Greatness series was introduced in 1966. Other titles with the Duell, Sloan and Pearce imprint included Eric Sloane's illustrated dictionary *The Folklore of American Weather* (1963), Ronald Reagan's autobiography *Where's the Rest of Me?* (1965), and Robert Silverberg's collection of science fiction tales *Earthmen and Strangers* (1966).

In its 1967 catalog Meredith announced that all new books were to be published under the imprint of Meredith Press and that all affiliated imprints, including Duell, Sloan and Pearce, were to be retired from use on backlist titles.

References:

"Duell, Sloan and Pearce Expands," *Publishers' Weekly*, 149 (13 April 1946): 2092-2093;

"Duell, Sloan & Pearce Receives Carey-Thomas Award . . .," *Publishers' Weekly*, 151 (25 January 1947): 406-407;

"Meredith Press: New Trade Book Division," *Publishers' Weekly*, 179 (29 May 1961): 37;

"Samuel Sloan [obituary]," *Publishers' Weekly*, 147 (7 April 1945): 1469.

—*Harry Thompson*

Photo by Kay-Hart

Photo by Eric Schaal

Photo by Mario Scacheri

C. Halliwell Duell (top left), Samuel Sloan (top right), and Charles A. Pearce in 1939, the year they founded their publishing firm

Duffield and Green
(New York: 1926-1934)

Duffield and Company
(New York: 1906-1926)

Fox, Duffield and Company
(New York: 1903-1906)

Fox, Duffield and Company was incorporated in 1903 at 36 East Twenty-first Street in New York by Rector Fox and Pitts Duffield; the firm later moved to 200 Madison Avenue. In 1906, when Fox retired, the firm's name was changed to Duffield and Company. Duffield withdrew in 1916, and after Horace Green became president in 1926 the house became Duffield and Green.

The first publication of Fox, Duffield was *Everyman* (1903). Other early titles included *The Autobiography of a Thief* (1903), edited by Hutchins Hapgood; *The Compromises of Life* (1903) by Henry Watterson; several works by Henrik Ibsen and a two-volume set of Maurice Maeterlinck's plays in 1906; and the first novels of H. G. Wells. In 1906 the firm purchased the list of Herbert S. Stone and Company of Chicago. *Three Weeks* (1907) by Elinor Glyn, a best-seller often reprinted, was banned in Boston by the Watch and Ward Society.

Duffield was the first publisher of the work of D. H. Lawrence and Katherine Anne Porter. Duffield's edition of Lawrence's *The White Peacock* (1911) preceded the British edition by one day. Though Porter later completely disavowed *My Chinese Marriage*, published by the firm in 1921, the book was in part ghost-written by her. The firm's other literary publications include several books by Martha Gilbert Dickinson Bianchi, among them *A Modern Prometheus* (1908), *The Cuckoo's Nest* (1909), *The Sin of Angels* (1912), and *The Point of View*

(1918). Two William Rose Benét titles, *Rip Tide* (1932) and *Starry Harness* (1933), appeared under the Duffield and Green imprint.

Of notable success for the firm was the publication of books for children and young adults, including those of Ada and Eleanor Skinner, illustrated by Jessie Willcox Smith; Nathaniel Hawthorne's *Wonder-Book and Tanglewood Tales for Girls and Boys* (1910), illustrated by Maxfield Parrish; Edward Lear's *The Complete Nonsense Book* (1912); and the stories of Emma Gelders Sterne.

In later years Duffield distinguished itself in the publication of historical fiction and biography, including the historical novels of General Krannoff; *Anton Chekhov* (1923) by William Gerhardie; *The Life of Calvin Coolidge* (1924) by Horace Green; *Memories of My Father* (1929) by Sir Henry F. Dickens; *Nelson, Man and Admiral* (1931) and *Napoleon's Autobiography* (1931) by Friedrich Max Kircheisen; and the autobiography of Thomas Johnstone Lipton, Bart. (1932). The quality of the firm's varied list was an asset to Dodd, Mead and Company, which purchased Duffield and Green in 1934.

Reference:
"Obituary Notes [Pitts Duffield]," *Publishers' Weekly*, 134 (20 August 1938): 503.

—*Laura Masotti Humphrey*

Inside cover of 1940 catalogue

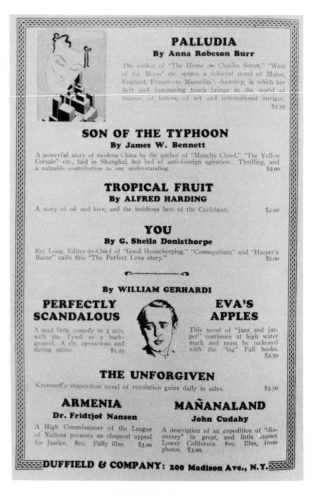

1928 advertisement

Ecco Press

(New York: 1971-   )

Ecco Press was founded in 1971 by Drue Heinz to publish fine quality fiction and poetry. Under editor in chief Daniel Halpern, managing editor Susan Dwyer, and contributing editor Paul Bowles, the firm has devoted its efforts primarily to literary productions. Two volumes from its American Poetry series have been nominated for significant awards: Stanley Plumly's *Out-of-the-Body Travel* for a National Book Critics Circle Award in 1978, and Sandra McPherson's *The Year of Our Birth* for a National Book Award in 1979. Ecco's quarterly *Antaeus* received the 1981 National Magazine Award for Fiction. Ecco published the Winner of the 1985 National Book Critics Circle Award for criticism, *Twentieth-Century Pleasures* by Robert Haas, and the 1986 winner of that award for poetry, *The Triumph of Achilles* by Louise Gluck.

Poets whose work has been published or reprinted by Ecco include John Ashbery, Louise Bogan, John Fowles, Louise Glück, Robert Hass, Laura Jensen, Al Lee, David McElroy, Lawrence Raab, John Crowe Ransom, James Reiss, Dennis Schmitz, Mark Strand, James Tate, and David Young. Noteworthy translations appearing under the Ecco imprint are Wolfgang Borchert's *The Sad Geraniums* (1973) and Czeslaw Milosz's *Bells in Winter* (1978).

A major project of the firm is its Neglected Books of the Twentieth Century series, featuring works by Sybille Bedford, Elizabeth Bowen, Italo Calvino, Caresse Crosby, and Ford Madox Ford.

Ecco Press books are distributed by W. W. Norton and Company. The address of Ecco Press in 18 West Thirtieth Street, New York 10001.

Reference:
David Lehman, "In Praise of the Independent," *Newsweek*, 102 (25 July 1983): 71-72.

—*Sharon Ann Jaeger*

M. Evans and Company

(New York: 1954-   )

M. Evans and Company, Incorporated was founded in 1954 by Melvin Evans and George C. deKay on East Forty-eighth Street, New York. Organized as a free-lance editorial service, Evans packaged nonfiction books for distribution by Doubleday, Random House, and McGraw-Hill. During the firm's first nine years, Evans, his wife Polly, deKay, and others edited fewer than ten titles per year. In 1963 the firm offered the first list of its own books. Evans left the company in 1964 and deKay became president, while continuing as an editor. In the same year Herbert M. Katz joined the firm as vice-president and editor. Evans's books were sold and distributed by J. B. Lippincott until 1978, and after that by E. P. Dutton. In 1981 Evans published twenty-seven titles, about a third of them fiction.

In addition to translations such as Marcel Clouzot's *The Walled City* (1973) and Christine de Rivoyre's *Boy* (1974), Evans published anthologies by Louis Untermeyer, mysteries by Donald E. Westlake, and the letters of Dalton Trumbo. Other Evans works include Ogden Nash's *The Animal Garden* (1965) and *The Cruise of the Aardvark* (1967), Thea Astley's *The Slow Natives* (1967), Dean R. Koontz's *Hanging On* (1973), and Brian Garfield's *Hopscotch* (1975).

From 1958 to 1963 the firm's address was 230 East Fiftieth Street. Since September 1963 Evans has been located at 216 East Forty-ninth Street, New York 10017.

—*David Dzwonkoski*

Fantasy Press Publishers
(Reading, Pennsylvania: 1946-1958)

One of the first American publishers to specialize in science fiction, Fantasy Press published works by great writers of the genre's golden age. The firm was begun by Lloyd Arthur Eshbach, A. J. Donnell, G. H. MacGregor, and L. H. Houck in Reading, Pennsylvania, in 1946. Fantasy Press published the first book about modern science fiction, *Of Worlds Beyond* (1947); edited by Eshbach, it included essays by John W. Campbell, Jr., Robert A. Heinlein, and A. E. Van Vogt. When Eshbach bought out his partners in 1950, he acquired an impressive list of publications; among them were the complete Lensman series of E. E. "Doc" Smith, *Triplanetary* (1948), *First Lensman* (1950), *Galactic Patrol* (1950), *Gray Lensman* (1951), *Second Stage Lensman* (1953), and *Children of the Lens* (1954). Fantasy Press also published two books in the earlier Skylark series by Smith, who is known as "the father of space opera."

There are three types of Fantasy Press books: the Special Edition, sold by subscription, numbered and bound in full cloth, with an extra page either signed by the author or bearing a photo and biography of a deceased author; the Regular Edition, identical in binding but without the special page; and the Greenberg Variant, bound in boards by Martin Greenberg of Gnome Press from unbound sheets of the original editions sold to Greenberg by Eshbach after 1958. Fantasy Press also attempted a line of reprinted pulp novels for collectors under the short-lived Polaris Press imprint. Among these was Campbell's *The Moon Is Hell!* (1950).

Heinlein had two novels published by Fantasy Press: *Beyond This Horizon* (1948) and *Assignment in Eternity* (1953). Other novels on the firm's list included Van Vogt's *The Book of Ptath* (1947) and *Masters of Time* (1950); Jack Williamson's *Darker than You Think* (1948), *The Cometeers* (1950), and *The Legion of Time* (1952); Eric Frank Russell's *Sinister Barrier* (1948), *Dreadful Sanctuary* (1951), and *Deep Space* (1954); L. Sprague de Camp's *Divide and Rule* (1948); Campbell's *The Incredible Planet* (1949); John Taine's (pseudonym of Eric Temple Bell) *Seeds of Life* (1951), *The Crystal Horde* (1952), and *G. O. G. 666* (1954); and Eshbach's *Tyrant of Time* (1955). Fantasy Press also published works by P. Schuyler Miller, Stanton A. Coblentz, and Murray

Leinster. In 1958 Eshbach sold his list to Gnome Press; by 1961 he had sold all of his backlist and moved from Reading.

Reference:
"The Growth of Science-Fiction and Fantasy Publishing in Book Form," *Publishers' Weekly,* 154 (25 December 1948): 2465.
                                   —*Martha A. Bartter*

Farrar and Rinehart
(New York: 1929-1945)

NINE EAST FORTY-FIRST STREET

NEW YORK

John Farrar and Stanley M. Rinehart both joined the George H. Doran Company in 1919; Rinehart was in sales and Farrar was an editor. Farrar eventually became editor of Doran's journal, the *Bookman,* while Rinehart became the *Bookman's* advertising manager.

In 1929, two years after Doran merged with Doubleday, Page to form Doubleday, Doran and Company, Farrar and Rinehart left to form their own publishing firm. Rinehart's brother Frederick, who had worked in book production at Doran, joined the new firm as its treasurer, with Farrar as vice-president and Stanley Rinehart as president. The firm was established at 12 East Forty-first Street in New York on 4 June 1929. First-month sales were only $26; by September the house had made $46,000. Farrar and Rinehart had taken about fifty Doubleday, Doran authors with them when they left to form their partnership. Among these authors were Hervey Allen; Stephen Vincent Benét; Floyd Dell; DuBose Heyward; and the Rinehart's' mother, the popular mystery writer Mary Roberts Rinehart. Farrar and Rinehart's first list in 1929 featured *Singermann* by Myron Brinig, *The Incredible Marquis, Alexandre Dumas* by Herbert Gorman, *The Half Pint Flask* by Heyward, and *The Romantics* by Mary Roberts Rinehart.

In 1930 Farrar and Rinehart initiated a dollar fiction program through which books on the firm's list would be reprinted in inexpensive cloth bindings or paper wrappers. The first books published under this program were titles that had proved successful in earlier editions: *The Door* by Mary

Roberts Rinehart; *Young Man of Manhattan* by Katharine Brush; and *Loyal Lover* by Margaret Widdemer. In 1931 the firm acquired the stock of the Cosmopolitan Book Corporation, along with authors Faith Baldwin, Rex Beach, and Louis Golding. In May of that year the firm moved into larger quarters at 9 East Forty-first Street. Publications in 1931 included Dell's *Love without Money,* Heyward's *Brass Ankle* and *Jasbo Brown and Selected Poems,* and Upton Sinclair's *Roman Holiday*—one of eight works by Sinclair published by Farrar and Rinehart during the 1930s. Heyward's *Peter Ashley* and Evelyn Waugh's *Black Mischief* appeared in 1932.

Farrar and Rinehart's first major success was Allen's *Anthony Adverse* (1933), a long, romantic novel set in Napoleonic times. The firm sent proofs to booksellers and offered them a twenty-five-cent rebate on the retail price on advance orders. By its publication date, 26 June 1933, *Anthony Adverse* had an advance sale of 15,000 to 20,000 copies. Carefully planned advertising and the Book-of-the-Month Club's selection of the novel as its July feature boosted 1933 sales to 275,000 copies. A film version in 1936 increased sales again; by the end of 1936 the book had sold 705,000 copies. It is estimated that, counting reprints and foreign sales, *Anthony Adverse* sold about two million copies by 1946. Benét was a reader for Farrar and Rinehart, and *Anthony Adverse* was published largely because of his support for it.

In 1934 the growing firm moved to 232 Madison Avenue; publications that year included Dell's *The Golden Spike* and Waugh's *A Handful of Dust.* In

John Farrar (top) and Stanley M. Rinehart, Jr., in 1939

By Dawn Powell

DANCE NIGHT

The story of a town—and of young love. Real characters; real places; they all live for you in as fine a novel as the author of She Walks in Beauty has written. A certain best-seller—publication October 10. $2.00

FARRAR AND RINEHART
AUTUMN BOOKS

"There is plenty of buried treasure . . . up and down the world . . . for those who are willing to seek it."

DOUBLOONS
The Story of Buried Treasure

From Block Island to the South Pacific the world is full of buried treasure. The author, an adventurer and authority, tells where they are, how they got there—the glamorous tales of old pirates and forgotten galleons and the exciting narrative of modern adventurers who sought what they lost! Illustrated by Cimino. October 10. $5.00

By Charles B. Driscoll

1930 advertisement

1935 the Feld-Crawford Fair Trade Act was passed to protect prices of books bought by retailers under contracts with publishers. Farrar and Rinehart was among the first New York publishers to sign a model contract drawn up by the American Booksellers Association; Stanley Rinehart was a member of the committee that drafted the contract. In 1936 Farrar and Rinehart tried to organize University Press Services, Incorporated, a distribution system for university press books, but the project failed due to lack of interest among university presses.

Farrar and Rinehart published Benét's *Thirteen O'Clock* (1937) and *Tales before Midnight* (1939) and Allen's *Action at Aquila* (1938). Henry Pringle's *The Life and Times of William Howard Taft* (1939) won a Pulitzer Prize, and the firm's Rivers of America series, conceived and edited by Constance Lindsay Skinner, won the first Carey-Thomas Award in 1942. Farrar and Rinehart brought out fourteen titles by Philip Wylie, including *Generation of Vipers* (1942). The firm continued to publish Allen's work in the 1940s, including *The Forest and the Fort* (1943) and *Bedford Village* (1944); it also published Charles Jackson's first and most important novel, *The Lost Weekend* (1944). Four of James Branch Cabell's later works were published by Farrar and Rinehart, and the firm was the American publisher of works by G. K. Chesterton and Frank Swinnerton. In 1944 the firm began publishing reprints under the Murray Hill Books imprint; the first of these was *The*

Great Bustard and Other People, an omnibus edition of two earlier books by the humorist Will Cuppy. Farrar and Rinehart also published a mystery series, begun in 1940 and overseen by Mary Roberts Rinehart, and the influential American Government in Action series.

Among the last publications under the Farrar and Rinehart imprint was Benét's *We Stand United, and Other Radio Scripts* in 1945. That year Farrar, who had left the firm in September 1944, joined Roger Straus to form Farrar, Straus and Company. Rinehart renamed the old firm Rinehart and Company and supervised its operations until it merged with Henry Holt and Company in 1959.

References:

"Cosmopolitan Book Corporation Sold to Farrar & Rinehart," *Publishers' Weekly,* 120 (26 September 1931): 1489-1490;

"Countryman Press Cooperates with Farrar and Rinehart," *Publishers' Weekly,* 131 (15 May 1937): 2014-2015;

"F. & R.'s Tenth Anniversary," *Publishers' Weekly,* 135 (28 January 1939): 351-354;

"F. & R. Establishes Murray Hill Imprint," *Publishers' Weekly,* 145 (3 June 1944): 2097;

Edith M. Stern, "Farrar and Rinehart," *Saturday Review of Literature,* 25 (21 March 1942): 11-13.

—*Deborah G. Gorman*

Farrar, Straus and Giroux
(New York: 1964-   )

Farrar, Straus and Cudahy
(New York: 1955-1962)

Farrar, Straus and Young
(New York: 1951-1955)

Farrar, Straus and Company
(New York: 1945-1951; 1962-1964)

John Farrar was born in Vermont in 1896. After serving as executive officer for the Air Service Intelligence during World War I, he graduated from Yale and wrote for the *New York World* before Christopher Morley and William Rose Benét recommended him to the George H. Doran Company. He joined Doran in 1921 to edit the company magazine, the *Bookman,* and there met Stanley Rinehart. In 1925 Farrar became editor in chief, and in 1927, when Doran merged with Doubleday, Page, Farrar and Rinehart were made directors of Doubleday,

Doran. They left in 1929 to start the firm of Farrar and Rinehart. Between 1943 and 1945 Farrar worked in the Psychological Warfare Branch of the Office of War Information. In 1944 he resigned from Farrar and Rinehart.

At the end of 1945 Rinehart changed the name of his firm to Rinehart and Company to avoid confusion with a new firm being formed by Farrar and Roger W. Straus, Jr. Straus, then twenty-eight, had studied at Hamilton College and taken a degree in journalism at the University of Missouri.

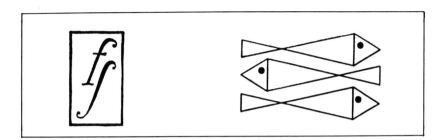

After writing for the *White Plains* (New York) *Daily Reporter,* he became an editor of *Current History and Forum* magazine and in 1941 started Book Ideas, a book-packaging firm. During the war he served in the navy's Office of Public Information. In late 1945 he and Farrar founded Farrar, Straus and Company at 580 Fifth Avenue, New York.

Farrar was chairman and Straus was president and chief executive officer of the new house. Also on the board were vice-president James H. Van Alen, treasurer E. Trevor Hill, secretary Allen H. Kempner, Stanley Young, and Julius Fleischmann. Margaret Petherbridge Farrar, Farrar's wife, served as mystery editor. The firm announced its interest in new writers, young writers, and the work of recent veterans. Its first list, which included James Branch Cabell's *There Were Two Pirates,* appeared in 1946.

By 1950 Farrar, Straus had a growing reputation for literary quality, having published Carlo Levi's *Christ Stopped at Eboli* (1947), Shirley Jackson's *The Road through the Wall* (1948) and *The Lottery* (1949), and Alberto Moravia's *The Woman of Rome* (1949). In 1949, after Random House turned down a collection of Edmund Wilson's essays, Straus contracted for them. The publication of *Classics and Commercials* (1950) began a relationship between Wilson and Farrar, Straus that lasted the rest of the author's life. Farrar, Straus had several early best-sellers, including Quentin Reynolds's *Courtroom* (1950) and Gayelord Hauser's *Look Younger, Live Longer* (1950); the latter work sold half a million copies by 1960.

Young had become more active in the firm over the years, and his name was added to the company's title in 1951. That year Farrar, Straus and Young acquired Creative Age Press from Eileen Garrett. In 1952 the firm joined Houghton Mifflin in subscribing to Ian Ballantine's plan for simultaneous publication of books in hardback by the trade publishers and in paperback by Ballantine Books. Pellegrini and Cudahy was acquired in 1953, and Sheila Cudahy joined the firm. Her name replaced Young's in the firm's imprint in

1955. Also in 1955 Robert Giroux joined the firm as vice-president and editor in chief. Born in 1914, Giroux graduated in 1936 from Columbia University. His first editing experience was on the *Columbia Review,* where he published work by Thomas Merton, John Berryman, and Mark Van Doren. As an editor at Harcourt, Brace, Giroux published Robert Lowell's first trade book, *Lord Weary's Castle,* which won the 1946 Pulitzer Prize. There he was also responsible for the first books of Randall Jarrell, Jean Stafford, Peter Taylor, William Gaddis, and Jack Kerouac. Giroux was editor in chief at Harcourt when he left for Farrar, Straus and Cudahy. Seventeen of his authors, including Berryman, Lowell, T. S. Eliot, Flannery O'Connor, and Bernard Malamud, followed Giroux to his new firm.

Farrar, Straus and Cudahy acquired L. C. Page and Company of Boston, with its large backlist of juvenile books, in 1957 and McMullen Books in 1958. The firm collected the first of its many National Book Awards in 1957 with Malamud's second novel, *The Assistant.* Eliot's poem *The Cultivation of Christmas Trees* (1956) was succeeded by two volumes of his criticism, *On Poetry and Poets* (1957) and *To Criticize the Critic, and Other Writings* (1965); a play, *The Elder Statesman* (1959); and a collection of early poems. Berryman's poetry at Farrar included *Homage to Mistress Bradstreet* (1956), *77 Dream Songs* (1964), *Berryman's Sonnets* (1967), *His Toy, His Dream, His Rest* (1968), and *Delusions, Etc.* (1972).

Other works that followed upon Giroux's arrival included Lowell's *Life Studies* (1959), *For the Union Dead* (1964), *Near the Ocean* (1967), *The Dolphin* (1973), and *Day by Day* (1977), as well as several works by Lowell's ex-wife, Jean Stafford; *The Collected Stories of Jean Stafford* (1969) was awarded the Pulitzer Prize. Works by O'Connor included *Everything That Rises Must Converge* (1965), a short story collection; *The Violent Bear It Away* (1960), a novel; *Mystery and Manners: Occasional Prose* (1969); and *The Complete Stories* (1971). Also published by the firm were the *Selected Writings* (1957) of Nobel laureate Juan Ramón Jiménez, Nathanael West's *The Complete Works* (1957), and Colette's *Chéri and The*

Robert Giroux (photo by Arthur W. Wang)

John Farrar and Roger W. Straus, Jr., in 1945, the year they founded their firm

THE FIRST FALL LIST FROM

Farrar, Straus

AND COMPANY, INC.

JULY 19	**INSIDE YOUR HOME** By Dan Cooper	Decorating	$3.95
AUG. 12	**THERE WERE TWO PIRATES** By James Branch Cabell	Novel	$3.00
AUG. 12	**DEADLY WEAPON** By Wade Miller	Mystery	$2.00
AUG. 16	**POWERFUL LONG LADDER** By Owen Dodson	Poetry	$2.50
SEPT. 16	**UNITED NATIONS** By Louis Dolivet	Handbook	$1.75
SEPT. 16	**NEVER LET WEATHER INTERFERE** By Messmore Kendall	Reminiscences	$3.75
SEPT. 23	**THE GIFTS OF LOVE** By Andrina Iverson	Novel	$2.50
SEPT. 27	**TELL YOUR SONS** By Willa Gibbs	Novel	$3.00
OCT. 1	**FORLORN SUNSET** By Michael Sadleir	Novel	$3.00
OCT. 7	**I MEET SUCH PEOPLE!** By Gurney Williams	Humor	$2.50
OCT. 9	**PUNCH WITH CARE** By Phoebe Atwood Taylor	Mystery	$2.50
OCT. 9	**RITUAL: PSYCHOANALYTIC STUDIES** By Theodore Reik	Psychoanalysis	$5.00
OCT. 14	**HOW MUCH DO YOU KNOW?** By Sylvan Hoffman	Quizzes	$2.50
OCT. 15	**THE ISLAND** By Francis Brett Young	Poetry	$3.50
OCT. 21	**THE DIM VIEW** By Basil Heatter	Novel	$2.50
OCT. 21	**FRANCIS** By David Stern	Humor	$2.50
OCT. 28	**ANNA ZENGER** By Kent Cooper	Novel	$3.75
NOV. 10	**SHIKAR AND SAFARI** By Edison Marshall	Adventure	$3.00
NOV. 15	**THE LAST CIRCLE** By Stephen Vincent Benét	Short stories and Poems	$3.00

Farrar, Straus and Company, Inc.
580 FIFTH AVENUE, N.Y. 19

IN CANADA:
Oxford University Press, Toronto

1946 advertisement

Last of Chéri (1953), *Claudine at School* (1957), and *Gigi* (1959). Elizabeth Bishop's translation of *The Diary of "Helena Morley"* (1957) was followed by *Questions of Travel* (1965), *The Complete Poems* (1969), and *The Collected Prose* (1984).

In 1960 Farrar, Straus and Cudahy bought the Noonday Press, a quality paperback line. Noonday had previously published a novel by Isaac Bashevis Singer, and since the purchase Farrar has published the Nobel Prize-winning writer's *The Spinoza of Market Street* (1961), *The Manor* (1967), *The Estate* (1969), *Enemies, a Love Story* (1972), *Passions, and Other Stories* (1975), and *Shosha* (1978). The Noonday imprint was dropped in the early 1980s.

Cudahy left the company in 1962. Two years later the publisher's imprint took its present form when Giroux became a full partner. The first book published by Farrar, Straus, and Giroux was Lowell's *For the Union Dead*. The quality of the list was maintained as the house added both established and new authors to its roster. Among its notable publications were Nobel laureate Salvatore Quasimodo's *Selected Writings* (1960); Jack Kerouac's *Big Sur* (1962) and *Visions of Gerard* (1963); Susan Sontag's first novel, *The Benefactor* (1963), which was followed by *Against Interpretation and Other Essays* (1966) and another novel, *Death Kit* (1967); and Thomas Merton's *Seeds of Destruction* (1965). Novels by the Mexican writer Carlos Fuentes included *Where the Air Is Clear* (1960), *The Death of Artemio Cruz* (1964), *Terra Nostra* (1976), and *The Old Gringo* (1985). Derek Walcott's *Selected Poems* (1964) was followed by *The Gulf* (1970), *Sea Grapes* (1976), and *The Star-Apple Kingdom* (1979).

Other works published by Farrar, Straus and Giroux include *A Sense of Where You Are* (1965), the first book by John McPhee; Jane Bowles's *Collected Works* (1966); and Walker Percy's second novel, *The Last Gentleman* (1966), which was followed by *Lancelot* (1977) and *The Second Coming* (1980). Works by Donald Barthelme include *Unspeakable Practices, Unnatural Acts* (1968), *Sadness* (1972), *Guilty Pleasures* (1974), *Dead Father* (1975), and *Great Days* (1979).

The firm's expansion continued with the acquisition of Octagon Books in 1968 and Hill and Wang in 1971. Farrar, Straus and Giroux consistently refused purchase offers from large corporations and sought to assure its continued financial independence by occasionally bringing out books with more commercial than literary interest. Its primary concern, though, remained literary excellence, as exemplified in Larry Woiwode's first novel, *What I'm Going to Do, I Think* (1969), and his

Beyond the Bedroom Wall: A Family Album (1975) and *Even Tide* (1977), a book of poems. Farrar reprinted Aleksandr Solzhenitsyn's *One Day in the Life of Ivan Denisovich* in 1971, before Solzhenitsyn was awarded the Nobel Prize, and followed it with his *August 1914* (1972) and *Lenin in Zurich* (1976); the firm had published his *Cancer Ward* in 1969. Other works of the 1970s include Grace Paley's *Enormous Changes at the Last Minute* (1974), John Steinbeck's *The Acts of King Arthur* (1976), and Allen Tate's *Collected Poems, 1919-1976* (1977).

Farrar retired in 1972 and died in 1974. A writer himself, he had founded the Bread Loaf Writers' Conference at Middlebury College, Vermont, in 1926 and had taught writing and publishing at New York University and Columbia University.

Straus, in addition to being president and chief executive officer of Farrar, Straus and Giroux, is also president of Hill and Wang. Straus is the principal shareholder. Giroux has been chairman of the board since 1973. The firm is among the few publishing houses to remain independent of large conglomerates. Its 1979 revenues were near $10 million, with profits of about $1 million. The house publishes about 100 trade books each year and maintains an extensive backlist. In 1981 Polish-exile Czeslaw Milosz, whose *Issa Valley* had just been published by Farrar, Straus and Giroux, was awarded the Nobel Prize. The next year, Elias Canetti received the Nobel Prize just as Farrar, Straus and Giroux was publishing his *The Torch in My Ear*. Two years later William Golding, whose works had been published by Farrar, Straus and Giroux since 1979, was honored by the Nobel Prize committee. Between 1945 and 1985 the firm published the work of thirteen Nobel laureates.

References:

"Farrar, Straus and Company Announces Officers and Staff," *Publishers' Weekly*, 149 (12 January 1946): 159-162;

"Farrar, Straus, and Cudahy Celebrates Tenth Anniversary," *Publishers' Weekly*, 169 (18 February 1956): 1024-1026;

Donald Hall, "Robert Giroux: Looking for Masterpieces," *New York Times Book Review*, 6 January 1980, p. 3;

"John Farrar [obituary]," *New York Times*, 7 November 1974, p. 48;

N. R. Kleinfield, "Roger Straus: Making It as an Independent," *New York Times Book Review*, 23 March 1980, p. 3.

—Jon Griffin

Fawcett Books

(New York: 1950-   )

The Fawcett Publications Group grew from a magazine publishing firm begun by Wilford H. Fawcett in Minneapolis in 1919. Its first magazine, *Captain Billy's Whiz Bang*, a joke book for hospitalized World War I veterans, sold 500,000 copies in a few months; later magazines included *True Confessions, Mechanix Illustrated, Motion Pictures*, and *True*. In 1935 Fawcett Publications moved its corporate headquarters to 22 West Putnam Avenue, Greenwich, Connecticut, with editorial and advertising offices at 67 West Forty-fourth Street, New York; the New York office later moved to 1 Astor Place, and finally to 1515 Broadway. Fawcett died in 1940; his four sons, Wilford, Jr., Roger, Gordon, and Roscoe, inherited the flourishing magazine firm. With editorial director Ralph Daigh, they made plans to enter the mass market paperback field in 1949.

Fawcett had been the distributor for New American Library's Mentor and Signet lines since 1948; the contract with NAL prohibited Fawcett from engaging in competitive reprint activities. Consequently, Daigh and Jim Bishop, a Fawcett editor, organized an entirely original line of fiction and nonfiction publications to be called Gold Medal Books—the first successful attempt at original paperback publishing on a large scale in America. The headquarters of Gold Medal Books was the Fawcett New York address. Early Gold Medal titles included *We Are the Public Enemies* (1950), essays on gangsters by Alan Hynd; Sax Rohmer's *Nude in Mink* (1950); and W. R. Burnett's *Stretch Dawson* (1950), on which the Twentieth Century-Fox movie *Yellow Sky* was based. Gold Medal Books sold for twenty-five cents; Red Seal Books, a similar line that was soon discontinued, sold for thirty-five cents. When Bishop resigned to write full time, William C. Lengel became the first editor in chief of Gold Medal Books. The early Gold Medals were considered no better than those published by the cheaper reprint lines—lurid, sensational, and violent, with cover art to match. Tereska Torres's *Women's Barracks* (1950) and Charles Williams's *Hill Girl* (1951) sold almost a million copies each in the first year, but it was *This Is Costello* (1951) by newspapermen Robert Prall and Norton Mockridge that earned national attention for the firm's publications. Gold Medal was by then publishing eight books a month.

Gold Medal's generous terms were attractive to authors. Fawcett offered a minimum royalty of $2,000—one cent per copy on the first run—and bought book rights only; the author could sell subsidiary rights and often earned royalties of one-and-a-half cents per copy on print runs beyond the initial 200,000. Like many Gold Medal books, Louis L'Amour's *Hondo* (1953) became a successful motion picture. Kurt Vonnegut, Jr.'s *Canary in a Cat House* (1961) and *Mother Night* (1962) were first published as Gold Medal Books, as were Taylor Caldwell's *Maggie, Her Marriage* (1953) and *Wicked Angel* (1965). Other Gold Medal authors included Mackinlay Kantor, Richard S. Prather, and John D. MacDonald.

When the NAL contract lapsed in 1955, Fawcett was free to start reprint publishing. Leona Nevler was hired as an associate editor for the new line, Crest Books, headed by Lengel, while Richard Carroll became editor in chief of Gold Medal Books. In 1957 Nevler bought *By Love Possessed* by James Gould Cozzens for $101,000, a record reprint bid for the time, and *Lolita* by Vladimir Nabokov for $100,000. These purchases established Fawcett's credentials as a serious bidder in the reprint market.

Premier Books, a fifty-cent reprint line emphasizing inspirational works, classics, and "solid" nonfiction, was established at the same time as Crest Books. *Rules of Games according to Hoyle* (1961) by Richard Frey, originally a Premier book, was later reprinted by Crest. The line between the Fawcett imprints was never hard and fast; in later years Gold Medal occasionally did a reprint if the Crest

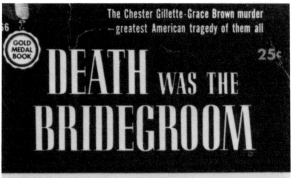

Cover of the 1955 book in the Gold Medal true crime series about the murder case on which Theodore Dreiser's American Tragedy *was based*

Cover of 1953 Fawcett paperback

schedule was full and time was important, and Crest often reprinted the backlist of an author whose current Gold Medal book was selling particularly well, such as those of John Updike and Joyce Carol Oates.

In 1961 William Shirer's *The Rise and Fall of the Third Reich* set records for cost, price, and size. Reprint rights cost Fawcett $400,000. The book was the biggest, most expensive paperback ever published up to that time, selling for $1.65—the first paperback to be priced at more than $1.00. Its publication was made possible only by a special machine capable of binding the 1,600 pages, almost two inches thick, into one volume. In 1968 Mario Puzo's *The Godfather* (1969) cost $410,000. It became a hit movie, and by 1977 over ten million copies of the book had been sold.

By 1962 the designation Fawcett World Library was used to include Crest, Premier, and Gold Medal Books. In 1967 Crest reprinted James Michener's *The Source*, purchased for $700,000, and in 1968 it published the first shrink-wrapped set of paperbacks, a five-volume set of Charles Schulz's "Snoopy" books that sold for $3.75. Crest authors Phyllis Whitney, Victoria Holt, Norah Lofts, Anya Seton, and Mary Stewart aimed at the women's market, while Helen MacInnes, Alistair Maclean, Harry Kemelman, and Isaac Bashevis Singer reached a wide readership. Arlene Friedman was editor in chief of Crest and Premier Books.

In 1972, 921,300 copies of Updike's *Rabbit Redux* (1971) were printed. In 1974 reprint rights to Michener's *The Drifters* (1971) and all but one of his earlier books were purchased for $1 million; in 1975 his *Centennial* became the first single book for which the reprint guarantee was $1 million. Michener's *Chesapeake* (1979) sold five million copies over three years in its Fawcett paperback edition, becoming the firm's all-time best-seller. Other popular books of the 1970s were *The Best and the Brightest* (1973) by David Halberstam, *Lady* (1974) by Tom Tryon, and *The Dreadful Lemon Sky* (1974) by John D. MacDonald.

When Daigh retired in 1974, Nevler became vice-president and publisher of Fawcett Books. In 1976 Fawcett was one of the last remaining family-owned publishing houses. None of the third generation of Fawcetts had entered the business, however, and the firm announced in September that the CBS/Publications Group had made an offer of acquisition. CBS, which had bought Holt, Rinehart and Winston in 1967 and Popular Library in 1971, wished to become "a major force" in paperback publishing. Its offer of $50 million in cash for the

Fawcett World Library, *Woman's Day,* and about thirty other magazines was accepted in January 1977. The firm's new identity was Fawcett Books, Incorporated, a unit of CBS/Publications Group; Popular Library was placed under the Fawcett umbrella. Fawcett's new address was 600 Third Avenue. Almost at once, the Justice Department began an investigation of the merger and, in June 1978, brought suit against CBS for tending to create a monopoly. According to the Justice Department, of the approximately twenty firms engaged in mass market paperback publication in the United States, the eight largest had accounted for about seventy-six percent and the four largest firms for fifty-one percent of total sales in 1973; in 1976 the eight largest accounted for eighty-one percent and the four largest for fifty-three percent of total sales, and also erected substantial barriers to new firms seeking to enter the field.

Fawcett Books bought the paperback rights to *Linda Goodman's Love Signs* for $2.25 million in 1978, tying the record sale price for fiction and breaking the nonfiction record. In August 1979 Fawcett announced that it would publish trade paperbacks on a regular basis under the Columbine imprint, and in October it entered into competition with Harlequin Books by bringing out a new line called Coventry Romances. Fawcett paid $500,000 for Robert A. Heinlein's *The Number of the Beast,* published in 1980 as a Columbine trade paperback. In January 1981 a line for young adults was started under the Juniper Books imprint with *A Matter of Feeling* by Janine Boissard.

Later that year vice-president and group publisher Kenneth B. Collins, who had headed the firm since the CBS acquisition, left for John Wiley and Sons. Nevler took over as head of the Fawcett Book Group, then the fourth largest paperback publisher in the United States, with Arlene Friedman as vice-president and editor in chief and Robert J. Granata as vice-president and managing director. In June 1981 CBS signed a consent decree with the Justice Department agreeing to sell Popular Library in order to retain the other Fawcett lines; but in March 1982 CBS announced the sale of the Fawcett paperback lines to Random House, a division of Newhouse Publications and publisher of Ballantine/Del Rey paperbacks. Popular Library was sold to Warner Books in November. The former Fawcett lines—Crest, Gold Medal, Juniper, and Premier—are now listed as imprints of Ballantine/Del Rey/Fawcett. The price for the Fawcett sale was rumored to have been $10 million up

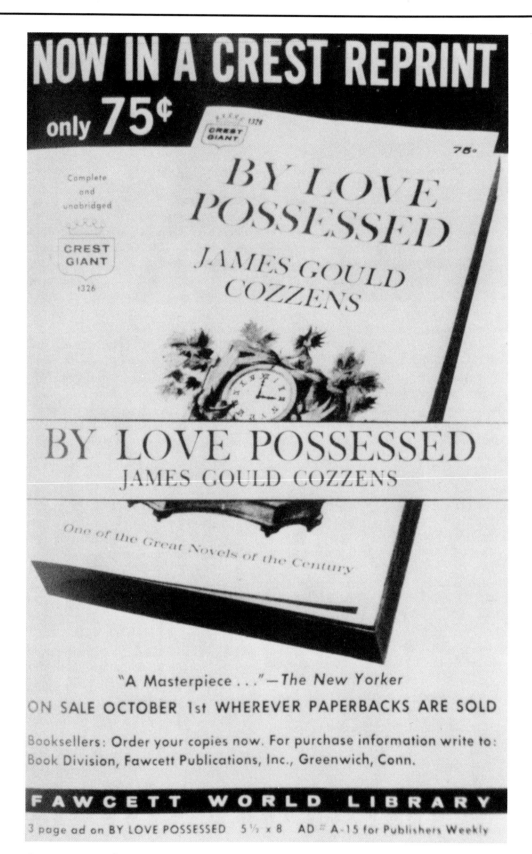

1959 advertisement. The $101,505 paid by Fawcett for paperback rights to Cozzens's novel was a record for the time.

front, and at least $17 million more over three years.

Nevler, who had resigned as Fawcett publisher in October 1981, joined Ballantine on 22 March 1982 as executive editor in charge of the Fawcett lines. The address of the Fawcett Book Group is 201 East Fiftieth Street, New York 10022.

References:

"CBS to Keep Fawcett, Sell Popular in Consent Decree," *Publishers Weekly*, 220 (3 July 1981): 17;

Ralph Daigh, *Maybe You Should Write a Book* (New York: Prentice-Hall, 1977);

Kenneth C. Davis, "The Building of Ballantine," *Publishers Weekly*, 225 (27 April 1984): 25-29;

Mildred Solà Neely, "25 Years of Fawcett: A Line That Began With Paperback Originals and Went on from There," *Publishers Weekly*, 207 (14 April 1975): 32-33;

"RH to Buy Fawcett Assets for Ballantine Books," *Publishers Weekly*, 221 (12 February 1982): 38, 40, 42;

"Three-Member Group to Run Fawcett as Nevler Resigns," *Publishers Weekly*, 220 (30 October 1981): 15;

"25-Cent Originals," *Newsweek*, 38 (20 August 1951): 92-93;

Susan Wagner, "Justice Department Sues CBS to Undo Fawcett Purchase," *Publishers Weekly*, 213 (12 June 1978): 18, 23;

"Wilford H. Fawcett [obituary]," *New York Times*, 8 February 1940, p. 23.

—*Martha A. Bartter*

Federal Writers' Project
(Washington, D.C.: 1935-1939)
Writers' Program
(1939-1943)

The Federal Writers' Project was created by executive order on 27 July 1935 as a unit of the Federal Arts Program of the Works Progress Administration, which also included the Art, Music, and Theater Projects. Although originally conceived as a relief measure for unemployed writers, it also employed jobless architects, professors, librarians, lawyers, photographers, and bankers. About ninety percent of the participants came from the relief rolls, in accordance with WPA regulations, and received monthly wages ranging from $103 in New York to $39 in Georgia and Mississippi.

The Federal Writers' Project was directed by Henry G. Alsberg, an ex-journalist, theater director, and dramatist who was responsible for the high literary standards set for the project's major books. Alsberg and his Washington staff established Writers' Project offices in every state and an additional one in New York City, creating one of the largest fact-gathering organizations ever assembled in the nation. In the seven-and-a-half years of its existence, first under federal sponsorship and—after 1939—under state sponsorship as the Writers' Program, the project employed an estimated 10,000 men and women (6,680 in its first year) and produced approximately 1,200 published books and

pamphlets as well as unpublished material.

The major achievement of the Writers' Project was the American Guide series. Volumes in the series range from the encyclopedic *Washington: City and Capital* (1937), which was 1,140 pages long in its original edition, to mimeographed pamphlets of a few pages. The series included guides for every state and for Puerto Rico; guides to about thirty large cities; several guides to major highways of historic interest, such as *U.S. One* (1938) and *The Oregon Trail* (1939); more than a score of regional guides, such as *Cape Cod Pilot* (1937), *Death Valley: A Guide* (1939), *Here's New England!* (1939), and *Monterey Peninsula* (1941); and hundreds of small-town and county guides, which Robert Cantwell characterized as "the living flesh and blood of American history."

The best known of the American Guide series are the state guides, most of which were published by fifteen commercial publishers at no expense to the government. Each guide discusses the state's natural setting, history, commerce, transportation, ethnic background, press, art, literature, music, theater, architecture, and chief cities. It also offers motor tours that follow the highways throughout the state, providing a wealth of detailed informa-

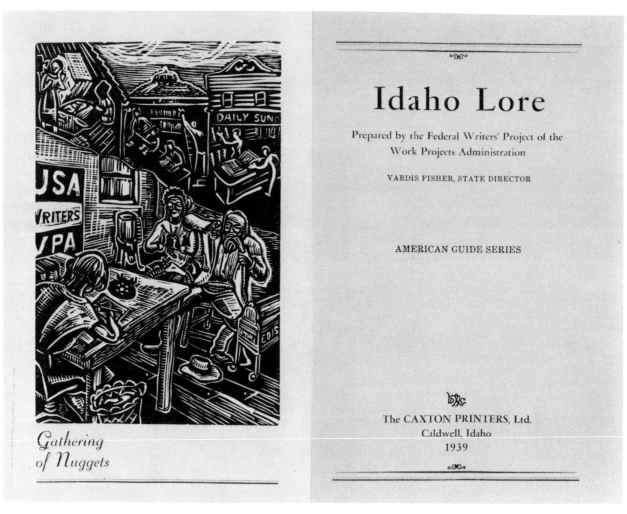

Frontispiece and title page for a state guide

tion and historical tidbits. Alfred Kazin, who recognized that the term *guide* was something of a misnomer, hailed the state books as "an extraordinary American epic . . . a repository and a symbol of the reawakened American sense of its own history."

The final determination as to whether or not manuscripts prepared in the field were ready for publication rested with Alsberg's Washington staff, which included Benjamin A. Botkin, John Cheever, Merle Colby, Harold Coy, George Cronyn, Katharine Kellock, Jerre Mangione (the project's national coordinating editor), Harold Rosenberg, Charles Edward Smith, and George T. Willison. The heaviest of the editorial burdens were borne by the state directors, whose roles as both editors and administrators one state director described as "a baffling combination of midwifery and the assembly line." Among the most successful of the state directors were the novelists Vardis Fisher, Harlan Hatcher, Ross Santee, and Lyle Saxon.

A valuable by-product of the American Guide series was the lesser-known Life in America series, some 150 volumes developed chiefly from the research conducted for the state guides. Published by Houghton Mifflin, these books included collections of folklore; studies of blacks, Indians, and white ethnic groups; maritime histories of Boston and New York; almanacs; songbooks; nature and animal studies, such as *Who's Who in the Zoo* (1937); histories of volunteer fire-fighting groups; a rapidly gathered documentation of the 1938 hurricane, *New England Hurricane* (1938), which became a best-seller; a book of spoken autobiographies by black and white Southern workers and farmers, *These Are Our Lives* (1939); and histories of place names.

The gathering of more than 2,000 narratives by ex-slaves in eighteen states in a period when the former slave population was rapidly dwindling is probably the Writers' Project's most valuable contribution to the literature of American minorities. The narratives were compiled first under the direction of John A. Lomax, the project's first folklore editor, and later under that of Sterling A. Brown, its national editor of Negro affairs; they were organized by Botkin into seventeen volumes, with hundreds of photographs, at the Library of Congress. The material has proved to be invaluable to scholars.

Before joining the staff of the Library of Congress Botkin served as the project's second folklore editor. During his brief tenure, the project shifted its sights from rural and traditional folklore to urban and contemporary material, which became known as Living Lore. Under Botkin's direction, New England Project workers investigated the lives of clock makers and munition workers in Connecticut, clam diggers in Maine, and Welsh slate workers and Italian granite workers in Vermont. From Montana and Arizona came stories told by copper miners; some were incorporated into a social history of the Montana copper mines, *Copper Camp* (1943). In Chicago, project workers recorded tales of railroad workers, sign painters, bricklayers, and steelworkers. In New York City a Living Lore unit of twenty-seven workers—among them Ralph Ellison, Saul Levitt, and May Swenson—gathered Jamaican, Irish, Serbian, Croatian, and Jewish lore, as well as children's street cries and games, and interviewed construction workers, needle trade employees, taxi drivers, and longshoremen. Most of the Living Lore material remains unpublished.

The Writers' Project was often criticized for not employing enough experienced writers; according to Bernard DeVoto, seventy percent of its employees were "writers by aspiration or appointment." Alsberg's response was that "a great variety of non-manual workers, research workers," were required to gather material for the project guides. Also, thousands of experienced writers, however poor, could not or, for reasons of pride, would not qualify for public relief. Among the published writers that the project hired from the relief rolls were Conrad Aiken, whose description of Deerfield in the Massachusetts state guide is considered one of the best pieces of writing in the American Guide series; Nelson Algren; Lionel Abel; Maxwell Bodenheim; Jack Conroy; Edward Dahlberg; Kenneth Fearing; Joe Gould; Zora Neale Hurston; Claude McKay; Kenneth Patchen; Kenneth Rexroth; Harry Roskolenko; and William Rollins, Jr. The professional writers were far outnumbered by aspiring writers, some of whom were able to use the Writers' Project as a launching pad for successful literary careers. Among them were Saul Bellow, Josef Berger (Jeremiah Digges), Loren Eiseley, William Gibson, David Ignatow, Weldon Kees, Isaac Rosenfeld, Studs Terkel, Margaret Walker, Richard Wright, and Frank Yerby. On the whole, the aspiring writers fared better in the Writers' Project than did their more experienced colleagues, who tended to feel that working on the project was an admission of poverty and defeat.

A frequent complaint of project writers was that they were not permitted to work on their own manuscripts during office time; some considered

Henry G. Alsberg (second from left), director of the Federal Writers' Project, with members of his staff: (left to right) Jerre Mangione, Roderick Seidenberg, and Joseph Gaer

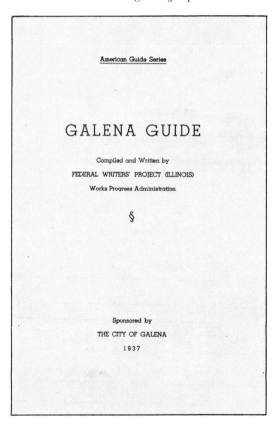

Title page for a city guide; Nelson Algren was a contributor to this volume

1947 advertisement

writing guidebooks a form of hackwork which contributed nothing to their literary development. To counteract such dissatisfaction, the project's administrators encouraged the state offices to establish literary publications that would print material written outside of office hours; *Shucks* (1936) by the Nebraska Project and *Material Gathered* (1936) by the San Francisco Project were two such ventures. Alsberg's office also arranged for the publication of a national anthology of off-time project writing titled *American Stuff* (1937). When its attempts to establish a federally sponsored magazine with that title failed, it persuaded *Frontier and Midland*, the *New Republic*, the *New Masses*, and *Poetry* to devote special issues or sections to the literary efforts of project writers. Despite employee complaints, administrative blunders, a hostile Congress, and the

constant and demoralizing threat of firings, the Writers' Project produced many more good books than its most sanguine champions could have expected.

The Writers' Project rapidly declined after the enactment of the Congressional Emergency Relief Act of 1939, which ended federal sponsorship and placed the Writers' Program, as it was then renamed, under state sponsorship. With its staff reduced to fewer than 2,000, it became a casualty of World War II early in 1943.

Reference:

Jerre Mangione, *The Dream and the Deal: The Federal Writers' Project, 1935-1943* (Boston & Toronto: Little, Brown, 1972).

—*Jerre Mangione*

Frederick Fell Publishers
(New York; Hollywood, Florida: 1943-   )

A World of Books That Fill a Need

Frederick Fell Publishers, Incorporated was founded in 1943 at 386 Park Avenue South, New York, by Frederick Fell, its president and editor in chief. Frederick Fell, as one of its earliest advertisements in *Publishers' Weekly* stated, was founded "on the principle of giving the public books that they want, books that they need, and books that will sell." Four major publication programs have evolved from this goal: the Western Americana series, Fell's Business Book Library, Fell's Personal Interest Library, and Fell's Self-Help Library. Other areas of publication include humor, biography, popular science, and pet care.

One of the firm's more noteworthy ventures into fiction was Fell's Science Fiction Library, which included both anthologies and novels. Among the latter were *The Last Space Ship* (1949) by William

Fitzgerald Jenkins under the pseudonym Murray Leinster and *City at World's End* (1951) by Edmond Hamilton. T. E. Dikty edited several compilations, including the annual *Best Science Fiction Stories and Novels*, while Donald A. Wollheim compiled *Flight into Space* (1950) and *Every Boy's Book of Science-Fiction* (1951).

Fell has published twenty to thirty new titles each year since the early 1960s. Not literary in emphasis, the list has included such fiction as Patricia Benton's *Cradle of the Sun* (1956), Natalja Wendel's *Summer in Spoleto* (1967), Irving Wallace's *The Sins of Philip Fleming* (1968), and Maurits I. Boas's *Preludes* (1978). One of the firm's best-known nonfiction titles was Lillian Roth's autobiography *I'll Cry Tomorrow* (1954). Fell sold the firm in 1981 to Thomas Flatt. It was sold again in August 1985 to

Donald Lessne, who moved it to 2500 Hollywood Boulevard, Hollywood, Florida 33020.

Reference:
William Goldstein, "Following a Well-Executed

Rescue Plan, The Fortunes of Frederick Fell Look Bright," *Publishers Weekly*, 222 (8 October 1982): 32-36.

—Anne Frascarelli

Follett Publishing Company
(Chicago: 1926-1982)

Charles W. Follett, a partner in J. W. Wilcox and Follett Company, Chicago schoolbook sellers, took over the firm in 1923 after J. W. Wilcox died. His four sons joined him in the business. In 1926 Follett created a publishing division by buying a publisher of foreign-language dictionaries; soon the division was producing school and college textbooks. The first address of Follett Publishing Company was 1257 South Wabash Avenue. After several moves, Follett settled in 1955 at 1010 West Washington Boulevard. During the 1960s trade publishing operated from 201 Wells Street, while educational publishing remained at West Washington Boulevard.

During World War II Dwight Follett, serving in the navy in the Pacific, wrote letters to his children about the adventures of a small dog caught up in the war. The letters were worked by Margaret Friskey into a book, *Scuttlebutt Goes to War* (1943), which became the first of a long line of Follett children's books. Dwight Follett became chairman of the firm at his father's death in 1952. He reorganized and expanded the company to form the Follett Corporation, with four divisions: Follett Publishing Company; Wilcox and Follett, wholesalers of new and used elementary and high school textbooks; Follett College Book Company, wholesalers of new and used college textbooks; and the Follett Library Book Company, providing books and, later, microcomputer programs for schools

and public libraries. The corporation also continued to operate the twelve college bookstores established by Charles Follett.

Two especially prominent Follett children's authors were Clara Ingram Judson and Irene Hunt. Best known for her biographies of famous Americans, such as *Abraham Lincoln* (1950), and her fictional series about immigrant groups in the United States, such as the Bohemians in *The Lost Violin* (1947), Judson received the Laura Ingalls Wilder award in 1960. Follett published Hunt's first book, *Across Five Aprils*, a Civil War story, in 1964. Her next book, *Up a Road Slowly* (1966), which follows a sensitive heroine from age seven to seventeen, won the Newbery Medal for 1967. Other Follett children's authors included Elizabeth Guilfoile, whose *Nobody Listens to Andrew* (1957) was the first book in Follett's Beginning-to-Read series, and Lynn Hall, popular writer of mysteries and animal stories for middle-grade children.

Most Follett titles for the adult trade market were sports or "how-to" books. Adult contemporary poetry appeared for a few years beginning in 1968 under the Big Table Books imprint. The series took its name and many of its poets from the Chicago literary magazine *Big Table*, which was published from 1959 until 1961. The most successful title in the series was an anthology edited by Paul Carroll, *The Young American Poets* (1968). Big Table also published some prose works on artistic subjects, including Claes Oldenburg's *Proposals for Monuments and Buildings, 1965-1969* (1969). Follett imprints included the Maxton Publishing Company and the Association Press; the latter was purchased from the YMCA in 1978. Under its various imprints, Follett published sixty new titles in 1980.

Robert J. R. Follett succeeded his father as chairman of the Follett Corporation in 1979. In 1981 the Follett Corporation sold its adult trade and reference book lists to the New Century Ed-ucation Corporation. On 30 December 1982 the assets and business of Follett Publishing Company were purchased by Esquire, Incorporated. The Follett Publishing Company's address is 1010 West Washington Boulevard, Chicago 60607.

Reference:

"Charles W. Follett [obituary]," *New York Times,* 20 December 1952, p. 17.

—*Margaret Becket*

Four Seas Company
(Sharon, Massachusetts; Boston: 1910-1930)

On graduating from Harvard in 1910, Edmund Randolph Brown founded the Four Seas Company at 313 Norwood Street in Sharon, Massachusetts. Brown derived the name of the firm from a statement by Confucius: "All men between the four seas are brothers." By 1922 the firm had moved to 188 Dartmouth Street in Boston; later it moved to 454 Stewart Street.

The Four Seas Company is important as the first or early publisher of several prominent American authors. The firm published Stephen Vincent Benét's first book, *Five Men and Pompey* (1915), and William Faulkner's first book, *The Marble Faun* (1924). Four Seas also published H. L. Mencken's *The Artist: A Drama without Words* (1912); Conrad Aiken's *The Jig of Forslin* (1916), *Nocturne of Remembered Spring* (1917), *The Charnel Rose* (1918), and

The House of Dust (1920); William Carlos Williams's *Al Que Quiere!* (1917); and Gertrude Stein's *Geography and Plays* (1922). Four Seas published new trade and limited editions of Harry Crosby's *Chariot of the Sun* in 1929, the year of Crosby's death. It also issued a magazine, the *Poetry Journal*.

In 1930 Four Seas, which had merged with other firms including John W. Luce and Company, Chapman and Grimes, and the Poet Lore Company, became Bruce Humphries, Incorporated. Brown left Bruce Humphries in 1965 to form the Branden Press, taking with him much of the Four Seas list as well as the Poet Lore titles. In 1971 Branden acquired what remained of the Bruce Humphries firm.

—*Lynne P. Shackelford*

Four Winds Press
(New York: 1966-1984)

FOUR WINDS PRESS

Four Winds Press was founded in 1966 at 50 West Forty-fourth Street, New York, by Scholastic, the educational publisher which produces *Scholastic* magazine and paperback reprints and originals. Scholastic established Four Winds Press to publish some of its paperback titles in hardcover editions. Under its first head, John A. Pope, Jr., Four Winds also began publishing adult titles. Under Judith R. Whipple, who took over as editor from Pope in 1968, the firm published between forty and fifty titles per year. In addition, Four Winds maintained an extensive backlist and in 1979 purchased the entire backlist of Parents' Magazine Press in order to reprint many of these titles under the Four Winds Press imprint.

Like Scholastic, Four Winds published both fiction and nonfiction primarily for children in elementary school. Titles were aimed at particular age and grade levels, though many were listed as suitable for "children of all ages." Over the years Four Winds Press publications won awards in children's publishing. Some of the better-known authors and illustrators who published with Four Winds include Eve Merriam, Gerald McDermott, Ezra Jack Keats, and Mercer Mayer. Four Winds Press was discontinued as an imprint of Scholastic in 1984.

—*Timothy D. Murray*

Franklin Library
(Franklin Center, Pennsylvania, and New York: 1974-   )

Founded in 1974, the Franklin Library is affiliated with the Franklin Mint, which produces various items for collectors. The Franklin Library offers deluxe "limited" editions of literary classics as well as reprints and first printings of works by living authors. The volumes are leatherbound, printed on paper of good quality, and sold by subscription only; the editions are heavily advertised and limited to the number of subscribers who have signed up by a set closing date. Franklin Library publications have included reprints of *Moby-Dick* (1974) and *Paradise Lost* (1979), signed reprints of Robert Penn Warren's *All the King's Men* (1976) and

Joseph Heller's *Catch-22* (1978), and first editions of Bernard Malamud's *Dubin's Lives* (1979) and Heller's *Good as Gold* (1979). The volumes are often signed by the author and often have new introductions by the author or by some other famous writer.

Neil Zelenetz is general manager and publisher of the Franklin Library; Darby Perry is vice-president, editorial. The firm's editorial offices are at 800 Third Avenue, New York 10022; it's headquarters are in Franklin Center, Pennsylvania 19091.

—*Peter Dzwonkoski*

Galaxy Science Fiction Novels
(New York: 1950-1961)

Galaxy Science Fiction Novels formed a paperback companion series to *Galaxy* magazine. The magazine, edited by Horace L. Gold, was published by World Editions, Incorporated, 105 West Fortieth Street, New York, from October 1950 to September 1951. It was then bought by Robert Guinn's Galaxy Publishing Corporation, 421 Hudson Street.

Galaxy Science Fiction Novels were sold on newsstands, as well as by mail order and subscription. The first thirty-one titles were published in a format similar to the magazine's—7 3/8 by 5 1/2 inches. Galaxy's first book, *Sinister Barrier* (1950) by Eric Frank Russell, was a reprint, as was its second, Jack Williamson's *The Legion of Space* (1950); but the third, Arthur C. Clarke's *Prelude to Space* (1951), was an original publication. The earliest titles were priced at twenty-five cents each; after book number eight, Galaxy Science Fiction Novels were published by the Galaxy Publishing Corporation, printed by the Guinn Company, and sold for thirty-five cents each. Other titles in the magazine format included reprints of *Odd John* (1951) by Olaf Stapledon, *Pebble in the Sky* (1953) by Isaac Asimov, *The Humanoids* (1954) by Jack Williamson, and *Shambleau* (1958) by C. L. Moore. *Shambleau* was the last title in magazine format. The four small-paperback-size books that followed, including Hal Clement's *Mission of Gravity* (1958), were also published by the Galaxy Publishing Corporation.

Guinn arranged with the Universal Publishing and Distributing Corporation, which put out the soft-core pornographic Beacon paperbacks, to publish a series called Galaxy Prize Selections, numbered as part of the Beacon line. The description of the books on the copyright page read: "*Galaxy Novels* are sturdy, inexpensive editions of choice works of imaginative suspense, both original and reprint, selected by the editors of *Galaxy Magazine* for Beacon Books." Some novels were slightly revised to include mild sex scenes and were given suggestive titles and cover art: A. E. Van Vogt's *The House That Stood Still* was revised as *The Mating Cry* (1960) and Cyril Judd's *Outpost Mars* was changed to *Sin in Space* (1961); Philip José Farmer's *Flesh* (1960) needed no title change. Later books in this series carried both Beacon Books and Galaxy Science Fiction Novels numbers. *Sin in Space* was the last of the series; discovering that the titles were poorly distributed at newsstands, Guinn sold them through the magazine until the stock was exhausted.

—*Martha A. Bartter*

Gambit
(Boston; Ipswich, Massachusetts: 1968-   )

Small, independently financed Gambit was founded at 53 Beacon Street in Boston by Lovell Thompson, retired vice-president of Houghton Mifflin, in January 1968. The whimsically chosen name, taken from the game of chess, means "a sacrifice of material for a gain of position." Gambit's first publication was a 250-copy edition of Richard Meryman's *Andrew Wyeth* (1969), selling at $2,500 per copy and reserved for Wyeth and the owners of his paintings. Houghton Mifflin published a $75 edition the same year. Among the titles on the firm's diversified backlist are caricaturist David Levine's *Pens and Needles* (1969), *No Known Survivors* (1970), and *The Fables of Aesop* (1975); *Munby, Man of Two Worlds* (1972), based on the diaries of the Victorian poet A. M. Munby; John Dos Passos's *The Fourteenth Chronicle* (1973), offered in both trade and limited editions, and *Century's Ebb* (1975); and *The Galbraith Reader* (1977), selections from the writings of John Kenneth Galbraith.

After a fire destroyed Gambit's first office, the firm moved to 27 North Main Street, Ipswich, Massachusetts. Gambit published the first volume of *Almanac of American Politics* in 1972, after this somewhat irreverent political manual by Michael Barone, Grant Ujifusa, and Douglas Matthews had been rejected by several other publishers.

Thompson, the company's managing editor, guides the firm in its role as "a testing ground for new tastes in editing and new approaches to understanding." The firm's intent to remain small gave it a few unprofitable years, especially in the

Cover for 1951 paperback

Catalogue back cover. The figure of Aesop is a caricature of Gambit founder Lovell Thompson.

Gambit

27 NORTH MAIN STREET
MEETING HOUSE GREEN
IPSWICH, MASSᵗᵗˢ 01938

late 1970s. By the early 1980s the firm's financial outlook had improved. In April 1984 Gambit was acquired by the Harvard Common Press, 535 Albany Street, Boston 02118. Gambit's editorial offices remain in Ipswich; the mailing address is Box 306, Ipswich, Massachusetts 01938.

References:

"Harvard Common Press Acquires Gambit," *Publishers Weekly*, 225 (27 April 1984): 23;

"Lovell Thompson Forms Gambit, Inc., Publisher," *Publishers' Weekly*, 193 (5 February 1968): 43.

—*Shirley Ricker*

Bernard Geis Associates
(New York: 1958-   )

Bernard Geis Associates, Incorporated was founded at 527 Lexington Avenue, New York, in 1958 by Bernard Geis, a former editor with *Coronet* and *Esquire* magazines, Grosset and Dunlap, and Prentice-Hall. Geis, the director and editor, was joined by twelve partners: Art Linkletter, who had come up with the idea for the firm; Ralph Edwards; Groucho Marx; Mark Goodson and William Todman of television's Goodson-Todman Productions; television producers John Guedel and Robert C. Temple; Esquire, Incorporated; Cowles Communications, Incorporated; attorney Jacques Leslie; and Diner's Club executives Ralph C. Schneider and Alfred Bloomingdale. Geis publications—never more than twenty titles a year—were distributed by Random House until the David McKay Company assumed distribution in 1972. Today Geis's titles are distributed by various publishing partners.

Geis publishes commercial fiction and non-fiction books with mass market appeal and promotes them heavily. Early titles included Linkletter's *The Secret World of Kids* (1959), Marx's autobiography *Groucho and Me* (1959), Abigail Van Buren's *Dear Teen-Ager* (1959), Harry S. Truman's autobiography *Mr. Citizen* (1960), Harpo Marx's

Harpo Speaks! (1961), and Jacqueline Susann's first book, *Every Night, Josephine!* (1963).

Six of Geis's partners withdrew in 1967 following the publication of books they considered too sensational. These books included Helen Gurley Brown's *Sex and the Single Girl* (1962), Susann's *Valley of the Dolls* (1966), and Henry Sutton's (pseudonym of David Slavitt) *The Exhibitionist* (1967)—the book which caused Bennett Cerf to end Random House's distribution for the firm. Particularly upsetting to Geis's Hollywood partners was Morton Cooper's *The King* (1967), a novel which was a thinly disguised biography of Frank Sinatra.

Those who remained undoubtedly made money, since some of these titles sold very well; and that is often characteristic of Geis's slim output. Geis published several relatively slow-selling novels during the early 1970s, however, including Hank Searls's *Pentagon* in 1970 and poet Karl Shapiro's only novel, *Edsel*, Lawrence Block's *Ronald Rabbit Is a Dirty Old Man*, and Gordon Merrick's *The Lord Won't Mind*, all in 1971. The slow sales might have played a part in the firm's reorganization in November 1971. Geis went on to publish Angela Davis's first book, *The Education of a Revolutionary* (1973), *Coal Miner's Daughter*, by Loretta Lynn and

Bernard Geis

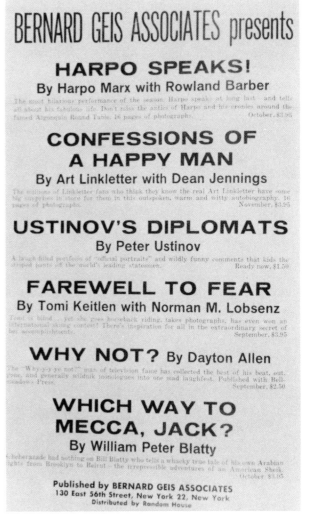

1960 advertisement

George Vecsey (1976), Andrew M. Greeley's novel *The Cardinal Sins* (1981) and subsequent Greeley best-sellers, and a series of novels by Nelson DeMille. The firm's output of titles has declined in the 1980s. The firm's address since 1960 has been 128 East Fifty-sixth Street, New York 10022.

References:

"Sex and the Singular Geis," *Time*, 90 (27 October 1967): 105;

"Shoes Off, Everyone," *Newsweek*, 70 (18 September 1967): 89.

—*Kathleen R. Davis*

David R. Godine, Publisher

(Brookline, Massachusetts; Boston: 1969-   )

DAVID R. GODINE · BOSTON

At the age of twenty, after a year studying books, typography, and graphic art on a fellowship, David R. Godine compiled *Lyric Verse: A Printer's Choice* (1966), which he produced at the Stinehour Press. After taking degrees from Dartmouth and Harvard, Godine incorporated David R. Godine, Publisher in 1969. He was twenty-four and his associates, Lance Hidy and Martha Rockwell, were also young. The firm's office was a barn at 282D Newton Street in Brookline, Massachusetts.

The firm's goals were to combine publishing and printing under one roof to insure that significant works were well printed and, at the same time, commercially successful. Early publications were mostly limited editions printed on rag or handmade paper; other materials, from fonts to inks, were of equally high quality. Most printing was done by letterpress, and many Godine books included original art work.

Godine's first list in 1970 consisted of five booklets in two series: the American Essays series included Henry David Thoreau's *Civil Disobedience* and *A Plea for Captain John Brown;* the Poems, Letters, Tracts, and Broadsides series included Andrew Marvell's *To His Coy Mistress,* James Agee's *The Last Letter . . . to Father Flye,* and Joel Barlow's *The Hasty-Pudding.* It was not long before full-scale books were produced: *John Wesley Powell: Selected Prose* appeared in 1970, and in 1971 the firm published its first trade title, Walt Whitman's *Specimen Days.* This book, the firm's first offset production, contained sixty-eight portraits of the author and fifty-seven Civil War photographs. The firm also began to publish original writing; in 1970 Godine published *Assays of Bias,* a book of poems by Arthur Freeman. The following year Howard Nemerov's *Stories Fables & Other Diversions* appeared, along with another volume of poetry, *This Body* (1971) by Nina Alonso. Early illustrators included Hidy, Fritz Kredel, Gillian Tyler, and Jacques Hnizdovsky. A reflection of Godine's interest in the art of printing was the series Typographic Explorations, starting with Jan Van Krimpen's *The Mechanical Cutting of Punches* (1971). In 1981 Joseph Blumenthal's *The Art of the Printed Book, 1455-1955* (1973) was in its fourth printing. Early Godine distributors were the Small Publishers' Company of New York and Barre Publishers of Massachusetts. In 1973 the firm moved from Brookline to Boston.

By 1974 Godine's specialty lines included a poetry chapbook series, Asian studies, and photography books. One of the earliest titles in this last category was Julia Margaret Cameron's *Victorian Photographs of Famous Men and Fair Women* (1973), which had originally been published in 1928. Godine's was an augmented edition with a new introduction and was published jointly with the Hogarth Press. Godine later strengthened this line with the Contemporary Photographers series. A 1976 book with copious photographs, *Two Hundred Years of American Sculpture,* was described by the publisher as "the most splendid book we have ever published." It was also the most successful commercially and remains a steady backlist seller.

Godine publishes many of its books in softcover, both after and simultaneously with hardcover publication. In 1978 the company initiated a quality paperback reprint series, Nonpareil Books;

David R. Godine

Dust jacket for 1936 Goldsmith novel

works of Edmund Wilson, William Gass, and Stanley Elkin have been reprinted in the Nonpareil line.

In 1980 Godine introduced a children's line with Dylan Thomas's *A Child's Christmas in Wales*, illustrated by Edward Ardizzone, and Sergei Prokofiev's *Peter and the Wolf*, with pictures by Erna Voigt. Recent years have seen an emphasis on translations. In 1980 Godine put out *Badenheim 1939*, the first novel to appear in English by Israeli author Aharon Appelfeld; the translation was by Dalya Bilu, who also translated Appelfeld's *The Age of Wonders* (1981). Other authors whose works have been translated into English and published by Godine include Friedrich Hölderlin, Ernesto Sábato, José Donoso, Jorge Amado, and Agustin Gomez-Arcos. Richard Howard's translation of Baudelaire's *Les Fleurs du Mal* won the American Book Award for translation in 1983.

After a decade in business Godine was publishing about 40 titles a year; had published about 250 titles, some in their fourth printing; and had increased its sales twentyfold. Most books were trade publications, although the firm continued its fine printing. For example, the limited edition of Anthony Hecht's *The Venetian Vespers* (1979) was set in monotype and printed by letterpress, while the Stinehour Press produced David Lance Goines's *A Constructed Roman Alphabet* (1981) in two colors by letterpress.

In 1983 Godine turned over its distribution and warehouse operations to Harper and Row. Looking back on ten years, Godine observed in a catalogue: "We have come this far by obeying two rules anathema to conventional business wisdom; we have stayed small, and we have deliberately tried to be as many things to as many people as possible." The firm's address is Horticultural Hall, 300 Massachusetts Avenue, Boston 02115.

References:

John F. Baker, "David Godine, Publisher," *Publishers Weekly*, 219 (30 January 1981): 32-34;

David R. Godine, "Young Publisher, Young Hands, Keep Fine Printing Alive," *Publishers' Weekly*, 199 (31 May 1971): 126-127;

David Lehman, "In Praise of the Independent," *Newsweek*, 102 (25 July 1983): 71-72.

—Vincent Prestianni

Goldsmith Publishing Company
(Chicago: circa 1931-circa 1939)

A publisher of low-cost hardcover books for preteen boys and girls, the Goldsmith Publishing Company was located at 727 South Dearborn in Chicago during most of the 1930s; from about 1937 to 1939 it shared space with M. A. Donohue Company at 711 South Dearborn. Goldsmith books were characterized by cheapness of format: low-quality paper, inexpensive cloth bindings, and comic-strip-quality dust jacket art. Authors of Goldsmith books for boys included Harold M. Sherman, Graham M. Dean, Ambrose Newcomb, and Wayne Whipple; series included Sherman's Tahara series and Dean's Tim Murphy Newspaper Mystery series. The idea, according to a dust jacket blurb, was to produce books that "will stir the imaginations of all boys," yet avoid "being nerve-wreckers." Like those for boys, the Goldsmith books for girls exploited popular stereotypes in offering stories of young romance and schoolgirl fiction.

—Peter Dzwonkoski

Laurence James Gomme
(New York: 1916-1917)
Vaughan and Gomme
(New York: 1914)
Gomme and Marshall
(New York: 1915-1916)

Born in 1882, Laurence James Gomme worked as an apprentice in the firm of Truslove and Hanson in London, and for A. T. Chapman and for Baker and Taylor in Montreal. He went to New York in 1907 and became chief stock clerk at Brentano's. The next year he began to manage Mitchell Kennerley's Little Book-Shop Around the Corner at 2 East Twenty-ninth Street in Manhattan, which had opened during the previous year. The bookshop had been established not to compete with larger bookshops but to showcase Kennerley's books and to serve as a locus for literary and artistic activity. The shop was frequented by actors, musicians, painters, photographers, and writers such as Richard Le Gallienne and Bliss Carman. With Donald Vaughan, Gomme bought the shop from Kennerley in 1912. In 1914 Vaughan and Gomme published pamphlet plays by writers including Kenneth Sawyer Goodman and Thomas Wood Stevens.

Vaughan withdrew from the shop's operation in 1914. Gomme joined briefly with John J. Marshall to publish the well-received *Anthology of Magazine Verse for 1914* (1915), edited by William Stanley Braithwaite, and Clinton Scollard's *Italy in Arms* (1915) under the Gomme and Marshall imprint, then went on to publish under his own name *Ballads, Patriotic and Romantic* (1916), edited by Scollard; Kilmer's *The Circus, and Other Essays* (1916); and *Eight Harvard Poets* (1917), in which the work of E. E. Cummings made its first appearance in book form. Gomme offered his bookshop as a meeting place and gallery for the new Society of Pictorial Photographers of America, which displayed the works of Edward Steichen, Alvin Langdon Coburn, and Clarence White. Gomme closed The Little Book-Shop Around the Corner and ended his publishing career in 1917; thereafter he was active in the antiquarian book field. He died in 1974.

References:

Laurence J. Gomme, "The Little Book-Shop Around the Corner," *Colophon*, new series 2 (Autumn 1937): 573-593;

Gomme, "My First Fifty Years in New York," *Antiquarian Bookman*, 22 (1958): 1587-1590;

"Laurence James Gomme [obituary]," *New York Times*, 5 February 1974, p. 40;

G. Thomas Tanselle, "The Laurence Gomme Imprint," *Papers of the Bibliographical Society of America*, 61 (1967): 225-240.

—*Deborah G. Gorman*

Greenberg: Publisher
(New York: 1924-1958)

Greenberg: Publisher was founded by Jacob (Jae) W. Greenberg in 1924 on East Fortieth Street in New York; later the firm moved to East Fifty-seventh Street. Greenberg published fiction, drama, essays, and children's books but emphasized nonfiction, including books on music, travel, cinema, theater, popular psychology, education, cooking, and "how-to" books.

In 1924, the year of its first trade list, Greenberg published George Gissing's *Critical Studies of the Works of Charles Dickens* with an introduction and bibliography of Gissing by Temple Scott. In 1925 Greenberg published Robert Graves's *The Meaning of Dreams,* which had been published in London in 1924. *Tony Sarg's Books for Children from Six to Sixty* (1924), *Tony Sarg's Book of Animals* (1925), and *Tony Sarg's New York* (1926) were the first three titles in a series of Sarg's illustrated books to be published by Greenberg.

In 1927 Greenberg published Alfred Adler's *Understanding Human Nature,* which eventually sold more than a million copies. Its success established the firm's reputation as a publisher of titles on popular psychology and mental health. Greenberg continued to publish works by Adler, including *The Science of Living* (1929). Several works by Joseph Jastrow appeared under the Greenberg imprint, including *Keeping Mentally Fit: A Guide to Everyday Psychology* (1928), *Piloting Your Life: The Psychologist as Helmsman* (1930), and *The House That Freud Built* (1932). Literary writers published and reprinted by Greenberg included Franklin P. Adams, Max Eastman, Lafcadio Hearn, Jack London, and Deems Taylor. Greenberg: Publisher was acquired by the Chilton Book Company in 1958.

References:

"Greenberg Marks Tenth Year," *Publishers' Weekly,* 126 (11 August 1934): 420;

"Greenberg: Publisher Celebrates Twenty-fifth Anniversary," *Publishers' Weekly,* 156 (1 October 1949): 1569-1571.

—Joseph Heininger

Green Tiger Press
(San Diego; La Jolla, California; San Diego: 1970-   )

Green Tiger Press was founded in 1970 by Harold and Sandra Darling in a spare bedroom of their San Diego home; the firm soon moved to larger quarters at 3620 Fifth Avenue. The first publications of the Green Tiger Press were reproduced illustrations by Edmund Dulac, Beatrix Potter, Arthur Rackham, and other artists in the form of notecards, stationery, posters, and calendars. In 1972 the firm began publishing paperbound books with Welleran Poltarnees's *All Mirrors Are Magic,* a historical appreciation of children's book art. Green Tiger also republished classic illustrated books, including Christina Rossetti's *Goblin Market* (1973) and Robert Louis Stevenson's *A Child's Garden of Verses* (1974), as well as collections of works by prominent book illustrators of the past, such as Henriette Willebeek Le Mair, Ernst Kreidolf, Kay Nielsen, and Sybille von Olfers.

In the mid-1970s Green Tiger Press moved to 7458 La Jolla Boulevard in La Jolla, California, and began publishing original titles. By adhering to high standards in the writing and illustrations of its books the firm has had commercial and critical success, and its publications are consistently nom-

Laurence James Gomme

Jacob (Jae) W. Greenberg in 1934

The founders of Greenwillow Books (left to right): Ava Weiss, Ada Shearon, Elizabeth Shub, and Susan Hirschman

inated for children's book awards. Contemporary Green Tiger authors and illustrators include Margery Bianco, Patrick Dowers, Cooper Edens, Michael Hague, and Jasper Tomkins. Green Tiger Press usually produces ten to twenty titles per year under the direction of Harold Darling, the editor/publisher, and Sandra Darling, the art director. In

1984 the firm moved to 1061 India Street, San Diego 92101.

Reference:

Patricia Holt, "The View from the West: Booksellers Turn Publishers," *Publishers Weekly*, 214 (17 July 1978): 143.

—*Timothy D. Murray*

Greenwillow Books

(New York: 1974-   )

 Greenwillow Books
A Division of
William Morrow & Company, Inc.
New York

Greenwillow Books, an autonomous children's book division of William Morrow and Company, Incorporated, was founded in late 1974 with Susan Hirschman as editor in chief. Since the first list of books was published in 1975, Greenwillow has published nearly 600 books. Author and/or illustrators who have written books for Greenwillow include Aliki and Franz Brandenburg, Donald Crews, Janina Domanska, Virginia Hamilton, Pat Hutchins, Ann Jones, Arnold Lobel, Anita Lobel,

Robin McKinley, Jack Prelutsky, Nancy Tafuri, and Vera Williams. In its eleven-year history, Greenwillow has been the publisher of one Newbery Medal Book, *The Hero and the Crown* by Robin McKinley (1985); two Newbery Honor Books; eight Caldecott Honor Books, the most recent being *Have You Seen My Duckling* by Nancy Tafuri (1985). Greenwillow Books is located at 105 Madison Avenue, New York 10016.

—*Theodora Mills*

Gregg Press

(Ridgewood, New Jersey; Boston: 1963-   )

Gregg Press

Gregg Press was founded in 1963 by Newton K. and Charles S. Gregg as the North American sales organization for Gregg Press, Limited England (now Gregg International Publishers). The firm was located at 171 East Ridgewood Avenue, Ridgewood, New Jersey. Chiefly a reprint house, Gregg Press published some original scholarship and reprinted standard works of American literature and science fiction. Through its successful Americans in Fiction series, the firm made available neglected works of American literature; among these were Mary E. W. Freeman's *A New England Nun, and Other Stories* (1967) and Charles W. Chestnutt's *The Conjure Woman* (1968). Among the firm's science fiction reprints were Andre Norton's Witch World series, Karel Capek's *The War with the Newts* (1975), and Brian Aldiss's *Hot House* (1976). Westerns and mysteries were also included in this rapidly expanded reprint program.

(Gregg Press, Incorporated, since 1971 a division of G. K. Hall, should not be confused with the Gregg Publishing Company—now a division of McGraw-Hill—originally begun in Chicago to publish and promote the Gregg shorthand materials, or with Newton K. Gregg of Rohnert Park, California.) Thomas T. Beeler is publisher and Elizabeth B. Kubik is editor in chief. The firm is now located at 70 Lincoln Street, Boston 02111.

—Martha A. Bartter

Grossman Publishers

(New York: 1962-1984)

Grossman Publishers was founded in 1962 in a basement at 125A East Nineteenth Street, New York. Richard L. Grossman, who had been a vice-president at Simon and Schuster since 1958, started his firm with a "philosophy of smallness" that nevertheless resulted in a diverse range of quality books. Among Grossman's first publications were Henri Cartier-Bresson's *Photographs* (1963); Ben Shahn's *Love and Joy about Letters* (1963), which earned an honorable mention in the Carey-Thomas Award competition; and Robert Capa's *Images of War* (1964).

In 1965 Grossman acquired Orion Press. Titles of distinction that year included *Rhymes for the Irreverent* by Edgar Y. Harburg and Grossman's most famous book, Ralph Nader's *Unsafe at Any Speed*. In the same year Grossman introduced a photography and graphics paperback line called Paragraphic Books and became the distributor for Gehenna Press.

1967 advertisement

1965 advertisement for Grossman's most famous book

Richard L. Grossman

*Barney Rosset, president of Grove Press (photo by
Arne C. Svenson)*

In 1968 the firm became the American distributor of Cape Editions, a series of unconventional and "neglected" classic fiction and nonfiction texts. Later that year, after publishing Pablo Neruda's *We Are Many*, Fidel Castro's *History Will Absolve Me*, Claude Levi-Strauss's *The Scope of Anthropology*, and Allen Ginsberg's *T. V. Baby Poems*, Grossman sold out to Viking Press and joined that firm as a vice-president. The Grossman imprint continued under Viking until 1984.

References:

David Dempsey, "Return of the Personal Publisher," *Saturday Review*, 46 (14 September 1965): 34-35;

"Viking Press Buys Grossman Publishers," *Publishers' Weekly*, 194 (16 September 1968): 51.

—Richard Horvath

Grove Press
(New York: 1949-)

Born in Chicago in 1922, Barnet (Barney) Lee Rosset, Jr., attended the city's Francis W. Parker School, a progressive institution which Rosset maintains had "a bigger influence on me than my parents or college." After a year at Swarthmore College and three months at the University of Chicago, he went to the University of California at Los Angeles. At the outbreak of World War II he enlisted in the infantry. Leaving the service in 1946 with the rank of first lieutenant, Rosset received his Ph.B. from the University of Chicago a year later, followed by a B.A. from the New School of Social Research in 1952. With money inherited from his father, a banker, Rosset acquired Grove Press for $3,000 in 1952, three years after its founding by John Balcomb and Robert Phelps. Balcomb and Phelps had published only three books—Melville's *The Confidence-Man* (1949), *The Verse in English of Richard Crashaw* (1949), and *Selected Writing of the Ingenious Mrs. Aphra Behn* (1950). At first, Rosset operated the firm from his apartment at 59 West Ninth Street in New York; a year later Grove moved to 795 Broadway.

From its beginning, Grove's publications have concentrated heavily on European—especially French—literature. Its first book after Rosset purchased the firm—*The Monk* (1952), a long-out-of-print work by the eighteenth-century English author Matthew G. Lewis—was followed by other out-of-print titles, such as Henry James's *The Golden Bowl* (1952). Grove's first catalogue in 1953 also included works by Arthur Rimbaud, Alfred de Vigny, Eugène Fromentin, Simone de Beauvoir, and John Skelton. In 1953 Grove acquired the Zodiac Library, which offered works by Trollope, Twain, Jane Austen, Dickens, and Thackeray. Grove also became the American publisher of the International Library of Sociology and Social Reconstruction.

Grove remained a struggling concern throughout the 1950s while nevertheless playing an important role in introducing major European authors to the American public. Soon after acquiring Grove, Rosset traveled to France in search of authors. As a result, Grove published *Waiting for Godot* (1954), the play which established Samuel Beckett's literary reputation in America. It was followed by his novels *Molloy* (1955), *Malone Dies* (1956), *Murphy* (1957), *The Unnamable* (1958), *Watt* (1959), and *How It Is* (1964) and the plays *All That Fall* (1957) and *Endgame* (1958).

Grove's main emphasis remained international. The firm published new works by Beckett, including *Happy Days* (1961), *Ends and Odds* (1976), and *Company* (1980). New titles by Brecht included *Mother Courage and Her Children* (1963), *The Threepenny Opera* (1964), *The Caucasian Chalk Circle* (1966), and *Galileo* (1966). Having introduced Ge-

SPRING 1953

NO NAME IN THE STREET by Kay Cicellis   **$3.00**

First novel by a fine young Greek writer whose stories have appeared in *Harper's Bazaar* and *Mademoiselle*.

THE MARQUIS DE SADE: A study by Simone de Beauvoir with selections from his writings   **$5.00**

Edmund Wilson said in the *New Yorker* of the study "Perhaps the very best thing which has yet been written on the subject." The extensive selections are from Sade's famous but unread writings.

THE SACRED FOUNT by Henry James   **$4.00**

The first new edition in many years of James' "definitive parable of life and the artist," with a new introductory essay by Leon Edel.

THE HOUSE BY THE MEDLAR TREE
by Giovanni Verga   **$3.50**

First translation of this great Sicilian classic. "Surely the greatest writer of Italian fiction..." D. H. Lawrence

THE MILITARY NECESSITY by Alfred de Vigny $3.00

Three deeply moving 'case histories' of life in the military service, written shortly after the campaigns of Napoleon, by one of the greatest French romantic poets, and himself a professional soldier.

COUNT D'ORGEL by Raymond Radiguet   **$3.00**

The last novel written by the author of *Devil in the Flesh*. With a preface by Jean Cocteau. "An astonishing evocation of Paris in the early nineteen-twenties."

EDWIN MUIR: COLLECTED POEMS, 1921-1951

The first publication in America of one of the finest living poets, long known in England.

RIMBAUD'S ILLUMINATIONS by Wallace Fowlie $4.00

A detailed analysis of *Les Illuminations* with a new translation and the French text of the poems.

FOLK TALES FROM KOREA
Collected by Zong In-Sob   **$4.50**

This collection of short novels, fairy tales, legends, and myths, shows us an important side of this people whose cultural attainments are considerable, yet who are now plunged in ruin.

59 West 9th St., New York City 11

Early advertisement

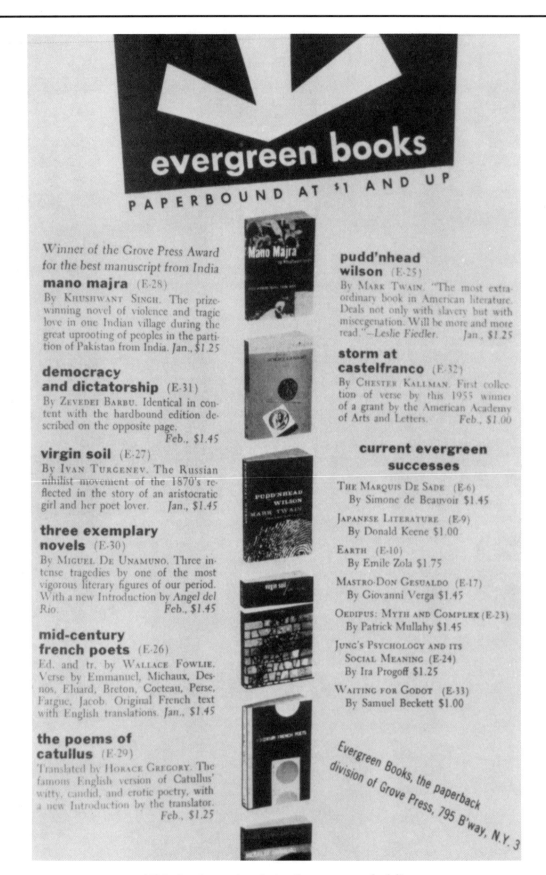

1956 advertisement introducing Evergreen paperback line

net to America through his plays, Grove published his novels *The Miracle of the Rose* (1966), *Funeral Rites* (1969), *The Thief's Journal* (1973), and *Our Lady of the Flowers* (1976). Grove also continued to publish Robbe-Grillet's works, including *The Erasers* (1964) and *Project for a Revolution in New York* (1972).

Grove's catalogue swelled with works by international writers during the 1960s and 1970s. Among new titles were Jorge Luis Borges's *Ficciones* (1962), Friedrich Durrenmatt's *The Visit* (1962) and *Play Strindberg* (1973), Rolf Hochhuth's *The Deputy* (1964), Yukio Mishima's *Madame de Sade* (1967) and *Sun & Steel* (1970), Mikhail Bulgakov's *The Master and Margarita* (1967) and *Flight* (1969), Fernando Arrabal's *Guernica and Other Plays* (1969), and several volumes of verse by Neruda. Not all of Grove's publications were entirely literary. The firm also offered such erotica as Frank Harris's *My Life and Loves* (1963), Pauline Réage's *Story of O* (1966), and the anonymous works *My Secret Life* (1967), *A Man with a Maid* (1968), and *The Lustful Turk* (1980).

Grove showed its sympathy for the Cuban revolution by publishing Regis Debray's *Revolution in the Revolution?* (1967), *Che Guevara Speaks* (1967), and, in the *Evergreen Review*, selections from Guevara's journals. On 26 July 1968 anti-Castro Cubans bombed the firm's offices. Seven years later, Grove filed suit against the Central Intelligence Agency, seeking $10 million in damages and access to the agency's files on the firm. Grove alleged that the agency was responsible for the bombing and had tapped the firm's phones and infiltrated its offices. One source of irritation to the CIA had been Grove's publication of double agent Kim Philby's *My Silent War* (1968). Although Grove failed in its efforts to obtain information from the agency, the firm is currently the plaintiff in a lawsuit against the CIA by the American Civil Liberties Union.

While the Cuban and Philby books caused problems for Grove, other nonfiction works brought financial success. Eric Berne's *Games People Play* (1964) became Grove's all-time best-seller. Nonfiction titles of literary significance include de Beauvoir's *The Marquis de Sade: With Selections from His Writings* (1953), Jean Cocteau's *Opium: The Diary of a Cure* (1957), Octavio Paz's *The Labyrinth of Solitude: Life and Thought in Mexico* (1962), and Allen Ginsberg's *Journals: Early Fifties, Early Sixties* (1977).

Rosset inaugurated the Evergreen Books paperback line in 1954. Usually, the paperbacks reprint Grove's hardcover titles. The *Evergreen Review* was launched in 1957. Edited by Rosset and Donald Allen, who were later joined by Richard Seaver and

Fred Jordan, the *Evergreen Review* became one of the best-known radical and avant-garde journals in America. Allen Ginsberg's poem *Howl*, although published in book form a few months earlier by City Lights, gained its first national exposure in the second issue of the *Evergreen Review*. Other writers featured in the journal during the 1950s and 1960s were Jack Kerouac, Lawrence Ferlinghetti, Norman Mailer, Jean-Paul Sartre, Pablo Neruda, Terry Southern, and Richard Brautigan. Beckett's play *Krapp's Last Tape* first appeared in the *Evergreen Review* in 1958 and was reprinted in paperback in 1960 under the Evergreen imprint as *Krapp's Last Tape and Other Dramatic Pieces*. Most works by Beckett were published in limited—occasionally signed—editions, as well as in Evergreen paperbacks and Grove hardcovers.

French writers distinguished Grove's list in the 1950s. Avant-garde theater was represented by Jean Genet's *The Maids. Death Watch* (1954) and *The Balcony* (1958). Grove published two drama collections by Eugène Ionesco: *Four Plays* (1958) included *The Bald Soprano, The Lesson, The Chairs*, and *Jack; or, the Submission; Plays* (1958) included *Amédée, The New Tenant*, and *Victims of Duty*. Typical of the French *nouveau roman* were Alain Robbe-Grillet's *The Voyeur* (1958) and *Jealousy* (1959).

Other international works published by Grove during the 1950s included Giovanni Verga's *The House by the Medlar Tree* (1953), Khushwant Singh's *Train to Pakistan* (1956), Lawrence Durrell's *Selected Poems* (1956), Miguel de Unamuno's *Three Exemplary Novels* (1956), Bertolt Brecht's *Threepenny Novel* (1956), Brendan Behan's *The Quare Fellow* (1957), and Shelagh Delaney's *A Taste of Honey* (1959). Because many of these works are read in college courses, Grove maintains a backlist of more than 400 titles.

In 1959 Grove launched the Evergreen Encyclopedia Editions, which included *The Journal of Eugène Delacroix* (1960) and André Maurois's *A History of France* (1960). Also in 1959 Grove created the Evergreen Gallery Editions, which included Jean Cathelin's *Jean Arp* (1959) and Oto Bihalji-Merin's *Modern Yugoslav Painting* (1960). A year later Grove inaugurated the Evergreen Profile Editions with André Francis's *Jazz*, Michael Hoffman's *Tchaikovsky*, Vladimir Jankelevitch's *Ravel*, and Pascal Pia's *Baudelaire*. These lines have all been discontinued.

Grove published the first unexpurgated American edition of D. H. Lawrence's *Lady Chatterley's Lover* on 4 May 1959. Two days later, inspectors at the New York Post Office refused to

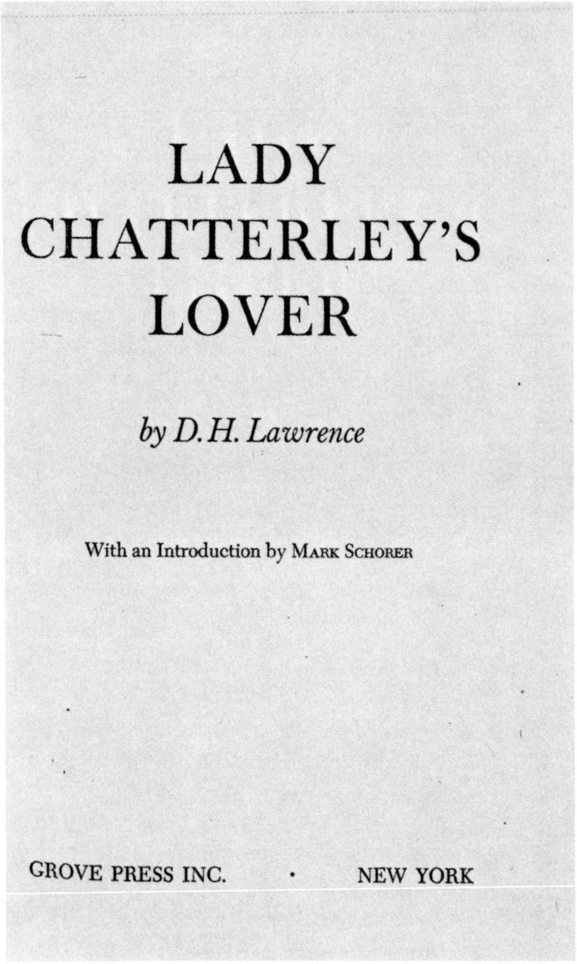

LADY
CHATTERLEY'S
LOVER

by D. H. Lawrence

With an Introduction by Mark Schorer

GROVE PRESS INC.   •   NEW YORK

*Title page for the first unexpurgated American edition of Law-
rence's novel, published in 1959. The novel was the subject of
a celebrated obscenity trial.*

HENRY MILLER

Tropic
of
Cancer

GROVE PRESS, INC. NEW YORK

*Title page for first American edition of Miller's novel, published
in 1961. The United States Supreme Court ruled in 1964 that
the novel was not obscene.*

ship the book and impounded 164 copies on grounds of obscenity. On 21 July Judge Frederick van Pelt Bryan of the United States District Court for the Southern District of New York ruled that *Lady Chatterley's Lover* was mailable and not obscene. He called it "an honest and sincere novel of literary merit." The novel was Grove's first major financial success.

Grove's output expanded from 50 titles in 1958 to a peak of 102 in 1961. Seaver, named managing editor in 1959; Allen, named associate editor in 1959; and Fred Jordan, sales manager since 1957, promotion and advertising manager after 1959, and later senior vice-president and senior editor, played key roles in this expansion. The firm moved to larger offices at 64 University Place in 1959. In June 1961 Grove inaugurated its Black Cat line of mass market paperbacks. Less expensive than the Grove Press or Evergreen Books volumes, these included Grove and Evergreen reprints, original titles, and reprints of titles originally published by other firms.

Grove's expansion included the addition of several important American writers to its list. Of the few American works published by Grove during the 1950s the most significant were Frank O'Hara's *Meditations in an Emergency* (1957) and Jack Kerouac's *The Subterraneans* (1958). During the early 1960s Grove published Charles Olson's *Distances: Poems* (1960); Robert Duncan's *The Opening of the Field* (1960); Robert Gover's first book, *One Hundred Dollar Misunderstanding* (1961); and John Rechy's first novel, *City of Night* (1963).

Two years after the publication of *Lady Chatterley's Lover*, Grove published the first American edition of Henry Miller's *Tropic of Cancer*. More than sixty censorship actions were instituted against the book, culminating in a 1964 United States Supreme Court ruling that it was not obscene. The notoriety produced by the censorship trials resulted in initial sales of over 100,000 clothbound copies of *Tropic of Cancer*. Total sales in hardcover and paperback editions now exceed three million copies. Grove followed with *Tropic of Capricorn* (1962) and *Black Spring* (1963), completing Miller's first trilogy. The second trilogy, *The Rosy Crucifixion*, comprised *Nexus* (1965), *Plexus* (1965), and *Sexus* (1965).

Grove's publication of William Burroughs's *Naked Lunch* (1962) was followed by his *Nova Express* (1964), *The Soft Machine* (1966), *The Ticket That Exploded* (1967), and *The Wild Boys* (1971). Seaver took Burroughs with him to Viking, where he started his own imprint, Richard Seaver Books, in 1971.

During the 1960s Grove published many of the major works of Imamu A. Baraka, the adopted name of LeRoi Jones, including *The Dead Lecturer* (1964), *The System of Dante's Hell* (1965), *The Baptism and The Toilet* (1967), and *Tales* (1967). Grove also published Michael McClure's *New Book: A Book of Torture* (1961) and *The Beard* (1967), Hubert Selby's *Last Exit to Brooklyn* (1964) and *The Room* (1971), and William Heyen's pseudonymous first book, *What Happens in Fort Lauderdale* (1968).

In 1969 Grove planned another expansion and borrowed heavily to finance its move to Mercer Street; but the economy went into a recession in 1971 and Grove's sales and profits sagged. Furthermore, as the 1970s progressed, Grove's erotic literature seemed tame compared to the blatant pornography that had become available largely because of the firm's own battles against censorship; readers interested only in titillation went elsewhere. A change in political and cultural attitudes also restricted the market for Grove's radical literature. The *Evergreen Review* was forced to close in 1973 due to Grove's financial difficulties. In order to cope with these problems, the firm accepted the 1971 offer of Random House to handle Grove's marketing. In 1978 the role of Random House was reduced to shipping, while Grove returned to handling its own sales.

Grove's involvement with the British theater, which had begun with Beckett, continued during the 1960s and 1970s with Harold Pinter and Tom Stoppard. Publication of Pinter's *The Birthday Party* and *The Caretaker* in 1961 was followed by *The Homecoming* (1966), *No Man's Land* (1975), *The Complete Works* (1977-1978) in three volumes, and *The Hot-house* (1980). Stoppard's works have included *Rosencrantz and Guildenstern Are Dead* (1967), *Enter a Free Man* (1972), *Travesties* (1975), and *Night and Day* (1979). American plays published by Grove have included David Mamet's *American Buffalo* (1977) and Bernard Pomerance's *The Elephant Man* (1979).

Grove published more works by Kerouac in the 1970s, including *Lonesome Traveler* (1970) and *Pic* (1971). *Mulligan Stew*, by former Grove editor Gilbert Sorrentino, appeared in 1979. Grove had a best-seller in the paperback edition of John Kennedy Toole's Pulitzer Prize-winning *A Confederacy of Dunces* (1981).

Grove, which was incorporated in 1964, seems to have survived the turmoil and decline of the 1970s and to have adjusted to a more modest level of productivity. While in 1968 Grove published 136 titles, in 1979 it produced 45 titles. The firm has shown a profit since 1975. In April 1985 Grove was sold to Wheatland Corporation, which is owned by George Weidenfeld and Ann Getty, for $2 million. Rosset remains in charge of Grove's management. Since 1976 Grove has been located at 196 West Houston Street, New York 10014.

References:

Randy Sue Coburn, "Barney Rosset, the Force be-

hind Grove Press," *Washington Star,* 12 August 1979;

"Grove Press," *Publishers' Weekly,* 164 (4 July 1953): 40;

Charles Rembar, *The End of Obscenity; The Trials of Lady Chatterley, Tropic of Cancer, and Fanny Hill* (New York: Random House, 1968).

—*David Dzwonkoski*

Haldeman-Julius Company
(Girard, Kansas: 1922-1964)
Appeal Publishing Company
(Girard, Kansas: 1919-1922)

Emanuel Julius was born in Philadelphia in 1889, the son of a Russian immigrant bookbinder. He left school at age thirteen but continued his education by reading. Julius developed a strong belief in socialism and worked for several radical and socialist newspapers, including the *Milwaukee Leader,* the *Chicago World,* the *Los Angeles Western Comrade,* and the *New York Call.* A coworker at the *Call,* Louis Kopelin, became managing editor of the socialist *Appeal to Reason* in Girard, Kansas, and Julius joined this paper's staff in 1915. In 1916, when Julius married Marcet Haldeman, a wealthy woman who shared his political beliefs, he changed his name to Haldeman-Julius.

In January 1919 Haldeman-Julius and Kopelin purchased the *Appeal to Reason* and its printing plant. In February 1919 the Appeal Publishing Company printed the first two titles in the Appeal's Pocket Series, *The Ballad of Reading Gaol* by Oscar Wilde and *The Rubáiyát of Omar Khayyám* with an introduction by Clarence Darrow. These works were followed by several titles on socialist themes, as well as additional reprints of classics. The series was known at various times as the Appeal Pocket Series, People's Pocket Series, Ten Cent Pocket Series, Five Cent Pocket Series, and Pocket Series. The firm became the Haldeman-Julius Company in 1922, and in 1923 the title of the series changed to Little Blue Books. The paperbound booklets in this popular series were 3 1/2 by 5 inches, 64 pages, not more than 15,000 words, printed on newsprint in eight-point type, and sold for five cents apiece. In 1925 Haldeman-Julius inaugurated the Big Blue Books, which were usually 30,000 words and 8 1/2 by 5 1/2 inches and priced at fifty cents. Haldeman-Julius's mass production techniques led to his being called the Henry Ford of publishing.

Most of the Little Blue Books and Big Blue Books were reprints of classics and literary works in the public domain. Authors included Shakespeare, Emerson, Longfellow, Poe, Ibsen, Wilde, Balzac, de Maupassant, Kipling, Hardy, Hugo, and Twain. The series also included original works, and more than a quarter of the firm's output consisted of radical books. Haldeman-Julius provided a publishing outlet for several liberal authors whose views he shared, among them Darrow, Upton Sinclair, Bertrand Russell, and Will Durant. The first edition of Louis Adamic's first book, *Yugoslav Proverbs,* was published by the firm in 1924; Durant's *The Story of Philosophy,* published in 1926 by Simon and Schuster, was originally published from 1922 to 1925 as eleven Pocket and Blue Books on philosophers. Although such works and reprints of classics accounted for the majority of the more than 3,000 titles in the Blue Books series, the firm's bestsellers concerned sex, love, and self-improvement. Haldeman-Julius also published his own works: *The Art of Reading* appeared in 1923, followed by *The Bunk Box* (1926) and *The Fun I Get out of Life* (1927). He and his wife wrote *Embers: A Play in One Act* (1923) and *Dust* (1928). In addition to the Little and Big Blue Books, Haldeman-Julius continued to publish the *Appeal to Reason* and its successor, the *Haldeman-Julius Weekly,* until 1951. The firm also published a monthly magazine, *Life and Letters,* from 1922 to 1925.

Haldeman-Julius was often criticized for his flamboyant marketing techniques. He regularly changed titles and subtitles of classic works in order to improve sales: de Maupassant's *The Tallow Ball* (1923) became *A French Prostitute's Sacrifice,* and Théophile Gautier's *The Fleece of Gold* (n.d.) was retitled *The Quest for a Blond Mistress.* Haldeman-

Emanuel Haldeman-Julius (Nation, *10 May 1952*)

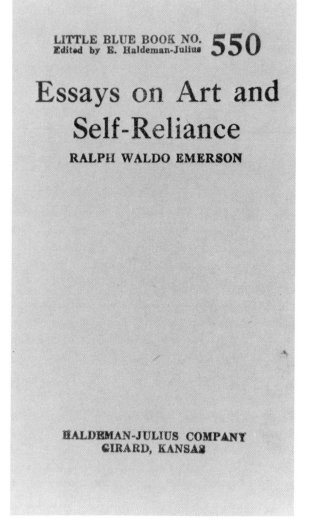

LITTLE BLUE BOOK NO. **550**
Edited by E. Haldeman-Julius

Essays on Art and Self-Reliance

RALPH WALDO EMERSON

HALDEMAN-JULIUS COMPANY
GIRARD, KANSAS

Little Blue Book cover

Julius was also accused of fraudulent advertising. For over five years the firm repeatedly stimulated sales by warning that the price of the Little Blue Books was about to be increased from five to ten cents. Advertisements also claimed that the classical and literary titles were about to be discontinued in favor of more popular works; this action was never taken, but many readers sent in orders thinking that it was their last chance to acquire good literature at low prices. The Little Blue Books and Big Blue Books sold more than 300 million copies before they were discontinued in 1964. The firm also published a few full-size books.

The firm began to have major problems in 1950, when Haldeman-Julius was convicted of nonpayment of income taxes. The claim was settled in 1954, nearly three years after Haldeman-Julius's death on 21 July 1951. Henry Haldeman succeeded his father as head of the firm and continued to publish the Little Blue Books until 1964, when he was convicted of advertising and selling obscene works by mail; the sex education titles in question had been sold by the company for years.

References:

"Emanuel Haldeman-Julius [obituary]," *New York Times*, 1 August 1951, p. 24;

Harry L. Golden, "Haldeman-Julius—The Success That Failed," *Midstream*, 3 (Spring 1957): 26-34;

Emanuel Haldeman-Julius, *The First Hundred Million* (New York: Simon & Schuster, 1928);

Richard Colles Johnson and G. Thomas Tanselle, "The Haldeman-Julius 'Little Blue Books' as a Bibliographical Problem," *Bibliographical Society of America Papers*, 64 (1970): 29-78.

—Judith Bushnell

Hallmark Editions
(Kansas City, Missouri: 1967-   )

Hallmark Cards, Incorporated was founded in Kansas City on 10 January 1910 by Joyce C. Hall. Book publishing was introduced fifty-seven years later, in 1967, primarily to produce "tasteful gifts" in the $2.00 to $2.50 range. Most Hallmark Editions are for the casual reader. About 110 volumes, only about twenty percent of which are literary, are published each year by a staff of twenty-five. The nonliterary productions deal with love, friendship, inspiration, and religion, with titles such as *The Gold of Friendship, So Many Kinds of Love, The Beauty of Motherhood,* and *God Is Everywhere.*

Popular literary books, usually twelvemos or sixteenmos, include selections from the writings of Anne Morrow Lindbergh, O. Henry, Peter Marshall, Will Rogers, Kahlil Gibran, Elizabeth Barrett Browning, and Boris Pasternak. In 1971 Hallmark published *Come Swiftly to Your Love,* a book of ancient Egyptian love poetry translated by Ezra Pound and Noel Stock, and Jesse Stuart's *Autumn Love Song.* Other literary publications include reprints of works by T. S. Eliot, John Keats, Rudyard Kipling, Archibald MacLeish, and Mark Twain. Children's books include *Mother Goose, Raggedy Ann and the Daffy Taffy Pull, Pet Parade,* and *Walt Disney World,* all of which have sold more than 200,000 copies each.

Joyce Hall died in 1982. Donald C. Hall is chairman of the board. Hallmark Cards, Incorporated is located at Twenty-fifth and McGee, Kansas City, Missouri 64108.

Reference:

"Joyce C. Hall [obituary]," *New York Times*, 30 October 1982, p. 35.

—Anuradha Mookerjee

Joyce C. Hall, founder of Hallmark Cards, publishers of Hallmark Editions

Alfred Harcourt (left) and Donald Brace in 1934

Harcourt Brace Jovanovich
(New York; San Diego: 1970-   )
Harcourt, Brace and World
(New York: 1960-1970)
Harcourt, Brace and Company
(New York: 1921-1960)
Harcourt, Brace and Howe
(New York: 1919-1921)

| Harcourt, Brace | Harcourt, Brace and World | 1960s | current Harcourt Brace Jovanovich |

Harcourt, Brace and Howe was launched on 29 July 1919 at 1 West Forty-seventh Street in New York after Alfred Harcourt and Donald Brace left Henry Holt and Company to found their own firm. Both had been employed at Holt for fifteen years since graduating from Columbia University. Harcourt had been in the editorial and trade sales departments; Brace had worked in book planning and manufacturing. The firm was to take an active role in textbook publishing under the direction of the third partner, Will D. Howe, head of the Indiana University English Department. The house was capitalized at $123,500. A key employee was Ellen Knowles Eayres, who had been Harcourt's secretary at Holt and later became his second wife. Harcourt had been encouraged to go into business on his own by Sinclair Lewis, whose *Free Air* was one of the first books published by the new house in the fall of 1919. Walter Lippmann and Louis Untermeyer served as consultants; Joel Spingarn, professor of comparative literature at Columbia, became a vice-president. After Howe's departure in 1921, at which time the firm became Harcourt, Brace and Company, S. Spencer Scott was responsible for the text department.

The firm's first best-seller was Lewis's *Main Street* (1920), followed by a string of successes in the 1920s: John Maynard Keynes's *The Economic Consequences of the Peace* (1920), Dorothy Canfield's *The Brimming Cup* (1921), Lytton Strachey's *Queen Victoria* (1921) and *Elizabeth and Essex* (1928), Giovanni Papini's *Life of Christ* (1923), E. M. Forster's *A Passage to India* (1924), Carl Sandburg's *Abraham Lincoln: The Prairie Years* (1926), and Virginia Woolf's *Orlando* (1928)—along with Lewis's *Babbitt*

(1922), *Arrowsmith* (1925), *Elmer Gantry* (1927), and *Dodsworth* (1929). In 1928 Harcourt, Brace became American publishers for the Pegasus Press of Paris, which published fine books on art—including the Pantheon series, planned for 200 volumes in several languages. The 1929 list included Robert Lynd's *Middletown*, Lewis Mumford's *Herman Melville*, and Vernon L. Parrington's *Main Currents of American Thought*. In 1930 Lewis became the first American to win the Nobel Prize for Literature and broke with the firm soon afterward in a dispute over the promotion of his books in relation to the prize.

In 1961 Jovanovich invited Kurt and Helen Wolff, the former proprietors of Pantheon, to come out of retirement and become his copublishers, thereby creating the first personal imprint arrangement in American publishing. The Wolffs—and later Mrs. Wolff alone after her husband's death—published works by such distinguished Continental figures as Italo Calvino, Max Frisch, Günter Grass, Amos Oz, Stanislaw Lem, and Georges Simenon. Similar copublishing arrangements were made with Hiram Haydn and Tony Godwin. Jovanovich also acquired Grune and Stratton (1968), Academic Press (1969), and Johnson Reprint (1969)—all publishers of scientific reference books and journals. Johnson is notable for its elaborate facsimile editions, such as the *Codex Atlanticus* of Leonardo Da Vinci, priced at $12,000. Harcourt, Brace and World was renamed Harcourt Brace Jovanovich in 1970. Pyramid Publications, a mass market paperback house, was purchased in 1973 and renamed Jove Books in 1977; it was sold to MCA in 1978. Other HBJ subsidiaries include

HBJ JOVE

A PROFILE OF HARCOURT BRACE JOVANOVICH

Harcourt Brace Jovanovich is today one of the world's largest publishers.

It was founded in 1919 with an extraordinary list that included Sinclair Lewis, Louis Untermeyer, Carl Sandburg, Walter Lippmann, W.E.B. DuBois, Dorothy Canfield and John Maynard Keynes. One of its first bestsellers was MAIN STREET by Sinclair Lewis, who went on to become America's first Nobel Prize winner in Literature. Over the years two other HBJ authors won the Nobel Prize, T.S. Eliot and St.-John Perse.

The list of notable authors and books we can recount with pride but, in respect of the reader's patience, we name only these:

Virginia Woolf	Paul de Kruif
Robert Merton	Diana Trilling
e.e. cummings	Pierre Teilhard
Lytton Strachey	de Chardin
Erich Maria Remarque	Arthur Clarke
E.M. Forster	Kingsley Amis
Ellen Glasgow	Leonardo da Vinci
James Gould Cozzens	Helen MacInnnes
William Faulkner	Lewis Mumford
Vernon Parrington	Jessamyn West
Leonard Woolf	W. Jackson Bate
Lincoln Steffens	S. I. Hayakawa
Charles A. Lindbergh	Richard Wilbur
Georges Simenon	Eudora Welty
Jan Struther	Jean Stafford
William Saroyan	Robert Lowell
Katherine Anne Porter	Brendan Gill
Robert Penn Warren	Randall Jarrell
Anne Morrow Lindbergh	Flannery O'Connor
James Thurber	Irving Howe
George Orwell	Jerzy Kosinski
Gunter Grass	Konrad Lorenz
Milovan Djilas	Cosima Wagner
Hannah Arendt	Thomas Merton
Peg Bracken	Edna O'Brien
Adelle Davis	Antoine
Mary Norton	de Saint-Exupery
P.L. Travers	Len Deighton
Mary McCarthy	Alice Walker

William Jovanovich
Chairman and President,
Harcourt Brace Jovanovich, Inc.

HBJ in 1976 published 139 scholarly journals, 7 magazines for farmers and stockmen, *Instructor* for teachers, 645 school textbooks and related materials, 688 scientific and technical books, 233 college instructional works, 68 medical books, 61 business periodicals, 98 publications in guidance and testing, 78 legal works, 13 newsletters, 107 trade hardcover books and 288 paperback books for popular audiences. HBJ manufactured graphic material and sold school supplies to fifty states and fifteen foreign countries; it underwrote and brokered and sold insurance; through Sea World, Inc., it managed three marine parks and conducted marine research; and it operated two successful bookclubs, five retail stores for school supplies, three campus bookmobiles and the HBJ Bookstore.

Our Company and the companies it has acquired over the years have been a part of the American culture for more than eighty years. We are to be found in San Diego, Los Angeles, San Francisco, Chicago, Cleveland, Boston, Dansville (N.Y.), Atlanta, Dallas, Lincoln, Denver, Sydney, Toronto, Quebec City, London, and, of course, New York City. Finally, we have grown exponentially—at the start there were five of us; today there are almost 7,000 of us.

© 1977 Harcourt Brace Jovanovich, Inc.

IN SEPTEMBER! JOVE/HBJ

1977 advertisement

the History Book Club and the Instructor Book Club. By 1977 the firm had reached $350 million in annual revenues.

Jovanovich's program of growth led to the acquisition of Sea World marine parks (1976), agriculture magazines, insurance companies, television stations, and professional and business periodicals. By 1979 corporate revenues had increased to $456.2 million, with net income of $23.8 million. In 1982 the HBJ trade department moved from New York to 1250 Sixth Avenue, San Diego, California 92101. Construction of a corporate headquarters building in Orlando, Florida, was completed in 1984. The company lists six headquarters cities: Orlando; San Diego; Cleveland; Battle Creek, Michigan; and Austin and San Antonio, Texas. In 1985 it employed 10,000 persons; its annual revenues were nearly $1 billion and its earnings exceeded $50 million. HBJ owns one of the richest and most diversified trade lists in publishing, with nine Nobel laureates (including Milton Friedman and Paul Samuelson in economics) and such recent successes as Alice Walker's *The Color Purple* (1982) and Umberto Eco's *The Name of the Rose* (1983). In 1984 the firm announced plans to publish four volumes of the letters of T. S. Eliot. Its Harvest series of the *Diaries of Virginia Woolf* received the Carey-Thomas Award for distinguished publishing in 1985. Despite his manifold corporate responsibilities, Jovanovich's primary commitment is to books, and he edited several of Djilas's books and assembled Charles A. Lindbergh's posthumously published *Autobiography of Values* (1978). Jovanovich has expressed his publishing credo: "The effort is dear, the results are uncertain, and the eye of eternity dims, but it shall all have been worthwhile if in the last hour the publisher holds in his hand that most singular of promises: a good book."

Harcourt, Brace and Company steadily created textbooks for colleges and high schools and began to make trade children's books profitable. Some distinguished adult trade titles during the 1930s were *The Autobiography of Lincoln Steffens* (1931), John Dos Passos's *U.S.A.* trilogy (1931, 1932, 1937), John O'Hara's *Appointment in Samarra* (1934), Ellen Glasgow's *Vein of Iron* (1935), and Anne Morrow Lindbergh's *North to the Orient* (1935). T. S. Eliot was first published by the house in 1932. Also in 1932 Brewer, Warren and Putnam was acquired with its list of 200 titles.

Harcourt resigned as president in 1942; Brace served as president until 1948, when he was succeeded by Scott. The 1940s brought publication of Robert Penn Warren's *All the King's Men* and Robert Lowell's *Lord Weary's Castle* (both Pulitzer Prize winners in 1946), James Gould Cozzens's *The Just and the Unjust* (1942) and *Guard of Honor* (1948) (another Pulitzer winner), and George Orwell's *Nineteen Eighty-four* (1949). The acquisition of Reynal and Hitchcock in 1948 brought Eugene Reynal to Harcourt, Brace as vice-president and head of the trade department. The Harbrace Modern Classics series was created to draw on the strong Harcourt, Brace backlist. The *Harbrace College Handbook*, first published in 1941, became one of the most widely adopted textbooks in America.

The 1950s and 1960s brought more prodigious sellers, Cozzens's *By Love Possessed* (1957) and Mary McCarthy's *The Group* (1963), and works by other notable authors, among them Milovan Djilas, E. E. Cummings, and Flannery O'Connor. The Harvest line of quality paperbacks commenced in the 1950s. Harbinger Books (nonfiction reprints for college use) and Voyager Books (paperbacks for the juvenile market) were instituted in the 1960s.

William Jovanovich, who had joined the text department in 1947, became president at the end of 1954 at the age of thirty-four. Under Jovanovich the house entered its period of greatest growth and expansion. Harcourt, Brace became a publicly traded stock on the New York Stock Exchange in 1960. That year Harcourt, Brace merged with World Book Company, a publisher of elementary school textbooks and standardized tests, and changed its imprint to Harcourt, Brace and World. Jovanovich also acquired the majority interest in the Canadian branch of Longmans, Green (which became Longmans Canada) and the English firm Rupert Hart-Davis (which was subsequently divested). HBW moved to its own building, a new twenty-seven-story structure at 757 Third Avenue, in 1963. During its first decade of Jovanovich's leadership, sales rose from $8 million in 1954 to over $51 million in 1964.

In 1961 Jovanovich invited Kurt and Helen Wolff, the former proprietors of Pantheon, to come out of retirement and become his copublishers, thereby creating the first personal imprint arrangement in American publishing. The Wolffs— and later Mrs. Wolff alone after her husband's death—published works by such distinguished Continental figures as Italo Calvino, Max Frisch, Günter Grass, Amos Oz, Stanislaw Lem, and Georges Simenon. Similar copublishing arrangements were made with Hiram Haydn and Tony Godwin. Jovanovich also acquired Grune and Stratton (1968), Academic Press (1969), and Johnson Reprint (1969)—all publishers of scientific reference books and journals. Johnson is notable for its elaborate facsimile editions, such as the *Codex Atlanticus* of Leonardo Da Vinci, priced at $12,000. Harcourt, Brace and World was renamed Harcourt Brace Jovanovich in 1970. Pyramid Publications, a mass market paperback house, was purchased in 1973 and renamed Jove Books in 1977; it was sold to MCA in 1978. Other HBJ subsidiaries include the History Book Club and the Instructor Book Club. By 1977 the firm had reached $350 million in annual revenues.

Jovanovich's program of growth led to the acquisition of Sea World marine parks (1976), agriculture magazines, insurance companies, television stations, and professional and business periodicals. By 1979 corporate revenues had increased to $456.2 million, with net income of $23.8 million. In 1982 the HBJ trade department moved from New York to 1250 Sixth Avenue, San Diego, California 92101. Construction of a corporate headquarters building in Orlando, Florida, was completed in 1984. The company lists six headquarters cities: Orlando; San Diego; Cleveland; Battle Creek, Michigan; and Austin and San Antonio, Texas. In 1985 it employed 10,000 persons; its annual revenues were nearly $1 billion and its earnings exceeded $50 million. HBJ owns one of the richest and most diversified trade lists in publishing, with nine Nobel laureates (including Milton Friedman and Paul Samuelson in economics) and such recent successes as Alice Walker's *The Color Purple* (1982) and Umberto Eco's *The Name of the Rose* (1983). In 1984 the firm announced plans to publish four volumes of the letters of T. S. Eliot. Its Harvest series of the *Diaries of Virginia Woolf* received the Carey-Thomas Award for distin-

guished publishing in 1985. Despite his manifold corporate responsibilities, Jovanovich's primary commitment is to books, and he edited several of Djilas's books and assembled Charles A. Lindbergh's posthumously published *Autobiography of Values* (1978). Jovanovich has expressed his publishing credo: "The effort is dear, the results are uncertain, and the eye of eternity dims, but it shall all have been worthwhile if in the last hour the publisher holds in his hand that most singular of promises: a good book."

References:

"Alfred Harcourt [obituary]," *New York Times*, 21 June 1954, p. 23;

Alfred Harcourt, "Publishing since 1900," *Bulletin of the New York Public Library*, 41 (1937): 895-905; reprinted in *Bowker Lectures on Book Publishing* (New York: Bowker, 1957), pp. 28-41;

Harcourt, *Some Experiences* (Riverside, Conn., 1951);

"Harcourt, Brace Completes 15 Years," *Publishers' Weekly*, 126 (28 July 1934): 274;

William Jovanovich, *In Art or Instruction* (New York: Harcourt, Brace & World, 1969);

Jovanovich, *Now, Barabbas* (New York: Harcourt, Brace & World, 1960);

Jovanovich, *Now, Barabbas* (New York: Harper & Row, 1964);

James M. Reid, *An Adventure in Textbooks, 1924-1960* (New York: Bowker, 1969);

"The Story of Harcourt, Brace & World, Inc.," *Book Production Magazine*, 76 (November 1962): 34-37; reprinted in *Profiles in Book Publishing* (New York: Freund, 1963), pp. 8-11.

—*Elizabeth Dzwonkoski*

Heritage Press
(New York: 1935-1970)

The Heritage Press was founded by George Macy in 1935 at 551 Fifth Avenue, New York, to publish "the classics which are our heritage from the past, in editions which will be the heritage of the future." Macy's aim was to sell beautiful editions of the classics at the relatively low price of about five dollars each. Less exclusive and expensive versions of Macy's Limited Editions Club volumes, Heritage Press books varied widely in size, typog-

raphy, design, and binding materials. The books were enclosed in slipcases.

Among early titles were *Romeo and Juliet*, illustrated by Sylvain Sauvage; *The Scarlet Letter*, bound in red leather and designed and illustrated by W. A. Dwiggins; *David Copperfield*, illustrated by John Austen; *A Shropshire Lad*, the first edition with color illustrations, which were done by E. A. Wilson; and the *Song of Solomon*, with illuminations in gold by Valenti Angelo—all in 1935. Later selections included an edition of *Mother Goose* (1936) with drawings by Roger Duvoisin; *The Adventures of Tom Sawyer* (1936) and *Adventures of Huckleberry Finn* (1943), illustrated from oil paintings by Norman Rockwell; and Irving Stone's *Lust for Life* (1937) with Van Gogh illustrations.

From 1937 to 1961 the Heritage Press's selections were distributed monthly through the Heritage Club, which, unlike the Limited Editions Club, did not limit the number of subscribers. The success of the club in attracting more than 9,000 subscribers by 1942 showed that there was a market for quality editions of the classics. Although Macy concentrated on subscription sales, Heritage Press books were also available, at slightly higher prices, from bookstores, and the firm billed itself as "the first American publishing house organized with the active cooperation of booksellers, and with the booksellers' needs primarily in mind." The board of directors included Adolph Kroch of Kroch's and Brentano's bookstores, Cedric Crowell of Doubleday Book Shops, and Frank Magel of Putnam. Heritage Press was the first publisher to sign a fair trade agreement with booksellers under the Feld-Crawford Act. Macy solicited the opinions of booksellers and subscribers about which titles should be published, but Bennett Cerf observed that it was Macy, "a one-man show," who ultimately made the selections.

Macy died in 1956. From 1961 to 1971 Heritage Press books were distributed through Dial Press and later through Atheneum. In 1970 the George Macy Companies, including Heritage, were purchased by Boise-Cascade. In 1980 and 1981 about 300 back titles were reprinted and sold on a subscription basis by the Danbury Mint of Connecticut.

References:

Bennett Cerf, "Trade Winds," *Saturday Review of Literature*, 25 (4 July 1942): 28-29;

"Dial Takes Over Trade Sale of Heritage Press Books," *Publishers' Weekly*, 167 (26 February 1955): 1299;

"Heritage Press Plans Classics With Retailers' Needs in Mind," *Publishers' Weekly*, 128 (28 September 1935): 1182-1183;

"Obituary Notes: George Macy," *Publishers' Weekly*, 169 (28 May 1956): 2256-2257.

—Christy Brown

Lawrence Hill and Company Publishers

(New York; Westport, Connecticut: 1972-   )

Lawrence Hill founded a publishing company under his own name in 1972 after Hill and Wang, which he co-owned, was acquired by Farrar, Straus and Giroux. For the first three years Hill maintained offices at 104 Fifth Avenue in New York City, where Hill and Wang had been located. In 1975 the firm moved to Westport, Connecticut.

Hill is interested in politics, and his lists reflect his sympathy with radicalism. "Many of my books are one-sided," he admitted in a 1985 interview; "my side against injustice, war and exploitation of the weak by the strong." In 102 titles published between 1972 and 1985, Hill showed his preference for radical thought, proletarian literature, and books about oppressed people, particularly in Africa and Latin America.

Among the firm's literary books are B. Traven's *The Death Ship* (1973); *Writers in Revolt: The Anvil Anthology, 1933-1940* (1973), edited by Jack Conroy and Curt Johnson; Langston Hughes's *Good Morning Revolution: Uncollected Writings of Social Protest* (1973), edited by Faith Berry; Nikki Giovanni's *Ego Tripping and Other Poems for Young Readers* (1974); Jack London's *The Iron Heel* (1980); Conroy's *The Disinherited* (1982) and *The Weed King and Other Stories* (1985); and *The Collected Poems of John Reed* (1985), edited by Corliss Lamont.

Hill's other interests are represented by *The Jazz Book: From Ragtime to Fusion and Beyond* (1982) by Joachim Berendt, *South Africa at War* (1983) by Richard W. Leonard, *Democracies and Tyrannies of the Caribbean* (1984) by William Krehm, and *Diary of the Twentieth Congress of the Communist Party of the Soviet Union* (1984) by Vittorio Vidali.

Most Hill books are published simultaneously in cloth and paperback. Independent Publishers Group is the firm's distributor. Hill's address is 520 Riverside Avenue, Westport, Connecticut 06880.

—Botham Stone

Lawrence Hill outside Toulouse-Lautrec's home in Albi, France

Vernon Ives, cofounder of Holiday House, in 1947

Hill and Wang

(New York: 1956-)

HILL AND WANG ∎ NEW YORK

Hill and Wang was founded in 1956 at 104 Fifth Avenue, New York, by Lawrence Hill and Arthur W. Wang, who had been sales manager and editor-in-chief, respectively, at A. A. Wyn, Incorporated. At the outset, the partners purchased eighty-eight backlist titles from Wyn, as well as outstanding contracts for future books. The new firm made its early reputation with its Dramabooks series, which was inaugurated in 1956. Originally, Dramabooks consisted of works of the great seventeenth century English playwrights, and also included works of drama criticism by Harley Granville-Barker, Stark Young, Bernard Shaw, G. K. Chesterton, Henri Fluchère, and books by Stanislavski, Richard Southern, Meyerhold, and Bertolt Brecht. Dramabooks offered collections of plays by modern dramatists, including Anouilh, Cocteau, Giraudoux, and Ghelderode. The series was expanded to include single contemporary plays, including Max Frisch's *Andorra* (1960) and *The Firebugs* (1963); Arthur Kopit's *Oh Dad, Poor Dad, Mamma's Hung You in the Closet and I'm Feelin' so Sad* (1960), *Indians* (1969), *Wings* (1978), and *End of the World* (1984); and Edward Bond's *Saved* (1968). Hill and Wang has published some ten volumes of Lanford Wilson plays, including *Hot l Baltimore* (1973) and the Talley series, as well as Marsha Norman's *'night, Mother* (1983) and Charles Fuller's *A Soldier's Play* (1982).

Hill and Wang began an extensive publishing program in the field of American literature and history in 1959 by purchasing from Thomas Yoseloff the rights to twenty-six titles in the American Century series. Hill and Wang added works by Langston Hughes such as *The Best of Simple* (1961), *Something in Common* (1962), *The Big Sea* (1963), and *I Wonder as I Wander* (1964). Since then, Hill and Wang has broadened the list to include some thirty interpretive works in American history, primarily intended for the college market. The firm also publishes a general list of trade paperbacks.

Among other works published by Hill and Wang are Elie Wiesel's *Night* (1960), *Dawn* (1961),

and *The Accident* (1962); B. Traven's *The Night Visitor and Other Stories* (1966), *The Treasure of the Sierra Madre* (1967), and Traven's jungle novels; Mark Van Doren's *Collected Stories* in three volumes, (1962, 1965, 1968), *Collected and New Poems 1924-1963* (1963), *The Narrative Poems of Mark Van Doren* (1964), and *Three Plays* (1966). Van Doren's *Good Morning: Last Poems* was published posthumously by Hill and Wang in 1973. Other literary works include Pär Lagerkvist's novel *The Dwarf* (1958), Siegfried Lenz's novels *The Lightship* (1962) and *The German Lesson* (1972), Wole Soyinka's *Idanre, and Other Poems* (1968), and Nikki Giovanni's *Spin a Soft Black Song* (1971). Among the firm's better-known nonfiction titles are David Ewen's *Encyclopedia of the Opera* (1955) and Wilson Follett's *Modern American Usage* (1966). Hill and Wang has also published translations of some eighteen books by Roland Barthes, including *Mythologies* (1972), *Elements of Semiology* (1977), *Writing Degree Zero* (1977), *Camera Lucida* (1981), and *The Grain of the Voice* (1984). Hill and Wang publishes works in contemporary politics, including numerous books prepared by the American Friends Service Committee—*Peace in Vietnam* (1967), *Struggle for Justice* (1971), and *A Compassionate Peace* (1982); K. S. Karol's *China: The Other Cummunism* (1968) and *Guerrillas in Power* (1970); works on the law by Marvin Frankel, such as *Criminal Sentences* (1973); and several books on military affairs by Richard A. Gabriel, among them *Military Incompetence* (1985).

The firm moved to 141 Fifth Avenue in 1961 and to 72 Fifth Avenue in 1969. In 1971 Hill and Wang was acquired by Farrar, Straus and Giroux and became a division of FSG. Its address is the same as that of the parent company: 19 Union Square West, New York 10003. Hill left Hill and Wang in 1971 to form his own publishing firm, Lawrence Hill and Company. Wang has remained at Hill and Wang as editor in chief of the imprint.

References:

"Farrar, Straus & Giroux Acquiring Hill & Wang,"

Publishers' Weekly, 200 (4 October 1971): 30; "Hill & Wang, New Publisher, Formed; Buys Titles

of Wyn," *Publishers' Weekly,* 169 (18 February 1956): 1034.

—*Botham Stone*

Holiday House
(New York: 1935-   )

HOLIDAY HOUSE

Holiday House is outstanding for its exclusive devotion to children's literature; for the artistic and technical quality of its works, many of which have won awards; and for the maintenance of this quality at competitive prices. Vernon Ives and Helen Gentry started Holiday House in 1935 from a corner of the pressroom of William E. Rudge's Sons at 225 Varick Street, New York. The founders each had experience in printing and publishing—Ives with William Edwin Rudge, Gentry with the Grabhorn Press in San Francisco. The first list of publications consisted of three nursery rhyme broadsides; two miniature "stocking books," *Cock Robin* and *Jack and the Beanstalk;* Hans Christian Andersen's *The Little Mermaid,* illustrated by Pamela Bianco; *Boomba Lives in Africa* by Caroline Singer and Cyrus LeRoy Baldridge; and *Jaufry the Knight and the Fair Brunissende,* an Arthurian tale translated from the medieval French by Ives and illustrated by John Atherton.

From the beginning, children's book critics noticed Holiday House, but bookstores and librarians were uneasy about the odd shapes and sizes of the broadsides and miniatures. In a 1947 interview Ives admitted that it took the firm a few years to live down the idea that it was a private press publishing collector's items. Even so, originality was not foresworn in the early years. Glen Rounds's *Lumbercamp* (1937) was bound in wood, and Irmengarde Eberle's *Spice on the Wind* (1940) was impregnated with oil of cloves. Miniature books

intended for use as Christmas cards were started by Holiday House, but the use of silk-screening and cloth in bookmaking were innovations that did not survive wartime shortages and postwar economies.

Rounds was Holiday House's first "discovery." His *Ol' Paul, the mighty Logger* (1936) was promoted on a cross-country trip by the author and his wife and followed by eighteen other tales of open country and horses. *Dive Bomber* (1939) by Robert Winston was the first Holiday House best-seller. Jim Kjelgaard was another Holiday House discovery. His first book, *Forest Patrol* (1941), was followed by *Rebel Siege* (1943), about the American Revolution, and in 1945 by *Big Red,* which sold 250,000 copies to become a best-seller for the house. His other Red books were close runners-up. Before his death in 1964, Kjelgaard had written twenty-three books for Holiday House. Ives wrote a factual children's book, *Russia* (1943), for the Lands and Peoples series for ages ten through fifteen. Nature themes are treated in The Life-Cycle series.

Holiday House moved in 1942 to 72 Fifth Avenue, and in 1947 to 513 Sixth Avenue. In 1951 the firm moved to an apartment at 8 West Thirteenth Street. Gentry retired from Holiday House in 1963 to live in New Mexico with her husband, David Greenhood, who had been an editor at Holiday House. Leslie Pap replaced Gentry as designer and production manager, and Marjorie Jones was hired as editor. Julian Scheer's *Rain Makes Applesauce* (1964), illustrated by Marvin Bileck, was the

Cover design by Valenti Angelo for firm's first catalogue (1935)

1967 advertisement

Dust jacket for 1973 Holt, Rinehart and Winston best-seller

firm's first Caldecott Honor Book.

Ives sold Holiday House in 1965 to John H. Briggs, Jr., who had worked for World Publishing Company, Farrar, Straus and Giroux, and Horizon Press; Ives remained as a paid consultant for the next three years. The firm moved to 18 East Fifty-sixth Street in 1966. Jones left Holiday House in 1971 and was replaced by Eunice Holsaert, who died in 1974; she was succeeded as editor by Margery Cuyler. Briggs has continued to keep Holiday House a small, specialized publishing firm devoted to producing quality books. It published thirty-nine titles in 1984. Since 1975, the company has been located at 18 East Fifty-third Street, New York 10022.

References:

Russell Freedman, *Holiday House: The First Fifty Years* (New York: Holiday House, 1985);

Muriel Fuller, "Vernon Ives of Holiday House," *Publishers' Weekly,* 151 (26 April 1947): 2206-2207.

—Theodora Mills

Holloway House Publishing Company
(Los Angeles: 1961-   )

An Original Holloway House Edition
HOLLOWAY HOUSE PUBLISHING CO.
LOS ANGELES, CALIFORNIA

Holloway House Publishing Company began in 1961 at 8762 Holloway Drive in Los Angeles when Masamori Kojima announced a line of special-interest paperback books on current or recent events. The first books to appear under the Holloway House imprint were *The Trial of Adolph Eichmann* (1961) by Dewey Linze and *Hemingway: Life and Death of a Giant* (1961) by Kurt Singer. The company then shifted its emphasis to erotica, such as Paul J. Gillette's *An Uncensored History of Pornography* (1965) and Dr. Hermann K. Wolff's *Role of the Dominant Female in American Society* (1966).

By 1967 Holloway House had a new address at 8060 Melrose Avenue, Los Angeles 90046, and a newly discovered market in the black mass audience. *Pimp: the Story of My Life* (1967) and *Trick Baby, the Biography of a Con Man* (1967), both by Iceberg Slim, the pseudonym of Robert Beck, immediately became popular. Holloway House continues to publish black-oriented fiction and nonfiction. The firm produces about thirty titles a year, almost all in paperback. It is the largest publisher in America of black experience literature.

Reference:

"Holloway House New Paperback Firm," *Publishers' Weekly,* 180 (18 September 1961): 36.

—Linda Quinlan

Holt, Rinehart and Winston
(New York: 1960-1985)
Henry Holt and Company
(New York: 1985-)

The New York firm of Holt, Rinehart and Winston, Incorporated was formed in 1960 when Henry Holt and Company, which had been founded in 1866 as Leypoldt and Holt, merged with Rinehart and Company of New York and the John C. Winston Company of Philadelphia. Former Holt president Edward T. Rigg was made chairman and chief executive officer; Alfred C. Edwards became president and chief administrative officer; and Charles F. Kindt, Jr., former president of Winston, and Stanley M. Rinehart, former president of Rinehart, became senior vice-presidents in the new firm. Rinehart died in 1969. Texas oilman Clinton W. Murchison was the dominant stockholder in Holt at the time of the merger; by 1966 his share of the firm had dropped from forty to eleven percent.

With Dudley Frazier and Howard I. Cady in charge of the trade department, Holt, Rinehart and Winston published Robert Ruark's *The Old Man's Boy Grows Older* (1961) and reprinted Kurt Vonnegut's *Cat's Cradle* (1963). After reprinting Christina Stead's most respected work, *The Man Who Loved Children* (1965), the firm published her *Dark Places of the Heart* (1966), the first novel by the Australian-born writer in fourteen years. It was followed by *The Puzzleheaded Girl* (1967) and *The Little Hotel* (1973). Perhaps spurred by President Kennedy's admiration for the poet, sales of Robert Frost's *In the Clearing* (1962) exceeded those of any previously published hardcover book of poetry in America, with more than 100,000 copies sold in four years. *Selected Poems of Robert Frost* followed in 1963.

During the mid-1960s the trade department was under the direction of Arthur A. Cohen as editor in chief and Samuel Stewart as managing editor. Published under the pseudonym Hannah Green, Joanne Greenberg's *I Never Promised You a Rose Garden* became a major best-seller in 1964. Holt, Rinehart and Winston also published Horace Gregory's *Collected Poems* (1964); Vonnegut's *God Bless You, Mr. Rosewater* (1965); John Ashbery's third book of poetry, *Rivers and Mountains* (1966); and Sarah Gainham's *Night Falls on the City* (1967).

The Winston Science Fiction series featured Lester del Rey's *Outpost of Jupiter* (1963) and *The Infinite Worlds of Maybe* (1966), Arthur C. Clarke's *Dolphin Island* (1963), Gordon R. Dickson's *Space Winners* (1965), and a reprint of Larry Niven's *Ringworld* (1977). Other series have included the Rinehart Editions of paperback texts, the Rinehart Suspense Novels, and the Rivers of America.

In 1967 Holt, Rinehart and Winston was acquired by CBS. Edwards assumed the chairmanship of Holt, Rinehart and Winston in 1968; Ross D. Sackett took his place as president. Among the many editors at Holt during the 1970s, Aaron Asher, Thomas Wallace, editor-in-chief, and Pace Barnes were perhaps the most important. Finally, an editing team consisting of Donald Hutter as executive editor of general books, Marion Wood as senior editor, and Jennifer Josephy as editor was formed in 1973. Although the instability of personnel at the beginning of the 1970s contributed to a decline in output, the firm quickly regained its momentum. From 1958 to 1968 the number of titles published annually had steadily risen from 101 to 508, but in 1971 only 225 titles were published. By 1976 the figure was up to 664 and by 1980 Holt could boast 850 new titles.

One of the more successful writers at Holt, Rinehart and Winston during the 1970s was Erica Jong. The firm published her first two books of poems, *Fruits & Vegetables* (1971) and *Half-Lives* (1973), and had a major best-seller in *Fear of Flying*

(1973). Holt, Rinehart and Winston published two more books of her poetry, *Loveroot* (1975) and the three-volume *The Poetry of Erica Jong* (1976), and another novel, *How to Save Your Own Life* (1977). Other titles of the 1970s included Mark Steadman's first novel, *McAfee County* (1971); Nicholas Gage's *The Bourlotas Fortune* (1975); André Malraux's *The Conquerors* (1976); Jack Higgins's *Storm Warning* (1976); Faith Baldwin's *Thursday's Child* (1976) and *Adam's Eden* (1977); Francis Steegmuller's *Silence at Salerno* (1978); and John Nichols's *The Magic Journey* (1978) and *A Ghost in the Music* (1979). Philip Roth moved from Random House to Holt for *The Breast* (1972), *The Great American Novel* (1973), and *My Life as a Man* (1974) before moving on to Farrar, Straus and Giroux. Holt has also published comic strip anthologies by Charles Schulz (*Peanuts*) and G. B. Trudeau (*Doonesbury*). Nonfiction authors have included Karl Barth, Philip Berrigan, Malcolm Boyd, John Dewey, Erich Fromm, Mark Lane, Maria Montessori, Lionel Trilling, and Wernher Von Braun.

Stanley D. Frank, who had been president during the mid-1970s, resumed the post in 1980.

Also in 1980 Richard Seaver, formerly of Grove Press and Viking, was made vice-president and publisher of general books, while Catherine Fallin became managing editor of general books. In November 1985 CBS sold the trade books division of Holt, Rinehart and Winston to Verlagsgruppe Georg von Holtzbrinck of Stuttgart, West Germany; CBS retained the firm's school and college divisions. The new trade house resumed the pre-1960 name Henry Holt and Company. Seaver continues as president and publisher of Henry Holt. The firm's address is 521 Fifth Avenue, New York 10175.

References:

"Court Dismisses $5 Million Libel Claim against Holt," *Publishers Weekly*, 212 (25 July 1977): 27-28;

"Holt, Rinehart, Winston Merger," *Publishers' Weekly*, 176 (28 December 1959): 45;

"The Story of Holt, Rinehart and Winston, Inc.," *Book Production Magazine*, 78 (July 1963): 30-34.

—David Dzwonkoski

John H. Hopkins and Son
(New York: 1934-1942?)

John H. Hopkins and Son, Incorporated was founded in January 1934 at 200 Fifth Avenue, New York. John H. Hopkins had been one of the founders of Barse and Hopkins, which had become Barse and Company when he left in 1928. Hopkins and Son published popular fiction for general readers. Romances predominated, and were given such suggestive titles as *Slandered* (1936) and *No Regrets* (1936) by Vida Hurst, and *Golden Goddess* (1935) and *Trapped by Love* (1936) by Rob Eden. The firm also offered westerns, as well as a mystery series

under the general title Green Shield Mysteries. Hopkins died in July 1939. The firm was no longer in business after his son, Irving G. Hopkins, entered the army in 1942.

Reference:

"Obituary Notes [John H. Hopkins]," *Publishers' Weekly*, 136 (22 July 1939): 237.

—Peter Dzwonkoski
Ruth Bennett

Advertisement from the firm's third year

Horizon Press
(New York: 1950-   )

Horizon Press
P U B L I S H E R S

Founded in 1950 at 1123 Broadway, New York, Horizon Press, Incorporated publishes trade books with an emphasis on art, photography, architecture, and general nonfiction. Ben Raeburn, president since 1961, has been an editor since the firm's founding.

Publishing fewer than ten titles a year during the 1950s, Horizon Press has increased its production to about fifty titles a year, ten to twenty percent of which are fiction. Chief among these have been works by the English author James Hanley, including *The Closed Harbour* (1953), *Another World* (1972), *A Dream Journey* (1976), and *A Kingdom* (1978). These titles were originally published in England. Other publications have included James T. Farrell's prose poem *When Time Was Born* (1966), Marc Kaminsky's *Birthday Poems* (1972) and *A New House* (1974), David Ignatow's notebooks, and volumes of poetry by Sir Herbert Read. Horizon's nonfiction authors include Martin Buber, Abba Eban, Oriana Fallaci, Paul Goodman, Herman Kahn, Peter Kro-

potkin, Henry Miller, Auguste Rodin, Frank Lloyd Wright, and Olgivanna Lloyd Wright.

A year after its founding, Horizon moved to 63 West Forty-fourth Street; in 1953 it moved to 220 West Forty-second Street. Since 1960 its address has been 156 Fifth Avenue, New York 10010. Tony Outhwaite was named managing editor in 1976; he was replaced in 1981 by John Brace Latham. Horizon Press has served as the distributor for several small publishers, including Foolscap Press, Imago Books, New Horizon, and The Smith.

References:

"Horizon Press' New Art Series," *Publishers' Weekly*, 187 (11 January 1965): 76;

"Horizon Press: New Poetry Series," *Publishers' Weekly*, 193 (18 March 1968): 42;

"Horizon Press to Have Another Feather in Its Cap," *Publishers Weekly*, 209 (17 May 1976): 32.

—*David Dzwonkoski*

Howell, Soskin and Company
(New York: 1940-1949)

Howell, Soskin and Company was founded in New York in January 1940 with Frank Mannheim as president, William Soskin as vice-president, Virginia Howell Mussey as treasurer, and Stanley Kunitz as secretary and editor. Within a month, the firm moved from 250 Park Avenue to 17 East Forty-fifth Street.

Among the few novels published by Howell, Soskin were Oskar Maria Graf's *The Life of My Mother* (1940), Agnes Boulton's *Ware Place* (1941), Alfred Hayes's *All Thy Conquests* (1946) and *Shadow of Heaven* (1947), and George Axelrod's *Beggar's Choice* (1947). The major emphasis was on nonfiction, including books by Eleanor Roosevelt, Low-

ell Thomas, Wyndham Lewis, and Sir Bernard Pares, and juveniles by Marion V. Ridgway, Florence Bibo Alexander, Marjorie Torrey, Eleanor Brown, and Madeleine Ley. The firm was also the sales representative for Stackpole Sons.

Howell, Soskin and Company was dissolved in 1949. Adult titles were sold to Crown Publishers and juveniles were taken over by Crown's subsidiary Lothrop, Lee and Shepard.

References:

"Crown to Act as Howell, Soskin Sales Representative," *Publishers' Weekly*, 155 (29 January 1949): 582;

"Howell, Soskin & Co. Organized," *Publishers' Weekly,* 137 (20 January 1940): 233;

P. E. G. Quercus, "Trade Winds," *Saturday Review* of Literature, 21 (27 January 1940): 24.

—*Vincent L. Tollers*

B. W. Huebsch
(New York: 1902-1925)

Benjamin W. Huebsch began his career in his brother Daniel's business as a printer of diaries, calendars, and yearbooks in New York. Setting up as a publisher at 150 Nassau Street, he published his first book, E. H. Griggs's *A Book of Meditations,* in 1902. He brought out his first list after moving to 225 Fifth Avenue in 1906; it included C. F. G. Masterman's *In Peril of Change* (1905) and Otto Pfleiderer's *Christian Origins* (1906). These iconoclastic books set the standard and tone for Huebsch's output. Christopher Morley contended that Huebsch's menorah device, designed by Charles B. Falls, "almost always marked a book that had some genuine reason for existence." Among the earlier titles Huebsch brought out were Maxim Gorky's novel *The Spy: The Story of a Superfluous Man* (1908), John Spargo's *Karl Marx: His Life and Work* (1910), Georges Sorel's *Reflections on Violence* (1912), and George Jean Nathan's *Another Book on the Theatre* (1915). Huebsch published Lola Ridge's first book, *The Ghetto, and Other Poems,* in 1918.

In the forefront of a small group of new publishers who brought new European writers to America, Huebsch published works by Gerhardt Hauptmann, August Strindberg, and Anton Chekhov. He established a strong relationship with James Joyce, placing several of his stories in H. L. Mencken's *Smart Set* and publishing the first American editions of *A Portrait of the Artist as a Young Man* (1916) and *Exiles* (1918). Though he declined *Ulysses* in 1920 for fear of censorship, Huebsch remained close to Joyce. (Later, when Huebsch worked for Viking Press, Joyce's contract with Viking stipulated that if Huebsch left, so would he.)

Huebsch also published D. H. Lawrence's *The Rainbow* (1915). Huebsch's journal, the *Freeman,* began in 1919. In 1922 Huebsch published Elizabeth Madox Roberts's second book, *Under the Tree,* and the first American edition of Daniel Corkery's *The Hounds of Banba.* Beginning with *Winesburg, Ohio* in 1919, Huebsch was the first publisher of six of Sherwood Anderson's works, including *Poor White* (1920), *The Triumph of the Egg* (1921), *Horses and Men* (1923), and *A Story Teller's Story* (1924). Around 1920 Huebsch moved to 116 West Thirteenth Street.

Huebsch's business declined during the 1920s, and in 1925 he merged his firm with the new Viking Press. Huebsch became vice-president of Viking and was in charge of editorial development. He brought from his own firm Joyce, Randolph Bourne, Van Wyck Brooks, and Thorstein Veblen and recruited Erskine Caldwell, Franz Werfel, and Alexander Woollcott. Huebsch retained his interest in Lawrence and published *Apocalypse* (1932), *Last Poems* (1933), and *Phoenix: The Posthumous Papers of D. H. Lawrence* (1936). He retired from Viking in May 1956 but continued as a consulting editor for the firm. He died on a trip to London in August 1964.

References:

"Benjamin W. Huebsch [obituary]," *New York Times,* 8 August 1964, p. 19;

"Huebsch and Viking Press to Combine," *Publishers' Weekly,* 108 (8 August 1925): 495;

B. W. Huebsch, "Footnotes to a Publisher's Life," *Colophon,* new series 2 (1936-1937): 406-426;

Benjamin W. Huebsch (photo by Meyer Studio)

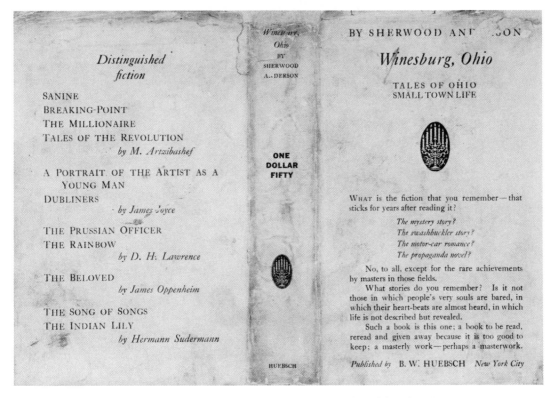

Dust jacket for 1919 publication. Huebsch was also the first publisher of five of Anderson's other works.

Christopher Morley, "The Bowling Green: The Sad Horn Blower," *Saturday Review of Literature*, 1 (15 August 1925): 43;

G. Thomas Tanselle, "In Memoriam: B. W. Huebsch," *Antiquarian Bookman*, 36 (30 August 1965): 727-728.

—Daniel Borus

International Publishers Company

(New York: 1924-   )

Alexander Trachtenberg's early political activities provided the basis for his career as a publisher. Born in Odessa, Russia, he came to New York in 1906 at twenty-two and studied at Trinity College and Yale University, where he was a leader of the Intercollegiate Socialist Society. In 1908 he was one of the founders of the *New York Call*, a Socialist daily. Trachtenberg's doctoral dissertation at Yale, "The History of Legislation for the Protection of Coal Miners in Pennsylvania," was accepted for publication by the United States Department of Labor in 1916. In 1915 he joined the faculty of the socialist Rand School of Social Science in New York. Trachtenberg was active in the movement to encourage the United States to recognize the Soviet government after the Russian Revolution, and in 1919 he helped found the American Labor Alliance for Recognition and Trade Relations with Russia. He remained a member of the Socialist party until 1921 and was a founding member of the United States Communist party.

International Publishers Company, Incorporated was established in 1924 by Trachtenberg, A. A. Heller, and A. H. Gross at 381 Fourth Avenue in New York. The founders intended to specialize in English translations of European radical literature, much of which had been inaccessible to American readers. The firm's earliest publications included Henri Barbusse's novel *Chains* (1925) and Leon Trotsky's *Literature and Revolution* (1925).

The output of International Publishers has reflected Trachtenberg's ideology. Titles in the so-

cial sciences, particularly political science and economics, have dominated International's lists. The firm's strengths in these subjects enabled the business to grow during the 1930s when scholars and workers sought information that would help them understand the Depression. Committed to providing its books at a low price, International retained the plates of its publications to facilitate the inexpensive reprinting of important works. Many bookstores did not carry International's books because of the small profit potential, so the firm reached its audience through academic libraries, political groups, labor unions, and bookstores specializing in radical literature.

International was the first firm to provide authoritative English editions of the works of Marx, Engels, Lenin, and Stalin. The company published the Labor Research Association's biennial *Labor Fact Books* and many monographs on labor, including Jack Hardy's *Labor and Textiles* (1931) and Philip Foner's *History of the Labor Movement in the United States* (1947). International has also published widely in black American history and issues; important titles include James W. Ford's *The Negro and the Democratic Front* (1938), Herbert Aptheker's *Essays in the History of the American Negro* (1945), and Foner's *The Life and Writings of Frederick Douglass* (1950). The firm's publications have included titles dealing with political issues in Ireland, Korea, Vietnam, and Ghana, and the works of political figures such as Samuel Adams, Franklin D. Roosevelt, and Kwame Nkrumah.

The firm has published translations of several

1928 advertisement

works by Ivan Pavlov, beginning with *Lectures on Conditioned Reflexes* in 1928. Other scientific titles have included Trofim Lysenko's *The Science of Biology Today* (1948) and James S. Allen's *Atomic Energy and Society* (1949). International has also published works in philosophy, literary criticism, art history, American history, American Indian issues, and women's studies. In 1945 International added a line of juvenile books under the Young World Books imprint.

Literary works, particularly translations of European poetry and novels with radical themes, have been a major part of International's lists. The firm has published translations of Soviet novels, including Dmitri Furmanov's *Chapayev* (1934), Nicholay Ostrovsky's *The Making of a Hero* (1937), and Petr Pavlinko's *Red Planes Fly East* (1938). International has also provided translations of literature from other countries, including the 1966 edition of *Rice Grains: Selected Poems*, the first English translation of the works of Filipino poet Amado V. Hernández. Many of the firm's literary works have reflected the founders' social and political philosophies: *Proletarian Literature in the United States: An Anthology* (1935); James Steele's *Conveyor* (1935), a novel about industrial working conditions; Ben Field's first book, *The Cock's Funeral* (1937), a collection of short stories about American farm workers; Richard Wright's *Bright and Morning Star* (1938); Aaron Kramer's book of verse *The Thunder of the Grass* (1948); Beth McHenry and Frederick N. Myers's novel about a militant union leader, *Home Is the Sailor* (1948); Philip Stevenson's *Old Father Antic* (1961), published under the pseudonym Lars Lawrence; and the anthology *Hear the Wind Blow! Poems of Protest & Prophecy* (1968). In 1974 International published *Voices from Wah' kontah: Contemporary Poetry of Native Americans*. Traditional American authors such as Twain, Cooper, Whitman, and Bryant have also been represented in the firm's output.

The radical nature of many of International's publications led to the 1951 arrest of Trachtenberg on charges of violating of the Smith Act. He was convicted of publishing documents which taught the doctrine and methods of overthrowing the United States government. In a statement to the court before his sentencing, Trachtenberg pointed out that "numerically, most of our books deal with specific problems of American life and the current world situation," but the strong anti-Communist sentiment of the day resulted in a prison term. Trachtenberg's conviction won him wide support among opponents of censorship, and his firm continued to publish the same kinds of works it always had. In 1955 Trachtenberg won a retrial after a key witness against him, Harvey Matusow, was found guilty of perjury. Trachtenberg's conviction was reversed in 1958. Four years later, he retired. He died in 1966.

In the early 1960s the firm moved to 381 Park Avenue South, Suite 1301, New York 10016. In 1962 it entered the quality paperback field with the New World and Little New World imprints. James S. Allen succeeded Trachtenberg as the company's editor and president; in 1973 Louis Diskin succeeded him; and in 1982, Diskin was succeeded by Betty M. Smith. The firm published 14 titles in 1984 and listed 200 titles in print.

References:

Books on Trial: The Case of Alexander Trachtenberg, Director, International Publishers (New York: The Committee to Defend Alexander Trachtenberg, 1952);

Sender Garlin, "Publisher on Trial: The Lifework of Alexander Trachtenberg," *Masses and Mainstream*, 5 (October 1952): 17-27;

"Obituary Notes [Alexander Trachtenberg]," *Publishers' Weekly*, 190 (26 December 1966): 65-66;

Alexander Trachtenberg, "Trial of Books," in *Looking Forward: Sections of Works in Progress by Authors of International Publishers on the Occasion of Its Thirtieth Anniversary* (New York: International Publishers, 1954).

—*Judith Bushnell*

Claude Kendall
(New York: 1929-1934; 1936)
Claude Kendall and Willoughby Sharp
(New York: 1934-1936)

Claude Kendall, a former United Press correspondent, founded a publishing house in 1929 at 70 Fifth Avenue in New York. Among the titles published under the Kendall imprint were Tiffany Thayer's *Thirteen Men* (1930) and Charles Fort's *Lo!* (1931). Willoughby Sharp joined the firm after a career as a Wall Street broker and author, having had two mysteries, *Murder in Bermuda* (1933) and *The Murder of the Honest Broker* (1934), published by Kendall. The first book published by the new house of Claude Kendall and Willoughby Sharp was Carman Barnes's *Young Woman* (1934). Maureen Fleming's *Elizabeth, Empress of Austria;* Marie Troubetzkoy's *Gallows' Seed;* and two novels of Henry B. L. Webb (John Clayton), *Dew in April* and *Gold of Toulouse,* were published in 1935.

In February 1936 the firm moved to 381 Fourth Avenue, and a month later its name was changed to Claude Kendall, Incorporated. Although Kendall announced a forthcoming monthly series of detective novels under a new imprint, The Clue Chasers' Club, bankruptcy forced the firm out of business later that year. Kendall was murdered in 1937.

Reference:

"Claude Kendall [obituary]," *Publishers' Weekly,* 132 (4 December 1937): 2150.

—Mary M. Huth

Mitchell Kennerley
(New York: 1906-1938)

Mitchell Kennerley came to New York from England in 1896 to work in the American office of John Lane. In 1902 he founded *Reader* magazine, which he sold to the Bobbs-Merrill Company in 1904. In April 1906 he founded a publishing house at 116 East Twenty-eighth Street. Between 1910 and 1916 he published the *Forum*.

Kennerley published more than 400 titles between 1906 and 1924. Of the 324 Kennerley books in print in 1914, 45 were drama, 52 were verse, and 102 were fiction. During its decade of greatest activity, 1907 to 1917, Kennerley published from 20 to 50 titles each year. During its period of decline, from 1918 to 1924, the firm published fewer than a dozen books annually.

Mitchell Kennerley built its reputation on new but promising authors and fine bookmaking. Authors whose first books were published by Kennerley included Van Wyck Brooks, Joseph Hergesheimer, Vachel Lindsay, and Walter Lippmann. The firm also introduced English writers to American readers. The Kennerley typeface was designed by Frederic W. Goudy for Kennerley's limited edition of H. G. Wells's *The Door in the Wall* (1911). Kennerley published D. H. Lawrence's *The Trespasser* in 1912 and his *Sons and Lovers* in 1913. The famous anthology *The Lyric Year* (1912) heralded the new voices in American poetry, including that of Edna St. Vincent Millay's "Renascence." Kennerley also published Lindsay's *General William Booth Enters into Heaven* (1913); Lawrence's *Love Poems and Others* (1913); Witter Bynner and Arthur Davison Ficke's satirical attack on poetic "schools," *Spectra* (1916); and Millay's first book, *Renascence and Other Poems* (1917).

In September 1913 Anthony Comstock, secretary of the New York Society for the Suppression of Vice, brought suit against Kennerley for publishing *Hagar Revelly* (1913), Daniel C. Goodman's novel about two poor girls in New York. Kennerley fought the charge and won a landmark censorship case. Also in 1913 the firm moved to 32 West Fifty-eighth Street.

Kennerley's Modern Drama series, edited by Edwin Bjorkman, published plays by Andreyev, Becque, Giacosa, Ibsen, and Schnitzler. Lawrence's play *The Widowing of Mrs. Holroyd* was published in 1914, preceding the English edition.

The firm's list of novels featured titles by Victoria Cross, Sewell Ford, Robert Hichens, Leonard Merrick, and Frank Richardson; Kennerley was also the principal American publisher for Frank Harris. Kennerley appealed to all sections of the reading public with such titles of contemporary interest as Marian Cox's *Spiritual Curiosities* (1911), F. A. Cook's *My Attainment of the Pole* (1913), Archibald Gracie's *The Truth about The Titanic* (1913), and Elsa Barker's *Letters from a Living Dead Man* (1919).

In 1915 Kennerley became president of Anderson Galleries, the New York auction house. Kennerley moved to the Anderson building at Madison Avenue and Fortieth Street in 1916 and to 489 Park Avenue in 1918. Kennerley published and campaigned strongly for two books by George D. Herron, a pacifist Christian socialist: *The Menace of Peace* (1917) and *Woodrow Wilson and the World's Peace* (1917). Kennerley also published Max Eastman's *Understanding Germany* (1916) and A. S. W. Rosenbach's *Unpublishable Memoirs* (1917). Goudy's *The Alphabet* appeared in 1918 and his *Elements of Lettering* in 1922. Millay's *Aria da Capo* and *Second April* were both published in 1921. The firm published only a few titles after 1924 as Kennerley

Claude Kendall (left) and Willoughby Sharp in 1934

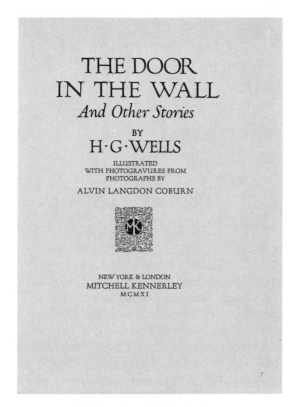

THE DOOR
IN THE WALL
And Other Stories
BY
H·G·WELLS

ILLUSTRATED
WITH PHOTOGRAVURES FROM
PHOTOGRAPHS BY
ALVIN LANGDON COBURN

NEW YORK & LONDON
MITCHELL KENNERLEY
MCMXI

Title page for 1911 publication   *Mitchell Kennerley (photo by Arnold Genthe)*

devoted himself to auctions and rare books; the last Kennerley title appeared in 1938. Kennerley committed suicide in 1950.

References:

Matthew J. Bruccoli, *The Fortunes of Mitchell Kennerley, Bookman* (New York & San Diego: Harcourt Brace Jovanovich, 1986);

Bruccoli, "Mitchell Kennerley, Entrepreneur of Books," *AB Bookman's Weekly,* 73 (19 March 1984): 2019-2020, 2080, 2084, 2086, 2088;

Special Kennerley Issue, *Monotype,* no. 70 (May 1924);

G. Thomas Tanselle, "The Mitchell Kennerley Imprint," *Book Collector,* 13 (1964): 185-193.

—Harry F. Thompson

Alfred A. Knopf
(New York: 1915-   )

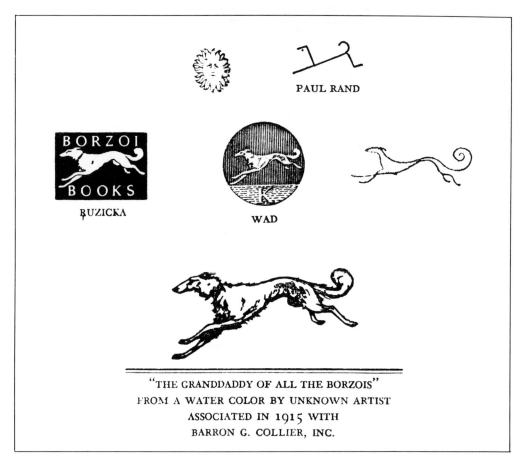

PAUL RAND

RUZICKA

WAD

"THE GRANDDADDY OF ALL THE BORZOIS"
FROM A WATER COLOR BY UNKNOWN ARTIST
ASSOCIATED IN 1915 WITH
BARRON G. COLLIER, INC.

Alfred A. Knopf was born on 12 September 1892 in New York. His father, Samuel Knopf, was a successful advertising executive and consultant; his mother died when Alfred was four years old. He attended public schools until he was sent to the MacKenzie School in Westchester County to prepare for Columbia University. In 1912 Knopf graduated with a B.A. degree and that summer went abroad for the first time.

While preparing an essay for Professor Joel Spingarn's comparative literature class, Knopf had written to John Galsworthy, who had invited the student to visit him in Devonshire. There Knopf was introduced to the works of Joseph Conrad and W. H. Hudson. After a stay in London and a taste of its literary life, young Knopf decided to abandon his plans to study law and to go into publishing instead.

In the fall of 1912 Knopf obtained, through paternal connections, a position with Doubleday, Page and Company in Garden City. Starting in accounting, he quickly moved on to manufacturing,

(Left to right): Alfred Knopf, Bennett Cerf, Blanche Knopf, and Donald Klopfer celebrating the merger of Alfred A. Knopf, Incorporated and Random House in April 1960

Alfred A. and Blanche Knopf in 1940

then to advertising, and finally to sales. His experience in the manufacturing department gave him an interest in the physical makeup of books. "I was able to frequent the composing room, play with cloth sample books, and try to improve the looks of bindings," he recalled later.

While working in the Doubleday sales division, Knopf was assigned to publicize Conrad's *Chance* (1913). Conrad's work was then relatively unknown in America. Knopf, a Conrad enthusiast, wrote to several prominent American writers and obtained their praise of Conrad's work. He prepared an illustrated booklet on Conrad which helped make *Chance* a success with American readers, selling over 50,000 copies and aiding sales of Conrad's earlier Doubleday books as well. "If you had not 'happened along,'" Conrad wrote Knopf later, "all these books would have remained on the back shelves of the firm where they have been reposing for the last ten years." For his achievement, Knopf received a salary increase from eight to twelve dollars a week. Knopf left Doubleday, Page in 1914 to join the publisher Mitchell Kennerley. When Kennerley discovered that his general assistant and traveling salesman was about to launch his own publishing firm, he fired Knopf in 1915.

In the spring of 1915 Knopf started work on his first list of books, using a desk in his father's office in the Candler Building at 220 West Forty-second Street in New York. By the end of the summer he had rented a small office on the nineteenth floor of the building, and his publishing operation was under way.

Blanche Wolf, Knopf's fiancée, joined him at the very beginning of the enterprise. They were married in 1916 and she was an integral part of the firm until her death in 1966. Born in New York in 1894, the daughter of a jeweler, Julius M. Wolf, and his wife Bertha, Blanche was educated by French and German governesses and at the Gardner School in New York. This cosmopolitan background enabled her to get along well with the foreign authors who became a major emphasis of the firm. Beginning as office manager at Knopf, Blanche assumed the office of director and vice-president in 1921.

The Knopf logo has always been a Borzoi, a long-haired Russian greyhound. It has appeared in many different styles by a variety of artists and type designers. In a *New Yorker* article in 1948, Geoffrey Hellman explained why the Borzoi was chosen: "Mrs. Knopf . . . was crazy about Borzois in 1915, or thought she was, and suggested that they use a drawing of one as a trademark. 'I bought

a couple of them later,' she says, 'and grew to despise them. One died and I gave the other to a kennel. I wished I'd picked a better dog for our imprint.'"

At twenty-five, Knopf had established a house that would achieve distinction among twentieth-century American publishers. The firm's success was due primarily to the forceful personalities of Alfred and Blanche Knopf and their unwavering belief in the virtue of publishing books worthy of the Borzoi imprint. Knopf's "Borzoi Credo" summarized his priorities: "*I believe that* a publisher's imprint means something, and that if readers paid more attention to the publisher of books they buy, their chances of being disappointed would be infinitely less. *I believe that* good books should be well made, and I try to give every book I publish a format that is distinctive and attractive. *I believe that* I have never knowingly published an unworthy book."

With his limited capital, Knopf built financial success upon an adherence to four principles outlined by Clifton Fadiman in 1965: "First, the Borzoi revolution in book design and manufacture, now an old story, in the twenties a radically new one. Second, the discovery of virtually a continentful of European high literature . . .—an act followed in later years by similar ones with respect to Latin America and Japan. Third, the organized effort to publish, often at a commercial loss, first-rate books in fields intimately tied to the personal interests of the Knopfs: historical scholarship, music, gastronomy, oenology, conservation. Finally, the sponsorship over an eleven-year period of *The American Mercury*, which, as the *Pequod* did for Ishmael, constituted the Harvard and Yale of a whole generation of young Americans."

The first Knopf book was *Four Plays* (1915) by Émile Augier, translated from the French by Barrett H. Clark. Of the remaining ten volumes on the initial list, all but one were translations from Russian, Polish, or French. The only book written in English was a new edition of Hudson's *Green Mansions* (1916) with a new introduction by Galsworthy. Though no American copyright was obtainable, Knopf received permission from Putnam for the new edition. The book became the first Knopf best-seller, and while not legally required to do so, Knopf paid royalties to the impoverished author.

The Knopfs were among the first American publishers to visit the Continent actively seeking the books of new writers for translation. "Certainly when in 1921 my wife and I first went to Germany,

Denmark, Sweden and Norway (as well as France), we found that very few if any American publishers had been there before us," Knopf wrote later. Attracted by the distinctive Knopf typographic style as well as by the uncompromising intellectual content of the Knopf books, American writers, too, were rapidly added to the list.

Joseph Hergesheimer became a Knopf author with his third book, *The Three Black Pennys* (1917). Knopf published Ezra Pound's *Lustra* (1917), which had been privately printed in London the year before; it was the first book of Pound's poetry to appear in the United States since 1912. In 1918 Knopf published T. S. Eliot's anonymous discussion of Pound's work, *Ezra Pound: His Metric and Poetry*—the first Eliot book published in America. Later the firm published Eliot's *Poems* (1920), which had previously been published in London.

Conrad Aiken first appeared on the Knopf list with *Scepticisms, Notes on Contemporary Poetry* (1919). His books of poetry published by Knopf included *Punch: The Immortal Liar* (1921) and *The Pilgrimage of Festus* (1923). Thomas Beer, who wrote novels, short stories, criticism, social history, and biography, had nearly all of his work published by Knopf. Among his best-known works are *Stephen Crane: A Study in American Letters* (1923) and *The Mauve Decade: American Life at the End of the Nineteenth Century* (1926). In 1920 Willa Cather, already a respected novelist, visited Knopf in his office and announced that she wanted him to publish her books. It was the beginning of a long, stable relationship based on mutual respect and admiration, one of many such relationships between the Knopf firm and its authors. Cather's first Knopf book was *Youth and the Bright Medusa* (1920); later ones included *A Lost Lady* (1923), *Death Comes for the Archbishop* (1927), and *Shadows on the Rock* (1931).

An important factor in establishing the literary prestige of the Knopf enterprise was the *American Mercury*, a monthly launched in January 1924. The joint editors and part owners of the magazine were George Jean Nathan and H. L. Mencken. During its years with Knopf, the *American Mercury* published outstanding work by established and unknown writers, many of whom later made their way to the Knopf list. Nathan and Mencken drifted apart after a few years, and Mencken continued alone as editor until the end of 1933. By that time he had lost interest, and Henry Hazlitt took over as editor in January 1934. Soon afterward Knopf ceased publishing the *American Mercury* and it became independent. But Mencken maintained an active role in the firm and became a member of the board of directors. Mencken's *The American Language* (1919), with later supplements and revisions, was the first systematic presentation of American as distinct from British English. His reminiscences, *Happy Days* (1940), *Newspaper Days* (1941), and *Heathen Days* (1943), were also published by Knopf.

An important Knopf poet was Wallace Stevens, from his first book, *Harmonium* (1923), to *The Collected Poems* (1954), which won the Pulitzer Prize for poetry in 1955. Although many deserving books, especially books of poetry, failed to return Knopf's investment, Kahlil Gibran's *The Prophet* (1923) and Walter Benton's *This Is My Beloved* (1943) were profitable experiments for the publisher. Enormously popular in a quite different vein was Clarence Day's *Life with Father* (1935) and other books about his eccentric parents.

Blanche Knopf introduced writers of crime and detective novels who won critical respect. All of Dashiell Hammett's major works were published by Knopf, including *Red Harvest* (1929), his first book, and *The Dain Curse* (1929), *The Maltese Falcon* (1930), *The Glass Key* (1931), and *The Thin Man* (1934). Raymond Chandler's first four books were published by Knopf: *The Big Sleep* (1939), *Farewell, My Lovely* (1940), *The High Window* (1942), and *The Lady in the Lake* (1943). Alfred Knopf worked with James M. Cain and Kenneth Millar (Ross Macdonald). Cain's first novel, *The Postman Always Rings Twice* (1934), was followed by *Serenade* (1937) and *Mildred Pierce* (1941). Nineteen of Millar's novels appeared with the Knopf imprint commencing with *Blue City* (1947) and including *The Galton Case* (1959), *The Far Side of the Dollar* (1965), *The Goodbye Look* (1969), and *The Underground Man* (1971).

Some important black writers had work published by the firm, most notably Langston Hughes, who was introduced in 1926 with *The Weary Blues*, a book of poetry. His Knopf books included another volume of poetry, *Fine Clothes to the Jew* (1927); a novel, *Not without Laughter* (1930); and a book of short stories, *The Ways of White Folks* (1934). James Weldon Johnson's *Black Manhattan*, a history and criticism of black literature in America, was published in 1930. Carl Van Vechten, a long-term Knopf author, recruited important black literary figures.

Conrad Richter's first Knopf book was his fourth, *Early Americana and Other Stories* (1936); it was followed by *The Sea of Grass* (1937). Richter's trilogy of novels about pioneer life in southeastern Ohio, *The Trees* (1940), *The Fields* (1946), and *The Town* (1950), were also published by Knopf. Among the respected poets introduced by Knopf in the 1940s was Theodore Roethke; his first book was *Open House* (1941). During the war years the first books of two prominent foreign correspondents were published by Knopf. William Shirer's *Berlin Diary* (1941) covered the years 1934 to 1941. John Hersey's first book was *Men on Bataan* (1942). Later Hersey accompanied American troops when they landed in Sicily; his insights into the developing relationships between Italians and Americans took fictional form in his extremely successful novel *A Bell for Adano* (1944). Knopf also published Hersey's classic *Hiroshima* (1946) and *The Wall* (1950).

After the war Knopf introduced several important novelists, including Walker Percy, Shirley Ann Grau, and John Updike. Percy's only Knopf book was his first, *The Moviegoer* (1961), but all of Grau's and Updike's best-known work was published by Knopf. Grau's first book was *The Black Prince and Other Stories* (1955); Updike's first Knopf book was his second published book and his first novel, *The Poorhouse Fair* (1959).

The new works of many foreign writers first came to Americans in Knopf editions. British figures included A. E. Coppard, Walter de la Mare, Robert Graves, Katherine Mansfield, T. F. Powys, and H. M. Tomlinson; other European authors included Mikhail Sholokhov, Albert Camus, Simone de Beauvoir, André Gide, Jean-Paul Sartre, Jean Giraudoux, Halldor Laxness, Knut Hamsun, and Oswald Spengler. Knopf published the first editions in English of two major works by Sigrid Undset, the Nobel Prize-winning novelist from Norway: *Kristen Lavransdatter* (1923), a trilogy, and *The Master of Hestviken* (1934), a tetralogy. Among the American first editions of Thomas Mann's work published by Knopf were *Buddenbrooks* (1924), *The Magic Mountain* (1924), and *Doctor Faustus* (1948). Blanche Knopf persuaded Sigmund Freud to sign with the firm for the American edition of his last book, *Moses and Monotheism* (1939). From non-European countries came works by Jorge Amado, Miguel Covarrubias, Gilberto Freyre, Yukio Mishama, Yasunari Kawabata, and Junichiro Tanizaki.

The Knopfs' interests in fields other than literature were reflected in the firm's lists. In the area of historical scholarship, Knopf published John Hope Franklin's *From Slavery to Freedom* (1947); Richard Hofstadter's *The American Political Tradition and the Men Who Made It* (1948), *The Age of Reform* (1955), *Anti-Intellectualism in American Life* (1963), and *The Paranoid Style in American Politics*

and Other Essays (1965); and Samuel Eliot Morison's *By Land and By Sea* (1953). American constitutional law and its role in American culture, another interest of the Knopfs, was the subject of *The Spirit of Liberty* (1952) by Learned Hand and *A Constitutional Faith* (1968) by Hugo Black. Books about music have played an important role at Knopf, notably Ernest Newman's four-volume *Life of Richard Wagner* (1933-1946). Knopf has also published successful books on wine and food—Alex Lichine's *Encyclopedia of Wines & Spirits* (1967) and Julia Child's *Mastering the Art of French Cooking* (1961)—as well as on photography and nature.

The designers of Knopf books contributed greatly to the firm's reputation. "The pioneering Knopf did in the production of good-looking books," according to Geoffrey Hellman, "made his early authors feel that they were in sympathetic hands and gave his list a certain cachet with the reading public." The firm's earliest books were designed by Knopf himself, but later the Rochester architect, designer, and writer Claude Bragdon became the first to prepare designs especially for Knopf. He was followed by Frederic W. Goudy and Bruce Rogers in 1923. Later that year, Elmer Adler was called upon to help design title pages, stationery, and advertisements. Adler's Pynson Printers printed some early Knopf books. Adler introduced Knopf and the Plimpton Press, the firm's principal printers, to the work of William A. Dwiggins, a calligrapher, typographer, and book designer. It was arranged that any Knopf manuscript given to Plimpton for manufacture would be designed by Dwiggins, whose first book for Knopf was Cather's *My Mortal Enemy* (1926). Until his death thirty years later, Dwiggins designed more than 320 volumes, including illustrations, endpapers, bindings, and jackets; many of the books were set in typefaces of his design with colophons written by him. Other notable designers who have worked for Knopf include George Salter, Louis J. Ansbacher, Warren Chappell, Rudolph Ruzicka, James Hendrickson, Guy Fleming, Herbert Bayer, and Vincent Torre.

Leading Knopf executives have included Knopf's father, who was the firm's treasurer until his death in 1931; Sidney R. Jacobs; William A. Koshland; and Joseph C. Lesser. Among important editors have been Harold Strauss, Judith Jones, Angus Cameron, Henry Robbins, and Herbert Weinstock. Blanche Knopf became president in 1957 when Alfred became chairman. Alfred, Jr., manager of the trade book department, left in 1959 to form a new publishing company, Atheneum.

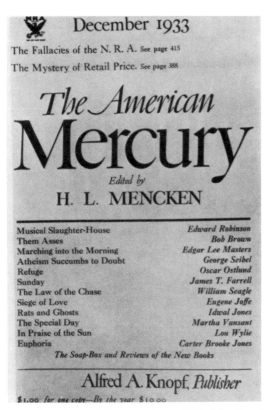

Cover of an issue of the magazine published by Knopf from
1924 to 1934

H. L. Mencken, editor of Knopf's American Mercury

1964 paperback edition of a title originally published by Street
and Smith in 1940

Title page for 1980 edition of a classic novel

In April 1960 Alfred and Blanche Knopf sold their company to Random House. In the *Borzoi Quarterly* they wrote:

> Bennett Cerf and Donald Klopfer were eager to work out some kind of association with us. Thus when a month or so ago Mr. Cerf broached the matter again, we suggested that he make a proposal. This he and Mr. Klopfer made to us on Monday, April 11. It seemed so fair in the financial sense and so ideal in every other that we came to an agreement in less than an hour. . . .
>
> The essential condition on which all four of us agreed is that the firm of Alfred A. Knopf, Incorporated, shall continue in the future as it has in the past as a separate and distinct imprint under the direction and editorial control of ourselves.

Vintage Books, a quality paperback imprint which had been started by Alfred, Jr., in 1954, was also acquired by Random House.

Blanche Wolf Knopf died in June 1966; the same year Random House, including Knopf, was purchased by RCA. In April 1967 Knopf married Helen Hedrick, whose novel *The Blood Remembers* had been published by the firm in 1941. By the late 1970s Knopf had largely retired from the company and had assumed the title of founding chairman; Robert A. Gottlieb was president and editor in chief of Alfred A. Knopf, Incorporated. Among the authors published under Gottlieb were Joseph Heller, Barbara Tuchman, and John Gardner. In 1980 RCA sold Random House and Knopf to Newhouse Publications. Nevertheless, the familiar Borzoi imprint endured, with 139 titles in 1980.

Knopf fiction titles still have an international flavor, and include some of the best of current fiction by women. Muriel Spark moved from Lippincott to Knopf with *The Girls of Slender Means* (1963), following it with *The Mandelbaum Gate* (1965). Doris Lessing came to Knopf in 1969 with *The Four-Gated City*. Toni Morrison's second novel, *Sula*, published by Knopf in 1974, was followed by a winner of the National Book Critics Circle Award, *Song of Solomon* (1977). Other writers whose works were published by Knopf in the 1960s, 1970s, and 1980s include Ray Bradbury, Len Deighton, Don DeLillo, William Kotzwinkle, Milan Kundera, John Le Carré, Alice Munro, and V. S. Naipaul.

Knopf died at his home in Purchase, New York, on 11 August 1984, at the age of ninety-one. During his life his firm had published the works of sixteen Nobel Prize winners and twenty-six Pulitzer Prize winners. The Knopf firm moved from its original address at 220 West Forty-second Street to the Heckscher Building at 730 Fifth Avenue in 1924. In the mid-1930s it moved to 501 Madison Avenue. In 1969 Knopf, together with Random House, moved to 201 East Fiftieth Street, New York 10022.

References:

Alfred A. Knopf, Quarter Century (Norwood, Mass: Plimpton Press, 1940);

Clifton Fadiman, ed., *Fifty Years: Being a Retrospective Collection of Novels, Novellas, Tales, Drama, Poetry, and Reportage and Essays (Whether Literary, Musical, Contemplative, Historical, Biographical, Argumentative, or Gastronomical) All Drawn from Volumes Issued during the Last Half-Century by Alfred and Blanche Knopf over This Sign and Device [the Borzoi]* (New York: Knopf, 1965);

"50 Years of the Borzoi," *Publishers' Weekly*, 187 (1 February 1965): 48-54;

Geoffrey T. Hellman, "Publisher: Alfred A. Knopf," *New Yorker*, 24 (20 November 1948): 44-57; (27 November 1948): 36-52; (4 December 1948): 40-53;

Alfred A. Knopf, "Book Publishing: The Changes I've Seen," *Atlantic*, 200 (December 1957): 155-156, 158, 160;

Knopf, "My First Job," *Atlantic*, 202 (August 1958): 79-80;

"Obituary Notes [Alfred A. Knopf]," *Publishers Weekly*, 226 (24 August 1984); 20-21;

Portrait of a Publisher, 1915-1965, 2 volumes (New York: The Typophiles, 1965).

—*Herbert H. Johnson*
Margaret Becket

Lancer Books

(New York: 1961-1973)

A LANCER BOOK

Lancer Books, a subsidiary of the Magnum Communications Corporation, was established in 1961 at 26 West Forty-seventh Street in New York with Irwin Stein and Walter Zacharius as publishers and Jack Hoffman as executive editor. Lancer's paperback line, marked by a black knight chesspiece logo, stressed genre fiction in attractive packaging. Its Science Fiction Library titles, with covers by Ed Emshwiller, were priced at sixty cents; its Limited Edition science fiction books were priced at seventy-five cents. Included in the Limited Edition series were reprints of *Martian Odyssey and Other Classics of Science Fiction* (1962) by Stanley G. Weinbaum and *The End of Eternity* (1963) by Isaac Asimov.

In 1963, under a new executive editor, Bernard Farbar, Lancer began to emphasize sex in private-eye adventure books by Henry Kane. Early titles in his Peter Chambers series included *Never Give a Millionaire an Even Break* and *Dead in Bed*, both in 1963. Later, this series was sold as "X-rated." In 1964 the Lancer Suspense Library was added to the line, with a logo of a red square with an arrow pointing to the book's title.

Also in 1964 Lancer discovered that the copyright to *Candy* by Terry Southern and Mason Hoffenberg (as "Maxwell Kenton"), first published in Paris in 1958 and rereleased by Putnam in 1964, was imperfect. Putnam planned to publish a paperback edition of the best-selling satire of pornographic novels in May 1965, but Lancer brought out an earlier edition of 500,000 copies priced at seventy-five cents. Putnam responded in January 1965 with its paperback edition of one million copies at ninety-five cents and a lawsuit, which Lancer countered. In February a judge denied both motions; the competing editions sold briskly.

In 1965 Lancer Books moved to 185 Madison Avenue and Larry T. Shaw became executive editor. The firm published 125 titles that year. The Suspense Library was upgraded: six of the twenty-four Suspense Library titles that year were by Michael Gilbert, while twelve were by Andrew Garve,

both well-regarded British mystery authors. Shaw also bought rights to the works of John Creasey; between 1966 and 1972 Lancer published nearly 100 Creasey titles, including books from most of his famous series: the Toff, Dr. Palfrey, the Baron, and Inspector West. Shaw added Ellery Queen mysteries and continued Kane's Peter Chambers books. But Shaw's main interest was science fiction; he had edited *If, Infinity,* and *Science Fiction Adventures* magazines in the 1950s and an anthology titled *Great Science Fiction Adventures* for Lancer in 1964. One of his first purchases was a trilogy of novels by Michael Moorcock under the pseudonym Edward P. Bradbury: *Warriors of Mars, Blades of Mars,* and *Barbarians of Mars,* all published by Lancer in 1966. Originally published in England, these novels were frankly based on the Martian world invented by Edgar Rice Burroughs, but Moorcock followed them with books that were far more inventive and original. Lancer published his Elric books, including *Stormbringer* (1967) and *The Stealer of Souls* (1967) and his Runestaff series. Other science fiction brought out under Shaw's editorship included a reprint of Poul Anderson's *The Corridors of Time* (1966).

In 1966 Lancer published several paperbacks based on early issues of Marvel Comics, including *The Amazing Spider-Man* and *The Fantastic Four.* Printed in black and white, the books proved unpopular with readers accustomed to color comics. Capitalizing on the success of heroic fantasy published by other firms, Lancer obtained the reprint rights to Robert E. Howard's Conan series, which Gnome Press had already revived. The Lancer books, starting in 1967 with *Conan* and *Conan the Conqueror,* included complete Howard stories as well as fragments completed by L. Sprague de Camp and Lin Carter. Eleven Conan books were published by Lancer between 1967 and 1971, all with striking pictorial covers by Frank Frazetta.

Also in 1967 Lancer initiated its line of Magnum Easy Eye books, with type thirty percent larger than usual on green-tinted, "no-glare" paper. Initially intended for students with poor eyesight, the line included *Adventures of Huckleberry Finn* and *The Red Badge of Courage;* but the firm found that many adults liked the format. After 1968 one-third of the Lancer line, including all the firm's gothics and westerns, came out in the Easy Eye format.

Lancer published 250 titles in 1968. When Shaw left that year to go to Dell, Evan Hayman and Robert Hoskins became the editors. Hoskins was especially helpful to new writers such as Dean R. Koontz and Barry Malzberg. In 1969 Lancer moved to 1650 Broadway. In 1971 the firm published 320 titles. The Johnny Morini series was initiated in 1972 with *Death Grip* by "Al Conroy" (Marvin H. Albert).

On 7 September 1973 Lancer Books sued Curtis Circulation Company and its parent group, Cadence Industries, for $7.5 million. Lancer accused Curtis of violating its book distribution con-

tract and of engaging in improper business procedures, including charging for expenses not incurred. Lancer suspended operations and furloughed its staff. Although Zacharius, president of the company, denied that Lancer was in bankruptcy and the firm was awarded damages, Lancer did not resume publishing.

References:

"Both Lancer and Putnam Injunctions Enjoined," *Publishers' Weekly*, 187 (22 February 1965): 132-133;

"Lancer Edition Starts 'Candy' Paperback Scramble," *Publishers' Weekly*, 187 (18 January 1965): 103-104;

"Lancer Suspends Operation and Files $7.5 Million Suit," *Publishers Weekly*, 204 (1 October 1973): 39-40.

—*Martha A. Bartter*

Limited Editions Club

(New York; Avon, Connecticut; Westport, Connecticut; New York: 1929-   )

The Limited Editions Club is a New York-based subscription book club which each year publishes twelve deluxe editions of classics, limited to not more than 2,000 numbered and signed copies. The club was founded in 1929 by George Macy, a bibliophile whose aim was to offer literary classics illustrated and printed by the most highly regarded contemporary artists and printers and thus to elevate standards of book production. For the next twenty-seven years Macy personally attended to every detail of the operation from title choice to binding. The club's first book was *The Travels of Lemuel Gulliver* (1929), with full-page monochromic illustrations by Alexander King.

Most of the club's books are published in large octavo or quarto formats in dust jackets and slipcases. They are distinguished in appearance, each volume differing from others but sharing a rec-

ognizable club quality. Club productions have ranged from ancient to modern classics, among them James Joyce's *Ulysses* (1935), illustrated by Henri Matisse; Aristotle's *Politics and Poetics* (1964), designed and printed by Roderick Stinehour and illustrated by Leonard Baskin; and John Steinbeck's *Of Mice and Men* (1970), with watercolors by Fletcher Martin. Other Limited Editions Club illustrators have included Pablo Picasso, John Sloan, Arthur Szyk, Lynd Ward, Thomas Hart Benton, Marie Laurencin, Miguel Covarrubias, Fritz Eichenberg, and Rockwell Kent. The watercolors for *Mask of Comus* (1954) were Edmund Dulac's final works.

Beautifully illustrated by the best American and foreign artists, the club's publications were also the labors of top book designers and printing houses, including Bruce Rogers, W. A. Dwiggins,

Will Ransom, Frederic Warde, C. P. Rollins, Peter Beilenson's Peter Pauper Press, D. B. Updike's Merrymount Press, the Spiral Press, Thistle Press, Marchbanks Press, William Edwin Rudge, Plantin Press, and Aldus Printers. The books are more than examples of excellence in craftsmanship: the unabridged texts, carefully selected for readability and literary value, are enhanced by introductions by such writers as André Maurois, Louis Untermeyer, and Van Wyck Brooks.

After Macy's death in 1956, the commitment to maintain a high standard of book production was continued by his wife until 1968 and then by his son Jonathan. In 1970 the Boise-Cascade Company (part of Communications/Research/Machines) bought the George Macy Companies, which included the Limited Editions Club; the Heritage Club, founded by Macy in 1937 to offer inexpensive editions of classics; and two other subsidiaries.

Between 1972 and 1979 the Limited Editions Club deteriorated, changing owners (the Cardavon Press, Ziff-Davis), locations (Avon, Connecticut; Westport, Connecticut), and directors (Heinz Eller, Gordon Carroll, Martin Simmons, and Louise Nelson). The only constant during this period was the editor, David Glixon. In 1979, Sidney Shiff purchased the club with the plan of returning it to its former standards. Relying primarily on his son, Benjamin Shiff, to design the club's books, Shiff

concentrated on contemporary works illustrated by noteworthy artists. Among his books are Arthur Miller's *Death of a Salesman*, illustrated by Leonard Baskin; Edgar Allan Poe's *The Fall of the House of Usher*, illustrated by Alice Neel; and *Poems of Octavio Paz*, illustrated by Robert Motherwell. In 1985 Limited Edition Club Books were sold by subscription, six books for $2000. The firm's address is 551 Fifth Avenue, New York, 10175.

References:

Paul A. Bennett, "The Man behind the Limited Editions Club—George Macy," *Linotype News*, 10 (September 1931): 5;

A Complete Catalogue: Forty Years of Limited Editions Club Books, 1929-1969 (New York: Philip C. Duschnes, 1970);

"George Macy [obituary]," *New York Times*, 21 May 1956, p. 25;

Ten Years and William Shakespeare: A Survey of the Publishing Activities of the Limited Editions Club from October 1929 to October 1940 (New York: Limited Editions Club, 1940);

Beatrice Warde, "George Macy and the Limited Editions Club," *Penrose Annual*, 48 (1954): 35-39.

—Margaret W. Fleming

Lion Books
(New York: 1949-1957)
Select Publications
(New York: 1949)

Martin Goodman, the owner of the Magazine Management Company and Atlas Magazines, entered the paperback publishing business in November 1949, calling his company Select Publications. He decided to market his paperbacks under the imprint Red Circle Books, primarily in candy stores and other retail outlets where his magazines and comic books sold well. With the publication of its eighth book, *Hungry Men* (1949) by Edward Anderson, the firm's name was changed to Lion Books, Incorporated, and the imprint to Lion Books; the Red Circle Books imprint was, however,

revived for the twelfth and thirteenth books, both published in 1949.

Lion's offices were at 350 Fifth Avenue (the Empire State Building), where Goodman's magazine companies were located. Arnold Hano was the editor of Lion Books. In 1950 the firm published a reprint of *Christ in Concrete* by Pietro di Donato, 250,000 copies of which were released to coincide with the movie version, *Give Us This Day*. In June 1950 William Goldberg was added to the staff as associate editor. In the same month Lion reprinted *The Continental Touch* by Joseph Wechsberg; *Ceylun*

PROUD SYMBOLS OF QUALITY
IN PAPERBACK BOOKS

Illustrated below are just a few of the outstanding LION BOOKS
and LION LIBRARY EDITIONS currently available

CANDIDE...
*an all-time bestseller,
complete and
unabridged.*
25¢

**THE HILLS
BEYOND...**
*by the incomparable
Thomas Wolfe. His only novel
available in a low-priced
paperbound.*
35¢

QUINTET...
*a collection of five of
the world's greatest
novels by outstanding
authors*
50¢

**THE TUNNEL
OF LOVE...**
*by Peter De Vries. A
laugh-provoking novel, soon
to be a Broadway comedy
starring Tom Ewell.*
35¢

*for a complete
listing of all*
LION BOOKS
and
**LION LIBRARY
EDITIONS,**

write to:
Al Dreyfuss
Lion Books
655 Madison Ave.
New York 21, N. Y.

LION BOOKS — *The Fastest-Growing Line of Paperback Books in America!*

1957 advertisement

212

by Margaret Rebecca Lay; and two westerns, *Guns of Arizona* by Charles N. Heckelmann and *Man Tracks* by Bennett Foster.

In May 1952 Lion, following the lead of Fawcett, began to publish occasional paperback originals. In many cases these were written to order from ideas or plots provided by Hano. The first book in this program was Louis Trimble's *Blondes are Skin Deep*. In June 1952 Lion Books moved to 270 Park Avenue. Its 1953 list included *His Great Journey*, a life of Christ by Manuel Komroff; *Sailor's Luck* by Basil Heatter; and *The Dream and the Flesh* by Vivian Connell.

In 1954 Lion moved to 655 Madison Avenue. That year it published *The Kidnapper*, an original novel by Robert Bloch. During the year the Lion Books imprint began to be replaced by the Lion Library imprint, although a few Lion Books were still published in 1955. Under the Lion Library imprint appeared the firm's popular series of regional anthologies: *Great Tales of the Deep South*

(1955), *Great Tales of City Dwellers* (1955), and *Great Tales of the Far West* (1956), as well as reprints of *Nineteen Stories* by Graham Greene (1955), *All Quiet on the Western Front* by Erich Maria Remarque in a thirty-five-cent edition (1956), and *Around the World in Eighty Days* by Jules Verne (1956). The last two were among Lion's best-selling books for 1956, along with *Quintet*, a collection of short novels by various authors. *House of Dolls* by Ka-Tzetnik and *Company K* by William March also made Lion's bestseller list for 1956. In August 1957 New American Library bought the publishing rights of Lion Books. The firm had published a total of 407 books. NAL brought out under the Signet imprint several titles that had been under development by Lion.

Reference:
"NAL Buying Rights to Some Lion Books," *Publishers' Weekly*, 172 (5 August 1957): 32.

—Martha A. Bartter

Loring and Mussey
(New York: 1933-1936)

J. Barrows Mussey
(New York: 1936-1937)

Loring and Mussey was founded in 1933 at 66 Fifth Avenue, New York, by Percy A. Loring and J. Barrows Mussey.

Loring and Mussey published popular fiction, a juvenile line, and some fine examples of the bookmaker's art. Chief among the latter is Warren Chappell's *Anatomy of Lettering*, which was selected as one of the Fifty Books of the American Institute of Graphic Arts for 1935. The firm's fiction lacked distinction. Representative titles include *Hunch* (1934) by Ray Humphreys, *Three Who Died* (1935) by August Derleth, and *Knights at Bay* by Philip Lindsay (1935). Other authors whose works were

published by the firm include Alexander Duffield, Francis MacManus, and Hugh Macmullan. Besides publishing books, the firm served as trade agent for other publishers, including Thomas Seltzer of New York and the Stephen Daye Press of Brattleboro, Vermont. Loring withdrew from the firm early in 1936, and Mussey continued under his own name at 100 Fifth Avenue for another year.

Reference:
"New House Announced," *Publishers' Weekly*, 124 (19 August 1933): 495.

—Peter Dzwonkoski

John W. Luce and Company
(Boston: 1904-1947)
Robinson, Luce Company
(Boston: 1904)

Early in 1904 the Robinson, Luce Company at 311 Washington Street in Boston advertised in *Publishers' Weekly* the publication of its humorous *The Foolish Dictionary* by Gideon Wurdz (Charles Wayland Towne). In September of that year the company, renamed John W. Luce and Company, again advertised the dictionary and added Hermann Sudermann's play *Fires of St. John*, translated by Charles Swickard, and Newton Newkirk's *Stealthy Steve: The Six-Eyed Sleuth*.

The firm slowly built up a list of literary titles, especially in drama and poetry, mostly by foreign authors. Among these were the poems and plays of Oscar Wilde; Lord Dunsany's *The Book of Wonder* (1913), *A Dreamer's Tales* (1916), and *Plays of Gods and Men* (1917); J. M. Synge's *Riders to the Sea* (1911); and two collections of Isaac Goldberg's translations of Yiddish plays. Other titles included William McDougall's *An Introduction to Social Psychology* (1909); Charles W. Eliot's *The Religion of the Future* (1909); H. L. Mencken's *The Artist: A Drama without Words* (1912); *The Technique of the One-Act Play* (1918), edited by Benjamin Roland Lewis; and Thorvald Solberg's *Copyright Miscellany* (1939).

Soon after opening, Luce moved to 31 Beacon Street and, in 1908, to 143 Federal Street. From about 1912 until 1945 the firm's address was 212 Summer Street. Just before the end of World War II the company merged with Manthorne and Burack, Incorporated and moved to the address of that small company at 30 Winchester Street. The merger increased Luce's book list by about a dozen titles, diversifying the subjects and adding a few juvenile titles. After 1947 Luce ceased listing its 105 titles in *The Publishers' Trade List Annual*. The firm disappeared from the publishing scene as demand for its backlist dropped off.

Reference:

"Manthorne and Burack Merge with John Luce Co.," *Publishers' Weekly*, 147 (24 February 1945): 928.

—*Theodora Mills*

Macaulay Company

(New York: 1909?-1941)

The earliest record of the Macaulay Company's existence is a 1909 advertisement for Hornor Cotes's Civil War novel *The Counterpart*. At that time the firm was located at 15-17 West Thirty-eighth Street, New York. In 1925 Macaulay moved to 115-117 East Twenty-third Street, and in 1928 to 257 Fourth Avenue. The firm specialized in histories, poetry, criticism, literary translations, and inexpensive popular literature. Nonfiction was published under the Gold Label Books imprint, established in 1931 at 381 Fourth Avenue.

Among Macaulay's more notable publications were William Carlos Williams's *A Voyage to Pagany;* Matthew Josephson's *Zola and His Time*, a premier selection of the newly formed Book League of America; and John Dos Passos's *Airways, Inc.*, all in 1928. Macaulay also published Malcolm Cowley's translations of Henri Barbusse's *Jesus* (1927) and Maurice Barrès's *The Sacred Hill* (1929); Robert M. Coates's *The Eater of Darkness* (1929) and *Yesterday's Burdens* (1933); and works by Michael Gold. Macaulay's anthology *American Caravan: A Yearbook of American Literature* appeared in 1927.

In 1939 Macaulay moved to 386 Fourth Av-

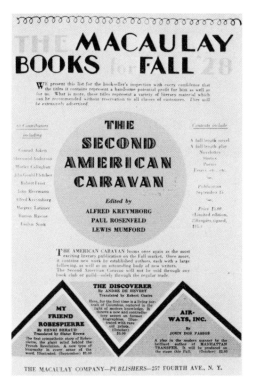

1928 advertisement

Durant L. Macrae (seated), president of Macrae Smith, and his staff in 1950. (Standing, left to right): Edward Shenton, vice-president and editor; Esther Weiss, office manager; Donald L. Macrae, production manager. (Seated, left to right): Helen Rotter, juvenile editor; Janet Hotson Baker, associate editor (photo by Swallow Studios).

enue. The firm's last fiction publication was the anonymously written *The Strange Death of Adolf Hitler* (1939). Macaulay declared bankruptcy in 1941;

the firm was acquired by J. J. Little and Ives printers, and its publications were sold to Citadel Press.

—*Alison Tanner Stauffer*

Macrae Smith Company

(Philadelphia; Turbotville, Pennsylvania: 1925-1977)

The Macrae Smith Company was founded on 1 January 1925 when Durant L. Macrae and Allan M. Smith bought the publishing operation of the George W. Jacobs Company, where they were employed. The firm was first located at 1712 Ludlow Street, Philadelphia. Jacobs continued to operate the firm's retail store at 1726 Chestnut Street. The Jacobs Company, which had been founded in 1892, had published multivolume sets of classics; the Macrae Smith Company took over three series of these reprints: the Rittenhouse Classics, the Washington Square Classics, and the Fairmount Classics.

Like the Jacobs Company, Macrae Smith concentrated on publishing genre fiction and works for young readers. Two of the early successful children's books remained in print for more than twenty-five years: Félicité LeFèvre's *The Cock, the Mouse and the Little Red Hen* (1907) and Constance Heward's *Ameliar-anne and the Green Umbrella* (1920), both originally published by Jacobs and illustrated by Tony Sarg. The LeFèvre book sold more than a quarter of a million copies. Other Macrae Smith children's books were illustrated by Manning deV. Lee, Frank E. Schoonover, and Charles Copeland.

Lida Larrimore was one of Macrae Smith's early best-selling novelists. Her first romantic novel, *Tarpaper Palace* (1928), sold fairly well, and it was followed in 1930 by *Mulberry Square*, a bestseller. In her long association with Macrae Smith, Larrimore's many books sold over a million copies. Rupert Sargent Holland's novels *Minot's Folly* (1925), *Yankee Ships in Pirate Waters* (1931), and *Wrecker's Reef* (1941) offered a blend of historical

romance and adventure that appealed to a wide audience. During the 1930s Katharine Newlin Burt's romances, such as *When Beggars Choose* (1937), *Safe Road* (1938), *If Love I Must* (1939), and *Captain Millett's Island* (1944), were among the more popular items on the Macrae Smith list. These and other romances focused on teenagers and young women as both readers and heroines—a market the firm cultivated. Other popular romance writers of the 1930s included Frances Shelley Wees, Jean Randall, and Joseph McCord. During the 1940s the firm published works by Robert S. Hichens, Constance W. Dodge, and Rosamund Du Jardin. The historical romances of Margaret Campbell Barnes sold well in these years. There is still a demand for the out-of-print works of Gladys Taber, whose novels *The Evergreen Tree* (1937) and *Give Us This Day* (1944) and nonfiction writings on nature, animals, and her own life—especially the books in the Stillmeadow series—were mainstays of the Macrae Smith list.

During the 1930s Macrae Smith published a few mysteries by Norman S. Bortner, Brian Flynn, and Adam Bliss. This genre was represented in the 1940s by works of William G. Schofield and Harry Lang and in the 1950s by Floyd Mahannah's books. Of greater profit to the firm, beginning with Edwin L. Sabin's *Rio Bravo* (1926), was western fiction. Harold Titus's *Black Feather* (1936) and Charles H. Snow's *Argonaut Gold* (1936) were followed during the 1940s by the works of Roy Manning, Bruce Douglas, E. E. Halleran, Brett Rider, and R. M. Hankins and during the 1950s by the sagas of Louis Trimble, Michael Carder, and Walker Tompkins.

1928 advertisement

Wave High the Banner: A Novel Based on the Life of Davy Crockett (1942) was Dee Brown's first book. In December 1943 the firm moved to 225 South Fifteenth Street. Smith died in 1947.

The firm's nonfiction consisted mainly of biographies and books on travel and the outdoors. During the 1960s and 1970s Macrae Smith's output diminished as it relied increasingly on its backlist. The company continued to publish short lists of fiction and juvenile works from its location at Routes 54 and Old 147 in Turbotville, Pennsylvania, where it moved in the late 1970s. Durant Macrae died in 1968, and Donald P. Macrae became president and treasurer. The firm went out of business in 1977.

References:
"Durant L. Macrae [obituary]," *Publishers' Weekly*, 194 (9 September 1968): 41;
"The Macrae Smith Co.," *Publishers' Weekly*, 107 (3 January 1925): 38.

—Arlene Shaner

Macy-Masius
(New York: 1926-1928)
Macy-Masius/Vanguard
(New York: 1928-1929)

Macy-Masius was begun in 1926 by twenty-six-year-old George Macy at 551 Fifth Avenue, New York. The firm's first title was *The Conning Tower Book,* a collection of verse from the newspaper columns of Franklin P. Adams. Although other works, such as *The Songs of Bilitis* by Pierre Louÿs, appeared in 1926, most of the firm's titles were published in 1927. Among the novels of that year were Herbert Asbury's *The Devil of Pei-Ling,* James B. Connolly's *Coaster Captain,* and Martin Feinstein's *The Drums of Panic.* In the same year, the company began a series of reprints, An American Bookshelf, edited by Mark Van Doren. Its first title was *Samuel Sewell's Diary.* Known and admired for their quality and fine design, Macy-Masius publications occasionally appeared in special limited editions.

When the firm was purchased by Vanguard Press in 1928, Macy continued to direct it, along with Jacob Baker, Vanguard's managing director. *The Plays of Ferenc Molnár,* including Edna St. Vincent Millay's translation of *Heavenly and Earthly Love,* appeared under the Macy-Masius/Vanguard imprint in 1929. Macy soon left to found the Limited Editions Club and, later, the Heritage Club.

Reference:
"Macy-Masius Merged with Vanguard Press," *Publishers' Weekly*, 113 (9 June 1928): 2375.

—David Dzwonkoski

1928 advertisement

Major Books
(Chatsworth, California; Canoga Park, California:
1975-1980)

Milton Luros founded Major Books, a division of Chatsworth Enterprises, Incorporated at 21322 Lassen Street, Chatsworth, California, in 1975. The mass market paperbacks—chiefly science fiction, westerns, and thrillers—were distributed by Kable News. Major Books published forty titles its first year and ninety-six in 1976. In 1979 the firm published ninety books, including E. R. Bixby's *Ambush Planet,* J. L. Bouma's *Slaughter at*

Crucifix Canyon, and Ursula Bloom's *The Fire and the Rose.* By that time Major Books had moved to 21335 Roscoe Boulevard in Canoga Park. By 1980 the firm, although still officially publishing, was putting out books dated in the previous year; its last book, J. B. Herman's *Black Sabbat,* probably appeared about mid-1980.

—*Martha A. Bartter*

Manor Books
(New York: 1972-1981)

Early in 1972 Manor Books, a newly formed corporation at 329 Fifth Avenue, New York, purchased the paperback division of the Macfadden-Bartell Corporation. The president of Manor Books was Walter Weidenbaum, formerly vice-president of Kable News. Donald A. Schrader was vice-president and editor in chief, and Joseph Greco, also from Kable News and Grove Press, was vice-president in charge of marketing. Manor Books planned to publish ten to twelve paperback books a month, both original and reprint fiction and nonfiction.

Among the 160 titles published by Manor Books in 1973 were Ted White's science fiction anthologies *The Best from Amazing Stories* and *The Best from Fantastic,* and the first books in the Blade series by "Jeffrey Lord." Beginning in January 1974 a "seal of guaranteed reader satisfaction" on Manor books offered readers a "different book in the same category at no charge" if the unsatisfactory book was returned with twenty-five cents for postage and handling. By 1975 Manor Books had moved to 432 Park Avenue and the president and publisher was David Young; in 1976 the publisher was Irwin Stein.

Manor Books reprinted some important science fiction titles, including *Now Wait for Last Year* (1976) by Philip K. Dick and *No Mind of Man* (1976), edited by Terry Carr and Robert Silverberg. Original Manor titles include westerns by Carter Travis Young and mysteries by William Harrison, Stephen Brett, Bob Garland, and G. P. Kennealy.

Henry M. McQueeney became president in 1977. Manor Books published 248 titles in 1978 and 500 titles in 1979 and again in 1980. These were mostly undistinguished works by obscure authors, released without publicity. By 1980 Manor Books had moved to 45 East Thirtieth Street, and in November books were still appearing with 1979 imprint dates. By 1981 the company was out of business.

Reference:

"The Manor Books Seal of Guaranteed Reader Satisfaction," *Publishers Weekly,* 204 (26 November 1973): 23.

—*Martha A. Bartter*

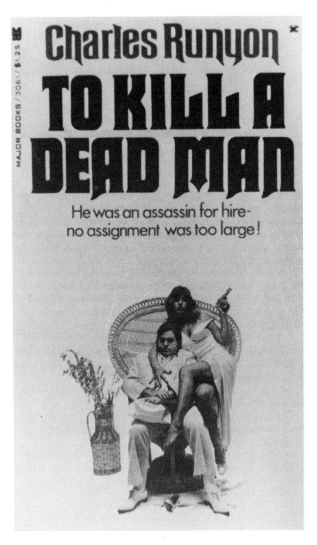

Cover for 1976 paperback

*Cover for a Manor Books paperback reprint, circa 1972, of a
1942 title*

Richard Marek Books
(New York: 1981-1985)
Richard Marek Publishers
(New York: 1977-1981)

RICHARD MAREK PUBLISHERS
NEW YORK

Richard Marek, editor in chief at Dial Press, left that company early in 1977 to establish Richard Marek Publishers, Incorporated, an autonomous imprint owned by the Putnam Publishing Group. From the Dial staff he brought Joyce Engelson as editor in chief and Ann Knauerhase and Deborah Zaitchik as senior editors. The new firm published sixty titles in 1981, about half of them fiction. Marek handled its own advertising while the parent company managed publicity, distribution, and other business matters.

Fiction writers published by Marek included Thomas Williams, Clark Howard, Barbara Traub, and Robert Ludlum. In 1979 Marek listed two titles by Yevgeny Yevtushenko, *The Face behind the Face* and *Ivan the Terrible and Ivan the Fool*. In 1979 Marek also published *How We Lived: A Documentary History of Immigrant Jews in America, 1880-1930* by Irving Howe and Kenneth Libo. Marek was the first house to sign a trade book agreement with the People's Republic of China; the agreement gave the firm world rights to 180 photographs of Chinese art, which appeared in 1981 as *The Treasures of China* by Annette Juliano.

In July 1981 Marek closed the firm. He and Engelson moved to St. Martin's Press, a New York subsidiary of Macmillan Publishers Limited of England, and established the St. Martin/Marek imprint there. In November 1985 Marek became president of E. P. Dutton. The Marek books imprint at St. Martin's Press was discontinued, and Marek has not arranged his own imprint at Dutton.

References:
"Additional Authors Sign with Marek," *Publishers Weekly*, 212 (28 November 1977): 34;

"Marek and Engelson Join St. Martin's," *Publishers Weekly*, 220 (10 July 1981): 14;

"Marek Signs Trade Book Agreement with China," *Publishers Weekly*, 217 (9 May 1980): 13;

"Richard Marek Talks about His First List," *Publishers Weekly*, 211 (25 April 1977): 50.

—*Theodora Mills*

Advertisement

Robert M. McBride and Company
(New York: 1915-1949)
McBride, Winston and Company
(New York: 1910-1911)
McBride, Nast and Company
(New York: 1911-1915)

Robert M. McBride and Company was originally incorporated in 1910 as McBride, Winston and Company; but by August 1911 Condé Nast, the magazine publisher, had acquired a principal financial interest in the firm and the name was changed to McBride, Nast and Company. Nast left McBride in June 1915. The new Robert M. McBride and Company published *Travel* magazine; *Lippincott's* magazine, a long-established, high-quality monthly, was absorbed by *Travel*. In these early years McBride was located at 31 Union Square North in New York, but by 1920 the firm had moved to 7 West Sixteenth Street. In 1928 McBride acquired the Dodge Publishing Company. The firm moved to 4 West Sixteenth Street in 1931 and to 116 East Sixteenth in 1935.

Robert Medill McBride has been characterized as a man without much literary intuition; most of the credit for his company's important publications is given to his editors, among whom were Robert O. Ballou, Tom Davin, Coburn Gilman, Richard Glaenzer, Guy Holt, and Jerre Mangione. Although McBride's lists were dominated by travel books, a few of which he wrote himself, the company published important works of fiction. McBride occasionally accepted, because of an astute editor's persistence, the work of a young writer destined for literary fame. One notable example is John Steinbeck's first book, *Cup of Gold* (1929), which received almost no attention following its publication.

Gilman convinced McBride to publish *The Shadow Before* (1934) by William Rollins; *Cat-Calls* (1935) by Peggy Bacon, the writer and illustrator of children's books; *Adventures in Error* (1936) by

the Arctic explorer Vilhjalmur Stefánsson; Thomas Hart Benton's *An Artist in America* (1937); and Jules Romains's *Les Copains*, translated as *The Boys in the Back Room* (1937). Mangione, a junior McBride editor in the 1930s, persuaded McBride to buy *Mr. Aristotle* (1935), a book of short stories by the Italian novelist Ignazio Silone. Mangione later proposed that McBride purchase Silone's novel-in-progress, *Bread and Wine;* but McBride's insensitivity to Silone's financial needs resulted in Harper's publishing it, with great success.

Other McBride publications included Hilaire Belloc's *The Green Overcoat,* illustrated by G. K. Chesterton (1913); a series of Fu Manchu mystery novels written by A. S. Ward under the pseudonym Sax Rohmer; August Strindberg's *In Midsummer Days* (1913), *The Growth of a Soul* (1914), and *Fair Haven and Foul Strand* (1914); Arthur Machen's *The Terror* (1917); Sir Richard F. Burton's *Kasîdah of Hâjî Abdû el-Yezdî* (1921); Maxim Gorky's *Fragments from My Diary* (1924), *The Judge* (1924), and *Decadence* (1927); Erskine Caldwell's *Some American People* (1935); and Chesterton's *On Running after One's Hat* (1933). McBride published the first books of two American poets: Louise Bogan, whose career began with *Body of This Death* (1923); and Leonie Adams, whose *Those Not Elect* appeared in 1925.

By far the most important author in the history of McBride was James Branch Cabell. Cabell's long relationship with McBride began in 1915 when his novel *The Rivet in Grandfather's Neck,* rejected by a dozen other publishers, caught the attention of the twenty-three-year-old Holt. McBride published approximately one Cabell novel a year through the 1920s and 1930s, among them *Figures*

1928 advertisement

James Branch Cabell, the most important McBride author

1900 advertisement (New York Times)

of Earth (1921) and The Silver Stallion (1926). Cabell's most famous novel, Jurgen, caused the greatest legal problem in McBride's history. Published on 17 September 1919, Jurgen at first drew little attention beyond literary circles, although it was highly praised by the critics. But on 3 January 1920 the New York Times published a letter by Walter J. Kinsley, who pointed out that by substituting sexual for poetic terminology one could "see the extreme sensuality that runs through" Jurgen. Soon afterward the New York Society for the Suppression of Vice obtained a warrant to seize all copies of Jurgen as well as the plates. Although some booksellers profited by selling copies under the counter, Jurgen was out of print for about two years while the legal battle was pending. When the case went to court, its dismissal brought Cabell and McBride a burst of recognition.

The firm moved to 200 East Thirty-seventh Street in 1946. In an attempt to improve its financial situation, McBride sold sixty titles to Dodd, Mead in June 1948; but the following June the firm was sold to Outlet Books. McBride formed a new company, Medill McBride, and attempted to carry on by purchasing the stock of some of the old Robert M. McBride titles. McBride resigned from Medill McBride in May 1951; the firm's new officers included Harold M. Metcalf, president, and Edward I. Metcalf, head of advertising and promotion. In April 1952 the firm changed its name to Metcalf Associates, with Edward I. Metcalf as president; in June it was in bankruptcy. Metcalf Associates was transferred to Outlet Books in February 1953.

References:

"Ballou Joins Robert M. McBride," Publishers' Weekly, 128 (20 July 1935): 156;

Jerre Mangione, An Ethnic at Large (New York: Putnam's, 1978), pp. 141-173;

"Publishing Hot off the Griddle," Publishers' Weekly, 136 (18 November 1939): 1911-1912.

—Chris M. Anson

McClure, Phillips and Company
(New York: 1900-1907)
The McClure Company
(New York: 1907-1908)

Samuel Sidney McClure was born in Indiana in 1857. He began his career in publishing in 1882 as editor of the Wheelman, the house organ of a Boston bicycle factory. In 1893 he founded The S. S. McClure Company, publisher of McClure's Magazine. In 1897 he went into partnership with Frank N. Doubleday to form the Doubleday and McClure Company. When Doubleday and McClure was dissolved at the end of 1899, Doubleday joined with L. C. Page to form Doubleday, Page and Company, while McClure founded McClure, Phillips and Company with John S. Phillips at 141-155 East Twenty-fifth Street in New York.

Although McClure lost several major authors to Doubleday, he retained Booth Tarkington, whose Monsieur Beaucaire appeared on McClure, Phillips's first list in 1900 along with Gertrude Brownell's April Sowing, Mary Crowinshield's The Archbishop and the Lady, Anna Katharine Green Rohlfs's The Circular Study, Elmore Elliott Peake's The Darlingtons, Norman Duncan's The Soul of the Street, and Arthur Conan Doyle's The Great Boer War. Doyle's Songs of Action had been published by Doubleday and McClure in 1898; McClure, Phillips went on to publish his The Return of Sherlock Holmes (1905) and Sir Nigel (1906).

Samuel Sidney McClure (left) and John S. Phillips

(Left to right) Ivan Obolensky and David McDowell

In 1902 McClure, Phillips added Joel Chandler Harris to its list; his *Gabriel Tolliver* (1902) was followed by *Wally Wanderoon and His Story-telling Machine* (1903), *A Little Union Scout* (1904), and *Told by Uncle Remus* (1905). The firm published Gelett Burgess and Will Irwin's *The Reign of Queen Isyl* (1903) and *The Picaroons* (1904); Joseph Conrad's *Falk; Amy Foster; To-Morrow* (1903), *Romance* (1904), and *The Point of Honor* (1908); George Ade's *In Babel* (1903) and *In Pastures New* (1906); Sir Anthony Hope's *Double Harness* (1904) and *The Great Miss Driver* (1908); Hildegard Brooks's *Daughters of Desperation* (1904); O. Henry's *Cabbages and Kings* (1904); and Edgar Jepson's *The Admirable Tinker* (1904) and *Lady Noggs, Peeress* (1905).

After 1904 McClure, Phillips signed few new authors, although it did publish *The Troll Garden* (1905) by Willa Cather, who worked for the firm. The company had never been a discoverer of new writers, preferring instead to attract established ones.

In 1907 the firm became The McClure Company as a result of the departure of Phillips in May

1906 to publish the *American Magazine*. McClure remained president of The McClure Company at its new location, 44 East Twenty-third Street. J. W. Corrigan served as vice-president and general manager, Harold Roberts as treasurer, and O. W. Brady as secretary. McClure's real interest was in his magazine, still published by The S. S. McClure Company, and in November 1908 he sold his book publishing firm to Doubleday, Page. McClure died in 1949.

References:

Robert E. Christin, Jr., "'McClure's Magazine,' 1893-1903: A Study of Popular Culture," Ph.D. dissertation, Ohio State University, 1958;

Peter Lyon, *Success Story: The Life and Times of S. S. McClure* (New York: Scribners, 1963);

S. S. McClure, *My Autobiography* (New York: Stokes, 1914);

"Samuel Sidney McClure [obituary]," *New York Times*, 23 March 1949, p. 27.

*—Nandita Batra
David Dzwonkoski*

McDowell, Obolensky
(New York: 1957-1960)
Ivan Obolensky
(New York: 1960-1967)
Astor-Honor
(New York: 1967-1968)

Astor-Honor, Inc.

McDowell, Obolensky, Incorporated was established on 1 February 1957 at 219 East Sixty-first Street in New York. Ivan Obolensky was a published novelist; David McDowell, a Kenyon College professor and secretary of the *Kenyon Review*, had worked for New Directions and Random House. The firm published its first book on 15 August 1957—*The Velvet Horn* by Andrew Lytle, which was nominated for a National Book Award. It was followed by Lytle's *A Novel, A Novella and Four Stories* (1958). Also on the company's first list was James Agee's *A Death in the Family* (1957), which was awarded the Pulitzer Prize for fiction. The firm

later published *Agee on Film* in two volumes (1958, 1960). Other early titles were William Carlos Williams's *The Selected Letters* (1957), Robie Macauley's *The End of Pity* (1957), and Hugh Kenner's *Gnomon* (1958). Other books nominated for National Book Awards were the revised, expurgated edition of *The Ginger Man* (1958) by J. P. Donleavy, *The Wheel of Earth* (1958) by Helga Sandburg, and *Happy Families Are All Alike* (1959) by Peter Taylor. In 1959 the house inaugurated its award-winning juvenile line, Astor Books, under the direction of Fabio Coen. Works by Anne Fremantle, Leo Lionni, and Joseph Tusiani have appeared under this imprint.

ALREADY PUBLISHED

The Velvet Horn

"A novel which is beautiful and terrible and utterly his own. I suspect that it is a landmark in American fiction."—CAROLINE GORDON $3.95

by ANDREW LYTLE

The End of Pity AND OTHER STORIES

"Wonderfully combine the absolutely real detail with the imaginative insight ... lively and humanly warm."—PAUL ENGLE $3.50

by ROBIE MACAULEY

Yallah A PHOTOGRAPHIC JOURNEY

A stunning text-and-picture book of the hill and desert dwellers of Northwestern Africa. 8¾" x 11". $10.00

by PAUL BOWLES

The Selected Letters of William Carlos Williams

The candid correspondence of a distinguished American poet. Edited by JOHN C. THIRLWALL. $5.00. Limited signed edition $15.00

COMING IN NOVEMBER

This Was Andersonville

An eye-witness account of the notorious prison camp. With 24 rare contemporary photographs and 24 full page drawings. Over 400 pages. 8½" x 11".
Pre-publication price $10.00. After November 11 $12.50

Edited by ROY MEREDITH

A Death in the Family

The last and greatest novel by one of the most talented writers of our time.
November 15 $3.50

by JAMES AGEE

McDOWELL OBOLENSKY Inc.
219 East 61st Street, New York 21, N. Y.
In Canada: George J. McLeod, Ltd., Toronto, Ont.

Advertisement for first list

On 1 June 1960 McDowell resigned from the company, and on 5 July the firm's name was changed to Ivan Obolensky, Incorporated. The company moved the following year to 341 East Sixty-second Street. In 1962 Obolensky published a limited edition of Rockwell Kent's *Greenland Journal* with six illustrations. Joan Didion's first novel, *Run River*, was published in 1963. Other prominent Obolensky authors included Chinua Achebe, John Betjeman, Burt Blechman, Edward Gorey, Christopher Logue, and Sacheverell Sitwell.

In 1967 the company was reorganized as Astor-Honor, Incorporated and moved to 48 East Forty-third Street. It continued for another year to publish the Astor Books for children, as well as adult titles under the Obolensky imprint. The firm also offered a paperback line, Honor Books. Astor-Honor went out of business in 1968.

References:

"McDowell Leaving McDowell, Obolensky; Firm to Continue," *Publishers' Weekly*, 177 (23 May 1960): 33;

"McDowell, Obolensky, Inc., New Trade Publishing House," *Publishers' Weekly*, 171 (11 February 1957): 111-112.

—Vincent Prestianni

McGraw-Hill
(New York: 1964-   )
McGraw-Hill Publishing Company
(New York: 1917-1964)
McGraw-Hill Book Company
(New York: 1909-1917)

James H. McGraw, an upstate New York schoolteacher, founded the McGraw Publishing Company in New York City in 1899 to publish technical journals. John Alexander Hill, a Colorado engineer turned editor, founded the Hill Publishing Company in New York in 1902. In 1907 Hill started a book publishing department with Martin M. Foss as manager; about the same time, McGraw established a book division under Edward Caldwell. In July 1909 Foss and Caldwell persuaded their employers to merge the two divisions into the McGraw-Hill Book Company. Hill was the first president of the company, which had offices in the McGraw Publishing Company Building at 239 West Thirty-ninth Street. Following the death of Hill on 24 January 1916 at fifty-seven, McGraw-Hill Book Company and Hill Publishing Company merged early in 1917 to form the McGraw-Hill Publishing Company with McGraw as president. The new firm was one of the largest technical publishing houses in the world; its properties included many engineering journals. The McGraw-Hill Book Company continued as a wholly-owned subsidiary of the newly merged firm.

The first McGraw-Hill book list consisted of 200 titles, but within ten years it comprised over 1,000. The firm gained a position as a major publisher of textbooks for technical, vocational, and engineering schools. During World War I McGraw-Hill published twenty textbooks for the aviation and submarine branches of the armed forces. Books on munitions manufacture were published for the Committee on Industrial Preparedness and the Council of National Defense. Among these was the revised second edition of Fred H. Colvin and Frank A. Stanley's *American Machinists' Handbook and Dictionary of Shop Terms* (1914), which set records for technical book sales. During the 1920s the list grew to include chemistry, accounting, scientific agriculture, mathematics, business administration,

The McGraw-Hill Building on Forty-second Street in New York

social sciences, medicine, and education books. This record was largely due to the efforts of Foss, Caldwell, and James S. Thompson. In 1921 the firm moved to 370 Seventh Avenue.

On 30 November 1925 Caldwell succeeded McGraw as president of the McGraw-Hill Book Company. On 29 December 1926 Caldwell retired and was replaced by Foss. In 1927 the College Department was established as a separate publishing unit. On 29 October 1928 McGraw resigned as president of McGraw-Hill Publishing Company and was replaced by Malcolm Muir. McGraw continued as chairman of the board. Also in 1928 came the acquisition of the A. W. Shaw Company, publishers of business magazines and books. Shaw's book division was consolidated with the McGraw-Hill Book Company.

In 1930 a trade department, Whittlesey House, was established under Guy Holt and, later, George Stewart. This department was formed because Foss wanted to avoid confusion that might result from including general trade books in a scientific and technical list. One of Whittlesey House's first books, *The World's Economic Dilemma* by Ernest Minor Patterson, was critical of business's disregard for social needs; but Walter B. Pitkin's *Life Begins at Forty* (1932) was an optimistic book for the Depression era. A vocational education department was also established at this time.

In 1931 the McGraw-Hill Building, thirty-eight stories of blue-green terra-cotta and glass, was opened at 342 West Forty-second Street. Seventy-five percent of the building became the home of the McGraw-Hill Publishing Company and its associated companies. The McGraw-Hill Book Company occupied three floors of this space. McGraw retired as chairman of the board in 1935 and was replaced by James H. McGraw, Jr. In 1937 Foss succeeded Muir as president of McGraw-Hill Book Company. By then the scientific and technical book publishing output of McGraw-Hill had become the largest in the country. In the 1940s the McGraw-Hill Book Company, led first by Thompson as president from 1944 to 1946 and then by Curtis G. Benjamin, established technical education, health education, and text-film (audio-visual) departments.

In 1945 McGraw-Hill entered literary publishing. Its first offering, published under the Whittlesey House imprint, was Adria Locke Langley's best-selling novel *A Lion Is in the Streets*. Soon to follow were the Boswell papers, commencing in 1950 with *The London Journal, 1762-1763*. With literary publications now included in the regular list,

the Whittlesey House imprint, which had been restricted to children's books during the 1940s, was discontinued.

In 1948 McGraw-Hill acquired the Gregg Publishing Company of Chicago and New York; in 1952 it became the Gregg Publishing Division, the business education department of the McGraw-Hill Book Company. The Blakiston Company, a long-established publisher of medical books, was acquired from Doubleday in 1954 and was reorganized as the Blakiston Division; the Blakiston imprint was discontinued in 1967. The F. W. Dodge Corporation was acquired in 1961. The 1960s brought the publication of the World University Library, a series of original paperbacks.

Among McGraw-Hill's literary publications of the 1950s and 1960s were Kay Boyle's *The Smoking Mountain: Stories of Postwar Germany* (1951); Edison Marshall's *The Heart of the Hunter* (1956); Richard Condon's *The Manchurian Candidate* (1959), *Some Angry Angel* (1960), and *A Talent for Loving* (1961); Jack Kerouac's *Lonesome Traveler* (1960); Elizabeth Spencer's *The Light in the Piazza* (1960); and Nathaniel Benchley's *Catch a Falling Spy* (1963). The firm was the first to publish work by Jerome Charyn, whose first book, *Once upon a Droshky* (1964), was followed by *On the Darkening Green* (1965). A Conrad Aiken collection, *3 Novels*, was published in 1965, and Edward Abbey's *Desert Solitaire* came out in 1968.

On 1 July 1963 McGraw-Hill instituted a policy that all books intended for library, reference, and scholarly use were to be printed on permanent paper. The older books had been made of paper sized with rosin-alum, resulting in a high-acid paper that disintegrated over the years. The new paper would have a useful life of about 300 years.

On 1 January 1964 McGraw-Hill Publishing Company, Incorporated changed its name to McGraw-Hill, Incorporated. The McGraw-Hill Book Company and the F. W. Dodge Corporation, previously wholly-owned subsidiaries, became divisions of McGraw-Hill, Incorporated. These, with the Publications Division, were the three major divisions of the parent company. The 1960s also brought changes in the administration of McGraw-Hill Book Company. Benjamin became chairman of the board and was replaced as president by Edward E. Booher in 1960. In 1968 Booher succeeded Benjamin as chairman; Harold W. McGraw, Jr., the grandson of James H. McGraw, became the new president. At the end of the 1960s the American Heritage Publishing Company was acquired to strengthen McGraw's efforts in the humanities.

The company moved from the McGraw-Hill Building to a skyscraper in the Rockefeller Center complex in 1972. Two years later McGraw was elected president of McGraw-Hill, Incorporated and Alexander J. Burke, Jr., became the new president of McGraw-Hill Book Company. McGraw became chairman of the board in 1976, retaining the office of president.

In 1979 the American Express Company tried to buy McGraw-Hill. The offer of $830 million, or $34 a share, was $8 per share higher than the New York Stock Exchange price the day before the offer. Harold McGraw, feeling that a takeover would compromise the company's editorial independence, rejected the offer, and the two companies traded public charges and filed lawsuits against each other. American Express persisted with a bid of $40 a share, or close to $1 billion, but management decided against accepting the offer.

In July 1981 Jon Gillett resigned as general manager of McGraw-Hill's trade books division to become president of Franklin Watts, Incorporated. McGraw-Hill immediately fired four editors and reorganized the trade division into the General Book Division, with Thomas Dembrofsky as general manager. Four new editors were hired in November and an editorial board was created. The reorganization suggested that McGraw-Hill was planning to de-emphasize the publication of fiction.

Harold McGraw was replaced as president of the firm in 1981 by Joseph L. Dionne. McGraw remained chairman. In November 1984 Dionne reorganized the company into nineteen "market-focus" groups, such as management, education, health, and construction, instead of the previous three major divisions.

McGraw-Hill's domestic operations are located in New York, Boston, Washington, D. C., Atlanta, Dayton, Dallas, San Francisco, and Hightstown, New Jersey. International operations are located in Toronto, London, Mexico City, and Tokyo. The success of the McGraw-Hill empire lies in the company's willingness to explore nontraditional means for collection, selection, and distribution of information; for example, the firm pioneered in electronic data-based information systems. McGraw-Hill has always been able to gear its publications to meet needs evolving from contemporary trends and events. As the owner of twenty-nine magazines, four television stations, and divisions involved in all aspects of communication, McGraw-Hill has been a giant in the publishing industry since the beginning of the century. In 1984, in terms of revenues, McGraw-Hill was the second-largest American book publisher after Simon and Schuster. Its address is 1221 Avenue of the Americas, New York 10020.

References:

Roger Burlingame, *Endless Frontiers: The Story of McGraw-Hill* (New York: McGraw-Hill, 1959);

"Gillett Leaves McGraw-Hill for Watts; Four in Trade Division Fired," *Publishers Weekly*, 220 (31 July 1981): 10, 16-17;

"James H. McGraw [obituary]," *New York Times*, 22 February 1948, p. 48;

"Joseph L. Dionne Named President of McGraw-Hill," *Publishers Weekly*, 220 (14 August 1981): 10;

N. R. Kleinfeld, "Turning McGraw-Hill Upside Down," *New York Times*, 2 February 1986, pp. F1, F27;

"McGraw-Hill Hires Four, Names New Editorial Board," *Publishers Weekly*, 220 (20 November 1981): 15;

James H. McGraw, *Teacher of Business: The Publishing Philosophy of James H. McGraw* (Chicago: Advertising Publications, 1944);

This Is McGraw-Hill (New York: McGraw-Hill, 1962);

Twenty-fifth Anniversary, 1909-1934 (New York: McGraw-Hill, 1934).

—*Carole B. Michaels-Katz*
Martha A. Bartter

Julian Messner
(New York: 1933-1966)
Julian Messner Division of Simon and Schuster
(New York: 1966-   )

1940

1970

Julian Messner, Incorporated was founded in August 1933 when Julian and Kathryn Grossman Messner rented a suite of offices at 8 West Fortieth Street in New York. Messner had been associated for fifteen years with Boni and Liveright, Horace Liveright, and Liveright, Incorporated; Mrs. Messner had operated the Kathryn Karn Bookshop in New York while doing editorial work for Liveright. Although Grace Metalious's *Peyton Place* (1956), with sales of 300,000 in the trade edition, was Messner's single most successful title, the company's reputation stems from its popular animal stories for children and biographies for high school students.

Messner's first list in the fall of 1933 consisted of four titles, all romantic fiction: Frances Parkinson Keyes's *Senator Marlowe's Daughter*, Madeline Woods's *Scandal House*, Sylvia Thalberg's *Too Beautiful,* and *Prescription for Marriage* by Kathryn Messner (as John Anders) in her only effort as a novelist.

Keyes, whom Messner brought with him from Liveright, proved to be the firm's most successful author. Sales of *Dinner at Antoine's* (1948) reached 250,000 copies. Keyes contributed more than two dozen titles to Messner's lists, including nonfiction works that received increased sales as selections by the Catholic Book Club, before she moved to another publisher in 1962.

Messner began to publish children's books in 1935 with Charles A. Beard's *The Presidents in American History.* Ruth Carroll's *Chessie* (1936) was extremely popular; *Chessie and Her Kittens* (1937) was advertised in *Publishers' Weekly* as further adventures of "the famous kitten who has already received over 60,000 fan letters." The juveniles list was expanded greatly after Helen Hoke joined Messner as children's book editor in 1939; she had previously held the same position at Henry Holt and brought several of Holt's popular authors with

her. Hoke developed the Julian Messner Shelf of Biographies, a highly successful series for teenagers. Gertrude Blumenthal succeeded Hoke in 1946 and originated other popular series, such as Romances for Young Moderns and Everyday Adventure Stories.

Messner built a reputation for publishing books of a liberal nature. Edwin Seaver's *Between the Hammer and the Anvil,* considered one of the best of the proletarian Depression novels, appeared in 1937. Daphne Greenwood's *Apollo Sleeps* (1937) claimed to treat the subject of homosexuality "with delicacy and distinction, yet with frankness." Among nonfiction titles were Raymond Gram Swing's *Forerunners of American Fascism* (1935) and George Seldes's *Lords of the Press* (1939). In 1946 the Julian Messner Award for the best book promoting racial or religious tolerance in America was awarded to Shirley Graham for *There Once Was a Slave: The Heroic Story of Frederick Douglass.*

Other authors published by Messner were Beatrix Beck, Ivy Compton-Burnett, Peter Freuchen, Ben Hecht, Harnett Kane, Stephen Longstreet, Minnie Hite Moody, J. Middleton Murry—including his *Autobiography* (1936) and *Heroes of Thought* (1938)—and Dale Van Every.

Messner intentionally remained small throughout its history. In 1935 it purchased Alfred H. King, Incorporated and acquired about 100 titles at the bankruptcy sale of Long and Smith, which it maintained as a separate corporation. After Julian Messner's death in 1948, Mrs. Messner became the firm's president until her own death in 1964. A group of Messner's employees attempted to retain control of the company, but they lost out to Leon Shimkin, president of Pocket Books, who bought Messner three months after Mrs. Messner's death. After Shimkin purchased fifty percent of

Kathryn G. Messner and Julian Messner in 1943

Melville Minton (left) and Earle H. Balch in 1938 (photo by Underwood & Underwood)

Simon and Schuster in 1966, he reorganized the parent company into divisions, one of which was the Julian Messner Division. The biography and adventure series were continued as Archway Books. Messner's Gilbert Press, a subsidiary formed in 1954 to publish nonfiction titles, was transferred to Simon and Schuster's mail order department; all other adult books were transferred to Simon and Schuster's list. The Julian Messner Division publishes hardcover books for children in the upper elementary grades through high school. The firm's address is 1230 Avenue of the Americas, New York 10020.

References:

"Julian Messner, Inc., Reaches Its Tenth Anniversary," *Publishers' Weekly*, 143 (8 May 1943): 1808-1814;

"Obituary. Julian Messner," *Publishers' Weekly*, 153 (21 February 1948): 1082-1083;

"Obituary. Kathryn G. Messner," *Publishers' Weekly*, 186 (17 August 1964): 28;

"25th Birthday for Julian Messner, Inc.," *Publishers' Weekly*, 174 (1 December 1958): 22-24.

                                                                    —Susan K. Ahern

Minton, Balch and Company
(New York: 1924-1938)

In 1924 Melville Minton, a salesman at Charles Scribner's Sons, and Earle H. Balch, advertising manager at G. P. Putnam's Sons, pooled their resources to set up Minton, Balch and Company at 11 East Forty-fifth Street, New York. By 1926 Minton, Balch had moved to 2 West Forty-fifth Street and adopted the black swan as its logo.

Although Minton, Balch was best known as a publisher of nonfiction, textbooks, and illustrated children's editions, the firm developed a small literary list. On its first list was Bernard De Voto's *The Crooked Mile* (1924), followed by novels by Dornford Yates, William Almon Wolff, Richard Connell, and Katharine Brush. The firm's most noteworthy literary achievements were the publication of Allen Tate's second book of poems, *Mr. Pope and Other Poems* (1928), and of his *Three Poems: Ode to the Confederate Dead, Message from Abroad, The Cross* (1930). Authors of juvenile fiction included Dorothy Aldis, Lois Lenski, and Susan Smith. Alice Grant Rosman was one of the firm's most popular novelists, writing for Minton, Balch *Visitors to Hugo* (1929) and *Mother of the Bride* (1936).

Minton, Balch brought out a popular series of biographies that included J. P. Marquand's *Lord Timothy Dexter* (1925), Leon Trotsky's *Lenin* (1925), and Allen Tate's *Stonewall Jackson* (1928) and *Jefferson Davis* (1929). The firm also built up a line of presidential biographies.

In August 1930 Minton, Balch merged with Putnam. Minton became Putnam's vice-president, and in 1932 he was elected president and Balch vice-president. Minton and Balch achieved financial control of Putnam in 1934. The Minton, Balch imprint was retained for some Putnam books until 1938. Balch left the firm in 1946; he died in 1977. Minton died in 1955.

References:

"Earle H. Balch [obituary]," *New York Times*, 3 July 1977, p. 32;

"New Members of Putnam Firm," *Publishers' Weekly*, 118 (30 August 1930): 765;

"A New Publishing House," *Publishers' Weekly*, 105 (26 January 1924): 241;

"Obituary Notes [Melville Minton]," *Publishers' Weekly*, 168 (6 August 1955): 533-534.

                                                                    —Edward J. Hall

1928 advertisement

Modern Age Books

(New York: 1937-1942)

Modern Age Books made an innovative attempt to enter the mass market and furnish quality paperbound books at low prices. Founded by economist Richard S. Childs in 1937, the company operated at 155 East Forty-fourth Street until 1938, at 432 Fourth Avenue from 1938 to 1941, and finally at 245 Fifth Avenue. Modern Age planned to publish original works and reprints in printings of 50,000 copies and to sell them through bookstores, drugstores, and newsstands for twenty-five, thirty-five, and fifty cents. Samuel Craig, the founder of the Literary Guild, was general manager; Louis Birk, a former Macmillan salesman, was managing editor.

While most of Modern Age's titles dealt with social and economic topics and current events, such as *Hitler Is No Fool* (1939) by Karl Billinger and *Business as Usual* (1941) by I. F. Stone, the firm also published novels, detective stories, and books for children. Modern Age published two collections of short stories by William Saroyan—*Love, Here Is My Hat* (1938) and *Peace, It's Wonderful* (1939)—as well as a reprint of *The Daring Young Man on the Flying Trapeze* (1937). Another collection of short stories published by Modern Age was *Babies without Tails* (1937) by Walter Duranty. Among novels published by the company were *Old Hell* (1937) by Emmett Gowen, *Bread and Stone* (1941) by Alvah Bessie, and *The Mysterious Mickey Finn* (1939) by Elliot Paul. Modern Age reprints included titles by Agatha Christie, E. M. Forster, and John Steinbeck.

Though the firm had a large sales staff and made energetic promotion efforts, including contests, a book club, and exhibits, the mass market distribution policy was a financial failure. Modern Age was forced to raise prices and cut the number of copies in a single printing. It also began publishing titles in cloth under a new imprint, the Starling Press; Starling was discontinued in January 1940, along with the practice of publishing the same title in both cloth and paper. In 1941 the firm's list included forty-seven titles in cloth and seventy-three in paper, but by 1942 Modern Age had abandoned the paperback format. World War II caused an exodus of the Modern Age management to the armed forces or other government service. The firm discontinued business in October 1942. Its assets were sold to other publishers, chiefly Viking Press.

Reference:

"Modern Age to Issue First List," *Publishers' Weekly*, 132 (3 July 1937): 35-36.

—*Jane Thesing*

1938 advertisement

Richard S. Childs, founder of Modern Age Books (photo by Nation-Wide)

497,127 sales
in 1927
a gain of
107,532
over 1926

MODERN LIBRARY
150 BEST SELLERS

keeps up its phenomenal growth because its titles are chosen from the whole range of literature, are supported within the bookstore by fine shelving, rack and displays, and are nationally advertised all through the year.

Spring Additions

THE ROMANCE OF LEONARDO DA VINCI
By Dmitri Merejkowski   No. 138

THE SEA AND THE JUNGLE
By H. M. Tomlinson   No. 99

A PORTRAIT OF THE ARTIST AS A YOUNG MAN
By James Joyce   No. 145

TWELVE MEN
By Theodore Dreiser   No. 148

THE EMPEROR JONES and THE STRAW
By Eugene O'Neill   No. 146

TRISTRAM SHANDY
By Laurence Sterne   No. 147

NANA
By Emile Zola   No. 142

THE THREE MUSKETEERS
By Alexandre Dumas   No. 143

FOURTEEN GREAT DETECTIVE STORIES
Edited by Vincent Starrett   No. 144

The MODERN LIBRARY, Inc.
20 East 57th Street   New York City

TOWARDS OUR
MILLION-A-YEAR GOAL
1928

1928 advertisement

The Modern Library
(New York: 1925-   )
The Modern Library of the World's Best Books
(New York: 1917-1925)

1920s

The Modern Library of the World's Best Books was founded in 1917 by Albert Boni and Horace Liveright as part of their new publishing firm, Boni and Liveright. Its offices were originally located at 105 West Fortieth Street in New York. Boni had earlier been involved with his brother Charles in The Little Leather Library, a series of thirty pocket-sized volumes of classics and abridgements that sold for $2.98 per set. Due to financial pressures the Bonis had had to sell their interest in The Little Leather Library, but Albert Boni still believed that a good reprint series could be successful. He convinced Liveright, who had no previous publishing experience, to become his partner in such an enterprise.

The Modern Library was to consist of reprints of English and European classics, including contemporary works otherwise unavailable in the United States. Included on the first Modern Library list were Oscar Wilde's *The Picture of Dorian Gray*, Rudyard Kipling's *Soldiers Three*, Robert Louis Stevenson's *Treasure Island*, and Friedrich Nietzsche's *Thus Spake Zarathustra*, as well as works by Dostoevski, Ibsen, and Schopenhauer. Each book was priced at sixty cents and bound in flexible imitation leather. This combination of price and quality made The Modern Library an immediate success. Boni and Liveright quickly added six more titles to the series. Eventually the list was expanded to include reprints of the work of American authors, including Henry James's *Daisy Miller* (1918), Sherwood Anderson's *Winesburg, Ohio* (1919), Stephen Crane's *Men, Women, and Boats* (1921), and Walt Whitman's *Leaves of Grass* (1921). By 1921 The Modern Library had a list of 104 titles priced at ninety-five cents apiece. Boni and Liveright en-

gaged distinguished authors, among them G. K. Chesterton, H. L. Mencken, John Reed, and William Butler Yeats, to write introductions for works in the series.

With the success of The Modern Library, Boni and Liveright began putting out original publications as well. Many of these were financially unsuccessful, and by 1925 Liveright, who had bought out Boni's interest in Boni and Liveright and who had made unsuccessful investments in the theater and in the stock market, found himself heavily in debt. Thus, when Bennett Cerf, then employed at Boni and Liveright, offered to buy The Modern Library, Liveright agreed to sell.

Cerf and his partner Donald Klopfer purchased The Modern Library for $215,000 and set up their new firm, The Modern Library, Incorporated at 73 West Forty-fifth Street. Klopfer was in charge of production and office management, while Cerf handled the editorial side, as well as advertising, publicity, and promotion. They divided the selling between them. One of the first things Cerf did was to weed out some of the less successful titles in the series. The partners then redesigned the books, abandoning the imitation leather in favor of sturdier, flexible bindings covered with balloon cloth. They added the logo of a girl carrying a torch, a creation of the German designer Lucien Bernhardt, and commissioned Rockwell Kent to design new endpapers.

Klopfer and Cerf also began to expand The Modern Library list. The first title they added was *Jungle Pearl* by William Beebe, followed by more enduring works such as Thomas Mann's *The Magic Mountain* and Willa Cather's *Death Comes for the Archbishop*. From 1925 to 1927 Cerf and Klopfer

THE MODERN LIBRARY
A DESCRIPTIVE CATALOGUE

*T*HE *MODERN LIBRARY* is a collection of the most significant, interesting, and thought provoking books in modern literature, hand bound, fully limp, and designed to sell at ninety-five cents a copy. The judicious selection of one new title a month has resulted, after eight years of strict adherence to a definite policy, in the notable list described in this catalogue. Most of the books have been written in the past thirty years, although there are also included a few works of earlier writers whose thought and spirit are so essentially modern, that the publishers feel they are properly embraced in the scope and aim of the series

THE MODERN LIBRARY · INC.
NEW YORK

Cover of first catalogue issued after the purchase of The Modern Library by Bennett Cerf and Donald Klopfer in 1925

A 1918 title page from Boni and Liveright's Modern Library

Title page redesigned after Cerf and Klopfer bought The Modern Library. The logo was designed by Lucien Bernhardt.

worked exclusively with The Modern Library series. In 1927, as they began to diversify and expand, they changed the name of their firm to Random House, Incorporated. The Modern Library became an imprint of Random House.

In 1931 longer works, known as Modern Library Giants and priced at a dollar, were added to the list. In 1939 page size was increased and the flexible bindings were replaced by stiff boards covered with smooth linen. A Modern Library paperback line was added in 1955.

Random House was acquired by the Radio Corporation of America in 1966; Cerf moved from president to chairman of the board. The following year, the Modern Library format was modernized with graphics by S. Neil Fujita. Cerf died in 1971. In 1980 RCA sold Random House, including The Modern Library, to the Newhouse publishing organization.

More than 600 titles have been published in The Modern Library, as many as 450 having been in print at one time. As of 1980, in spite of competition from paperback publishers, there were 211 titles in The Modern Library's list. Klopfer is chairman of the board of Random House; Jason Epstein is vice-president in charge of The Modern Library. The firm's address is 201 East Fiftieth Street, New York 10022.

References:

Bennett Cerf, *At Random: The Reminiscences of Bennett Cerf* (New York: Random House, 1977);

Walker Gilmer, *Horace Liveright: Publisher of the Twenties* (New York: Lewis, 1970).

—Timothy D. Murray

Moffat, Yard and Company
(New York: 1905-1924)

In 1905 William David Moffat and his brother-in-law Robert Sterling Yard founded the publishing house Moffat, Yard and Company, with offices at 289 Fourth Avenue in New York. The firm's president, Moffat, a Princeton graduate, had worked for twenty years for Charles Scribner's Sons, where he served on the staffs of the *Book Buyer* and *Scribner's Magazine*, managed the education department, and finally became business manager. Yard, also a Princeton graduate, had been a reporter and Sunday editor of the *New York Herald*. He had also worked for the publisher R. H. Russell for two years and for four years with Scribner, where he was head of book advertising and subsequently editor of the *Lamp*. While with Moffat, Yard as editor in chief, Yard contributed articles on publishing to the *Saturday Evening Post* which were collected into a book, *The Publisher* (1913).

Moffat, Yard's first offering was *Drawings* (1905) by the illustrator Howard Chandler Christy; other Christy books included *The American Girl* (1906), *Our Girls* (1907), the *Christy Book of Drawings* (1908), and *Songs of Sentiment* (1910). *Port Arthur* by Richard Barry also appeared in 1905; early fiction included Edward Peple's *Semiramis*, William Frederick Dix's *The Lost Princess*, Constance Smedley's *Conflict*, George S. Viereck's *The House of the Vam-*

pire, and Richard Le Gallienne's *Little Dinners with the Sphinx*, all in 1907, followed by Frederick Palmer's *The Big Fellow* in 1908.

In January 1908 the house acquired American rights to the *Burlington Magazine*, a prestigious British art monthly. The firm published two popular series of children's books: Our American Holidays, edited by Robert Schauffler, and the Mother Lets Us books, edited by Constance Johnson. The firm's strong juvenile list included an edition of Frances Hodgson Burnett's *The Good Wolf* (1908) and her *Barty Crusoe and His Man Saturday*, *The Children's Book*, and *The Land of the Blue Flower*, all in 1909.

Moffat, Yard commissioned Reginald Wright Kauffman to write *The House of Bondage* (1910), a fictional account of white slavery in New York City, during a grand jury investigation of the problem. As Kauffman finished a chapter the text was checked against the current findings of the grand jury to ensure accuracy and authenticity.

Between 1908 and 1920 the firm published ten books by William Winter, including *Other Days* (1908), the "author's edition" of *The Poems of William Winter* (1909), *The Life of David Belasco* (1918), and the multivolume *Shakespeare on the Stage* (1911-1916). Moffat, Yard published Elwood Worcester's *Religion and Medicine* (1908), *The Christian Religion*

1908 advertisement (New York Times)

Lawrence Hughes, president of William Morrow and Company

as a Healing Power (1909), and *The Issues of Life* (1915). Psychology, psychotherapy, and social work were represented on the house's list. *Social Service and the Art of Healing* by Richard C. Cabot was first published in 1909 and reprinted several times. The firm published Sigmund Freud's *Leonardo da Vinci: A Psychosexual Study of an Infantile Reminiscence* (1916), *Delusion and Dream* (1917), and *Totem and Taboo* (1918). Carl Jung's *Analytical Psychology* (1916), *Psychology of the Unconscious* (1916), and *Collected Papers on Analytical Psychology* (1916) appeared under the Moffat, Yard imprint. William James's *The Energies of Man* was published by the firm in 1908 and released in a new edition in 1913.

The Modern American Writers series made its debut in 1918 with Grant Overton's *The Women Who Make Our Novels* and Howard W. Cook's *Our Poets of Today*. It continued in 1919 with George Gordon's *The Men Who Make Our Novels* and in 1920 with Blanche C. Williams's *Our Short Story Writers*.

In the earliest days of the motion picture industry Moffat, Yard developed mechanisms to make it easier for authors to deal with filmmakers.

In 1914 a department was established under the direction of Anna Archibald to market plays, motion picture synopses, and dramatizations of novels, and to act as liaison between authors and motion picture companies.

Yard left the firm in 1911 to devote himself to environmental causes. Thomas R. Smith managed the firm from 1911 until 1914. Moffat left the company in 1922 to become editor of the *Mentor*. Howard C. Cook was editorial manager and John H. Apeler was business manager when Moffat, Yard was acquired by Dodd, Mead in 1924. Yard died in 1945; Moffat died in 1946.

References:
"Robert Sterling Yard [obituary]," *New York Times*, 19 May 1945, p. 19;
"William David Moffat [obituary]," *New York Times*, 1 October 1946, p. 23;
Robert Sterling Yard, *The Publisher* (Boston & New York: Houghton Mifflin, 1913).

—Nancy Hill Evans

William Morrow and Company
(New York: 1926-   )

William Morrow and Company was founded on 1 January 1926 at 303 Fifth Avenue in New York by William Morrow, who had been with Frederick A. Stokes for nineteen years. The firm's first list was published in September 1926 and was headed by Honoré Willsie Morrow's *On to Oregon!*, a children's book by Morrow's wife. The following month Morrow published Rupert Hughes's controversial *George Washington: The Human Being and the Hero*. This biography, one of the first to take a realistic look at Washington, was publicly burned in Chicago but nevertheless sold well and prompted other attempts to debunk formerly sacrosanct figures. Other early Morrow titles were Honoré Morrow's trilogy about Abraham Lincoln, *Forever Free* (1927), *With Malice toward None* (1928), and *The Last*

Full Measure (1930); Thomas C. Hinkle's *Tawny* (1927), a popular juvenile book; Margaret Mead's *Coming of Age in Samoa* (1928); James Gould Cozzens's *Cock Pit* (1928); Frank Kent's *Political Behavior* (1928); René Lacoste's *Lacoste on Tennis* (1928); Norah James's *Sleeveless Errand* (1929); and Charles Yale Harrison's *Generals Die in Bed* (1930).

Morrow died in 1931 at fifty-eight and was praised by the *New York Times* as a "progressive" publisher. Thayer Hobson, who had come to the firm from Dodd, Mead in 1927, became president. The firm was notable at this time for the relative youth of its executives and for the active role that women, such as editorial director Frances Phillips and treasurer Eva Colby, played in its development. Morrow had established a solid list and managed

Thayer Hobson, president of William Morrow and Company from 1931 to 1958

William Morrow

to maintain its quality during the Depression. Nevil Shute's *Lonely Road* (1932) was followed by his *Kindling* (1938) and *Ordeal* (1939); later, Morrow published his *The Chequer Board* (1947), *No Highway* (1948), *The Legacy* (1950), and *On the Beach* (1957). James Hilton's *And Now Good-Bye* was published in 1932, with Edgar Mowrer's provocative *Germany Puts Back the Clock* and Isabel Paterson's novel *Never Ask the End* following in 1933. Perry Mason was introduced in 1933 in Erle Stanley Gardner's *The Case of the Velvet Claws*. Hilton's *Lost Horizon* was republished in 1934 with great success. Enid Bagnold's *"National Velvet"* and *A Diary without Dates* appeared the following year. William Morrow and Company published 465 books in its first decade.

In late 1946 Morrow agreed with Swallow Press in Denver to publish belles lettres under a joint imprint. *Anchor in the Sea* (1947), a collection of psychological fiction edited by Alan Swallow, was the first book. The arrangement was discontinued twenty titles later in 1951. Between 1946 and 1952 Morrow bought Jefferson House, Women's Press, William Sloane Associates, M. S. Mill, and M. Barrows. In 1958 Hobson became chairman of the board and was succeeded as president by D. M. Stevenson. The following year, Hobson sold his stock in the company to a group headed by John T. Lawrence, who then became president. In 1961 Morrow, Dodd, Mead, and Thomas Y. Crowell launched a quality paperback line for college students, Apollo Editions; later, the Dial Press joined in the venture.

Lawrence Hughes became president in 1965. Two years later Morrow acquired Reynal and Company, and in 1967 became a wholly-owned subsidiary of the Chicago textbook publisher Scott, Foresman and Company, with Hughes retaining his position. Lothrop, Lee and Shepard, publishers of juveniles, was already a subsidiary of Scott, Foresman when Morrow was acquired; the two subsidiaries worked closely together, strengthening Morrow's output of juveniles. Late in 1969 Morrow, Lothrop, Lee and Shepard, and Fielding Publications, the travel guidebook publisher distributed by Morrow, all moved to 105 Madison Avenue. In 1974 Greenwillow Books, another juvenile division, was formed.

During the 1960s Morrow published Morris L. West's *The Shoes of the Fisherman* (1963) and *The Tower of Babel* (1968), as well as the first published plays of Imamu Amiri Baraka (LeRoi Jones), *Dutchman and The Slave* (1964). In the 1970s Morrow helped the poet Nikki Giovanni gain her first wide exposure with *Black Feeling, Black Talk, Black Judgement* (1970). The firm also published *The New Yorker Book of Poems* (1974) and Pablo Neruda's *Song of Protest* (1976). Robert Pirsig's *Zen and the Art of Motorcycle Maintenance: An Inquiry into Values* (1974) and Jean-Paul Sartre's *Between Existentialism and Marxism* (1976) were published under the Morrow Paperback Editions imprint. Morrow has also published a substantial list of juveniles under the Morrow Junior Books imprint, including Beverly Cleary's books since 1951. In 1981 Scott, Foresman—by then known as SFN Companies—sold Morrow to the Hearst Corporation for $25.25 million.

References:

"First Decade of William Morrow & Co.," *Publishers' Weekly*, 130 (12 December 1936): 2294-2295;

"Lawrence Hughes, President of William Morrow, on His Company's 50-Year Past, Its Present and Future," *Publishers Weekly*, 209 (12 January 1976): 32-35;

Madalynne Reuter, "Hearst Agrees to Acquire Morrow for $25,250,000," *Publishers Weekly*, 219 (27 February 1981): 68, 70;

"The Story of William Morrow and Company, Inc.," *Book Production Magazine*, 80 (December 1964): 22-25;

"William Morrow [obituary]," *Publishers' Weekly*, 120 (14 November 1931): 2229-2230.

—*Christopher Camuto*

The New American Library
(New York: 1965-)
The New American Library of World Literature
(New York: 1948-1965)

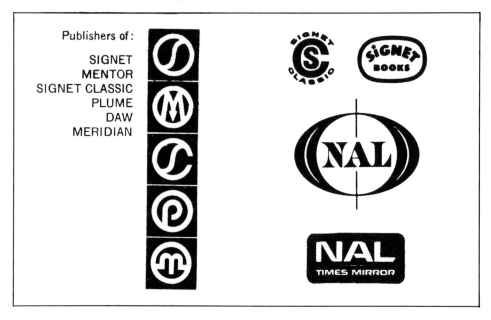

The New American Library of World Literature was founded on 25 February 1948 at 501 Madison Avenue in New York by Kurt Enoch and Victor Weybright. Enoch had been a publisher in Germany, where he was a founder of Albatross Books, a line of inexpensive paperbacks which was later combined with Tauchnitz, the English-language reprint series published in Germany. A refugee from the Nazis, Enoch came to the United States in 1942 as head of production for the American branch of the English Penguin Books. Weybright, an author and editor, had held a diplomatic post in England during World War II, after which he joined Enoch at the American Penguin branch, with responsibility for editorial matters. In 1948, due to problems brought about by British trade restrictions, competition between British and American Penguins on the world market, and policy disputes with the founder of the English Penguin, Allen Lane, Enoch, and Weybright formed The New American Library of World Literature (NAL) to take over the assets of the American Penguin branch. Enoch was president of the new firm; Weybright was chairman of the board and editor in chief.

Enoch and Weybright believed that readers would pay slightly more for fiction and nonfiction of better quality than was usually found in paperback books. At a time when a typical paperback sold for twenty-five cents, NAL books were priced at thirty-five cents, and occasionally higher. Enoch and Weybright chose the Signet imprint to designate contemporary fiction and the Mentor imprint for classics and nonfiction. These imprints paralleled the Penguin and Pelican lines, respectively, of Penguin Books; and for a while in 1948 NAL titles carried a joint Penguin-Signet or Pelican-Mentor imprint. From 1948 until 1955 NAL books were distributed by Fawcett Publications.

One of the first Signet successes was Erskine Caldwell's *God's Little Acre*, which Enoch and Weybright had reprinted in 1946 while still at Penguin. They carried the title with them to NAL; by 1973 it had sold over nine million copies. Other bestselling Signet reprints have included Mickey Spillane's *I, the Jury* (1948), Ayn Rand's *The Fountainhead* (1952) and *Atlas Shrugged* (1959), Mac Hyman's *No Time for Sergeants* (1956), George Orwell's *Animal Farm* (1959), and Ian Fleming's *Goldfinger* (1960) and *Thunderball* (1962). Mentor books include *America in Perspective* (1948), edited by Henry Steele Commager; Rachel Carson's *The Sea around Us* (1954); and Bertrand Russell's *Human Society in Ethics and Politics* (1962). *The Iliad, The Odyssey,* and

1954 advertisement

Cover for 1953 volume. The New American Library paid a record $100,000 for paperback rights to the work.

Cover for 1953 paperback

Cover for 1951 paperback

Great Dialogues of Plato, all translated by W. H. D. Rouse, were published in 1956; *Dante's Inferno,* translated by John Ciardi, was published in 1962. Over the years, other lines were added, including Signet classics for literature after the Renaissance; Plume for trade paperbacks appealing to the college market; and NAL BOOKS, a hardcover line.

Besides being one of America's foremost modern reprinters of literary works, The New American Library has also been the first publisher of works by recent authors. Sometimes these first publications took the form of paperback originals: for example, Henry Miller's *A Devil in Paradise* appeared first in 1956 as a Signet paperback. Norman Mailer has had several paperback originals published by The New American Library, often under the Signet imprint. These include *Miami and the Siege of Chicago* and *The Armies of the Night,* both published in 1968 in paperback editions which preceded hardcover publication, also by The New American Library. Another Mailer NAL paperback original is *Maidstone* (1971). Mostly as paperback originals, The New American Library has published modern science fiction. Robert Heinlein's *The Day after Tomorrow* appeared in 1951. Beginning with *The Horn of Time* in 1968, the firm published six of Poul Anderson's novels, including *Beyond the Beyond* (1969) and *The People of the Wind* (1973). Roger Zelazny's *Today We Choose Faces* (1973) and *Bridge of Ashes* (1976) were also published by NAL.

In hardcover editions The New American Library has often been the first publisher of works of modern literature. Two important contemporary novelists had their first books published by the firm: John Gardner's *The Resurrection* and William Gass's *Omensetter's Luck* both appeared in 1966 and were among the firm's first hardcover publications. They were followed by Wright Morris's *In Orbit* (1967) and Malcolm Lowry's *Dark as the Grave Wherein My Friend Is Laid* (1968), as well as works by Caldwell and by Terry Southern.

Other authors whose works have been published by NAL, either as reprints or as originals, include James Baldwin, Pearl S. Buck, Truman Capote, E. L. Doctorow, James T. Farrell, William Faulkner, E. M. Forster, John Fowles, James Joyce, D. H. Lawrence, Sinclair Lewis, John O'Hara, J. D. Salinger, Georges Simenon, Irving Stone, William Styron, Irving Wallace, and Herman Wouk.

In 1952 NAL established *New World Writing,* a "little magazine" in paperback book form. The first number included work by Christopher Ish-

erwood, Flannery O'Connor, Tennessee Williams, Gore Vidal, and Wright Morris. In 1959 *New World Writing* was taken over by Lippincott. In September 1967 NAL began a somewhat similar publication, *New American Review;* this publication was sold in 1970 to Simon and Schuster, who in turn sold it in 1972 to Bantam Books, where it was retitled *American Review* and published until 1977.

In 1957 NAL bought Lion Books; unpublished works under contract to Lion were brought out under the Signet imprint. In 1960 The Times Mirror Company, publisher of the *Los Angeles Times* and other newspapers, bought NAL. Four years later Enoch left the presidency of NAL to head the Times Mirror book division; he was succeeded as president of NAL by John P. R. Budlong. The firm moved in June 1965 to 1301 Avenue of the Americas; the same year, the name was shortened to The New American Library, Incorporated. Weybright departed in 1966 to become a partner in the publishing house of Weybright and Talley; Sidney B. Kramer became president of NAL. In May 1970 NAL established a second office at 120 Woodbine Street in Bergenfield, New Jersey, to handle sales, order processing, and accounting. Kramer was replaced in 1972 by Herbert K. Schnall. Also in 1972 NAL entered into a copublishing agreement with DAW Books, a line of science fiction and fantasy published by Donald A. Wollheim. When another Times Mirror subsidiary, World Publishing Company, folded in 1974, NAL took over its Meridian Books line of trade paperbacks. Robert G. Diforio became president of NAL in 1981.

In its first year of operation, the firm had had a total staff of 20; by 1981 NAL employed over 400 people, including at least 80 salesmen in the field. It has been estimated that from its founding to 1981 NAL published around 8,300 titles. Of these, about sixty-five percent are literary, including westerns, Gothics, romances, and the like. More serious literary works amount to about forty percent of the firm's total output.

In November 1983 NAL was purchased from Times Mirror by a group of investors which included Ira J. Hechler, Lester Pollack, Leon Levy, and Jack Nash, as well as some of NAL's senior management: Diforio, who by then was chairman and chief executive officer; Elaine Koster, publisher; and Marvin Brown, president and chief administrative officer. The purchase price was reportedly over $50 million. In February 1985 The New American Library bought E. P. Dutton, Incorporated, acquiring in the transaction Dial Books

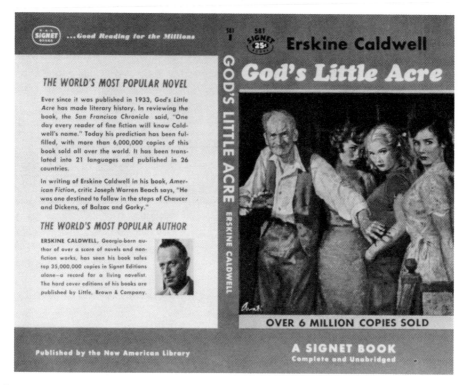

Cover for one of NAL's first best-sellers, which Kurt Enoch and Victor Weybright brought with them when they left Penguin Books to form their own company

Cover for 1959 reprint of Benedict's 1946 anthropological work

for Young Readers and Lodestar. NAL's editorial offices have been located at 1633 Broadway, New York 10019 since October 1979.

References:

Good Reading for the Millions: A Brief History of Signet and Mentor Imprints, 1948-1958 (New York, 1958);

"The Story of the New American Library of World Literature, Inc.," *Book Production Magazine,* 79 (June 1964): 46-49;

Victor Weybright, *The Making of a Publisher: A Life in the 20th Century Book Revolution* (New York: Reynal-Morrow, 1967).

—*Philip A. Metzger*

New Directions Publishing Corporation

(Cambridge, Massachusetts; Norfolk, Connecticut; Boston; New York: 1936-   )

The history of New Directions is inseparable from the biography of its founder and publisher, James Laughlin. For many years Laughlin has personally brought to light the work of unknown or underrated writers. He was an early publisher of Henry Miller, Dylan Thomas, Thomas Merton, and Tennessee Williams; once considered avant-garde, these authors are today in the mainstream of modern literature.

Laughlin has observed that "The name New Directions (which was suggested by Gorham Munson) is as often as not misleading in its implication of the experimental, the avant-garde and the offbeat. From the first there was an emphasis on these areas, . . . yet many of the most important books have been works written in traditional, even conventional forms, or have been translations of classic texts from other languages. . . ." Laughlin has been innovative not only in what he has published but in how he has published it. New Directions produces books in large-house volume while maintaining a small-press ethic in its use of fine printers, designers, and artists. The firm has also steadfastly supported its authors. New Directions has developed a reputation for not remaindering books and, often in spite of limited sales, has managed to keep the works of significant authors in print. Nearly twenty percent of its output consists of foreign works in translation.

Although New Directions put out its first book in 1936, the company's roots go back to 1934 when Laughlin, heir to the Jones and Laughlin Steel fortune and a sophomore on leave from Harvard, spent a year in Europe studying with Gertrude Stein and Ezra Pound. At Pound's suggestion, Laughlin returned to Cambridge and began publishing.

From the late 1930s through the early 1940s New Directions was in search of office space. Laughlin's first office was the trunk of his car. An aunt in Norfolk, Connecticut, offered the use of a stable, which was converted to offices and warehouse space. Five sites in the Boston area also served as offices, among them a house owned by Merrill Moore in South Boston, the apartment of Delmore and Gertrude Schwartz at 41 Bowdoin Street in Cambridge, and Albert Erskine's apartment at 1 Craigie Street, Cambridge. In 1942 New Directions moved to 67 West Forty-fourth Street in New York.

The first New Directions publication was a sixteen-page chapbook, *Pianos of Sympathy* (1936), a surrealist fantasy by Wayne Andrews under the pseudonym Montagu O'Reilly. It was followed by *New Directions in Prose and Poetry* (1936), the first of the New Directions "annuals." The 198-page anthology reprinted pieces that Laughlin had published as guest literary editor of Munson's *New*

Wayne Andrews' <u>Pianos of Sympathy</u> by "Montagu O'Reilly"
was the first New Directions "book," preceding the first volume
in the "New Directions in Prose and Poetry" anthology series
by some months.

The actual beginning of New Directions had been an occasional
literary section of a few pages in Gorham Munson's magazine
<u>New Democracy</u>. It was Gorham who thought up the name "New Directions"
for this section, and, with his blessing, it later was carried
over to the independent publishing venture. <u>New Democracy</u> was the
organ of the American wing of the Social Credit movement--to which
I had been exposed (along with so much else) by Pound when I got
leave of absence from Harvard in 1935 to attend the "Ezuversity"
in Rapallo.

Since <u>Pianos</u> there have been well on toward three hundred
books of all kinds and sizes under the New Directions imprint,
but this was the firstborn, and, reading it again today--twenty-five
years later--I find it still just as engaging in itself as it was
then, and as good an example of what has interested me above
everything in publishing--the work of the unique individual who
breaks away from the herd.

Part of a statement by James Laughlin describing the early years of New Directions (Manuscripts Department, Lilly Library)

James Laughlin, founder of New Directions, in 1940

Laughlin with Frances Steloff of the Gotham Book Mart

Democracy before the magazine went out of business, and included contributions by Stein, Robert Fitzgerald, Elizabeth Bishop, and Lorine Neidecker. Laughlin intended to publish another anthology each year, but intervals of as long as three years separated issues during World War II. Currently one issue of *New Directions* appears each year.

The first full-length New Directions book by a single author was William Carlos Williams's *White Mule* (1937). In 1938 the firm published twelve new titles, including *The Complete Collected Poems of William Carlos Williams, 1906-1938.* Another 1938 title was Delmore Schwartz's first book, *In Dreams Begin Responsibilities,* which contained a story, verse, and a play. New Directions published Miller's *The Cosmological Eye* in 1939; other Miller volumes were *Wisdom of the Heart* (1941), *Sunday after the War* (1944), and *The Air-Conditioned Nightmare* (1945). Pound's *Culture* (1938)—reprinted in 1952 under its intended title, *Guide to Kulchur* —was followed by his *Cantos LII-LXXI* (1940); *The Pisan Cantos* (1948); *Diptych, Rome-London* (1958); *A Lume Spento and Other Early Poems* (1965); and *Drafts & Fragments of Cantos CX-CXVII* (1969). A collection of Pound's letters to and essays about James Joyce, *Pound/Joyce,* appeared in 1967. Kenneth Patchen's second book, *First Will & Testament* (1939), began a long association between Patchen and New Directions.

Before the war, Laughlin made yearly trips to Europe in search of new writers and printers. These trips yielded manuscripts from George Orwell, André Breton, Denis de Rougemont, and Hugh MacDiarmid. Another discovery, Dylan Thomas, enjoyed a fruitful relationship with New Directions which began with *The World I Breathe* in 1939 and continued with fourteen more books (seven published posthumously after 1953), among them *Portrait of the Artist as a Young Dog* (1940), *Under Milk Wood* (1954), and *Adventures in the Skin Trade* (1955).

In 1939 New Directions reprinted William Carlos Williams's *In the American Grain;* this work inaugurated the New Classics series, reprints of out-of-print works, translations, and significant new collections of writings by New Directions authors. The series comprised about three dozen titles, among them works of prose and poetry by D. H. Lawrence, novels by Henry James and E. M. Forster, Stein's *Three Lives* (1941), F. Scott Fitzgerald's *The Great Gatsby* (1945), Djuna Barnes's *Nightwood* (1946), and Carson McCullers's *Reflections in a Golden Eye* (1950). The series also included translations of the selected poems of Garcia Lorca and Mallarmé, as well as Hermann Hesse's *Siddhartha*

(1951), a book that Miller had recommended. The Poet of the Month series, started in 1941 and changed to Poets of the Year in 1943, alternately presented the work of new poets, established contemporary poets, and classic writers of the past. Among the poets presented in the series were Malcolm Cowley, Robert Penn Warren, John Wheelwright, Yvor Winters, Josephine Miles, John Donne, and Robert Herrick; and in translation, Rimbaud, Rilke, Baudelaire, and Brecht. The pamphlets were sold cheaply, with the idea that subscription backing for the series would underwrite most of the cost of production. The series, which terminated in 1944, was remarkable for the quality of its editing and production. Each pamphlet was printed at a fine press; designers included Peter Beilenson, Carl Rollins, Victor Hammer, Ned Thompson, Josef Blumenthal, Ward Ritchie, and Margaret Evans.

The Makers of Modern Literature series, consisting of critical works devoted to the elucidation of the writings of modern authors, began with books by Harry Levin on Joyce (1941), Vladimir Nabokov on Nikolai Gogol (1944), and Yvor Winters on E. A. Robinson (1946). The Modern Readers series began in the late 1940s with reprints of works by Louis-Ferdinand Céline, William Faulkner, and Italo Svevo. An annual magazine, *Pharos,* was begun in 1945 but lasted only three years. Each issue was devoted to a single work, the first being Tennessee Williams's *Battle of Angels,* his first separately published play. This publication began a relationship between New Directions and the playwright that resulted in nearly two dozen books, including *A Streetcar Named Desire* (1947) and *Cat on a Hot Tin Roof* (1955).

New Directions has produced a steadily growing number of fine-press limited editions. The firm's first illustrated book, an edition of the King James version of Ecclesiastes with drawings by Emlen Etter, was designed by Beilenson in 1940. André Gide's *Theseus* and Thomas's *Twenty-Six Poems* were printed by the Officina Bodoni in Verona in 1949. Edward Dahlberg's *The Sorrows of Priapus* (1957), in a limited edition, featured forty-two drawings by Ben Shahn.

In 1941 New Directions published *The Real Life of Sebastian Knight,* the first work written in English by Nabokov. He also wrote translations, works of criticism, and a collection, *Nine Stories* (1947), for New Directions. *The Crack-Up,* a collection of short pieces and notebooks by F. Scott Fitzgerald edited by Edmund Wilson, was published in 1945 and revived interest in Fitzgerald's work.

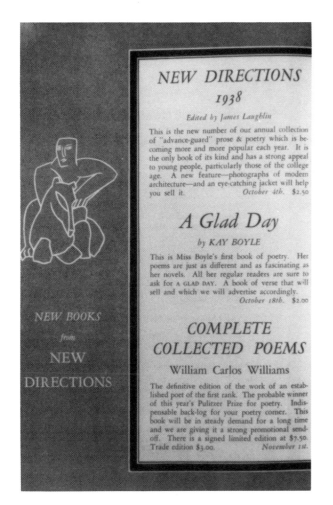

1938 advertisement

The firm moved to 500 Fifth Avenue in 1945. Two years later New Directions marked its tenth anniversary with the publication of *Spearhead: 10 Years of Experimental Writing in America*, a collection of writings selected from previous publications, with additions from important little magazines of the period. Also in the 1940s New Directions began publishing works by Thomas Merton and John Hawkes. Merton's *Thirty Poems* (1944) was followed by *Seeds of Contemplation* (1949), *Raids on the Unspeakable* (1966), and *Zen and the Birds of Appetite* (1968). The posthumous *The Asian Journals* (1973) was edited by Laughlin. Hawkes's first novel, *The Cannibal,* was published by New Directions in 1949; other Hawkes novels published by New Directions included *Second Skin* (1964), *The Blood Oranges* (1971), *Death, Sleep & the Traveler* (1974), and *Travesty* (1976).

The firm moved to 333 Sixth Avenue in 1949. That year Laughlin, in partnership with Richard T. Smyth, established a college textbook department specializing in history, the social sciences, and the humanities. In the next decade popular success came to writers whose works New Directions had published during its first fifteen years; in order to make its books more accessible to a wider public and to keep titles in print, the firm began a line of quality paperbacks in 1955. Over 450 titles have appeared in this format. Laughlin's travels to the Orient in the early 1950s resulted in the appearance of Asian authors, including Li Ch'ing-Chao and Yukio Mishima, on the New Directions list.

Laughlin joked that he had begun New Directions "to provide employment for writers," and he did so not only by publishing their works but by hiring them. Among the writers the firm employed were Schwartz, Patchen, Robert Lowry, Horace Gregory, Hayden Carruth, and Donald M. Allen. Foremost among the firm's designers was the graphic artist Alvin Lustig, whose award-winning designs had a strong influence on book art in the 1950s and 1960s.

During those decades a second generation of modern writers came into the New Directions fold. Kenneth Rexroth took on a role similar to Pound's and acted as an informal acquisitions editor. Rexroth had come to the firm in 1944 with his second book of poems, *The Phoenix and the Tortoise* (1944); in addition to publishing Rexroth's work, New Directions accepted his recommendations for publication of the work of a group of younger writers, most of them from the San Francisco area. The first was Lawrence Ferlinghetti, author of *A Coney Island of the Mind* (1958), one of the best-selling New

Directions titles. In 1960 the firm published a numbered and signed edition of Jack Kerouac's *Excerpts from Visions of Cody.* Since the publication of *With Eyes at the Back of Our Heads,* also in 1959, the poet Denise Levertov has been a regular at New Directions. The Beat poet Gregory Corso's *The Happy Birthday of Death* (1960) was followed by *Long Live Man* (1962) and *Elegiac Feelings American* (1970). In 1961 Lippincott took over distribution of New Directions books.

New Directions published Hayden Carruth's second book, *Journey to a Known Place* (1961), as well as his *For You* (1970) and *From Snow and Rock, from Chaos* (1973). Richard Eberhart won the Pulitzer Prize for his *Selected Poems 1930-1965* (1965). New Directions has reprinted several works by Robert Creeley, as well as his edition of Charles Olson's *Selected Writings* (1966). Michael McClure's *September Blackberries* appeared in 1974. In the mid-1970s three new novelists had work published by the firm: Frederick Busch, Coleman Dowell, and Robert Nichols. The firm entered the 1980s with a PEN/Faulkner Award-winning novel, Walter Abish's *How German It Is* (1980).

The strength of New Directions lies as much in its translations of foreign writing and its reprints of modern classics as in its publishing of contemporary American writers. Its list included the work of Edouard Dujardin, Jean Cocteau, Federico Garcia Lorca, Henri Michaux, Pablo Neruda, Octavio Paz, Alfred Jarry, and Christopher Isherwood. New Directions books are now distributed by W. W. Norton and Company.

Vice-president and managing director Griselda J. Ohannessian works with a staff of five at 80 Eighth Avenue, New York 10011.

References:

D. J. Beard, "New Directions Publishing Corporation, 1936-64," M. A. thesis, University of North Carolina, 1966;

Miriam Berkley, "The Way It Was: James Laughlin and New Directions," *Publishers Weekly,* 228 (22 November 1985): 24-29;

"New Directions Completes Its First Decade," *Publishers' Weekly,* 150 (24 August 1946): 803-807;

Richard Ziegfeld, "The Art of Publishing I," *Paris Review,* 25 (Summer 1984): 154-193; (Winter 1984): 112-151.

—D. W. Faulkner
John Harrison
David Dzwonkoski

Noonday Press
(New York: 1951-1960)

One of the earliest firms in the United States to specialize in higher-priced paperbacks, Noonday Press was founded at 77 Irving Place in New York in 1951 by Arthur Cohen and Cecil Hemley. The firm's first book was a volume of poems by Hemley, *Porphry's Journey* (1951). Subsequent titles included fiction and nonfiction. In 1955 Noonday began a new series of lower-priced reprints, Meridian Books. The following year Noonday and Meridian separated, with Hemley retaining the editorship of Noonday and Cohen assuming control of Meridian. In April 1960 Meridian became a subsidiary of World Publishing Company.

Noonday was purchased by Farrar, Straus and Cudahy in 1960. Noonday had developed a list of sixty paperback titles, including works by Jean-Paul Sartre, which Farrar, Straus and Cudahy continued for a time to publish under the Noonday imprint. Noonday also began a series of Reader's Guides, which includes John Unterecher's *A Reader's Guide to William Butler Yeats* (1959) and George Williamson's *A Reader's Guide to T. S. Eliot* (1966).

Noonday, a semiannual literary magazine edited by Hemley, was discontinued after the acquisition by Farrar, Straus and Cudahy, and the Noonday paperback imprint was gradually phased out. Hemley left soon after the sale to join the Ohio University Press; he died in 1966.

References:

"Cecil Hemley [obituary]," *Publishers' Weekly,* 189 (21 March 1966): 52;

"Noonday Press, Meridian Books Separate Their Operations," *Publishers' Weekly,* 169 (4 February 1956): 751.

—Carol Kuniholm

North Point Press
(Berkeley, California: 1980-   )

The goal of North Point Press of Berkeley, California, is to fill the gap between the small press and the mass market publisher. Literary titles—American and foreign, contemporary and classic, originals and reprints—are the firm's major products. Fine design and durability are emphasized in paper, printing, and binding; dust jackets appear on most paperback editions. All titles are marketed aggressively, and backlists are maintained indefinitely. Average print runs are 4,000 to 10,000 copies.

North Point grew out of a six-year reading binge. William D. Turnbull, a civil engineer who had made a fortune in real estate, decided to take time out to "read every book I had missed in my practical and pragmatic college training." He started with the Greeks and Romans and worked his way forward through 2,000 books to contemporary literature. Seeking new books to read, he took special note of independent publishers such as City Lights and New Directions, and thought about starting a firm of his own. He asked Jack Shoemaker, a bookseller who had done some work with Sand Dollar Books, to be his editor in chief. Turnbull chose the name North Point because "if you know which way north is you can't get lost."

North Point opened in January 1980. The firm's first list carried twelve titles, including *Saint Augustine's Pigeon* (1980) by Evan S. Connell and *The Geography of the Imagination* (1981) by Guy Davenport. By the end of 1984 the list had more than ninety titles, among them William Bronk's *Life Sup-*

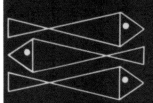
1953 advertisement

Back to Press

WEST WITH THE NIGHT *by Beryl Markham*

*First published in 1942 and long out-of-print, Beryl Markham's
eloquent memoir describes her life as a racehorse trainer and
pioneer aviator in Africa in the 20s and 30s.*

"Did you read Beryl Markham's book WEST WITH THE NIGHT? *I knew her
fairly well in Africa and never would have suspected that she would put
pen to paper except to write in her flyer's log book. As it is, she has written so
well, and marvelously well that I was completely ashamed of myself as a
writer . . . I wish you would get it and read it because it is really a bloody,
wonderful book."* —ERNEST HEMINGWAY *(in a letter to Maxwell Perkins)*

Paper, $12.50

NORTH POINT PRESS, 850 Talbot Avenue, Berkeley, CA 94706

1983 advertisement

*Storer Lunt, president of W. W. Norton and Company from
1951 to 1958; chairman of the board from 1958 to 1976*

William Warder Norton

ports: New and Collected Poems (1981); Samuel Hazo's novel *The Wanton Summer Air* (1982); Gilbert Sorrentino's novel *Blue Pastoral* (1983); and North Point's first best-seller, Connell's *Son of the Morning Star* (1984). This critically acclaimed account of George Custer had sold 150,000 hardcover copies by mid-1985.

North Point has also published new editions of works by Montaigne, Ovid, Petrarch, Goethe, the French novelist Jean Giono, and the Chinese poet Li He. In 1982 the firm received a Carey-Thomas Honor Citation from *Publishers Weekly* for its "enterprise in publishing new work and reviving works from the past in beautifully made editions." The firm's address is 850 Talbot Avenue, Berkeley, California 94706.

References:

"Carey-Thomas Award Winners Honored," *Publishers Weekly*, 222 (23 July 1982): 68;

Patricia Holt, "North Point Press Aims High," *Publishers Weekly*, 220 (6 November 1981): 50-53;

David Lehman, "In Praise of the Independent," *Newsweek,*102 (25 July 1983): 71-72;

Edwin McDowell, "Publishing: A Best Seller for Connell," *New York Times*, 28 December 1984, p. C32;

Herbert Mitgang, "Keeping Quality in Print," *New York Times Book Review*, 5 October 1980, p. 51;

"Publishing Rises in the West," *Time*, 125 (24 June 1985): 78-81.

—Margaret Becket

W. W. Norton and Company
(New York: 1925-   )
People's Institute Publishing Company
(New York: 1924-1925)

William Warder Norton founded the People's Institute Publishing Company in 1924 to publish the People's Institute lecture series that was then being given at the Cooper Union in New York. The firm was located at 70 Fifth Avenue. The first publication in the People's Institute Lecture-in-Print series was Everett Dean Martin's *Psychology* (1924) in twenty pamphlets collected in a package for subscribers. It was followed by H. A. Overstreet's *Influencing Human Behavior* (1925), Charles S. Myers's *Industrial Psychology* (1925), and John B. Watson's *Behaviorism* (1925).

Though Norton's venture was a success, he found that booksellers wanted the lectures to be published in one volume rather than as twenty or more pamphlets in a package. This situation, together with Norton's desire to expand the business, prompted him to reorganize the firm in 1925 as W. W. Norton and Company. He adopted the sea-

gull as the firm's logo and "Books That Live" as its motto. In 1927 Norton brought in Elling Aarmestad as his assistant; the following year he hired George Stevens as an associate. Another important early staff member was Storer Lunt, formerly of Doubleday, who became sales manager in 1930. The firm established its textbook division the same year.

Norton always retained his belief that publishing should educate as well as entertain; his goal was to help "modern men and women know more about themselves and their world, and to feel they understand something of what it is all about." One of the firm's initial ventures was its New Science series, edited by C. K. Ogden and including Bronislaw Malinowski's *Myth in Primitive Psychology* (1926), I. A. Richards's *Science and Poetry* (1926), and Charles Judson Herrick's *Fatalism or Freedom: A Biologist's Answer* (1926). Other early titles in-

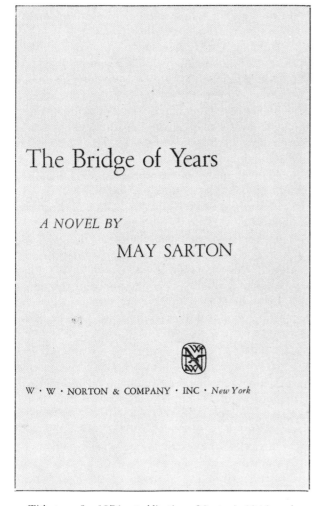

Title page for 1971 republication of Sarton's 1946 work

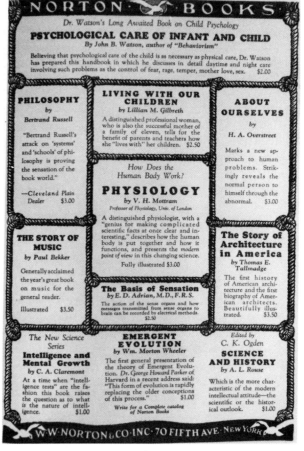

1928 advertisement

cluded Benjamin C. Gruenberg's *Modern Science and People's Health* (1926), Herbert Spencer Jennings's *The Biological Basis of Human Nature* (1930), Walter Cannon's *The Wisdom of the Body* (1932) and *Digestion and Health* (1936), Lancelot Hogben's *Mathematics for the Million* (1937), and Crane Brinton's *The Anatomy of Revolution* (1938).

A subject which especially interested Norton, and which became one of the firm's strengths, was psychology, particularly psychoanalysis. Norton followed Franz Alexander's *The Medical Value of Psychoanalysis* (1932) with Sigmund Freud's *New Introductory Lectures* (1933) and early work by Karen Horney, Otto Fenichel, and Wilhelm Stekel.

The firm did not neglect the humanities and the arts during its early years. Norton personally obtained the right to Bertrand Russell's *Philosophy* (1927), as well as several other Russell works. An important early title in political philosophy was José Ortega y Gasset's *Revolt of the Masses* (1932). One of Norton's most important discoveries among writers in the humanities was Edith Hamilton, whose *The Roman Way* (1932), *Three Greek Plays* (1937), and *The Greek Way* (1942) were among the firm's most popular titles. Due largely to the efforts of Norton's wife Mary, the Norton music/musicology list grew into one of the most prestigious in American publishing. Norton acquired the English-language rights to works by the German musicologist Paul Bekker, including *The Story of Music* (1927) and *The Changing Opera* (1935), and published books by the distinguished music authors Gustave Reese, Curt Sachs, Walter Piston, and Paul Henry Láng. Norton eventually hired Láng as the firm's music editor. The visual arts were represented by Lázló Moholy-Nagy's *The New Vision* (1938) and Malvina Hoffman's *Sculpture Inside and Out* (1939).

Literature did not occupy as prominent a place on the firm's early lists as it does today. Mary Norton was responsible for the firm's acquiring English-language rights to works by the German poet Rainer Maria Rilke, several of which she translated. No contemporary American poets appeared on Norton's early lists and the firm did not publish much fiction. The exceptions included mysteries by Phoebe Atwood Taylor, who also wrote under the pseudonym Alice Tilton; *Far Wandering Men* (1929), a book of short stories by John Russell; and the surprisingly popular *Ultima Thule* (1929) by the Australian novelist Mrs. J. G. Richardson, who wrote under the pseudonym Henry Handel Richardson. Literary criticism was represented with books by John Cowper Powys, Enid Starkie, Lionel

Trilling, John Mason Brown, Elizabeth Drew, and Malcolm Cowley, whose memoir *Exile's Return: A Narrative of Ideas* was published in 1934.

During World War II Norton chaired the Council on Books in Wartime and coined its slogan, "Books are weapons in the war of ideas." The firm contributed to the war effort with the Citizens series, books on war-related topics. Norton's most successful trade title during the war was Dr. Gordon Seagrave's *Burma Surgeon* (1943), which sold 140,000 copies in its first year.

Norton died on 7 November 1945; Lunt succeeded him as president. The firm moved to 101 Fifth Avenue in 1951. Lunt became chairman of the board in 1958 and was replaced as president by George Brockway, who became chairman in 1976 and was succeeded as president by Donald S. Lamm. Under Lunt and his successors W. W. Norton has grown steadily. The firm retains the educational goals of its founder and has continued to bring out successful titles in music, art, science, literature, and psychology. In psychology, Erik Erikson's *Childhood and Society* (1950) was one of the most important and influential books of its time.

Under the management of R. H. MacMurphey, Norton's college sales more than doubled during the 1950s; *The American Tradition in Literature* (1956) and *The Norton Anthology of English Literature* (1962) have become standard texts in college literature survey courses. Norton has also been successful with several reprint series which, while not part of the textbook division, are aimed primarily at college students. In 1955, the same year it moved to 55 Fifth Avenue, W. W. Norton launched its Seagull Editions of hardbound reprints from its backlist; three years later the firm initiated the Norton Library of paperback reprints of classic works, quality editions at prices that students can afford. The paperback Norton Critical Editions of classics, with eighty-seven titles in print by 1980, have become standard classroom texts.

The firm's trade division has constantly expanded; best-selling books have included William Lederer and Eugene Burdick's *The Ugly American* (1958), Lederer's *A Nation of Sheep* (1961), Betty Friedan's *The Feminine Mystique* (1963), Douglas Wallop's *The Year the Yankees Lost the Pennant* (1963), Joseph P. Lash's *Eleanor: The Years Alone* (1972), and Vincent Bugliosi's *Helter Skelter* (1974).

Perhaps the most significant development since World War II has been Norton's literary publishing. Prior to the war fiction, poetry, literary biography, and criticism were overshadowed by Norton's other publishing interests; since the war fiction, especially popular fiction, has flourished. Novelist Gerald Warner Brace had most of his later work published by Norton. Norton also obtained American publishing rights to works by the English novelists Anthony Burgess, whose *Enderby* Norton published in 1968, and Jean Rhys. Since the late 1950s the firm has built a strong list of books by American poets; perhaps the best known of these is May Sarton, almost all of whose output has been published by Norton. In 1965 Norton published *Plain Song,* a volume of poems, the first book by poet and novelist Jim Harrison. Bollingen Prize-winner A. R. Ammons has had his last five major books published by Norton, beginning with *Uplands* in 1970 and including *Collected Poems 1951-1971* (1972). Another important Norton poet is Adrienne Rich; the firm has published five of her books, including *Poems: Selected and New, 1950-1974* (1975). Other noteworthy poets with books published by Norton include Richard Hugo, Louis Zukofsky, Audre Lorde, Robert L. Peters, Christopher Middleton, Raymond Roseliep, Margaret Avison, Gilbert Sorrentino, Helen Wolfert,

John Ciardi, John Hollander, Gordon Parks, and Linda Pastan.

In 1974 Norton purchased the Liveright Publishing Company. Norton itself has resisted being taken over by larger firms and remains one of the few independent major American publishing houses. Since 1974 it has been located at 500 Fifth Avenue, New York 10110.

References:

George P. Brockway, "Warder Norton's Idea," *Bulletin of the American Library Association*, 51 (1957): 20-22;

"Norton's First Twenty-five Years," *Publishers' Weekly*, 156 (10 December 1949): 2373-2374;

"Norton's Tenth Anniversary," *Publishers' Weekly*, 125 (13 January 1934): 146-147;

"William Warder Norton [obituary]," *New York Times*, 9 November 1945, p. 19;

Howard P. Wilson, "Norton's Ingredients for Success," *Columbia Library Columns*, 18 (February 1969): 3-15.

—Timothy D. Murray

Outing Publishing Company
(New York: 1905-1918)

Outing Publishing Company was founded by James K. Reeve in 1905 after he assumed control of the popular *Outing Magazine.* The company's address was 35-37 West Thirty-first Street, New York.

Books published by Outing appealed to the public's appetite for stories of the American West, romance, and tales of the out-of-doors. Its list included books by some of the most popular adventure writers of the period, including Albert Bigelow Paine's *The Lucky Piece* (1906), Alfred Henry Lewis's *The Throwback* (1906), Ralph D. Paine's *The Praying Skipper* (1906), and Emerson Hough's *The Way of a Man* (1907). In 1907 Outing published Clarence Mulford's *Bar-20,* in which Hopalong Cassidy made his first appearance. This and several other Outing books were illustrated by N. C. Wyeth. An early Zane Grey novel, *The Last of the Plainsmen,*

with illustrations by Grey, appeared in 1908.

Heavy expenses and labor problems resulted in Outing's bankruptcy in April 1909. The firm was reorganized in October at 315 Fifth Avenue. It continued to publish the same type of books as before—for example, Charles A. Seltzer's *The Range Riders* (1911)—but new titles were fewer and emphasis fell upon publication of several magazines in addition to *Outing,* including *Yachting, Brains,* and two fiction monthlies, *Bohemian Magazine* and *Gray Goose.* In March 1918 Macmillan acquired Outing's book list.

References:

"MacMillan Takes Over Outing Publishing Company," *Publishers' Weekly,* 93 (30 March 1918): 1012;

"*Outing Magazine* Reorganized as Publishing Com-

1908 advertisement

pany," *Publishers' Weekly,* 76 (2 October 1909): 963;

"The Outing Publishing Company in Receivers'

Hands," *Publishers' Weekly,* 75 (17 April 1909): 1423.

—*Gary R. Treadway*

The Overlook Press
(Woodstock, New York; New York: 1971-   )

The Overlook Press was founded by Peter Mayer in 1971 in a converted apple shed in Woodstock, New York City. Later it established editorial offices at 625 Madison Avenue, then at 667 Madison Avenue, New York. Its sales, distribution, and billing are handled largely through Viking Penguin, although special sales are occasionally organized at Woodstock, where the firm has moved into larger quarters on the outskirts of town.

At first Mayer operated the press part time while continuing his work as publisher and editor in chief of Avon Books. He later persuaded his father, Alfred, a successful glove manufacturer, to run Overlook. Alfred Mayer became president in 1976 when his son left Avon to become president and publisher at Pocket Books. Since 1978 Peter Mayer has been chief of Penguin International in London, but he still exerts considerable influence on the Overlook Press.

Overlook specializes in hardcover books on art and design, but frequently publishes general nonfiction, fiction, and poetry. The first Overlook title was *Aufbau* (1972), an untranslated collection of articles from a German-language newspaper; the book was edited by Will Schaber. Overlook literary publications (in both original and reprint editions) have included Lawrence Durrell's *Pope Joan* (1972) and *Vega and Other Poems* (1973), Martin

Esslin's *The Theatre of the Absurd* (1973), Joseph Roth's *The Radetzky March* (1974) and *Flight without End* (1977), and Philip Larkin's *A Girl in Winter* (1976) and *Jill* (1976). A surprising success was achieved with Miyamoto Musashi's *A Book of Five Rings* (1974), a martial arts guide which had sold over 95,000 copies by 1981.

As its main source of income, Overlook has drawn on the talents of the artistic community in Woodstock to offer a wide range of illustrated books on art, handicrafts, industrial and graphic design, and carpentry, as well as encyclopedias and dictionaries of architecture and gastronomy. The first such book was Milton Glaser's *Graphic Design* (1973), which received wide acclaim and had sold 25,000 copies by 1981 despite its sixty-dollar price. Glaser also designed Overlook's winged elephant logo. The firm's current address is 12 West Twenty-first Street, New York 10010.

References:

Joann Davis, "The First 10 Years Are the Hardest," *Publishers Weekly,* 220 (30 October 1981): 46-47, 49;

"Overlook Press, New Academic Imprint," *Publishers Weekly,* 201 (14 February 1972): 47.

—*Xinmin Liu*

Padell Publishing Company
(New York: circa 1938-1981)

Padell Publishing Company was founded by Max Padell around 1938 in New York; for most of its publishing years the firm's offices were at 830 Broadway. During his lifetime Max Padell was involved in a variety of publishing and book-related activities. He was one of the founders in 1922 of Bookazine, a large New York wholesaler and distributor which is still in business. He also started the Padell Book and Magazine Company, under which imprint he published Guy de Maupassant's *Tales of French Love and Passion* (1943), John Dillon's *From Dance Hall to White Slavery* (n.d.) and H. M. Lytle's *The Tragedies of the White Slaves* (1945). He was the founder, as well, of the Key Publishing Company. Padell's publishing interests were eclectic. He published magazines, titillating fiction, and a variety of how-to and self-help books.

Padell was actively involved in literary publishing, too, and his main contribution to literature was publishing the work of the poet Kenneth Patchen. During the 1940s Padell published several Patchen titles in either original or reprint editions, including *Journal of Albion Moonlight* (1941); *They Keep Riding Down All the Time* (1947); *Pictures of Life and of Death* (1947); *A Letter to God,* published with Henry Miller's essay *Patchen; Man of Anger and of Light* (1947); *Sleepers Awake* (1946); *CCCLXXIV Poems* (1948); and *See You in the Morning* (1948).

After Max Padell's death, Padell Publishing Company continued under the direction of Padell's grandson, Avram C. Freedberg, with offices at 2115 Avenue K, Brooklyn, New York. The firm discontinued operations in 1981.

—Timothy D. Murray

Pantheon Books
(New York: 1942-   )

Kurt Wolff founded a successful publishing house, Kurt Wolff Verlag, in Leipzig in 1913; the firm published works by Franz Kafka, Franz Werfel, and Heinrich Mann. Wolff also founded an art publishing house, Pantheon Casa Editrice, in 1924. Fleeing Nazi Germany for the United States in 1941, Wolff brought with him a small amount of capital, with which he began his new publishing firm, Pantheon, in 1942. The firm was originally housed in his Washington Square apartment in New York. From there, Pantheon moved to an office at 41 Washington Square South. The original officers of Pantheon Books were Wolff, who served as editor and as vice-president; Kyrill Schabert, president and sales manager; and Wolff's wife, Helen, who handled editorial work and promotion. A year after the firm began, Wolff accepted a partner, Jacques Schiffrin, founder of Bibliothèque de la Pléiade in Paris.

From its inception, Pantheon Books was distinctive for its commitment to bringing European works to the American market. The firm's first book was Charles Péguy's *Basic Verities* (1943), translated by Ann and Julian Green. This was followed by Erich Kahler's *Man the Measure* (1943) and Hermann Broch's *The Death of Virgil* (1945). After Schiffrin's arrival, Pantheon published translations of works of some of the leading French authors with whom he had worked in France: André Gide, Joseph Kessel, and Jean Vercors. In the 1950s and 1960s Pantheon published more works by foreign authors, including *Doctor Zhivago* (1958) by Boris Pasternak, *The Leopard* (1960) by Giuseppe di Lampedusa, and *The Tin Drum* (1962) by Günter Grass. The firm also published several of the historical novels of the British writer Bryher, including *Gate to the Sea* (1958) and *Ruan* (1960).

In addition to providing translations of Eu-

1943 advertisement

1968 advertisement

ropean works, Pantheon also offered bilingual editions of poetry, among them Paul Claudel's *Coronal* (1943). Some of the firm's successes were American works, including Anne Morrow Lindbergh's *Gift from the Sea* (1955).

In 1943 Pantheon began to publish the Bollingen series, a line of scholarly books dealing with art, myth, comparative religion, psychology, and related subjects. Sponsored by the Mellon Foundation, the series was published by Pantheon until 1967 and continued by the Princeton University Press.

In May 1959 Kurt and Helen Wolff sold their stock in Pantheon and moved to Locarno, Switzerland. They maintained an association with the firm until 1961, when they assumed their own imprint at Harcourt, Brace; Kurt Wolff died in an auto accident in 1963, but Helen Wolff continues to direct the imprint at Harcourt Brace Jovanovich. Schabert left Pantheon in 1960 to join the American Book Publishers Council. In 1961 Pantheon became a division of Random House but remained editorially autonomous under the editorship of André Schiffrin, Jacques Schiffrin's son.

Since 1961 Pantheon has emphasized social and cultural analysis, characterized by books such as Estes Kefauver's examination of the welfare system, *In a Few Hands* (1965). Two series developed in the 1960s reflect this new social interest: Studies in Social History began with the publication of Edward Thompson's *The Making of the English Working Class* (1964), and the first title of the Anti-Textbooks series was Theodore Roszak's *The Dissenting Academy* (1968).

References:
"Kurt Wolff [obituary]," *New York Times*, 23 October 1963, p. 41;

Herbert Mitgang, "Profiles: Helen Wolff," *New Yorker* (2 August 1982): 41-73;

[Pantheon Books Announces Pictorial Record of Great Masterpieces of Art and Architecture Destroyed in World War II], *Publishers Weekly*, 149 (2 February 1946): 876;

"Pantheon Books Expands on First Anniversary," *Publishers' Weekly*, 145 (8 April 1944): 1449-1452;

Thomas Weyr, "Helen Wolff," *Publishers Weekly*, 203 (5 February 1973): 30-32.

—Carol Kuniholm

Paperback Library
(New York: 1961-1972)

PAPERBACK LIBRARY

Morris S. Latzen, president of the Sterling Group, Incorporated, and Hy Steirman, president and publisher of *Bluebook* magazine, founded the Paperback Library early in 1961 at 152 West Forty-second Street, New York. The firm brought out a line of paperbacks, both reprints and originals, in three editions: Bronze, at thirty-five cents; Silver, at fifty cents; and Gold, at seventy-five cents. Titles from the firm's first year were *Lady Blanche Farm* by Frances Parkinson Keyes, a Bronze reprint; and *Boarding House Blues* and *Side Street and Other Stories* by James T. Farrell and *The Inspiring Life and Thoughts of Billy Graham* by Glenn Daniels, Silver originals.

In December 1961 the firm moved to 260 Park Avenue South. It soon developed a strong line of science fiction and fantasy, including the first printing of Harlan Ellison's *Ellison Wonderland* (1962) and the first paperback edition of Clifford D. Simak's *Cosmic Engineers* (1964); L. Sprague de Camp's *The Tritonian Ring* (1968) and *The Glory That Was* (1971), both reprints; C. L. Moore's *Jirel of Joiry* (1969); and a reprint of Philip K. Dick's *A Maze of Death*. Paperback Library also published three of Lin Carter's Thongor books. The firm reprinted Abraham Merritt's fantasy *Dwellers in the Mirage* in 1962. That year also saw the republication of Irving Stone's *Adversary in the House* (Gold edition); Bill Mauldin's *Army* (Silver edition); Farrell's *Sound of a City* (Silver); and Paul Evan Lehman's *Texas Vengeance* (Bronze). From the first, the longest list was in the Silver price range. In 1963 Owen Wister's

The Virginian came out in a Gold sixty-cent edition; Philip Wylie and Edwin Balmer's *When Worlds Collide*, Gypsy Rose Lee's *The G-String Murders* and *Mother Finds a Body*, and Ernest Haycox's *Border Trumpet* and *Trouble Shooter* were published in Silver format; and Balzac's *The Girl with the Golden Eyes* came out as a Bronze edition. The firm also published serious works about sex, as well as books on the occult, Gothic and historical novels, westerns, and mysteries. Among Paperback Library's best-known books was *My Life with Jacqueline Kennedy* (1970) by Mary Barelli Gallagher, which sold over two million copies.

In 1969 Steirman, owner not only of Paperback Library but also of *Coronet* magazine and Coronet Books, a newly formed hardcover line, merged the three firms into Coronet Communications, Incorporated, at 315 Park Avenue South, which had been the address of Paperback Library since 1968. Warner Communications Company bought Paperback Library in 1972 and moved its offices to 75 Rockefeller Plaza on 27 July 1973. The firm became Warner Books in 1975.

—*Martha A. Bartter*

Parents' Magazine Press
(New York: 1962-   )

George J. Hecht was a civic-minded, innovative man whose achievements included the founding of the United Neighborhood Houses of New York, the Welfare Council of New York, and, with others, the Greater New York Fund, now the United Fund. He established the American Parents Committee, Incorporated, the only full-time professional organization in Washington working solely for legislation on behalf of children. The same interest in the public welfare motivated his establishment in 1926 of Parents' Magazine Enterprises at 52 Vanderbilt Avenue in New York. *Parents' Magazine*, devoted to advising parents on child rearing, was unique among periodicals at the time of its inception and is considered the forerunner of all such magazines.

In the late 1950s Parents' Magazine Enterprises began distributing books for children through its book clubs, which included the Read Aloud Book Club for Little Readers, the Beginning Readers Book Club, the Calling All Girls Book Club, and the American Boy Book Club. In 1962 Parents' Magazine Enterprises started Parents' Magazine Press, which eventually provided the majority of the books these clubs distributed. The first editor of Parents' Magazine Press was Harold Schwartz. The firm's first list consisted of twenty titles for the two-to-seven-year-old group. Although the firm emphasized the publication of quality hardcover picture books for children from two to twelve, its list was expanded under Schwartz's successors, among whom were Alvin Tresselt, Selma Lane, and Barbara Francis. These editors introduced nonfiction books for older read-

ers at the elementary and high school levels, cookbooks, books on child behavior and development, and Pippin Paperbacks, a line of quality picture books in softcover. Many of the firm's books became the subjects of filmstrips developed for educational use by Parents' Magazine Enterprises.

Parents' Magazine Press books are intended to make reading fun for children and thereby to encourage the development of reading skills. Many PMP books tell amusing stories using animal characters; Beatrice Schenk De Regniers's *Miss Suzy* (1964), illustrated by Arnold Lobel, and *How Joe the Bear and Sam the Mouse Got Together* (1965) are typical. PMP also developed the idea of basing stories on real-life situations and themes, such as that of a mother going back to work, as in *The Terrible Thing That Happened at Our House* (1975), or life on a farm, as in *Grandpa Had a Windmill, Grandma Had a Churn* (1977).

In 1978 Hecht sold Parents' Magazine Enterprises to Gruner and Jahr USA, Incorporated. In 1979 most of the press's backlist was sold to Four Winds Press, a division of Scholastic Magazines, Incorporated. Hecht died in 1980. Under the direction of children's book editor Christopher Medina, Parents' Magazine Press publishes ten to fifteen hardcover books a year for the Parents' Magazine Read Aloud Book Club. Parents' Magazine Press is now located at 685 Third Avenue, New York 10017.

References:
"George J. Hecht [obituary]," *Publishers Weekly*, 217 (9 May 1980): 17;

George J. Hecht, founder of Parents' Magazine Press　　　　　　　　　*William Farquhar Payson*

1928 advertisement

"Parents' Magazine Enters Children's Book Publishing," *Publishers' Weekly*, 182 (2 July 1962): 171-172;

"Scholastic Gets Parents' Magazine Press Backlist," *Publishers Weekly*, 216 (26 November 1979): 10;

Sybil Steinberg, "The Many Children of Parents' Magazine," *Publishers Weekly*, 210 (19 July 1976): 83-84.

—*Deborah G. Gorman*

Peter Pauper Press

(Larchmont, New York; Mt. Vernon, New York; New York; White Plains, New York: 1928-   )

The Peter Pauper Press was begun in the spring of 1928 in the basement of Peter Beilenson's home in Larchmont, New York, in order "to print books as beautifully as a craftsman might, and sell them as cheaply as only a pauper could." The firm is known for its high-quality printing, attractive bindings, and reasonable prices. Beilenson was born in 1905 and graduated from the College of the City of New York in 1925. He became fascinated with the art of fine printing and worked briefly for the William Edwin Rudge printing firm and the Village Press before beginning his own firm. The first book of the Peter Pauper Press was a limited edition of *With Petrarch* (1928), a translation by J. M. Synge of several of Petrarch's sonnets. This edition was chosen by the American Institute of Graphic Arts (AIGA) as one of the fifty best-designed books of 1928. Most of the firm's publications were reprints of classics, selected for their wide appeal. Beilenson's publication of several of John Donne's works in the early 1930s is thought to have been responsible for renewed interest in Donne.

In 1929 the imprint "At the Sign of the Blue-Behinded Ape" first appeared. Beilenson explained its occasional use as being "for things too odoriferous or unrespectable for Peter Pauper." Beilenson's wife, Edna, became an active participant in Peter Pauper's operations after their marriage in 1930. In 1934 Peter Pauper began a series of limited editions, including *A Shropshire Lad* by A. E. Housman and *The Love Poems of John Donne*. In 1935 the firm moved its offices to Mt. Vernon, New York. Between 1936 and 1938 the AIGA recognized six more Peter Pauper publications.

In the 1940s the firm began publishing the Deluxe Artists Editions. Among these were Emerson's *Select Essays* (1941), *Robinson Crusoe* (1945), and Franklin's *Autobiography* (1945). Generally,

publications of the firm are in thin sixteenmos or, less frequently, quartos and octavos. Peter Pauper editions include small anthologies of poetry, epigrams, recipes, and selections from standard authors. These are customarily illustrated or decorated with woodcuts and issued in dust jackets which reproduce the designs of the covers.

After Peter Beilenson's death in 1962, Edna Beilenson continued the operation of the Peter Pauper Press. In 1978 she moved the firm's offices to those of the Van Nostrand Reinhold Company at 135 West Fiftieth Street, New York. This firm had taken over distribution for Peter Pauper five years earlier. In 1984 Peter Pauper Press moved to White Plains, New York, and arranged for distribution by Kampmann and Company. Since Edna Beilenson's death in 1981 the firm's affairs have been handled by Evelyn and Nick Beilenson. The address is 202 Mamaroneck Avenue, White Plains, New York 10601.

References:

Peter Beilenson, "The Walpole Printing Office, The Peter Pauper Press, Not to Mention the Blue-Behinded Ape," in *The Annual of Bookmaking: 1927-1937* (N.p.: The Colophon, 1938);

Gizella P. Callender, "The Peter Pauper Press," *American Book Collector*, 12 (March 1962): 15-24;

"Edna Beilenson [obituary]," *New York Times*, 4 March 1981, IV: 23;

Paul McPharlin, "Peter Pauper Classics," *Publishers' Weekly*, 150 (7 September 1946): 1215-1219;

"Peter Beilenson [obituary]," *New York Times*, 21 January 1962, p. 88.

—*Ronelle K. H. Thompson*

PETER PAUPER PRESS, INC.
1984 CATALOGUE

Dear Bookseller:

Peter Pauper Press has published hardcover collectors' editions and gift books for 55 years. However, THE OLYMPICS — A BOOK OF LISTS, due to arrive in March, will be our first ever paperback.

THE OLYMPICS is packed full of fascinating information about the Olympics from ancient times to Los Angeles. Of course, you will find the world's fastest human and greatest athlete listed, but the reader also will discover feminine fact, boycotts and scandals, politics, family feats and "strange but true." You won't want to miss it! 96 pages; paperback; $4.95. Available in 10-pack and 24-pack.

Peter Pauper books in general are available in best seller and other selections in 24-packs and 54-packs; and our discount schedule makes these pre-packs particularly good bargains.

Our best wishes to you in 1984!

Nick Beilenson

Also New For 1984!

STEPPING STONES: MEDITATIONS IN A GARDEN. Author Lillian Marshall's meditative teachings are "stepping stones" to spiritual tranquility. For example: "Advancing begins with the first step forward . . . What road shall you follow?" $3.95. Hardcover with jacket. 32 pp. January.

Cover of catalogue

Payson and Clarke

(New York: 1924-1929)

In 1924 William Farquhar Payson and James L. Clarke entered into the partnership of Payson and Clarke, Limited, with offices at 385 Madison Avenue, New York. A graduate of Columbia University, Payson had been on the editorial staff of the *New York Times* and had gone on to become a managing editor and director of *Vogue*. With short stories, travel sketches, and novels to his credit, he came to the newly established firm with the background of both author and editor. Years spent in London as a publisher's representative had given him contacts to acquire partial ownership of the distinguished British collector's magazine *Connoisseur*, which was first published in America by Payson and Clarke in February 1926. It was followed by the firm's first book, *Contemporary Scale Models of Vessels of the Seventeenth Century* by Henry B. Culver, published in a numbered edition of 1,000 copies in 1926.

In this same year Edward K. Warren and Joseph Brewer joined the company. Clarke sold his holdings in 1927. He was succeeded as vice-president and treasurer by Warren, a Harvard graduate and son of a distinguished New York clergyman. Brewer, the company secretary, was a Dartmouth man who had done graduate work at Oxford and had been on the staff of the *Spectator* in London.

Early Payson and Clarke publications were chiefly art books, but European connections gave the young firm priority in receiving new fiction from abroad. Its lists included a significant number of foreign works in translation, as well as original works by American authors. In 1927 an arrangement with Victor Gollancz of London ensured international publishing programs for both firms.

Payson and Clarke published several noteworthy literary titles, including Felix Hollander's *The Sins of the Fathers* (1927), André Savignon's *The Sorrows of Elsie* (1927), Blaise Cendrar's *The African Saga* (1927), and Gertrude Stein's *Useful Knowledge* (1928). In 1928 Payson left the company to begin publishing under the William Farquhar Payson imprint. Brewer became president of Payson and Clarke. At the time of his appointment the firm had become well known in the trade for the modern decor of its new quarters at 6 East Fifty-third Street. In 1929, the last year of the Payson and Clarke imprint, the firm's publications included Robert Penn Warren's first book, *John Brown: The Making of a Martyr;* Lola Ridge's *Firehead* in a trade as well as a limited edition of 225 signed copies; Clement Ripley's *Dust and Sun;* Achmed Abdullah and Faith Baldwin's *Broadway Interlude;* and George Seldes's *You Can't Print That!* On New Year's Day 1930 the firm was renamed Brewer and Warren.

References:

"Joseph Brewer Heads Payson and Clarke," *Publishers' Weekly*, 114 (15 September 1928): 850;

"Payson and Clarke Make Close Contact with Gollancz," *Publishers' Weekly*, 112 (3 December 1927): 2034;

"Radio Broadcasting [Payson and Clarke Ltd. advertised broadcasting . . . will now be Wednesday evenings, station WOR]," *Publishers' Weekly*, 113 (31 March 1928): 1448;

"William F. Payson [obituary]," *New York Times*, 16 April 1939, III: 6.

—Joan Gillen Conners
Anne Ludlow

Peachtree Publishers, Limited

(Atlanta: 1978-   )

Peachtree Publishers was founded in Atlanta, Georgia, in 1978 by Helen L. Elliott, who had been publishing audiovisual instructional courses for keyboard and guitar through her company, Educational Products. Feeling that talented Southern writers should not have to go to New York for publication, Mrs. Elliott decided to provide a trade publishing house devoted to regional literature. In its first year Peachtree published one book, Ann Ashford's verse-story *If I Found a Wistful Unicorn: A Gift of Love.* In the next seven years Peachtree sold over 100,000 copies of Ashford's book and steadily expanded its list.

In 1979 Peachtree published the first book by *Atlanta Constitution* columnist and humorist Lewis Grizzard, *Kathy Sue Loudermilk, I Love You.* The firm published seven books by Grizzard in the next six years with total sales of over one million copies.

Another of Peachtree's successful discoveries was Georgia physician-novelist Ferrol Sams. Sams's two novels, *Run with the Horsemen* (1982) and *The Whisper of the River* (1984), sold over 150,000 copies and received critical acclaim.

In 1985 Peachtree published thirteen titles, bringing its total of published books to seventy-eight, including *Chitlin Strut & Other Madrigals* (1983) by William Price Fox; *The Black & White Stories of Erskine Caldwell* (1984); three books by Celestine Sibley; and *A Collection of Classic Southern Humor* (1984) and *A Collection of Classic Southern Humor II* (1985), both edited by George William Koon.

After his mother's death, Wayne T. Elliott became president of Peachtree in 1983; his sister Nancy Elliott has been vice-president since 1980. The firm is located at 494 Armour Circle, N.E., Atlanta, Georgia 30324.

—*Christopher T. Lee*

Helen L. Elliott, founder of Peachtree Publishers

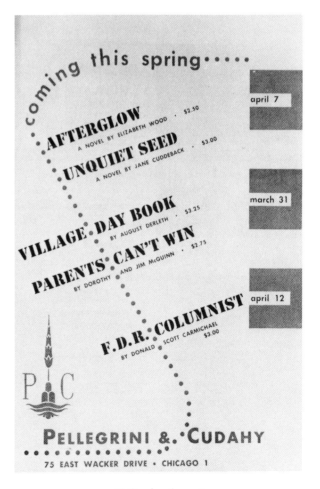

1947 advertisement

Pellegrini and Cudahy
(Chicago; New York: 1947-1953)

children's books

Pellegrini and Cudahy was founded in 1947 by George Pellegrini and his wife Sheila Cudahy at 75 East Wacker Drive in Chicago. The firm moved to 65 Fifth Avenue, New York, in 1948, and to 41 East Fiftieth Street in 1952. Pellegrini and Cudahy published approximately 135 titles between 1947 and 1953, including fiction, science fiction, biography, poetry, philosophy, and books on art, religion, music, and travel.

The firm's fiction titles included Charles Williams's *All Hallows' Eve* (1948); Giovanni Guareschi's *The Little World of Don Camillo* (1950) and its sequels; and books by the Nobel Prize winner François Mauriac, including *The Desert of Love* (1951) and *The Loved and the Unloved* (1952). Art books published by Pellegrini and Cudahy included Selden Rodman's *Renaissance in Haiti* (1948) and MacKinley Helm's biography of John Marin (1948). The juvenile list, published under the Ariel Books imprint and edited by Jean Poindexter Colby, included Leonard Wibberley's *The King's*

Beard (1952) and Josephine Balfour Payne's *The Stable That Stayed* (1952). The firm's science fiction anthologies were edited by August Derleth. These collections, with stories by J. Sheridan Le Fanu, H. P. Lovecraft, and A. E. van Vogt, were published annually.

Pellegrini died in 1952, and Cudahy continued to run the firm until it merged with Farrar, Straus the following year.

References:

"New Publishing Firm, Ariel Books, to Open in Chicago," *Publishers' Weekly*, 149 (25 May 1946): 2752;

"Obituary, George Pellegrini," *Publishers' Weekly*, 162 (September 1952): 1443;

"Pellegrini and Cudahy Completely Established," *Publishers' Weekly*, 151 (17 May 1947): 2508.

—*Kathleen R. Davis*

Penguin Books
(New York: 1939-1948; 1951-1975)
Viking Penguin
(New York: 1975-   )

In August 1939, four years after Allen Lane founded Penguin Books, Limited in Harmondsworth, Middlesex, England (the name *Penguin* had "a dignified flippancy," according to Lane), an American branch of the firm was established. The American Penguin was managed by Ian Ballantine, who held a forty-nine percent share of the new imprint. Offices were established at 3 East Seventeenth Street in New York. Ninety-eight imported, out-of-copyright paperback titles, including fifty Penguin Books, twenty nonfiction Pelicans, ten illustrated classics, and eighteen volumes of Shakespeare, were introduced at twenty-five cents each. Included in the first group of plain orange and white paperbacks, each marked with the silhouette of the Antarctic bird, were Anton Chekhov's *Three Plays*, Arnold Bennett's *The Grand Babylon Hotel*, P. G. Wodehouse's *My Man Jeeves*, and H. G. Wells's *The Invisible Man*. The Puffin, Peregrine, and Ptarmigan lines of books for juveniles were eventually introduced. Most successful in the early years were *The Odyssey, Don Quixote,* and various plays of George Bernard Shaw. About a third of all shops carrying Penguin Books in these years were college bookstores, and the college connection has remained important for Penguin in the American market.

At first, all American Penguin books were produced in England and imported. When World War II restricted trade routes, the American imprint was threatened and Lane turned to German immigrant Kurt Enoch for the obvious solution: American production of American books. If Enoch, in association with Ballantine, could raise the necessary capital to arrange the domestic manufacture of Penguin books, he would be rewarded with a five percent share of the company. The effort was successful, and Penguin prospered during the war with a series of titles designed to capitalize on military interest, including books published in cooperation with the unofficial army magazine *Infantry Journal*.

By the end of the war American Penguin was functioning as an independent company. When Lane attempted to regain control, Ballantine left to establish his own paperback house, Bantam Books. In the disruption and reorganization that followed, Enoch was promised a forty percent share of Penguin in America if he could successfully restructure the company. The problems were primarily editorial, because Ballantine had taken the best of the editorial staff with him. Enoch solved his problem by entering into partnership with Victor Weybright, a friend of Lane's with an impressive knowledge of American publishing.

Enoch and Weybright reasserted the independence of Penguin in America, introducing pictorial covers "revelatory of female anatomy and amatory desire," in Lane's words, and publishing authors Lane found vulgar—John O'Hara, James M. Cain, Erskine Caldwell, and William Faulkner, for example. This circumstance and Lane's attempt to renege on his promise of a forty percent share of the company's stock to Enoch (who had in turn promised half of his interest to Weybright) forced a break in 1948. Enoch and Weybright bought out Lane's interest in American Penguin and reorganized the company as the New American Library of World Literature. The Penguin and Pelican imprints were combined with New American Library's Signet and Mentor imprints for a year; after that the names Penguin and Pelican were dropped by Enoch and Weybright, though they had exclusive rights to those names for three years.

Lane reentered American publishing in January 1950 with Allen Lane, Incorporated in Baltimore. The next year, as soon as the terms of his agreement with Enoch and Weybright permitted, he reincorporated in New York as Penguin Books, Incorporated.

Alan Lane (left) and Ian Ballantine of Penguin Books

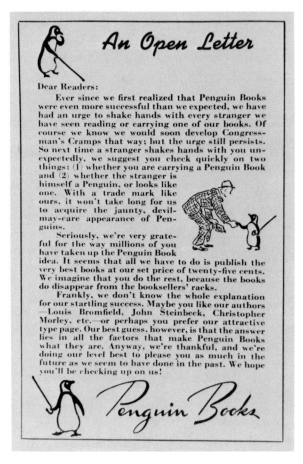

One of the letters to readers printed at the end of early Penguin volumes

1946 advertisement

Immediately after Lane's death in 1970 the British firm was taken over by S. Pearson and Son, a conglomerate with extensive international oil, manufacturing, real estate, and publishing interests, including ownership of the *Financial Times* of London. In 1975 American Penguin acquired two-thirds of Viking Press for an estimated $9 million, resulting in Viking Penguin, Incorporated. The Penguin imprint continues as a division of Viking Penguin. The American and British Penguins have separate lists, although some titles appear on both.

Penguin still reaps the rewards of its backlist, from which it derives some sixty percent of its annual sales. Penguin's top sellers include Arthur Miller's *Death of a Salesman,* John Steinbeck's *The Grapes of Wrath,* James Joyce's *A Portrait of the Artist as a Young Man,* Plato's *The Last Days of Socrates,* and the firm's perennial money-makers, *The Odyssey* and *The Canterbury Tales.* Penguin has also introduced its Contemporary American Fiction series with reprints of Thomas McGuane's *Panama* (1979), Edmund White's *Nocturnes for the King of Naples* (1980), and Jessamyn West's *The Life I Really Lived* (1981). An example of Penguin's response to contemporary concerns is its Virago imprint, which is devoted to distinguished fiction by and about women. Viking Penguin publisher and president Allan Kellock summarizes Penguin's tradition: "Solidly belletristic, with a literary richness and variety unparalleled in paperback publishing." Viking Penguin's address is 40 West Twenty-third Street, New York 10010.

References:

Penguins, a Retrospect, 1935-1951 (Harmondsworth, U.K.: Penguin, 1952);

Dennis Traut, *Penguin's Penguins* (New York: Penguin, 1982);

Sir William E. Williams, *The Penguin Story, MCMXXXV-MCMLVI* (Harmondsworth, U.K.: Penguin, 1956).

—*Gregory P. Ames*

Permabooks
(New York: 1948-1973)

Permabooks was established in September 1948 as an imprint of Garden City Publishing Company, a reprint subsidiary of Doubleday. For its first two years, during which 101 titles were published under the editorship of George DeKay, Permabooks were bound in boards and sold for thirty-five cents. About eighty percent of the early lists were nonfiction; early titles included *Best Loved Poems; The Male Hormone* by Paul de Kruif; *Stories for Men,* edited by Charles Grayson; *Best Short Stories of Jack London;* and *South Sea Stories* by W. Somerset Maugham.

In 1951 Permabooks switched from hardbound to paperback books. At the same time, Permabooks began to publish more fiction, though such titles as Patrick Duffy's *The Standard Bartender's Guide, The Perma Cross-Word Puzzle Dictionary,* and Fulton Oursler's *The Greatest Story Ever Told* still provided the foundation for the list. During the early 1950s Permabooks reprinted works by F. Scott Fitzgerald, Ernest Hemingway, James Gould Cozzens, Nancy Hale, Vicki Baum, Frank G. Slaughter, and Michael Avellone.

In fall 1953 Permabooks introduced two new imprints—Perma Stars, fiction titles priced at twenty-five cents; and Perma Specials, longer, more sophisticated books that sold for fifty cents. That year distribution of Permabooks, which had been handled by Macfadden Publications, a magazine publisher and distributor, was taken over by Doubleday. Within nine months Doubleday sold Permabooks to Pocket Books. The merger was to have

1953 advertisement

resulted in the new imprint Perma-Pocket Books; it was never used, however, and Pocket Books continued to offer Permabooks as a separate section of its lists. In 1966 Pocket Books merged with Simon and Schuster, taking the Permabooks imprint with it. This imprint continued to be listed in the Simon and Schuster catalogue until 1973.

References:

"Permabooks Becomes Separate Doubleday Division," *Publishers' Weekly,* 161 (3 May 1952): 1850;

"Permabooks Line Merges With Pocket Books," *Publishers' Weekly,* 161 (3 May 1952): 1850.

—*Ronelle K. H. Thompson*

Philosophical Library
(New York: 1941-   )

Dagobert D. Runes, an immigrant from Rumania, founded the Philosophical Library in New York in 1941. Runes's *Dictionary of Philosophy* (1942) was the firm's first publication; a revised and enlarged edition was published in 1982. Runes also edited *Who's Who in Philosophy* (1942), a biographical dictionary of over 500 living thinkers. The firm later published the anthologies *Living Schools of Philosophy* (1947), *The Treasury of Philosophy* (1955), and *Classics in Logic* (1962), all edited by Runes, as well as Runes's *On the Nature of Man* (1956) and Jean-Paul Sartre's *Being and Nothingness* (1956) and *The Philosophy of Existentialism* (1965).

Literary titles have been scant but include Paul Claudel's *Poetic Art; Ivan Franko, the Poet of*

Western Ukraine, translated by Percival Cundy; and Pablo Picasso's play *Desire,* all in 1948. Among later titles was Boris Pasternak's *The Adolescence of Zhenya Luvers* (1961). By 1986 the Philosophical Library had published works by twenty-two Nobel Prize winners.

Runes died in 1982. Rose Morse Runes is general manager of Philosophical Library, Incorporated. The firm is located at 200 West Fifty-seventh Street, New York 10019.

Reference:

"Dagobert D. Runes [obituary]," *New York Times,* 27 September 1982, IV: 9.

—*Edward J. Hall*

Dagobert D. Runes, founder of Philosophical Library

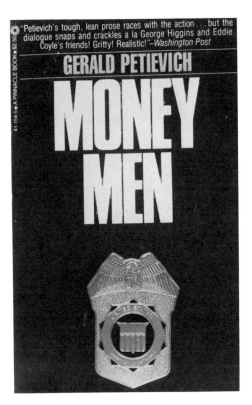

Cover for 1981 paperback

Stanley J. Corwin, president and publisher of Pinnacle Books from 1976 to 1980

Pinnacle Books

(New York; Los Angeles; New York: 1969-)

A TOM DOHERTY ASSOCIATES BOOK

TOR
science
fiction

PINNACLE BOOKS
NEW YORK

Pinnacle Books was founded in New York in 1969 by David Zentner. The first book of the firm was Don Pendleton's *The Executioner: War against the Mafia* (1969); it was followed by other books in the Executioner series as well as science fiction by Pendleton. By 1971 Pinnacle Books had expanded its list to emphasize publications in series, which included Alan Caillou's Colonel Tobin and Warren Murphy's Destroyer series. The firm continued to publish original science fiction, including Michael Elder's *Paradise Is Not Enough* and Harris Moore's *Slater's Planet,* both in 1971.

The firm's action series and science fiction met with commercial success. In 1972 Pinnacle's estimated sales exceeded $4 million. When Stanley J. Corwin became president and publisher of Pinnacle Books in 1976, he started Corwin Books, a hardcover line, and moved Pinnacle to 1 Century Plaza, 2029 Century Park East, Los Angeles, with Patrick O'Connor as editor in chief. From that location Pinnacle published, in addition to its usual output, books with movie tie-ins, such as Graham Masterton's *The Manitou* (1976).

To augment its scanty science fiction line (only 10 titles out of almost 150 in 1977), Pinnacle conceived a short-lived science fiction series, Futurian Science Fiction, with Roger Elwood, followed by Robert Silverberg, as consulting editor. The project collapsed in 1978 with Silverberg's resignation from Pinnacle.

In 1977 *Love's Avenging Heart* by Patricia Matthews sold a million copies. Pinnacle immediately began to publish historical romances, including more by Matthews. Harlequin Enterprises, a publisher of romance novels, proposed a merger with Pinnacle in February 1979. Justice Department threats to lodge an antitrust complaint caused Harlequin to terminate discussions.

In December 1980 Pinnacle returned to New York. With Ira G. Corn as chairman of the board and Stanley L. Reisner as president and chief executive officer, Pinnacle undertook a new science fiction line. By 1981 the Pinnacle imprint was appearing on four books per month. Early titles included Andre Norton's *Forerunner,* Fred Saberhagen's *Water of Thought,* Poul Anderson's *The Psychotechnic League,* and Keith Laumer's *The Breaking Earth.* The firm is the distributor for Tor Books.

At the end of 1985 Pinnacle Books filed for reorganization under Chapter 11 of the Federal Bankruptcy Act, with liabilities to secured creditors of $1.5 million. The firm is a subsidiary of First Tarent Corporation; Sondra T. Ordover is president and publisher. Pinnacle Books, Incorporated is located at 1430 Broadway, New York 10018.

References:

"Ballantine and Pinnacle Tie Up with British Firms," *Publishers Weekly* (15 March 1976): 20, 24;

"Pinnacle Appoints Corwin, Eyes Hardcover Expansion," *Publishers Weekly,* 209 (8 March 1976): 20-21;

Marianne Yen, "Pinnacle Authors Fight to Regain Contracts," *Publishers Weekly,* 228 (20 December 1985): 25.

—Martha A. Bartter

Platt and Munk Company

(New York: 1921-   )

George Edmund Platt, treasurer of Platt and Nourse Company and Hurst Company, sold his interest in these firms and started the George E. Platt Company in April 1920. On 1 January 1921 he joined forces with the brothers Arnold and Alexander Munk, who had been salesmen for the Saalfield Publishing Company, to form the children's book publishing firm of Platt and Munk at 118-120 East Twenty-fifth Street, New York. When Platt died in 1923 Arnold Munk assumed the presidency of Platt and Munk.

Harry E. Harrison joined Platt and Munk in 1924 and worked with Arnold Munk on most of the books from idea to production, bringing out as many as thirty-eight new titles a year. Sales and promotion were the responsibility of Alexander Munk, who established a nationwide reputation for the firm before his death at the age of forty-three in 1937.

Beginning in 1927, the year the firm moved to 200 Fifth Avenue, anthologies and picture books prepared in-house and, occasionally, public domain reprints were attributed to Watty Piper, a house pseudonym. By far the most popular Watty Piper title was *The Little Engine That Could* (1930), published originally with drawings by Lois Lenski; by 1976 over five million copies had been sold. Arnold Munk discovered the tale in the 1920s and published a copyrighted version. In 1955 the house offered a $1,000 reward to anyone who could "furnish authentic proof conclusively establishing the identity of the original author." The offer of this reward followed claims by Elizabeth McKinney Chmiel that her relative, Frances M. Ford, wrote the original story in 1912. No evidence was received that positively showed the author's identity, and the money was divided among three people. It was ascertained that the story had been told and retold under different titles and had first appeared in a printed version as *The Pony Engine* by Mabel C. Bragg in 1910.

Other successful Platt and Munk productions included the Tasha Tudor books, Holly Hobbie and Cricket Book series, *Uncle Wiggily's Puzzle Book* (1928) by Howard Roger Garis, and *Stories That Never Grow Old* (1938). Many of the firm's items were blends of books and toys—panorama, paper doll, punch-out, and puzzle books. Platt and Munk also had a reprint series, the Great Writers Collection, consisting of short story collections by authors including Edgar Allan Poe, Jack London, Jules Verne, and O. Henry.

The firm bought the juvenile series Wee Books for Wee Folks from the Henry Altemus Company in 1926, and added the Cupples and Leon imprint in 1956 by taking over that children's book firm. Arnold Munk died in 1957 and was succeeded as president by his wife, Edna Munk. In March 1969 Platt and Munk became a division of Child Guidance, a producer of educational toys and games and part of the Questor Corporation. Platt and Munk's offices moved to 1055 Bronx River Avenue, Bronx. Questor sold this division to Gabriel Industries in 1977 and in 1978 Grosset and Dunlap acquired the imprint from Gabriel. At that time Platt and Munk had approximately 165 active juvenile titles. Grosset and Dunlap was acquired by the Putnam Publishing Group in 1982. Platt and Munk continues as an imprint of The Putnam Young Readers Group. The firm's address is 200 Madison Avenue, New York 10016.

References:

"Little Engine Award Split; Origin Not Identified," *Publishers' Weekly*, 169 (14 April 1956): 1727-1728;

"News from Publishers," *Publishers' Weekly*, 129 (28 March 1936): 1333;

"News Items of the New Year," *Publishers' Weekly*, 99 (1 January 1921): 28;

"Platt and Munk Completes a Quarter-Century," *Publishers' Weekly*, 149 (27 April 1946): 2297-2298.

—Kathleen McGowan

Arnold H. Munk

1928 advertisement

Playboy Press
(Chicago: 1962-1982)

PLAYBOY PRESS
PAPERBACKS

₽¥P

A Playboy Press Book

Playboy Press was founded in 1962 as a division of the HMH Publishing Company by Hugh M. Hefner, its first president, editor, and publisher. With offices at 919 North Michigan Avenue, Chicago, the company's original purpose was to reprint in book form material from *Playboy* magazine. In 1970 the firm was reorganized with Robert A. Gutwillig as director of publishing development and Michael Cohn as manager; both were former executives at the World Publishing Company. By this time, the parent company had been renamed Playboy Enterprises, Incorporated. After a distribution agreement with Simon and Schuster, Playboy Press's output increased from eight titles in 1969 to sixty-four in 1971. The firm used the imprints Playboy Paperbacks for mass market books, Playboy Press and Seaview for hardcover titles, and Wideview for trade paperbacks. Successful titles included Henry Miller's *My Life and Times* (1971), J. Paul Getty's *How to Be a Successful Executive* (1971), Howard Cosell's *Cosell* (1973), and Spiro Agnew's novel *The Canfield Decision* (1976). The firm's books were sold through its Playboy Book Club as well as in retail outlets.

In September 1979 Playboy Press switched its distribution to Harper and Row for its hardcover books and International Circulation Distributors for its paperbacks. It also announced a new science fiction program, beginning that year with a reprint of Philip José Farmer's *The Image of the Beast* and an original title, George Takei and Robert Asprin's *Mirror Friend, Mirror Foe*. The Playboy Book Club had over 100,000 members by 1980. In 1981 the firm reprinted four widely acclaimed recent novels: Shirley Hazzard's *Transit of Venus*, Anne Tyler's *Morgan's Passing*, Alberto Moravia's *Time of Desecration*, and Lynn Sharon Schwartz's *Rough Strife*.

In June 1982 Playboy Enterprises sold its book publishing operations, not including the Playboy name, to the Berkley-Jove subsidiary of the Putnam Publishing Group for an undisclosed sum. Derick J. Daniels, president and chief operating officer of Playboy, said that "publishing industry economics today make it difficult for medium-to-small houses such as ours to earn an adequate return on investment." The sale agreement allows Playboy to continue selling books with Playboy titles, such as *The Playboy Host and Bar Book,* and to produce compilations of material from *Playboy* magazine.

References:

"Playboy Acquires Reprint Rights to Four New Novels," *Publishers Weekly*, 218 (7 November 1980): 44;

Madalynne Reuter, "Berkley-Jove to Acquire Playboy Book Operations," *Publishers Weekly*, 221 (18 June 1982): 16.

—Edward J. Hall

1972 advertisement

Pocket Books
(New York: 1938-   )

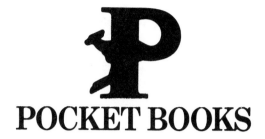

1939   1943   1945   1962   1964

Robert F. de Graff is generally considered the man most responsible for starting the modern paperback book revolution in America. He was involved with Doubleday, Page's Garden City Publishing Company from 1925 to 1936 and Blue Ribbon Books from 1936 to 1938; both firms specialized in cheap clothbound reprints, usually priced in the one- to two-dollar range. Influenced by the success of German and British paperback publishers, de Graff left Blue Ribbon Books in 1938 to begin an extensive study of how to produce the cheapest possible book of acceptable quality. When he was convinced that he could accomplish his goal, he approached Richard Simon, M. Lincoln Schuster, and Leon Shimkin, the top executives of Simon and Schuster, who agreed to become partners in Pocket Books, Incorporated.

De Graff proposed to publish only reprints, paying a royalty of one cent per copy to be split between the original publisher and the author. De Graff sent a sample book, Pearl Buck's *The Good Earth*, to a test group of 1,000 readers. The results were favorable, and in June 1939 Pocket Books published its first list of ten titles. The firm's distinctive logo, Gertrude the Kangaroo, was designed by Frank J. Lieberman; it was later redesigned by Walt Disney Studios. Pocket Books was first located in Simon and Schuster's offices at 386 Fourth Avenue, New York.

The books in the initial list were priced at twenty-five cents apiece. Each had a sturdy four-color cover, colored end sheets, stained edges, high-grade paper, and a sewn binding, and measured 4 1/4 by 6 1/2 inches. The first list included James Hilton's *Lost Horizon; Wake Up and Live*, a self-help book; Emily Brontë's *Wuthering Heights; Five Tragedies* by Shakespeare; Agatha Christie's *The Murder of Roger Ackroyd;* Thornton Wilder's *The Bridge of San Luis Rey;* and Felix Salten's *Bambi.* Despite the predictions of fellow publishers that book-buying Americans did not want paperbound books and that the American masses were not readers, the first Pocket Books list was a spectacular success, with several titles selling out almost immediately.

Pocket Books sales manager Wallis E. Howe developed a unique distribution system: rather than relying solely on bookstores and department stores, Pocket Books also used magazine and newspaper wholesalers to distribute its books. Pocket Books were sold in almost every conceivable retail outlet: newsstands, cigar stores, grocery stores, drugstores, and subway, train, and bus stations. Although the books on the initial list were distributed only in the New York City area, in a few weeks Pocket Books were being sold all over the United States and, by 1949, all over the world. Sales in 1939 were 1.5 million copies.

Philip Van Doren Stern, Simon and Schuster's manufacturing director, soon became editorial consultant for Pocket Books and created some of the early Pocket Book original or "made" books, usually anthologies of humor, short stories, or verse. Pocket Books published new books on a regular schedule, usually five to ten titles a month. The variety of material on the first list was repeated on later lists—reprints of best-sellers, popular fiction, self-help books, classics, mysteries, and original anthologies became Pocket Books staples. The firm generally avoided "high brow" authors such as Ernest Hemingway or William Faulkner. Dale Carnegie's *How to Win Friends and Influence People* (1940) became one of its early best-sellers; sales reached 1.3 million copies by April 1941, despite the fact that the hardbound edition published by Simon and Schuster in 1936 had already sold over one million copies.

Pocket Books faced its first major competition in November 1941 when Joseph Meyers's Avon Pocket-Size Books appeared in a format similar to that of Pocket Books. Pocket Books brought suit; after a year of litigation, which included two appeals, Avon was allowed to continue publishing but agreed to drop the word *Pocket-Size* from its name. Pocket established a Canadian subsidiary, Pocket Books of Canada, Limited, in 1943.

In 1944 Pocket Books was acquired by Marshall Field Enterprises. By the end of World War II annual sales had reached 35 million volumes.

In 1946 Lewis Freeman, formerly director of Blue Ribbon Books and later of Triangle Books, a thirty-nine-cent hardcover reprint division of Doubleday, became executive vice-president. In 1950 de Graff became chairman of the board of the firm and was replaced as president by Shimkin, who also remained executive vice-president of Simon and Schuster. In the early 1950s Pocket Books moved to 630 Fifth Avenue.

Pocket Books started its thirty-five-cent Cardinal Editions line in 1951; in 1953 the Cardinal Giants and the Pocket Book of Great Art series, both priced at fifty cents, appeared. De Graff retired in 1954. The same year, Pocket Books started the Pocket Library series of classics priced at thirty-five and fifty cents and also acquired Permabooks from Doubleday. In 1955 Pocket Books founded its own distribution service, Affiliated Publishers, which soon began to distribute books for other houses as well. The firm was bought back from Field Enterprises in 1957 by Shimkin and James M. Jacobson, executive vice-president in charge of sales. The following year, Pocket Books acquired Simon and Schuster's Golden Books.

In 1961 Pocket Books instituted a short-lived hardcover line, Trident Press, mainly to lure author Harold Robbins from Knopf. The same year, the firm acquired Washington Square Press and All Saints Press and also became a publicly owned company, placing twenty percent of its shares on the market. By 1964 Pocket Books was selling almost 300 million books a year. The firm of Julian Messner was acquired in 1965; the following year, Pocket Books itself became a division of Simon and Schuster. Affiliated Publishers ceased operation in the late 1960s. In 1975 Pocket Books was acquired, along with Simon and Schuster, by Gulf & Western Industries, a conglomerate. Pocket Books and Simon and Schuster have occasionally shared the Archway imprint for juvenile books and the Timescape imprint for fantasy and science fiction.

Pocket Books considers its backlist to be a crucial factor in its financial success. In both units and dollars, backlist titles account for between forty and fifty percent of total annual sales. *Lost Horizon* is the oldest title on this extensive list, which includes books by such perennial best-selling authors as Robbins, Agatha Christie, Erle Stanley Gardner, and Zane Grey. Partly because of this backlist emphasis, Pocket Books did not participate in the fierce competition for titles in the paperback business in the 1960s and so lost ground to other houses, such as Dell and Bantam. To bring Pocket Books back to life, Peter Mayer, editor and publisher of Avon Books, was hired in 1976. Wallaby, a trade paperback line, was started in 1977. Mayer was replaced in 1978 by Ronald Busch, president of Ballantine Books. At the end of the 1970s Pocket Books projected a fresh image as an aggressive promoter of best-selling fiction by Herman Wouk, Richard Brautigan, Bernard Malamud, Morris West, Joan Didion, Judith Rossner, and John Irving, in addition to Robbins. In 1982 Pocket Books launched another hardcover imprint, Poseidon Press, giving the company access to a wider range of material and allowing its authors to be reviewed as hardcover authors. Judith Michael's *Deceptions*, V. C. Andrew's *My Sweet Audrina,* and Henry Bean's *False Match* were all published in 1982 by Poseidon.

Pocket Books publishes more than 300 titles per year and has over 2,000 titles actively in print. Some Pocket Books titles are among the best-selling books of all time; these include Dr. Benjamin Spock's *Baby and Child Care,* the *Merriam-Webster Dictionary*, and the *University of Chicago Spanish-English Dictionary.* The firm's address since 1976 has been 1230 Avenue of the Americas, New York 10020.

References:

Lewis Freeman, *A Brief History of Pocket Books, 1939-1967* (New York: Pocket Books, 1967);

"The Story of Pocket Books, Inc.," *Book Production Magazine,* 78 (August 1963): 42-45.

—Timothy D. Murray

Robert F. de Graff, founder of Pocket Books, with a model of Gertrude the Kangaroo (Thomas L. Bonn, UnderCover: An Illustrated History of American Mass Market Paperbacks, *p. 45)*

Cover for the first Pocket Book, published in 1939

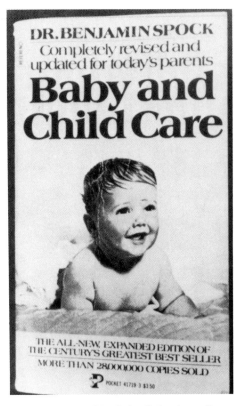

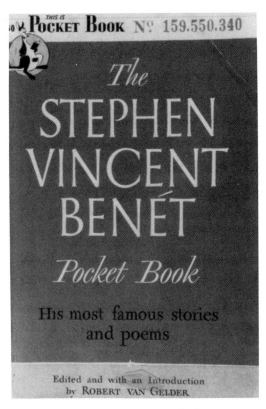

Cover for one of Pocket's all-time best-sellers

Cover for 1946 paperback

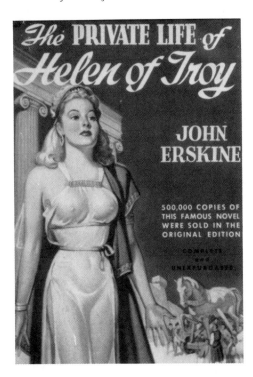

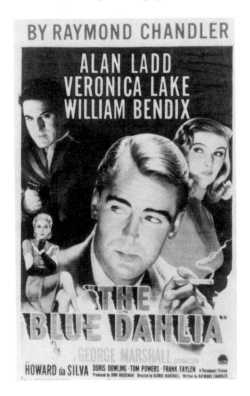

Cover for a 1948 Popular Library reprint of Erskine's 1925 novel. The illustration by Earle Bergey became known as the "nipple cover."

Cover for 1976 Popular Library paperback, featuring poster from 1946 film

Popular Library
(New York: 1942-1982)

P O P U L A R ⬆ L I B R A R Y   50¢
LITHO IN U.S.A.

In 1942 Ned L. Pines, founder and publisher of Pines Publications, added a mass market paperback line to his group of magazines. Under editorial director Leo Margulies and editor in chief Charles N. Heckelmann, Popular Library followed the format of the pioneering paperback publisher, Pocket Books. The first seventy-six books were twenty-five-cent reprints of mystery novels, including *The Saint Overboard* by Leslie Charteris, *Danger in the Dark* by Mignon Eberhart, *Crime of Violence* by Rufus King, *Murder in the Madhouse* by Jonathan Latimer, and *Miss Pinkerton* by Mary Roberts Rinehart. Popular Library's first offices were at 45 West Forty-fifth Street; the firm moved to 11 East Thirty-ninth Street in 1944, and to 10 East Fortieth Street in 1945.

In January 1946 Popular Library expanded its line to include serious novels, westerns, swashbucklers, short story anthologies, cartoons, humor, and current affairs. The first titles under the new program included *Buckaroo* by Eugene Cunningham, *Timbal Gulch Trail* by Max Brand, *The Sea Hawk* by Rafael Sabatini, *The Mortal Storm* by Phyllis Bottome, and *The Mystery Companion*, edited by A. L. Furman. In 1946 the firm published reprints of *Lummox* by Fannie Hurst, *Trouble Shooter* by Ernest Haycox, *Stella Dallas* by Olive Higgins Prouty, *Dr. Hudson's Secret Journal* by Lloyd C. Douglas, and *Dividend on Death* by Brett Halliday. One of Popular Library's biggest sellers was *Duel in the Sun* by Niven Busch, published in December 1946. The cover featured a still from the movie showing Gregory Peck and Jennifer Jones. By 1957 three million copies had been sold. Hal Ellson's *Duke* (1950) sold over 750,000 copies in its first year, and over 1.5 million by 1958. In 1951 William L. Shirer's *Traitor* was brought out with a major promotion in conjunction with Farrar, Straus and Young, the hardcover publisher.

Following the lead of Fawcett's Gold Medal, Popular Library began a line of original paperbacks in 1952. By 1955 the firm was publishing an average of two originals a month, mostly mysteries and westerns. Reprints continued to be important;

in 1955 Popular Library published *A Time to Love and a Time to Die* by Erich Maria Remarque, *The World in the Evening* by Christopher Isherwood, *Sigmund Freud for Everybody* by Rachel Baker, and *I'll Cry Tomorrow* by Lillian Roth with Mike Connolly and Gerold Frank. A 1956 best-seller was Saul Bellow's *The Adventures of Augie March*, winner of the 1954 National Book Award for fiction. In 1957 Popular Library brought out Patrick Dennis's *Auntie Mame;* by 1958 more than two million copies had been sold. That year the firm published 120 titles, with an average print order per title of 200,000 to 250,000 copies.

In 1958 Popular Library paid the World Publishing Company a $100,000 advance for *Webster's New World Dictionary of the American Language*, which it published in a seventy-five-cent edition. In 1975 it was still one of the firm's most-ordered school titles, with sales exceeding twenty million copies. Heckelmann left in 1958 to help found Monarch Books; James A. Bryans replaced him. Under Bryans's direction, Popular Library paid more attention to books for women, gradually phasing out original westerns and mysteries and adding love stories, historical epics, and biographies. A set of mystery reprints, Joan Kahn—Harper Novels of Suspense, was also started.

In 1962 Pines sold 127,000 shares of Popular Library stock, representing about a quarter of his interest in the company. Within four years, Frank P. Lualdi was president, publisher, and director. In 1967 the Perfect Film and Chemical Corporation acquired nearly all the outstanding stock of the company. Popular Library published almost 200 titles that year.

In October 1971 the Columbia Broadcasting System—which had already bought Holt, Rinehart and Winston—acquired Popular Library for $9.65 million. Popular Library became a unit of the CBS/Education and Publishing Group at 355 Lexington Avenue. Patrick O'Connor was made editor in chief in 1972. Under O'Connor Popular Library combined category fiction with literary titles, including the Lost American Fiction series from Southern

Illinois University Press. In 1973 Popular Library published 270 titles, including John Le Carré's *The Naive and Sentimental Lover,* for which it paid $150,000. O'Connor received the Carey-Thomas Award in 1976 for publishing distinguished fiction in mass market paperbacks.

In 1977 CBS acquired Fawcett Publications, including Gold Medal, Crest, and Premier Books. Popular Library, which had stopped bidding for major titles and made much of its income from its backlist, including Marjorie Kellogg's *Tell Me That You Love Me, Junie Moon* and Harper Lee's *To Kill a Mockingbird,* continued to operate on a severely limited budget. O'Connor left in 1979 and was re-placed by Arlene Friedman; by this time Popular Library was little more than a unit of CBS Publications, virtually a subsidiary of the Fawcett Books line. In November 1982 most of Popular Library's assets were sold to Warner Books, and the imprint was discontinued.

References:

"CBS/Holt and Popular Library," *Publishers' Weekly,* 200 (30 August 1971): 240;

"Warner Books Buys Most of Popular Library Assets," *Publishers Weekly,* 222 (12 November 1982): 10.

—Martha A. Bartter

Praeger Publishers
(New York: 1969-   )
Frederick A. Praeger
(New York: 1950-1969)

1969

FREDERICK A. PRAEGER, *Publishers*

New York • Washington • London

Born into a publishing family in Vienna in 1915, Frederick Praeger fled from the Nazis to the United States in 1938. After traveling across the country and working in a series of menial jobs, he served the United States military in Germany in intelligence and editorial positions. Praeger founded Frederick A. Praeger, Incorporated in New York in 1950, using $6,000 of his savings and $4,000 borrowed from friends. The firm is best known for its art paperbacks, reference books on international affairs, and strongly anticommunist works in current history. The few works of fiction Praeger has published include *The Apartment and The Fortune Cookie: Two Screenplays* (1971) by Billy Wilder and I. A. L. Diamond, and *Russia's Other Writers: Selections from Samizdat Literature* (1971). The firm has also published a few works of nonfiction by writers of fiction; among these were Milovan Djilas's *The New Class* (1957), Alan Paton's *Hope for South Africa* (1959) and *The Long View* (1968), and William Saroyan's autobiographical *Places Where I've Done Time* (1972).

Praeger moved from 15 West Forty-seventh Street to 64 University Place in 1960 and to 111 Fourth Avenue in 1964. Encyclopædia Britannica acquired Frederick A. Praeger, Incorporated in 1966. Praeger left the company in 1968 and George Aldor succeeded him as president. The firm's name was changed to Praeger Publishers in 1969. David R. Replogle served as president from 1972 until 1974, when Charles Van Doren assumed the presidency.

Praeger series include Praeger World Affairs Atlases, Praeger Library of Chinese Affairs, Praeger Library of U.S. Government Departments and Agencies, and World of Art. The five-volume *Praeger Encyclopedia of Art* was published in 1971. Begun in 1964, the Praeger Special Studies series presents research in international economics and politics. The Young Readers Department, initiated in 1969, produces the How They Live and Work and Voices from the Nation series. College paperbacks are published in the Praeger University series and Praeger Paperbound Texts. In 1959 Praeger launched a trade paperback series, Praeger Paperbacks. Since acquiring Phaidon Press, Limited, a British art publishing house, in 1969, Praeger has distributed Phaidon's titles in the United States.

Praeger Publishers moved to 200 Park Avenue in 1977. In December of that year Britannica sold Praeger to the CBS Educational and Professional Publishing Group; Praeger moved to 383 Madison Avenue in 1978. On 1 January 1986 CBS sold Praeger to Greenwood Press of Westport, Connecticut, a subsidiary of Congressional Information Service, Incorporated, which is owned by the Dutch publisher Elsevier. Ronald Chambers was appointed editorial director and general manager of Praeger. Since 1980, Praeger has been located at 521 Fifth Avenue, New York 10175.

References:

"Britannica Buys Frederick A. Praeger, Inc.," *Publishers' Weekly*, 189 (2 May 1966): 31;

"Praeger Observes Double Anniversary," *Publishers' Weekly*, 188 (11 October 1965): 40;

"Praeger Plans Major Series on Federal Government," *Publishers' Weekly*, 189 (14 March 1966): 41;

Madalynne Reuter, "Greenwood Press to buy Praeger from CBS," *Publishers Weekly*, 229 (3 January 1986): 12.

—Jutta Willman

Prentice-Hall

(New York; Englewood Cliffs, New Jersey; New York: 1913-)

1950

Prentice-Hall, Incorporated was started in 1913 by Charles W. Gerstenberg and Richard P. Ettinger, economics professors at New York University. The name was derived from their mothers' maiden names. The firm's first publications were Gerstenberg's textbook *Materials of Corporation Finance* (1915) and Ettinger and David Golieb's *Credits and Collections* (1917). Prentice-Hall's first office consisted of a single room at 70 Fifth Avenue, New York; the company gradually occupied more and more space and finally purchased the entire building in 1945.

After more than two decades of successful development of its college texts and reference materials, primarily in business and economics, Prentice-Hall inaugurated its trade department, headed by David Dunlap, in 1937 with the publication of Anita Leslie's *Rodin, Immortal Peasant*. In 1945, under the direction of Gorham Munson, the trade department began to publish popular fiction. Eliot Taintor's *September Remember* (1945), Prentice-Hall's first novel, was followed by Helen Haberman's *How About Tomorrow Morning?* (1945) and Emery Bekessy and A. Hemberger's *Barabbas* (1946). Prentice-Hall's first fiction best-seller, Rosamond Marshall's *Dutchess Hotspur* (1946), sold over 100,000 copies. Gerstenberg died in 1948.

Noteworthy novels published by Prentice-Hall include Louis Auchincloss's first novel, *The Indifferent Children* (1947), published under the pseudonym Andrew Lee; John Hewlett's *Harlem Story* (1948); *Most Likely to Succeed* (1954) by John Dos Passos; E. R. Braithwaite's *To Sir, With Love* (1959); Bel Kaufman's *Up the Down Staircase* (1965); and Louise Meriwether's *Daddy Was a Number Runner* (1970). In the early 1950s Prentice-Hall published the first American editions of translations of several Georges Simenon novels. Even more successful than fiction were inspirational and self-help books such as Norman Vincent Peale's *The Power of Positive Thinking* (1952), which enjoyed an eventual sale of more than two million copies, and others by Pat Boone, Art Linkletter, and Abigail Van Buren.

Prentice-Hall has developed course materials for the study of literature, from Hoxie Neale Fairchild's *An Approach to Literature* (1929) and Edwin Burgum's anthology of essays *The New Criticism* (1930) to Kenneth Burke's *A Grammar of Motives* (1945) and *A Rhetoric of Motives* (1950) and Allen Tate's collection of essays on Southern literature and culture, *A Southern Vanguard* (1947). Prentice-Hall acquired the firm of Allyn and Bacon in 1951 and established a subsidiary, Hawthorn Books, Incorporated, in 1952. In 1954 Prentice-Hall moved to a sprawling office complex in Englewood Cliffs, New Jersey. Ettinger became chairman of the board in 1955 and was succeeded as president by John G. Powers, who instituted a program of acquisitions: Charles E. Merrill Books in 1957, Iroquois Publishing Company and the National Foremen's Institute in 1960, and the New York Institute of Finance in 1962. Powers also formed two subsidiaries, Atherton Press and Wadsworth Publishing Company.

Two series of publications in literature, Twentieth Century Views and Twentieth Century Interpretations, are under the general editorship of Maynard Mack. Each volume in the Twentieth Century Views series, which was begun in 1962, is a collection of critical essays on a literary figure, while the Twentieth Century Interpretations series, which started in 1968, is devoted to the critical examination of particular literary works.

Powers resigned in 1962 and was replaced as president by Carroll Newsome, who was succeeded in 1964 by Paul R. Andrews. Andrews sold off Atherton Press, Hawthorn Books, Allyn and Bacon, and Wadsworth but established three textbook subsidiaries: Winthrop Publishers, Goodyear Publishing Company, and Reston Publishing Company. Andrews moved up to chairman of the board when Ettinger died in 1971, and Frank J. Dunnigan became president. Three departments were acquired

from Appleton-Century-Crofts in 1973, including a line of medical and nursing texts. In creating the largest textbook empire in current publishing, Prentice-Hall acquired and established many smaller enterprises for specific markets, from elementary, high school, and college students to specialized fields such as nursing, environmental science, and tax law. In 1985 Prentice-Hall was acquired by Gulf + Western Industries, Incorporated and became part of Simon and Schuster, Incorporated. Prentice-Hall operations comprise a substantial part of Simon and Schuster's Education Publishing Group and play a major role in the General Reference Group. Prentice-Hall's address is the Simon and Schuster Building, 1230 Avenue of the Americas, New York 10020.

References:

"Charles W. Gerstenberg [obituary]," *New York Times*, 16 September 1948, p. 29;

"The Prentice-Hall Story," *Book Production Magazine*, 76 (October 1962): 54-57;

"Prentice-Hall Takes Over Entire Building at 70 Fifth Avenue," *Publishers' Weekly*, 150 (2 November 1946): 2606;

"Richard P. Ettinger [obituary]," *New York Times*, 25 February 1971, p. 40;

"Ten Years of Trade Books at Prentice-Hall," *Publishers' Weekly*, 151 (5 April 1947): 1916-1919.

—Stephen Elwell

Pyramid Books
(New York: 1949-1977)

 PYRAMID BOOKS • ***NEW YORK***

In 1949 Alfred R. Plaine, president, and Matthew Huttner, secretary and treasurer, founded the Almat Publishing Company with its paperback imprint, Pyramid Books, at 185 Madison Avenue in New York. The sensational nature of the firm's earliest publications is evident in such titles as Gordon Sample's *Reckless Passion* (1949) and Thomas Stone's *Shameless Honeymoon* (1950)—both small twenty-five-cent paperbacks—as well as Allan Seager's *Cage of Lust* (1952) and C. R. Cooper's *Teenage Vice!* (1952), thirty-five-cent Pyramid Giants.

Pyramid moved to 444 Madison Avenue in 1952. Plaine and Huttner each assumed the title of copublisher. Also in 1952, Pyramid began publish-

ing original works; these included William Rohde's *The Heel* (1953) and *Give Me a Little Something* (1956). The majority of titles were mysteries, westerns, and romances, but Pyramid also published *Quintet* (1961), edited by Richard Wright. In 1956 the firm introduced a line of better-quality paperbacks, Pyramid Royals, offering reprints of John Gunther's *Death Be Not Proud* (1957) and Arthur Conan Doyle's *The Lost World* (1958).

In 1962 Almat became Pyramid Publications, Incorporated, with Plaine as chairman and Huttner as president. Pyramid began to emphasize science fiction and fantasy, including Philip José Farmer's *Tongues of the Moon* (1964) and Philip K. Dick's *The*

1955 advertisement

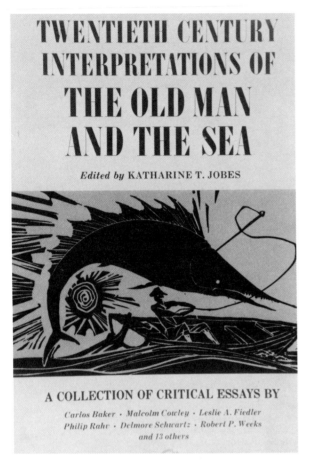

Cover for 1968 Prentice-Hall paperback

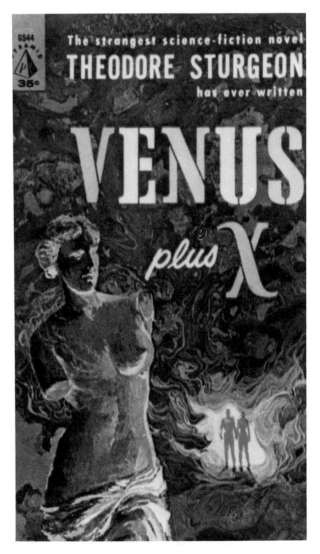

Cover for 1960 paperback original

Zap Gun (1967). In the 1960s Pyramid developed several imprints, including Hi-Lo and Willow Books for children and Little Paperback Classics.

In 1969 Pyramid became a division of the Walter Reade Organization, Incorporated at 444 Madison Avenue. In the 1970s Pyramid began the Weird Heroes series, edited by Byron Preiss and featuring science fiction, mysteries, and other genre fiction in anthology form. Pyramid started the Pyramid Specials, a series of oversized paperbacks, in 1972.

Acquired by Harcourt Brace Jovanovich in 1974, Pyramid moved to 919 Third Avenue, where it continued with Huttner in charge. It had its big-gest sellers in John Jakes's Bicentennial series, beginning with *The Bastard* (1974), and Barbara Cartland's romance novels. A religious line, Pillar Books, was started in 1975.

The Pyramid imprint came to an end in 1977 when Harcourt Brace Jovanovich replaced it with the Jove imprint. Its final address was 757 Third Avenue.

Reference:

"HBJ to Buy Pyramid; Huttner to Continue Post," *Publishers Weekly*, 211 (4 April 1977): 68.

—David Dzwonkoski

Harlin Quist Books
(New York: 1966-   )

Harlin Quist Books, specializing in children's books and posters, was founded by Harlin Quist in 1966 at 252 East Forty-ninth Street in New York. Many of the firm's publications have won awards for the high quality of their illustrations. *The Tree* (1966) by Eleonore Schmid and Etienne Delessert won a special award for graphic design at the International Children's Book Fair in Bologna, Italy, and a silver medal from the Society of Illustrators. The Society of Illustrators also awarded silver medals to Schmid's *Horns Everywhere* (1968), which was illustrated by Schmid, and to *Story Number 1* (1968) by Eugene Ionesco, which was illustrated by Delessert.

From an office at 13 rue du Cherche Midi in Paris, Harlin Quist books published children's titles which were well received in England and on the Continent. Some of these titles were brought to the United States, where they were distributed by Crown Publishers. These included *Two Wise Children* (1966) by Robert Graves and *Gertrude's Child* (1974) by Richard Hughes. In turn, Harlin Quist Books introduced the works of American authors and illustrators to the European market, among them *Famous Sally* (1966) by Shirley Jackson, illustrated by Charles B. Slackman; *Somebody Came* (1966) by Mark Van Doren, illustrated by Lorraine Fox; and *He Was There from the Day We Moved In* (1969) by Rhoda Levine, with illustrations by Edward Gorey. Harlin Quist Books subsequently established offices at 1 Dag Hammarskjold Plaza, New York 10017. Its books are sold and distributed by Dial/Delacorte Sales.

—Karin S. Mabe

Title page for 1966 publication

The Geographical History
of America
or the Relation of Human Nature
to the Human Mind

By GERTRUDE STEIN

With an Introduction by
THORNTON WILDER

PUBLISHER'S NOTE

This space is usually reserved for a brief description of a book's contents. In this case, however, I must admit frankly that I do not know what Miss Stein is talking about. I do not even understand the title.

I admire Miss Stein tremendously, and I like to publish her books, although most of the time I do not know what she is driving at. That, Miss Stein tells me, is because I am dumb.

I note that one of my partners and I are characters in this latest work of Miss Stein's. Both of us wish that we knew what she was saying about us. Both of us hope, too, that her faithful followers will make more of this book than we are able to!

President

RANDOM HOUSE

Dust jacket flap for Stein's 1936 book

Random House

(New York: 1927-   )

In 1925 Bennett Cerf and Donald S. Klopfer bought The Modern Library from Horace Liveright. Cerf had been working for Boni and Liveright for only two years; Klopfer was a friend of Cerf's with no publishing experience. The purchase price of $215,000 was a bargain for one of the most valuable properties in publishing: in 1925 The Modern Library, a line of 108 reprints of modern classics, sold about 300,000 copies without serious promotion from Liveright. Cerf and Klopfer established offices at 73 West Forty-fifth Street in New York and commissioned Lucien Bernhardt to design a new logo, the running figure with a torch. Income from the increasingly successful Modern Library soon allowed Cerf and Klopfer to diversify their interests. By 1928 a million volumes had been sold at ninety-five cents each.

In 1927 the partners decided to publish a few books "at random." Rockwell Kent drew the cottage logo, which made its first appearance on a February 1927 pamphlet announcing seven titles under a joint imprint: Random House of New York and Nonesuch Press of London. In contrast to The Modern Library concept of convenient, durable reprints at a modest price, these were elegant limited editions aimed at the opposite end of the book-buying market. The first book under the joint imprint was a 1,650-copy edition of Herman Melville's *Benito Cereno*. The firm moved to larger quarters at 20 East Fifty-seventh Street in 1928.

In spring 1928 appeared the first book to be published exclusively by Random House—an edition of Voltaire's *Candide* illustrated by Kent and limited to 1,470 copies, of which 95 had hand-colored illustrations; it was priced at $15 and $75. In 1929 Random House published 475 copies of the first edition of Edwin Arlington Robinson's *The Prodigal Son*.

Since the expensive limited editions were successful, often being oversubscribed by three or four times, Random House began offering trade editions of its books in 1929. The trade edition of *Candide* was a Literary Guild selection that year, and in 1930 the Book-of-the-Month Club offered the Random House edition of Melville's *Moby-Dick*, also illustrated by Kent.

The firm published William Faulkner's *Idyll in the Desert* (1931) in a limited edition of 400 signed copies. From that point Random House published all of Faulkner's important works, including *Absalom, Absalom!* (1936), *The Unvanquished* (1938), and *Intruder in the Dust* (1948). In 1962 Random House published his last novel, *The Reivers*, for which he won the Pulitzer Prize.

The booming market for limited editions in the 1920s was severely reduced by the Depression, and in the early 1930s Random House became exclusively a trade imprint. The firm weathered the Depression well, supported by its Modern Library books.

In 1932 Random House captured public attention and won increased respect from other publishing houses when Cerf and Klopfer launched a legal battle for the right to publish James Joyce's *Ulysses* in the United States. Originally published by Sylvia Beach in Paris under the imprint of Shakespeare and Company, *Ulysses* had been declared obscene in America. Travelers returning from abroad often smuggled copies of the Paris edition in their suitcases—a practice that inspired Cerf and Klopfer's legal strategy. Inside the covers of a smuggled copy of *Ulysses* they pasted excerpts of favorable criticism in several languages, since only material inside a copy of the book could be admitted as evidence in court. Next they found someone to take the book abroad and bring it back in a suitcase through New York customs. An agent for Random House was at the scene to insist that the customs inspector check this traveler's suitcase. The copy was seized and the landmark case was underway. In December 1933 U.S. District Court Judge John M. Woolsey declared *Ulysses* not obscene, and Random House published the first American edition in 1934.

In 1934 Random House began publishing the work of Gertrude Stein, whose *The Autobiography of Alice B. Toklas* (Harcourt, Brace, 1933) had recently made her a popular figure after years of limited-edition obscurity. Random House's Stein titles in 1934 were *Four Saints in Three Acts* and *Portraits and Prayers*. Cerf persuaded Stein to come to the United States for a lecture tour in the fall of that year; it was her first visit home in thirty-one years. The tour made her the public's favorite literary eccentric for a time and enhanced her reputation with critics. Random House remained her chief publisher until she died in 1946. Cerf and Stein enjoyed a friendship typified by Cerf's dust jacket copy for Stein's *The Geographical History of America or the Relation of Human Nature to the Human Mind* (1936):

> . . . I must admit frankly that I do not know what Miss Stein is talking about. I do not even understand the title.
>
> I admire Miss Stein tremendously and I like to publish her books, although most of the time I do not know what she is driving at. That, Miss Stein tells me, is because I am dumb.
>
> I note that one of my partners and I are characters in this latest work of Miss Stein's. Both of us wish that we knew what she was saying about us. Both of us hope, too, that her faithful followers will make more of this book than we are able to!

Story magazine, launched in 1931 and devoted exclusively to short stories, was bought by Random House and the Book-of-the-Month Club in 1933. They sold it two years later, but meanwhile the magazine had discovered new writers for Random House, including William Saroyan. Random House published his first two books, *The Daring Young Man on the Flying Trapeze and Other Stories* (1934) and *Inhale & Exhale* (1936).

After Liveright died in 1933 some of his best writers came to Random House because they knew Cerf from his Boni and Liveright days. Among them was Eugene O'Neill, who was already considered America's greatest living playwright and whose works—in contrast to most published plays—always sold well. O'Neill insisted that Random House hire Saxe Commins, with whom he had worked at Boni and Liveright, as his editor. O'Neill and Commins remained with Random House for the rest of their lives. O'Neill titles published by the firm included *Ah, Wilderness!* (1933), *The Iceman*

Cometh (1946), and *A Moon for the Misbegotten* (1952).

People at Random House loved the theater and indulged themselves in drama publishing despite the trade's conviction that people wanted to see plays, not read them. Play-reading groups bought a modest number of the Broadway comedies of the 1930s, such as George S. Kaufman and Moss Hart's *Merrily We Roll Along* (1934) and *The Man Who Came to Dinner* (1939). Much later, Hart's autobiography *Act One* (1959) became a Random House best-seller. Another playwright sought out by Random House was Irwin Shaw, whose first play, *Bury the Dead*, opened in New York in 1936. Random House published it in 1936 and another play, *The Gentle People*, in 1939. The short story collections *Sailor off the Bremen* (1939) and *Welcome to the City* (1942) followed. In 1948 Shaw's first novel, *The Young Lions*, was a best-seller. Other plays published by Random House included Clifford Odets's *Golden Boy* (1937) and *Clash by Night* (1942) and Lillian Hellman's *The Little Foxes* (1939) and *Watch on the Rhine* (1941).

Robinson Jeffers, a former Boni and Liveright author, came to Random House in the 1930s; the firm published his poetry collections *Give Your Heart to the Hawks* (1933), *Solstice* (1935), and *Such Counsels You Gave to Me* (1937). In 1946 Random House published his adaptation of Euripides' tragedy *Medea*. The British poets Stephen Spender and W. H. Auden both had collections titled *Poems* published by the firm in 1934, and Random House remained the American publisher of these poets for years. Of the many other British and continental writers published by Random House, among the most prominent were George Bernard Shaw, Robert Graves, André Malraux, and Isak Dinesen.

In 1936 Random House merged with Smith and Haas, a small firm with a prestigious list, and Harrison Smith and Robert Haas became partners with Cerf and Klopfer in Random House. Smith was bought out a year later by the other three; Haas retained part ownership of Random House until 1956, when he retired and Cerf and Klopfer bought his stock. With Smith and Haas came Louise Bonino, under whose leadership Random House began to develop a substantial children's list. Early children's titles included *Palaces on Monday* (1936) by Marjorie Fischer, *Up Creek and Down Creek* (1936) by Esther Greenacre Hall, and *The Shoemaker's Son: The Life of Hans Christian Andersen* (1941) by Constance Buel Burnett.

In 1939 Random House signed a contract with Theodor Geisel (Dr. Seuss); among his biggest Random House successes were *Horton Hatches the*

Egg (1940), *How the Grinch Stole Christmas* (1957), and *Yertle the Turtle* (1958). In the late 1950s Cerf's wife Phyllis joined Theodor and Helen Geisel to form Beginner Books, an independent line for new readers. The enterprise was successful and became a Random House subsidiary in 1960. Mrs. Cerf started two other successful series: Step-Up Books for children just beyond the Beginner Books level, and Take-Along Books to be read to preschoolers.

Probably the best-known Random House children's series was Landmark Books. Written for readers in their early teens, Landmark Books told the stories of important episodes in American history. An unusual feature of the series was the decision to seek respected writers in the adult field, rather than children's writers, as authors for the books. Early titles included Dorothy Canfield Fisher's *Paul Revere and the Minute Men* (1950) and Samuel Hopkins Adams's *The Pony Express* (1950), *The Santa Fe Trail* (1951), and *The Erie Canal* (1953).

In adult books, World War II brought several Random House best-sellers. Elliot Paul's *The Last Time I Saw Paris* (1942) was a nostalgic portrait of Paris before the war. In *Guadalcanal Diary* (1943), Richard Tregaskis, a foreign correspondent, recorded the long struggle of American marines to take the Pacific island. Another correspondent, Quentin Reynolds, described the war on several fronts in *The Curtain Rises* (1944).

In 1944 Random House joined Scribner, the Book-of-the-Month Club, Harper, and Little, Brown in the purchase of Grosset and Dunlap. Random House moved to 457 Madison Avenue in 1946.

Among new novelists Random House introduced in the 1940s was Budd Schulberg, whose first book, *What Makes Sammy Run?* (1941), showed Hollywood as a place of bitter competition and unlimited fraud. A later Schulberg novel, *The Disenchanted* (1950), presumably based on the life of F. Scott Fitzgerald, was a best-seller. Random House published John Cheever's first book, a short story collection called *The Way Some People Live*, in 1943. Other Random House novelists of the 1940s included Adams, with *Canal Town* (1944), *Banner by the Wayside* (1947), and *Plunder* (1948); and Sinclair Lewis, who came to Random House with *Gideon Planish* (1943). Lewis's *Cass Timberlane* (1945) and *Kingsblood Royal* (1947) were best-sellers. John O'Hara moved to Random House with *Hellbox* (1947) and remained with the firm until his death. His score of books included *A Rage to Live* (1949), *Ten North Frederick* (1955), and *From the Terrace* (1958).

Continued expansion of the firm in the 1950s and 1960s was aided by frequent best-sellers. One factor in this success was James Michener. He had already had a few books published by other firms, but Random House published his first novel, *The Fires of Spring*, in 1949. It was a best-seller, as were most of his later books, including *Return to Paradise* (1951), *Hawaii* (1959), *The Source* (1965), and *Centennial* (1974). Novelist Ayn Rand, whose philosophy of "objectivism" was a controversial topic of the 1950s, wrote one of the firm's best-sellers: *Atlas Shrugged* (1957), her only Random House book. Even more controversial was a nonfiction best-seller, Whittaker Chambers's *Witness* (1952), his account of his work in a communist spy ring in the 1930s, his repudiation of communism, and his role as a prosecution witness in the espionage trial of Alger Hiss.

Among literary writers, one of the firm's chief figures in this period was Robert Penn Warren. His first Random House title was *World Enough and Time* (1950), followed by *Band of Angels* (1955); a book of poems, *Promises* (1957); *The Cave* (1959); and *Wilderness* (1961). Poet Karl Shapiro began appearing on the Random House list with *Poems 1940-1953* (1953), followed by *Poems of a Jew* (1958) and *The Bourgeois Poet* (1964).

Random House editors played a vital role in attracting and developing good writers. Commins was editor in chief from 1933 to 1958 and director of The Modern Library for many years. He was known for pushing his writers to perfect their work. Albert Erskine, who had come from Reynal and Hitchcock in 1947, took over the editing of Faulkner's books after Commins's death in 1958. Erskine's authors also included O'Hara, Michener, Shapiro, Ralph Ellison, and Robert Penn Warren. Other highly respected editors were Harry Maule, who came from Doubleday with Sinclair Lewis in 1937, and Hiram Haydn, formerly of Bobbs-Merrill, who arrived in 1955.

In October 1959 Random House offered its stock to the public for the first time, selling 222,060 shares, or thirty percent of the total shares in the company. On 17 April 1960 Random House acquired Alfred A. Knopf, Incorporated, with Knopf and his wife Blanche retaining editorial control of books published under their respected Borzoi imprint. Acquired with Knopf was the Vintage line of quality paperbacks. The next year Random House purchased the distinguished Pantheon imprint which, like Knopf, remained editorially independent. Pantheon had been founded by Kurt and Helen Wolff in 1942.

A 1965 Random House title that attracted considerable attention was Truman Capote's "nonfiction novel" *In Cold Blood*. Random House had introduced Capote in 1948 with *Other Voices, Other Rooms*.

In 1965 Cerf stepped down as president of Random House, and he and Klopfer chose Robert Bernstein to succeed him. Cerf became chairman of the board. In January 1966 RCA took over control of Random House for an exchange of sixty-two percent of a share of RCA for each share of Random House. This worked out to a purchase price of $40 million.

A surprise best-seller in 1966 was *The Random House Dictionary of the English Language,* which sold out its first printing of 150,000 copies in the two months before Christmas. Like an earlier Random House product, *The American College Dictionary* (1947), it offered an important challenge to the Merriam-Webster dominance in the dictionary field.

William Styron's *The Confessions of Nat Turner,* a novel about the Virginia slave insurrection of 1831, was a controversial Random House best-seller in 1967. The following year the firm published Jerzy Kosinski's novel *Steps.* In 1969 Random House's list included Philip Roth's *Portnoy's Complaint,* which was number one on the fiction best-seller list for the year. Continuing its tradition of publishing drama, Random House has offered plays and screenplays by Woody Allen, including *Don't Drink the Water* (1967) and *Play It Again, Sam* (1969).

Cerf stepped down as chairman of Random House in 1970 and Klopfer assumed that role. Cerf died in 1971. In 1973 Bernstein announced the acquisition of Ballantine Books. Random House bought the mass market paperback imprint from Intext, Incorporated for $6.4 million. Ballantine remains an editorially independent subsidiary. Grosset and Dunlap was sold to Filmways, Incorporated in 1974.

Important Random House authors of the 1970s included Gore Vidal, Eudora Welty, and E. L. Doctorow. Vidal's *Burr* (1973) was a best-seller; his other Random House novels include *Myron* (1974), *1876* (1976), and *Creation* (1981). Welty's titles include *Losing Battles* (1970), *One Time, One Place: Mississippi in the Depression: A Snapshot Album* (1971), and *The Optimist's Daughter* (1972). Doctorow's *Ragtime* (1975) was a best-selling novel in which historical and fictional characters and incidents were skillfully interwoven.

In April 1980 RCA sold Random House to Newhouse Publications for $65 million; two years later Random House acquired Fawcett Books from CBS. Random House remains one of the biggest publishers in the world and has retained its reputation for quality. In some fifty years it has built perhaps the most important backlist of modern authors in the trade. Klopfer is chairman emeritus; Bernstein is chairman, president, and chief executive officer. In August 1984 Howard Kaminsky, former president of Warner Books, was named publisher and president of the adult trade division. Since 1968 Random House has been located at 201 East Fiftieth Street, New York 10022.

References:

"Bennett Cerf [obituary]," *New York Times,* 29 August 1971, p. 1;

Bennett Cerf, *At Random: the Reminiscences of Bennett Cerf* (New York: Random House, 1977);

"Modern Library at 20," *Newsweek,* 14 (16 October 1939): 36-37;

"Random House Celebrates Its Twenty-fifth Birthday," *Publishers' Weekly,* 158 (21 October 1950): 1844-1848;

Richard L. Simon, "Trade Winds: Bennett Cerf," *Saturday Review of Literature,* 33 (23 December 1950): 4-6, 40;

Edith M. Stern, "Random House," *Saturday Review of Literature,* 24 (6 December 1941): 18, 20, 24.

—*Margaret Becket*

Bennett Cerf (left) and Donald Klopfer at the time of their acquisition of The Modern Library in 1925

Random House offices in the north wing of a brownstone mansion at 457 Madison Avenue, New York. The firm occupied these offices from 1946 until 1968.

(Left to right) Klopfer, Cerf, and Robert K. Haas, partners in Random House from 1936 until 1956, when Haas sold his interest to the other two

(Left to right) Random House editor Albert Erskine, author John O'Hara, and Cerf admiring O'Hara's Rolls-Royce

Louise Bonino, Random House children's book editor

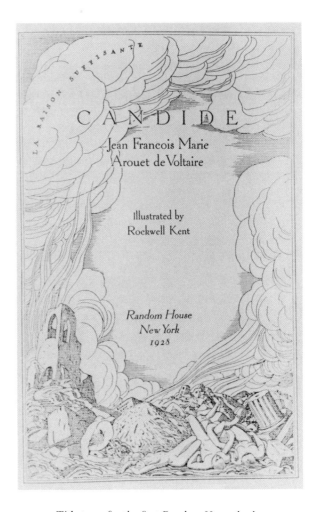

Title page for the first Random House book

Reader's Digest
Condensed Books
(Pleasantville, New York: 1950-   )

Reader's Digest Condensed Books grew directly out of *Reader's Digest* magazine, which had been publishing a book condensation in each issue for years. The plan to expand this program into a separate division of the company was that of Ralph Henderson and A. L. Cole, both now retired. In the spring of 1950 the first volume was mailed to 183,000 charter subscribers. The company's present distribution averages 2 million copies per volume in the United States; in addition to the American edition eleven separate editions, with a total of 1.5 million copies per volume, are published in Europe and Asia. The firm publishes six volumes a year, each containing condensations of four or five books. Since its founding Reader's Digest Condensed Books has condensed over 700 titles, and adds twenty to twenty-five each year. Approximately eighty percent of these are novels, the rest general nonfiction. Condensed Books does not publish poetry or drama.

Condensed Books Projects, part of the Condensed Books Department, concentrates on publishing one-shot and series books. Among the more important Condensed Books Projects series have been Best Loved Books for Young People in fourteen volumes (1966), Great Biographies in twelve volumes (1970), Best of the West in two volumes (1976), and several two-volume sets of Great Stories of Mystery and Suspense. Between 1973 and 1979 Reader's Digest Condensed Books published the Today's Non-Fiction Best Sellers series in seventeen volumes with a total of fifty-two titles. In 1982 the Condensed Books Department published *The Reader's Digest Condensed Bible*. Condensed Books are published by the Reader's Digest Association, Incorporated. John S. Zinsser, Jr., is vice-president and editor in chief; Barbara J. Morgan is executive editor. The address of Reader's Digest Condensed Books is Pleasantville, New York 10570.

Reference:

James P. Wood, *Of Lasting Interest: The Story of the Reader's Digest* (Garden City: Doubleday, 1958).

—*Nandita Batra*

Henry Regnery Company
(Hinsdale, Illinois; Chicago: 1947-1977)
Contemporary Books
(Chicago: 1977-   )

REGNERY GATEWAY, INC.

A Communications Company   Since 1947

Henry Regnery founded the Henry Regnery Company in 1947 in Hinsdale, Illinois. In 1949 the firm moved to 20 West Jackson Boulevard in Chicago. Its reputation was built on its publication of books critical of Allied policies in the reconstruction of Germany following World War II. The growing threat of communism was another focus of Regnery's early publishing activities, and political conservatism was championed in William F. Buckley's *God and Man at Yale* (1951), Russell Kirk's *The Conservative Mind* (1953), and Robert Welch's *The Life of John Birch* (1954).

Regnery also published studies of twentieth-century American literature, notably Louise Bogan's *Achievement in American Poetry, 1900-1950* (1951); American editions of Wyndham Lewis's novels *Revenge for Love* (1952), *Rotting Hill* (1952), and *Self-Condemned* (1955); Richard Weaver's *The Ethics of Rhetoric* (1953); Allen Tate's collection of essays *The Forlorn Demon* (1953); and Ezra Pound's *Impact* (1960). During the 1950s and early 1960s the firm developed a strong and successful list of titles on Roman Catholic theology and religious philosophy.

In 1957 Regnery bought the Reilly and Lee Company, a Chicago firm whose reputation as a children's publisher was based primarily on its series of Oz books by L. Frank Baum and his successors. Reilly and Lee also published Edgar Guest's poetry. The 1971 acquisition of the Cowles Book Company, a general trade and juvenile house, provided Regnery with additional diversification.

Regnery's son-in-law, Harvey Plotnick, became president in 1968 when Regnery assumed the chairmanship of the firm. In 1977 Regnery sold his interest in the firm, which became Contemporary Books, still headed by Plotnick. Contemporary Books is located at 180 North Michigan Avenue, Chicago 60601. Within months, Regnery purchased the firm's paperback line and founded Gateway Editions, Limited. In 1979 this firm was renamed Regnery Gateway, Incorporated; it publishes hardcover and paperback books, mostly nonfiction. Its address is 940-950 North Lake Shore Drive, Lake Bluff, Illinois 60044.

References:

Cleveland Amory, "Trade Winds," *Saturday Review*, 55 (22 April 1972): 10-11;

Rudolph C. Ellsworth, "Henry Regnery Company," *Catholic Library World*, 25 (1963-1964): 295-299;

"Personal Publisher," *Time*, 66 (12 December 1955): 108;

Henry Regnery, "Henry Regnery Company," *Catholic Library World*, 28 (1956-1957): 327-329;

Regnery, *Memoirs of a Dissident Publisher* (New York: Harcourt Brace Jovanovich, 1979).

—Stephen Elwell

John S. Zinsser, Jr., editor of Reader's Digest Condensed Books

Program for testimonial dinner in honor of Henry Regnery

1968 advertisement

Reilly and Lee Publishing Company
(Chicago: 1919-1977)
Reilly and Britton Publishing Company
(Chicago: 1904-1919)
Madison Book Company
(Chicago: 1902-1904)

1920s

1940s

Frank K. Reilly and Sumner C. Britton founded the Madison Book Company, sole selling agency for *Webster's Unabridged Dictionary,* in Chicago in 1902. In March 1904 the name was changed to the Reilly and Britton Publishing Company. Reilly and Britton was first located in a one-room office at 84 Adams Street and was incorporated with capital of $2,500.

The first book published under the Reilly and Britton imprint was L. Frank Baum's *The Marvelous Land of Oz* (1904), a sequel to *The Wonderful Wizard of Oz,* which had been published by the G. M. Hill Company in 1900. The publishers sponsored several promotional devices, including a contest, a sample Oz newspaper, and buttons, which popularized the Oz series and made it the strongest selling item on the trade list for many years. Twelve Oz books, written by Baum and illustrated by John R. Neill, were published before Baum's death in 1919; the series was then continued by Ruth Plumly Thompson and Jack Snow and reached a total of thirty-nine volumes by the 1950s.

In addition to the Oz books, Reilly and Britton published a large list of juveniles, general literature, and gift books. Early juvenile series included Aunt Jane's Nieces (1906), Boy Fortune Hunters (1907), and—capitalizing on current inventions—the Airship Boys and Aeroplane Boys series (1910). Books for adults ranged from the Miss Minerva series of humorous Southern tales (1910) to the serious novels of Joseph Medill Patterson, *A Little Brother of the Rich* (1908) and *Rebellion* (1911).

Reilly and Britton moved to larger quarters at 258 Wabash Avenue in 1908; a London office opened the same year. The company had increased its capital stock to $200,000 by 1911; the next year it moved to the Graphic Arts Building at 1006 South Michigan Avenue, where it occupied the entire fifth floor. During this period Britton served as president and Reilly as secretary-treasurer; in 1913 the two men exchanged titles. Three years later Britton resigned to form his own publishing house in New York. Samuel H. Darst succeeded him as secretary of Reilly and Britton, and William F. Lee, who had joined the firm in 1910, was named vice-president and member of the board of directors.

The most important new author of the decade 1910 to 1919 was Edgar A. Guest, whose first collection of poems, *A Heap o' Livin',* was published in 1916. This began a long list of Guest books, which attained huge sales over the next forty years. Another staple for the firm, *Diet and Health* by Dr. Lulu Peters, was first published in 1918. Popular novelists of this period included Opie Read, whose *The New Mr. Howerson* appeared in 1914, as well as Leona Dalrymple and Maria Thompson Daviess. In 1919 Lee became a full partner, and the firm's name was changed to Reilly and Lee. People in the book trade considered the the Reilly and Lee partnership "an ideal combination."

Reilly and Lee fiction of the 1920s frequently combined romance and mystery with social consciousness. *Peewee* (1922) by William MacHarg and *Saturday Nights* (1922) by Earl G. Curtis dealt with problems faced by poor residents of the Chicago slums. Patriotism in the aftermath of World War I marked the juvenile fiction of Roy J. Snell, whose mystery stories for boys contained "little lessons against radicalism." Gen. Leonard Wood's *America's*

Duty (1921) taught readers lessons learned from the war.

Lee died in 1924. In 1927 the firm moved to larger offices at 536 Lake Shore Drive. Steady expansion of the business outside of Chicago resulted in the opening of a New York office at 51 East Forty-second Street the same year.

Reilly and Lee promoted its publications of the 1920s through a variety of special advertising campaigns and contests. Thompson wrote a play, *A Day in Oz,* with songs by Norman Sherrerd, to publicize Children's Book Week in 1925. Reilly and Lee furnished costumes, and the play was performed in many cities under the sponsorship of local booksellers. In 1928 Reilly and Lee announced a contest, with a prize of $1,000, for the best title submitted for Guest's new book of verse. The winner was a Detroit clergyman who suggested *Harbor Lights of Home.*

Reilly died in 1932, the same year the firm moved to 325 West Huron Street. Frank J. O'Connell became president. Reilly and Lee survived the Depression by relying on its established authors and its lines of cookbooks, graduation books, and baby books. Reference works were added, including the revised *Webster's Unabridged Dictionary* (1928) and the *New Pictorial Atlas* (1933). R. E. Pinkerton's novels *The Test of Donald Norton* (1924) and *The Fourth Norwood* (1925) and adventure books such as Sterling North's *Tiger* (1933) were also successful.

Esther Gould was made literary editor in 1934 with the responsibility of expanding the fiction list. Western titles were added during the late 1930s,

including the illustrated books of cowboy-artist Dan Muller. In 1940 Reilly and Lee began handling sales and distribution of the books of the Caxton Printers of Caldwell, Idaho. Caxton had built up a long list of Western Americana and travel books. After World War II Reilly and Lee continued to keep in print many of its popular series and added new volumes of Guest and Oz. Biographies of Guest and Baum were published in 1955 and 1962, respectively.

In 1957 Reilly and Lee was acquired by the Henry Regnery Company. Regnery retained the Reilly and Lee imprint for juveniles and reprints, including juvenile biographies by Edwin Hoyt; fiction by Enid Blyton; an anthology of poems for young people, *The Golden Journey* (1965), edited by Louise Bogan and William Jay Smith; and the Oz books. The Reilly and Lee imprint was dropped when Regnery became Contemporary Books, Incorporated in 1977.

References:

"Frank K. Reilly [obituary]," *Publishers' Weekly,* 121 (4 June 1932): 2261;

"The Reilly and Britton Co. of Wabash Avenue, Chicago," *Canadian Bookseller & Newsagent & Stationers' Journal* (October 1908): 25;

"The Reilly & Lee Co. Celebrate Their Twenty-fifth Anniversary," *Publishers' Weekly,* 111 (9 April 1927): 1500-1501;

"William F. Lee [obituary]," *New York Times,* 8 March 1924, p. 11.

                                                          —*Annie E. Stevens*

1928 advertisement

Reynal and Hitchcock
(New York: 1933-1948)

Reynal and Hitchcock was established in October 1933 by Eugene Reynal and Curtice Hitchcock with the intent of publishing "a small distinguished list covering many fields." Most of the works published by the firm were nonfiction, but its list included some quality fiction. Educated at Harvard and Oxford, Reynal had started his publishing career in the shipping room at Harper; he quickly moved up to become manager of Blue Ribbon Books, a publisher of cheap hardcover reprints which was owned by a consortium of publishers. Reynal bought Blue Ribbon Books in 1933. Hitchcock had been an editor at Macmillan and at Stokes. In their new firm, Reynal was primarily responsible for business matters, while Hitchcock dealt with editorial concerns.

Initially the firm occupied offices at 448 Fourth Avenue, where it shared sales, advertising, and bookkeeping staffs with Blue Ribbon Books. Within a year the firm moved to 386 Fourth Avenue.

In 1934, in order to ensure their mutual survival during the Depression, Reynal and Hitchcock formed an association with the John Day Company. Each firm maintained a separate editorial department, but all other publishing operations were handled by Reynal and Hitchcock. The arrangement was terminated in 1938 when Day entered into a similar association with Putnam.

In January 1934 Reynal and Hitchcock issued its first list of fifty-four titles, nearly all of which were nonfiction. The few literary titles included Elizabeth Corbett's *Mr. Underhill's Progress* and *The House across the River* and Tex Harding's *The Devil's Drummer*. Subsequent fiction included Rosamond Lehmann's *The Weather in the Streets* (1936) and the popular Mary Poppins series by P. L. Travers. Lin Yutang's *The Importance of Living* (1937) was a bestselling nonfiction title. In its first five years of existence the firm published 100 titles which sold an average of 9,000 copies each. By 1940 it was publishing the works of Otto W. Tolchius, George Fielding Eliot, Francis Brett Young, Thurman Arnold, and Gustav Stolper.

In 1939, by arrangement with Houghton, Mifflin, the firm published Hitler's *Mein Kampf;* by the time Reynal and Hitchcock returned the property in 1942, it had sold over 280,000 copies. In 1940 the firm organized a college division under T. J. Wilson, who had come from Henry Holt and Company; but when he left in 1941 to enter military service, no replacement was hired. The twelve texts in the list were leased to Houghton, Mifflin and later sold to Holt.

During World War II Reynal and Hitchcock published a few fiction titles, including Antoine de Saint-Exupéry's *Flight to Arras* (1942); Lillian Smith's *Strange Fruit* (1944); and Arthur Miller's first book, *Situation Normal* (1944). In 1944 the firm started the Labor Book Club and in 1945 began the Pamphlet Press, both short-lived endeavors. Also in 1945 Reynal and Hitchcock moved to 8 West Fortieth Street.

The last few years of the firm's existence saw the publication of Lehmann's *The Ballad and the Source* (1945); Noel Houston's *The Great Promise* (1946); Roald Dahl's second book, *Over to You: 10 Stories of Flyers and Flying* (1946); Josephine Miles's *Local Measures* (1946); and Francis Steegmuller's *States of Grace* (1946).

In May 1946, at the peak of the firm's literary output, Hitchcock died of a heart attack. Several important literary titles were published over the next two years, including Miller's *All My Sons* (1947); Malcolm Lowry's *Under the Volcano* (1947); Charles Olson's first book, *Call Me Ishmael* (1947); and Alfred Kazin's *The Open Street* (1948). Reynal, feeling the lack of his partner's editorial expertise, arranged a merger in 1948 with Harcourt, Brace and Company, where he took over the trade department.

Reynal left Harcourt, Brace in 1955 to establish Reynal and Company at 221 East Forty-ninth Street. Viking Press handled the firm's sales and distribution until William Morrow and Company took over in 1962. Among Reynal's first publications were Alan Valentine's *Vigilante Justice* and Reginald Arkell's *The Miracle of Merriford*, both in 1956. Reynal published several books on art, including *The Complete Work of Michelangelo* (1965) and Charles H. Morgan's *George Bellows, Painter of America* (1965). After Reynal died in 1968 the company was absorbed by William Morrow.

References:

"Curtice N. Hitchcock [obituary]," *Publishers' Weekly*, 149 (11 May 1946): 2564-2565;

318

It isn't the size of the list or the individual best seller that counts—it's the batting average and the length of book life. Out of the 12 new titles† on the REYNAL & HITCHCOCK 1935 fall list . . .

1 sold over 25,000
1 sold over 20,000
1 sold 17,000
1 sold 9,000
2 sold between 6,000 and 9,000
2 sold between 4,000 and 6,000
2 (published in late November, both expensive books), sold between 2,000 and 3,000

The remaining 2 fell between 1,000 and 2,000 and could be classed as commercial failures.

Out of the total, at least half, we confidently predict, will sell as many copies in 1936 as in their first season. Some will sell more.

And on the same principle is built the following short list for the first three months of the spring season.

January

THE NEXT HUNDRED YEARS by C. C. Furnas   A Book-of-the-Month Club Selection $3.00
WHERE LIFE IS BETTER by James Rorty $3.00*
THE WHOLE WORLD & COMPANY by Gretchen Green $3.00*

February

THE EXILE by Pearl S. Buck $2.50*
MOUNT ROYAL by Elizabeth Corbett $2.00
HOLY IRELAND, A Novel by Norah Hoult $2.50
THE ACTIVITY PROGRAM by A. Gordon Melvin $3.50*

March

THE YANKEE BODLEYS, A Novel by Naomi Lane Babson $2.50

In late March or April, we shall publish THE WEATHER IN THE STREETS, the new novel by Rosamond Lehmann, author of Dusty Answer and Invitation to the Waltz.

*JOHN DAY Books

†Titles and exact figures supplied on request.

Reynal & Hitchcock
386 FOURTH AVENUE, NEW YORK

1936 advertisement

Eugene Reynal (left) and Curtice Hitchcock

Stanley M. Rinehart, Jr.

"Eugene Reynal [obituary]," *Publishers' Weekly,* 193 (1 April 1968): 21-22;

"John Day Makes Arrangements to Publish through R. & H.," *Publishers' Weekly,* 126 (1 December 1934): 1990;

"Reynal and Hitchcock Combines with Harcourt, Brace," *Publishers' Weekly,* 153 (3 January 1948): 38.

—*Philip A. Metzger*

Rinehart and Company
(New York: 1945-1959)

Rinehart and Company was founded by Stanley M. Rinehart, Jr., in December 1945, after the resignation of John Farrar from Farrar and Rinehart. The firm retained the titles and series originally published under the Farrar and Rinehart imprint and built up strong new lists in both the college and trade departments. Officers of the new company included Rinehart as president, his brother Frederick as first vice-president, Ranald P. Hobbs as vice-president in charge of the college department, and H. Stahley Thompson as vice-president for production. Theodore Amussen became vice-president and head of the trade book department in 1953.

The Rivers of America series, initiated by Farrar and Rinehart in 1937, was Rinehart's most successful publishing sequence, with every volume continuously in print through 1959. The first volume, *Kennebec* (1937) by Robert P. Tristram Coffin, was followed by fifty-one others, representing every region of the United States, over the next seventeen years.

New publications on Rinehart's first list in 1946 included *The Hucksters* by Frederic Wakeman, chosen as a Book-of-the-Month Club selection; other authors on the list were Stephen Vincent Benét, Erich Fromm, Archibald MacLeish, Hervey Allen, and Mary Roberts Rinehart. Faith Baldwin's *Woman on Her Way* and *No Private Heaven* and Philip Wylie's *An Essay on Morals* all appeared in 1947.

Rinehart actively promoted its publications and encouraged the development of new writers through contests and publicity campaigns. In 1947 Rinehart, in cooperation with Paul Engle and the Writers Workshop of the University of Iowa, established an annual fellowship for young writers; the first award of $750 went to Flannery O'Connor. Winners of the Rinehart-sponsored Mary Roberts Rinehart Mystery Novel Contest and the U. S. Army Short Story Contest received publishing contracts. In December 1948 Rinehart became the first publisher to contribute books as prizes on a radio quiz program, "Hit the Jackpot": the library of over 300 titles, valued at $1,000, included most of the books on the Rinehart trade list.

In 1948 Rinehart published Norman Mailer's *The Naked and the Dead; The Lion and the Rose,* a book of poems by May Sarton; and a biography of Nathaniel Hawthorne by Robert Cantwell. The success of *The Naked and the Dead* was especially noteworthy in view of its major handicaps: it was a war novel, published when booksellers were sure a war novel would not sell; it was a first novel by an unknown author; and it was high priced at four dollars. George C. Bartter, director of advertising and publicity, credited daily advertisements in the newspapers of ten major cities for the rapid success of the book. *The Naked and the Dead* topped the bestseller list within six weeks of publication; it sold 100,000 copies in five months and over 180,000 by the end of the year. In 1949 Rinehart published Wylie's *Opus 21,* Gertrude Stein's *Last Operas and Plays,* and Francine Findler's *The Root and the Bough.* The first 20 volumes of the Rinehart Editions, a paperback series of literary classics published by Rinehart's college department, appeared in 1950; the series eventually numbered over 100 titles. Also in 1950 Rinehart published David Daiches's biography of Robert Burns and Sarton's *Shadow of a Man.*

Innovative book design and the use of new technology made Rinehart well known in the trade. The American Institute of Graphic Arts chose Rinehart as the winner of the 1949 *Bookbinding and Book Production* magazine award for "consistent excellence in trade book design." A factor in the selection was Rinehart's successful application of good design to new techniques in production. Composition by IBM typewriter, instead of standard printing, halved the costs involved in publishing Hans Letz's *Music for the Violin and Viola* (1948). In 1953 Rinehart published *The Wonderful World of Insects* by Albro T. Gaul, the first book composed by electronic photo-composer. Printed by offset, the book had a new type of binding—plasticized paper—and was printed in two colors and lacquered. Rinehart's second photo-composed book, *The New Testament in Cadenced Form* (1954), represented the first use of the photo-composer for a book printed by letterpress and the first book printed from Dow Rapid-Etch magnesium plates.

In 1951 Rinehart acquired a controlling interest in A. S. Barnes and Company, which had been in business since 1838 chiefly as a publisher of nonfiction. Rinehart controlled basic publishing operations and the Barnes editors moved into Rinehart's offices at 232 Madison Avenue, but the two companies remained editorially and financially independent. In 1955 Rinehart sold its interest to John Lowell Pratt, president of A. S. Barnes.

Rinehart publications of the 1950s included Mailer's *Barbary Shore* (1951); Wylie's *The Disappearance* (1951); Sarton's *A Shower of Summer Days* (1952), *The Land of Silence* (1953), *Faithful Are the Wounds* (1955), *In Time Like Air* (1958), and *I Knew a Phoenix* (1959); William March's *The Bad Seed* (1954); *Hear Me Talkin' to Ya* (1955), a popular history of jazz by Nat Shapiro and Nat Hentoff; Leo

W. Schwarz's *Feast of Leviathan* (1956); May Swenson's *A Cage of Spines* (1958); and the *Peanuts* cartoon series by Charles M. Schulz. Writers of juvenile works included Elizabeth Enright, Leon Dean, and Helen Girvan.

Mary Roberts Rinehart, the mother of Stanley and Frederick Rinehart and the author of fifty-five books, died in 1959 at eighty-two. Her first book, *The Circular Staircase*, originally published by Bobbs-Merrill in 1908, was Rinehart's all-time top seller, with a fifty-year sales record of 400,000 in hardcover and 800,000 in paperback. Sales of all of her books totaled over 20 million copies. She had actively participated in her sons' publishing business as a writer and a member of the board of directors.

In December 1959 Rinehart and Company and the John C. Winston Company, publishers of elementary school textbooks, merged with Henry Holt and Company to form Holt, Rinehart and Winston. At the time of the merger the total sales volume of the three companies was estimated at $35 million. The firm was purchased by CBS, Incorporated in 1967. Stanley Rinehart served as senior vice-president and member of the board of directors of Holt, Rinehart and Winston until his death in 1969.

References:

Rinehart Editions, the First 100: A Report by the Publishers (New York: Rinehart, 1960);

"Stanley M. Rinehart, Jr. [obituary]," *New York Times*, 27 April 1969, p. 92;

"The Story of Holt, Rinehart, and Winston, Inc.," *Book Publishers Monthly*, 78 (July 1963): 30-34;

John T. Winterich, "Rinehart Celebrates on September 3 Its Twenty-fifth Anniversary," *Publishers' Weekly*, 166 (4 September 1954): 826-832.

—Annie E. Stevens

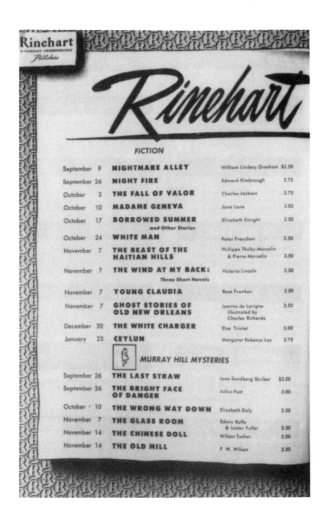

1946 advertisement

The Saalfield Publishing
Company
(Akron, Ohio: 1900-1977)

When the Werner Company, a book manufacturing and publishing company in Akron, Ohio, decided to dispose of its book publishing department in late 1899, the manager of the department, Arthur J. Saalfield, purchased the business. On 1 January 1900 he started what was to become one of the largest publishers of children's books, activity books, and reprints in the world.

The Saalfield Publishing Company's early stock consisted of books originally published by Werner, including Fanny Lemira Gillette's *White House Cook Book* (1900), Bibles, dictionaries, and a host of subscription and premium books, but Saalfield soon began to publish original works. Among these were *Mr. Bunny, His Book* (1900) and *Teddy Bears* (1907) by Saalfield's wife, Adah Louise Sutton; James Ball Naylor's *Ralph Marlowe* (1901), *In the Days of St. Clair* (1902), and *Under Mad Anthony's Banner* (1903); Frances Trego Montgomery's *Billy Whiskers* (1903), the first book in the popular Billy Whiskers series; James A. Braden's *The Lone Indian* (1903), *The Cabin in the Clearing* (1904), *The Trail of the Seneca* (1907), and Auto Boys series; and Matthew Stanley Kemp's proletarian novel *Boss Tom* (1904).

By 1906 the company needed more space than it had at the Werner plant and Saalfield bought the Globe Sign Company at South High Street and Miller Avenue. This facility enabled Saalfield to produce children's books made of muslin, which became important in the firm's line. The company began to specialize in the production of children's books, concentrating on low-priced reprints of popular classics or recently out-of-print titles. These books had great success in five-and-ten-cent stores.

Albert G. Saalfield, Saalfield's oldest son, had joined the company in 1905. Albert was important in the development of inexpensive children's books and is credited with beginning another line for which the company was famous, paper doll and activity books. The years before World War I were marked by a steady improvement in production and marketing methods, expansion in the international market, and the purchase of additional office and production space. Business boomed during the war with an increase in demand for children's books. A new building was erected next to the Globe building in 1917, the year Arthur J. Saalfield, Jr., entered the business; another building was added in 1926.

The Saalfield Publishing Company's search for new markets led it into a publishing enterprise that proved to be a great success: "royalty properties," involving the acquisition of exclusive rights to publications related to motion picture stars and other entertainers. In 1933 the firm secured the rights to publications featuring Shirley Temple. Six weeks after the introduction of Shirley Temple books and paper dolls, sales exceeded four million, fifteen times the return ordinarily considered acceptable, and the demand kept climbing. A new building had to be erected in 1937 to handle the volume. Many motion picture personalities, cartoon characters, and later, television figures were added to the Saalfield list, among them Mary Martin, Bing Crosby, Jane Arden, the Quiz Kids, Ann Sothern, Jane Russell, Marilyn Monroe, Mickey Mouse, Li'l Abner, Peanuts, Woody Woodpecker, and assorted characters from *Finian's Rainbow, Gulliver's Travels, Goodbye, Mr. Chips,* "The Cisco Kid," "Wyatt Earp," and "Bonanza."

The company maintained its specialization in books, games, and activity books for children throughout the rest of its existence. Albert Saalfield's son, Henry R. Saalfield, who had joined the firm in 1936, was president when the company ceased operations in 1977.

References:

"Albert G. Saalfield [obituary]," *New York Times*, 10 February 1959, p. 33;

"Fiftieth Anniversary Observed by Saalfield," *Publishers' Weekly*, 157 (11 March 1950): 1350-1351;

Viola A. Smith, "History of the Saalfield Publishing Company, Akron, Ohio," M. A. thesis, Kent State University, 1951.

—Dean H. Keller

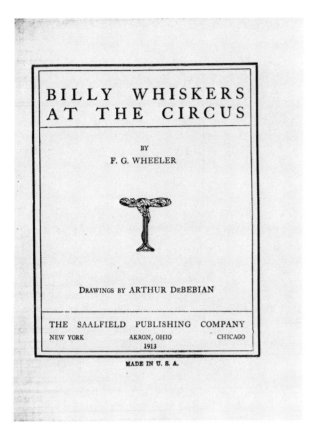

Title page for a book in the popular children's series about the goat Billy Whiskers

1928 advertisement

St. Martin's Press
(New York: 1952-   )

1955

Macmillan and Company, Limited of London established St. Martin's Press at 103 Park Avenue, New York, in 1952 as a distributor for those Macmillan books for which American rights were not held by other publishers. The following year St. Martin's was also designated as the American distributor of selected books published in England by Edward Arnold, Limited. St. Martin's early lists were dominated by English reference works (the most successful of which was *Grove's Dictionary of Music and Musicians*), textbooks, and trade reprints.

St. Martin's relationship with Macmillan has shifted over the years toward a more flexible arrangement which allows it to publish its own books and to negotiate with other British houses for reprint and joint publication rights. Most of the company's trade list, however, still originates in England. Ian MacKenzie, who took over the direction of St. Martin's from Daniel Macmillan in 1956, was instrumental in introducing titles of American origin into St. Martin's trade list. Robert Traver's *Anatomy of a Murder* (1958) was one of the most successful titles published during MacKenzie's tenure. But when St. Martin's experienced financial difficulties in 1962, MacKenzie was replaced by Frank Upjohn, and the firm fell back on established reference books such as the British *Who's Who*, the *Annual Register of World Events*, the *Statesman's Yearbook*, and *Roget's Thesaurus*.

St. Martin's development as a domestic trade publisher really began in 1970, when Thomas J. McCormack, who had joined the firm a year earlier as director of its trade department, became president. In his first ten years, McCormack increased the firm's output ten times. Profits also increased dramatically. McCormack's concentration on extending St. Martin's list resulted in the publication of Fay Weldon's novels *Down among the Women*

(1972) and *Female Friends* (1974) and James Herriot's best-selling autobiographical quartet *All Creatures Great and Small* (1972), *All Things Bright and Beautiful* (1974), *All Things Wise and Wonderful* (1977), and *The Lord God Made Them All* (1981). M. M. Kaye's *The Far Pavilions*, a 1978 best-seller, was followed by Jerzy Kosinski's *Passion Play* (1979).

Category fiction, a house staple, has included romantic novels by Pamela Hill and Rosamunde Pilcher, mysteries by Duncan Kyle, and the work of prominent science fiction writers Frederik Pohl, Gordon Dickson, and Joseph W. Haldeman, whose *The Forever War* (1974) won the Nebula and Hugo awards. In 1979 the company published G. Gordon Liddy's first novel, *Out of Control*, and in the spring of 1980 it brought out Liddy's autobiography, *Will*. In 1981 Richard Marek established his imprint, Richard Marek Books, at St. Martin's; the imprint ceased when Marek left in November 1985 to become president of E. P. Dutton.

While St. Martin's has concentrated on increasing its general trade list, it has also continued its development of school and college texts for the American market in the areas of composition, drama, fiction, poetry, science, reading, and language study. The firm published 750 titles in 1984. McCormack remains president of St. Martin's Press; Alexander Macmillan is chairman of the board. The firm is currently located at 175 Fifth Avenue, New York 10010.

Reference:

Madalynne Reuter, "All Things Bright and Exuberant: St. Martin's Press Is 25 Years Old," *Publishers Weekly*, 212 (8 August 1977): 30-33.

—Stephen Elwell

Thomas J. McCormack, president of St. Martin's Press

David I. Rome, president of Schocken Books
(photo ©Marvin Moore)

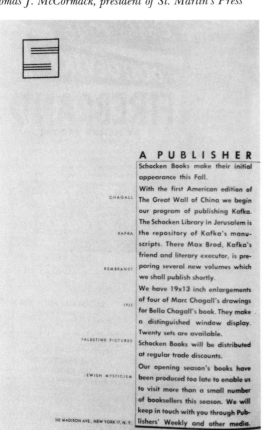

A PUBLISHER

CHAGALL

KAFKA

REMBRANDT

1933

PALESTINE PICTURES

JEWISH MYSTICISM

312 MADISON AVE. NEW YORK 17, N.Y.

Schocken Books make their initial appearance this Fall.

With the first American edition of The Great Wall of China we begin our program of publishing Kafka. The Schocken Library in Jerusalem is the repository of Kafka's manuscripts. There Max Brod, Kafka's friend and literary executor, is preparing several new volumes which we shall publish shortly.

We have 19x13 inch enlargements of four of Marc Chagall's drawings for Bella Chagall's book. They make a distinguished window display. Twenty sets are available. Schocken Books will be distributed at regular trade discounts.

Our opening season's books have been produced too late to enable us to visit more than a small number of booksellers this season. We will keep in touch with you through Publishers' Weekly and other media.

SCHOCKEN BOOKS

PRESENTS HIS FIRST LIST

IN TIME AND ETERNITY: A JEWISH READER. An anthology of eighteen centuries of Jewish life and thought. With new translations of old documents and prayers. Edited by Nahum N. Glatzer. 256 pages. November. $2.75

BELLA CHAGALL: BURNING LIGHTS. With 36 original drawings by Marc Chagall. The wife of the great painter tells folk stories of her Russian-Jewish childhood. 268 pages. October. $3.00

GERSHOM G. SCHOLEM: MAJOR TRENDS IN JEWISH MYSTICISM. "Will at once take its place in the list of the most significant books on Mystical Religion and withal he knows how to write effectively."—Rufus M. Jones in the Harvard Theological Review. 460 pages. November. $5.50

FRANZ KAFKA: THE GREAT WALL OF CHINA. Stories and Reflections. Translated by Willa and Edwin Muir. 316 pages. October 25. $3.00

KARL WOLFSKEHL: 1933: POEMS. For 30 years Wolfskehl was a central figure in German literary and artistic life. Driven out of a cherished culture, he responded in these poems. Both German and English text. January. $2.75

ROMAN VISHNIAC: POLISH JEWS. Last pictorial record of people and places destroyed. On the eve of the war the photographer took pictures of Jewish life from the Baltic to the Carpathians. With an introductory essay by Abraham Joshua Heschel. Spring. $4.50

MARTIN BUBER: HASIDIC TALES. For forty years Buber has been retelling stories of the Hasidic movement. He presents here his final version. This volume deals with the founder and his disciples. 280 pages. Translated by Olga Marx. January. $3.00

MAX BROD: FRANZ KAFKA. A Biography. A lifelong friend who has introduced Kafka to the literary world, Brod's authority and knowledge are unique. Translated by G. Humphrey Roberts. With illustrations. About 250 pages. January. $3.00

A. REIFENBERG: ANCIENT HEBREW ARTS. Over 200 illustrations show the relics of Hebrew culture in biblical and talmudic times in Palestine and the Hellenic and Roman world. This volume presents the findings of modern archaeology. About 250 pages. Spring. $4.50

J. ROSNER: A PALESTINE PICTURE BOOK. A photographer who has lived in Palestine for twenty years shows the landscape of the country and the life of its settlers. 130 photographs. Spring. $5.50

REMBRANDT'S DRAWINGS FROM THE BIBLE. Thirty-two drawings of biblical scenes by the Dutch master, faithfully reproduced in original size. Collotype. 10x12½ inches. Portfolio. Spring. $7.50

FRANZ KAFKA: COLLECTED WORKS IN GERMAN. A second, revised edition with additional material of the "Gesammelte Schriften." Edited by Max Brod. Volumes I-V. Average 330 pages. October. Each volume $3.00

1946 advertisement

Saturday Review Press
(New York: 1971-1977)
McCall Books
(New York: 1968-1971)

McCall Books was founded in New York in 1968 by Norton Simon. When Saturday Review Industries, headed by Nicholas Charney and John Veronis, took over the *Saturday Review* magazine and McCall Books in 1971, the firm became Saturday Review Press. In 1973 the firm was sold to E. P. Dutton and Company with the agreement that the name Saturday Review Press could be used only for a limited time. In 1977 the division was merged into the Dutton adult division. Among novels published by the Saturday Review Press were Robert Rossner's *A Hero Like Me: A Hero Like You* (1972), Marvin Kaye's *A Lively Game of Death* (1972) and *The Grand Ole Opry Murders* (1974), Jack Pearl's *Callie Knight* (1974), and Noel B. Gerson's *Special Agent* (1976).

—*Carole Michaels-Katz*

Schocken Books
(New York: 1945-   )

Salman Schocken founded Schocken Verlag in Berlin in 1928 to publish books of particular interest to the German Jewish population. Schocken established an impressive list of authors, including S. Y. Agnon, who in 1966 won the Nobel Prize for literature; Martin Buber, who did editorial work for the firm; and Franz Kafka, to whose works Schocken acquired world rights in 1934.

The rise of Nazism in Germany incited Schocken to increase the publication of Judaica, and in 1938 the firm was closed by the Gestapo. Schocken moved its headquarters to Palestine, where it had already established a branch. In 1945 Schocken established Schocken Books, Incorporated as the American branch of the firm. The American Schocken offered literature of Jewish interest, mostly by Jewish writers. The firm published Bella Chagall's *Burning Lights* (1946), Max Brod's biography of Kafka (1947), Buber's *Tales of the Hasidim* in two volumes (1947-1948), Kafka's *The Penal Colony* (1948), *The Diaries of Franz Kafka* in two volumes (1948-1949), *The Collected Poems of Isaac Rosenberg* (1949), and Kafka's *Dearest Father* (1954). Roman Vishniac, Shalom Aleichem, and Yitzhak Shenberg are other writers whose work has been published by the firm. Salman Schocken died in New York in 1959.

Under the leadership of Schocken's son-in-law, T. Herzl Rome, and then of Schocken's son, Theodore, Schocken Books continued publishing Judaica and Kafka in the 1960s and 1970s; but it also expanded its list to include psychology, art, history, women's studies, and literary criticism. In addition it developed an extensive paperback list. Schocken Books is noted for its publications in ecology and for its reprints of Maria Montessori's educational works. The Montessori books were a special interest of Eva Schocken Glaser, who became head of the house after Theodore Schocken's death in 1975.

The firm relies heavily on its backlist of over 1,000 titles and tries to keep its books in print as long as possible. In the early 1980s Schocken began to increase its publication of original works, as opposed to reprints. The firm had best-sellers in Kit Williams's *Masquerade* (1980) and Harold S. Kushner's *When Bad Things Happen to Good People* (1981), each of which had sold over 400,000 copies in hardcover by 1984. In 1984 it published a translation of a 500-year-old Spanish novel, *Tirant lo Blanc* by Joanot Martorell and Martí Joan de Galba. The firm published eighty-four titles that year. In 1985 Schocken published, to unprecedented critical acclaim, Raymond Rosenthal's translation of *The Periodic Table* by Primo Levi—the first English translation of a work by the Italian chemist and

Auschwitz survivor to appear in twenty years.

David I. Rome is president of Schocken Books, which is located at 62 Cooper Square, New York 10003.

References:
"Salman Schocken [obituary]," *New York Times*, 8 August 1959, p. 17;

"Schocken Books to Issue First Titles in October,"

Publishers' Weekly, 150 (19 October 1946): 2350;

"Schocken Publishing House," *Publishers Weekly*, 215 (19 March 1979): 44-45;

"Small Publisher With Big Literary Ideas," *New York Times*, 21 July 1984, I: 13;

"Theodore Schocken [obituary]," *New York Times*, 21 March 1975, p. 40.

                                                                        —*Deborah G. Gorman*

William R. Scott
(New York: 1938-1970)

The firm of William R. Scott, Incorporated was founded in New York by William R. Scott and his wife Ethel McCullough Scott, a teacher and organizer of progressive primary schools in New York and in Bennington, Vermont, in the fall of 1938 when they wrote and handcrafted *Cotton Tails: A Tactile Book*. With encouragement from a New York bookseller, demand for the book outran the supply even when the price rose, and the Scotts were kept busy for a while sewing the books by hand. The next year the firm introduced the first of its Noisy Book series, similar in concept to its first book but not handcrafted.

The three original stockholders and editors of the firm were the Scotts and her brother John G. McCullough. Its address was 248 West Eleventh Street. In 1940 the business office was moved to North Bennington, Vermont, but the editorial office remained in New York. In April 1942 the firm moved to 72 Fifth Avenue. Lillian Lustig joined the firm in March 1944 and became president within two years. In 1946 William Scott was elected chairman of the board, McCullough became vice-president and treasurer, and Ethel Scott became secretary. About this time the firm moved to 513 Sixth Avenue.

In 1943 William R. Scott, Incorporated listed 32 children's titles by 19 authors, along with a single adult book. By 1970 there were 165 titles, all for children, by 67 authors. Many books remained on Scott's lists for years, in part because the firm did not require large sales for books to be kept in print.

Most of the books were for children of eight years and younger. The books explained the world in terms suitable to a child's age level, as in *The Man in the Manhole and the Fix-It Men* (1946) by Juniper

Sage and Bill Ballantine and *Dark Is Dark* (1947) by McCullough. The award-winning *Stick-in-the-Mud* (1953), written and illustrated by Jean and Fred Ketchum, respectively, combined explanatory information with fantasy, humor, and storytelling. Nature and science books, such as *How Big Is Big—From Stars to Atoms* (1946) by Herman and Nina Schneider and *Thanks to Trees—Their Use and Conservation* (1952) by Irma E. Webber, frequently appeared in the lists. The firm published songbooks; cookbooks; how-to-do-it books; how-to-say-it books in English, French, and Spanish; and books about other cultures. Manuscripts were pretested on children before publication.

Illustrators of Scott books were well-known artists; among them were Jean Charlot, Esphyr Slobodkina, Lucienne Bloch, and Leonard Weisgard. Margaret Wise Brown was the Scott author with the greatest number of titles. The Schneiders, Webber, Miriam Schlein, and May Garelick also wrote many books for the firm.

Scott continued to grow slowly, moving to 8 West Thirteenth Street in 1950 and to 333 Avenue of the Americas in 1965. In 1970 the firm was acquired by Addison-Wesley Publishing Company in Reading, Massachusetts. Young Scott Books became an imprint of Addison-Wesley.

References:
"Don't Push It Please," *Publishers' Weekly*, 136 (26 August 1939): 689;

"Ten Years of Studied Growth," *Publishers' Weekly*, 153 (24 April 1948): 1801-1802.

                                                                        —*Theodora Mills*

1942 advertisement

Sears Publishing Company
(New York: 1929-1934)
J. H. Sears Company
(New York: 1922-1929)

After having been president of Appleton from 1904 to 1918, Joseph H. Sears started his own publishing firm, J. H. Sears Company, in 1922 at 17 East Fifty-fourth Street in New York. In 1925 the company moved to 40 West Fifty-seventh Street.

Sears published books on domestic subjects, such as gardening, housekeeping, and etiquette, as well as reference volumes and vocational books. In 1926 Sears, in collaboration with the Kingsport Press of Tennessee, introduced a line of small ten-cent cloth-bound books known as The American Home Classics. The series included works by Bunyan, Defoe, Dickens, and Hawthorne, as well as such popular fiction as Ouida's *Under Two Flags* and Marie Corelli's *Thelma*. Another Sears reprint line was The Royal Blue Library, which also offered cheap editions of classics. Millions of these books were sold between 1926 and 1929, largely through displays in Woolworth and Sears, Roebuck stores.

In 1929 the firm was reincorporated as Sears Publishing Company; the following year it moved to 114 East Thirty-second Street. In 1930 Sears published Samuel Hopkins Adams's *The Godlike Daniel* and James G. Dunton's *The Counterfeit Wife;* Arthur Somers Roche's *The Gracious Lady* appeared in 1932.

In 1934, following a gradual decrease in production, Sears Publishing Company was bought by Frank C. Dodd and incorporated into Dodd, Mead. Sears retired, and died in 1946.

Reference:
"Joseph H. Sears [obituary]," *New York Times,* 17 February 1946, p. 42.

—David W. Raymond

New Spring Publications of
SEARS PUBLISHING CO., Inc.
114 East 32nd Street   New York

NEW FICTION

Music in the Street   *By Vera Caspary* $2.00
Rich with the ecstacy of young love and secret hopes and desires.

Contact   *By Elliot White Springs* $2.50
A powerful novel which draws a vivid picture of a flying man's psychology.

The Perfect Leaf   *By Frank A. Fortescue* $2.00
Nobody will ever be able to explain woman to mankind.

Narcissus   *By John Hawley Roberts* $2.50
The story of a young man who held that his body should not be defiled.

The Age of Youth   *By Arthur Somers Roche* $2.00
The charming romance of a girl who borrowed $25,000 from a man.

The Passionate Angel   *By Ferrin L. Fraser* $2.00
She was rich and good to look at, went too far and came a cropper.

They Tell No Tales   *By Lee Thayer* $2.00
Peter Clancy, the super-detective, follows a hunch.

The Cowled Menace   *By Willard E. Hawkins* $2.00
Something new in detective fiction. The murder of a dead man.

The Pitcher of Romance   *By Richard Washburn Child* $2.00
A collection of dramatic and absorbing short fiction.

BIOGRAPHY AND NON-FICTION

Famous Duels and Assassinations   *By Lewis Melville and*
                                      Reginald Hargreaves $4.00
Duels and assassinations that have made history. Illustrated.

Manhattan Fever   *By Sally Brookes* $2.50
A girl's own intimate story. True, poignant and utterly frank.

Prayer for Profit   *By Robert Collyer Washburn* $3.00
The "debunking" of the Mayflower and the truth about the Pilgrim Fathers.

Confessions in Art   *By Harrison S. Morris* $3.50
A volume of intimately told recollections of great artists.

O Rare Content   *By Henry W. Lanier* $2.50
A delightful humorous story of the victory of a farm. Illustrated.

JUVENILES

**The Young Birdmen Across the
Continent, or The Coast-to-Coast
Flight of the Night Mail**   *By Keith Russell* $1.00
The second volume of the Young Birdmen Series telling the further adventures of
the three young birdmen, Jerry McRae, Peter O'Brien and Danersk. Illustrated.

*Have you sufficient
stock of these inter-
esting books?*

*Send for catalogue of
our complete line of
publications.*

1930 advertisement

Thomas Seltzer
(New York: 1920-1926)
Scott and Seltzer
(New York: 1919-1920)

Thomas Seltzer brought to his publishing career experience as a translator of German, Polish, and Russian literature and as an assistant to Albert and Charles Boni in the establishment of The Modern Library. Seltzer, an uncle of the Bonis, held one-third interest in the Boni firm and was its vice-president as well as an editor of The Modern Library; he left the firm in November 1918. Temple Scott, an Englishman whose real name was Isaac Henry Solomon Isaacs, had been head of Brentano's publishing department for thirteen years when he resigned in the summer of 1918. The two men soon discovered that they had similar ideas about publishing, and on 19 July 1919 they started the firm of Scott and Seltzer at 5 West Fiftieth Street in New York.

Scott and Seltzer published six books, all in 1919: Stefan Zweig's *The Burning Secret*, published under the pseudonym Stephen Branch; Douglas Goldring's *The Fortune;* William Henry Warner's *The Bridge of Time;* Scott's *The Silver Age and Other Dramatic Memories;* Albert Rhys Williams's *Lenin: The Man and His Work;* and *A Landscape Painter*, the first American book appearance of four short stories by Henry James.

Scott and Seltzer ended their partnership in 1920 and Seltzer opened his own business. His first undertaking was the New Library of Social Science, which began with Ramsay MacDonald's *Parliament and Revolution* (1920). This book still bore the imprint of Scott and Seltzer along with that firm's logo, a triangle that included the partners' initials. The logo was soon redesigned so that the initials would be a T and an S and the imprint was changed to read "Thomas Seltzer." The first book with the new logo and imprint was Edwin Arlington Robinson's seventh book of poetry, *Lancelot* (1920), which was also published by the Lyric Society.

Seltzer's most important literary author was D. H. Lawrence. The firm published twenty of Lawrence's books, eleven of them before their publication in England. The first Lawrence work published by Seltzer was *Touch and Go* (1920); others included *Women in Love*, in a limited edition without Seltzer's imprint in 1920, and again in a trade edition in 1922; *Aaron's Rod* (1922); *Kangaroo* (1923); *The Rainbow* (1924); and *Little Novels of Sicily* (1925), translated by Lawrence from the Italian of Giovanni Verga. Other noteworthy Seltzer publications included the first edition of James's *Master Eustace* (1920), Gilbert Murray's *Our Great War and the Great War of the Ancient Greeks* (1920), and Zweig's *Jeremiah: A Drama in Nine Scenes* (1922).

In July 1922 John S. Sumner of the New York Society for the Suppression of Vice seized two Seltzer books from Brentano's bookstore and from several branches of the Womrath bookstores. The books were a limited edition of Arthur Schnitzler's *Casanova's Homecoming* (1921) and the anonymous *A Young Girl's Diary* (1921), with a foreword by Sigmund Freud. Seltzer won the obscenity case, but Sumner persuaded a grand jury to indict the firm on the same charges. The case dragged on for two years.

In 1923 Seltzer published E. E. Cummings's first book of poetry, *Tulips and Chimneys*, and John Howard Lawson's first book, *Roger Bloomer*. The following year the firm published Anton Chekhov's *The Cherry Orchard, and Other Plays*, Martha Ostenso's *A Far Land*, and Nathalia Crane's *The Janitor's Boy, and Other Poems*.

Also in 1924 Seltzer published the first American edition of *Within a Budding Grove*, the second volume of Marcel Proust's *Remembrance of Things Past*. Henry Holt and Company had published the first volume, *Swann's Way*, in 1922 but had let Proust go due to modest sales. Seltzer brought out the third volume, *The Guermantes Way*, in 1925. All three volumes were translated by C. K. Scott Moncrieff. The remainder of *Remembrance of Things Past* was published by Albert and Charles Boni. Crane's *Lava Lane, and Other Poems* appeared in 1925. In

Seltzer's first edition of Lawrence's 1921 work

Thomas Seltzer (photo by Alexandra Levin)

February of that year Seltzer agreed to destroy the plates of *Casanova's Homecoming* and *A Young Girl's Diary,* and Sumner dropped the obscenity charges against the firm. By that time, the legal fees in the case had nearly bankrupted the firm. Seltzer's last publication was David George Plotkin's *Ghetto Gutters and Other Poems* (1926).

In 1926 Seltzer's publishing line was purchased by Albert and Charles Boni. During its brief existence the firm had published 219 books, including more than 90 novels and more than 30 poetry volumes. Its other books were mainly in economics, politics, and sociology. Seltzer's imprint appeared occasionally during the 1930s on such books as J. Middleton Murry's *The Necessity of Communism*

(1933) and Jeanette E. Talcott's *Passing Moods* (1936). He died in 1943.

References:

Gerald M. Lacy, ed., *D. H. Lawrence Letters to Thomas and Adele Seltzer* (Santa Barbara: Black Sparrow Press, 1976);

G. Thomas Tanselle, "The Thomas Seltzer Imprint," *Papers of the Bibliographical Society of America,* 58 (1964): 380-448;

"Thomas Seltzer [obituary]," *Publishers' Weekly,* 144 (25 September 1943): 1179;

Thomas Seltzer: The First Five Years (New York: The Committee, 1925).

—*Neal L. Edgar*

Sharon Publications

(Closter, New Jersey; Cresskill, New Jersey; Teaneck, New Jersey: 1976-   )

Sharon Publications, Incorporated was founded in 1976 by Michael Edrei at 631 Closter Dock Road, Closter, New Jersey. In its first year Sharon published seventy titles, targeted primarily at the adolescent and children's market; the size and character of the firm's annual lists have remained constant since then.

Sharon Publications includes five imprints. Starbooks are popular biographies of rock stars, movie stars, and other celebrities, along with illustrated books about fads such as break dancing. Bambi Books are for young children and include Classics (unabridged reprints of classic children's fiction), Pic-a Books (retellings of traditional stories), activity books, and preschool wordbooks. Contemporary Teens Books are original novels dealing with typical adolescent problems. Sharon

Romances are novels about young lovers. Back-to-School Books are reference books for junior high and high school students. About ten percent of Sharon's books are published in hardcover; the rest are paperbacks.

In 1983 Sharon Books was merged with Edrei Communications Corporation, which is active in magazine publishing, and moved to 105 Union Avenue, Cresskill, New Jersey. Edrei's D. S. Magazines publishes fifteen specialty magazines for the adolescent market.

Sharon Books are distributed by New American Library and Warner Publisher Services. In 1986 the firm moved into new corporate offices at 1086 Teaneck Road, Teaneck, New Jersey 07666.

—*Botham Stone*

Michael S. Edrei, founder and president of Sharon Publications

Frank Shay (second from right) and friends on the beach at Provincetown, Massachusetts, in 1921. Eugene O'Neill is on the left (photo by Nickolas Muray).

Frank Shay

(New York: 1916-1923)

Frank Shay started in the book business as manager of Schulte's Book Store in New York in 1912. He subsequently worked in the Washington Square Book Store, owned by Albert and Charles Boni. In 1915 the Bonis sold the store to Shay. The Theatre Guild was formed in the store, and the store later gave space to the Provincetown Players, of which Shay was a member. Both groups were intimately related to Shay's publishing interests.

From 17 West Eighth Street, Shay published the first three series of the Provincetown Plays in 1916. The first volume included Eugene O'Neill's *Bound East for Cardiff;* the second volume included Susan Glaspell's *Suppressed Desires,* which Shay published separately in 1917; the third volume included O'Neill's *Before Breakfast,* which Shay also published in 1916 as a separate volume. Shay collaborated with George Cram Cook on a combined edition of the Provincetown Plays, which was published in Cincinnati by Stewart and Kidd in 1921. Shay was planning to publish a reprint of Theodore Dreiser's *Sister Carrie* (1900) when he was drafted into the army. He introduced Dreiser to Horace Liveright, and the firm of Boni and Liveright published the book in 1917.

After war service, Shay opened the Frank Shay Book Shop at 4 Christopher Street in Greenwich Village. In 1920 he published Edna St. Vincent Millay's *A Few Figs From Thistles,* followed by her *Aria da Capo* in 1921.

Shay became increasingly interested in the Cape Cod area and opened a Provincetown branch of his bookshop in 1922. The following year he sold the New York shop to Robert A. Hicks, moved permanently to Cape Cod, and soon became a leader of the summer art colony in Provincetown. Although Shay retired from the bookselling and publishing business in the 1920s, he continued to write and compile books of plays and songs, including *Five Plays for Strolling Mummers* (1926) and *My Pious Friends and Drunken Companions, Songs and Ballads of Conviviality* (1927). In 1930 he married Edith Foley, and together they wrote *Sand In Their Shoes: A Cape Cod Reader* (1951). Shay died in 1954.

Reference:

"Frank Shay [obituary]," *New York Times,* 15 January 1954, p. 19.

—Neal L. Edgar

Sheed and Ward

(New York: 1933-1973)

Frank J. Sheed and his wife, Maisie Ward, founded Sheed and Ward in London in 1926 to publish good Catholic literature. In February 1933 the firm opened an American office at 63 Fifth Avenue, New York. Sheed and Ward introduced to American readers some of the great figures of the Catholic literary movement in England between World Wars I and II, notably Hilaire Belloc, G. K. Chesterton, Ronald Knox, and Christopher Dawson. Other authors on the firm's list included Jacques Maritain, George Bernanos, Sigrid Undset, and François Mauriac.

Sheed and Ward aggressively promoted its publications. In 1934 the company began a series of public debates on current thought in fields of Catholic interest. The same year saw the publication of *A Sheed and Ward Survey,* a 400-page omnibus of selections from sixty-one recent Sheed and Ward titles. The Sheed and Ward Book Society, modeled after the Catholic Book-a-Month Club in England, was organized in 1935. For eighteen dollars a year members received ten books, all published by Sheed and Ward. In May 1936 the publishers announced three contests in which readers were invited to submit reviews of certain Sheed and Ward books.

Important books of the 1930s included Belloc's *The Autobiography of G. K. Chesterton* (1936), *Characters of the Reformation* (1936), *The Great Heresies* (1938), *Sonnets and Verse* (1939), and Maritain's *Introduction to Logic* (1937). Sheed and Ward sought to appeal to non-Catholic readers with *Pilgrim's Regress* (1935) by C. S. Lewis, *Communism and Man* (1938) by Sheed, *Beyond Politics* (1939) by Dawson, and biographies of Voltaire, Philip II, Dostoevski, and Mozart.

Frank J. Sheed and Maisie Ward

1934 advertisement

The business was plagued by financial troubles during its first twenty years. In the 1930s both proprietors went on lecture tours to raise money. After heavy losses due to a swindle in 1943, the firm recovered and relocated at 830 Broadway.

After World War II Sheed and Ward added more books of literary criticism to its list. In 1947 the firm announced a new critical biography series, Great Writers of the World, with volumes on Horace, Boccaccio, Rabelais, de Maupassant, Dante, Newman, and St. Paul. The first American edition of Mauriac's *Vipers' Tangle* was published in 1947, followed by *Renaissance in the North: Ibsen to Undset* (1947) by W. Gore Allen, a biography of the nineteenth-century Irish novelist William Carleton by Benedict Kiely in 1948, and *Immortal Diamond: Studies in Gerard Manley Hopkins* (1949), edited by Norman Weyand.

In January 1951 a fire destroyed the firm's entire stock of backlist books. That September new editorial offices were opened at 840 Broadway. Larger offices were established at 64 University Place in 1959.

Sheed retired as president of the company in 1962 to become chairman of the board; Louise Wijnhausen, a former vice-president, succeeded him. Under her leadership Sheed and Ward began a new fiction program not restricted to Catholic audiences. The program began with the publication of a controversial novel, *Vessel of Dishonor* (1962) by Paul Roche. Books on contemporary issues during the 1960s included *The Crisis of Western Education* (1961) by Christopher Dawson; *The Council, Reform and Reunion* (1961), a seminal book on the ecumenical movement by Hans Küng; *The New*

Orpheus; Essays Toward a Christian Poetic (1964), edited by Nathan Scott; and *The Crucible of Change* (1968) by Andrew Greeley. Sheed continued to publish his own books of theology, and the Roman Catholic Church awarded him an honorary doctorate of sacred theology in 1956; he was the first layman to be so honored.

Robert J. Meinke succeeded Wijnhausen as president in 1969. In March 1973 Sheed and Ward was sold to the Universal Press Syndicate in New York, headed by James F. Andrews, a former Sheed and Ward editor, and John P. McMeel. The new owners changed the imprint to Sheed, Andrews and McMeel, then to Andrews and McMeel, and finally to Andrews, McMeel and Parker; moved the firm's offices to 4400 Johnson Drive, Fairway, Kansas 66205; and reduced the Catholic emphasis in favor of general trade publishing. Ward died in 1975; Sheed died in 1981.

References:

"Frank J. Sheed [obituary]," *New York Times*, 21 November 1981, p. 19;

"Maisie Ward [obituary]," *New York Times*, 29 January 1975, p. 38;

Frank Sheed, "Aiming a Little above the Middle Brow, Frank Sheed on the Travails of a Catholic Publisher," *Publishers Weekly*, 206 (9 September 1974): 35-37;

Sheed, *The Church and I* (New York: Doubleday, 1974);

Wilfred Sheed, "Sheed and Ward, Inc.," *Catholic Library World*, 28 (1956-1957): 13-15.

—Annie E. Stevens

Simon and Schuster

(New York: 1924-   )

1927

Richard Leo Simon and Max Lincoln Schuster founded their publishing company on 2 January 1924 with $4,000, a one-room office at 37 West Fifty-seventh Street, New York, and no books. The founders created publishing ideas and looked for authors to carry them out.

Both partners were graduates of Columbia University. Schuster had been a journalist, had worked in advertising, and had edited a trade magazine for the Motor and Accessory Manufacturers Association. Simon had been involved in the importing business, had sold pianos, and had been a salesman for Boni and Liveright. Though both partners participated in all phases of the business, Schuster concentrated on editing and was also gifted at writing advertising copy. His column "From the Inner Sanctum of Simon and Schuster," carried in the *New York Times* and *Publishers' Weekly* and signed "Essandess," discussed the publishing business in a lively and informal manner. Simon was a salesman with boundless energy, but he also wrote and edited books.

The firm's first book, the world's first crossword puzzle book, originally carried the imprint of the Plaza Publishing Company, a name created to disguise the identities of the fledgling publishers in case the book was a failure. By October the book was so successful that Simon and Schuster acknowledged the product as theirs and published several more crossword books. The books were written by F. Gregory Hartswick, Prosper Buranelli, and Margaret Petherbridge, editors of the *New York World's* puzzle page.

The firm was joined in August 1924 by seventeen-year-old Leon Shimkin, who contributed his business acumen and worked as office manager, bookkeeper, and business manager. His appointment as secretary-treasurer of the company was delayed only by the New York State requirement that a person in that capacity be twenty-one years old. He soon became a partner. Shimkin later

brought to the firm Dale Carnegie's *How to Win Friends and Influence People* (1936) and J. K. Lasser's *Your Income Tax* (1936), which were huge best-sellers.

The company's early successes were nonfiction titles, including Will Durant's *The Story of Philosophy* (1926), Robert Ripley's *Believe It or Not!* (1929), and *Van Loon's Geography* (1932) by Hendrik Willem Van Loon, as well as two books that purported to be nonfiction but were widely believed to be hoaxes—Ethelreda Lewis's *Trader Horn* (1927) and Joan Lowell's *The Cradle of the Deep* (1929). In its first ten years Simon and Schuster published 251 books, of which about 50 were very successful. The firm developed the practice of carefully analyzing what the public was likely to read and mixing popular titles with serious works of more limited appeal. Simon and Schuster moved to larger offices at 386 Fourth Avenue in 1930.

Another key to the success of Simon and Schuster was advertising. Under Jack A. Goodman, who became advertising manager in 1935, the firm carried out extensive campaigns to promote its titles. In 1936 and 1937 Simon and Schuster's advertising account with the *New York Times* for 100,000 lines of copy was the largest among publishers. The firm was the first to use opinion poll techniques to pretest books and was constantly probing and testing new merchandising methods. The company also took risks, such as giving an unheard-of advance of $250,000 to twenty top *Life* magazine photographers to produce *A Treasury of Art Masterpieces* (1939), a ten-dollar gift book which became a best-seller. The success of the Treasury series, which included Schuster's *A Treasury of the World's Great Letters* (1940), demonstrated the firm's skill in recognizing and meeting public interest.

Though its early fiction was not successful, Simon and Schuster always included literary titles on its lists. Beginning with *Wolf Solent* in 1929, the firm published the novels and nonfiction of John

340

M. Lincoln Schuster (left) and Richard L. Simon with their first book, published in 1924

The "Inner Sanctum" between Simon's and Schuster's offices

from THE INNER SANCTUM *of*

SIMON *and* SCHUSTER

Publishers • *Rockefeller Center* • *New York*

*An apparently naïve
but actually devilishly canny
free offer*

We address ourselves this morrow to Shining Youth, for whom we have gifts. Mature members of the audience, however awash with wisdom and charm, are not eligible and are requested to pass on to the financial pages.

O Youth, carefree and lyrical, trembling on the brink of a 9-to-5 job with one hour for lunch, you are about to begin the great adventure of Growing Up and Older. You will have your first kiss and know ecstasy. You will attend your first dance and know worldliness. You will be stood up on Saturday night and know tragedy.

And if you are lucky, you will discover the novels of P. G. WODEHOUSE (over which the older blokes have been purpling with laughter these many years) and learn the meaning of untrammeled hilarity.

By way of doing our bit to introduce WODEHOUSE to *la jeunesse*, we are going to Give Away 100 copies of his latest novel, *Bertie Wooster Sees It Through* (just published, $3.50) to qualified parties. More about qualifications in a sec.

Of this new WODEHOUSE novel *Punch* says:

"The plot is as complex and adroitly manipulated as ever, the figures of speech as outrageous, the literary allusions as wildly misapplied. In comic invention, in sheer writing ability, it ranks with the author's best."

Only a conscienceless worm would reveal the details of the demmed ingenious plot — a masterly structure built on the solid foundation of (1) Bertie Wooster's mustache, (2) Jeeves, the gentleman's gentleman, and (3) the giant conflicts these two fundamentally opposed elements engender.

Now, lads, Your Correspondents have 100 free copies of this book for those of you who meet the following requirements:

1. You must not be more than 26 years old.

2. You must not remember when Skeezix was a baby.

3. You must not have ever said "hotcha!", "voh-doh-dee-oh-doh!" or "wock-a-doo, wock-a-doo, wock-a-*doo!*"

4. You must have no recollection of seeing, hearing or shaking hands with Peaches Browning, Chandu the Magician, or Singing Sam the Barbasol Man.

If you fulfill these conditions and would like a free copy of the new WODEHOUSE novel, just write to us and ask for it. Send proof, however flimsy, of your age. Proof may be anything or anybody but must not exceed 11 x 14½ inches in size or weigh more than 32 pounds. (It is quite all right for you yourself to weigh more than 32 pounds.) Remember, neatness will get you nowhere. The important thing is to be among the best 100 petitioners. We are judge and jury, and there is no appeal. Write to Simon and Schuster, Dept. PG, 630 Fifth Avenue, New York 20, N. Y. Entries must be postmarked no later than Monday, February 28th.

You are not morally obliged to let us know what you thought of the book and why, on the handy form enclosed with each copy. However, if you feel that to remain silent would be an act of churlish ingratitude, send us your opinion.

We regret that oldsters get short shrift in this offer. All we can say to them is: hard cheese, old tops, we'll have something for you later — in the interim, hie to your bookseller's, buy *Bertie Wooster Sees It Through* by P. G. WODEHOUSE, and cheer up.

— ESSANDESS

"Inner Sanctum" column for 23 February 1955

Cowper Powys, including *In Defense of Sensuality* (1930), *A Glastonbury Romance* (1932), *The Art of Happiness* (1935), and *Owen Glendower* (1940). *Little Man, What Now?* (1933) by the German author Hans Fallada was the firm's first literary work to sell well. Howard Fast's *Conceived in Liberty* was published in 1939.

In the 1930s the company began publishing deserving first novels, including *Bottom Dogs* (1930) by Edward Dahlberg and *They Shoot Horses, Don't They?* (1935) by Horace McCoy. It also started a long-lived series, the Inner Sanctum Mysteries, in 1936 with the publication of works by Elizabeth Curtiss and Esther Tyler. Anthony Boucher, who wrote *The Case of the Crumpled Knave* (1939) and *The Case of the Baker Street Irregulars* (1940), was one of the firm's successful early mystery writers. The Inner Sanctum series reached its peak in the 1940s and 1950s under Lee Wright, who was widely acknowledged as among the best editors in the field. In 1939 Simon, Schuster, Shimkin, and Robert F. de Graff launched Pocket Books, the first successful paperback imprint in twentieth-century America.

In 1940 Simon and Schuster moved into larger offices at 1230 Sixth Avenue. In 1942 Simon and Schuster and Western Printing and Lithographing Company, which was producing comic books and other novelty items, published the first twelve Little Golden Books, which were distributed through the mass market outlets of Pocket Books and through toy stores. Though Simon and Schuster had not been in children's publishing prior to this time, the executives recognized the potential market for inexpensive children's books which were of high quality and well illustrated. A large advertising campaign was planned for Little Golden Books, but demand for the titles was so great that the only ad placed was an apology that the number of books available could not keep up with demand. By the end of the decade Little Golden Books had sold over 300 million copies of over 200 titles.

In 1944 Marshall Field Enterprises purchased Simon and Schuster and Pocket Books for about $3 million, but the publishers continued to operate with complete autonomy. The Field financial strength provided stability for Simon and Schuster, especially in dealing with a flood of unsold books in the late 1940s.

Simon and Schuster expanded the volume of its publishing in the 1940s, and literary titles became a more important facet of the firm's business. Simon and Schuster published Mary McCarthy's first novel, *The Company She Keeps* (1942); Kay

Boyle's *Primer for Combat* (1942), *Avalanche* (1944), and *1939* (1948); Laura Z. Hobson's *Gentleman's Agreement* (1947); and Herman Wouk's first novel, *Aurora Dawn* (1947). It also published the early novels of Jerome Weidman, including *I'll Never Go There Anymore* (1941); Weidman later wrote a novel about publishing, *The Center of the Action* (1969), using Simon and Schuster as the setting. In the 1950s the firm published *The Cardinal* (1950) by Henry Morton Robinson; *The Man in the Grey Flannel Suit* (1955) and *A Summer Place* (1958) by Sloan Wilson; and *The Blackboard Jungle* (1954) and *Strangers When We Meet* (1958) by Evan Hunter, who also wrote the mystery novel *The 87th Precinct* (1959) under the pseudonym Ed McBain. Another of the firm's mystery writers of the 1950s was Richard Powell, with *A Shot in the Dark* (1952). Simon and Schuster moved to 630 Fifth Avenue in December 1951.

During this period Simon and Schuster also published American editions and translations of works by prominent foreign writers, among them Nikos Kazantzakis's *Zorba the Greek* (1953) and *The Greek Passion* (1954). The books of French novelists Romain Gary, Jean Dutourd, and Michel Butor were also published by Simon and Schuster. The firm published the early work of South African Nadine Gordimer, including her first novel, *The Lying Days* (1953), and translations of the works of Swedish novelist Vilhelm Moberg, including *The Emigrants* (1951) and *Unto a Good Land* (1954). Simon and Schuster became a prolific publisher of humor with works by James Thurber, P. G. Wodehouse, S. J. Perelman, Ludwig Bemelmans, and Edward Streeter. The works of cartoonists Peter Arno and Walt Kelly, the creator of Pogo, were also published by the firm.

After Marshall Field died in 1957, Simon, Schuster, and Shimkin bought the firm back from Field Enterprises for $1 million. Shimkin and James M. Jacobson bought Pocket Books at the same time. Simon retired the same year, and Schuster and Shimkin bought his stock and became equal partners. Simon died in 1960. In January 1961 Pocket Books became a public company, selling twenty percent of its shares to outside investors, and in 1964 Western Publishing Company—which had changed its name from Western Printing and Lithographing Company in 1960—became the sole owner of Golden Books. Though formal ties have varied, Simon and Schuster has continued to be involved in publishing Golden Books through personnel as well as corporate connections. When Schuster retired in 1966 the company purchased his shares for $2 million, and Shimkin gained control of the firm. He turned over his new shares to Pocket Books, of which he already owned forty-six percent, then merged the two companies and came out with more than fifty percent of the consolidated firm. By the end of 1966 Shimkin was head of the publishing combine, which was the world's largest distributor of books.

In the following years the firm added divisions which are creatively autonomous but share finance and distribution. Besides Simon and Schuster and Pocket Books, imprints of the company include Touchstone Books (trade paperbacks); Washington Square Press (paperbacks); Julian Messner (children's books); Archway Books (original fiction for children); Monarch Press (high school and college study outlines); Collins (reference books); Silhouette (paperback romances); and Kenan Press, Linden Books, Summit, and Wyndam Books (all hardcover imprints). Schuster died in 1970. In January 1973 Shimkin became chairman of the board and Seymour Turk became president. In June 1975 Simon and Schuster was purchased by the conglomerate Gulf + Western Industries. Richard E. Snyder was appointed president of the corporation, publisher of Simon and Schuster, and head of the trade division. Michael Korda remained editor in chief, a position he had held since 1968.

During the 1960s and 1970s the company maintained a large volume of literary publications, always remaining eclectic and oriented toward public taste. Simon and Schuster published one of the most important first novels in American literature, Joseph Heller's *Catch-22*, in 1961 and brought out Harold Robbins's best-selling *The Carpetbaggers* the same year. The firm published Doris Lessing's *The Golden Notebook* (1962) and *Children of Violence* (1964); Irving Wallace's *The Prize* (1962), *The Seven Minutes* (1969), and *The Word* (1972); and Chaim Potok's *The Chosen* (1967). Simon and Schuster has published little science fiction, but it brought out a hardcover edition of Ray Bradbury's *Fahrenheit 451* in 1967. Louis Untermeyer's *The Pursuit of Poetry* was published in 1969. The firm had great success with historical romances, especially R. F. Delderfield's *God Is an Englishman* (1970) and *Theirs Was the Kingdom* (1971) and Susan Howatch's *Penmarric* (1971). Simon and Schuster published Richard Brautigan's *The Abortion* (1971) and *The Hawkline Monster* (1974); Graham Greene's *The Honorary Consul* (1973) and *The Human Factor* (1978); Margaret Atwood's *Surfacing* (1973) and *Lady Oracle* (1976); Judith Rossner's *Looking for Mr. Goodbar*

(1975); Thomas Berger's *Sneaky People* (1975); Mary Higgins Clark's mystery novel *Where Are the Children?* (1975); Marilyn French's *The Women's Room* (1977); Joan Didion's *A Book of Common Prayer* (1977) and *The White Album* (1979); and Kate Millett's *The Basement* (1979).

The firm also published important nonfiction titles, including *The Rise and Fall of the Third Reich* (1960) by William Shirer. Watergate journalists Carl Bernstein and Bob Woodward, anthropologist-mystic Carlos Casteneda, and philosopher Bertrand Russell have also appeared on the firm's list.

In the 1980s the firm maintains its image as a house that sells books exceptionally well. On the 27 April 1980 *New York Times Book Review* best-seller list, Simon and Schuster had eight titles—five nonfiction and three fiction. The firm published Greene's *Doctor Fischer of Geneva, or the Bomb Party*, Larry Collins and Dominique Lapierre's *The Fifth Horseman*, Howatch's *Sins of the Fathers*, and Clark's *The Cradle Will Fall*—all in 1980—and Didion's *Salvador* in 1983. Simon and Schuster has also published most of the novels of Larry McMurtry.

In 1985 Gulf + Western acquired Prentice-Hall, making that company, with its strong business and textbook lines, a subsidiary of Simon and Schuster. Since 1976 Simon and Schuster has been located in the Simon and Schuster Building, 1230 Avenue of the Americas, New York 10020.

References:

"Essandess—Aetat 10 Ann.," *Publishers' Weekly*, 125 (6 January 1934): 40-41;

Lawrence Fertig, M. Lincoln Schuster, and Albert Leventhal, *Richard Simon: Words Spoken in Memory, August 1st, 1960* (New York, 1960);

"M. Lincoln Schuster [obituary]," *New York Times*, 21 December 1970, p. 38;

"The Making of a Best Seller: The Story of Book Manufacture at Simon and Schuster," in *The Annual of Bookmaking* (New York: Colophon, 1938);

"Richard L. Simon [obituary]," *New York Times*, 30 July 1960, p. 17;

M. Lincoln Schuster, "Publishing," in *Publishers on Publishing*, edited by Gerald Gross (New York: Grosset & Dunlap, 1961): 404-406;

Peter Schwed, *Turning the Pages: An Insider's Story of Simon & Schuster, 1924-1984* (New York: Macmillan, 1984);

"The Story of Simon and Schuster, Inc.," *Book Production Magazine*, 79 (March 1964): 36-39.

—Jane I. Thesing

Former Simon and Schuster executives Leon Shimkin (front),
Emil Staral (middle), and Albert Leventhal

Richard E. Snyder, chairman of the board and president of
Simon and Schuster (photo by George Chinsee, M Magazine)

Upton Sinclair

Cover for 1923 self-published work

Upton Sinclair

(Pasadena, California; Monrovia, California:
1918-1949)

Sinclair Press

(New York: 1901)

See also the Sinclair entry in *DLB 9, American Novelists, 1910-1945*.

Upton Sinclair first published one of his own writings under the Sinclair Press imprint in New York in 1901, after several publishers had rejected the manuscript of his first novel, *Springtime and Harvest*. Sinclair was so convinced of the book's merit that he borrowed $200 from an uncle and, with another $200 from his savings, he had 1,000 copies printed. He sold them at $1.00 a copy to his family and acquaintances. Even though Sinclair was interviewed about the book by two of the largest New York dailies, he sold only two copies to "strangers."

After moving from New York to Pasadena, California, in 1914, Sinclair published *The Profits of Religion: An Essay in Economic Interpretation* (1918). A socialist, Sinclair was convinced that commercial publishers were inordinately concerned with profits and unwilling to risk the libel suits that could result from his more radical muckraking. He wanted to distribute books of marginal marketability at the lowest prices, to disseminate ideas rather than to make a profit. Sinclair published his own books and pamphlets from 1918 until 1949. The books and some of the pamphlets were brought out simultaneously by trade publishers, including Boni and Liveright, which published *Jimmie Higgins* (1919), the second title published by Sinclair in California, and *They Call Me Carpenter: A Tale of the Second Coming* (1922); Albert and Charles Boni, which published five Sinclair titles, including *Oil!* (1927) and *Mental Radio* (1930); and Farrar and Rinehart, which published *Roman Holiday* (1931) and *The Wet Parade* (1931).

In 1920, after his attack upon "the big business press in America" was published serially in the *Appeal*, Sinclair discovered that his printer could not get any more paper from wholesalers. Suspecting a conspiracy to silence his criticism, Sinclair quietly purchased a carload of Kraft brown wrapping paper and had *The Brass Check: A Study of American Journalism* printed on it.

Many of the titles published by Sinclair alone were experimental. Among these were *Hell: A Verse Drama and Photoplay* (1923), *Singing Jailbirds: A Drama in Four Acts* (1924), *Bill Porter: A Drama of O. Henry in Prison* (1925), and *Oil!* (1929), a four-act play based on his novel.

The Flivver King: A Story of Ford-America (1937) was based on the life of Henry Ford. When the CIO was on strike against the Ford Motor Company, Sinclair offered 200,000 copies of *The Flivver King* to the strikers at fifty cents a copy. He was proud to learn that the auto workers had folded the pamphlet lengthwise and stuck it in their pockets, where it was visible as a symbol of protest.

Sinclair moved to Monrovia, California, in 1943 and continued to publish his works from there, ending with *O Shepherd, Speak!* in 1949. He died in 1968.

References:

William A. Bloodworth, Jr., *Upton Sinclair* (Boston: Twayne, 1977);

Leon Harris, *Upton Sinclair, American Rebel* (New York: Crowell, 1975);

Upton Sinclair, *American Outpost: A Book of Reminiscences* (New York: Farrar & Rinehart/Pasadena: Upton Sinclair, 1932);

Sinclair, *The Autobiography of Upton Sinclair* (New York: Harcourt, Brace, 1962);

"Upton Sinclair [obituary]," *New York Times*, 26 November 1968, p. 1.

—Earl G. Ingersoll

William Sloane Associates
(New York: 1946-1952)

William Sloane Associates was founded in 1946 by William Sloane, Norman Hood, Keith Jennison, and Helen Taylor at 93 Park Avenue, New York; the firm later moved to 119 West Fifty-seventh Street. The founders had worked together at Henry Holt and Company but had left Holt in protest against its new owner, Texas oilman and financier Clinton Murchison. They planned the new firm as a trade venture.

The firm's first list included *Thunder out of China* (1946) by Theodore H. White and Annalee Jacoby, a Book-of-the-Month Club selection; *The Quiet Center* (1946), a first volume of poetry by Edith Heinrich; and books by Ernie Pyle and Mark Van Doren. In 1947 Sloane Associates added Bill Mauldin and Marion Hargrove and published A. B. Guthrie's *The Big Sky*. Later that year Henry Holt and Company sold the yet-unpublished American Men of Letters series—originally planned by Sloane and Taylor—to William Sloane Associates. This series, edited by Van Doren, Joseph Wood Krutch, Lionel Trilling, and Margaret Marshall, received the Carey-Thomas Award in 1949. The first volume, *Edwin Arlington Robinson* (1948) by Emery Neff, was followed by ten more, including *Henry David Thoreau* (1948) by Krutch, *Nathaniel Hawthorne* (1949) by Van Doren, *Jonathan Edwards* (1949) by Perry Miller, *Emily Dickinson* (1951) by Richard Chase, and *Theodore Dreiser* (1951) by F. O. Matthiessen. Newton Arvin's 1950 study of Herman Melville won the National Book Award.

In the spring of 1947 Sloane Associates released *Off Broadway*, Maxwell Anderson's collection of essays on the theater. In 1948 Sloane Associates began to publish and distribute Anderson's plays, which had previously been published under the playwright's own imprint. These included *Anne of the Thousand Days* (1948) and *Barefoot in Athens* (1951). The firm also published *Lost in the Stars* (1950), a dramatization by Anderson and Kurt Weill of Alan Paton's novel *Cry, the Beloved Country* (1948). Sloane Associates published the first major volumes of poetry by John Frederick Nims—*The Iron Pastoral* (1947)—and John Berryman—*The*

Dispossessed (1948). A novel by Guthrie, *The Way West* (1949), won the Pulitzer Prize in 1950. Other important publications were *Road to Survival* (1948), an ecological study by William Vogt; and *Human Fertility: The Modern Dilemma* (1951), a controversial description of modern genetics by Robert Cook.

Personal and financial troubles during the late 1940s and early 1950s led to the failure of the firm. In 1948 Sloane Associates engaged James Van Toor to organize the college textbook department, an effort which proved to be very costly. The textbook list included titles in economics, education, English, political science, psychology, and sociology. In 1949 Taylor and Jennison resigned because of differences with Sloane.

Sloane was attacked as a Communist sympathizer by the columnist Walter Winchell in January 1951 because of the firm's publication of *The Federal Bureau of Investigation* (1950) by Max Lowenthal. Sloane strongly denied the charge, and the Anti-Censorship Committee of the American Book Publishers Council released a statement severely criticizing Winchell for his attack upon freedom of the press.

In February 1951 Sloane Associates and Franklin Watts, a publisher of children's books, combined their business, manufacturing, and sales departments. Sloane Associates' continued financial problems resulted in the sale of the college textbook department to Dryden Press in June 1952. Shortly afterwards, William Sloane Associates was acquired by William Morrow. In 1955 Sloane became director of Rutgers University Press; he died in 1974.

William Morrow maintained an active backlist of Sloane publications, and the Sloane imprint appeared in new books until 1966. New works by Krutch during this period included *The Best of Two Worlds* (1953), *More Lives than One* (1962), and *If You Don't Mind My Saying So* (1964); White wrote *Fire in the Ashes: Europe in Mid-Century* (1953), *The Mountain Road* (1958), and *The View from the Fortieth Floor* (1960). The Sloane imprint also appeared on

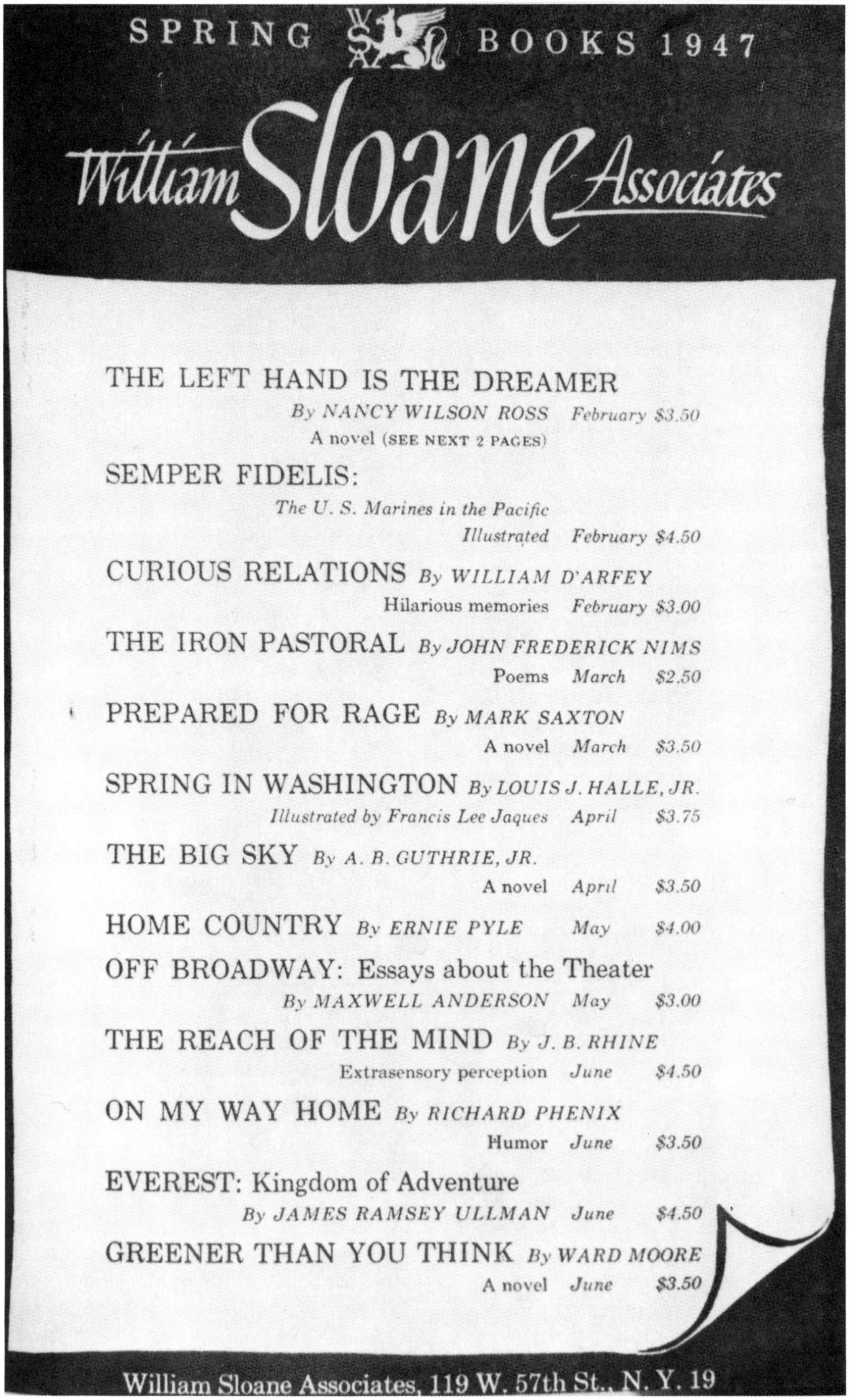

Early advertisement

translations of *The Last of the Bohemians* (1954) by André Beucler, *A Roman Affair* (1957) by Ercole Pati, and *Dance on the Volcano* (1959) by Marie Chauvet. Nonfiction works included *The Road to Harper's Ferry* (1959), a study of abolition by J. C. Furnas; and *The Seven Deadly Sins* (1962), essays by Angus Wilson and others. Novels by Barbara Jefferis, Nicholas Monsarrat, and Merle Miller were also published by Morrow under the Sloane imprint.

References:
"The New Sloane Offices Arranged for Convenience and Efficiency," *Publishers' Weekly*, 151 (29 March 1947): 1793;

"Sloane's Men of Letters Series Wins the Carey-Thomas Award," *Publishers' Weekly*, 155 (5 February 1949): 804;

"William Sloane [obituary]," *Publishers Weekly*, 206 (7 October 1974): 15.

—*Annie E. Stevens*

Harrison Smith and Robert Haas
(New York: 1932-1936)
Harrison Smith
(New York: 1931-1932)

1932

Harrison Smith worked for the Century Company, the *New York Tribune*, and the Foreign Press Service before becoming chief editor at Harcourt, Brace. Smith recommended William Faulkner's *Sartoris* to Harcourt, Brace in 1929. When Harcourt declined to publish Faulkner's *The Sound and the Fury*, however, Smith joined with the English publisher Jonathan Cape to form Jonathan Cape and Harrison Smith, Incorporated and published the book in 1929.

Relations between Cape and Smith were often stormy, and the partnership dissolved in 1931. Smith started his own firm, Harrison Smith, Incorporated, at 17 East Forty-ninth Street in New York in November and published Faulkner's *Light in August* in May 1932. Smith published only a few other titles under his imprint, among them Ward Greene's *Weep No More* (1932), General Rafael de Nogales's *Memoirs of a Soldier of Fortune* (1932), and Irina Skariatina's *A World Begins* (1932). In March 1932 Robert K. Haas joined the firm as vice-president and treasurer, and the name Harrison Smith

and Robert Haas, Incorporated was adopted. A former classmate of Smith's at Yale, Haas had distributed the Little Leather Library with Harry Scherman and had been one of the founders and president of the Book-of-the-Month Club.

Smith had brought several authors besides Faulkner with him from Cape and Smith, including Evelyn Scott and Lynd Ward. Ward's *Wild Pilgrimage: A Novel in Woodcuts* was published by Smith and Haas in 1932. Like Ward's other early "novels," it consisted entirely of woodcut illustrations arranged to tell a story without words.

During the four years of its existence, Smith and Haas published Faulkner's *A Green Bough* (1933), *Doctor Martino and Other Stories* (1934), and *Pylon* (1935); Antoine de Saint-Exupéry's *Southern Mail* (1933); Kay Boyle's *The First Lover and Other Stories* (1933) and *Gentlemen, I Address You Privately* (1933); William March's first three books, *Company K* (1933), *Come in at the Door* (1934), and *The Little Wife and Other Stories* (1935); and Isak Dinesen's first book, *Seven Gothic Tales* (1934). Two books by

WARD GREENE'S

Weep No More

Second printing, $2.50

General RAFAEL De NOGALES'

Memoirs

of a Soldier of Fortune

Already published. Illustrated, $3.75

IRINA SKARIATINA'S

A World Begins

March 31st. Illustrated, $3.50

WILLIAM FAULKNER'S

Light in August

May, $2.50

CLAIRE SPENCER'S

The Quick and the Dead

April, $2.50

KAY BOYLE'S

Year Before Last

May, $2.50

URSULA PARROTT'S

Tumult and the Shouting

May, $2.00

HELEN GRACE CARLISLE'S

We Begin

April, $2.50

CHARLES BEAHAN'S

Night for a Lady

April, $2.00

MILDRED GILMAN'S

Love for Two

April 7th, $2.00

HARRISON SMITH, Inc. 17 EAST 19th STREET NEW YORK

1932 advertisement

André Malraux, *Man's Fate* (1934) and *The Royal Way* (1935), were first published in America by Smith and Haas.

When Smith and Haas was acquired by Random House in 1936, both men continued their publishing careers there. They also brought their juvenile editor, Louis Bonino, under whose supervision Smith and Haas had published Jean de Brunhoff's Babar books.

References:

Joseph Blotner, *Faulkner: A Biography* (New York: Random House, 1974);

Bennett Cerf, *At Random* (New York: Random House, 1977);

"News from Publishers," *Publishers' Weekly*, 129 (28 March 1936): 1334;

"Robert Haas Enters Firm of Harrison Smith, Inc.," *Publishers' Weekly*, 121 (26 March 1932): 1483.

—Arlene Shaner

Stein and Day Publishers

(New York; Briarcliff Manor, New York: 1962-   )

Stein and Day Publishers was founded in 1962 by Sol Stein and his wife, Patricia Day, at 149 East Forty-ninth Street, New York; due to rapid expansion, the firm moved before the end of its first year to 7 East Forty-eighth Street, New York. Stein and Day publishes in hardcover general fiction, belles lettres, drama, biography, history, physical and behavioral sciences, practical books, and medical books for the layman. It also publishes trade and mass-market paperbacks.

The firm has always catered to the best-seller market, having been represented for nineteen consecutive years on the best-seller list. About half of Stein and Day's titles have been book club selections. The film also maintains an active backlist of 405 titles, the most successful of which are childcare, health, and how-to-do-it books. Among Stein and Day's successful and notable fiction titles are Elia Kazan's *America America* (1962) and *The Arrangement* (1967); Dylan Thomas's *The Beach of Falesá* (1963); Leslie A. Fiedler's *Back to China* (1965) and *Nude Croquet* (1969); Helen Tucker's first two books, *The Sound of Summer Voices* (1969) and *The Guilt of August Fielding* (1971); Susan Howatch's *Call in the Night* (1973); Gordon Thomas and Max Morgan Witt's *Voyage of the Damned* (1974); Joachim G. Joachim's *The Dice of God* (1975); Malachi Martin's *The Final Conclave* (1978); *To Catch a King* (1979) and *Solo* (1980) by Jack Higgins, a pseudonym of

Henry Patterson; and E. Howard Hunt's *The Hargrave Deception* (1980).

Nonfiction best-sellers for Stein and Day include Barbara Howar's *Laughing All the Way* (1973) and *The Memory Book* by Harry Lorayne and Jerry Lucas (1975). Among other well-known authors are lawyer F. Lee Bailey and J. B. Priestley. The firm began a line of children's books, the Really Truly Stories, in 1964, but it was short-lived.

During its first two years Stein and Day published 50 books. The firm intended to maintain a small business by publishing 30 books per year. By 1974, however, its output had increased to nearly 100 books a year, leading to competition with major publishing houses. On 6 July 1979, after operating at a loss for a year, Stein and Day was sold to the Dutch firm Kluwer N. V. of Deventer; on 30 August 1979 control of the company was returned to Stein and Day stockholders. The firm published 111 titles in 1984. Stein is president and editor in chief; Day is vice-president and editor. The firm's address since 1973 has been Scarborough House, Briarcliff Manor, New York 10510.

Reference:

"Stein and Day: 'It's Like a Personal Bookshop,'" *Publishers' Weekly*, 186 (2 November 1964): 40-41.

—Kathleen R. Davis

Stewart and Kidd Company

(Cincinnati: 1910-1924)

The Stewart and Kidd Company, usually called "Stewart Kidd" in its imprint, was formed in 1910 when K. K. Stewart and John G. Kidd, Cincinnati booksellers, purchased the Robert Clarke Company, a publisher primarily of Americana. The Stewart and Kidd Company was also trade agent for the book publications of *Field and Stream* magazine. Its main literary activities were in the publication of drama and, to a lesser extent, poetry. Among the firm's earlier offerings were Everard Jack Appleton's *The Quiet Courage, and Other Songs of the Unafraid* (1912) and *With the Colors: Songs of the American Service* (1917); Madison Cawein's poetry volumes *Minions of the Moon* (1913) and *The Republic* (1913); Mary MacMillan's *Short Plays* (1913) and *The Little Golden Fountain, and Other Verses* (1916); and Margaret Douglas Rogers's *The Gift: A Poetic Drama* (1914).

Starting in 1919 the firm published translations of August Strindberg's plays and fiction, and in 1920 Frank Shay and Pierre Loving edited *Fifty Contemporary One-Act Plays*. The Stewart Kidd Modern Plays series included Eugene O'Neill's *The Emperor Jones* (1921), Stark Young's *Three One-Act Plays: Madretta; At the Shrine; Addio* (1921), Edna St. Vincent Millay's *Two Slatterns and a King* (1921), Christopher Morley's *Thursday Evening* (1922), and Booth Tarkington's *The Ghost Story* (1922) and *The Trysting Place* (1923). In the early 1920s the firm was the selling agent for Frank Shay, also a publisher of drama. Steward and Kidd also published a line of sporting books, mostly on fishing.

The company was located at 121 East Fifth Street in Cincinnati until 1919, when it moved to 19-23 East Fourth Street. It was purchased by Appleton in 1924.

Reference:

"Appleton Takes Over Stewart Kidd Publishing," *Publishers' Weekly*, 105 (1 March 1924): 663.

—David Dzwonkoski

Sol Stein, Patricia Day, and their children

1962 advertisement

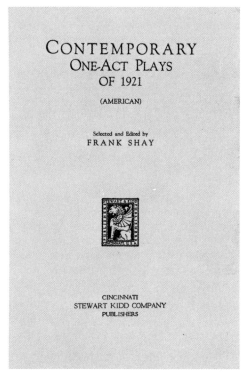

Title page for one of several anthologies of plays edited by Shay for Stewart and Kidd. This volume included plays by Eugene O'Neill and Edna St. Vincent Millay and one coauthored by Ben Hecht.

Lyle Stuart
(New York; Secaucus, New Jersey: 1956-   )

Lyle Stuart, the "bad boy of publishing," began his publishing career in 1951 with *Exposé—* soon retitled *The Independent—* a monthly tabloid labeled "iconoclastic" by some and "sensational" by others. In 1956 he launched his book publishing venture, Lyle Stuart, Incorporated, with the proceeds from a libel judgment against newspaper columnist Walter Winchell. The firm's first title was *The Pulse Test* by Arthur Coca.

Stuart is best known for nonfiction publications such as *The Sensuous Woman* (1969) by "J" and *The Sensuous Man* (1971) by "M"; *Casino Gambling for the Winner* (1978) by Stuart; and *Dirty Work: The CIA in Western Europe* (1978), edited by Philip Agee and Louis Wolf. The firm's relatively few fiction titles include the republication of Dalton Trumbo's antiwar novel *Johnny Got His Gun* (1959); and *Naked Came the Stranger* (1969), an erotic best-seller collaborated on by several journalists under the pseudonym Penelope Ashe.

Lyle Stuart, Incorporated has three imprints: Lyle Stuart; Citadel Press, which specializes in film books; and University Books, Incorporated. In April 1972 the firm moved from 239 Park Avenue South, New York, to 120 Enterprise Avenue, Secaucus, New Jersey 07094.

Reference:

Sarah Crichton, "Lyle Stuart," *Publishers Weekly*, 213 (29 May 1978): 12.

—Donna Nance

Swallow Press
(Denver; Chicago: 1954-   )
Alan Swallow, Publisher
(Baton Rouge; Albuquerque; Gunnison, Colorado; Denver: 1940-1954)

From 1940 until his death in 1966, Alan Swallow published approximately 400 books distinguished for their carefully selected titles, attractive formats, and affordable prices. The firm was especially noted for its literary works, both creative and critical; bibliographies and other reference works; and books about the West. Operating his firm almost single-handedly, Swallow was involved in editing, designing, printing, promoting, and shipping.

In 1939, while a graduate student at Louisiana State University, Swallow purchased a second-hand Kelsey handpress and set it up in a garage. In 1940 he published a collection of writings by his fellow graduate students, *Signets: An Anthology of* *Beginnings;* and *First Manifesto,* a collection of poems by Thomas McGrath, which was the first number in the Swallow Pamphlets series. From 1940 to 1954 Swallow combined teaching with occasional publishing while serving on the faculties of three western colleges. Lincoln Fitzell's book of poems *In Plato's Garden* (1940) and Ray West's edition of *Rocky Mountain Stories* (1941), which Swallow published under the Sage Books imprint, were two early efforts.

In May 1946, while teaching at the University of Denver, Swallow arranged to publish selected titles jointly with William Morrow and Company. Two critical works, Yvor Winters's *In Defense of Reason* (1947) and Allen Tate's *On the Limits of Poetry*

(1948), were among the books published by the two firms. The arrangement lasted for four years and produced twenty-one books before it was dissolved because sales of the Swallow titles were not covering Morrow's costs of production and distribution.

Swallow published several bibliographies, among them George Arm's *Poetry Explication* (1950). While the first edition sold poorly, later editions of the work and other checklists of criticism published by Swallow, including Jarvis Thurston's *Short Fiction Criticism* (1960), Donna Gerstenberger's *The American Novel* (1961), and Arthur Coleman's *Drama Criticism* (1966), sold out. Swallow's *Index to Little Magazines* (1949) was an early effort to provide a bibliography of that type of publishing. Swallow was associated with a variety of little magazines, serving as a member of editorial boards, as editor, or as publisher. In 1954 Swallow quit teaching to devote his full time to publishing. In 1955 he founded *Twentieth Century Literature;* an annotated "Current Bibliography" appeared in each issue.

Poetry published under the Alan Swallow imprint included Janet Lewis's *Poems, 1924-1944* (1950), Winters's *Collected Poems* (1952), and J. V. Cunningham's *The Exclusions of a Rhyme* (1960) and *To What Strangers, What Welcome* (1964). Swallow fiction titles included Frederick Manfred's *Morning Red* (1956), *Arrow of Love* (1961), and *Wanderlust* (1962); Vardis Fisher's *A Goat for Azazel* (1956), *My Holy Satan* (1958), and *Orphans in Gethsemane* (1960)—parts of the Testament of Man series; and the first American edition of Maude Hutchins's *Victorine* (1959). Swallow published Tate's *Collected Essays* in 1959. In 1966 Swallow published with Harcourt, Brace the first volume of *The Diary of Anaïs Nin;* the second volume appeared from Swallow Press in 1967. Before the appearance of Nin's diary, Swallow had reprinted much of her fiction and had published the first American edition of her *D. H. Lawrence* (1964).

Swallow continued the Sage Books imprint for books about the American West—science, biography, guidebooks, history, and cookbooks, as well as some fiction. Sales of the firm's Western Americana line—including Orrin Bonney's *Guide to the Wyoming Mountains and Wilderness Areas* (1960)—supported the publication of poetry and fiction. Swallow and Sage books appeared in both paperback and hardcover.

At the peak of his career just before his death in 1966 at fifty-one, Swallow was publishing fifty to sixty titles a year. In 1967 Mae Swallow sold her husband's firm to Durrett Wagner, who moved it to South Wabash Street in Chicago. Wagner wished to retain Swallow's "little publisher" values. The firm published thirty-seven books in 1969, reflecting the original Swallow subject interests. In 1973 Wagner became vice-president and editor in chief; Morton Weisman, former president of A. C. McClurg, became president of Swallow.

In 1979 Weisman concluded a licensing agreement with Ohio University Press in Athens. The agreement was to run for 100 years, renewable every 10 years. Swallow remained in Chicago and retained its imprints. The acquisition and editing of Swallow and Sage Books manuscripts remained the prerogative of Weisman; manufacturing, sales, shipping, and warehousing were handled by the university press. Since 1970 Swallow Press has published between twenty-five and thirty titles per year and has expanded its list to include social science books. Swallow Press has been located since 1976 at 811 West Junior Terrace, Chicago 60613.

References:

"Alan Swallow [obituary]," *New York Times,* 28 November 1966, p. 39;

Donna Ippolito and Shirley Kopatz, "Alan Swallow: Platten Press Publisher," *Journal of the West,* 8 (1969): 477-483;

Alan Swallow, "Story of a Publisher," *New Mexico Quarterly,* 36 (Winter 1966-1967): 301-324;

Norma N. Yueh, "Alan Swallow, Publisher," *Library Quarterly,* 39 (1969): 223-232.

—*Phyllis Andrews*

September 1932 advertisement

Lyle Stuart

Ticknor and Fields

(New Haven, Connecticut, and New York;
New York: 1979-)

In May 1979 Houghton Mifflin Company of Boston announced the establishment of a trade book subsidiary that would revive the nineteenth-century imprint Ticknor and Fields. Chester Kerr, retiring as director of the Yale University Press, was chosen to head the subsidiary, which had offices in New Haven, Connecticut, and in New York. The firm added children's books to its list of fiction and general nonfiction when the Clarion Books imprint was moved from Houghton Mifflin's school division to Ticknor and Fields in 1980. Corlies M. Smith, formerly senior editor at Viking, replaced Kerr early in 1984, and the New Haven location was discontinued. The firm published eighteen titles in 1984.

Publications of the twentieth-century Ticknor and Fields include Meira Chand's first three novels, *The Gossamer Fly* (1980), *Last Quadrant* (1982), and *The Bonsai Tree* (1983); Gloria Naylor's *Linden Hills* (1985); Carolyn Chute's *The Beans of Egypt, Maine*

(1985); and Eugene O'Neill's *Poems, 1912-1944* (1980) and his play *The Calms of Capricorn* (1982). Nonfiction includes John Hersey's *Aspects of the Presidency* (1980); Calvin Trillin's *Uncivil Liberties* (1982), *Killings* (1984), and *With All Disrespect* (1985); and Frances Spalding's *Vanessa Bell: A Bloomsbury Portrait* (1983). The firm's address is 52 Vanderbilt Avenue, New York 10017.

References:

"Chester Kerr to Head New Houghton Mifflin Subsidiary," *Publishers Weekly,* 215 (7 May 1979): 34;

"Ticknor and Fields' Debut Described by Chester Kerr," *Publishers Weekly,* 271 (18 January 1980): 94;

Joann Davis, "Corlies Smith at the Helm," *Publishers Weekly,* 227 (12 April 1985): 46.

—Theodora Mills

Time-Life Books

(New York; Alexandria, Virginia: 1961-)

Established as a subsidiary of Time, Incorporated in 1961, Time-Life Books, Incorporated was developed from the pictorial books published by Time in the late 1950s and from articles in *Life* magazine. Time-Life Books contain original material in such areas as art, history, nature, food, and photography. Among the Time-Life series are the Great Ages of Man, the American Wilderness, the Life Nature Library, the Life World Library, and The Old West.

The firm ventured into literary book publishing with its Time Reading Program book club, which, from April 1962 to August 1966, published reprints of Graham Greene's *The Power and the Glory* (1962), Albert Camus's *The Plague* (1962), and John Cheever's *The Wapshot Chronicle* (1965). The club was started and operated by Max Gissen, book editor of *Time* magazine. It was revived, with some of the same titles, in September 1980. The Time Reading Program editions, published in stiff, pictorial wrappers, often feature new introductions by

the author, as in the case of Vladimir Nabokov's *Bend Sinister* (1964), or original introductions by well-known writers—for example, Peter DeVries's for Jerome K. Jerome's *Three Men in a Boat* (1964).

Time-Life Books are sold by subscription and, since 1966, also in bookstores. From 1969 to 1974 Time, Incorporated owned the Book Find Club and the Seven Arts Book Society and, from 1971 to 1974, the Sports Illustrated Book Club. In 1977 it acquired the Book-of-the-Month Club for $63 million; the Fortune Book Club is a subsidiary of the Book-of-the-Month Club.

Time-Life Books published 51 titles in 1984 and had 641 titles in print. Its high sales volume places the firm among the top ten publishers in the United States.

Joan D. Manley is chairman of the board of Time-Life Books; Reginald Brack, Jr., is president and chief executive officer. The firm was established in New York; in the 1970s it moved to 777 Duke Street, Alexandria, Virginia 22314.

References:

Robert T. Elson, *Time, Inc.: The Intimate History of a Publishing Enterprise, 1923-1941* (New York: Atheneum, 1968);

Elson, *The World of Time, Inc.: The Intimate History of a Publishing Enterprise. Volume Two: 1941-1960* (New York: Atheneum, 1973);

Herbert R. Lottman, "Around the World with Time-Life Books," *Publishers Weekly*, 208 (8 December 1975): 22-25;

"Time, Inc. Forms Book Club: The Time Reading Program," *Publishers' Weekly*, 181 (1 January 1962): 39.

—*Neal L. Edgar*

Times Books
(New York: 1977-   )
Quadrangle/The New York Times Book Company
(New York: 1967-1977)
Quadrangle Books
(Chicago: 1959-1967)

Times Books originated in Chicago as Quadrangle Books in 1959. The firm was bought by the *New York Times* in 1967, but the name was not changed to Times Books until 1977. Other book publishing imprints of the *Times* were Arno Press, Cambridge Book Company, and Truman Talley Books. Times Books primarily published nonfiction, and about half of the titles were written by members of the newspaper's staff. Among the most successful Times titles were Fox Butterfield's *China* (1982), Hedrick Smith's *The Russians* (1983), and David Shipler's *Russia* (1983).

Quadrangle/The New York Times Book Company was reorganized in 1976 after financial losses and management problems. The firm became a subsidiary of Random House in 1984 with Jonathan B. Segal as the editorial director. Times Books is based in the Random House building at 201 East Fiftieth Street, New York 10022.

—*Christopher Surr*

Tor Books
(New York: 1980-   )

Tor Books was founded in 1980 by Thomas Doherty—who had been publisher of Ace Books and Tempo Books and sales manager of Simon and Schuster—to publish science fiction, fantasy, horror, and thrillers in mass market paperbacks. His intention was "to publish better science fiction than anybody else in the country." The original staff consisted of Barbara Doherty (now vice-president, secretary, and comptroller), Harriet McDougal (now vice-president and editorial director), and James Baen (who has since left to found Baen Books). Tor had $1.7 million in sales during its first year; it now generates twelve times that figure. In 1985 164 titles were published, including a few trade paperbacks and hardcovers. Tor authors include Richard Hoyt, Isaac Asimov, Ben Bova, and Orson Scott Card; Piers Anthony's *Race against Time* (1985) was a mass market best-seller. The firm's address is 49 West Twenty-fourth Street, New York 10010.

Reference:

Marianne Yen, " 'There Isn't Any One Big Mass Market Anymore': How Tom Doherty Succeeded with Tor Books," *Publishers Weekly*, 228 (15 November 1985): 27-28.

—*Christopher Surr*

Reviving a famous imprint

Ticknor & Fields — the publishers of Emerson, Thoreau,
Hawthorne and Dickens — was acquired by Houghton
Mifflin Company in 1880. Now, 100 years later, the imprint is back
in the marketplace with a First List of exceptional quality.

JOHN HERSEY
Aspects of The Presidency:
Truman and Ford in Office
Introduction by Robert A. Dahl
*In this election year — closeups of two
Presidents*. Unique, first-hand accounts
of the aggressive Truman, the passive
Ford, in a book that illuminates
America's toughest job.
$10.95 May (012-X)

EUGENE O'NEILL
Poems 1912-1944
Edited with an introduction
by Donald C. Gallup
*Barred from publication during the
O'Neills' lifetime — the first edition
of poems by America's greatest
playwright*. From early, entertaining
verse to mature, beautiful love poems.
$9.95 June (007-3)

STEPHEN SPENDER
Mary Stuart
Freely translated and adapted from
Schiller's play with a new preface by
Mr. Spender
*From England's most respected poet
— the first American edition of a
major work*.
$8.95 cloth (008-1) $4.95 paper May (013-8)

JAMES GRAHAM-CAMPBELL
The Viking World
Foreword by David M. Wilson
*In time for the 1980 exhibition at the
Metropolitan Museum of Art — the
most definitive, spectacular, and
commanding volume ever published on
the Vikings*. The brutal splendor of 300
years, in a lavish re-creation of Viking
life from shipbuilding to domestic arts.
*130 color photographs • 80 b&w photographs
• 98 b&w illustrations • 51 color illustrations •
224 pages • 8½" x 11" • A Main Selection of
the History Book Club • A Selection of the
Macmillan Book Clubs • A Selection of the
Dolphin Book Club* • $25 April (005-7)

R.B. CUNNINGHAME GRAHAM
Reincarnation: The Best Short Stories
of Cunninghame Graham
*The wild Scotsman of whom George
Bernard Shaw said, "He'd wipe the
floor with us all if he often wrote like
that."* He often did. $8.95 May (004-9)

MEIRA CHAND
The Gossamer Fly
*Eastern and Western cultures clash
in an exquisite novel of love and loss*.
A Japanese husband, an English wife,
push their daughter to the gossamer
edge of madness. $8.95 April (002-2)

AUBREY BURL
Rings of Stone:
The Prehistoric Stone Circles of
Britain and Ireland
Photographs by Edward Piper
*A traveler's uncommon guide to the
mysterious Stone Circles of the British
Isles*. Country by country, color photo-
graphs explore Stonehenge, Avebury,
48 other sites • *32 color photographs
• 150 b&w photographs • 28 maps and ground
plans • A Selection of the Macmillan Book
Clubs* • $19.95 March (000-6)

DERVLA MURPHY
Wheels Within Wheels:
Unraveling an Irish Past
*The difficult journey from good
daughter to fulfilled woman — by
Ireland's foremost travel writer*. With
pain and humor, the author of *Full Tilt*
unravels 30 years of rage and love that
bound her to an ailing mother.
$10.95 April (006-5)

For full ISBN's, add prefix 0-89919-.

TO ORDER call Houghton Mifflin Company,
toll-free, 800-225-3362, or write
Houghton Mifflin Company,
Wayside Road, Burlington, Mass. 01803

TICKNOR & FIELDS

A Houghton Mifflin Company
383 Orange Street, New Haven, Conn. 06511 and
52 Vanderbilt Avenue, N.Y., N.Y. 10017

1980 advertisement

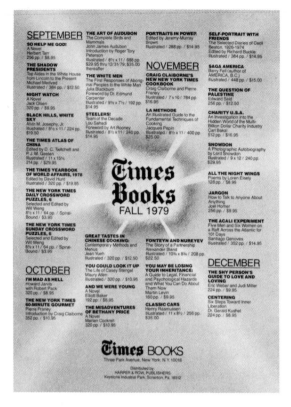

Advertisement

The staff of Tor Books: (standing) Ralph Arnote, circulation director; (back row, left to right) Harriet P. McDougal, vice-president and editorial director; Tom Doherty, president, publisher, and treasurer; Barbara Doherty, vice-president, secretary, and comptroller; Nancy Wiesenfeld, managing editor; Beth Meacham, senior editor; Michael Seidman; (front row, left to right) Amanda Dwyer; Melissa Ann Singer; David Hartwell

Tower Publications
(New York: 1960-1973; 1975-1982)
Belmont-Tower Books
(New York: 1973-1975)

TOWER 43-251

With Harry Shorten as publisher and president, Tower Publications was founded at 185 Madison Avenue, New York, in 1960. One of its early paperback novels was *Girl of the Streets* (1960) by Orrie Hitt, under the Midwood imprint. Early Midwood and Tower books emphasized erotica. It is often difficult to distinguish Midwood from Tower Books productions during this period: *Don't Bet on Blondes* (1963) by Walter Dyer, another original novel, is described as a Midwood-Tower Book on the title page but as a Midwood Book on the cover and spine.

By 1965 Tower was advertising for easily readable, topical nonfiction; Midwood Books also wanted nonfiction, but only of a sensational nature. *Hemingway's Paris* (1965) by Morrill Cody was a serious nonfiction Tower Book. Tower continued to publish fiction and retained an emphasis on sexual themes, as shown by *Friends and Lovers* by Oscar Pinkus, *The Pagan Empress* by Kevin Mathews, and *Cry into the Wind* by Eugenie Gaffney, all published in the early 1960s. Tower also emphasized movie tie-ins, especially sexually oriented titles such as *Love à la Carte* by George St. George.

In 1969 Tower Books published a series of westerns about a gunman known only as Lassiter; the series was written by various authors under the house name Jack Slade. The firm also published original science fiction, including *Three Faces of Time* (1969) by Frank Belknap Long.

Tower Books purchased Belmont Books in 1969. The imprints remained separate until 1973, when they were combined into Belmont-Tower Books. In 1971 Tower Books published over 300 fiction and nonfiction titles, both reprints and originals; fiction series included The Marksman and Peter McCurtin's Soldier of Fortune titles. In 1973, with McCurtin as editor in chief, the number of books published was 288; but it declined thereafter.

In 1976 or 1977 Tower Publications moved to 2 Park Avenue. By 1979 Belmont-Tower Books was publishing only nonfiction—both originals and hardcover reprints—in public affairs, feminism, the occult, wildlife, and cooking. Midwood Books was publishing only erotica by this time. The assets of Tower Publications were sold at a bankruptcy auction in August 1982, and the firm was liquidated.

Reference:
"Court Approves Auction of Tower Books Assets," *Publishers Weekly*, 222 (17 September 1982): 61.

—*Martha A. Bartter*

Cover for paperback, circa 1969

1928 advertisement

Universal Publishing and Distributing Corporation

(New York; Eastchester, New York: 1947-1978)

United Publishers

(New York: 1945-1947)

Arnold E. Abramson, vice-president of Farrell Publishing Corporation, began United Publishers in 1945 at 117-119 East Thirty-seventh Street in New York to explore what was then called hobby publishing and is now known as special-interest publishing. In 1947 United Publishers, which had published some magazines and cartoon collections, was incorporated and its name was changed to the Universal Publishing and Distributing Corporation. In 1950 Abramson resigned from Farrell to spend his full time with UPD. The firm's first major success was *Family Handyman* magazine, started in 1950, and UPD was soon publishing "how-to" magazines dealing with activities ranging from golf and skiing to knitting. The firm published books on the same subjects as spin-offs from its magazines. UPD soon became one of the largest special-interest publishers in the United States.

In the early 1950s UPD began publishing oversized paperback books called Uni Giants; one of these was *Aphrodite's Lover* (1953) by Arthur MacArthur. In 1954 it began publishing Beacon Books and Beacon-Envoy Books (not to be confused with publications of the Boston-based Beacon Press), paperback lines featuring erotica. Beacon Books also published some of the Galaxy Science Fiction Novels, including Poul Anderson's *Virgin Planet* (1960). By the time UPD offered its stock to the public in 1961, the number of books published under the Beacon or Beacon-Envoy imprints had increased from one title a month to eight.

In 1963 UPD began two paperback lines, Award Books and Nova Books. Some Award Books were drawn from UPD magazines, and many were of the "how-to" type. Award also published titles in Nick Carter's Killmaster series, including *Seven against Greece* and *A Korean Tiger*, both in 1967; and works by John Creasey, including *The Smog* (1972)

in the Dr. Palfrey series and *The Killers of Innocence* (1973). Many Award Books stressed the occult and the sensational—for example, Brad Steiger's *ESP—Your Sixth Sense* (1966) and *Flying Saucers Are Hostile* (1967). Some were by well-known writers, including *The River War* (1964) by Winston Churchill and *August 22nd* (1965) by Upton Sinclair. Award also reprinted *My Life* (1966) by Isadora Duncan. The Award imprint was used for both original and reprint fiction and nonfiction. Nova Books were reprints for young readers.

From 800 Second Avenue, its location since 1956, UPD moved in 1967 to 235 East Forty-fifth Street. By this time the Beacon-Envoy Books had been renamed Beacon-Signal. In 1969 UPD acquired two major science fiction magazines, *Galaxy* and *If*, and incorporated the latter into the former in 1975. More science fiction was added to the Award Books list, including reprints of *Conjure Wife* (1970) by Fritz Leiber, *The Invasion of the Body Snatchers* (1973) by Jack Finney, *The Rithian Terror* (1972) and *Off Center* (1973) by Damon Knight, several anthologies edited by Robert Silverberg, and the *Best from Galaxy* series.

Despite the success of its magazines and books, UPD found itself in financial trouble at the beginning of the 1970s. Outside assistance was necessary to pay some writers; *Ski* and *Golf* magazines were sold to the Times Mirror Company in 1972, *Family Handyman* was sold to the Webb Company in 1977, and *Galaxy* was discontinued. The UPD offices were moved to 720 White Plains Post Road, Eastchester, New York, in 1975. By 1977 the firm had been restructured and all imprints other than Award Books had been discontinued. Universal Publishing and Distributing Corporation went out of business in 1978.

—Martha A. Bartter

Vanguard Press

(New York: 1926-)

1927

1935

Charles Garland, believing that no one was entitled to any wealth beyond that required for his basic needs, petitioned to refuse a $1 million inheritance from the estate of his father, a stockbroker. When the courts denied his petition, he used the money to start the philanthropic American Fund for Public Service, also known as the Garland Fund. Upton Sinclair, among others, urged the Garland Fund to support the dissemination of reading material to the working class. Accordingly, the fund apportioned $100,000 to start the Vanguard Press in 1926. The firm was controlled by the Garland Foundation, whose first managing director was Jacob Baker. The first offices of the Vanguard Press were at 80 Fifth Avenue in New York.

The goal of the Vanguard Press was to produce inexpensive books which would spread what Sinclair termed "the ideas of social justice." The titles in the initial list of the Vanguard Series were priced at fifty cents apiece. *Kropotkin's Revolutionary Pamphlets* (1927) and Veblen's *The Theory of the Leisure Class* (1927), as well as books by Marx, Lenin, Proudhon, and Sinclair, reflected the political ideas of Garland and the board members of the American Fund. Eighty titles were published in the Vanguard Series, and over 400,000 copies were sold. The most popular title in the series was *Heavenly Discourse* (1927), a book of satirical dialogues by California poet Charles Erskine Scott Wood.

In 1928 Vanguard entered trade publishing. In May the firm acquired the Macy-Masius publishing house and, along with the low-cost books in the Vanguard Series, began publishing more commercial books. Shortly after the merger with Macy-Masius, James Henle, a former journalist, bought a half interest in Vanguard from the American Fund. A few years later Henle acquired complete control of the firm, and the Garland Foundation was dissolved.

Though he committed the Vanguard Press to commercial publishing, Henle retained the firm's emphasis on social and topical issues. John K. Winkler's *John D.: A Portrait in Oils* (1929) and John T. Flynn's *Graft in Business* (1931) were typical of the muckraking titles on Henle's early lists. The most successful of these topical books was the 1932 publication *100,000,000 Guinea Pigs,* an exposé of dangerous consumer products by Arthur Kallet and F. J. Schlink, engineers at Consumers' Research. The book went into dozens of printings.

As a publisher of controversial books, Vanguard Press actively fought censorship. In 1929 Henle and Vanguard sponsored a bill in the New York State legislature to make publishers, as well as authors, liable in obscenity prosecutions; the idea was to force publishers to take a more active role in the battle against censorship, but the bill was never passed. Vanguard also published *Who's Obscene?* (1930) by Mary Ware Dennett, two of whose education pamphlets had been suppressed by the government. The firm resisted the suppression of Donald Henderson Clarke's novel *Female* (1933) and won a dismissal of the case.

Under Henle, Vanguard continued to publish controversial political tracts such as *What Is Communism?* (1936) by Earl Browder, secretary of the American Communist party. Works by socially conscious novelists Nelson Algren, William Cunningham, Meridel Le Suer, and Daniel Fuchs were published by Vanguard in the 1930s. Vanguard published James T. Farrell's *Young Lonigan* in 1932 and, with the publication of *Studs Lonigan: A Trilogy* in 1935, Farrell became a major American literary figure. He eventually had more than thirty books published under the Vanguard imprint, including *A World I Never Made* (1936), *My Days of Anger* (1943), and *Bernard Clare* (1946).

Vanguard was the first publisher of the novels of Saul Bellow, whose *Dangling Man* and *The Victim* appeared in 1944 and 1947. Vardis Fisher had several titles published by Vanguard, among them *The Mothers* (1943), *The Golden Rooms* (1944), and *Intimations of Eve* (1946).

Evelyn Shrifte became president of Vanguard in 1952. The firm acquired Thames and Hudson in 1953. Vanguard published French novelist Pierre Boulle's best-known work, *The Bridge over the River Kwai,* in 1954 and *Auntie Mame* by Patrick Dennis (Edward E. Tanner) in 1955.

While Vanguard has moved away from radical or avant-garde works, it has continued to be a significant literary publisher. Farrell remained a highly regarded author until his death in 1979. Joyce Carol Oates was another Vanguard author whose books combined literary merit with high sales. *By the North Gate* (1963), *Expensive People* (1968), *Wonderland* (1971), and *Do with Me What You Will* (1973) are among the twenty-one Oates

titles published by Vanguard before the author discontinued her association with the firm in 1980. Vanguard has published most of poet William Heyen's major books, including *Noise in the Trees* (1974), *The Swastika Poems* (1977), and *Long Island Light* (1979).

Vanguard published 12 titles in 1984 and had 500 titles in print. Since 1936 Vanguard has been located at 424 Madison Avenue, New York 10017.

Reference:

"Vanguard's First Ten Years," *Publishers' Weekly,*
    129 (13 June 1936): 2348-2350.

—Timothy D. Murray

The Viking Press
(New York: 1925-1975)
Viking Penguin
(New York: 1975-   )

Children's Books

Harold K. Guinzburg and George S. Oppenheimer founded The Viking Press, Incorporated at 30 Irving Place, New York, on 1 March 1925. The firm's name and its logo, a Viking ship drawn by Rockwell Kent, were chosen as symbols of enterprise, adventure, and exploration in publishing. The founders announced that they planned to limit their offerings "to a few each season and make those few represent the best—to cultivate home soil yet seek foreign lands. . . ." Guinzburg, the president of Viking, was a graduate of Harvard and had spent the previous year visiting authors and publishers in Europe for Simon and Schuster. Oppenheimer, the secretary-treasurer, a graduate of Williams College, had served as advertising and promotion manager for Knopf.

In August 1925, before any titles had been published, Viking acquired the twenty-three-year-old firm of B. W. Huebsch; Huebsch became vice-president of Viking, bringing with him a backlist of titles by James Joyce, D. H. Lawrence, Gelett

Burgess, Sherwood Anderson, Wilfred Owen, and Romain Rolland. The first Viking list in the fall of 1925 included *The Book of American Negro Spirituals,* edited by James Weldon Johnson; *The Confessions of a Fool* by August Strindberg; and *Prairie,* a first novel by Walter J. Muilenburg.

Later publications included Siegfried Sassoon's *Satirical Poems* (1926), biographies by Vita Sackville-West and Carl Van Doren, and other nonfiction by Bertrand Russell, Thorstein Veblen, and Mohandas Gandhi. Viking also published several posthumous first American editions of the works of Saki (H. H. Munro): *The Square Egg and Other Sketches, with Three Plays* (1924), *The Short Stories of Saki* (1930), and *The Novels and Plays of Saki Complete in One Volume* (1933). Through Huebsch, the firm gained ten popular works by Elizabeth Madox Roberts, including *The Time of Man* (1926), *My Heart and My Flesh* (1927), *The Haunted Mirror* (1932), *He Sent Forth a Raven* (1935), and *Not by Strange Gods* (1941).

In 1929 Viking moved to larger quarters at 32 East Forty-eighth Street. From the start, the company pursued an active sales policy: as Oppenheimer stated in 1930, "We believe that in a dull year the best plan is to throw all possible power into advertising . . . [to] maintain volume." Two years later Viking offered bookstores ninety percent credit on return of all books ordered before the publication date; this policy was later known as the Viking Protection Plan.

As the 1930s began, Viking added new authors who were or became popular or literary successes. Dorothy Parker's *Laments for the Living* (1930) was followed by a book of poems, *Death and Taxes* (1931); a collection of stories, *After Such Pleasures* (1933); and her collected poems, *Not so Deep as a Well* (1936). Six of Lawrence's books—*Etruscan Places* (1932), *The Letters of D. H. Lawrence* (1932), *Last Poems* (1933), *Love among the Haystacks & Other Pieces* (1933), *The Lovely Lady* (1933), and *A Modern Lover* (1934)—were posthumously published by Viking in first American editions. The first edition of Irish writer Sean O'Faoláin's first book, *Midsummer Night Madness and Other Stories* (1932), and his three novels, *A Nest of Simple Folk* (1934), *Bird Alone* (1936), and *Come Back to Erin* (1940), were published by Viking. Viking published Erskine Caldwell's *God's Little Acre* (1933), *We Are the Living* (1933), *Journeyman* (1935), and *Southways* (1938) after luring Caldwell away from Scribner.

In 1933 Oppenheimer, who had turned over his duties as secretary to Marshall A. Best in 1928, resigned from the firm. The same year, May Massee, formerly head of juvenile books for Doubleday, was hired to build a children's department. The books were to be "clear-minded and beautiful . . . [to] make young Americans think and feel more vividly . . . [and be] more aware of the world around." The first catalogue contained twelve titles by authors including Maud and Miska Petersham, Kurt Weise, and Marjorie Flack. Books brought out under Massee's guidance won nine Newbery and five Caldecott Medals. *The Story of Ferdinand* (1936) by Munro Leaf sold more than 400,000 copies in thirty years. Other children's books published by Viking include Robert McCloskey's *Make Way for Ducklings* (1941), Wesley Dennis's *Flip* (1941), William Pène Du Bois's *The Twenty-one Balloons* (1947), and titles by Kate Seredy, Dorothy Kunhardt, and Ludwig Bemelmans, author of the popular Madeline series.

By Viking's tenth anniversary in 1935, the firm's average annual output was forty adult titles and ten juveniles. Three years later, when Pascal

Covici, who had been a partner in Covici-Friede, joined the editorial staff, Viking also acquired John Steinbeck, Covici's longtime friend. Steinbeck's first book for Viking was *The Long Valley* (1938), followed the next year by *The Grapes of Wrath*, of which 56,181 copies were shipped in one week and more than 90,000 were ordered before publication. *The Grapes of Wrath* was banned from the Buffalo Public Library and protested by California farmers, but more than 350,000 copies were in print by the end of the year. Other Steinbeck books published by Viking include *The Wayward Bus* (1947) and *East of Eden* (1952).

During the 1930s and 1940s Viking published works by Sylvia Townsend Warner, Franz Werfel, Roger Martin du Gard, Ben Hecht, Ernest K. Gann, Laura Hobson, Stefan Zweig, Richard Wright, and Muriel Rukeyser. The first trade edition of Joyce's *Collected Poems* was published by Viking in 1937, followed two years later by the first American edition of *Finnegans Wake*. With *Brighton Rock* (1938), Graham Greene began a long line of publications at Viking that included *The Confidential Agent* (1939); *The Labyrinthine Ways* (1940), republished in 1946 under its better-known British title *The Power and the Glory*; *The Heart of the Matter* (1948); *The Third Man* (1950); *The Comedians* (1966); and *Collected Stories* (1973). The success of these works created a need for additional space, and Viking took over two floors at 18 East Forty-eighth Street in 1939.

In 1943 the noted book designer and publisher Robert O. Ballou joined the firm. The same year, Viking launched the Viking Portable Library. The first book in the series, *As You Were*, an anthology edited by Alexander Woollcott, was planned especially for members of the armed forces. It was followed by volumes of Steinbeck, Hemingway, Shakespeare, Lawrence, and Joyce. In 1949 a copy of *Voltaire*, the forty-first title in the series, was the one-millionth Viking Portable printed. In 1954 some of the volumes were published in paperback for the first time. The seventy-fifth Viking Portable, *Graham Greene*, appeared in 1973. The Viking Portable Library format was designed by Milton Glick, who had joined the firm as director of production in 1928.

In the 1940s Helen Taylor and Keith Jennison joined the firm as editors and Malcolm Cowley and Mark Schorer became advisers. Viking published Lillian Hellman's *Another Part of the Forest* in 1947. Major additions to the list were Arthur Miller and Rumer Godden. Formerly at Reynal and Hitchcock, Miller switched to Viking for the publication of his most celebrated drama, *Death of a Salesman*, in 1949. Godden was a prolific author of fiction for both adults and children, as well as adult nonfiction. Viking published the Nero Wolfe mysteries of Rex Stout and a distinguished list of nonfiction by Ruth Benedict, George Gamow, Alex Comfort (who also wrote fiction for the firm), Norman Cousins, W.E.B. Du Bois, and Lionel Trilling. By 1950 Viking was putting out about sixty titles a year.

Cowley began a long career as an author at Viking in 1951 with *Exile's Return: A Literary Odyssey of the 1920s*, followed by *The Literary Situation* (1954) and *—And I Worked at the Writer's Trade* (1978). Viking also published Herbert Gold's first novel, *Birth of a Hero* (1951), and Harvey Swados's first novel, *Out Went the Candle* (1955), but neither of these authors remained with the firm. Viking published John Masters's *Bhowani Junction* (1954) and Peter Matthiessen's *Partisans* (1955), *Wildlife in America* (1959), and *Raditzer* (1961).

Saul Bellow's long tenure at Viking began in 1953 with his third novel, *The Adventures of Augie March*, his first real success. It was followed by *Seize the Day* (1956), *Henderson the Rain King* (1959), *Herzog* (1964), and *Mr. Sammler's Planet* (1970). Bellow was awarded a Pulitzer Prize for *Humboldt's Gift* (1975), his last book with Viking, and a year later he was awarded the Nobel Prize. He then moved to Harper and Row.

Marianne Moore came to Viking in 1955 with her first prose collection, *Predilections*, and followed it with three books of poetry: *Like a Bulwark* (1956), *O To Be a Dragon* (1959), and *Tell Me, Tell Me: Granite, Steel, and Other Topics* (1966). Iris Murdoch's second novel, *The Flight from the Enchanter*, was published by Viking in 1956. Viking also published Murdoch's *The Unicorn* (1963), *The Red and the Green* (1965), and *The Sacred and Profane Love Machine* (1974).

The classic novel of the Beat generation, Jack Kerouac's *On the Road*, was published by Viking in 1957, followed a year later by *The Dharma Bums*. Kerouac then moved to other publishers. Also in 1957 Viking published Evan S. Connell, Jr.'s first book, *The Anatomy Lesson and Other Stories*. His next three books, including *Mrs. Bridge* (1959), also bore the Viking imprint. The firm published Shirley Jackson's *The Haunting of Hill House* in 1959.

In 1955 Viking started a paperback reprint series, Compass Books, which offered titles from its hardcover list. Viking nonfiction of the 1950s included Joseph Campbell's *The Columbia Viking Desk Encyclopedia* (1955) and the first of five volumes of *Writers at Work: The Paris Review Interviews* (1958). In 1956 Huebsch resigned as vice-president but retained his positions as director and editor. Best moved up from secretary and general manager to replace Huebsch as vice-president. In 1956 Viking moved to 625 Madison Avenue. When Guinzburg died in October 1961 his son Thomas, who had joined the company in 1953 and had become vice-president in 1960, was elected president.

During the 1960s Viking published nonfiction by Hannah Arendt, Edward Crankshaw, Nat Hentoff, André Maurois, Barbara Tuchman, Samuel P. Huntington, Zbigniew Brzezinski, Theodore Draper, Karl Menninger, and Barry Commoner, as well as fiction by Ian Fleming, Wallace Stegner, Ken Kesey, Hamilton Basso, and Jimmy Breslin. Viking also published Peter S. Beagle's first three books, *A Fine and Private Place* (1960), *I See by My Outfit* (1965), and *The Last Unicorn* (1968). Beginning with *Friday's Footprint: Twelve Stories and a Novella* (1960), Viking published several novels by Nadine Gordimer.

Two authors Viking had published since the 1930s, Rebecca West and Patrick White, became especially prominent during the 1960s and 1970s. West's *The Birds Fall Down* came out in 1966, but she had been writing nonfiction for the firm since *The Thinking Reed* (1936). Viking had been White's sole American publisher since *Happy Valley* (1940), and his later works, including *The Aunt's Story* (1948), *Voss* (1957), *The Solid Mandala* (1966), and *The Eye of the Storm* (1973), earned him the Nobel Prize in 1973.

Viking bought Grossman Publishers in 1968, acquiring the Orion Press of Howard Greenfield as a subsidiary of Grossman. The Seafarer paperback series for children was launched in the same year. By the 1970s Viking's series or imprints also included The Viking Critical Library, Viking Large Type Books, and the Modern Masters series of biographies. The firm also published screenplays by Ingmar Bergman, Federico Fellini, and Luchino Visconti, and fiction by writers perhaps better known for their work for the screen, including George Axelrod, Penelope Gilliatt, and Richard Matheson.

Viking and Richard Seaver, formerly of Grove Press, reached an agreement in 1971 under which Seaver would publish with Viking twenty to thirty titles, mostly by foreign authors, under his own imprint. Seaver assembled a list that included Flann O'Brien, Octavio Paz, Eugène Ionesco, William S. Burroughs, John Rechy, and William Eastlake. Seaver left in 1978 to become head of general books at Holt, Rinehart and Winston. Jacqueline Kennedy Onassis was a consulting editor for Viking from 1975 until 1977.

Between 1969 and 1973 Viking's output increased from 184 to 342 titles per year, but then steadily declined; in 1979 the firm published only 154 titles. One trend of the 1970s was a new, though modest, emphasis on poetry. Under the Cape Editions imprint, the firm published translations of poetry or essays by Pablo Neruda, André Breton, and George Trakl. In addition, Viking published the work of contemporary American poets, including Daniel Halpern's *Traveling on Credit* (1972) and *Street Fire* (1975) and Greg Kuzma's *Good News: Poems* (1973). John Ashbery's *Self-Portrait in a Convex Mirror* (1975), a National Book Award winner, was followed by his *Houseboat Days* (1977).

Viking's fiction list during the 1970s included Frederick Forsyth's *The Day of the Jackal* (1971), *The Odessa File* (1972), and *The Dogs of War* (1974); Peter Maas's *Serpico* (1973); Thomas Pynchon's *Gravity's Rainbow* (1973); Judith Guest's *Ordinary People* (1976); Muriel Spark's *The Abbess of Crewe* (1974); Lawrence Durrell's *Monsieur* (1975), *Sicilian Carousel* (1977), and *Livia; or, Buried Alive* (1979); Kingsley Amis's *The Alteration* (1977) and *Jake's Thing* (1979); Robert Coover's *The Public Burning* (1977); and Dalton Trumbo's *Night of the Aurochs* (1979).

In 1975 Penguin Books took over Viking. Thomas Guinzburg commented, "The marriage is ideal. Each partner brings an enviable dowry to the other." Hardcover books are published under the Viking imprint, softcover under Penguin. Guinzburg continued as president and chief executive officer of Viking Penguin, Incorporated until he was succeeded by Irving Goodman, the former head of trade books at Holt, in September 1978. The current president is Alan Kellock, who was formerly vice-president in charge of the Penguin Books division. Viking Penguin's address is 40 West Twenty-third Street, New York 10010.

References:

M. S. Bean, "A History and Profile of the Viking Press," M.A. thesis, University of North Carolina, 1969;

Paul A. Bennett, "Milton Glick Does the Viking Books," *Linotype News*, 9 (January 1931): 5;

" 'Enterprise . . . and Exploration'; Viking's 25th Anniversary," *Publishers' Weekly*, 158 (9 December 1950): 2426-2429;

Daisy Maryles, "Viking and Penguin: Big U.S. Move from U.K., Worldwide PB Distribution for Americans," *Publishers Weekly*, 208 (17 November 1975): 14-15;

"The Viking Ship," *Bulletin of the American Library Association*, 50 (1956): 493-497.

—*Elizabeth A. Dzwonkoski*

James Henle, former president of Vanguard Press

Former Viking Press executives (from left): Benjamin W. Huebsch, vice-president and head of the trade department; Harold Guinzburg, cofounder and president; and Marshall A. Best, secretary, manager, and later vice-president

Page from catalogue

May Massee, former Viking Press children's book editor

P. F. Volland Company
(Chicago; Joliet, Illinois: 1908-1934)

1928

The P. F. Volland Company was founded at 58 West Washington Street, Chicago, in 1908 with Paul F. Volland as president, W. R. Anderson as vice-president, and F. J. Clampitt as secretary-treasurer. Limited in capital, Volland began by offering an original American product to compete in the European-dominated greeting card market. The firm's success in sales of cards and inspirational mottoes led to the publication of inspirational verse and prose booklets and eventually of gift books. Further expansion took the firm into the publication of children's books, which became its specialty. Selection of material was based on "The Volland Ideal," printed in each book, which promised "to give children only the best. Books for children should contain nothing to cause fright, suggest fear, glorify mischief, excuse malice or condone cruelty." Volland adapted the usual slogan of "good books for children" into its own motto, "Books Good for Children." Among the firm's early titles were Madison Cawein's *So Many Ways* (1911) and *The Message of the Lilies* (1913) and Ring Lardner's *Bib Ballads* (1915). In addition, Volland published *Flower Children* (1910) by Elizabeth Gordon, *Animal Children* (1913) by Edith Brown Kirkwood, and *A Year with the Fairies* (1914) by Ann Scott, all illustrated by M. T. Ross. Volland's most significant author of children's books was Johnny Gruelle, creator of the popular Raggedy Ann and Andy books. The first Raggedy Ann book, *Raggedy Ann Stories*, was published in 1918, and *Raggedy Andy* was added two years later. Volland continued to publish Gruelle's works for nearly twenty years.

In 1919 Vera Trepagnier, who claimed she had been cheated out of royalties, entered the office and shot Volland to death. Clampitt then became president. In 1924 Volland merged with the Gerlach/Barlow greeting card company; the Volland name was retained, as were its Chicago offices. Branches were also established in New York, Boston, and San Francisco, with manufacturing in Joliet, Illinois. In 1925 the company headquarters moved to Joliet. In the 1920s and early 1930s Volland listed more than 120 titles, including *Fairy Tales from France* (1920), illustrated by John Rae; Dixie Willson's *Honey Bear* (1923); Wilbur Nesbit's *In Tumbledown Town* (1926); and Alexander Key's *The Red Eagle* (1930). In addition to the Raggedy Ann and Andy series, the firm published Sunny Books, Hug Me Toy Books, Fairy Children Books, and Happy Children Books.

By 1935 Volland was out of business. The Gruelle series, Mother Goose, and Old, Old Tales Retold had been acquired by M. A. Donohue and Company, 711 South Dearborn Street, Chicago; all other Volland publications were in the hands of the Wise Book Company, 386 Fourth Avenue, New York, and were published under the Wise-Volland imprint.

References:

"Originality—The Volland Co.'s Watchword," *Publishers' Weekly*, 93 (29 June 1918): 1971;

"Paul F. Volland [obituary]," *New York Times*, 6 May 1919, p. 10.

—*Elizabeth A. Dzwonkoski*

Henry Z. Walck

(New York: 1958-   )

Established in New York at 101 Fifth Avenue in 1958, Henry Z. Walck, Incorporated specializes in books for boys and girls from cradle to college. The firm took over the juvenile titles of the Oxford University Press of New York, of which Walck had been president. Walck brought to his new firm Patricia C. Lord and Dorothea Wheelock, both of whom had been employed in Oxford's children's book division. Henry Z. Walck, Incorporated became a division of the David McKay Company in 1973. Walck is no longer associated with the firm.

Books published by Henry Z. Walck, Incorporated include Pelagie Doane's *A Small Child's Bible* (1959), *St. Francis* (1960), and *The Boy Jesus* (1963); Lois Lenski's *When I Grow Up* (1960); and Edward Ardizzone's *Tim's Last Voyage* (1972). The firm is located at the McKay offices, 2 Park Avenue, New York 10016.

Reference:

"Walck Buys Oxford Juvenile Department," *Publishers' Weekly,* 172 (2 December 1957): 22.

—Peter Dzwonkoski

Walker and Company

(New York: 1959-   )

Walker and Company was founded by Samuel S. Walker, Edmund Stillman, and John Kirk in May 1959 at 35 West Fifty-third Street, New York. Walker had previously worked for Time, Incorporated and had been the director of the Free Europe Press from 1951 to 1959. Walker and Company publishes books on current events, history, popular science, and art; it also publishes fiction, particularly mysteries. Under the Philip Hofer Press imprint, Walker publishes books illustrated with the work of famous artists.

In announcing its Connoisseur Mystery series in the winter of 1961, the company declared its intention to avoid the "tough-talking private eyes, pointless sadism, and sensational eroticism" typically associated with American mystery writers, and instead to concentrate its efforts on the "so-called English school." That policy led to the publication of works by Sarah Gainham, Desmond Cory, John Creasy, William Haggard, Simon Harvester, and Elizabeth LeMarchand, as well as John Le Carré's *Call for the Dead* (1962) and *A Murder of Quality* (1963).

Science fiction, a minor specialty taken up by the firm in the late 1960s, includes Ursula Le Guin's *The Left Hand of Darkness* (1969), Robert Silverberg's *Thorns* (1969) and *Nightwings* (1970), Roger Zelazny's *Jack of Shadows* (1971), and Andre Norton's *The Day of the Ness* (1975). Among Walker's other publications in fiction have been *At Swim—Two Birds* (1961) and *The Third Policeman* (1967) by Flann O'Brien (pseudonym of Brian O'Nolan);

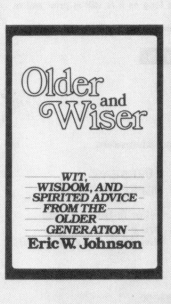

Catalogue cover

Malcolm Muggeridge's *Affairs of the Heart* (1961); and Richard Wright's *Lawd Today* (1963). The firm published 214 titles in 1984. It is currently located at 720 Fifth Avenue, New York 10019.

Reference:

"Walker & Co., New House, Issues First Books in Feb.," *Publishers' Weekly*, 179 (9 January 1961): 39-40.

—*Stephen Elwell*

Warner Books
(New York: 1974-　)
Warner Paperback Library
(New York: 1972-1974)

In 1972 the Warner Communications subsidiary of the Kinney National Services conglomerate purchased Coronet Communications, the publisher of the Paperback Library. The Paperback Library was renamed Warner Paperback Library and subsumed, along with several comic publishing and distributing firms owned by Warner Communications, under the newly created Warner Publishing, Incorporated at 909 Third Avenue in New York. William Sarnoff was chairman of Warner Publishing and Howard Kaminsky was president of Warner Paperback Library. In 1974 Warner Paperback Library was renamed Warner Books, Incorporated.

At the time of the takeover, Paperback Library was a small publisher of mass market paperbacks. With an initial budget of $3 million, Kaminsky set out to expand the firm's offerings. In 1973 Warner paid a $700,000 advance for Robert Crichton's *The Camerons* (1974), published by Alfred A. Knopf, and promoted the book heavily with television commercials. The following year the firm paid a $1 million advance for Bob Woodward and Carl Bernstein's *All the President's Men* (1975). Also in 1974 Warner began publishing books compiled from *Mad* magazine, which is published by E. C. Communications, another Warner Communications subsidiary. (The *Mad* series had first been published by Ballantine, then by The New American Library.) In 1978 Warner Books moved into the trade field, and in 1980 the firm began publishing hardcover books. In 1982 Warner bought Popular Library from CBS, and reprinted under its own imprint the 2,000 titles so acquired.

Warner Books reprints a diverse range of genre fiction, including westerns by Max Brand; mysteries; the espionage novels of William F. Buckley; Gothic romances by Phyllis A. Whitney, Dorothy Daniels, and Jennifer Wilde; and science fiction by Gordon Dickson and Poul Anderson.

Fiction best-sellers for the firm have included paperback reprints of Alison Lurie's *The War between the Tates* (1975), Elia Kazan's *The Arrangement* (1976) and *The Understudy* (1976), Bob Randall's *The Fan* (1978), Judith Krantz's *Scruples* (1979), and Sidney Sheldon's *Bloodline* (1979) and *A Rage of Angels* (1981). Warner Books has also reprinted John Cheever's *The World of Apples* (1974) and several titles by Iris Murdoch. Nonfiction reprints have included Dan Rather and Gary P. Gates's *The Palace Guard* (1975) and Richard Nixon's *Six Crises* (1981) and the two-volume *RN: The Memoirs of Richard Nixon* (1981).

Warner Books publishes only about ten hardcover books a year, but it has had some best-sellers among them. These include *Richard Simmons's "Never-Say-Diet" Book* (1980); Durk Pearson and Sandy Shaw's *Life Extension* (1982); Andrew Greeley's novels *Thy Brother's Wife* (1982), *Ascent into Hell* (1984), and *Lord of the Dance* (1984); and John Naisbitt's *Megatrends* (1983).

Warner Books published 241 titles in 1984. In August of that year Kaminsky left Warner Books to become publisher and chief executive officer of the trade department of Random House. Laurence J. Kirshbaum succeeded him as president of Warner Books. The firm's present address is 666 Fifth Avenue, New York 10103.

References:
Edwin McDowell, "Warner Chief to Lead Unit at Random House," *New York Times*, 29 August 1984, III: 22;
"Warner Books Buys Most of Popular Library Assets," *Publishers Weekly*, 222 (12 November 1982): 10;

"Warner Paperback Library Tests the Power of Television in Building a Best Seller," *Publishers Weekly*, 205 (25 March 1974): 41;
"Warner's Goes For Big Numbers," *Publishers Weekly*, 222 (13 August 1982): 30.

—*David Dzwonkoski*

W. J. Watt and Company
(New York: 1908-1928)

William J. Watt was the son of John Watt, who ran the Madison Avenue Bookstore in New York. Watt was a traveling salesman for the Robert M. McBride publishing house until 1908, when he started W. J. Watt and Company at 43 West Twenty-seventh Street. His list was limited to light fiction by American and English authors, romantic novels, spy and detective stories, and westerns. Of the twenty or so authors whose work was published by the company, none was famous except P. G. Wodehouse. His novel *The Intrusion of Jimmy* was published by Watt in 1910, followed by *The Prince and Betty* in 1912 and *The Little Nugget* in 1914.

Watt persuaded Robert Aitken, whose first romantic novel was published by McBride, to switch to his imprint for his next three titles. *When Tragedy Grins* (1912), the tale of a penniless American girl in Paris who "goes upon the boulevards as a night beggar to earn a living," was one of Grace Miller White's novels for Watt. *The Tigress* (1916) was

Anne French's last novel and the only one that Watt published by the author of the Susan Clegg novels. Charles Neville Buck wrote four westerns for Watt, including *The Code of the Mountains* (1915) and *Destiny* (1916). *The Bishop's Emeralds* (1908) was the first of three Watt detective novels by Houghton Townley. British writer Cecily Ullman Sidgwick's *Salt of the Earth* was published in 1917. Chauncey Cory Brainerd and Mrs. Edith R. Brainerd, writing jointly under the pseudonym E. J. Rath, contributed humorous novels to the list, among them *Too Much Efficiency* (1917).

In 1920 W. J. Watt and Company moved to 31 West Forty-third Street. The firm went out of business in 1928. Watt died in 1948 at sixty-seven.

Reference:
"William J. Watt [obituary]," *New York Times*, 19 July 1948, p. 19.

—*Theodora Mills*

Catalogue cover

Howard Kaminsky, president of Warner Books from 1972 to 1984. He is currently publisher and chief executive officer of the trade department at Random House.

Franklin Watts

Franklin Watts, Inc.

FOR BOYS & GIRLS $1

LITTLE MOO *by Helen Sterling*
Pictures by **DENISON BUDD.** The hilarious adventures of a calf that got into a circus by mistake and made the hit of the show! *Full color on every page. 7½" x 10½"*—larger than *Little Choo Choo.* First printing 50,000, or more.
July. $1.00

INTO THE ARK *by Marjorie Hartwell*
A full color illustration on every page with 26 pairs of animals moving into the ark. 7½" x 10½", First printing 50,000, or more.
April. $1.00

THE FIRST BOOK OF BOATS *by Campbell Tatham*
Illustrated by **JEANNE BENDICK.** Scores of little pictures of all kind of boats, done in "rebus" style. Three colors. Uniform with *First Flying Book.*
April. $1.00

SET THE CLOCK *by Dorothy King*
Illustrated by **WILL ANDERSON.** Telling time is fun when we follow a bright, happy child through a whole day. With clock face and movable hands. (Formerly published at $1.50 by *Harcourt, Brace.*) Full color. First printing 25,000, or more.
March. $1.00

MAJOR AND THE KITTEN *by Helen Hoke*
Illustrated by **DIANA THORNE.** A gay, amusing story of Mopsy, a ragamuffin kitten, and Old Major, a dignified St. Bernard dog. (Formerly published at $2.00 by *Holt.*) Full color. First printing 25,000, or more.
March. $1.00

FOR BOYS & GIRLS 50¢

RAILROAD ABC *Pictures by Denison Budd*
A tremendous value with full four-color illustrations on every page. First printing 25,000.
Ready. 50¢

FIND THE TOYS *by Marion Vannett Ridgway*
Illustrated by **HELEN SMITH.** A delightful book, in full color, with a flap on each page, which, when lifted, reveals a toy. First printing 40,000, or more.
July. 50¢

WHAT ARE THEY SAYING *by Helen Blake*
Illustrated by **HILDEGARD HOPKINS.** Full color book with flaps showing what the animals say—a book for the youngest. First printing 40,000, or more.
July. 50¢

FRANKLIN WATTS, Inc., 285 Madison Ave.,

1945 advertisement

Franklin Watts
(New York: 1942-   )

1950s

1965

FRANKLIN WATTS
New York / Toronto
1980

Franklin Watts, Incorporated was founded in 1942 by Franklin Watts at 285 Madison Avenue, New York; later it moved to 730 Fifth Avenue. Watts had begun his career in 1925 as a bookseller in Kansas; after that he had been a department store book buyer in Indiana. Since 1932 he had been a sales representative for a group of publishers. His firm's first book, *Voices of History,* a collection of speeches and papers edited by Watts, was published in October 1942. In the first year Watts also began its self-help series of 8 1/2-inch-by-11-inch paperbacks. The most successful of these, *Touch Typing in Ten Easy Lessons,* sold over one million copies.

In 1944 Watts entered the children's book market with the publication of *Little Choo Choo* by his wife, Helen Hoke, under her pseudonym of Helen Sterling. This popular book was followed by the development of the First Books series for young children. One of the best-known contributors to this series was Langston Hughes with *The First Book of Negroes* (1952) and *The First Book of Rhythms* (1954), as well as First Books on jazz (1955), the West Indies (1956), and Africa (1960). Children's books by Ogden Nash also bear the Watts imprint; these include *A Boy Is a Boy* (1960), *Girls Are Silly* (1962), and *A Boy and His Room* (1963). In 1948 Hoke became vice-president of Franklin Watts, Incorporated and helped to develop another children's line, the Terrific Triple Title books; these were anthologies with titles such as *Riddles, Riddles, Riddles* (1953), compiled by Joseph Leeming.

Watts became a subsidiary of the Grolier Company in 1957. Franklin Watts retired from the firm in 1969 and was succeeded as president by

Howard B. Graham. Watts moved to London, where he founded Franklin Watts, Limited. In 1973 Watts expanded into Europe with the creation of RSW Verlag in Esslingen, West Germany, a partnership between Watts, Rizzoli Editore of Milan, and J. F. Schreiber Verlag of Esslingen. Since 1975 Franklin Watts, Incorporated has attempted to increase its selection of adult books, but it continues to be most widely known for its many nonfiction series designed for elementary and high school students. These include Let's Find Out Books, Focus Books, World Focus Books, the Sports Action Books series begun by Edward Radlauer in 1971, and the Science Experience series edited by Jeanne Bendick from 1968 to 1978. A new series, The International Library, nonfiction books for teens, is printed in four languages and in five countries.

In 1976 Franklin Watts returned to the United States to establish the Frank Book Corporation at 10 Waterside Plaza, New York. He died in New York on 21 May 1978 at seventy-four. Jonathan N. Gillett, formerly general manager of McGraw-Hill's trade book division, succeeded Graham as president of Franklin Watts, Incorporated in August 1981. The firm's current address is 387 Park Avenue South, New York 10016.

References:

"Obituary Notes [Franklin Watts]," *Publishers Weekly,* 213 (5 June 1978): 20;

"Watts Marks Tenth Anniversary," *Publishers' Weekly,* 162 (25 October 1952): 1777-1779.

—Carol Kuniholm

A. Wessels and Company
(New York: 1900-1911)

Founded in 1900 at 7-9 West Eighteenth Street, New York, A. Wessels and Company published classics, children's books, fiction, literary criticism, and art criticism, as well as books on exploration and history. Among its first titles were Sarah Warner Brooks's *Poverty Knob* (1900), William Burton's *History and Description of English Porcelain* (1902), and reprints of works of Omar Khayyám and Lewis Carroll. The firm moved in 1903 to 43-45 East Nineteenth Street and in 1907 to 156 Fifth Avenue, where it published George Bancroft's *Abraham Lincoln* (1908) and Ada Carter's *The Seamless Robe* (1909). Most of Wessels's publications were reprints. Nearing bankruptcy in 1911, the firm was liquidated by a committee of New York publishers.

—Theodora Mills

Western Publishing Company
(Racine, Wisconsin: 1960-   )
Western Printing and Lithographing Company
(Racine: 1910-1960)
West Side Printing Company
(Racine: 1907-1910)

 Golden Press
Publications

Western Publishing Company, Incorporated is a worldwide organization that traces its roots to a small printing shop in Racine, Wisconsin. Edward Henry Wadewitz was born in Waubeka, Wisconsin, on 22 February 1878. He did not speak English until his family left this primarily German community to live in Iron Mountain, Michigan. He was forced to drop out of school at fifteen after his father died. Wadewitz then traveled to Racine in search of full-time employment. He held jobs as a store clerk, farmer, factory hand, and machinist before additional schooling enabled him to secure several jobs as a bookkeeper. The last of these was at the West Side Printing Company at 618 State Street. In 1907 Wadewitz and his brother William purchased the company for $2,500. Knowing little of the printing trade, Wadewitz hired Roy A. Spencer, a printer at the *Racine Journal*, to run the presses of his newly acquired company. Spencer also invested in the business. William Wadewitz eventually sold his interest to his brother and Spencer.

In their first year of operation Wadewitz and Spencer had an income of $5,000, mostly from commercial printing. In 1908 they moved to larger quarters at 548-550 State Street. In 1910 they bought their first lithographic press, incorporated the firm with a capital of $75,000, and changed its name to Western Printing and Lithographing Company. Sales reached $19,000 that year.

By 1914 annual sales were up to $100,000. Western's main work continued to be custom and commercial printing for local businesses. In 1916 Western entered book publishing when Hamming-Whitman Publishing Company of Chicago defaulted on bills due to Western for the printing of children's books. To recover its expenses, Western sold the books. The success of this venture inspired Wadewitz and Spencer to enter the children's literature field. On 9 February 1916 Western Printing and Lithographing Company bought out Hamming-Whitman, including all work in progress, unprinted stock, copyrights, and drawings, and formed Whitman Publishing Company, which became the largest publisher of juvenile books and games in the world. After acquiring Whitman, Western moved to larger facilities at 208-222 Second Street. In 1928, with sales in excess of $2.5 million, Wadewitz was able to build modern headquarters, specially designed as a center for graphic arts, at 1220 Mound Avenue.

In 1932 Whitman Publishing Company acquired exclusive rights to reproduce the Walt Disney characters for juveniles, coloring books, and comic books. The association with Disney eventually led to the acquisition of rights to the cartoon characters of Walter Lantz, Warner Brothers, and Sesame Street. Continuing to expand, Western established an office in Poughkeepsie, New York, in 1934 where in 1936 Dell Publishing Company made arrangements for Western to edit and print Dell's comic magazines, pocket-size mysteries, and paperback adventure books. This arrangement continued until 1962.

In 1935 the Artists and Writers Guild was established as a subsidiary of Western to foster new ideas in children's books. Guild members were hired to prepare new designs and formats, often for other companies. In 1942 the guild created the Little Golden Books for Simon and Schuster, which in 1958 sold the series to the Golden Press, owned jointly by Western and Affiliated Publishers, Incorporated, a subsidiary of Pocket Books. The Artists and Writers Guild also produced works for Harper and Row, Doubleday, Random House, Grosset and Dunlap, and Macmillan. Western eventually opened two new offices in New York to house both the guild and the newsstand division of Whitman Publishing.

In the 1950s Western formed the Guild Press

and entered into the planning, design, and production of religious books and greeting cards and readers for parochial schools. American Yearbook Company of Owatonna, Minnesota, a publisher of high school and college annuals, also became a subsidiary of Western during this time. In 1951 Western established a branch at 9916 Santa Monica Boulevard in Los Angeles. Wadewitz died in 1955. In 1960 the present name, Western Publishing Company, Incorporated, was adopted. Becoming sole owner of Golden Press in 1964, Western began marketing the successful line of Golden Book volumes, which included the Golden Nature Guides, Golden Picture Dictionaries, Disney Golden Books, and Betty Crocker Cook Books. Under the imprint of Golden Press, Western has offered the work of some of America's foremost illustrators of children's books. Feodor Rojankovsky illustrated Marie Colmont's *Christmas Bear* (1969) and his own *Rojankovsky's Wonderful Picture Book* (1972). The highly detailed scenes of Richard Scarry appear in his *Best Storybook Ever* (1968) and *All Year Long* (1976). Garth Williams illustrated several volumes for Western, including Margaret Wise Brown's *The Sailor Dog* (1969). Mercer Mayer produced *One Monster after Another* (1974) and *Herbert the Timid Dragon* (1980). Western acquired Odyssey Press and Capitol Publishing Company in 1961. Odyssey, which specialized in textbooks, was sold to Bobbs-Merrill in 1970. Capitol, a publisher of activity books and games for children, was discontinued in 1969. In 1979 Western became a subsidiary of the Mattel toy company. With offices all over the United States and branches in France, Australia, and Canada, Western Publishing Company is a major publisher of children's literature. A. Joseph Marino is the current president and chief executive officer. The firm's headquarters are still at 1220 Mound Avenue, Racine, Wisconsin 53404.

References:

Don H. Black, *E. H.: The Life Story of E. H. Wadewitz* (Racine, Wisconsin, 1955?);

"Edward H. Wadewitz [obituary]," *New York Times,* 16 January 1955, p. 92;

The Story of Western: Fifty Years of Progress (Racine, Wisconsin, 1957).

—*Karin S. Mabe*

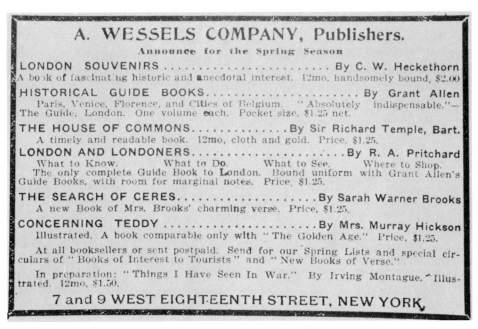

1903 advertisement (New York Times)

Covers for two 1943 Whitman Publishing Company Better Little Books

1937 advertisement

Whitman Publishing Company

(Racine, Wisconsin: 1916-)

In early 1916 the Hamming-Whitman Company of Chicago defaulted on its bills and was taken over by its chief creditor, Western Printing and Lithographing Company of Racine, Wisconsin. Western renamed the firm Whitman Publishing Company and moved its offices to Western's headquarters in Racine.

Under Western, Whitman quickly became known for its inexpensive juvenile books printed on pulp paper and sold in five-and-ten-cent stores. The firm's series of popular Big Little Books, initiated in 1932 with Chester Gould's *The Adventures of Dick Tracy*, set the standard for books of their kind and became the generic term for similar publications by other firms. Little Orphan Annie, Tarzan, Buck Rogers, and Popeye books were among the most popular of the series. By 1936 Whitman was publishing thirty-six million books a year, probably more than its closest competitors—Saalfield, Goldsmith, and Rand McNally—combined. Whitman was an innovator in modern market research for children's books.

In 1932 Whitman acquired rights to Walt Disney's Snow White, Donald Duck, and Mickey Mouse. Later it acquired the license to publish books featuring other comic strip and motion picture cartoon characters, including Woody Woodpecker, Bugs Bunny, and the denizens of Sesame Street.

Whitman Publishing Company is no longer in use as an imprint for books. The Whitman line today comprises games, coloring books, comic books, play money, jigsaw puzzles, coin albums, and numismatic guides manufactured by Western, which became Western Publishing Company in 1960. The firm is located at 1220 Mound Avenue, Racine, Wisconsin 53404.

Reference:

"Testing, Testing, Western Style," *Publishers' Weekly*, 190 (28 November 1966): 10.

—*Gregory P. Ames*

Albert Whitman and Company

(Chicago; Niles, Illinois: 1919-)

JUNIOR PRESS BOOKS

ALBERT WHITMAN & CO
CHICAGO

1939

Albert Whitman began publishing in Chicago around the turn of the century with a street guide for New York City. He later cofounded the Hamming-Whitman Company, which defaulted on its bills and was taken over by its chief creditor, Western Printing and Lithographing Company, in 1916.

In 1919 Whitman started Albert Whitman and Company at 560 West Lake Street, Chicago. Although the firm acquired the trade publications of Laird and Lee and the Laidlaw Brothers in 1932, thereby adding a series of reference titles to its list, Whitman has published almost exclusively for preschool- and grade-school-age readers. Whitman sold the company to five of his employees in 1949 but remained with the firm until his death in 1962.

Among Whitman's most popular titles are the books in Gertrude Chandler Warner's Boxcar Children Mysteries. *The Box-Car Children*, the first in the series, was originally published by Rand, McNally in 1924; Scott, Foresman later acquired the series and sold Whitman rights to all the Boxcar titles in 1950. Florence Parry Heide's mysteries, coauthored variously with Carole Smith, Sylvia Van Clief, and Roxanne Heide, include *The Hidden Box Mystery* (1973) and *Mystery of the Forgotten Island* (1980).

Maj Lindman's tales of Swedish children in the Snipp, Snapp, Snurr and Flicka, Ricka, Dicka series, published by Whitman during the 1930s and 1940s, enjoyed both critical and popular acclaim, as did Laura Bannon's tale of a Seminole family, *When the Moon Is New* (1953). Bannon illustrated another Whitman favorite, *Pecos Bill: The Greatest Cowboy of All Time* (1937) by James Cloyd Bowman. Other popular titles include *The Boy Who Cried Wolf* (1960) by Katherine Evans, *One More Thing, Dad* (1980) by Susan L. Thompson, and Joan L. Nixon's *Christmas Eve Mystery* (1981). Whitman also pub-

lishes Concept Books, designed to teach children about life and help them develop a positive self-image; titles include *Who Is a Stranger and What Should I Do?* (1985) by Linda Walvoord Girard and *I'll Never Love Anything Ever Again* (1985) by Judy Delton. Just for Fun Books include Virginia Mueller's *A Playhouse for Monster* (1985) and Norma Simon's *Oh, That Cat!* (1985).

Richard Pugh is the president of Albert Whitman and Company, which has been located since 1982 at 5747 West Howard Street, Niles, Illinois 60648.

References:

"Albert Whitman & Co.," *Publishers' Weekly*, 96 (9 August 1919): 396;

"Albert Whitman [obituary]," *Publishers' Weekly*, 182 (19 November 1962): 34.

—*Gregory P. Ames*

Whittlesey House
(New York: 1930-1965)

McGraw-Hill Publishing Company created Whittlesey House in 1930 to publish nonfiction for the general reader, as distinct from the scientific and technical books with which McGraw-Hill was identified. Later the division also published some adult fiction and many children's books. Whittlesey House was named for Curtis E. Whittlesey, the first treasurer of the old McGraw Company. Whittlesey House shared offices with McGraw-Hill at 370 Seventh Avenue in New York until both firms moved in 1932 to 330 West Forty-second Street. Guy Holt, a former managing editor of *Lippincott's Magazine*, was the first director of Whittlesey House. His successors included George W. Stewart, Hugh J. Kelly, and William E. Larned.

The World's Economic Dilemma (1930) by Ernest Minor Patterson was the first Whittlesey House title. A criticism of the social irresponsibility of big business, it was well suited to the mood of the nation after the stock market crash. Throughout the 1930s Whittlesey House practical knowledge, current affairs, and self-help books sold well. The firm's biggest success was Walter B. Pitkin's *Life Begins at Forty* (1932). Another widely read title was Stuart Chase's *Rich Land, Poor Land* (1936), a warning against wasting American natural resources. Anthropologist Clyde Kluckhohn's *Mirror for Man* (1949) won a Whittlesey House contest for the best manuscript

on a scientific subject written for the ordinary reader. Whittlesey House also published books on astronomy, aviation, psychology (especially child rearing), and hobbies.

Whittlesey House's first venture into adult fiction, *A Lion Is in the Streets* (1945) by Adria Locke Langley, was an instant best-seller. Other Whittlesey House novels included Kay Boyle's *His Human Majesty* (1949), Elizabeth Ogilvie's *Rowan Head* (1949), and Jesse Stuart's *Hie to the Hunters* (1950).

Whittlesey House editor in chief Edward C. Answell contracted with Yale University in 1949 to publish its huge collection of James Boswell's private papers; but in 1950 McGraw-Hill restricted the Whittlesey House imprint to its children's books and a few specialized items, so the Boswell papers were published with the McGraw-Hill imprint. Whittlesey House had been publishing children's books since the mid-1930s, but most had been science or hobby titles. After 1950 more titles of literary and artistic interest appeared, including Ellen McGregor's *Miss Pickerell Goes to Mars* (1951), Louise Fatio's *The Happy Lion* (1954), and Eve Titus's *Anatole* (1956). All three books became series. Paul Galdone illustrated the Miss Pickerel and Anatole books; Roger Duvoisin was the artist for the Happy Lion series. Duvoisin also illustrated the 1952 adaptation of Gian-Carlo Menotti's television

*The Whittlesey House staff in 1940: (left to right) Catherine D. Mahon, William E. Larned, George Brockway, Hugh J. Kelly,
Clinton Simpson, William Poole, Claire Gray*

Guy Holt, first director of Whittlesey House

Alfred Cahen, founder of World Publishing Company

opera *Amahl and the Night Visitors.* The firm also published Frances Frost's *The Little Whistler* (1949) and *Fireworks for Windy Foot* (1956).

In the mid-1960s the Whittlesey House imprint was phased out and replaced by the designation Junior Books. Today McGraw-Hill uses its own imprint for juvenile books.

References:

Roger Burlingame, *Endless Frontiers: The Story of McGraw-Hill* (New York: McGraw-Hill, 1959);

"Whittlesey House: Its Ten Years of Publishing," *Publishers' Weekly,* 138 (21 September 1940): 1103-1105.

—*Margaret Becket*

World Publishing Company
(Cleveland and New York: 1940-1974)
World Syndicate Publishing Company
(Cleveland: 1929-1940)
Commercial Bookbinding Company
(Cleveland: 1905-1929)

Alfred Cahen was born in Poland in 1880. He became an apprentice bookbinder at thirteen, traveling to cities in Poland, Russia, Germany, and the Netherlands before settling in London in 1898. Four years later he moved to Cleveland and worked for various publishing companies before setting up the Commercial Bookbinding Company in his home. Among his customers was the World Syndicate Company, publishers of inexpensive Bibles and dictionaries. Cahen bought World Syndicate in 1929 and the newly combined firm, located at 2231 West 110th Street in Cleveland, became World Syndicate Publishing Company; "Syndicate" was dropped from the name in 1940. World continued to publish Bibles and dictionaries; by 1935 it was turning out six million volumes annually.

In 1933 Benjamin David Zevin, business manager of the *New York Daily Food News,* married Cahen's daughter. Zevin moved to Cleveland in 1934 and was appointed advertising manager for World. Two years later he became director of sales and advertising; by 1939 he was vice-president. Zevin

was the driving force in the development of World from a Bible and dictionary publisher to a major trade and reprint house.

Zevin introduced Tower Books, a series of forty-nine-cent hardbound nonfiction reprints, in 1939. This innovation proved instantly successful—one million copies of forty-two titles were sold in 1941, two million the next year, and four million in 1943.

Tower Books were mainly books on self-help, hobbies, health, and popular psychology. Biggest sellers were *The Hygiene of Marriage* (1940) by Millard Everett, *Roget's Thesaurus* (1941), and *A Complete History of the United States* (1941) by Clement Wood. Fiction was added in 1942; the list included reprints of James T. Farrell's *Young Lonigan* (1943), with a new introduction by the author; Richard Wright's *Uncle Tom's Children: Five Long Stories* (1943); Christopher Morley's *Kitty Foyle* (1944); and Oscar Wilde's *The Picture of Dorian Gray* (1944). The books were marketed at newsstands and beauty parlors as well as through bookstores.

1941 advertisement

In 1942 Zevin launched Forum Books, a hardbound nonfiction reprint series "selected for the discriminating reader." These sold for eighty-nine cents and later for one dollar. The fifteen 1942 titles included *The Story of America* by Hendrik Willem Van Loon, *The Voice of America* by Mark Van Doren, and *The Complete Works of William Shakespeare*. Forum added fiction reprints to its list in 1944; titles included *The Virgin and the Gipsy* (1944) by D. H. Lawrence and *The Human Comedy* (1945) by William Saroyan.

In 1942 Zevin hired William Targ, a Chicago antiquarian bookseller, as editor of the Tower and Forum lines. Especially interested in crime fiction, Targ secured rights to novels by James M. Cain, Dashiell Hammett, Ellery Queen, Eric Ambler, Raymond Chandler, Agatha Christie, and Erle Stanley Gardner.

In 1945 Zevin was made president of the firm when Cahen became chairman of the board. Rather than compete with the postwar paperback boom, World discontinued the Tower and Forum lines. Targ went to New York to establish a trade book department and expand the reprint line; he set up offices at 14 West Forty-ninth Street, moving the next year to 107 West Forty-third Street. In 1952 World's New York office relocated to 119 West Fifty-seventh Street. The headquarters remained in Cleveland. In 1952 Targ was appointed editor in chief and vice-president.

In 1946 World established a new reprint line: The Living Library, quality reprints of American classics introduced by well-known authors, illustrated by contemporary artists, and sold for one dollar each. Carl Van Doren was hired as editor. Among the first titles reprinted in The Living Library was Theodore Dreiser's *An American Tragedy* (1948), with an introduction by H. L. Mencken. Targ negotiated reprint rights to all of Dreiser's works from his widow, and in 1951 World published Helen Dreiser's *My Life with Dreiser*. Other Living Library reprints included Sinclair Lewis's *Main Street* (1946), Carl Sandburg's *Poems of the Midwest* (1946), and Leo Tolstoy's *Anna Karenina* (1946).

Also in 1946 World began a children's book series, Rainbow Classics, with May Lamberton Becker, children's book editor of the *New York Herald Tribune*, as general editor. The first titles in the series included *Robin Hood*, *Heidi*, *Black Beauty*, and *A Child's Garden of Verses*.

World continued to publish Bibles and dictionaries. During World War II the firm produced forty percent of the seventeen million government-issued Bibles; by 1955 World claimed to have published more King James Bibles than any other firm. These ranged in price from $1.00 to $225 for the *Bruce Rogers World Bible* (1949), of which only 975 copies were printed. *Webster's New World Dictionary of the American Language, College Edition* (1953) took David R. Guralnik and a staff of 101 twelve years to prepare. World also became well known for its anthologies, including George Jean Nathan's *World's Great Plays* (1944), James M. Cain's *For Men Only* (1944), Targ's *The American West* (1946), and Alfred Kazin's *F. Scott Fitzgerald: The Man and His Work* (1951).

World published its first successful trade list in 1954. Among the titles were Herbert Gold's *The Prospect before Us*, MacKinlay Kantor's *God and My Country*, Simone de Beauvoir's *She Came to Stay*, M. F. K. Fisher's *The Art of Eating*, and Andre Norton's *The Stars Are Ours!* In 1955 World published *Party of One: The Selected Writings of Clifton Fadiman*, de Beauvoir's *All Men Are Mortal*, and Kantor's *Andersonville*. In the late 1950s World's trade titles included Harry Golden's *Only in America* (1958) and Yaël Dayan's *New Face in the Mirror* (1959).

In the spring of 1960 World acquired Meridian Books, one of the first publishers of higher-priced paperbacks. Zevin announced that Meridian would have full editorial autonomy under its founder and president, Arthur A. Cohen. Meridian published both reprints and original works by Isaac Babel, Jean Piaget, Jacques Maritain, Alan Watts, Alfred North Whitehead, José Ortega y Gasset, Mercea Eliade, and Bronislaw Malinowski. It also reprinted classics by Henry James, Montesquieu, Lewis Carroll, and John Locke. The Meridian Books imprint continued until 1974.

In 1962 Zevin became chairman of World and Leonard A. Charpie assumed the presidency. Cahen, the founder of the company, died in 1963. In the early 1960s the firm continued to publish large and profitable trade lists. Targ edited Richard Wright's *Eight Men* (1961); other noteworthy titles included *The Collected Short Stories of Conrad Aiken* (1960), François Mauriac's *The Son of Man* (1960), de Beauvoir's *The Prime of Life* (1962), and Brigid Brophy's *Flesh* (1962).

World's sales in 1963 totaled more than $14 million. A leading Bible publisher and the second largest publisher of dictionaries in the United States, the firm also had substantial adult and juvenile trade lists. In 1963 the Times-Mirror Company of Los Angeles acquired World through an exchange of stock. It was announced that World was to remain an autonomous publishing subsidi-

Benjamin D. Zevin, president of World Publishing Company from 1945 to 1962; chairman of the board from 1962 to 1965

Editors and executives of World Publishing Company in 1955 (from left): Donald Friede, William Targ, Benjamin D. Zevin,
Eleanor Kask, and Abe Lerner

ary of Times-Mirror with no management changes. Before the sale was concluded, however, the new owners asked World personnel to sign contracts allowing employees to be shifted to different assignments.

Times-Mirror had recently acquired The New American Library of World Literature (NAL), a paperback publisher, and NAL began to control the trade department of World. Targ resigned to become senior editor of G. P. Putnam's Sons, taking many of his authors, including de Beauvoir, Golden, and Lin Yutang, with him. Most of the trade department personnel eventually left the firm as NAL exerted more and more control. In January 1965 Zevin resigned as chairman and Dexter E. Robinson was elected president. The firm moved to 110 East Fifty-ninth Street in 1969.

In 1973 World began to reduce its trade publishing activity and to return to its earliest specialization, Bible and dictionary publishing. In January 1974 the British publisher William Collins Company bought World's Bibles and dictionaries, and the next month Times-Mirror announced that Meridian Books would be published by New American

Library. The dissolution of the World Publishing Company was complete, although the name continued to exist for another five years as the William Collins Company renamed itself William Collins + World Publishing Company. On 1 January 1979 the firm became William Collins Publishers.

(The World Publishing Company is not to be confused with the World Book Company, publisher of educational materials, which merged with Harcourt, Brace in 1960.)

References:

"Alfred Cahen [obituary]," *New York Times*, 5 September 1963, p. 31;

R. M. Miller, "Brief History of the World Publishing Company, Cleveland, Ohio," M.A. thesis, Case Western Reserve University, 1957;

William A. Targ, *Indecent Pleasures* (New York: Macmillan, 1975);

Thirty Years After (Cleveland: World Syndicate, 1935);

John T. Winterich, "The World Publishing Company's First Half-Century," *Publishers' Weekly*, 167 (14 May 1955): 2164-2170.

—Kathleen McGowan

Thomas Yoseloff
(New York: 1955-1978)

Thomas Yoseloff, Incorporated was founded in 1955 at 11 East Thirty-sixth Street, New York, by Thomas Yoseloff. Within its first three years the firm acquired the Story Classics Press, the Sagamore Press, and A. S. Barnes and Company. Yoseloff's first book was Charles Angoff's *H. L. Mencken: A Portrait from Memory* (1956). A four-volume reprint of *Battles and Leaders of the Civil War* (1956), the most successful publication of Yoseloff's first year, helped establish Civil War history as an important focus of the firm's publishing activities. Equally significant was Yoseloff's interest in Judaica. Among the firm's major publications in this area were Eliezer Ben Yehuda's eight-volume *Dictionary and Thesaurus of the Hebrew Language* (1959) and Meyer Waxman's six-volume *History of Jewish Literature* (1960). The firm also published fiction by Jewish authors, including Saul Davis's *Adventures of Shlomele* (1956); Mendele Mocher Seforim's *The Nag* (1957), translated by M. Speigel; and Seforim's *Fishke the Lame* (1960), translated by Gerald Stillman.

Yoseloff published the first American edition of Robert Graves's *Adam's Rib* (1958). Several well-known American poets, including Kenneth Patchen, Galway Kinnell, and William Carlos Williams collaborated on the translation of Yvann Goll's *Jean Sans Terre* (1958). The firm also published some juveniles, among them Yoseloff's translation of *The Further Adventures of Till Eulenspiegel* (1957), with illustrations by Jane Frank.

After the acquisition of A. S. Barnes and Company in 1958, Yoseloff became chief executive officer of that company and the name Thomas Yoseloff became an imprint of Barnes. In 1966 Barnes moved from New York to Cranbury, New Jersey. Yoseloff and his son Julien remained in control of the firm until 1978, when it was acquired by Leisure Dynamics, Incorporated of San Diego, California. Thomas Yoseloff, Limited, an English subsidiary established in 1957, is a leading publisher of books on the cinema, including the annual *International Film Guide* edited by Peter Cowie.

Advertisement

Advertisement

References:
"Yoseloff Acquires Major Interest in A. S. Barnes," *Publishers' Weekly*, 173 (10 March 1958): 36;

"Thomas Yoseloff Buys Story Classics Press," *Publishers' Weekly*, 170 (20 August 1956): 789.

                                                                  —*Stephen Elwell*

Zebra Books
(New York: 1975-   )

The Zebra Books imprint had belonged to Grove Press and to Pinnacle Books before it was acquired by Kensington Publishing Corporation in 1975. This mass market paperback house specializes in historical romances but publishes originals and reprints in all genres. Two of Zebra's million-copy sellers are Hugh McDonald's *Appointment in Dallas* (1977) and David Abodaher's *Iacocca* (1985). Walter Zacharius is the chairman of the board and Roberta Bender Grossman is the president and publisher. The firm's address is 475 Park Avenue South, New York 10016.

                                                                  —*Christopher Surr*

Roberta Grossman, president and publisher of Zebra Books, with Walter Zacharius, chairman of the board

Appendix

Trends in Twentieth-Century Mass
Market Publishing

Main Trends in Twentieth-Century
Book Clubs

Trends in Twentieth-Century Mass Market Publishing

Kenneth C. Davis

In the United States, the paperback book is a fixture in everyday life as commonplace as record albums, sporting goods, or kitchen appliances. From children's books to high school and college textbooks, from romances for reading in the summer sun to the classics of literature, the books read by Americans today are most likely to be bound in paper covers. But that has not always been the case: the paperback book is a relative newcomer as American products go.

The modern paperback book made its debut in the American marketplace in 1939. During its forty-odd years of existence the paperback has made an enormous contribution to the country's social, cultural, educational, and literary life. Before these inexpensive, widely distributed books came along, most books sold no more than a few thousand copies and million-sellers were rare. In the early 1930s there were only about 500 legitimate bookstores in the United States, mostly in the nation's twelve largest cities; these stores catered to the wealthy "carriage trade." Stationery stores stocked limited numbers of popular novels and Bibles, but that was all. Two-thirds of America's counties had no bookstores at all. Only half of all the books published by American publishing houses sold more than 2,500 copies. Public libraries were not as widespread and well funded as they would later become with increased federal support. Consequently, many Americans had no direct access to books.

Overnight, the paperback changed that forever. Suddenly, a book could reach not hundreds or thousands of readers, but millions, many of whom had never owned—or perhaps even read—a book before.

When the modern paperback book first appeared the standard price was twenty-five cents. These "quarter books" were sold on street corner newsstands, in bus and train stations, in hotel lobbies, and in drugstores—the "mass market" outlets where books had never been sold before and which gave the books the name "mass market paperbacks."

With their low price and widespread availability, paperbacks "democratized" reading in America; that is, reading was no longer only for the wealthy who could afford hardcover books or for students with access to a school or public library. Great books, popular novels, science fiction, romance, cookbooks, and philosophy were made available to a mass audience for the first time. This was the beginning of what came to be known as the Paperback Revolution, which resulted in more Americans reading more books than ever before in the country's history.

This revolution began in the United States in June 1939 when Robert F. de Graff, a veteran publisher, started a company called Pocket Books that would mass produce paperbound books. This idea was neither new nor untried. Paperbacks had a long history in America, going back to colonial times when sermons and religious tracts were published with paper bindings. There were numerous attempts during the nineteenth century to publish books in paper covers, but for a variety of economic and legal reasons, none of these experiments lasted more than a few years. In Europe, on the other hand, paper bindings had been used for hundreds of years. In Germany, for example, millions of English-language paperbacks had been sold by Tauchnitz Editions. Also in Germany, Reclam's Universal Bibliothek had set even larger sales records with German-language editions of Greek and Roman classics and philosophical works. In the 1930s another German company, The Albatross Modern Continental Library, had great success with its paperbound reprints of English-language books.

In 1935 an even more influential and successful British company, Penguin Books, was founded by Allen Lane, who felt that readers would pay a few pence for quality books bound in paper covers. The success of Penguin was immediate and startling. In just three years more than 25 million

Banner Books was one of the lines launched by the Hearst Corporation

Beacon began in 1954 and published more than 300 titles

With its early volumes Handi-Books (1941-1951) tried to undersell the larger paperback lines. It published mainly mysteries and westerns.

The Pennant line was a Bantam spin-off in the 1950s

Penguin Books were sold, far beyond the wildest expectations of anyone connected with the British book business and certainly beyond even Lane's imaginings.

De Graff watched the success of Penguin Books with admiration and a little envy. Why couldn't the same thing be done in the United States? he wondered. Surely there were many Americans who would be willing to spend a small amount of money for good reading. Most other publishers disagreed with de Graff, saying that what worked in Europe would not work in the United States because Americans were not interested in reading, whatever the price of a book—an elitist point of view that de Graff simply dismissed. Perhaps more significant was the attitude of publishers and booksellers who feared that these inexpensive books would spell disaster for the sale of more profitable hardcover books. In the face of this pessimism, de Graff found willing partners in the young firm of Simon and Schuster, whose founders, Richard Simon and M. Lincoln Schuster, shared his belief that there was a mass audience of Americans eager for books that were affordable and available.

De Graff's plans for Pocket Books were modest, and it was unlikely that he knew he was embarking on a course that would change the world of books forever. He started off with a list of ten books that were to be sold on an experimental basis in New York City. Initially, he planned cautious printings of no more than 10,000 copies per title. In making the choice of his first ten books, de Graff was also cautious. In an attempt to discern exactly what the public was interested in reading, he selected a few proven sellers from various subject categories. To remove the doubts of skeptical readers who might not believe that these small, inexpensive books could possibly be the same as the original edition, the cover of each Pocket Book carried the promise "Complete and Unabridged."

(The first ten Pocket Books were *Lost Horizon* by James Hilton, *Wake Up and Live* by Dorothea Brande, *Five Great Tragedies* by Shakespeare, *Topper* by Thorne Smith, *The Murder of Roger Ackroyd* by Agatha Christie, *Enough Rope* by Dorothy Parker, *Wuthering Heights* by Emily Brontë, *The Way of All Flesh* by Samuel Butler, *The Bridge of San Luis Rey* by Thornton Wilder, and *Bambi* by Felix Salten.)

The success of Pocket Books was instantaneous and unprecedented in the annals of American publishing. These books, with their plastic laminated covers and bright red endpapers, took first New York City and then the rest of the country by storm.

The keys to success, de Graff and his partners knew, were to cut operating and production costs and to radically increase sales volume through wider distribution. The first step taken to cut costs was to reduce royalty payments. Almost all books are sold on a royalty basis, which means that the author is paid a percentage of the cover price of the book. In traditional hardcover publishing, the starting royalty was ten percent, with increases based upon sales volume. With paperbacks, which were often reprints of books originally published in hardcover, the royalty paid on the sale of the books was split between the author and the originating hardcover publisher. This paperback royalty is part of what is known as subsidiary rights income, which also includes book club sales, magazine serializations, and movie or other dramatic rights. Often it is the income from these subsidiary rights that makes a book profitable. Pocket Books cut the royalty from ten percent to four percent.

Another element of the plan was to create original books; it was less expensive for Pocket Books to publish a book it had commissioned than to buy rights to a reprint from a hardcover publisher. So among the early Pocket Books were many anthologies of poetry and short stories, collections of humor, and original reference volumes such as *The Pocket Dictionary*.

By cutting the royalty rate by more than half and relying less on reprints of successful hardcovers for their material, de Graff and his partners had gone a long way in reducing their costs. Substantial savings also resulted when the founders of Pocket Books reduced their discounts to dealers and booksellers. (The discount is the percentage of the cover price that the dealer keeps as profit.) Further economies were achieved by reducing the size of the books; printing them on less expensive paper; using the original publisher's printing plates whenever possible; and utilizing a process known as "perfect binding," in which the pages of books are bound together with glue rather than sewn, as hardcover books were at that time. (Today almost all paperbacks and many hardcovers are glued.) Finally, the single most important factor in reducing production costs was the ability to increase the size of printings to ten times the size of a typical hardcover print run: the larger the size of the print run, the lower the cost per book, or unit cost.

All of these cost-saving measures resulted in profit margins of as little as a half cent per book, a margin that would only prove profitable if

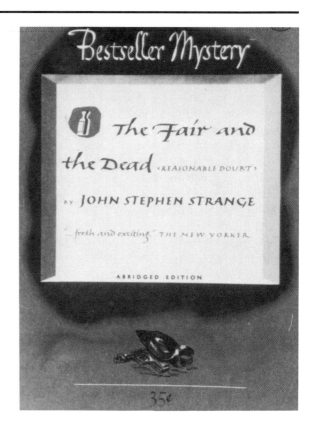

The Mercury, Bestseller, and Jonathan Press mystery series were published by Lawrence Spivak in the 1940s and 1950s. In 5 1/2"
x 7 3/4" format, they resembled magazines more than pocket books.

those large paintings could be sold in sufficient quantities. Rather than relying on the small network of book outlets that already existed, de Graff saw that he would have to get Pocket Books into places that had never sold books before. He was able to do this by reaching out to the people who delivered newspapers and magazines to their sales outlets around the country. The magazine distributors had access to over 100,000 locations. It was this marriage of paperback books to the magazine distribution system that opened the way for Pocket Books and the Paperback Revolution. Within a very short time, Pocket Books were being sold in newsstands, cigar stores, stationery shops, food stores, drugstores, five-and-dime stores, and just about anywhere a small rack of books could be squeezed in. The scheme was unprecedented in American publishing history, and it worked better than even the most optimistic forecaster could have predicted.

After the initial offering of ten books, Pocket Books soon broadened its editorial menu. Along with popular novels Pocket Books published plays, biographies, reference books, humor and joke books, and nonfiction how-to books on such popular subjects as gardening and cooking. Literary classics and children's books were also published, but with slightly less success as people still preferred to own these types of books in hardcover. It did not take long for Pocket Books to publish its first million-seller, a sales level rarely reached even today by hardcover books. In the spring of 1940 Pocket Books published a paperback edition of Dale Carnegie's inspirational guide to personal and business success, *How to Win Friends and Influence People*, a big best-seller in its hardcover edition. It sold close to a million paperback copies in six months and went on to become one of the best-selling books of all time.

The book that lays claim to being *the* best-seller of all time (apart from all the editions of the Holy Bible) was also a Pocket Books product of this early period. Written in the late 1940s at the suggestion of a Pocket Books editor, *Baby and Child Care* (1946) by Dr. Benjamin M. Spock has become a landmark in American childcare, a once controversial book that has become an institution. In its first ten years Dr. Spock's guide, with its simple and calm approach to child raising, sold about one million copies per year. By 1985 Pocket Books had lost count of the exact number of copies it had sold but the figure was estimated at well past 30 million copies and still climbing.

The success of Pocket Books did not go unnoticed by other publishers. The phenomenal sales rate of the "quarter books" and the proven existence of an eager audience for a wide range of inexpensive reading soon brought a rash of competitors into the paperback field. Just two months after the first Pocket Books appeared, they were joined in the racks by imports of the British Penguins brought to the United States by Ian Ballantine, who later founded both Bantam Books and Ballantine Books. Several enterprising magazine publishers also saw the success of Pocket Books and wanted to imitate it by setting up paperback imprints. The most important of these were Joseph Meyers, who launched Avon Books in 1941; Ned Pines, who founded Popular Library in 1942; and George Delacorte, who started Dell Books in 1943.

These new companies quickly proved successful, even during World War II when paper was in short supply. But throughout the war and well into the next decade, Pocket Books was head and shoulders above the competition, a dominance reflected by the fact that for many years people called all paperbacks "pocket books."

As the paperback industry entered the 1950s, the business was far different from the novelty it had been just a few years earlier. Paperback sales in 1950 totaled some 200 million copies with revenues estimated at $46 million. The changes in paperback publishing could be seen in the upward movement in cover prices. For nearly ten years, the twenty-five-cent price had ruled supreme; publishers felt that if they charged more, customers would balk. But prices gradually began to edge up as one publisher after another introduced first thirty-five-cent books, then fifty-cent books, and, by 1952, seventy-five-cent books. (An exception to the rule—briefly—was Dell Books, which introduced a ten-cent line in 1951; the experiment was discontinued after thirty-six titles had been published.) This was the beginning of a spiral that continued slowly for several years and then accelerated during the inflationary 1970s, bringing the industry to its current levels, far beyond anything de Graff had envisioned.

The increases in cover prices were not just a way to make higher profits. Rising costs were making it impossible to publish long books, including many best-selling novels, at twenty-five cents. The higher prices also reflected a new level of competition for paperback rights to the most desirable hardcover books. Where Pocket Books once held a near monopoly on the acquisition of reprint rights, the success of rival publishers, especially Bantam Books (founded in 1945) and New American Library (founded in 1948), meant that the

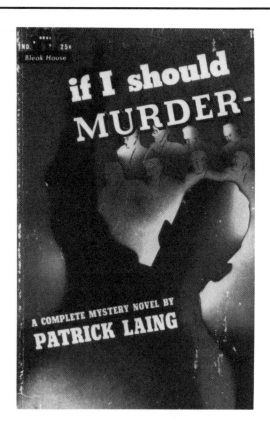

Some imprints did not survive: (this page) Airmont, Bleak House, Book Company of America; (next page) MacFadden, Monarch, Zenith

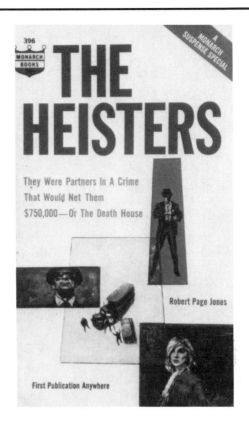

jockeying for rights to major novels was becoming fiercer.

The system of acquiring paperback reprints had evolved out of a formula devised at the turn of the century, when books were reprinted in inexpensive hardcover editions. Under the usual agreement, the paperback publisher received for a limited time the right to publish a paperbound edition of a book at a certain price and to sell it in specified parts of the world. The paperback publisher guaranteed a stated amount of money called the advance, which was payable whether the book earned back the money or not. Reprint rights were acquired through a simple sealed-bid auction: the winner was the publisher who offered the largest advance without any knowledge of what his competitors were offering. Paperback houses were beginning to offer increasingly large sums of money as advances. In order to cover the cost of these advances, which reached $102,000 in 1952 for James Jones's *From Here to Eternity*, publishers had to raise cover prices.

The pace of paperback sales was unhurt by the doubling and tripling of cover prices. The American consumer had spoken. Readers wanted the best books and were prepared to pay more for them, which meant more profits and power for the paperback houses.

Besides the profitability of the paperback, the industry was attracting more attention for what it was publishing. Because the 1950s was a conservative era socially, politically, and sexually, paperback houses soon came under fire from church groups, elected officials, and civic leaders for the types of books that were being published and the style in which they were published. With stiffening competition among paperback houses, many publishers began to resort to lurid, suggestive cover art and misleading blurbs to arouse the interest of book buyers. Soon it was a rare paperback that did not feature a partially undressed woman on its cover. Even classics and the most innocent of novels attempted to lure readers with titillating artwork and suggestive cover copy. This era of sensationalistic illustration gave paperback fiction its reputation as "trashy" or "second-rate literature," a reputation which cast the paperback in a tawdry light for many years.

In addition to the racy covers, the subject matter of popular paperbacks helped foster this disreputable public image. Mysteries and stories of crime dominated the paperback racks. The two most successful practitioners of this genre during the 1950s were Erle Stanley Gardner, the creator of the famous attorney-detective Perry Mason, and Mickey Spillane, whose most famous creation was the hard-boiled private eye Mike Hammer. These two writers sold tens of millions of paperbacks during the 1950s.

Adding to the lurid image that the paperback was acquiring was the success of Gold Medal Books, a paperback imprint begun in 1950 by the Fawcett magazine publishers, which specialized in original paperback fiction—that is, books that had not appeared earlier in hardcover. Gold Medal Books were mainly westerns, mysteries, and thrillers aimed at male readers. The company introduced two of the giants of the mass market field, John D. MacDonald with his Travis McGee mysteries and Louis L'Amour, the best-selling western writer of all time. For the most part Gold Medal Books were violent action novels with extremely daring covers; people pointed to them as the worst example of the paperback's preoccupation with "trash."

This is not to say that paperbacks of the 1950s were limited to stories of murder and mayhem. Paperbacks of the period also provided some of America's most important writers with a wide audience. Perhaps the two best examples are J. D. Salinger, whose novel *The Catcher in the Rye* (New American Library, 1953) was one of the best-selling paperbacks of the 1950s and remains required reading for young people, and Jack Kerouac, whose *On the Road* (New American Library, 1958) sent a generation off in search of the "Beat" lifestyle. Although both books appeared in hardcover editions, it was the paperback editions that made Salinger and Kerouac, along with Norman Mailer, William Styron, James Baldwin, John Steinbeck, and Flannery O'Connor, known to a broad American audience. At the same time, the availability in paperback of works by earlier writers, such as William Faulkner and D. H. Lawrence, brought new recognition and readership to these literary giants. For the first time in American publishing history, access to the best writing was not limited to the elite.

Of course, many of these writers were controversial at that time, and the paperback suffered the consequences. Throughout the 1950s paperbacks were banned and censored in communities across the country—sometimes because of their covers, but more often because of their content. Paperback publishers fought dozens of censorship battles during this time, culminating in 1959 with the landmark ruling in favor of the publication by Grove Press of the notorious Lawrence novel *Lady Chatterley's Lover*. The ruling opened the way for a new generation of First Amendment freedoms and set the stage for the loosening of attitudes that lay ahead in the 1960s. Yet even today, paperback books are censored in schools and communities across the country.

It was during the 1960s that the paperback truly became a fixture in American life, graduating beyond its small beginnings to have a major economic impact upon the publishing world. With school and college enrollment on the rise as the children of the baby boom grew up, the paperback became a major educational tool. To meet the demand for college material, the "trade," "quality," or "oversized" paperback appeared. In the first days of their existence, these paperbacks were usually limited to highly academic titles that were printed in smaller quantities than the mass market paperbacks. Among the earliest trade paperback imprints was Hayward Cirker's Dover Books, founded in 1942 and specializing in out-of-print technical and scientific books. By far the most influential trade paperback imprint was Doubleday's Anchor Books, established by Jason Epstein, a young Doubleday editor, in 1952. With many academic, scholarly, and literary titles, Anchor Books proved an enormous success. Other new trade paperback imprints soon followed, including Alfred A. Knopf's Vintage Books, Arthur Cohen's Meridian Books, and Sol Stein's Beacon Press Paperbacks.

Instead of being sold through mass market outlets, this generation of paperbacks was primarily sold through college stores and retail bookstores, hence the name "trade" paperback. The name "quality paperback" was given to them because they tended to be more serious and academically oriented than most mass market paperbacks were, although this was not always true. They were called "oversized" because they were usually larger than the rack-sized paperbacks that Pocket Books had pioneered. Today, the lines between mass market and trade paperbacks have become blurred and most consumers are not aware of any difference.

The 1960s saw dynamic, often violent, social changes sweeping America; the paperback reflected these changes and, in some respects, helped bring them about. Many of the books responsible for shaping ideas about such issues as the civil rights movement were widely read in paperback. Among these were *Black Like Me* (New American Library, 1961) by John Howard Griffin, a white man's account of disguising himself as a black and traveling through the South; *The Autobiography of Malcolm X* (Grove Press, 1965); and *Soul on Ice* (Dell, 1969) by

Eldridge Cleaver. Similarly, the modern feminist movement owes much of its inspiration to the enormous paperback success of Betty Friedan's *The Feminine Mystique* (Dell, 1963), which reached millions of readers. On a more whimsical note, one could look at the popularity of J. R. R. Tolkien's *Lord of the Rings* trilogy (Ballantine, 1969) and see how a generation that rebelled against the Establishment found inspiration in this epic battle of good against evil.

One of the most significant accomplishments of the paperback industry in this period was the perfection of the "instant books," in-depth treatments of major news stories which were often published within days of the event. Although quick publishing had existed since the early days of the industry, it was during the 1960s, with technology's assistance, that books truly became "instant." The first of these was *The Report of the Warren Commission on the Assassination of President Kennedy*, which was published by Bantam in 1964 just days after the massive and controversial report was released to the public. Combining the speed of a newspaper with the book's ability to cover a topic more thoroughly than any newspaper could, the instant book became a new form of journalism that, when used properly, contributed to wider understanding of major issues faced by America during the 1960s and 1970s. Other instant books included *The Report of the Commission on Obscenity and Pornography* (Bantam, 1970), *The Pentagon Papers* (Bantam, 1971), *The Watergate Hearings* (Bantam, 1973), and *The White House Transcripts* (Bantam, Dell, 1974).

The 1960s also saw a new emphasis on the best-seller; Jacqueline Susann, Ian Fleming, Harold Robbins, Arthur Hailey, and Philip Roth became household words in America, propelled to new heights of fame and riches by the wide exposure they received through paperbacks. By the beginning of the 1970s new sales records were being compiled by *The Godfather* (Fawcett, 1970) by Mario Puzo, *The Exorcist* (Bantam, 1973) by William Peter Blatty, and *Jaws* (Bantam, 1975) by Peter Benchley. The paperback industry seemed to be more successful and profitable than ever. As in the 1950s the success was not limited to popular novels. Serious writers, past and present, were reaching millions of readers. Some examples are the works of Hermann Hesse; Alvin Toffler's *Future Shock* (Bantam, 1971); and newly rediscovered writers such as Kurt Vonnegut, whose audience seemed to read his works almost exclusively in paperback.

The tremendous profits such books generated for publishers brought other changes to the industry. Large corporations without experience in the book world began to look at publishing as a ripe area for investment. During the late 1960s and early 1970s many paperback houses, once run independently by the men and women who had founded them, came under the control of large firms such as Gulf + Western, which owns Pocket Books and Simon and Schuster; CBS, which bought and later sold Fawcett Books; RCA, the former owner of Ballantine Books; and Warner Communications, owner of Warner Books. The presence of these corporate giants meant new infusions of cash for paperback companies, and the bidding for best-selling books reached a new level.

By the mid-1970s million-dollar paperback auctions had become almost commonplace. Of course, the only way to pay for these auction bids, along with other rising costs during an inflationary period, was through dramatic increases in cover prices. But the readers' breaking point had been reached. Sales of paperbacks, which had climbed steadily since their introduction, began to level off as price resistance set in. People who were willing to pay a dollar or two for paperbacks slowed their purchases when prices rose to three and four dollars. For publishers, the answer seemed to be concentration on trying to promote more of the blockbuster best-sellers. Much of the diversity that had characterized the Paperback Revolution during its first three decades was disappearing, a victim of bottom-line decisionmaking. The new style of publishing management and the high stakes involved led to the collapse of several paperback houses in the late 1970s and early 1980s.

In the mid-1980s hardcover and paperback publishers have evolved complex relationships that have completely altered the way the paperback business operates. Paperback houses are now owned by hardcover houses or, in some cases, publish hardcover books themselves. The distinctions between hardcover, mass market, and trade paperback have all but disappeared. No longer does the hardcover house acquire and produce a book which will later be sold to a paperback house. Increasingly, books are acquired by publishers who control both hardcover and paperback rights. The auctions have been replaced by complicated long-term deals between publishers and writers. Many more books are now published in original paperback editions, either trade or mass market, with the potential audience determining the best format. The industry is larger and more complicated, but not necessarily more efficient. The guesswork of trying to determine what Americans want to read still underlies much of what happens in book publishing. As always in publishing, mistakes are more common than successes.

The revolutionary days of the paperback are over. The qualities of idealism and willingness to experiment that characterized the founders of many of the great paperback houses have been diminished. There is little reason to believe that a return to a commitment to quality and seriousness on a mass scale is possible. Serious books continue to be published, but it seems unlikely that they will ever reach a mass market of many millions of readers, despite a growing American population. Instead, these books tend to be published under quality imprints for a shrinking elite readership. The ideal of the most books of the highest quality for the most people at the lowest price—the guiding principle of the Paperback Revolution—has been lost and will never be regained.

Main Trends in Twentieth-Century Book Clubs

John Tebbel

Book clubs became an important factor in publishing and merchandising during the latter half of the twentieth century, but their origins predate the Civil War and their general practices were similar to subscription bookselling after 1865.

The idea of a book club was born in the imagination of S. V. S. Wilder, first president of the American Tract Society, founded in 1825 as the result of a merger between tract societies in New York and New England; at least forty other such societies had been formed in America since 1803. All of them were descendants of the Religious Tract Society formed in London in 1799.

Wilder demonstrated what religious proselytizing could do in the hands of a shrewd, aggressive businessman. His "Tract of the Month" program gave readers book dividends, and his products were advertised in a monthly magazine similar to those of modern book clubs. Printing was consolidated in a plant in New York City, and Wilder undercut his competitors by selling all the society's books and pamphlets at cost.

Wilder's agents in the field represented "one of the most ambitious, aggressive and successful promotion enterprises ever realized by an American publisher," in the words of historian Lawrance Thompson. The society's sales figures were in the millions by the late nineteenth century. Its efforts were by this time part of a broad subscription book market, which sold books through traveling salesmen or by mail order to people who had no library or bookstore service.

All of this was an anticipation of the book clubs of our time. The actual origin of the modern book club, however, can be traced to Germany, after the First World War, where an intellectually impoverished generation, hungry for reading matter, created a series of book guilds in 1919. The book club as we know it came to America when entrepreneurs saw that magazine subscription and mail-order methods could be combined and adapted to market contemporary books.

At least two of these entrepreneurs disputed the German origin. Harry Scherman, founder of the Book-of-the-Month Club, asserted in a 1927 article that neither the German guilds nor any other person or organization had anything to do with the inception of his club. It was, he said, an idea that he conceived himself in 1916, whose "main outlines . . . had been worked out and . . . kept in reserve for about ten years . . . because its later sponsors were deep in the worries of another book business during that period."

A similar assertion came from Samuel Craig, founder with Harold Guinzburg of the Literary Guild, which followed the BOMC by only a few months. Craig asserted that he first formulated the Guild plan in 1921 and officially incorporated it as the Literary Guild in April 1922, but failed to obtain the capital to put it into operation. Hearing in 1926 of the success of the German clubs, he reincorporated as the Literary Guild of America in November 1926, beginning actual operations two months later.

One fact not in dispute is that Scherman launched the modern American book club idea in 1926 with the Book-of-the-Month Club. He came to it by way of advertising. In 1913 he was working for a new agency, Ruthrauff and Ryan, writing booklets, direct mail letters, and circulars, and found that he was particularly good at selling books by mail. "I had always noticed," he said later, "how people could be influenced to read books by what was said about them." He had a chance to pursue his new interest by transferring his talents to the mail-order department of the J. Walter Thompson agency.

Scherman's book club career seems to have originated in Pleasantville, a suburb of New York, where he lived with his wife, an English teacher in a nearby orphanage. The orphanage's art teacher, George Cronyn, had his own salon, which was inhabited by such intellects as Walter Lippman, Lawrence Langner, and the Boni brothers, Charles and Albert. The Bonis told Scherman about the Little Leather Library they were starting and showed him a dummy of their first book, *Romeo and Juliet.*

As a man who dealt with new products, Scherman was captivated by this one and saw its commercial possibilities at once. He remembered that a

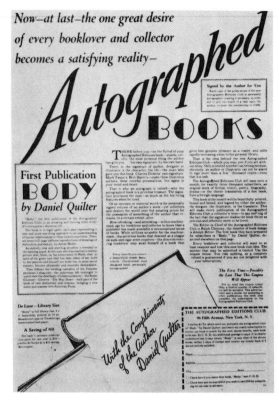

Advertisement for the Autographed Editions Club, established
in 1931 (New York Times Book Review)

Advertisement for the Classics Club, established in
1941 (Esquire)

Advertisement for The Book League of America, established in
1928 (New York Times Book Review)

tobacco company had produced a minute volume of Shakespeare which was inserted in cigarette packs. He suggested that the Bonis offer the Whitman Candy Company the opportunity to put copies of *Romeo and Juliet* into their candy boxes. Whitman's advertising department seized on the idea with delight and created a new product called the "Library Package," which would contain fifteen of Shakespeare's plays in the Little Leather Library format. Whitman ordered a thousand copies at ten cents net. The Bonis had to borrow $5,000 to fill the order, since they had no capital, nor in fact any books.

Seeing that his idea was going to work, Scherman resigned from J. Walter Thompson, taking with him one of the agency's best copywriters, Maxwell Sackheim. Together they promoted the Little Leather Library to the point where these books could be found not only in candy boxes but in bookstores and drugstores everywhere, along with a large mail-order sale. At some point after the sales totals had passed twenty-five million, the Bonis decided to try another kind of publishing and sold their interest in the Library to Scherman and Sackheim.

Sackheim did not want to pursue the retail store possibilities of the Little Leather Library; he thought the books would do better if they were sold only by mail order, provided a repeat-sale feature could be added. As a result, the partners launched a Book-of-the-Week Club, an idea using techniques employed by the magazine subscription business. For five dollars a year, patrons could provide themselves with culture on the installment plan, buying a classic every week. Apparently that was too much culture; the plan failed.

With their efforts divided between the Library and an advertising agency they had started, Scherman and Sackheim needed a partner. One soon arrived in the person of Robert K. Haas, then at the start of his remarkable publishing career. Haas bought a seventy-five percent interest in the Library and became its chief executive at a time when its sales had declined to the point where it had become necessary to sell tablecloths and doilies in order to survive. But Haas persuaded Arthur Brisbane, the noted Hearst columnist, to contribute a set of thirty short biographies, which helped, and he also set up a subsidiary called the National Music Library to sell record albums. If the coming of radios had not temporarily depressed phonograph and record sales, this side effort might have surpassed its annual gross of a million dollars.

Radio was one of the changing social factors that began to affect the Little Leather Library seriously by 1925; but the partners had good reason to be satisfied, since it had already sold more than forty-eight million volumes. Furthermore, the basic concept was a proven success, and it was not difficult for Scherman to make it the vehicle for his book club idea. Scherman believed that both publishers and booksellers were grossly underestimating the size of their audience. It was reasonable, he thought, to assume that if he could persuade millions of readers to buy the Little Leather Library, he might do even better with regular trade books. Since retailers were obviously not capable of reaching a market of this size, he was convinced that mail order was the answer.

Scherman's idea in establishing the BOMC was to close the gap between publishers and the potential market of readers by using the mails. Clearly, people could not be expected to choose easily from the thousands of titles publishers were making available to them every year, so Scherman set up a board of judges who would do it for them, choosing as members people who were well known for their literary activities. Continuity and volume would be assured by employing the subscription method.

As a good advertising man, Scherman tested the market first, and the results encouraged him to incorporate the BOMC. He named Haas its first president and chose Silvia Townsend Warner's *Lolly Willowes* as the first selection. It was sent to an initial list of 4,750 members in April 1926. The results were gratifying. By the end of the year 46,539 members had signed on. BOMC showed a loss the first year of $24,054 but it was the last deficit the club ever had. In the worst year of the Depression, 1932, the club still made a profit of $48,000.

The notion of using judges to make the selections was an important factor in the club's early success. Patrons trusted such people as Dorothy Canfield, Henry Seidel Canby, Christopher Morley, William Allen White, and Heywood Broun to do their choosing for them. Over the next forty years, only twelve judges would serve.

There was some opposition at first from retailers, who were afraid that their sales would suffer; but in actual practice, they benefited. For example, Esther Forbes's *Genteel Lady* was expected by its publisher, Houghton Mifflin, to achieve a 5,000-copy advance sale in the stores; but the book sold another 14,000 copies after the club made it the third selection, and such stimulation became a common occurrence.

Advertisement for the Detective Book Club, established in 1942 (Esquire)

Advertisement for the Fine Editions Club, established circa 1956 (Esquire)

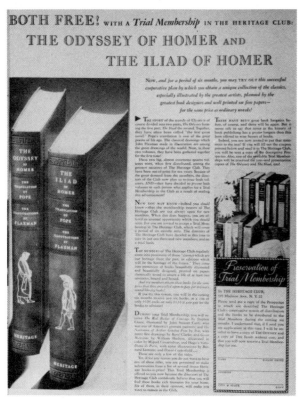

Advertisement for The Heritage Club, established in 1935 (Esquire)

Advertisement for The Literary Guild of America, established in 1926 (New York Times Book Review)

Meanwhile, Scherman was about to have a rival. Craig had announced the advent of the Literary Guild in the spring of 1926, but it had taken him several months to raise the money and organize a jury, with Carl Van Doren as chairman and Zona Gale, Elinor Wylie, and Joseph Krutch—soon to be joined by Hendrik Willem Van Loon and Glenn Frank—as members. Craig eventually dropped the jury.

Craig and his partner, Harold Guinzburg, approached the club idea with some variations on Scherman's methods. They began with a national campaign of display advertising and followed it up by using the bookstores, acting as agents, to solicit members. Members got twelve books a year for twenty-eight dollars, including delivery. To obtain books, the Guild paid the publishers a flat sum and published its own edition before the trade edition appeared. Unlike BOMC books, Guild books had special title pages.

But the Guild introduced a new element that set off an immediate controversy. It would not only supply its customers with books before the trade edition appeared, but would sell them below the retail price. Answering the outcry that arose, Craig pointed out that word of mouth was the most important factor in selling books, and the 50,000 or so copies of a book sent out by the Literary Guild would certainly generate a further demand in the bookstores. Publishers did not accept this reasoning. Frank Dodd wrote: "The trade is against the Literary Guild. . . . It will disturb not only trade relations but the public." Eighteen publishers announced that they would not submit books to the Guild, and John Macrae, the president of E. P. Dutton, launched a personal campaign against both clubs, particularly the BOMC, with the intention of destroying them if he could.

But, as one might expect from so individualistic an industry, not all publishers refused to do business with the clubs, and it was increasingly clear that the reading public did not share the hostility of the trade. A measure of peace was achieved in 1927 when Guinzburg, who had bought out Craig's interest in the Guild, signed an agreement with the American Booksellers Association, making some concessions on the price-cutting issue.

The trade was still alarmed, however, by the remarkable growth of book clubs. By the summer of 1928, nine of them were thriving, although some—including the First Editions Club, which was founded in 1927 and then bought up by the BOMC—had already disappeared. Publishers of children's books had been among the first to sense

the new possibilities. The Junior Monthly Book Service was exploring them as early as 1926, although it quickly expired. In 1928 *Junior League* magazine launched the Junior Book-of-the-Month Club—the name was changed to the Junior Book Club at the insistence of the BOMC—and others followed in 1929. All these early efforts, however, were eclipsed in March 1929 when the Literary Guild announced that it was forming the Junior Literary Guild. Competing clubs were dismayed to read that 100,000 circulars had been sent out in the first direct-mail campaign, and that these were to be backed by a $250,000 advertising program, with display ads in leading magazines.

In 1928 Craig had begun the Book League of America, which offered the opportunity for members to get books both in magazine form and in regular hardcover. As their initial choice, customers were advised that they could have Matthew Josephson's *Zola and His Times* either in a large octavo of 560 pages or in a magazine format, with an introduction by Van Wyck Brooks, who was on the selection board. Those who subscribed found, however, that in practice they were offered twelve new books in the magazine format, while the hardcover volumes were all reprints.

Religious book clubs appropriated another segment of the market. After the first venture, the Religious Book Club, appeared to be successful, three Catholic book clubs began operations in 1928, followed by the Ministers' Selective Book Service, a creation of the Methodist Publishing House, and the Free Thought Book of the Month Club.

Still other variations on the club idea proliferated, largely in the direction of specialization. Most successful of these was Doubleday's Crime Club, organized in 1928 and still in operation today, but other noteworthy, although briefer, starts included the Business Book League and the Scientific Book Club, both begun in 1929. There was even a Texas Book Club (1928), organized by the department store entrepreneur Stanley Marcus in 1928, and, remarkably, the American Booksellers Association's own Book Selection Club, founded in 1927 as a defensive measure. It was unsuccessful and soon disappeared.

Among the subscription clubs, the ventures originated by George Macy were outstanding and destined for a long life. Macy began with the Limited Editions Club, classics in fine bindings and illustrated by eminent artists, filling out his limited subscription list at high prices even in the depths of the Depression. He followed this with a lower-priced line, the Heritage Club Editions, another

Advertisement for Marboro Book Club, established circa
1956 (Esquire)

Advertisement for Reader's Digest Condensed Book Club,
established in 1950 (Esquire)

Advertisement for Young Readers of America, established by the
Book-of-the-Month Club circa 1953 (Esquire)

series done with the help of noted designers and artists.

The war against the clubs came to a climax in 1929 when the BOMC sued Macrae and Dutton for $200,000 for various charges Macrae had made against the club, but the suit was quickly withdrawn when the publisher retracted some of his accusations. This was the beginning of a long series of truces which left only Dutton, Stokes, and Brentano's publishing department refusing to submit books to the clubs. As a result of the war, BOMC toned down the emphasis on lower prices in its advertising, and opposition melted away as it became obvious that the book club was an idea whose time had come. Eventually even Macrae was delighted when the BOMC took one of his books.

Charles Boni produced a cheaper version of the subscription book in May 1929 with his Paper Books, paperbacks with well-designed formats and cover designs executed by Rockwell Kent. They were sold for a five-dollar yearly subscription and were delivered every month, at a cost of forty-two cents per book. Boni, who had excellent connections, was able to hire some of the best designers in the business, and he called on some of his numerous friends to constitute his editorial board: Everett Dean Martin, an author and educator; the poet and critic Louis Untermeyer; Padraic Colum, one of the best-known Irish writers; and Lincoln Colcord, journalist and short-story writer.

But Paper Books were not welcomed by either the old-line publishers or the booksellers. They saw this scheme as just another form of price-cutting. The club's first selection was *The Golden Wind* by Takashi Ohta and Margaret Sperry, which not even Colum's introduction could make into an "important" book. The plan might have succeeded even so, except for the economic problems of the 1930s, the shifting currents in Boni's own life, and the competitive pressures from so many other clubs. If nothing more, Paper Books was another demonstration of the vitality and imagination that the Bonis, particularly Charles, brought to publishing in their era. By early 1931, the Paper Books club was dead.

As the Depression deepened, surviving clubs began to feel the pressure from dollar reprints and cheap book lines developed by publishers to meet the needs of a crippled economy. In the melancholy climate of 1930, an unusual rate of subscription cancellations and a sharp increase in the cost of getting new subscribers compelled the BOMC to take action. Beginning with its July 1930 selection, the club abandoned the practice of buying a book

from the publisher in the latter's own regular edition. Now the BOMC would pay $14,000 outright for the plates and make its own edition of 42,500 to 70,000 copies. An adjustment would be made in the payment if the size of the edition was higher or lower. The club also stopped giving free books to subscribers for joining, offering instead a discount of twenty percent.

The Literary Guild took a somewhat different approach. It began to work through the retailers in 1930, soliciting orders both for selections for the current month and for those of past months. It sent canvassers to sell public libraries the notion of taking a Guild Book every month for every branch. Guild salesmen offered magazines a plan to give three of the club's books free with every $5.95 two-year subscription. The Guild bought the Book League of America in 1932 even while it was starting another club, the Guild Dollar Book Club. The Dollar Book Club was an ingenious scheme to unload overstock left from regular distribution—in other words, it was a form of remaindering.

Responding to these moves, the BOMC offered its mail order customers the current selection free, with no obligation to subscribe and only a quarter for packing and postage. While all of this was legitimate competition, it continued to provoke irritation in the trade, which protested what it could only believe was more price-cutting. The clubs paid no attention, except to point out that they were only trying to protect themselves from hard times, as the publishers had done. Business, in fact, was good.

Robert Haas, now in partnership with Robert Smith as Smith and Haas, conceived in the fall of 1934 a new club which would sell hardcover books at the lowest prices yet seen: ninety-five cents per book. Blanket subscriptions for fifteen books of fiction a year would be solicited; customers would pay $2.75 in advance for the first three volumes, although they were given a return privilege with full credit. New Books, Incorporated, as Haas called his plan, encountered so much hostility in the trade that it died before it was born.

Macy's plan to sell quality books at low prices was a better idea. He offered twelve fine books a year for a twenty-seven-dollar subscription price when he began his Heritage Club in 1935, and in five years he had signed up more than 9,000 members. For some reason, subscriptions jumped by more than 2,000 in the six months after Pearl Harbor. In March 1941 Macy had begun a dollar reprint operation called the Readers Club, based on his conviction that many books were not getting the attention they deserved. He also introduced something new in his selection board: his judges got a cent-a-copy royalty for every volume sold. Eventually Macy consolidated all his clubs—Limited Editions, Heritage, Readers, and Junior Heritage—as the George Macy Companies. From 1940 onward, business for the book clubs continued to be progressively better. Even World War II was not able to slow down or inhibit club growth. During the war years, the BOMC increased its circulation by nearly 100 %, tripled its net sales, and increased its profits after taxes by more than 100 %, to nearly $1.5 million.

Even so, the club had to go through a brief period of readjustment in the postwar period, as rising costs added to the problems of mail-order bookselling. Membership also declined briefly in 1947, but it did not do so again. Along with so many other enterprises, the company went public in 1947; 2,600 investors took advantage of the stock offering.

The great growth of the book clubs occurred in the postwar period and continues relatively unabated today. Proliferating even during the Depression, the clubs needed only the expansion that occurred after 1945 to become big business.

Book clubs continued to prosper because they were able to take advantage of the failure of the publishing community to solve its oldest problem: distribution. As Scherman had been astute enough to realize, there was a gap between the bookstores and readers' needs, and increasingly that gap was being filled by the clubs. Magazines, too, were offering new competition to the bookstores. Some of them started book clubs of their own, as *Playboy* did, or even subsidiary publishing houses, using their subscription lists as a basis for solicitation. The book club idea began to have its definitions blurred somewhat by mail-order publishing that was closely related to the clubs. It was, for example, a short selling step from Time-Life Books and the American Heritage Publishing Company to the genuine clubs, which themselves could be divided into three general categories: independently operated, as the BOMC; an adjunct of a magazine, like the Reader's Digest Book Club; or part of a general publishing house, as in the case of Doubleday's many club enterprises. As time went on, the clubs broadened their spectrum to provide books for a wide range of specialists, such as social scientists, academicians, business executives, doctors, lawyers, psychologists, engineers, and natural scientists.

A legal problem arose for the clubs when their use of the word free in their advertising and promotion efforts brought them under the scrutiny of the Federal Trade Commission, which brought a complaint in July 1948 against the BOMC, Walter J. Black, Incorporated (owners of the Classics Club and the Detective Book Club), the Cadillac Publishing Company, Incorporated, and Doubleday. The charge was "false, misleading, and deceptive practices," but the commission by its three-to-two decision in the matter showed how uncertain it was about just what constituted these practices. Taking his cue from this indecision, Meredith Wood, then president of BOMC, signified his intention not to comply. Wood was also aware that the commission had no power to assess damages or impose criminal penalties, so defiance would cost him no more than court costs. BOMC lost the legal contest after appeals had carried the case into 1952. By the court decision handed down then, which applied to other clubs as well, BOMC had to sign a cease and desist order which prevented it from advertising dividend books as "free." The club carried its case to the Supreme Court, which was not required to rule because the FTC reversed itself in 1953 and dismissed its own complaint, this one specifically against the Doubleday clubs. Competitive life among the clubs then went on as before.

Most of the other clubs could not afford to compete with the BOMC in some ways, particularly its expansion of services. It had offered Christmas cards as early as 1943, and in 1947 it sold magazine subscriptions to its customers. New members were added in 1948 with the acquisition of the Non-Fiction Book Club from Henry Holt and Company, bringing in 11,000 new accounts. The club had been selling art reproductions since September 1943, but in November 1948 it made a profitable deal with the Metropolitan Museum of Art in New York to distribute the museum's "Metropolitan Miniatures," sets of twenty-four full-color reproductions of great art works priced at one dollar per set. By May 1953 the club was circulating 126,360 of these sets; by 1956 more than five millions sets had been distributed. Later the club added the Quality Paperback Book Club and the distribution of record albums.

After thirty-four years of existence, book clubs by 1960 were an important part of the publishing scene. The BOMC alone during that period had distributed about 160 million books to subscribers; total distribution by all clubs was estimated to be more than 700 million books. That was more than all the books in all the public and university libraries of the United States, including the holdings of the Library of Congress.

There had been a few failures along the way. The Travelers Book Club was begun as a subsidiary of the BOMC in 1948 to explore the possibilities of reviving the nineteenth-century business of selling books to passengers on trains and other public vehicles. It lasted less than a year. Practical and Educational Books, Incorporated was set up as a wholly owned subsidiary of the club in 1948 to sell "functional books" by direct mail, but it, too, was discontinued a year later.

Pollster George Gallup was able to draw a profile of book club subscribers in the late 1950s: "They are usually youngish people just married. They have been accustomed to intellectual influences, in their homes and then during their higher education. They have gone out into the world and have become immersed in the demanding social and economic activities that characterize our society. The arrival of children makes for still more complicated living. They adjust as well as they can to these living difficulties, but gradually begin to feel that they are backsliding intellectually, as the result of the fast tempo of life. They are keenly conscious, in particular, that they are reading fewer and fewer books, and they have always looked to books, more than in any other direction, for intellectual stimulation and satisfaction. The impulsion to a bookclub is natural in the circumstances, if only because the sheer convenience makes it seem the most promising solution to their backsliding. . . ." By the 1970s book clubs accounted for about 8.5 % of total book sales in the United States. In 1979 there were more than 200 clubs, with sales of 250 million books, or 8.7 % more than the year before. The dollar value of those sales was estimated at $503 million, an 11.3 % rise from 1978, and the advance continued into the 1980s. Total membership of all the clubs has been estimated at about seven million.

But in their success, the clubs were not without problems. The worst of these was rising postal rates, a difficulty they shared with the remainder of the industry. Another problem was the decline in population growth during the decade before 1980, along with a decline in the college population. It was assumed that the rapidly increasing older population would make a positive difference, and that some customers might be added as higher pricing in the retail market made bargains more attractive. That advantage for the clubs, however, was offset wherever the big discount chains were operating. Growing illiteracy in America was still another factor, as was the increasing number of people who could read but watched television in-

stead. Book club executives also worried about what many publishers saw as a turning away from traditional books by customers, since traditional books had always been the clubs' stock in trade.

But in the 1980s paperback books were beginning to represent larger shares of club sales, and in the general diversifying of publishing that was taking place, the specialized clubs were beginning to do even better than they had before. In a sense, what had happened to magazines—the decline of the general magazine and the rise of the specialized periodical—was repeating itself in the club business. The BOMC and the Literary Guild were still the giants, but the Reader's Digest Book Club had risen to parity with them and there were other competitors. The Guild, for example, was only one of Doubleday's more than thirty book clubs. Of one thing, however, there could be little doubt: in 1985 book clubs were such an important part of book merchandising that any decline in their fortunes, if it occurred, could only mean that the book business itself was declining; and in spite of all the adverse factors that might be cited, there was no sign that such a development was imminent.

MAJOR BOOK CLUBS

Adult Book Clubs

Autographed Editions Club

The Book League of America

Book-of-the-Month Club, Incorporated

Catholic Book Club

Christian Quality Paperback Book Club

Classics Club

Cooking & Crafts Club

Detective Book Club

Dolphin Book Club (BOMC)

Doubleday Book Club

Fine Editions Club

Fireside Theater

Fortune Book Club

The Heritage Club

History Book Club

Limited Editions Club

The Literary Guild of America

Marboro Book Club

Military Book Club

Mystery Guild

Nature Science Book Club

Nostalgia Book Club

Popular Science Book Club

Quality Paperback Book Club (BOMC)

Reader's Digest Condensed Book Club

Reader's Subscription Book Club

Religious Book Club

Science Fiction Book Club

Word Book Club

Young Readers of America

Children's Book Clubs

Arrow Book Club

Buddy Books Paperback Book Club

Discovering Books Paperback Book Club

Disney's Wonderful World of Reading

Junior Literary Guild

Literary Guild, Young Adults Division

Teen Age Book Club

Books for Further Reading

Blumenthal, Joseph. *The Printed Book in America*. Boston: David R. Godine, 1977.

Bonn, Thomas L. *Undercover: An Illustrated History of American Mass Market Paperbacks*. Harmondsworth, U.K. & New York: Penguin, 1982.

Crider, Allen Billy. *Mass Market Publishing in America*. Boston: G. K. Hall, 1982.

Davis, Kenneth C. *Two-Bit Culture: The Paperbacking of America*. Boston: Houghton Mifflin, 1984.

Gross, Gerald, ed. *Publishers on Publishing*. New York: Bowker, 1961; New York: Grosset & Dunlap, 1961.

Kurian, George Thomas. *The Directory of American Book Publishing from Founding Fathers to Today's Conglomerates*. New York: Simon & Schuster, 1975.

Lehmann-Haupt, Hellmut, Lawrence C. Worth, and Rollo G. Silver. *The Book in America: A History of the Making and Selling of Books in the United States*. 2nd ed. New York: Bowker, 1951.

Madison, Charles A. *Book Publishing in America*. New York: McGraw-Hill, 1966.

Madison. *Jewish Publishing in America; The Impact of Jewish Writing on American Culture*. New York: Sanhedrin Press, 1976.

Mott, Frank Luther. *Golden Multitudes: The Story of Best Sellers in the United States*. New York: Macmillan, 1947.

Reginald, R., and M. R. Burgess. *Cumulative Paperback Index 1939-1959*. Detroit: Gale Research, 1973.

Schick, Frank L. *The Paperbound Book in America; The History of Paperbacks and Their European Background*. New York: Bowker, 1958.

Schreuders, Piet. *Paperbacks, U.S.A.: A Graphic History, 1939-1959*. San Diego: Blue Dolphin, 1981.

Tanselle, G. Thomas. *Guide to the Study of United States Imprints*. 2 vols. Cambridge: Harvard University Press, 1971.

Tebbel, John. *A History of Book Publishing in the United States*. 4 vols. New York: Bowker, 1972-1981.

Tebbel. *Paperback Books: A Pocket History*. New York: Pocket Books, 1964.

University of Illinois Library School. *Brief Studies of General Book Publishing Firms of the United States*. Urbana: University of Illinois, 1931.

Walters, Ray. *Paperback Talk*. Chicago: Academy Chicago Publishers, 1985.

Contributors

Susan K. Ahern .... *University of Houston*
Gregory P. Ames .... *University of Rochester*
Phyllis Andrews .... *University of Rochester*
Chris M. Anson... *University of Minnesota*
Martha A. Bartter .... *Ohio State University*
Nandita Batra... *University of Rochester*
Margaret Becket... *University of Rochester*
Ruth Bennett .... *Rochester, New York*
Robert Bertholf... *State University of New York at Buffalo*
Ernest Bevan, Jr. .... *Bates College*
Daniel Borus... *New York, New York*
Christy Brown .... *Indiana University*
Judith Bushnell.......................... *State University of New York College at Geneseo*
Christopher Camuto .... *University of Virginia*
Joan Gillen Conners .... *Rochester, New York*
Alma Burner Creek (deceased) .... (formerly *University of Rochester*)
Kathleen R. Davis .... *Syracuse, New York*
Kenneth C. Davis... *New York, New York*
Philip Dematteis... *Columbia, South Carolina*
David Dzwonkoski... *Virginia Beach, Virginia*
Elizabeth A. Dzwonkoski .... *Rochester, New York*
Peter Dzwonkoski .... *University of Rochester*
Neal L. Edgar... *Kent State University*
Stephen Elwell... *Indiana University*
Nancy Hill Evans... *Carnegie-Mellon University*
Ada Fan... *Phillips Academy, Andover, Massachusetts*
D. W. Faulkner .... *New Haven, Connecticut*
Alan J. Filreis .... *University of Virginia*
Margaret W. Fleming .... *Rochester, New York*
Anne Frascarelli .... *University of Rochester*
Christine Garrison... *University of Rochester*
Deborah G. Gorman .... *Philadelphia, Pennsylvania*
Jon Griffin .... *University of Rochester*
Edward J. Hall... *Kent State University*
John Harrison .... *University of Arkansas*
Joseph Heininger... *University of Rochester*
Elizabeth Hoffman... *University of Rochester*
Richard Horvath .... *University of Rochester*
Laura Masotti Humphrey .... *Honeoye Falls, New York*
Mary M. Huth .... *University of Rochester*
Earl G. Ingersoll.......................... *State University of New York College at Brockport*
Sharon Ann Jaeger... *Anchorage, Alaska*
Herbert H. Johnson... *Rochester Institute of Technology*
Dean H. Keller .... *Kent State University*
Carol Kuniholm .... *University of Pennsylvania*
Christopher T. Lee... *Columbia, South Carolina*
Xinmin Liu .... *Beijing, China*
Anne Ludlow .... *Rochester, New York*

419

Karin S. Mabe .... *Manlius, New York*

Jerre Mangione .... *Philadelphia, Pennsylvania*

Kathleen McGowan .... *University of Rochester*

Philip A. Metzger .... *Southern Illinois University*

Carole B. Michaels-Katz .... *University of Rochester*

Theodora Mills .... *Rochester, New York*

Anuradha Mookerjee .... *Cincinnati, Ohio*

Timothy D. Murray .... *Washington University, St. Louis*

Donna Nance .... *University of South Carolina*

Bill Oliver .... *University of Virginia*

Vincent Prestianni .... *Monroe Community College, Rochester, New York*

Elizabeth Scott Pryor .... *Atlanta, Georgia*

Linda Quinlan .... *University of Rochester*

David W. Raymond .... *University of Rochester*

Shirley Ricker... *University of Rochester*

Carmen R. Russell .... *University of Florida*

Lynne P. Shackelford .... *University of North Carolina*

Arlene Shaner .... *Portland, Oregon*

Alison Tanner Stauffer .... *University of Rochester*

Annie E. Stevens .... *University of Rochester*

Botham Stone.. *Columbia, South Carolina*

Christopher Surr .... *Columbia, South Carolina*

John Tebbel.. *Southbury, Connecticut*

Jane I. Thesing .... *University of South Carolina*

Harry F. Thompson .... *University of Rochester*

Ronelle K. H. Thompson.. *Rochester, New York*

Vincent L. Tollers .... *State University of New York College at Brockport*

Gary R. Treadway.. *University of South Carolina*

Carol Ann Wilkinson.. *University of Rochester*

Jutta Willman .... *Bloomington, Indiana*

Cumulative Index

Dictionary of Literary Biography, Volumes 1-46
Dictionary of Literary Biography Yearbook, 1980-1984
Dictionary of Literary Biography Documentary Series, Volumes 1-4

Cumulative Index

DLB before number: *Dictionary of Literary Biography,* Volumes 1-46
Y before number: *Dictionary of Literary Biography Yearbook,* 1980-1984
DS before number: *Dictionary of Literary Biography Documentary Series,* Volumes 1-4

A

The Abbey Theatre and Irish
    Drama, 1900-1945 .... DLB10

Abbot, Willis J. 1863-1934 .... DLB29

Abbott, Jacob 1803-1879 .... DLB1

Abbott, Robert S. 1868-1940 .... DLB29

Abelard-Schuman DLB46

Abell, Arunah S. 1806-1888 .... DLB43

Abercrombie, Lascelles 1881-1938 .... DLB19

Abse, Dannie 1923- DLB27

Academy Chicago Publishers DLB46

Ace Books DLB46

Actors Theatre of Louisville DLB7

Adair, James 1709?-1783? DLB30

Adamic, Louis 1898-1951 .... DLB9

Adams, Brooks 1848-1927 .... DLB47

Adams, Charles Francis, Jr. 1835-1915 .... DLB47

Adams, Douglas 1952- Y83

Adams, Franklin P. 1881-1960 .... DLB29

Adams, Henry 1838-1918 .... DLB12, 47

Adams, Herbert Baxter 1850-1901 .... DLB47

Adams, James Truslow 1878-1949 .... DLB17

Adams, John 1734-1826 .... DLB31

Adams, John Quincy 1767-1848 .... DLB37

Adams, Samuel 1722-1803 .... DLB31,43

Adams, William Taylor 1822-1897 .... DLB42

Adcock, Fleur 1934- DLB40

Ade, George 1866-1944 .... DLB11, 25

Adeler, Max (see Clark, Charles Heber)

AE 1867-1935 .... DLB19

Aesthetic Poetry (1873), by Walter Pater DLB35

Afro-American Literary Critics:
    An Introduction DLB33

Agassiz, Jean Louis Rodolphe 1807-1873 .... DLB1

Agee, James 1909-1955 .... DLB2, 26

Aiken, Conrad 1889-1973 .... DLB9, 45

Ainsworth, William Harrison 1805-1882 .... DLB21

Akins, Zoë 1886-1958 .... DLB26

Alba, Nanina 1915-1968 .... DLB41

Albee, Edward 1928- DLB7

Alcott, Amos Bronson 1799-1888 .... DLB1

Alcott, Louisa May 1832-1888 .... DLB1, 42

Alcott, William Andrus 1798-1859 .... DLB1

Alden, Isabella 1841-1930 .... DLB42

Aldington, Richard 1892-1962 .... DLB20, 36

Aldis, Dorothy 1896-1966 .... DLB22

Aldiss, Brian W. 1925- DLB14

Aldrich, Thomas Bailey 1836-1907 .... DLB42

Alexander, James 1691-1756 .... DLB24

Alger, Horatio, Jr. 1832-1899 .... DLB42

Algonquin Books of Chapel Hill DLB46

Algren, Nelson 1909-1981 .... DLB9; Y81, 82

Alldritt, Keith 1935- DLB14

Allen, Ethan 1738-1789 .... DLB31

Allen, Hervey 1889-1949 .... DLB9, 45

Allen, James 1739-1808 .... DLB31

Allen, Jay Presson 1922- DLB26

Allen, Samuel W. 1917- DLB41

Allen, Woody 1935- DLB44

Allingham, William 1824-1889 .... DLB35

Allott, Kenneth 1912-1973 .... DLB20

Allston, Washington 1779-1843 .... DLB1

Alsop, George 1636-post 1673 .... DLB24

Alsop, Richard 1761-1815 .... DLB37

Alvarez, A. 1929- DLB14, 40

America: or, a Poem on the Settlement of the British Colonies (1780?), by Timothy Dwight DLB37

American Conservatory Theatre DLB7

American Fiction and the 1930s DLB9

American Humor: A Historical Survey
 East and Northeast
 South and Southwest
 Midwest
 West DLB11

The American Writers Congress (9-12 October 1981) Y81

The American Writers Congress: A Report on Continuing Business Y81

Ames, Fisher 1758-1808 .... DLB37

Ames, Mary Clemmer 1831-1884 .... DLB23

Amini, Johari M. 1935- DLB41

Amis, Kingsley 1922- DLB15, 27

Amis, Martin 1949- DLB14

Ammons, A. R. 1926- DLB5

Amory, Thomas 1691?-1788 .... DLB39

Anderson, Margaret 1886-1973 .... DLB4

Anderson, Maxwell 1888-1959 .... DLB7

Anderson, Paul Y. 1893-1938 .... DLB29

Anderson, Poul 1926- DLB8

Anderson, Robert 1917- DLB7

Anderson, Sherwood 1876-1941 .... DLB4, 9; DS1

Andrews, Charles M. 1863-1943 .... DLB17

Angelou, Maya 1928- DLB38

The "Angry Young Men" DLB15

Anhalt, Edward 1914- DLB26

Anthony, Piers 1934- DLB8

Anthony Burgess's *99 Novels:* An Opinion Poll Y84

Antin, Mary 1881-1949 .... Y84

Appleton-Century-Crofts DLB46

Apple-wood Books DLB46

Arbor House Publishing Company DLB46

Arcadia House DLB46

Archer, William 1856-1924 .... DLB10

Arden, John 1930- DLB13

Arena Stage DLB7

Arensberg, Ann 1937- Y82

Arlen, Michael 1895-1956 .... DLB36

Armed Services Editions DLB46

Arno Press DLB46

Arnold, Edwin 1832-1904 .... DLB35

Arnold, Matthew 1822-1888 .... DLB32

Arnow, Harriette Simpson 1908- DLB6

Arp, Bill (see Smith, Charles Henry)

Arthur, Timothy Shay 1809-1885 .... DLB3, 42

As I See It, by Carolyn Cassady DLB16

Asch, Nathan 1902-1964 .... DLB4, 28

Ash, John 1948- DLB40

Ashbery, John 1927- DLB5; Y81

Asher, Sandy 1942- Y83

Ashton, Winifred (see Dane, Clemence)

Asimov, Isaac 1920- DLB8

Atheneum Publishers DLB46

Atherton, Gertrude 1857-1948 .... DLB9

Atkins, Josiah circa 1755-1781 .... DLB31

Atkins, Russell 1926- DLB41

The Atlantic Monthly Press DLB46

Aubert, Alvin 1930- DLB41

Aubin, Penelope 1685-circa, 1731 .... DLB39

Auchincloss, Louis 1917- DLB2; Y80

Auden, W. H. 1907-1973 .... DLB10, 20

Austin, Alfred 1835-1913 .... DLB35

Austin, Mary 1868-1934 .... DLB9

Authors and Newspapers Association DLB46

The Author's Apology for His Book (1684), by John Bunyan DLB39

An Author's Response, by Ronald Sukenick Y82

Avalon Books DLB46

Avon Books DLB46

Ayckbourn, Alan 1939- DLB13

Aytoun, William Edmondstoune 1813-1865 .... DLB32

B

Bache, Benjamin Franklin 1769-1798 . . . . DLB43

Bacon, Delia 1811-1859 . . . . DLB1

Bacon, Thomas circa 1700-1768 . . . . DLB31

Bage, Robert 1728-1801 . . . . DLB39

Bagnold, Enid 1889-1981 . . . . DLB13

Bailey, Paul 1937- DLB14

Bailey, Philip James 1816-1902 . . . . DLB32

Baillie, Hugh 1890-1966 . . . . DLB29

Bailyn, Bernard 1922- DLB17

Bainbridge, Beryl 1933- DLB14

Bald, Wambly 1902- DLB4

Balderston, John 1889-1954 . . . . DLB26

Baldwin, James 1924- DLB2, 7, 33

Baldwin, Joseph Glover 1815-1864 . . . . DLB3, 11

Ballantine Books DLB46

Ballard, J. G. 1930- DLB14

Ballou, Robert O. [publishing house] DLB46

Bambara, Toni Cade 1939- DLB38

Bancroft, George 1800-1891 . . . . DLB1, 30

Bancroft, Hubert Howe 1832-1918 . . . . DLB47

Bangs, John Kendrick 1862-1922 . . . . DLB11

Bantam Books DLB46

Banville, John 1945- DLB14

Baraka, Amiri 1934- DLB5, 7, 16, 38

Barber, John Warner 1798-1885 . . . . DLB30

Barbour, Ralph Henry 1870-1944 . . . . DLB22

Baring, Maurice 1874-1945 . . . . DLB34

Barker, A. L. 1918- DLB14

Barker, George 1913- DLB20

Barker, Harley Granville 1877-1946 . . . . DLB10

Barker, Howard 1946- DLB13

Barker, James Nelson 1784-1858 . . . . DLB37

Barker, Jane 1652-1727? DLB39

Barks, Coleman 1937- DLB5

Barlow, Joel 1754-1812 . . . . DLB37

Barnard, John 1681-1770 . . . . DLB24

Barnes, Djuna 1892-1982 . . . . DLB4, 9, 45

Barnes, Margaret Ayer 1886-1967 . . . . DLB9

Barnes, Peter 1931- DLB13

Barnes, William 1801-1886 . . . . DLB32

Barnes and Noble Books DLB46

Barney, Natalie 1876-1972 . . . . DLB4

Baron, Richard W., Publishing Company DLB46

Barrax, Gerald William 1933- DLB41

Barrie, James M. 1860-1937 . . . . DLB10

Barry, Philip 1896-1949 . . . . DLB7

Barse and Hopkins DLB46

Barstow, Stan 1928- DLB14

Barth, John 1930- DLB2

Barthelme, Donald 1931- DLB2; Y80

Bartlett, John 1820-1905 . . . . DLB1

Bartol, Cyrus Augustus 1813-1900 . . . . DLB1

Bartram, John 1699-1777 . . . . DLB31

Bartram, William 1739-1823 . . . . DLB37

Basic Books DLB46

Bass, T. J. 1932- Y81

Bassett, John Spencer 1867-1928 . . . . DLB17

Bassler, Thomas Joseph (see Bass, T. J.)

Baum, L. Frank 1856-1919 . . . . DLB22

Baumbach, Jonathan 1933- Y80

Bawden, Nina 1925- DLB14

Bax, Clifford 1886-1962 . . . . DLB10

Bayer, Eleanor (see Perry, Eleanor)

Beach, Sylvia 1887-1962 . . . . DLB4

Beagle, Peter S. 1939- Y80

Beal, M. F. 1937- Y81

Beale, Howard K. 1899-1959 . . . . DLB17

Beard, Charles A. 1874-1948 . . . . DLB17

A Beat Chronology: The First Twenty-five
    Years, 1944-1969 . . . . DLB16

Beattie, Ann 1947- Y82

Becker, Carl 1873-1945 . . . . DLB17

Beckett, Samuel 1906- DLB13, 15

Beckford, William 1760-1844 . . . . DLB39

Beckham, Barry 1944- DLB33

Beecher, Catharine Esther 1800-1878 . . . . DLB1

Beecher, Henry Ward 1813-1887 . . . . DLB3, 43

Beer, George L. 1872-1920 . . . . DLB47

Beer, Patricia 1919- DLB40

Beerbohm, Max 1872-1956 .... DLB34

Behan, Brendan 1923-1964 .... DLB13

Behn, Aphra 1640?-1689 .... DLB39

Behrman, S. N. 1893-1973 .... DLB7, 44

Belasco, David 1853-1931 .... DLB7

Belitt, Ben 1911- DLB5

Belknap, Jeremy 1744-1798 .... DLB30, 37

Bell, Marvin 1937- DLB5

Bellamy, Edward 1850-1898 .... DLB12

Bellamy, Joseph 1719-1790 .... DLB31

Belloc, Hilaire 1870-1953 .... DLB19

Bellow, Saul 1915- DLB2, 28; Y82; DS3

Belmont Productions DLB46

Bemelmans, Ludwig 1898-1962 .... DLB22

Bemis, Samuel Flagg 1891-1973 .... DLB17

Benchley, Robert 1889-1945 .... DLB11

Benedictus, David 1938- DLB14

Benedikt, Michael 1935- DLB5

Benét, Stephen Vincent 1898-1943 .... DLB4

Benét, William Rose 1886-1950 .... DLB45

Benford, Gregory 1941- Y82

Benjamin, Park 1809-1864 .... DLB3

Bennett, Arnold 1867-1931 .... DLB10, 34

Bennett, Charles 1899- DLB44

Bennett, Hal 1930- DLB33

Bennett, James Gordon 1795-1872 .... DLB43

Bennett, James Gordon, Jr. 1841-1918 .... DLB23

Bennett, John 1865-1956 .... DLB42

Benson, Stella 1892-1933 .... DLB36

Benton, Robert 1932-   and Newman,
    David 1937- DLB44

Beresford, Anne 1929- DLB40

Berg, Stephen 1934- DLB5

Berger, John 1926- DLB14

Berger, Meyer 1898-1959 .... DLB29

Berger, Thomas 1924- DLB2; Y80

Berkeley, George 1685-1753 .... DLB31

The Berkley Publishing Corporation DLB46

Bernard, John 1756-1828 .... DLB37

Berrigan, Daniel 1921- DLB5

Berrigan, Ted 1934-1983 .... DLB5

Berry, Wendell 1934- DLB5, 6

Bessie, Alvah 1904- DLB26

Bester, Alfred 1913- DLB8

The Bestseller Lists: An Assessment Y84

Betjeman, John 1906-1984 .... DLB20; Y84

Betts, Doris 1932- Y82

Beveridge, Albert J. 1862-1927 .... DLB17

Beverley, Robert circa 1673-1722 .... DLB24, 30

Bierce, Ambrose 1842-1914? DLB11, 12, 23

Biggle, Lloyd, Jr. 1923- DLB8

Biglow, Hosea (see Lowell, James Russell)

Billings, Josh (see Shaw, Henry Wheeler)

Bingham, Caleb 1757-1817 .... DLB42

Binyon, Laurence 1869-1943 .... DLB19

Biographical Documents I Y84

Bird, William 1888-1963 .... DLB4

Bishop, Elizabeth 1911-1979 .... DLB5

Bishop, John Peale 1892-1944 .... DLB4, 9, 45

Black, David (D. M.) 1941- DLB40

Black, Walter J. [publishing house] DLB46

Black, Winifred 1863-1936 .... DLB25

The Black Arts Movement, by Larry Neal DLB38

Black Theaters and Theater Organizations in
    America, 1961-1982: A Research List DLB38

Black Theatre: A Forum [excerpts] DLB38

Blackamore, Arthur 1679-? DLB24, 39

Blackburn, Paul 1926-1971 .... DLB16; Y81

Blackburn, Thomas 1916-1977 .... DLB27

Blackmore, R. D. 1825-1900 .... DLB18

Blackwood, Caroline 1931- DLB14

Blair, Francis Preston 1791-1876 .... DLB43

Blair, James circa 1655-1743 .... DLB24

Blair, John Durburrow 1759-1823 .... DLB37

Bledsoe, Albert Taylor 1809-1877 .... DLB3

Blish, James 1921-1975 .... DLB8

Bloch, Robert 1917- DLB44

Block, Rudolph (see Lessing, Bruno)

Blunden, Edmund 1896-1974 .... DLB20

Blunt, Wilfrid Scawen 1840-1922.............. DLB19

Bly, Nellie (see Cochrane, Elizabeth)

Bly, Robert 1926- DLB5

The Bobbs-Merrill Company DLB46

Bodenheim, Maxwell 1892-1954..............DLB9, 45

Boehm, Sydney 1908- DLB44

Boer, Charles 1939- DLB5

Bogan, Louise 1897-1970..................... DLB45

Bogarde, Dirk 1921- DLB14

Boland, Eavan 1944- DLB40

Bolling, Robert 1738-1775.................... DLB31

Bolt, Robert 1924- DLB13

Bolton, Herbert E. 1870-1953 .... DLB17

Bond, Edward 1934- DLB13

Boni, Albert and Charles [publishing house] ... DLB46

Boni and Liveright DLB46

The Book League of America DLB46

Boorstin, Daniel J. 1914- DLB17

Booth, Philip 1925- Y82

Borrow, George 1803-1881.................... DLB21

Botta, Anne C. Lynch 1815-1891............... DLB3

Bottomley, Gordon 1874-1948................. DLB10

Bottoms, David 1949- Y83

Bottrall, Ronald 1906- DLB20

Boucher, Anthony 1911-1968 .... DLB8

Bourjaily, Vance Nye 1922- DLB2

Bourne, Edward Gaylord 1860-1908 .... DLB47

Bova, Ben 1932- Y81

Bovard, Oliver K. 1872-1945 .... DLB25

Bowen, Elizabeth 1899-1973.................. DLB15

Bowen, Francis 1811-1890..................... DLB1

Bowen, John 1924- DLB13

Bowers, Claude G. 1878-1958 .... DLB17

Bowers, Edgar 1924- DLB5

Bowles, Paul 1910- DLB5, 6

Bowles, Samuel III 1826-1878................. DLB43

Boyd, James 1888-1944...................... DLB9

Boyd, John 1919- DLB8

Boyd, Thomas 1898-1935 .... DLB9

Boyesen, Hjalmar Hjorth 1848-1895 .... DLB12

Boyle, Kay 1902- DLB4, 9

Brackenbury, Alison 1953- DLB40

Brackenridge, Hugh Henry 1748-1816..... DLB11, 37

Brackett, Charles 1892-1969................... DLB26

Brackett, Leigh 1915-1978....................DLB8, 26

Bradbury, Malcolm 1932- DLB14

Bradbury, Ray 1920- DLB2, 8

Braddon, Mary Elizabeth 1835-1915 .... DLB18

Bradford, Andrew 1686-1742 .... DLB43

Bradford, Gamaliel 1863-1932 .... DLB17

Bradford, John 1749-1830 .... DLB43

Bradford, William 1590-1657.............. DLB24, 30

Bradford, William III 1719-1791.............. DLB43

Bradley, David 1950- DLB33

Bradley, Marion Zimmer 1930- DLB8

Bradley, William Aspenwall 1878-1939......... DLB4

Bradstreet, Anne 1612 or 1613-1672........... DLB24

Bragg, Melvyn 1939- DLB14

Braine, John 1922- DLB15

Branagan, Thomas 1774-1843................. DLB37

Branden Press................................. DLB46

Brautigan, Richard 1935-1984....... DLB2, 5; Y80, 84

Braxton, Joanne M. 1950- DLB41

Bray, Thomas 1656-1730..................... DLB24

Braziller, George [publishing house] DLB46

The Bread Loaf Writers' Conference 1983........ Y84

The Break-Up of the Novel (1922),
    by John Middleton Murry.................. DLB36

Breasted, James Henry 1865-1935.............. DLB47

Bremser, Bonnie 1939- DLB16

Brenton, Howard 1942- DLB13

Bresmer, Ray 1934- DLB16

Brewer, Warren and Putnam.................. DLB46

Bridges, Robert 1844-1930 .... DLB19

Bridie, James 1888-1951....................... DLB10

Briggs, Charles Frederick 1804-1877 .... DLB3

Brighouse, Harold 1882-1958 .... DLB10

Brimmer, B. J., Company DLB46

Brisbane, Albert 1809-1890.................... DLB3

Brisbane, Arthur 1864-1936................... DLB25

Broadway Publishing Company.................. DLB46

Brock, Edwin 1927- DLB40

Brodhead, John R. 1814-1873................. DLB30

Bromfield, Louis 1896-1956..................DLB4, 9

Broner, E. M. 1930- DLB28

Brontë, Anne 1820-1849 .... DLB21

Brontë, Charlotte 1816-1855 .... DLB21

Brontë, Emily 1818-1848.................. DLB21, 32

Brooke, Frances 1724-1789................... DLB39

Brooke, Henry 1703?-1783................... DLB39

Brooke, Rupert 1887-1915 .... DLB19

Brooke-Rose, Christine 1926- DLB14

Brooks, Charles Timothy 1813-1883 .... DLB1

Brooks, Gwendolyn 1917- DLB5

Brooks, Jeremy 1926- DLB14

Brooks, Mel 1926- DLB26

Brooks, Noah 1830-1903 .... DLB42

Brooks, Richard 1912- DLB44

Brooks, Van Wyck 1886-1963 .... DLB45

Brophy, Brigid 1929- DLB14

Brossard, Chandler 1922- DLB16

Brother Antoninus (see Everson, William)

Brougham, John 1810-1880 .... DLB11

Broughton, James 1913- DLB5

Broughton, Rhoda 1840-1920 .... DLB18

Broun, Heywood 1888-1939.................. DLB29

Brown, Bob 1886-1959.....................DLB4, 45

Brown, Cecil 1943- DLB33

Brown, Charles Brockden 1771-1810.......... DLB37

Brown, Christy 1932-1981.................... DLB14

Brown, Dee 1908- Y80

Brown, Fredric 1906-1972.................... DLB8

Brown, George Mackay 1921- DLB14, 27

Brown, Harry 1917- DLB26

Brown, Margaret Wise 1910-1952............. DLB22

Brown, Oliver Madox 1855-1874.............. DLB21

Brown, T. E. 1830-1897 .... DLB35

Brown, William Hill 1765-1793............... DLB37

Brown, William Wells 1813-1884............... DLB3

Browne, Charles Farrar 1834-1867............ DLB11

Browne, Michael Dennis 1940- DLB40

Browne, Wynyard 1911-1964................... DLB13

Browning, Elizabeth Barrett 1806-1861 .... DLB32

Browning, Robert 1812-1889................... DLB32

Brownjohn, Allan 1931- DLB40

Brownson, Orestes Augustus 1803-1876........ DLB1

Bruce, Philip Alexander 1856-1933 .... DLB47

Bruce Humphries [publishing house] DLB46

Bruckman, Clyde 1894-1955 .... DLB26

Bryant, William Cullen 1794-1878........... DLB3,43

Buchan, John 1875-1940 .... DLB34

Buchanan, Robert 1841-1901.............. DLB18, 35

Buchman, Sidney 1902-1975 .... DLB26

Buck, Pearl S. 1892-1973..................... DLB9

Buckley, William F., Jr. 1925- Y80

Buckminster, Joseph Stevens 1784-1812........ DLB37

Buckner, Robert 1906- DLB26

Budd, Thomas ?-1698........................ DLB24

Budrys, A. J. 1931- DLB8

Buechner, Frederick 1926- Y80

Bukowski, Charles 1920- DLB5

Bullins, Ed 1935- DLB7, 38

Bulwer-Lytton, Edward (also Edward Bulwer)
    1803-1873................................ DLB21

Bumpus, Jerry 1937- Y81

Bunting, Basil 1900- DLB20

Bunyan, John 1628-1688 .... DLB39

Burgess, Anthony 1917- DLB14

Burgess, Gelett 1866-1951.................... DLB11

Burgess, John W. 1844-1931 .... DLB47

Burgess, Thornton W. 1874-1965 .... DLB22

Burk, John Daly circa 1772-1808............... DLB37

Burke, Kenneth 1897- DLB45

Burnett, Frances Hodgson 1849-1924 .... DLB42

Burnett, W. R. 1899-1982 .... DLB9

Burney, Fanny 1752-1840 .... DLB39

Burns, Alan 1929- DLB14

Burroughs, Edgar Rice 1875-1950.............. DLB8

Burroughs, Margaret T. G. 1917- DLB41

Burroughs, William S., Jr. 1947-1981 .... DLB16

Burroughs, William Seward 1914-
.... DLB2, 8, 16; Y81

Burroway, Janet 1936- DLB6

Burton, Virginia Lee 1909-1968............... DLB22

Busch, Frederick 1941- DLB6

Busch, Niven 1903- DLB44

Butler, Octavia E. 1947- DLB33

Butler, Samuel 1835-1902 .... DLB18

Butterworth, Hezekiah 1839-1905............. DLB42

B. V. (see Thomson, James)

Byatt, A. S. 1936- DLB14

Byles, Mather 1707-1788 .... DLB24

Byrd, William II 1674-1744 .... DLB24

Byrne, John Keyes (see Leonard, Hugh)

C

Cabell, James Branch 1879-1958 .... DLB9

Cable, George Washington 1844-1925......... DLB12

Cahan, Abraham 1860-1951.............DLB9, 25, 28

Cain, George 1943- DLB33

Caldwell, Ben 1937- DLB38

Caldwell, Erskine, 1903- DLB9

Calhoun, John C. 1782-1850 .... DLB3

Calisher, Hortense 1911- DLB2

Calmer, Edgar 1907- DLB4

Calverley, C. S. 1831-1884.................... DLB35

Calvert, George Henry 1803-1889............. DLB1

Camm, John 1718-1778 .... DLB31

Campbell, John 1653-1728 .... DLB43

Campbell, John W., Jr. 1910-1971.............. DLB8

Campbell, Roy 1901-1957 .... DLB20

Candour in English Fiction (1890),
by Thomas Hardy....................... DLB18

Cannan, Gilbert 1884-1955.................... DLB10

Cannell, Kathleen 1891-1974 .... DLB4

Cannell, Skipwith 1887-1957 .... DLB45

Cantwell, Robert 1908-1978 .... DLB9

Cape, Jonathan, and Harrison Smith
[publishing house] DLB46

Capen, Joseph 1658-1725 .... DLB24

Capote, Truman 1924-1984 ....DLB2; Y80, 84

Carey, Mathew 1760-1839...................... DLB37

Carroll, Gladys Hasty 1904- DLB9

Carroll, John 1735-1815....................... DLB37

Carroll, Lewis 1832-1898 .... DLB18

Carroll, Paul 1927- DLB16

Carroll, Paul Vincent 1900-1968................ DLB10

Carroll and Graf Publishers DLB46

Carruth, Hayden 1921- DLB5

Carryl, Charles E. 1841-1920.................. DLB42

Carswell, Catherine 1879-1946 .... DLB36

Carter, Angela 1940- DLB14

Carter, Henry (see Leslie, Frank)

Carter, Landon 1710-1778 .... DLB31

Carter, Lin 1930- Y81

Caruthers, William Alexander 1802-1846 .... DLB3

Carver, Jonathan 1710-1780................... DLB31

Carver, Raymond 1938- Y84

Cary, Joyce 1888-1957....................... DLB15

Casey, Juanita 1925- DLB14

Casey, Michael 1947- DLB5

Cassady, Carolyn 1923- DLB16

Cassady, Neal 1926-1968 .... DLB16

Cassill, R. V. 1919- DLB6

Castlemon, Harry (see Fosdick, Charles Austin)

Caswall, Edward 1814-1878 .... DLB32

Cather, Willa 1873-1947...................DLB9; DS1

Catton, Bruce 1899-1978 .... DLB17

Causley, Charles 1917- DLB27

Caute, David 1936- DLB14

The Caxton Printers, Limited DLB46

Center for the Book Research................... Y84

Challans, Eileen Mary (see Renault, Mary)

Chalmers, George 1742-1825.................. DLB30

Chamberlain, Samuel S. 1851-1916............. DLB25

Chamberlin, William Henry 1897-1969........ DLB29

Chambers, Charles Haddon 1860-1921........ DLB10

Chandler, Harry 1864-1944 .... DLB29

Channing, Edward 1856-1931.................. DLB17

Channing, Edward Tyrrell 1790-1856.......... DLB1

Channing, William Ellery 1780-1842 .... DLB1

Channing, William Ellery II 1817-1901......... DLB1

Channing, William Henry 1810-1884........... DLB1

Chaplin, Charlie 1889-1977 .... DLB44

Chappell, Fred 1936- DLB6

Charles, Gerda 1914- DLB14

The Charles Wood Affair: A Playwright Revived.. Y83

Charyn, Jerome 1937- Y83

Chase, Borden 1900-1971 .... DLB26

Chase-Riboud, Barbara 1936- DLB33

Chauncy, Charles 1705-1787 .... DLB24

Chayefsky, Paddy 1923-1981 .... DLB7, 44; Y81

Cheever, Ezekiel 1615-1708 .... DLB24

Cheever, John 1912-1982.............. DLB2; Y80, 82

Cheever, Susan 1943- Y82

Chelsea House................................. DLB46

Cheney, Ednah Dow (Littlehale) 1824-1904 ..... DLB1

Cherry, Kelly 1940 .... Y83

Cherryh, C. J. 1942- Y80

Chesnutt, Charles Waddell 1858-1932......... DLB12

Chesterton, G. K. 1874-1936 .... DLB10, 19, 34

Cheyney, Edward P. 1861-1947 .... DLB47

Child, Francis James 1825-1896 .... DLB1

Child, Lydia Maria 1802-1880................... DLB1

Childress, Alice 1920- DLB7, 38

Childs, George W. 1829-1894 .... DLB23

Chilton Book Company....................... DLB46

Chittenden, Hiram Martin 1858-1917......... DLB47

Chivers, Thomas Holley 1809-1858 .... DLB3

Chopin, Kate 1851-1904...................... DLB12

Christie, Agatha 1890-1976................... DLB13

Church, Benjamin 1734-1778 .... DLB31

Churchill, Caryl 1938- DLB13

Ciardi, John 1916- DLB5

City Lights Books............................. DLB46

Clapper, Raymond 1892-1944............... DLB29

Clark, C. M., Publishing Company DLB46

Clark, Charles Heber 1841-1915 .... DLB11

Clark, Eleanor 1913- DLB6

Clark, Lewis Gaylord 1808-1873............... DLB3

Clark, Walter Van Tilburg 1909-1971........... DLB9

Clarke, Austin 1896-1974................... DLB10, 20

Clarke, Gillian 1937- DLB40

Clarke, James Freeman 1810-1888 .... DLB1

Clarke, Rebecca Sophia 1833-1906 .... DLB42

Clausen, Andy 1943- DLB16

Clay, Cassius Marcellus 1810-1903............. DLB43

Cleland, John 1710-1789 .... DLB39

Clemens, Samuel Langhorne 1835-1910
.... DLB11, 12, 23

Clement, Hal 1922- DLB8

Clemo, Jack 1916- DLB27

Clifton, Lucille 1936- DLB5, 41

Clode, Edward J. [publishing house] DLB46

Clough, Arthur Hugh 1819-1861.............. DLB32

Coates, Robert M. 1897-1973.................DLB4, 9

Coatsworth, Elizabeth 1893- DLB22

Cobb, Jr., Charles E. 1943- DLB41

Cobb, Frank I. 1869-1923 .... DLB25

Cobb, Irvin S. 1876-1944................... DLB11, 25

Cobbett, William 1762-1835 .... DLB43

Cochran, Thomas C. 1902- DLB17

Cochrane, Elizabeth 1867-1922................. DLB25

Cockerill, John A. 1845-1896................... DLB23

Coffee, Lenore J. 1900?-1984 .... DLB44

Coffin, Robert P. Tristram 1892-1955.......... DLB45

Cogswell, Mason Fitch 1761-1830 .... DLB37

Cohen, Arthur A. 1928- DLB28

Colden, Cadwallader 1688-1776........... DLB24, 30

Cole, Barry 1936- DLB14

Colegate, Isabel 1931- DLB14

Coleman, Emily Holmes 1899-1974 .... DLB4

Coleridge, Mary 1861-1907..................... DLB19

Collins, Mortimer 1827-1876 .... DLB21, 35

Collins, Wilkie 1824-1889....................... DLB18

Collyer, Mary 1716?-1763? DLB39

Colman, Benjamin 1673-1747 .... DLB24

Colter, Cyrus 1910- DLB33

Colum, Padraic 1881-1972.................... DLB19

Colwin, Laurie 1944- Y80

Comden, Betty 1919- and Green,
Adolph 1918- DLB44

The Comic Tradition Continued
[in the British Novel]..................... DLB15

Commager, Henry Steele 1902- DLB17

The Commercialization of the Image of
Revolt, by Kenneth Rexroth DLB16

Community and Commentators: Black
Theatre and Its Critics................... DLB38

Compton-Burnett, Ivy 1884?-1969 .... DLB36

Congreve, William 1670-1729 .... DLB39

Connell, Evan S., Jr. 1924- DLB2; Y81

Connelly, Marc 1890-1980.................DLB7; Y80

Connor, Tony 1930- DLB40

Conquest, Robert 1917- DLB27

Conrad, Joseph 1857-1924 .... DLB10, 34

Conroy, Jack 1899- Y81

Conroy, Pat 1945- DLB6

The Consolidation of Opinion: Critical
Responses to the Modernists.............. DLB36

Constantine, David 1944- DLB40

A Contemporary Flourescence of Chicano
Literature.................................... Y84

A Conversation with Chaim Potok................ Y84

Conversations with Publishers I: An Interview
with Patrick O'Connor Y84

Conway, Moncure Daniel 1832-1907 .... DLB1

Cook, Ebenezer circa 1667-circa 1732 .... DLB24

Cooke, John Esten 1830-1886 .... DLB3

Cooke, Philip Pendleton 1816-1850 .... DLB3

Cooke, Rose Terry 1827-1892................. DLB12

Coolidge, Susan (see Woolsey, Sarah Chauncy)

Cooper, Giles 1918-1966 .... DLB13

Cooper, James Fenimore 1789-1851............. DLB3

Cooper, Kent 1880-1965 .... DLB29

Coover, Robert 1932- DLB2; Y81

Coppel, Alfred 1921- Y83

Coppola, Francis Ford 1939- DLB44

Corelli, Marie 1855-1924 .... DLB34

Corman, Cid 1924- DLB5

Corn, Alfred 1943- Y80

Cornish, Sam 1935- DLB41

Corrington, John William 1932- DLB6

Corso, Gregory 1930- DLB5, 16

Cortez, Jayne 1936- DLB41

Corvo, Baron (see Rolfe, Frederick William)

Cory, William Johnson 1823-1892............. DLB35

Cosmopolitan Book Corporation DLB46

Costain, Thomas B. 1885-1965................. DLB9

Cotton, John 1584-1652 .... DLB24

Coventry, Francis 1725-1754 .... DLB39

Covici-Friede DLB46

Coward, Noel 1899-1973 .... DLB10

Coward, McCann and Geoghegan............. DLB46

Cowles, Gardner 1861-1946 .... DLB29

Cowley, Malcolm 1898- DLB4; Y81

Cox, Palmer 1840-1924....................... DLB42

Coxe, Louis 1918- DLB5

Coxe, Tench 1755-1824 .... DLB37

Cozzens, James Gould 1903-1978..... DLB9; Y84; DS2

Craddock, Charles Egbert (see Murfree, Mary N.)

Cradock, Thomas 1718-1770 .... DLB31

Craig, Daniel H. 1811-1895 .... DLB43

Craik, Dinah Maria 1826-1887 .... DLB35

Cranch, Christopher Pearse 1813-1892.......DLB1, 42

Crane, Hart 1899-1932........................ DLB4

Crane, Stephen 1871-1900 .... DLB12

Craven, Avery 1885-1980...................... DLB17

Crawford, Charles 1752-circa 1815............. DLB31

Crayon, Geoffrey (see Irving, Washington)

Creative Age Press........................... DLB46

Creel, George 1876-1953 .... DLB25

Creeley, Robert 1926- DLB5, 16

Creelman, James 1859-1915................... DLB23

Cregan, David 1931- DLB13

Crèvecoeur, Michel Guillaume Jean de
1735-1813................................ DLB37

Crews, Harry 1935- DLB6

Crichton, Michael 1942- Y81

A Crisis of Culture: The Changing Role
of Religion in the New Republic DLB37

Cristofer, Michael 1946- DLB7

Criticism In Relation To Novels (1863),
     by G. H. Lewes............................ DLB21

Crockett, David 1786-1836 ....DLB3, 11

Croly, Jane Cunningham 1829-1901............ DLB23

Crosby, Caresse 1892-1970 and Crosby,
     Harry 1898-1929........................... DLB4

Crossley-Holland, Kevin 1941- DLB40

Crothers, Rachel 1878-1958 .... DLB7

Crowley, John 1942- Y82

Crowley, Mart 1935- DLB7

Crown Publishers............................. DLB46

Croy, Homer 1883-1965........................ DLB4

Crumley, James 1939- Y84

Cruz, Victor Hernández 1949- DLB41

Cullen, Countee 1903-1946..................... DLB4

Cummings, E. E. 1894-1962 .... DLB4

Cummings, Ray 1887-1957 .... DLB8

Cummins, Maria Susanna 1827-1866.......... DLB42

Cunningham, J. V. 1911- DLB5

Cuomo, George 1929- Y80

Cupples and Leon........................... DLB46

Cuppy, Will 1884-1949 .... DLB11

Currie, Mary Montgomerie Lamb Singleton,
     Lady Currie (see Fane, Violet)

Curti, Merle E. 1897- DLB17

Curtis, George William 1824-1892...........DLB1, 43

D

D. M. Thomas: The Plagiarism Controversy....... Y82

Dale, Peter 1938- DLB40

Dall, Caroline Wells (Healey) 1822-1912........ DLB1

The Dallas Theater Center DLB7

D'Alton, Louis 1900-1951 .... DLB10

Daly, T. A. 1871-1948........................ DLB11

Damon, S. Foster 1893-1971................... DLB45

Dana, Charles A. 1819-1897.................DLB3, 23

Dana, Richard Henry, Jr. 1815-1882 .... DLB1

Dane, Clemence 1887-1965.................... DLB10

Danforth, John 1660-1730.................... DLB24

Danforth, Samuel I 1626-1674 .... DLB24

Danforth, Samuel II 1666-1727 .... DLB24

Dangerous Years: London Theater,
     1939-1945................................ DLB10

Daniel, John M. 1825-1865.................... DLB43

Daniels, Josephus 1862-1948 .... DLB29

Danner, Margaret Esse 1915- DLB41

Daryush, Elizabeth 1887-1977 .... DLB20

Dashwood, Edmée Elizabeth Monica
     de la Pasture (see Delafield, E. M.)

d'Aulaire, Edgar Parin 1898- and
     d'Aulaire, Ingri 1904- DLB22

Daves, Delmer 1904-1977 .... DLB26

Davidson, Avram 1923- DLB8

Davidson, Donald 1893-1968 .... DLB45

Davidson, John 1857-1909.................... DLB19

Davidson, Lionel 1922- DLB14

Davie, Donald 1922- DLB27

Davies, Samuel 1723-1761 .... DLB31

Davies, W. H. 1871-1940 .... DLB19

Daviot, Gordon 1896-1952 .... DLB10

Davis, Charles A. 1795-1867................... DLB11

Davis, Clyde Brion 1894-1962 .... DLB9

Davis, Dick 1945- DLB40

Davis, H. L. 1894-1960 .... DLB9

Davis, John 1774-1854........................ DLB37

Davis, Margaret Thomson 1926- DLB14

Davis, Ossie 1917- DLB7, 38

Davis, Richard Harding 1864-1916........ DLB12, 23

Davis, Samuel Cole 1764-1809................. DLB37

Davison, Peter 1928- DLB5

Davys, Mary 1674-1732....................... DLB39

DAW Books DLB46

Dawson, William 1704-1752 .... DLB31

Day, Benjamin Henry 1810-1889............... DLB43

Day, Clarence 1874-1935 .... DLB11

Day, Dorothy 1897-1980...................... DLB29

Day, The John, Company DLB46

Day Lewis, C. 1904-1972 .... DLB15, 20

Day, Thomas 1748-1789....................... DLB39

Deal, Borden 1922- DLB6

de Angeli, Marguerite 1889- DLB22

De Bow, James D. B. 1820-1867 .... DLB3

de Camp, L. Sprague 1907- DLB8

The Decay of Lying (1889),
     by Oscar Wilde [excerpt] DLB18

Dedication, *Ferdinand Count Fathom* (1753),
     by Tobias Smollett DLB39

Dedication, *Lasselia* (1723), by Eliza
     Haywood [excerpt] DLB39

Dedication, *The History of Pompey the
     Little* (1751), by Francis Coventry DLB39

Dedication, *The Wanderer* (1814),
     by Fanny Burney DLB39

Defense of *Amelia* (1752), by Henry Fielding ... DLB39

Defoe, Daniel 1660-1731 .... DLB39

de Fontaine, Felix Gregory 1834-1896 .... DLB43

De Forest, John William 1826-1906 .... DLB12

de Graff, Robert 1895-1981 .... Y81

Delafield, E. M. 1890-1943 .... DLB34

de la Mare, Walter 1873-1956 .... DLB19

Delaney, Shelagh 1939- DLB13

Delany, Samuel R. 1942- DLB8, 33

Delbanco, Nicholas 1942- DLB6

DeLillo, Don 1936- DLB6

Dell, Floyd 1887-1969 .... DLB9

Dell Publishing Company DLB46

del Rey, Lester 1915- DLB8

Demby, William 1922- DLB33

Dennie, Joseph 1768-1812 .... DLB37,43

Dennis, Nigel 1912- DLB13, 15

Dent, Tom 1932- DLB38

Denton, Daniel circa 1626-1703 .... DLB24

Derby, George Horatio 1823-1861 .... DLB11

Derleth, August 1909-1971 .... DLB9

The Derrydale Press DLB46

De Tabley, Lord 1835-1895 .... DLB35

Deutsch, Babette 1895-1982 .... DLB45

Deveaux, Alexis 1948- DLB38

The Development of Lighting in the Staging
     of Drama, 1900-1945 [in Great Britain].... DLB10

de Vere, Aubrey 1814-1902 .... DLB35

The Devin-Adair Company DLB46

De Voto, Bernard 1897-1955 .... DLB9

De Vries, Peter 1910- DLB6; Y82

de Young, M. H. 1849-1925 .... DLB25

The Dial Press DLB46

Diamond, I. A. L. 1920- DLB26

Dick, Philip K. 1928- DLB8

Dickens, Charles 1812-1870 .... DLB21

Dickey, James 1923- DLB5; Y82

Dickey, William 1928- DLB5

Dickinson, Emily 1830-1886 .... DLB1

Dickinson, John 1732-1808 .... DLB31

Dickinson, Jonathan 1688-1747 .... DLB24

Dickinson, Patric 1914- DLB27

Dickson, Gordon R. 1923- DLB8

Didion, Joan 1934- DLB2; Y81

Di Donato, Pietro 1911- DLB9

Dillard, Annie 1945- Y80

Dillard, R. H. W. 1937- DLB5

Dintenfass, Mark 1941- Y84

Diogenes, Jr. (see Brougham, John)

DiPrima, Diane 1934- DLB5, 16

Disch, Thomas M. 1940- DLB8

Disney, Walt 1901-1966 .... DLB22

Disraeli, Benjamin 1804-1881 .... DLB21

Dix, Dorothea Lynde 1802-1887 .... DLB1

Dix, Dorothy (see Gilmer, Elizabeth Meriwether)

Dixon, Richard Watson 1833-1900 .... DLB19

Dobell, Sydney 1824-1874 .... DLB32

Dobson, Austin 1840-1921 .... DLB35

Doctorow, E. L. 1931- DLB2, 28; Y80

Dodd, William E. 1869-1940 .... DLB17

Dodge, B. W., and Company DLB46

Dodge, Mary Mapes 1831?-1905 .... DLB42

Dodgson, Charles Lutwidge (see Carroll, Lewis)

Doesticks, Q. K. Philander, P. B. (see Thomson,
     Mortimer)

Donald, David H. 1920- DLB17

Donleavy, J. P. 1926- DLB6

Donnelly, Ignatius 1831-1901 .... DLB12

Dooley, Ebon (see Ebon)

Doolittle, Hilda 1886-1961 .... DLB4, 45

Doran, George H., Company DLB46

Dorn, Edward 1929- DLB5

Dorr, Rheta Childe 1866-1948 . . . . DLB25

Dos Passos, John 1896-1970 . . . . DLB4, 9; DS1

Doughty, Charles M. 1843-1926 . . . . DLB19

Douglas, Keith 1920-1944 . . . . DLB27

Douglas, Norman 1868-1952 . . . . DLB34

Douglass, Frederick 1817?-1895 . . . . DLB1,43

Douglass, William circa 1691-1752 . . . . DLB24

Dover Publications DLB46

Dowden, Edward 1843-1913 . . . . DLB35

Downing, J., Major (see Davis, Charles A.)

Downing, Major Jack (see Smith, Seba)

Dowson, Ernest 1867-1900 . . . . DLB19

Doyle, Arthur Conan 1859-1930 . . . . DLB18

Doyle, Kirby 1932- DLB16

Drabble, Margaret 1939- DLB14

Dramatists Play Service DLB46

Draper, John W. 1811-1882 . . . . DLB30

Draper, Lyman C. 1815-1891 . . . . DLB30

Dreiser, Theodore 1871-1945 . . . . DLB9, 12; DS1

Drinkwater, John 1882-1937 . . . . DLB10, 19

The Drue Heinz Literature Prize
     Excerpt from "Excerpts from a Report
        of the Commission," in David
        Bosworth's *The Death of Descartes*
     An Interview with David Bosworth Y82

Duane, William 1760-1835 . . . . DLB43

Du Bois, W. E. B. 1868-1963 . . . . DLB47

Duell, Sloan and Pearce DLB46

Duffield and Green DLB46

Duffy, Maureen 1933- DLB14

Dugan, Alan 1923- DLB5

Dukes, Ashley 1885-1959 . . . . DLB10

Dumas, Henry 1934-1968 . . . . DLB41

Duncan, Robert 1919- DLB5, 16

Duncan, Ronald 1914-1982 . . . . DLB13

Dunlap, John 1747-1812 . . . . DLB43

Dunlap, William 1766-1839 . . . . DLB30, 37

Dunn, Douglas 1942- DLB40

Dunne, Finley Peter 1867-1936 . . . . DLB11, 23

Dunne, John Gregory 1932- Y80

Dunne, Philip 1908- DLB26

Dunning, Ralph Cheever 1878-1930 . . . . DLB4

Dunning, William A. 1857-1922 . . . . DLB17

Plunkett, Edward John Moreton Drax,
     Lord Dunsany 1878-1957 . . . . DLB10

Duranty, Walter 1884-1957 . . . . DLB29

Durrell, Lawrence 1912- DLB15, 27

Duyckinck, Evert A. 1816-1878 . . . . DLB3

Duyckinck, George L. 1823-1863 . . . . DLB3

Dwight, John Sullivan 1813-1893 . . . . DLB1

Dwight, Timothy 1752-1817 . . . . DLB37

Dyer, Charles 1928- DLB13

Dylan, Bob 1941- DLB16

E

Eager, Edward 1911-1964 . . . . DLB22

Eastlake, William 1917- DLB6

Eastman, Carol ?- DLB44

Ebon 1942- DLB41

Ecco Press DLB46

Edes, Benjamin 1732-1803 . . . . DLB43

Edgar, David 1948- DLB13

Edmonds, Walter D. 1903- DLB9

Edwards, Jonathan 1703-1758 . . . . DLB24

Edwards, Jonathan, Jr. 1745-1801 . . . . DLB37

Edwards, Junius 1929- DLB33

Effinger, George Alec 1947- DLB8

Eggleston, Edward 1837-1902 . . . . DLB12

Eighteenth-Century Aesthetic Theories DLB31

Eighteenth-Century Philosophical
     Background DLB31

Eigner, Larry 1927- DLB5

Eklund, Gordon 1945- Y83

Elder, Lonne III 1931- DLB7, 38, 44

Eliot, George 1819-1880 . . . . DLB21, 35

Eliot, John 1604-1690 . . . . DLB24

Eliot, T. S. 1888-1965 . . . . DLB7, 10, 45

Elkin, Stanley 1930- DLB2, 28; Y80

Ellet, Elizabeth F. 1818?-1877 . . . . DLB30

Elliott, Janice 1931- DLB14

Elliott, William 1788-1863 .... DLB3

Ellis, Edward S. 1840-1916 .... DLB42

Ellison, Harlan 1934- DLB8

Ellison, Ralph 1914- DLB2

Emanuel, James Andrew 1921- DLB41

Emerson, Ralph Waldo 1803-1882 .... DLB1

Emerson, William 1769-1811 .... DLB37

Empson, William 1906-1984................... DLB20

The End of English Stage Censorship,
    1945-1968................................. DLB13

The English Renaissance of Art (1908),
    by Oscar Wilde............................ DLB35

Enright, D. J. 1920- DLB27

Enright, Elizabeth 1909-1968.................. DLB22

L'Envoi (1882), by Oscar Wilde............... DLB35

Epstein, Julius 1909- and
    Epstein, Philip 1909-1952................. DLB26

Equiano, Olaudah circa 1745-circa 1801........ DLB37

Erskine, John 1879-1951 .... DLB9

Ervine, St. John Greer 1883-1971 .... DLB10

Eshleman, Clayton 1935- DLB5

Essay on Chatterton (1842),
    by Robert Browning DLB32

Estes, Eleanor 1906- DLB22

Ets, Marie Hall 1893- DLB22

Eugene O'Neill Memorial Theater Center....... DLB7

Evans, George Henry 1805-1856 .... DLB43

Evans, M., and Company..................... DLB46

Evans, Mari 1923- DLB41

Evans, Mary Ann (see Eliot, George)

Evans, Nathaniel 1742-1767 .... DLB31

Evans, Sebastian 1830-1909.................... DLB35

Everett, Edward 1794-1865.................... DLB1

Everson, William 1912- DLB5, 16

Every Man His Own Poet; or, The
    Inspired Singer's Recipe Book (1877),
    by W. H. Mallock DLB35

Ewart, Gavin 1916- DLB40

Ewing, Juliana Horatia 1841-1885............. DLB21

Exley, Frederick 1929- Y81

Experiment in the Novel (1929),

by John D. Beresford DLB36

F

"F. Scott Fitzgerald: St. Paul's Native Son
    and Distinguished American Writer":
    University of Minnesota Conference,
    29-31 October 1982.......................... Y82

Faber, Frederick William 1814-1863........... DLB32

Fair, Ronald L. 1932- DLB33

Fairfax, Beatrice (see Manning, Marie)

Fancher, Betsy 1928- Y83

Fane, Violet 1843-1905....................... DLB35

Fantasy Press Publishers....................... DLB46

Fante, John 1909-1983 .... Y83

Farley, Walter 1920- DLB22

Farmer, Philip José 1918- DLB8

Farquharson, Martha (see Finley, Martha)

Farrar and Rinehart........................... DLB46

Farrar, Straus and Giroux..................... DLB46

Farrell, James T. 1904-1979............. DLB4, 9; DS2

Farrell, J. G. 1935-1979...................... DLB14

Fast, Howard 1914- DLB9

Faulkner, William 1897-1962....... DLB9, 11, 44; DS2

Faust, Irvin 1924- DLB2, 28; Y80

Fawcett Books DLB46

Fearing, Kenneth 1902-1961 .... DLB9

Federal Writers' Project DLB46

Federman, Raymond 1928- Y80

Feiffer, Jules 1929- DLB7, 44

Feinstein, Elaine 1930- DLB14, 40

Fell, Frederick, Publishers DLB46

Felton, Cornelius Conway 1807-1862........... DLB1

Fenno, John 1751-1798....................... DLB43

Fenton, James 1949- DLB40

Ferber, Edna 1885-1968.....................DLB9, 28

Ferdinand, Vallery III (see Salaam, Kalamu ya)

Ferguson, Sir Samuel 1810-1886 .... DLB32

Ferguson, William Scott 1875-1954........... DLB47

Ferlinghetti, Lawrence 1919- DLB5, 16

Fern, Fanny (see Parton, Sara

Payson Willis)

Fiction Best-Sellers, 1910-1945 .... DLB9

Fiction into Film, 1928-1975: A List of Movies
  Based on the Works of Authors in
  British Novelists, 1930-1959 .... DLB15

Fiedler, Leslie 1917- DLB28

Field, Eugene 1850-1895 .... DLB23, 42

Field, Rachel 1894-1942 ....DLB9, 22

Fielding, Henry 1707-1754 .... DLB39

Fielding, Sarah 1710-1768.................... DLB39

Fields, James Thomas 1817-1881................ DLB1

Fields, Julia 1938- DLB41

Fields, W. C. 1880-1946 .... DLB44

Figes, Eva 1932- DLB14

Filson, John circa 1753-1788 .... DLB37

Finlay, Ian Hamilton 1925- DLB40

Finley, Martha 1828-1909 .... DLB42

Finney, Jack 1911- DLB8

Finney, Walter Braden (see Finney, Jack)

Firbank, Ronald 1886-1926.................... DLB36

Firmin, Giles 1615-1697 .... DLB24

First Strauss "Livings" Awarded to Cynthia
  Ozick and Raymond Carver
  An Interview with Cynthia Ozick
  An Interview with Raymond Carver Y83

Fisher, Dorothy Canfield 1879-1958............ DLB9

Fisher, Roy 1930- DLB40

Fisher, Sydney George 1856-1927.............. DLB47

Fisher, Vardis 1895-1968...................... DLB9

Fiske, John 1608-1677........................ DLB24

Fiske, John 1842-1901........................ DLB47

Fitch, Thomas circa 1700-1774 .... DLB31

Fitch, William Clyde 1865-1909 .... DLB7

FitzGerald, Edward 1809-1883 .... DLB32

Fitzgerald, F. Scott 1896-1940 ..... DLB4, 9; Y81; DS1

Fitzgerald, Penelope 1916- DLB14

Fitzgerald, Robert 1910- Y80

Fitzgerald, Thomas 1819-1891 .... DLB23

Fitzgerald, Zelda Sayre 1900-1948................ Y84

Fitzhugh, William circa 1651-1701.............. DLB24

Flanagan, Thomas 1923- Y80

Flanner, Janet 1892-1978...................... DLB4

Flavin, Martin 1883-1967...................... DLB9

Flecker, James Elroy 1884-1915 .... DLB10, 19

Fleeson, Doris 1901-1970...................... DLB29

The Fleshly School of Poetry and Other
  Phenomena of the Day (1872), by Robert
  Buchanan DLB35

The Fleshly School of Poetry: Mr. D. G.
  Rossetti (1871), by Thomas Maitland
  (Robert Buchanan)........................ DLB35

Fletcher, John Gould 1886-1950..............DLB4, 45

Flint, F. S. 1885-1960....................... DLB19

Follen, Eliza Lee (Cabot) 1787-1860 .... DLB1

Follett, Ken 1949- Y81

Follett Publishing Company DLB46

Foote, Horton 1916- DLB26

Foote, Shelby 1916- DLB2, 17

Forbes, Calvin 1945- DLB41

Forbes, Ester 1891-1967...................... DLB22

Force, Peter 1790-1868....................... DLB30

Forché, Carolyn 1950- DLB5

Ford, Charles Henri 1913- DLB4

Ford, Corey 1902-1969........................ DLB11

Ford, Ford Madox 1873-1939 .... DLB34

Ford, Jesse Hill 1928- DLB6

Ford, Worthington C. 1858-1941............... DLB47

Foreman, Carl 1914-1984 .... DLB26

Fornés, María Irene 1930- DLB7

Forrest, Leon 1937- DLB33

Forster, E. M. 1879-1970 .... DLB34

Fortune, T. Thomas 1856-1928 .... DLB23

Fosdick, Charles Austin 1842-1915 .... DLB42

Foster, Hannah Webster 1758-1840 .... DLB37

Foster, John 1648-1681....................... DLB24

Foster, Michael 1904-1956.................... DLB9

Four Essays on the Beat Generation,
  by John Clellon Holmes.................... DLB16

Four Seas Company DLB46

Four Winds Press............................ DLB46

Fowles, John 1926- DLB14

Fox, John, Jr. 1862 or 1863-1919 .... DLB9

Fox, William Price 1926- DLB2; Y81

Fraenkel, Michael 1896-1957 .... DLB4

France, Richard 1938- DLB7

Francis, Convers 1795-1863 .... DLB1

Frank, Melvin (see Panama, Norman)

Frank, Waldo 1889-1967 .... DLB9

Franken, Rose 1895?- Y84

Franklin, Benjamin 1706-1790 .... DLB24,43

Franklin, James 1697-1735 .... DLB43

Franklin Library............................. DLB46

Frantz, Ralph Jules 1902-1979................. DLB4

Fraser, G. S. 1915-1980...................... DLB27

Frayn, Michael 1933- DLB13, 14

Frederic, Harold 1856-1898 .... DLB12, 23

Freeman, Douglas Southall 1886-1953......... DLB17

Freeman, Legh Richmond 1842-1915 .... DLB23

Freeman, Mary Wilkins 1852-1930 .... DLB12

Freneau, Philip 1752-1832................... DLB37,43

Friedman, Bruce Jay 1930- DLB2, 28

Friel, Brian 1929- DLB13

Friend, Krebs 1895?-1967? DLB4

Fringe and Alternative Theater
   in Great Britain......................... DLB13

Frothingham, Octavius Brooks 1822-1895....... DLB1

Froude, James Anthony 1818-1894............. DLB18

Fry, Christopher 1907- DLB13

Fuchs, Daniel 1909- DLB9, 26, 28

Fuller, Charles H., Jr. 1939- DLB38

Fuller, Henry Blake 1857-1929................ DLB12

Fuller, John 1937- DLB40

Fuller, Roy 1912- DLB15, 20

Fuller, Samuel 1912- DLB26

Fuller, Sarah Margaret, Marchesa
   D'Ossoli 1810-1850...................... DLB1

Fulton, Robin 1937- DLB40

Furness, William Henry 1802-1896............. DLB1

Furthman, Jules 1888-1966................... DLB26

The Future of the Novel (1899),
   by Henry James........................ DLB18

G

Gaddis, William 1922- DLB2

Gág, Wanda 1893-1946....................... DLB22

Gaine, Hugh 1726-1807 .... DLB43

Gaines, Ernest J. 1933- DLB2, 33; Y80

Galaxy Science Fiction Novels DLB46

Gale, Zona 1874-1938 .... DLB9

Gallico, Paul 1897-1976....................... DLB9

Galsworthy, John 1867-1933............... DLB10, 34

Galvin, Brendan 1938- DLB5

Gambit DLB46

Gannett, Frank E. 1876-1957................... DLB29

Gardam, Jane 1928- DLB14

Garden, Alexander circa 1685-1756 .... DLB31

Gardner, John 1933-1982 ....DLB2; Y82

Garis, Howard R. 1873-1962 .... DLB22

Garland, Hamlin 1860-1940................... DLB12

Garnett, David 1892-1981 .... DLB34

Garraty, John A. 1920- DLB17

Garrett, George 1929- DLB2, 5; Y83

Garrison, William Lloyd 1805-1879..........DLB1, 43

Gascoyne, David 1916- DLB20

Gaskell, Elizabeth Cleghorn 1810-1865........ DLB21

Gass, William Howard 1924- DLB2

Gates, Doris 1901- DLB22

Gay, Ebenezer 1696-1787..................... DLB24

The Gay Science (1866),
   by E. S. Dallas [excerpt].................. DLB21

Gayarré, Charles E. A. 1805-1895 .... DLB30

Geddes, Virgil 1897- DLB4

Geis, Bernard, Associates...................... DLB46

Gelber, Jack 1932- DLB7

Gellhorn, Martha 1908- Y82

Gems, Pam 1925- DLB13

A General Idea of the College of Mirania (1753),
   by William Smith [excerpts]................ DLB31

Genovese, Eugene D. 1930- DLB17

Gent, Peter 1942- Y82

George, Henry 1839-1897..................... DLB23

Gerhardie, William 1895-1977................. DLB36

Gernsback, Hugo 1884-1967 .... DLB8

Gerrold, David 1944- DLB8

Geston, Mark S. 1946- DLB8

Gibbons, Floyd 1887-1939..................... DLB25

Gibson, Wilfrid 1878-1962.................... DLB19

Gibson, William 1914- DLB7

Gillespie, A. Lincoln, Jr. 1895-1950 .... DLB4

Gilliam, Florence ?-?.......................... DLB4

Gilliatt, Penelope 1932- DLB14

Gillott, Jacky 1939-1980 .... DLB14

Gilman, Caroline H. 1794-1888 .... DLB3

Gilmer, Elizabeth Meriwether 1861-1951 .... DLB29

Gilmer, Francis Walker 1790-1826 .... DLB37

Gilroy, Frank D. 1925- DLB7

Ginsberg, Allen 1926- DLB5, 16

Giovanni, Nikki 1943- DLB5, 41

Gipson, Lawrence Henry 1880-1971........... DLB17

Gissing, George 1857-1903 .... DLB18

Glanville, Brian 1931- DLB15

Glasgow, Ellen 1873-1945 ....DLB9, 12

Glaspell, Susan 1882-1948....................DLB7, 9

Glass, Montague 1877-1934 .... DLB11

Glück, Louise 1943- DLB5

Goddard, Morrill 1865-1937................... DLB25

Goddard, William 1740-1817 .... DLB43

Godfrey, Thomas 1736-1763 .... DLB31

Godine, David R., Publisher DLB46

Godwin, Gail 1937- DLB6

Godwin, Parke 1816-1904 .... DLB3

Godwin, William 1756-1836 .... DLB39

Gogarty, Oliver St. John 1878-1957 .... DLB15, 19

Goines, Donald 1937-1974.................... DLB33

Gold, Herbert 1924- DLB2; Y81

Gold, Michael 1893-1967....................DLB9, 28

Goldberg, Dick 1947- DLB7

Golding, William 1911- DLB15

Goldman, William 1931- DLB44

Goldsmith, Oliver 1730 or 1731-1794 .... DLB39

Goldsmith Publishing Company DLB46

Gomme, Laurence James [publishing house] ... DLB46

The Goodman Theatre........................ DLB7

Goodrich, Frances 1891-1984 and
    Hackett, Albert 1900- DLB26

Goodrich, Samuel Griswold 1793-1860 ....DLB1, 42

Goodwin, Stephen 1943- Y82

Gookin, Daniel 1612-1687...................... DLB24

Gordon, Caroline 1895-1981 .... DLB4, 9; Y81

Gordon, Giles 1940- DLB14

Gordon, Mary 1949- DLB6; Y81

Gordone, Charles 1925- DLB7

Goyen, William 1915-1983.................DLB2; Y83

Grady, Henry W. 1850-1889 .... DLB23

Graham, W. S. 1918- DLB20

Grahame, Kenneth 1859-1932.................. DLB34

Gramatky, Hardie 1907-1979.................. DLB22

Granich, Irwin (see Gold, Michael)

Grant, Harry J. 1881-1963 .... DLB29

Grant, James Edward 1905-1966 .... DLB26

Grasty, Charles H. 1863-1924 .... DLB25

Grau, Shirley Ann 1929- DLB2

Graves, John 1920- Y83

Graves, Richard 1715-1804.................... DLB39

Graves, Robert 1895-1985 .... DLB20

Gray, Asa 1810-1888 .... DLB1

Gray, David 1838-1861 .... DLB32

Gray, Simon 1936- DLB13

Grayson, William J. 1788-1863 .... DLB3

The Great War and the Theater, 1914-1918
    [Great Britain] DLB10

Greeley, Horace 1811-1872................... DLB3, 43

Green, Adolph (see Comden, Betty)

Green, Duff 1791-1875....................... DLB43

Green, Gerald 1922- DLB28

Green, Henry 1905-1973 .... DLB15

Green, Jonas 1712-1767 .... DLB31

Green, Joseph 1706-1780..................... DLB31

Green, Julien 1900- DLB4

Green, Paul 1894-1981 .... DLB7, 9; Y81

Greenberg: Publisher......................... DLB46

Green Tiger Press DLB46

Greene, Asa 1789-1838....................... DLB11

Greene, Graham 1904- DLB13, 15

Greenhow, Robert 1800-1854 .... DLB30

Greenough, Horatio 1805-1852 .... DLB1

Greenwell, Dora 1821-1882.................... DLB35

Greenwillow Books DLB46

Greenwood, Grace (see Lippincott, Sara Jane Clarke)

Greenwood, Walter 1903-1974 .... DLB10

Greer, Ben 1948- DLB6

Gregg Press................................... DLB46

Persse, Isabella Augusta,
    Lady Gregory 1852-1932................. DLB10

Grey, Zane 1872-1939 .... DLB9

Grieve, C. M. (see MacDiarmid, Hugh)

Griffith, Elizabeth 1727?-1793 .... DLB39

Griffiths, Trevor 1935- DLB13

Grigson, Geoffrey 1905- DLB27

Griswold, Rufus 1815-1857.................... DLB3

Gross, Milt 1895-1953 .... DLB11

Grossman Publishers DLB46

Grove Press................................... DLB46

Grubb, Davis 1919-1980 .... DLB6

Gruelle, Johnny 1880-1938................... DLB22

Guare, John 1938- DLB22

Guest, Barbara 1920- DLB5

Guiterman, Arthur 1871-1943................. DLB11

Gunn, Bill 1934- DLB38

Gunn, James E. 1923- DLB8

Gunn, Neil M. 1891-1973 .... DLB15

Gunn, Thom 1929- DLB27

Guthrie, A. B., Jr. 1901- DLB6

Guthrie, Ramon 1896-1973.................... DLB4

The Guthrie Theater.......................... DLB7

Guy, Rosa 1925- DLB33

Gwynne, Erskine 1898-1948................... DLB4

Gysin, Brion 1916- DLB16

H

H. D. (see Doolittle, Hilda)

Hackett, Albert (see Goodrich, Frances)

Hailey, Arthur 1920- Y82

Haines, John 1924- DLB5

Hake, Thomas Gordon 1809-1895 .... DLB32

Haldeman, Joe 1943- DLB8

Haldeman-Julius Company..................... DLB46

Hale, Edward Everett 1822-1909 .... DLB1, 42

Hale, Leo Thomas (see Ebon)

Hale, Lucretia Peabody 1820-1900 .... DLB42

Hale, Nancy 1908- Y80

Hale, Sarah Josepha 1788-1879 .... DLB1, 42

Haley, Alex 1921- DLB38

Haliburton, Thomas Chandler 1796-1865 ...... DLB11

Hall, Donald 1928- DLB5

Hallam, Arthur Henry 1811-1833.............. DLB32

Halleck, Fitz-Greene 1790-1867 .... DLB3

Hallmark Editions DLB46

Halper, Albert 1904-1984 .... DLB9

Halstead, Murat 1829-1908.................... DLB23

Hamburger, Michael 1924- DLB27

Hamilton, Alexander 1712-1756............... DLB31

Hamilton, Alexander 1755?-1804.............. DLB37

Hamilton, Cicely 1872-1952 .... DLB10

Hamilton, Edmond 1904-1977 .... DLB8

Hamilton, Ian 1938- DLB40

Hamilton, Patrick 1904-1962 .... DLB10

Hamilton, Virginia 1936- DLB33

Hammon, Jupiter 1711-died between
    1790 and 1806........................... DLB31

Hammond, John ?-1663....................... DLB24

Hamner, Earl 1923- DLB6

Hampton, Christopher 1946- DLB13

Handlin, Oscar 1915- DLB17

Hankin, St. John 1869-1909.................. DLB10

Hanley, Clifford 1922- DLB14

Hannah, Barry 1942- DLB6

Hannay, James 1827-1873.................... DLB21

Hansberry, Lorraine 1930-1965 .... DLB7, 38

Harcourt Brace Jovanovich.................... DLB46

Hardwick, Elizabeth 1916- DLB6

Hardy, Thomas 1840-1928 .... DLB18, 19

Hare, David 1947- DLB13

Hargrove, Marion 1919- DLB11

Harness, Charles L. 1915- DLB8

Harper, Michael S. 1938- DLB41

Harris, Benjamin ?-circa 1720 ....DLB42,43

Harris, George Washington 1814-1869.......DLB3, 11

Harris, Joel Chandler 1848-1908 .... DLB11, 23, 42

Harris, Mark 1922- DLB2; Y80

Harrison, Harry 1925- DLB8

Harrison, Jim 1937- Y82

Harrison, Paul Carter 1936- DLB38

Harrison, Tony 1937- DLB40

Harrisse, Henry 1829-1910...................DLB47

Harsent, David 1942- DLB40

Hart, Albert Bushnell 1854-1943..............DLB17

Hart, Moss 1904-1961 ....DLB7

Hart, Oliver 1723-1795.......................DLB31

Harte, Bret 1836-1902.......................DLB12

Hartley, L. P. 1895-1972 ....DLB15

Harwood, Lee 1939- DLB40

Harwood, Ronald 1934- DLB13

Haskins, Charles Homer 1870-1937 ....DLB47

A Haughty and Proud Generation (1922),
    by Ford Madox Hueffer DLB36

Hauser, Marianne 1910- Y83

Hawker, Robert Stephen 1803-1875............DLB32

Hawkes, John 1925- DLB2; Y80

Hawthorne, Nathaniel 1804-1864 ....DLB1

Hay, John 1838-1905.....................DLB12, 47

Hayden, Robert 1913-1980....................DLB5

Hayes, John Michael 1919- DLB26

Hayne, Paul Hamilton 1830-1886 ....DLB3

Haywood, Eliza 1693?-1756 ....DLB39

Hazzard, Shirley 1931- Y82

Headley, Joel T. 1813-1897 ....DLB30

Heaney, Seamus 1939- DLB40

Heard, Nathan C. 1936- DLB33

Hearn, Lafcadio 1850-1904...................DLB12

Hearst, William Randolph 1863-1951 ....DLB25

Heath, Catherine 1924- DLB14

Heath-Stubbs, John 1918- DLB27

Hecht, Anthony 1923- DLB5

Hecht, Ben 1894-1964............. DLB7, 9, 25, 26, 28

Hecker, Isaac Thomas 1819-1888 ....DLB1

Hedge, Frederic Henry 1805-1890 ....DLB1

Heidish, Marcy 1947- Y82

Heinlein, Robert A. 1907- DLB8

Heller, Joseph 1923- DLB2, 28; Y80

Hellman, Lillian 1906-1984.................DLB7; Y84

Hemingway, Ernest 1899-1961 .... DLB4, 9; Y81; DS1

Henchman, Daniel 1689-1761 ....DLB24

Henderson, David 1942- DLB41

Henderson, Zenna 1917- DLB8

Henley, William Ernest 1849-1903 ....DLB19

Henry, Buck 1930- DLB26

Henry, Marguerite 1902- DLB22

Henry, Robert Selph 1889-1970...............DLB17

Henty, G. A. 1832-1902 ....DLB18

Hentz, Caroline Lee 1800-1856................DLB3

Herbert, Alan Patrick 1890-1971 ....DLB10

Herbert, Frank 1920- DLB8

Herbert, Henry William 1807-1858.............DLB3

Herbst, Josephine 1892-1969.................DLB9

Hercules, Frank E. M. 1917- DLB33

Hergesheimer, Joseph 1880-1954 ....DLB9

Heritage Press..................................DLB46

Hernton, Calvin C. 1932- DLB38

The Hero as Poet. Dante; Shakspeare (1841),
    by Thomas Carlyle........................DLB32

Herrick, Robert 1868-1938..................DLB9, 12

Herrick, William 1915- Y83

Herrmann, John 1900-1959...................DLB4

Hersey, John 1914- DLB6

Hewat, Alexander circa 1743-circa 1824........DLB30

Hewitt, John 1907- DLB27

Hewlett, Maurice 1861-1923..................DLB34

Heyen, William 1940- DLB5

Heyward, Dorothy 1890-1961 and
    Heyward, DuBose 1885-1940 ....DLB7

Heyward, DuBose 1885-1940.............DLB7, 9, 45

Higgins, Aidan 1927- DLB14

Higgins, Colin 1941- DLB26

Higgins, George V. 1939- DLB2; Y81

Higginson, Thomas Wentworth 1822-1911...... DLB1

Hildreth, Richard 1807-1865 .... DLB1, 30

Hill, Geoffrey 1932- DLB40

Hill, "Sir" John 1714?-1775.................... DLB39

Hill, Lawrence, and Company Publishers....... DLB46

Hill, Susan 1942- DLB14

Hill, Walter 1942- DLB44

Hill and Wang.................................. DLB46

Hilton, James 1900-1954 .... DLB34

Himes, Chester 1909-1984.................... DLB2

The History of the Adventures of Joseph Andrews
(1742), by Henry Fielding [excerpt]........ DLB39

Hoagland, Edward 1932- DLB6

Hoagland, Everett H. III 1942- DLB41

Hobsbaum, Philip 1932- DLB40

Hobson, Laura Z. 1900- DLB28

Hochman, Sandra 1936- DLB5

Hodgman, Helen 1945- DLB14

Hodgson, Ralph 1871-1962.................... DLB19

Hoffenstein, Samuel 1890-1947 .... DLB11

Hoffman, Charles Fenno 1806-1884............ DLB3

Hoffman, Daniel 1923- DLB5

Hofmann, Michael 1957- DLB40

Hofstadter, Richard 1916-1970................ DLB17

Hogan, Desmond 1950- DLB14

Holbrook, David 1923- DLB14, 40

Holcroft, Thomas 1745-1809................. DLB39

Holden, Molly 1927-1981..................... DLB40

Holiday House DLB46

Hollander, John 1929- DLB5

Holley, Marietta 1836-1926.................... DLB11

Hollo, Anselm 1934- DLB40

Holloway, John 1920- DLB27

Holloway House Publishing Company......... DLB46

Holme, Constance 1880-1955................. DLB34

Holmes, Oliver Wendell 1809-1894............ DLB1

Holmes, John Clellon 1926- DLB16

Holst, Hermann E. von 1841-1904 .... DLB47

Holt, John 1721-1784 .... DLB43

Holt, Rinehart and Winston................... DLB46

Home, Henry, Lord Kames 1696-1782........ DLB31

Home, William Douglas 1912- DLB13

Homes, Geoffrey (see Mainwaring, Daniel)

Honig, Edwin 1919- DLB5

Hooker, Jeremy 1941- DLB40

Hooker, Thomas 1586-1647................... DLB24

Hooper, Johnson Jones 1815-1862 .... DLB3, 11

Hopkins, Gerard Manley 1844-1889........... DLB35

Hopkins, John H., and Son.................... DLB46

Hopkins, Lemuel 1750-1801................... DLB37

Hopkins, Samuel 1721-1803................... DLB31

Hopkinson, Francis 1737-1791 .... DLB31

Horizon Press DLB46

Horne, Richard Henry (Hengist) 1802
or 1803-1884............................. DLB32

Horovitz, Israel 1939- DLB7

Hough, Emerson 1857-1923................... DLB9

Houghton, Stanley 1881-1913 .... DLB10

Housman, A. E. 1859-1936................... DLB19

Housman, Laurence 1865-1959 .... DLB10

Howard, Maureen 1930- Y83

Howard, Richard 1929- DLB5

Howard, Roy W. 1883-1964 .... DLB29

Howard, Sidney 1891-1939.................. DLB7, 26

Howe, E. W. 1853-1937 .... DLB12, 25

Howe, Henry 1816-1893 .... DLB30

Howe, Julia Ward 1819-1910.................. DLB1

Howell, Clark, Sr. 1863-1936................. DLB25

Howell, Evan P. 1839-1905................... DLB23

Howell, Soskin and Company DLB46

Howells, William Dean 1837-1920............. DLB12

Hoyem, Andrew 1935- DLB5

Hubbard, Kin 1868-1930...................... DLB11

Hubbard, William circa 1621-1704 .... DLB24

Huebsch, B. W. [publishing house]............ DLB46

Hughes, David 1930- DLB14

Hughes, Langston 1902-1967................. DLB4, 7

Hughes, Richard 1900-1976................... DLB15

Hughes, Ted 1930- DLB40

Hughes, Thomas 1822-1896................... DLB18

Hugo, Richard 1923-1982 .... DLB5

Hugo Awards and Nebula Awards DLB8

Hulme, T. E. 1883-1917..................... DLB19

Humorous Book Illustration................... DLB11

Humphrey, William 1924- DLB6

Humphreys, David 1752-1818................ DLB37

Humphreys, Emyr 1919- DLB15

Huncke, Herbert 1915- DLB16

Hunter, Evan 1926- Y82

Hunter, Jim 1939- DLB14

Hunter, Kristin 1931- DLB33

Hunter, N. C. 1908-1971 .... DLB10

Huston, John 1906- DLB26

Hutchinson, Francis 1694-1746................ DLB31

Hutchinson, Thomas 1711-1780........... DLB30, 31

Huxley, Aldous 1894-1963 .... DLB36

I

The Iconography of Science-Fiction Art......... DLB8

Ignatow, David 1914- DLB5

Imbs, Bravig 1904-1946 .... DLB4

Inchbald, Elizabeth 1753-1821................. DLB39

Inge, William 1913-1973 .... DLB7

Ingelow, Jean 1820-1897 .... DLB35

The Ingersoll Prizes Y84

Ingraham, Joseph Holt 1809-1860 .... DLB3

International Publishers Company............. DLB46

Introductory Essay: *Letters of Percy Bysshe Shelley* (1852), by Robert Browning......... DLB32

Introductory Letters from the Second Edition of *Pamela* (1741), by Samuel Richardson ... DLB39

Irving, John 1942- DLB6; Y82

Irving, Washington 1783-1859 ....DLB3, 11, 30

Irwin, Will 1873-1948 .... DLB25

Isherwood, Christopher 1904-1986 .... DLB15

The Island Trees Case: A Symposium on School Library Censorship...................... Y82

    An Interview with Judith Krug Y82

An Interview with Phyllis Schlafly............ Y82

An Interview with Edward B. Jenkinson...... Y82

An Interview with Lamarr Mooneyham....... Y82

An Interview with Harriet Bernstein......... Y82

J

Jackmon, Marvin E. (see Marvin X)

Jackson, Angela 1951- DLB41

Jackson, Helen Hunt 1830-1885............ DLB42, 47

Jackson, Shirley 1919-1965 .... DLB6

Jacob, Piers Anthony Dillingham (see Anthony, Piers)

Jacobson, Dan 1929- DLB14

Jakes, John 1932- Y83

James, Henry 1843-1916 .... DLB12

James, John circa 1633-1729 .... DLB24

James Joyce Centenary: Dublin, 1982 .... Y82

Jameson, J. Franklin 1859-1937 .... DLB17

Jameson, Storm 1891- DLB36

Jay, John 1745-1829.......................... DLB31

Jeffers, Lance 1919-1985 .... DLB41

Jeffers, Robinson 1887-1962................... DLB45

Jefferson, Thomas 1743-1826 .... DLB31

Jellicoe, Ann 1927- DLB13

Jenkins, Robin 1912- DLB14

Jenkins, William Fitzgerald (see Leinster, Murray)

Jennings, Elizabeth 1926- DLB27

Jensen, Merrill 1905-1980 .... DLB17

Jerome, Jerome K. 1859-1927 .... DLB10, 34

Jewett, Sarah Orne 1849-1909................. DLB12

Jewsbury, Geraldine 1812-1880................ DLB21

Joans, Ted 1928- DLB16, 41

Johnson, B. S. 1933-1973................... DLB14, 40

Johnson, Charles R. 1948- DLB33

Johnson, Diane 1934- Y80

Johnson, Edward 1598-1672................... DLB24

Johnson, Fenton 1888-1958 .... DLB45

Johnson, Gerald W. 1890-1980................ DLB29

Johnson, Lionel 1867-1902 .... DLB19

Johnson, Nunnally 1897-1977 .... DLB26

Johnson, Pamela Hansford 1912- DLB15

Johnson, Samuel 1696-1772 .... DLB24

Johnson, Samuel 1709-1784 .... DLB39

Johnson, Samuel 1822-1882 .... DLB1

Johnston, Annie Fellows 1863-1931 .... DLB42

Johnston, Denis 1901-1984 .... DLB10

Johnston, Jennifer 1930- DLB14

Johnston, Mary 1870-1936 .... DLB9

Johnstone, Charles 1719?-1800? DLB39

Jolas, Eugene 1894-1952 .... DLB4, 45

Jones, Charles C., Jr. 1831-1893 .... DLB30

Jones, David 1895-1974 .... DLB20

Jones, Ebenezer 1820-1860 .... DLB32

Jones, Ernest 1819-1868 .... DLB32

Jones, Gayl 1949- DLB33

Jones, Glyn 1905- DLB15

Jones, Gwyn 1907- DLB15

Jones, Henry Arthur 1851-1929 .... DLB10

Jones, Hugh circa 1692-1760 .... DLB24

Jones, James 1921-1977 .... DLB2

Jones, LeRoi (see Baraka, Amiri)

Jones, Lewis 1897-1939 .... DLB15

Jones, Major Joseph (see Thompson, William
    Tappan)

Jones, Preston 1936-1979 .... DLB7

Jong, Erica 1942- DLB2, 5, 28

Jordan, June 1936- DLB38

Joseph, Jenny 1932- DLB40

Josephson, Matthew 1899-1978 .... DLB4

Josiah Allen's Wife (see Holley, Marietta)

Josipovici, Gabriel 1940- DLB14

Josselyn, John ?-1675 .... DLB24

Joyce, Adrien (see Eastman, Carol)

Joyce, James 1882-1941 .... DLB10, 19, 36

Judd, Sylvester 1813-1853 .... DLB1

June, Jennie (see Croly, Jane Cunningham)

Justice, Donald 1925- Y83

K

Kalechofsky, Roberta 1931- DLB28

Kaler, James Otis 1848-1912 .... DLB12

Kandel, Lenore 1932- DLB16

Kanin, Garson 1912- DLB7

Kantor, Mackinlay 1904-1977 .... DLB9

Kaplan, Johanna 1942- DLB28

Katz, Steve 1935- Y83

Kaufman, Bob 1925- DLB16, 41

Kaufman, George S. 1889-1961 .... DLB7

Kavanagh, Patrick 1904-1967 .... DLB15, 20

Kavanagh, P. J. 1931- DLB40

Kaye-Smith, Sheila 1887-1956 .... DLB36

Keane, John B. 1928- DLB13

Keble, John 1792-1866 .... DLB32

Keeble, John 1944- Y83

Keeffe, Barrie 1945- DLB13

Keeley, James 1867-1934 .... DLB25

Kelley, Edith Summers 1884-1956 .... DLB9

Kelley, William Melvin 1937- DLB33

Kellogg, Ansel Nash 1832-1886 .... DLB23

Kelly, George 1887-1974 .... DLB7

Kelly, Robert 1935- DLB5

Kemble, Fanny 1809-1893 .... DLB32

Kemelman, Harry 1908- DLB28

Kendall, Claude [publishing company] DLB46

Kendell, George 1809-1867 .... DLB43

Kennedy, Adrienne 1931- DLB38

Kennedy, John Pendleton 1795-1870 .... DLB3

Kennedy, Margaret 1896-1967 .... DLB36

Kennedy, X. J. 1929- DLB5

Kennelly, Brendan 1936- DLB40

Kennerley, Mitchell [publishing house] DLB46

Kent, Frank R. 1877-1958 .... DLB29

Kerouac, Jack 1922-1969 .... DLB2, 16; DS3

Kerouac, Jan 1952- DLB16

Kerr, Orpheus C. (see Newell, Robert Henry)

Kesey, Ken 1935- DLB2, 16

Kiely, Benedict 1919- DLB15

Kiley, Jed 1889-1962 .... DLB4

Killens, John Oliver 1916- DLB33

Kilmer, Joyce 1886-1918 .... DLB45

King, Clarence 1842-1901 .... DLB12

King, Francis 1923- DLB15

King, Grace 1852-1932 .... DLB12

King, Stephen 1947- Y80

King, Woodie, Jr. 1937- DLB38

Kingsley, Charles 1819-1875............... DLB21, 32

Kingsley, Henry 1830-1876.................... DLB21

Kingsley, Sidney 1906- DLB7

Kingston, Maxine Hong 1940- Y80

Kinnell, Galway 1927- DLB5

Kinsella, Thomas 1928- DLB27

Kipling, Rudyard 1865-1936 .... DLB19, 34

Kirkland, Caroline 1801-1864 .... DLB3

Kirkland, Joseph 1830-1893.................... DLB12

Kirkup, James 1918- DLB27

Kizer, Carolyn 1925- DLB5

Klappert, Peter 1945- DLB5

Klass, Philip (see Tenn, William)

Knickerbocker, Diedrich (see Irving, Washington)

Knight, Damon 1922- DLB8

Knight, Etheridge 1931- DLB41

Knight, John S. 1894-1981 .... DLB29

Knight, Sarah Kemble 1666-1727 .... DLB24

Knoblock, Edward 1874-1945 .... DLB10

Knopf, Alfred A. 1892-1984..................... Y84

Knopf, Alfred A. [publishing house] DLB46

Knowles, John 1926- DLB6

Knox, Frank 1874-1944 .... DLB29

Knox, John Armoy 1850-1906................. DLB23

Kober, Arthur 1900-1975 .... DLB11

Koch, Howard 1902- DLB26

Koch, Kenneth 1925- DLB5

Koenigsberg, Moses 1879-1945................. DLB25

Koestler, Arthur 1905-1983 .... Y83

Komroff, Manuel 1890-1974 .... DLB4

Kopit, Arthur 1937- DLB7

Kops, Bernard 1926?- DLB13

Kornbluth, C. M. 1923-1958.................... DLB8

Kosinski, Jerzy 1933- DLB2; Y82

Kraf, Elaine 1946- Y81

Krasna, Norman 1909-1984 .... DLB26

Kreymborg, Alfred 1883-1966.................. DLB4

Krim, Seymour 1922- DLB16

Krock, Arthur 1886-1974...................... DLB29

Kubrick, Stanley 1928- DLB26

Kumin, Maxine 1925- DLB5

Kunjufu, Johari M. (see Amini, Johari M.)

Kupferberg, Tuli 1923- DLB16

Kuttner, Henry 1915-1958 .... DLB8

Kyger, Joanne 1934- DLB16

L

Ladd, Joseph Brown 1764-1786................ DLB37

La Farge, Oliver 1901-1963 .... DLB9

Lafferty, R. A. 1914- DLB8

Laird, Carobeth 1895- Y82

Lamantia, Philip 1927- DLB16

L'Amour, Louis 1908?- Y80

Lancer Books.................................. DLB46

Landesman, Jay 1919- and
   Landesman, Fran 1927- DLB16

Lane, Charles 1800-1870 .... DLB1

Lane, Pinkie Gordon 1923- DLB41

Laney, Al 1896- DLB4

Lanham, Edwin 1904-1979 .... DLB4

Lardner, Ring 1885-1933.................. DLB11, 25

Lardner, Ring, Jr. 1915- DLB26

Larkin, Philip 1922- DLB27

Lathrop, Dorothy P. 1891-1980 .... DLB22

Lathrop, John, Jr. 1772-1820.................. DLB37

Latimore, Jewel Christine McLawler (see Amini,
   Johari M.)

Laumer, Keith 1925- DLB8

Laurents, Arthur 1918- DLB26

Laurie, Annie (see Black, Winifred)

Lavin, Mary 1912- DLB15

Lawrence, David 1888-1973 .... DLB29

Lawrence, D. H. 1885-1930 .... DLB10, 19, 36

Lawson, John ?-1711 .... DLB24

Lawson, Robert 1892-1957 .... DLB22

Lawson, Victor F. 1850-1925 .... DLB25

Lea, Henry Charles 1825-1909 .... DLB47

Lea, Tom 1907- DLB6

Leacock, John 1729-1802...................... DLB31

Lear, Edward 1812-1888 .... DLB32

Leary, Timothy 1920- DLB16

Lectures on Rhetoric and Belles Lettres (1783),
    by Hugh Blair [excerpts].................. DLB31

Lederer, Charles 1910-1976 .... DLB26

Ledwidge, Francis 1887-1917.................. DLB20

Lee, Don L. (see Madhubuti, Haki R.)

Lee, Harper 1926- DLB6

Lee, Harriet (1757-1851) and
    Lee, Sophia (1750-1824) DLB39

Lee, Laurie 1914- DLB27

Le Fanu, Joseph Sheridan 1814-1873 .... DLB21

Leffland, Ella 1931- Y84

Le Gallienne, Richard 1866-1947............... DLB4

Legare, Hugh Swinton 1797-1843.............. DLB3

Legare, James M. 1823-1859 .... DLB3

Le Guin, Ursula K. 1929- DLB8

Lehman, Ernest 1920- DLB44

Lehmann, John 1907- DLB27

Lehmann, Rosamond 1901- DLB15

Leiber, Fritz 1910- DLB8

Leinster, Murray 1896-1975................... DLB8

Leitch, Maurice 1933- DLB14

Leland, Charles G. 1824-1903 .... DLB11

Lennart, Isobel 1915-1971..................... DLB44

Lennox, Charlotte 1729 or 1730-1804......... DLB39

Lenski, Lois 1893-1974 .... DLB22

Leonard, Hugh 1926- DLB13

Lerner, Max 1902- DLB29

Leslie, Frank 1821-1880 .... DLB43

Lessing, Bruno 1870-1940..................... DLB28

Lessing, Doris 1919- DLB15

Letter to [Samuel] Richardson on *Clarissa*
    (1748), by Henry Fielding.................. DLB39

Lever, Charles 1806-1872 .... DLB21

Levertov, Denise 1923- DLB5

Levi, Peter 1931- DLB40

Levien, Sonya 1888-1960...................... DLB44

Levin, Meyer 1905-1981................ DLB9, 28; Y81

Levine, Philip 1928- DLB5

Levy, Benn Wolfe 1900-1973............. DLB13; Y81

Lewis, Alfred H. 1857-1914 .... DLB25

Lewis, Alun 1915-1944 .... DLB20

Lewis, C. Day (see Day Lewis, C.)

Lewis, Charles B. 1842-1924.................. DLB11

Lewis, C. S. 1898-1963 .... DLB15

Lewis, Henry Clay 1825-1850 .... DLB3

Lewis, Matthew Gregory 1775-1818 .... DLB39

Lewis, Richard circa 1700-1734................ DLB24

Lewis, Sinclair 1885-1951.................. DLB9; DS1

Lewis, Wyndham 1882-1957................... DLB15

Lewisohn, Ludwig 1882-1955............. DLB4, 9, 28

The Library of America DLB46

Liebling, A. J. 1904-1963 .... DLB4

Limited Editions Club DLB46

Lindsay, Jack 1900- Y84

Linebarger, Paul Myron Anthony (see
    Smith, Cordwainer)

Link, Arthur S. 1920- DLB17

Linn, John Blair 1777-1804 .... DLB37

Linton, Eliza Lynn 1822-1898 .... DLB18

Linton, William James 1812-1897 .... DLB32

Lion Books DLB46

Lippincott, Sara Jane Clarke 1823-1904 .... DLB43

Lippmann, Walter 1889-1974 .... DLB29

Lipton, Lawrence 1898-1975 .... DLB16

Literary Effects of World War II
    [British novel]............................. DLB15

Literary Prizes [British]....................... DLB15

Literary Research Archives: The Humanities
    Research Center, University of Texas........ Y82

Literary Research Archives II: Berg
    Collection of English and American Literature
    of the New York Public Library.............. Y83

Literary Research Archives III:
The Lilly Library............................ Y84

Literature at Nurse, or Circulating Morals (1885),
by George Moore DLB18

Littlewood, Joan 1914- DLB13

Lively, Penelope 1933- DLB14

Livings, Henry 1929- DLB13

Livingston, Anne Howe 1763-1841 .... DLB37

Livingston, William 1723-1790 .... DLB31

Llewellyn, Richard 1906-1983 .... DLB15

Lochridge, Betsy Hopkins (see Fancher, Betsy)

Locke, David Ross 1833-1888.............. DLB11, 23

Locke, John 1632-1704........................ DLB31

Locke, Richard Adams 1800-1871.............. DLB43

Locker-Lampson, Frederick 1821-1895........ DLB35

Lockridge, Ross, Jr. 1914-1948 .... Y80

Lodge, David 1935- DLB14

Lodge, Henry Cabot 1850-1924 .... DLB47

Loeb, Harold 1891-1974........................ DLB4

Logan, James 1674-1751 .... DLB24

Logan, John 1923- DLB5

Logue, Christopher 1926- DLB27

London, Jack 1876-1916.....................DLB8, 12

Long, Haniel 1888-1956....................... DLB45

Longfellow, Henry Wadsworth 1807-1882....... DLB1

Longfellow, Samuel 1819-1892 .... DLB1

Longley, Michael 1939- DLB40

Longstreet, Augustus Baldwin 1790-1870 ....DLB3, 11

Lonsdale, Frederick 1881-1954................ DLB10

A Look at the Contemporary Black Theatre
Movement................................ DLB38

Loos, Anita 1893-1981................DLB11, 26; Y81

Lopate, Phillip 1943- Y80

The Lord Chamberlain's Office and Stage
Censorship in England.................... DLB10

Lorde, Andre 1934- DLB41

Loring and Mussey........................... DLB46

Lossing, Benson J. 1813-1891 .... DLB30

Lothrop, Harriet M. 1844-1924 .... DLB42

The Lounger, no. 20 (1785), by Henry
Mackenzie.............................. DLB39

Lovingood, Sut (see Harris, George Washington)

Low, Samuel 1765-? DLB37

Lowell, James Russell 1819-1891 ....DLB1, 11

Lowell, Robert 1917-1977 .... DLB5

Lowenfels, Walter 1897-1976................... DLB4

Lowry, Malcolm 1909-1957..................... DLB15

Loy, Mina 1882-1966........................... DLB4

Luce, John W., and Company DLB46

Lucie-Smith, Edward 1933- DLB40

Ludlum, Robert 1927- Y82

Luke, Peter 1919- DLB13

Lurie, Alison 1926- DLB2

Lyon, Matthew 1749-1822..................... DLB43

Lytle, Andrew 1902- DLB6

Lytton, Edward (see Bulwer-Lytton, Edward)

Lytton, Edward Robert Bulwer 1831-1891 ..... DLB32

M

Mac A'Ghobhainn, Iain (see Smith, Iain Crichton)

MacArthur, Charles 1895-1956..........DLB7, 25, 44

Macaulay, Rose 1881-1958..................... DLB36

Macaulay, Thomas Babington 1800-1859....... DLB32

Macaulay Company........................... DLB46

MacBeth, George 1932- DLB40

MacCaig, Norman 1910- DLB27

MacDiarmid, Hugh 1892-1978 .... DLB20

MacDonald, George 1824-1905................. DLB18

MacDonald, John D. 1916- DLB8

Macfadden, Bernarr 1868-1955 .... DLB25

Machen, Arthur Llewelyn Jones 1863-1947 .... DLB36

MacInnes, Colin 1914-1976.................... DLB14

Macken, Walter 1915-1967 .... DLB13

Mackenzie, Compton 1883-1972............... DLB34

Mackenzie, Henry 1745-1831.................. DLB39

Mackey, William Wellington 1937- DLB38

MacLean, Katherine Anne 1925- DLB8

MacLeish, Archibald 1892-1982 ..... DLB4, 7, 45; Y82

Macleod, Norman 1906- DLB4

MacNamara, Brinsley 1890-1963 .... DLB10

MacNeice, Louis 1907-1963 .... DLB10, 20

Macpherson, Jeanie 1884-1946 . . . . DLB44

Macrae Smith Company DLB46

Macy-Masius DLB46

Madden, David 1933- DLB6

Maddow, Ben 1909- DLB44

Madhubuti, Haki R. 1942- DLB5, 41

Madison, James 1751-1836 . . . . DLB37

Mahan, Alfred Thayer 1840-1914 . . . . DLB47

Mahin, John Lee 1902-1984 . . . . DLB44

Mahon, Derek 1941- DLB40

Mailer, Norman 1923-
. . . . DLB2, 16, 28; Y80, 83; DS3

Main Selections of the Book-of-the-Month Club,
1926-1945 . . . . DLB9

Main Trends in Twentieth-Century
Book Clubs DLB46

Mainwaring, Daniel 1902-1977 . . . . DLB44

Major, Clarence 1936- DLB33

Major Books DLB46

Makemie, Francis circa 1658-1708 . . . . DLB24

Malamud, Bernard 1914- DLB2, 28; Y80

Mallock, W. H. 1849-1923 . . . . DLB18

Malone, Dumas 1892- DLB17

Malzberg, Barry N. 1939- DLB8

Mamet, David 1947- DLB7

Manfred, Frederick 1912- DLB6

Mangan, Sherry 1904-1961 . . . . DLB4

Mankiewicz, Herman 1897-1953 . . . . DLB26

Mankiewicz, Joseph L. 1909- DLB44

Mankowitz, Wolf 1924- DLB15

Manley, Delarivière 1672?-1724 . . . . DLB39

Mann, Abby 1927- DLB44

Mann, Horace 1796-1859 . . . . DLB1

Manning, Marie 1873?-1945 . . . . DLB29

Mano, D. Keith 1942- DLB6

Manor Books DLB46

March, William 1893-1954 . . . . DLB9

Marcus, Frank 1928- DLB13

Marek, Richard, Books DLB46

Marion, Frances 1886-1973 . . . . DLB44

The Mark Taper Forum DLB7

Markfield, Wallace 1926- DLB2, 28

Marquand, John P. 1893-1960 . . . . DLB9

Marquis, Don 1878-1937 . . . . DLB11, 25

Marryat, Frederick 1792-1848 . . . . DLB21

Marsh, George Perkins 1801-1882 . . . . DLB1

Marsh, James 1794-1842 . . . . DLB1

Marshall, Edward 1932- DLB16

Marshall, Paule 1929- DLB33

Marston, Philip Bourke 1850-1887 . . . . DLB35

Martin, Abe (see Hubbard, Kin)

Martineau, Harriet 1802-1876 . . . . DLB21

Martyn, Edward 1859-1923 . . . . DLB10

Marvin X 1944- DLB38

Marzials, Theo 1850-1920 . . . . DLB35

Masefield, John 1878-1967 . . . . DLB10, 19

Massey, Gerald 1828-1907 . . . . DLB32

Mather, Cotton 1663-1728 . . . . DLB24, 30

Mather, Richard 1596-1669 . . . . DLB24

Matheson, Richard 1926- DLB8, 44

Mathews, Cornelius 1817-1889 . . . . DLB3

Mathias, Roland 1915- DLB27

Mathis, June 1892-1927 . . . . DLB44

Mathis, Sharon Bell 1937- DLB33

Matthews, Jack 1925- DLB6

Matthews, William 1942- DLB5

Matthiessen, Peter 1927- DLB6

Maugham, W. Somerset 1874-1965 . . . . DLB10, 36

Maury, James 1718-1769 . . . . DLB31

Mavor, Elizabeth 1927- DLB14

Mavor, Osborne Henry (see Bridie, James)

Maxwell, William 1908- Y80

May, Elaine 1932- DLB44

Mayer, O. B. 1818-1891 . . . . DLB3

Mayes, Wendell 1919- DLB26

Mayfield, Julian 1928-1984 . . . . DLB33; Y84

Mayhew, Henry 1812-1887 . . . . DLB18

Mayhew, Jonathan 1720-1766 . . . . DLB31

Mayor, Flora Macdonald 1872-1932 . . . . DLB36

Mazursky, Paul 1930- DLB44

McAlmon, Robert 1896-1956 . . . . DLB4, 45

McBride, Robert M., and Company DLB46

McCaffrey, Anne 1926- DLB8

McCarthy, Cormac 1933- DLB6

McCarthy, Mary 1912- DLB2; Y81

McCay, Winsor 1871-1934.................... DLB22

McClatchy, C. K. 1858-1936.................. DLB25

McCloskey, Robert 1914- DLB22

McClure, Joanna 1930- DLB16

McClure, Michael 1932- DLB16

McClure, Phillips and Company.............. DLB46

McCluskey, John A., Jr. 1944- DLB33

McCorkle, Samuel Eusebius 1746-1811........ DLB37

McCormick, Anne O'Hare 1880-1954 .... DLB29

McCormick, Robert R. 1880-1955 .... DLB29

McCoy, Horace 1897-1955 .... DLB9

McCullagh, Joseph B. 1842-1896.............. DLB23

McCullers, Carson 1917-1967 ....DLB2, 7

McDonald, Forrest 1927- DLB17

McDowell, Obolensky.......................... DLB46

McEwan, Ian 1948- DLB14

McGahern, John 1934- DLB14

McGeehan, W. O. 1879-1933 .... DLB25

McGill, Ralph 1898-1969 .... DLB29

McGinley, Phyllis 1905-1978................... DLB11

McGough, Roger 1937- DLB40

McGraw-Hill................................... DLB46

McGuane, Thomas 1939- DLB2; Y80

McGuckian, Medbh 1950- DLB40

McGuffey, William Holmes 1800-1873 .... DLB42

McIlvanney, William 1936- DLB14

McIntyre, O. O. 1884-1938................... DLB25

McKay, Claude 1889-1948...................DLB4, 45

McKean, William V. 1820-1903................ DLB23

McLaverty, Michael 1907- DLB15

McLean, John R. 1848-1916................... DLB23

McLean, William L. 1852-1931 .... DLB25

McMaster, John Bach 1852-1932 .... DLB47

McMurtry, Larry 1936- DLB2; Y80

McNally, Terrence 1939- DLB7

McPherson, James Alan 1943- DLB38

Mead, Matthew 1924- DLB40

Mead, Taylor ?- DLB16

Medill, Joseph 1823-1899...................... DLB43

Medoff, Mark 1940- DLB7

Meek, Alexander Beaufort 1814-1865........... DLB3

Meinke, Peter 1932- DLB5

Meltzer, David 1937- DLB16

Melville, Herman 1819-1891 .... DLB3

Mencken, H. L. 1880-1956 .... DLB11, 29

Mercer, David 1928-1980...................... DLB13

Mercer, John 1704-1768....................... DLB31

Meredith, George 1828-1909 .... DLB18, 35

Meredith, Owen (see Lytton, Edward Robert Bulwer)

Meredith, William 1919- DLB5

Meriwether, Louise 1923- DLB33

Merrill, James 1926- DLB5

Merton, Thomas 1915-1968 .... Y81

Merwin, W. S. 1927- DLB5

Messner, Julian [publishing house] DLB46

Mew, Charlotte 1869-1928...................... DLB19

Mewshaw, Michael 1943- Y80

Meyer, Eugene 1875-1959...................... DLB29

Meynell, Alice 1847-1922...................... DLB19

Micheline, Jack 1929- DLB16

Michener, James A. 1907?- DLB6

Micklejohn, George circa 1717-1818............ DLB31

Middleton, Christopher 1926- DLB40

Middleton, Stanley 1919- DLB14

Milius, John 1944- DLB44

Millar, Kenneth 1915-1983 ....DLB2; Y83

Millay, Edna St. Vincent 1892-1950 .... DLB45

Miller, Arthur 1915- DLB7

Miller, Caroline 1903- DLB9

Miller, Eugene Ethelbert 1950- DLB41

Miller, Henry 1891-1980 .... DLB4, 9; Y80

Miller, Jason 1939- DLB7

Miller, May 1899- DLB41

Miller, Perry 1905-1963 .... DLB17

Miller, Walter M., Jr. 1923- DLB8

Miller, Webb 1892-1940 .... DLB29

Millhauser, Steven 1943- DLB2

Millican, Arthenia J. Bates 1920- DLB38

Milne, A. A. 1882-1956........................ DLB10

Milner, Ron 1938- DLB38

Milnes, Richard Monckton (Lord Houghton)
    1809-1885................................. DLB32

Minton, Balch and Company DLB46

Mitchel, Jonathan 1624-1668 .... DLB24

Mitchell, Adrian 1932- DLB40

Mitchell, Donald Grant 1822-1908............. DLB1

Mitchell, James Leslie 1901-1935 .... DLB15

Mitchell, Julian 1935- DLB14

Mitchell, Langdon 1862-1935.................. DLB7

Mitchell, Loften 1919- DLB38

Mitchell, Margaret 1900-1949 .... DLB9

Modern Age Books........................... DLB46

The Modern Language Association of America
    Celebrates Its Centennial.................... Y84

The Modern Library DLB46

Modern Novelists—Great and Small (1855), by
    Margaret Oliphant DLB21

The Modernists (1932), by Joseph Warren
    Beach DLB36

Moffat, Yard and Company DLB46

Monkhouse, Allan 1858-1936.................. DLB10

Monro, Harold 1879-1932.................... DLB19

Monsarrat, Nicholas 1910-1979................ DLB15

Montague, John 1929- DLB40

Montgomery, John 1919- DLB16

Montgomery, Marion 1925- DLB6

Moody, Joshua circa 1633-1697 .... DLB24

Moody, William Vaughn 1869-1910............ DLB7

Moorcock, Michael 1939- DLB14

Moore, Catherine L. 1911- DLB8

Moore, Clement Clarke 1779-1863 .... DLB42

Moore, George 1852-1933.................. DLB10, 18

Moore, Marianne 1887-1972 .... DLB45

Moore, T. Sturge 1870-1944 .... DLB19

Moore, Ward 1903-1978....................... DLB8

Morgan, Berry 1919- DLB6

Morgan, Charles 1894-1958 .... DLB34

Morgan, Edmund S. 1916- DLB17

Morgan, Edwin 1920- DLB27

Morison, Samuel Eliot 1887-1976.............. DLB17

Morley, Christopher 1890-1957 .... DLB9

Morris, Lewis 1833-1907 .... DLB35

Morris, Richard B. 1904- DLB17

Morris, William 1834-1896 .... DLB18, 35

Morris, Willie 1934- Y80

Morris, Wright 1910- DLB2; Y81

Morrison, Toni 1931- DLB6, 33; Y81

Morrow, William, and Company............... DLB46

Morse, Jedidiah 1761-1826 .... DLB37

Morse, John T., Jr. 1840-1937................. DLB47

Mortimer, John 1923- DLB13

Morton, Nathaniel 1613-1685 .... DLB24

Morton, Sarah Wentworth 1759-1846 .... DLB37

Morton, Thomas circa 1579-circa 1647........ DLB24

Mosley, Nicholas 1923- DLB14

Moss, Arthur 1889-1969....................... DLB4

Moss, Howard 1922- DLB5

The Most Powerful Book Review in America
    [*New York Times Book Review*] Y82

Motion, Andrew 1952- DLB40

Motley, John Lothrop 1814-1877............DLB1, 30

Mottram, R. H. 1883-1971.................... DLB36

Movies from Books, 1920-1974.................. DLB9

Mowrer, Edgar Ansel 1892-1977 .... DLB29

Mowrer, Paul Scott 1887-1971................. DLB29

Muhajir, El (see Marvin X)

Muhajir, Nazzam Al Fitnah (see Marvin X)

Muir, Edwin 1887-1959 .... DLB20

Muir, Helen 1937- DLB14

Muldoon, Paul 1951- DLB40

Munby, Arthur Joseph 1828-1910............. DLB35

Munford, Robert circa 1737-1783 .... DLB31

Munro, H. H. 1870-1916..................... DLB34

Munroe, Kirk 1850-1930 .... DLB42

Munsey, Frank A. 1854-1925................. DLB25

Murdoch, Iris 1919- DLB14

Murfree, Mary N. 1850-1922................. DLB12

Murphy, Richard 1927- DLB40

Murray, Albert L. 1916- DLB38

Murray, Gilbert 1866-1957 .... DLB10

Murray, Judith Sargent 1751-1820 .... DLB37

Murray, Pauli 1910-1985 .... DLB41

Myers, Gustavus 1872-1942................... DLB47

Myers, L. H. 1881-1944 .... DLB15

Myers, Walter Dean 1937- DLB33

N

Nabokov, Vladimir 1899-1977 .... DLB2; Y80; DS3

Nabokov Festival at Cornell Y83

Nasby, Petroleum Vesuvius (see Locke, David Ross)

Nash, Ogden 1902-1971...................... DLB11

Nathan, Robert 1894- DLB9

The National Theatre and the Royal Shakespeare
Company: The National Companies DLB13

Naughton, Bill 1910- DLB13

Neagoe, Peter 1881-1960...................... DLB4

Neal, John 1793-1876 .... DLB1

Neal, Joseph C. 1807-1847 .... DLB11

Neal, Larry 1937-1981........................ DLB38

Neihardt, John G. 1881-1973................... DLB9

Nelson, William Rockhill 1841-1915........... DLB23

Nemerov, Howard 1920- DLB5, 6; Y83

Neugeboren, Jay 1938- DLB28

Nevins, Allan 1890-1971....................... DLB17

The New American Library DLB46

New Directions Publishing Corporation DLB46

New Forces at Work in the American Theatre:
1915-1925................................ DLB7

The New *Ulysses* Y84

A New Voice: The Center for the Book's First
Five Years................................... Y83

The New Wave [Science Fiction] DLB8

Newbolt, Henry 1862-1938.................... DLB19

Newby, P. H. 1918- DLB15

Newcomb, Charles King 1820-1894 .... DLB1

Newell, Peter 1862-1924...................... DLB42

Newell, Robert Henry 1836-1901.............. DLB11

Newman, David (see Benton, Robert)

Newman, Frances 1883-1928 .... Y80

Newman, John Henry 1801-1890........... DLB18, 32

Newspaper Syndication of American Humor... DLB11

Nichols, Dudley 1895-1960 .... DLB26

Nichols, John 1940- Y82

Nichols, Mary Sargeant (Neal) Gove
1810-1884................................. DLB1

Nichols, Peter 1927- DLB13

Nichols, Roy F. 1896-1973..................... DLB17

Nicholson, Norman 1914- DLB27

Ní Chuilleanáin, Eiléan 1942- DLB40

Nicolay, John G. 1832-1901 and
Hay, John 1838-1905 .... DLB47

Niebuhr, Reinhold 1892-1971 .... DLB17

Nieman, Lucius W. 1857-1935.................. DLB25

Niggli, Josefina 1910- Y80

Niles, Hezekiah 1777-1839 .... DLB43

Nims, John Frederick 1913- DLB5

Nin, Anaîs 1903-1977 ....DLB2, 4

Nissenson, Hugh 1933- DLB28

Niven, Larry 1938- DLB8

Nobel Prize in Literature
The 1982 Nobel Prize in Literature
Announcement by the Swedish Academy
of the Nobel Prize Y82
Nobel Lecture 1982: The Solitude of Latin
America............................... Y82
Excerpt from *One Hundred Years of
Solitude* Y82
The Magical World of Macondo......... Y82
A Tribute to Gabriel García Márquez Y82
The 1983 Nobel Prize in Literature
Announcement by the Swedish
Academy Y83
Nobel Lecture 1983 .... Y83
The Stature of William Golding Y83
The 1984 Nobel Prize in Literature.......... Y84
Announcement by the Swedish
Academy Y84
Jaroslav Seifert Through the Eyes of the
English-Speaking Reader.............. Y84
Three Poems by Jaroslav Seifert......... Y84

Noel, Roden 1834-1894 .... DLB35

Nolan, William F. 1928- DLB8

Noland, C. F. M. 1810?-1858 .... DLB11

Noonday Press..................................DLB46

Noone, John 1936- DLB14

Nordhoff, Charles 1887-1947 ....DLB9

Norman, Marsha 1947- Y84

Norris, Charles G. 1881-1945..................DLB9

Norris, Frank 1870-1902 ....DLB 12

Norris, Leslie 1921- DLB27

Norse, Harold 1916- DLB16

North Point Press.............................DLB46

Norton, Alice Mary (see Norton, Andre)

Norton, Andre 1912- DLB8

Norton, Andrews 1786-1853 ....DLB1

Norton, Caroline 1808-1877...................DLB21

Norton, Charles Eliot 1827-1908 ....DLB1

Norton, John 1606-1663.......................DLB24

Norton, W. W., and Company..................DLB46

A Note on Technique (1926), by Elizabeth
    A. Drew [excerpts].........................DLB36

Nourse, Alan E. 1928- DLB8

The Novel in [Robert Browning's] "The Ring
    and the Book" (1912), by Henry James DLB32

Novel-Reading: *The Works of Charles Dickens,*
    The Works of W. Makepeace Thackeray (1879),
    by Anthony Trollope......................DLB21

The Novels of Dorothy Richardson (1918), by
    May Sinclair.............................DLB36

Novels with a Purpose (1864), by Justin M'Carthy
    ....DLB21

Noyes, Alfred 1880-1958 ....DLB20

Noyes, Crosby S. 1825-1908 ....DLB23

Noyes, Nicholas 1647-1717 ....DLB24

Noyes, Theodore W. 1858-1946................DLB29

Nugent, Frank 1908-1965 ....DLB44

Nye, Bill 1850-1896 ....DLB11, 23

Nye, Robert 1939- DLB14

O

Oakes, Urian circa 1631-1681 ....DLB24

Oates, Joyce Carol 1938- DLB2, 5; Y81

Oberholtzer, Ellis Paxson 1868-1936 ....DLB47

O'Brien, Edna 1932- DLB14

O'Brien, Kate 1897-1974 ....DLB15

O'Brien, Tim 1946- Y80

O'Casey, Sean 1880-1964......................DLB10

Ochs, Adolph S. 1858-1935....................DLB25

O'Connor, Flannery 1925-1964.............DLB2; Y80

Odell, Jonathan 1737-1818 ....DLB31

Odets, Clifford 1906-1963...................DLB7, 26

O'Faolain, Julia 1932- DLB14

O'Faolain, Sean 1900- DLB15

O'Flaherty, Liam 1896-1984...............DLB36; Y84

Off Broadway and Off-Off-Broadway...........DLB7

Off-Loop Theatres DLB7

O'Grady, Desmond 1935- DLB40

O'Hara, Frank 1926-1966 ....DLB5, 16

O'Hara, John 1905-1970 ....DLB9; DS2

O. Henry (see Porter, William S.)

Older, Fremont 1856-1935 ....DLB25

Oliphant, Laurence 1829-1888 ....DLB18

Oliphant, Margaret 1828-1897 ....DLB18

Oliver, Chad 1928- DLB8

Oliver, Mary 1935- DLB5

Olsen, Tillie 1913?- DLB28; Y80

Olson, Charles 1910-1970 ....DLB5, 16

On Art in Fiction (1838), by Edward Bulwer ... DLB21

On Some of the Characteristics of Modern
    Poetry and On the Lyrical Poems of Alfred
    Tennyson (1831), by Arthur Henry
    Hallam...................................DLB32

O'Neill, Eugene 1888-1953 ....DLB7

Oppen, George 1908-1984 ....DLB5

Oppenheim, James 1882-1932.................DLB28

Oppenheimer, Joel 1930- DLB5

Optic, Oliver (see Adams, William Taylor)

Orlovitz, Gil 1918-1973......................DLB2, 5

Orlovsky, Peter 1933- DLB16

Ormond, John 1923- DLB27

Ornitz, Samuel 1890-1957 .... DLB28, 44

Orton, Joe 1933-1967 .... DLB13

Orwell, George 1903-1950 .... DLB15

The Orwell Year Y84

Osbon, B. S. 1827-1912 .... DLB43

Osborne, John 1929- DLB13

Osgood, Herbert L. 1855-1918 .... DLB47

O'Shaughnessy, Arthur 1844-1881 .... DLB35

Oswald, Eleazer 1755-1795 .... DLB43

Otis, James (see Kaler, James Otis)

Otis, James, Jr. 1725-1783 .... DLB31

Ottendorfer, Oswald 1826-1900 .... DLB23

Ouida 1839-1908 .... DLB18

Outing Publishing Company DLB46

Outlaw Days, by Joyce Johnson DLB16

The Overlook Press DLB46

Overview of U.S. Book Publishing, 1910-1945 ... DLB9

Owen, Guy 1925- DLB5

Owen, Wilfred 1893-1918 .... DLB20

Owsley, Frank L. 1890-1956 .... DLB17

Ozick, Cynthia 1928- DLB28; Y82

P

Pack, Robert 1929- DLB5

Padell Publishing Company DLB46

Padgett, Ron 1942- DLB5

Page, Thomas Nelson 1853-1922 .... DLB12

Pain, Philip ?-circa 1666 .... DLB24

Paine, Robert Treat, Jr. 1773-1811 .... DLB37

Paine, Thomas 1737-1809 .... DLB31, 43

Paley, Grace 1922- DLB28

Palfrey, John Gorham 1796-1881 .... DLB1, 30

Palgrave, Francis Turner 1824-1897 .... DLB35

Paltock, Robert 1697-1767 .... DLB39

Panama, Norman 1914- and
    Frank, Melvin 1913- DLB26

Pangborn, Edgar 1909-1976 .... DLB8

"Panic Among the Philistines": A Postscript,

An Interview with Bryan Griffin Y81

Panshin, Alexei 1940- DLB8

Pansy (see Alden, Isabella)

Pantheon Books DLB46

Paperback Library DLB46

Paperback Science Fiction DLB8

Parents' Magazine Press DLB46

Parke, John 1754-1789 .... DLB31

Parker, Dorothy 1893-1967 .... DLB11, 45

Parker, James 1714-1770 .... DLB43

Parker, Theodore 1810-1860 .... DLB1

Parkman, Francis, Jr. 1823-1893 .... DLB1, 30

Parks, Gordon 1912- DLB33

Parks, William 1698-1750 .... DLB43

Parley, Peter (see Goodrich, Samuel Griswold)

Parrington, Vernon L. 1871-1929 .... DLB17

Parton, James 1822-1891 .... DLB30

Parton, Sara Payson Willis 1811-1872 .... DLB43

Pastan, Linda 1932- DLB5

Pastorius, Francis Daniel 1651-circa 1720 ...... DLB24

Patchen, Kenneth 1911-1972 .... DLB16

Patmore, Coventry 1823-1896 .... DLB35

Paton, Joseph Noel 1821-1901 .... DLB35

Patrick, John 1906- DLB7

Patterson, Eleanor Medill 1881-1948 .... DLB29

Patterson, Joseph Medill 1879-1946 .... DLB29

Pattillo, Henry 1726-1801 .... DLB37

Paul, Elliot 1891-1958 .... DLB4

Paulding, James Kirke 1778-1860 .... DLB3

Paulin, Tom 1949- DLB40

Pauper, Peter, Press DLB46

Paxton, John 1911-1985 .... DLB44

Payn, James 1830-1898 .... DLB18

Payne, John 1842-1916 .... DLB35

Payne, John Howard 1791-1852 .... DLB37

Payson and Clarke DLB46

Peabody, Elizabeth Palmer 1804-1894 .... DLB1

Peachtree Publishers, Limited DLB46

Pead, Deuel ?-1727 .... DLB24

Peake, Mervyn 1911-1968 .... DLB15

Peck, George W. 1840-1916 .... DLB23, 42

Pellegrini and Cudahy.......................... DLB46

Penguin Books DLB46

Penn, William 1644-1718...................... DLB24

Penner, Jonathan 1940- Y83

Pennington, Lee 1939- Y82

Percy, Walker 1916- DLB2; Y80

Perelman, S. J. 1904-1979 .... DLB11, 44

Periodicals of the Beat Generation DLB16

Perkins, Eugene 1932- DLB41

Perkoff, Stuart Z. 1930-1974 .... DLB16

Permabooks DLB46

Perry, Eleanor 1915-1981 .... DLB44

Peterkin, Julia 1880-1961..................... DLB9

Petersham, Maud 1889-1971 and
    Petersham, Miska 1888-1960.............. DLB22

Pharr, Robert Deane 1916- DLB33

Phillips, David Graham 1867-1911 ....DLB9, 12

Phillips, Jayne Anne 1952- Y80

Phillips, Stephen 1864-1915 .... DLB10

Phillips, Ulrich B. 1877-1934 .... DLB17

Phillpotts, Eden 1862-1960 .... DLB10

Philosophical Library DLB46

Phoenix, John (see Derby, George Horatio)

Pickard, Tom 1946- DLB40

Pinckney, Josephine 1895-1957................. DLB6

Pinero, Arthur Wing 1855-1934............... DLB10

Pinnacle Books DLB46

Pinsky, Robert 1940- Y82

Pinter, Harold 1930- DLB13

Piper, H. Beam 1904-1964 .... DLB8

Piper, Watty.................................. DLB22

Pisar, Samuel 1929- Y83

Pitkin, Timothy 1766-1847 .... DLB30

Pitter, Ruth 1897- DLB20

The Place of Realism in Fiction (1895), by
    George Gissing............................ DLB18

Plante, David 1940- Y83

Plath, Sylvia 1932-1963.....................DLB5, 6

Platt and Munk Company DLB46

Playboy Press................................ DLB46

Playwrights and Professors, by Tom Stoppard.. DLB13

Plomer, William 1903-1973..................... DLB20

Plumly, Stanley 1939- DLB5

Plumpp, Sterling D. 1940- DLB41

Plunkett, James 1920- DLB14

Plymell, Charles 1935- DLB16

Pocket Books DLB46

Poe, Edgar Allan 1809-1849.................... DLB3

Poe, James 1921-1980 .... DLB44

Pohl, Frederik 1919- DLB8

Poliakoff, Stephen 1952- DLB13

Polite, Carlene Hatcher 1932- DLB33

Pollard, Edward A. 1832-1872................. DLB30

Polonsky, Abraham 1910- DLB26

Poole, Ernest 1880-1950...................... DLB9

Poore, Benjamin Perley 1820-1887............. DLB23

Popular Library DLB46

Porter, Eleanor H. 1868-1920 .... DLB9

Porter, Katherine Anne 1890-1980...... DLB4, 9; Y80

Porter, Peter 1929- DLB40

Porter, William S. 1862-1910................. DLB12

Porter, William T. 1809-1858.................DLB3, 43

Portis, Charles 1933- DLB6

Postscript to [the Third Edition of] *Clarissa*
    (1751), by Samuel Richardson.............. DLB39

Potok, Chaim 1929- DLB28; Y84

Potter, David M. 1910-1971 .... DLB17

Pound, Ezra 1885-1972......................DLB4, 45

Powell, Anthony 1905- DLB15

Pownall, David 1938- DLB14

Powys, John Cowper 1872-1963 .... DLB15

Powys, T. F. 1875-1953....................... DLB36

The Practice of Biography: An Interview with
    Stanley Weintraub Y82

The Practice of Biography II: An Interview with
    B. L. Reid.................................. Y83

The Practice of Biography III: An Interview with
    Humphrey Carpenter....................... Y84

Praeger Publishers............................ DLB46

Pratt, Samuel Jackson 1749-1814.............. DLB39

Preface to *Alwyn* (1780), by Thomas Holcroft .. DLB39

Preface to *Colonel Jack* (1722), by Daniel
 Defoe DLB39

Preface to *Evelina* (1778), by Fanny Burney DLB39

Preface to *Ferdinand Count Fathom* (1753), by
 Tobias Smollett DLB39

Preface to *Incognita* (1692), by William
 Congreve.................................. DLB39

Preface to *Joseph Andrews* (1742), by
 Henry Fielding........................... DLB39

Preface to *Moll Flanders* (1722), by Daniel
 Defoe DLB39

Preface to *Poems* (1853), by Matthew Arnold ... DLB32

Preface to *Robinson Crusoe* (1719), by Daniel
 Defoe DLB39

Preface to *Roderick Random* (1748), by Tobias
 Smollett DLB39

Preface to *Roxana* (1724), by Daniel Defoe DLB39

Preface to *St. Leon* (1799), by William Godwin.. DLB39

Preface to Sarah Fielding's *Familiar Letters*
 (1747), by Henry Fielding [excerpt]....... DLB39

Preface to Sarah Fielding's *The Adventures of
 David Simple* (1744), by Henry Fielding DLB39

Preface to *The Cry* (1754), by Sarah Fielding.... DLB39

Preface to *The Delicate Distress* (1769), by
 Elizabeth Griffin DLB39

Preface to *The Disguis'd Prince* (1733), by Eliza
 Haywood [excerpt]........................ DLB39

Preface to *The Farther Adventures of Robinson
 Crusoe* (1719), by Daniel Defoe............ DLB39

Preface to the First Edition of *Pamela* (1740), by
 Samuel Richardson....................... DLB39

Preface to the First Edition of *The Castle of
 Otranto* (1764), by Horace Walpole......... DLB39

Preface to *The History of Romances* (1715), by
 Pierre Daniel Huet [excerpts].............. DLB39

Preface to *The Life of Charlotta du Pont* (1723),
 by Penelope Aubin........................ DLB39

Preface to *The Old English Baron* (1778), by
 Clara Reeve DLB39

Preface to the Second Edition of *The Castle of
 Otranto* (1765), by Horace Walpole......... DLB39

Preface to *The Secret History, of Queen Zarah, and
 the Zarazians* (1705), by Delarivière
 Manley.................................... DLB39

Preface to the Third Edition of *Clarissa* (1751),

by Samuel Richardson [excerpt]............ DLB39

Preface to *The Works of Mrs. Davys* (1725), by
 Mary Davys DLB39

Preface to Volume 1 of *Clarissa* (1747), by
 Samuel Richardson....................... DLB39

Preface to Volume 3 of *Clarissa* (1748), by
 Samuel Richardson....................... DLB39

Prentice, George D. 1802-1870 .... DLB43

Prentice-Hall DLB46

Prescott, William Hickling 1796-1859.........DLB1, 30

The Present State of the English Novel (1892),
 by George Saintsbury DLB18

Price, Reynolds 1933- DLB2

Price, Richard 1949- Y81

Priest, Christopher 1943- DLB14

Priestley, J. B. 1894-1984 ....DLB10, 34; Y84

Prime, Benjamin Young 1733-1791 .... DLB31

Prince, F. T. 1912- DLB20

Prince, Thomas 1687-1758 .... DLB24

Pritchett, V. S. 1900- DLB15

Procter, Adelaide Anne 1825-1864 .... DLB32

The Progress of Romance (1785), by Clara Reeve
 [excerpt] DLB39

The Proletarian Novel........................ DLB9

Propper, Dan 1937- DLB16

The Prospect of Peace (1778), by Joel Barlow..... DLB37

Proud, Robert 1728-1813..................... DLB30

Prynne, J. H. 1936- DLB40

The Public Lending Right in America
 Statement by Sen. Charles McC. Mathias, Jr.
 PLR and the Meaning of Literary Property
 Statements on PLR by American Writers Y83

The Public Lending Right in the United Kingdom
 Public Lending Right: The First Year in the
 United Kingdom........................... Y83

Publications and Social Movements
 [Transcendentalism] DLB1

Pulitzer, Joseph 1847-1911 .... DLB23

Pulitzer, Joseph, Jr. 1885-1955 .... DLB29

Pulitzer Prizes for the Novel, 1917-1945........ DLB9

Purdy, James 1923- DLB2

Putnam, George Palmer 1814-1872............. DLB3

Putnam, Samuel 1892-1950.................... DLB4

Puzo, Mario 1920- DLB6

Pyle, Ernie 1900-1945 .... DLB29

Pyle, Howard 1853-1911 .... DLB42

Pym, Barbara 1913-1980 .... DLB14

Pynchon, Thomas 1937- DLB2

Pyramid Books DLB46

Pyrnelle, Louise-Clarke 1850-1907 .... DLB42

Q

Quad, M. (see Lewis, Charles B.)

Quin, Ann 1936-1973 .... DLB14

Quincy, Samuel of Georgia ?-? DLB31

Quincy, Samuel of Massachusetts 1734-1789 ... DLB31

Quist, Harlin, Books.......................... DLB46

R

Rabe, David 1940- DLB7

Radcliffe, Ann 1764-1823 .... DLB39

Raine, Craig 1944- DLB40

Raine, Kathleen 1908- DLB20

Ralph, Julian 1853-1903....................... DLB23

Ralph Waldo Emerson in 1982 .... Y82

Rambler, no. 4 (1750), by Samuel Johnson
    [excerpt] DLB39

Ramée, Marie Louise de la (see Ouida)

Ramsay, David 1749-1815 .... DLB30

Randall, Dudley 1914- DLB41

Randall, Henry S. 1811-1876.................. DLB30

Randall, James G. 1881-1953.................. DLB17

Random House............................... DLB46

Ransom, John Crowe 1888-1974 .... DLB45

Raphael, Frederic 1931- DLB14

Raphaelson, Samson 1896-1983 .... DLB44

Rattigan, Terence 1911-1977.................. DLB13

Rawlings, Marjorie Kinnan 1896-1953........DLB9, 22

Raworth, Tom 1938- DLB40

Ray, David 1932- DLB5

Raymond, Henry 1820-1869................... DLB43

Read, Herbert 1893-1968...................... DLB20

Read, Opie 1852-1939......................... DLB23

Read, Piers Paul 1941- DLB14

Reade, Charles 1814-1884..................... DLB21

Reader's Digest Condensed Books.............. DLB46

Reading, Peter 1946- DLB40

Rechy, John 1934- Y82

Redgrove, Peter 1932- DLB40

Redmond, Eugene B. 1937- DLB41

Reed, Henry 1914- DLB27

Reed, Ishmael 1938- DLB2, 5, 33

Reed, Sampson 1800-1880...................... DLB1

Reese, Thomas 1742-1796..................... DLB37

Reeve, Clara 1729-1807 .... DLB39

Regnery, Henry, Company DLB46

Reid, Alastair 1926- DLB27

Reid, Christopher 1949- DLB40

Reid, Helen Rogers 1882-1970 .... DLB29

Reid, James ?-? DLB31

Reid, Mayne 1818-1883 .... DLB21

Reid, Thomas 1710-1796...................... DLB31

Reid, Whitelaw 1837-1912..................... DLB23

Reilly and Lee Publishing Company........... DLB46

Reisch, Walter 1903-1983...................... DLB44

"Re-meeting of Old Friends": The Jack Kerouac
    Conference.................................. Y82

Remington, Frederic 1861-1909 .... DLB12

Renault, Mary 1905-1983....................... Y83

Representative Men and Women: A Historical
    Perspective on the British Novel,
    1930-1960................................. DLB15

Review of [Samuel Richardson's] *Clarissa* (1748),
    by Henry Fielding.......................... DLB39

The Revolt (1937), by Mary Colum [excerpts].. DLB36

Rexroth, Kenneth 1905-1982.............DLB16; Y82

Rey, H. A. 1898-1977.......................... DLB22

Reynal and Hitchcock DLB46

Reynolds, G. W. M. 1814-1879 .... DLB21

Reynolds, Mack 1917- DLB8

Reznikoff, Charles 1894-1976 .... DLB28, 45

Rhett, Robert Barnwell 1800-1876.............. DLB43

Rhodes, James Ford 1848-1927 . . . . DLB47

Rhys, Jean 1890-1979 . . . . DLB36

Rice, Elmer 1892-1967 . . . . DLB4, 7

Rice, Grantland 1880-1954 . . . . DLB29

Rich, Adrienne 1929- DLB5

Richards, George circa 1760-1814 . . . . DLB37

Richards, I. A. 1893-1979 . . . . DLB27

Richards, Laura E. 1850-1943 . . . . DLB42

Richardson, Dorothy M. 1873-1957 . . . . DLB36

Richardson, Jack 1935- DLB7

Richardson, Samuel 1689-1761 . . . . DLB39

Richter, Conrad 1890-1968 . . . . DLB9

Rickword, Edgell 1898-1982 . . . . DLB20

Riddell, John (see Ford, Corey)

Ridler, Anne 1912- DLB27

Riis, Jacob 1849-1914 . . . . DLB23

Riley, John 1938-1978 . . . . DLB40

Rinehart and Company DLB46

Ripley, Arthur 1895-1961 . . . . DLB44

Ripley, George 1802-1880 . . . . DLB1

The Rising Glory of America: Three Poems DLB37

The Rising Glory of America: Written in 1771
(1786), by Hugh Henry Brackenridge and
Philip Freneau DLB37

Riskin, Robert 1897-1955 . . . . DLB26

Ritchie, Anna Mowatt 1819-1870 . . . . DLB3

Ritchie, Anne Thackeray 1837-1919 . . . . DLB18

Ritchie, Thomas 1778-1854 . . . . DLB43

Rites of Passage [on William Saroyan] Y83

Rivers, Conrad Kent 1933-1968 . . . . DLB41

Rivington, James circa 1724-1802 . . . . DLB43

Rivkin, Allen 1903- DLB26

Robbins, Tom 1936- Y80

Roberts, Elizabeth Madox 1881-1941 . . . . DLB9

Roberts, Kenneth 1885-1957 . . . . DLB9

Robinson, Casey 1903-1979 . . . . DLB44

Robinson, James Harvey 1863-1936 . . . . DLB47

Robinson, Lennox 1886-1958 . . . . DLB10

Robinson, Mabel Louise 1874-1962 . . . . DLB22

Rodgers, Carolyn M. 1945- DLB41

Rodgers, W. R. 1909-1969 . . . . DLB20

Roethke, Theodore 1908-1963 . . . . DLB5

Rogers, Will 1879-1935 . . . . DLB11

Roiphe, Anne 1935- Y80

Rolfe, Frederick William 1860-1913 . . . . DLB34

Rolvaag, O. E. 1876-1931 . . . . DLB9

Roosevelt, Theodore 1858-1919 . . . . DLB47

Root, Waverley 1903-1982 . . . . DLB4

Rose, Reginald 1920- DLB26

Rosen, Norma 1925- DLB28

Rosenberg, Isaac 1890-1918 . . . . DLB20

Rosenfeld, Isaac 1918-1956 . . . . DLB28

Rosenthal, M. L. 1917- DLB5

Ross, Leonard Q. (see Rosten, Leo)

Rossen, Robert 1908-1966 . . . . DLB26

Rossetti, Christina 1830-1894 . . . . DLB35

Rossetti, Dante Gabriel 1828-1882 . . . . DLB35

Rossner, Judith 1935- DLB6

Rosten, Leo 1908- DLB11

Roth, Henry 1906?- DLB28

Roth, Philip 1933- DLB2, 28; Y82

Rothenberg, Jerome 1931- DLB5

Rowe, Elizabeth 1674-1737 . . . . DLB39

Rowlandson, Mary circa 1635-circa 1678 . . . . DLB24

Rowson, Susanna Haswell circa 1762-1824 . . . . . DLB37

The Royal Court Theatre and the English Stage
Company DLB13

The Royal Court Theatre and the New
Drama DLB10

Royall, Anne 1769-1854 . . . . DLB43

Rubens, Bernice 1928- DLB14

Rudkin, David 1956- DLB13

Rumaker, Michael 1932- DLB16

Rumens, Carol 1944- DLB40

Runyon, Damon 1880-1946 . . . . DLB11

Rush, Benjamin 1746-1813 . . . . DLB37

Russ, Joanna 1937- DLB8

Russell, Benjamin 1761-1845 . . . . DLB43

Russell, Charles Edward 1860-1941 . . . . DLB25

Russell, George William (see AE)

Rutherford, Mark 1831-1913 . . . . DLB18

Ryan, Michael 1946- Y82

Ryskind, Morrie 1895- DLB26

S

The Saalfield Publishing Company DLB46

Saberhagen, Fred 1930- DLB8

Sackler, Howard 1929-1982 .... DLB7

Sackville-West, V. 1892-1962 .... DLB34

Saffin, John circa 1626-1710.................. DLB24

Sage, Robert 1899-1962 .... DLB4

St. Johns, Adela Rogers 1894- DLB29

St. Martin's Press DLB46

Saki (see Munro, H. H.)

Salaam, Kalamu ya 1947- DLB38

Salemson, Harold J. 1910- DLB4

Salinger, J. D. 1919- DLB2

Salt, Waldo 1914- DLB44

Sanborn, Franklin Benjamin 1831-1917 .... DLB1

Sanchez, Sonia 1934- DLB41

Sandburg, Carl 1878-1967..................... DLB17

Sanders, Ed 1939- DLB16

Sandoz, Mari 1896-1966...................... DLB9

Sandys, George 1578-1644 .... DLB24

Santmyer, Helen Hooven 1895- Y84

Sargent, Pamela 1948- DLB8

Saroyan, William 1908-1981 .... DLB7, 9; Y81

Sarton, May 1912- Y81

Sassoon, Siegfried 1886-1967.................. DLB20

Saturday Review Press........................ DLB46

Saunders, James 1925- DLB13

Saunders, John Monk 1897-1940.............. DLB26

Savage, James 1784-1873..................... DLB30

Savage, Marmion W. 1803-1872............... DLB21

Sawyer, Ruth 1880-1970...................... DLB22

Sayers, Dorothy L. 1893-1957 .... DLB10, 36

Sayles, John Thomas 1950- DLB44

Scannell, Vernon 1922- DLB27

Schaeffer, Susan Fromberg 1941- DLB28

Scharf, J. Thomas 1843-1898.................. DLB47

Schlesinger, Arthur M., Jr. 1917- DLB17

Schmidt, Michael 1947- DLB40

Schmitz, James H. 1911- DLB8

Schocken Books DLB46

Schouler, James 1839-1920.................... DLB47

Schrader, Paul 1946- DLB44

Schreiner, Olive 1855-1920.................... DLB18

Schulberg, Budd 1914- DLB6, 26, 28; Y81

Schurz, Carl 1829-1906....................... DLB23

Schuyler, George S. 1895-1977 .... DLB29

Schuyler, James 1923- DLB5

Schwartz, Delmore 1913-1966................. DLB28

Schwartz, Jonathan 1938- Y82

Science Fantasy.............................. DLB8

Science-Fiction Fandom and Conventions DLB8

Science-Fiction Fanzines: The Time Binders DLB8

Science-Fiction Films DLB8

Science Fiction Writers of America and the
   Nebula Awards........................... DLB8

Scott, Evelyn 1893-1963 .... DLB9

Scott, Harvey W. 1838-1910................... DLB23

Scott, Paul 1920-1978........................ DLB14

Scott, Sarah 1723-1795 .... DLB39

Scott, Tom 1918- DLB27

Scott, William Bell 1811-1890 .... DLB32

Scott, William R. [publishing house]........... DLB46

Scott-Heron, Gil 1949- DLB41

Scripps, E. W. 1854-1926..................... DLB25

Scudder, Horace E. 1838-1902 .... DLB42

Scupham, Peter 1933- DLB40

Seabrook, William 1886-1945.................. DLB4

Seabury, Samuel 1729-1796 .... DLB31

Sears Publishing Company DLB46

Seaton, George 1911-1979..................... DLB44

Seaton, William Winston 1785-1866........... DLB43

Sedgwick, Catharine Maria 1789-1867.......... DLB1

Seeger, Alan 1888-1916 .... DLB45

Seid, Ruth (see Sinclair, Jo)

Seidel, Frederick Lewis 1936- Y84

Selby, Hubert, Jr. 1928- DLB2

Selected English-Language Little Magazines and
   Newspapers [France, 1920-1939]........... DLB4

Selected Humorous Magazines (1820-1950) DLB11

Selected Science-Fiction Magazines and
    Anthologies DLB8

Seligman, Edwin R. A. 1861-1939 .... DLB47

Seltzer, Thomas [publishing house]............ DLB46

Sensation Novels (1863), by H. L. manse DLB21

Seredy, Kate 1899-1975 .... DLB22

Serling, Rod 1924-1975........................ DLB26

Settle, Mary Lee 1918- DLB6

Sewall, Joseph 1688-1769..................... DLB24

Sewell, Samuel 1652-1730 .... DLB24

Sex, Class, Politics, and Religion [in the British
    Novel, 1930-1959]........................ DLB15

Sexton, Anne 1928-1974 .... DLB5

Shaara, Michael 1929- Y83

Shaffer, Anthony 1926- DLB13

Shaffer, Peter 1926- DLB13

Shairp, Mordaunt 1887-1939................. DLB10

Shange, Ntozake 1948- DLB38

Sharon Publications.......................... DLB46

Sharpe, Tom 1928- DLB14

Shaw, Bernard 1856-1950 .... DLB10

Shaw, Henry Wheeler 1818-1885.............. DLB11

Shaw, Irwin 1913-1984 ....DLB6; Y84

Shaw, Robert 1927-1978.................... DLB13, 14

Shay, Frank [publishing house]................ DLB46

Shea, John Gilmary 1824-1892 .... DLB30

Shebbeare, John 1709-1788 .... DLB39

Sheckley, Robert 1928- DLB8

Sheed, Wilfred 1930- DLB6

Sheed and Ward............................ DLB46

Sheldon, Alice B. (see Tiptree, James, Jr.)

Sheldon, Edward 1886-1946.................. DLB7

Shepard, Sam 1943- DLB7

Shepard, Thomas I 1604 or 1605-1649........ DLB24

Shepard Thomas II 1635-1677................ DLB24

Sheridan, Frances 1724-1766................. DLB39

Sherriff, R. C. 1896-1975.................... DLB10

Sherwood, Robert 1896-1955...............DLB7, 26

Shiels, George 1886-1949..................... DLB10

Shillaber, Benjamin Penhallow 1814-1890....DLB1, 11

Shine, Ted 1931- DLB38

Shirer, William L. 1904- DLB4

Shockley, Ann Allen 1927- DLB33

Shorthouse, Joseph Henry 1834-1903 .... DLB18

Shulman, Max 1919- DLB11

Shute, Henry A. 1856-1943 .... DLB9

Shuttle, Penelope 1947- DLB14, 40

Sidney, Margaret (see Lothrop, Harriet M.)

Sigourney, Lydia Huntley 1791-1865.........DLB1, 42

Silkin, Jon 1930- DLB27

Silliphant, Stirling 1918- DLB26

Sillitoe, Alan 1928- DLB14

Silman, Roberta 1934- DLB28

Silverberg, Robert 1935- DLB8

Simak, Clifford D. 1904- DLB8

Simcox, George Augustus 1841-1905........... DLB35

Simmons, Herbert Alfred 1930- DLB33

Simmons, James 1933- DLB40

Simms, William Gilmore 1806-1870 ....DLB3, 30

Simon, Neil 1927- DLB7

Simon and Schuster DLB46

Simons, Katherine Drayton Mayrant 1890-1969... Y83

Simpson, Louis 1923- DLB5

Simpson, N. F. 1919- DLB13

Sims, George R. 1847-1922.................... DLB35

Sinclair, Andrew 1935- DLB14

Sinclair, Jo 1913- DLB28

Sinclair, May 1863-1946...................... DLB36

Sinclair, Upton 1878-1968..................... DLB9

Sinclair, Upton [publishing house]........ DLB46

Singer, Isaac Bashevis 1904- DLB6, 28

Singmaster, Elsie 1879-1958.................... DLB9

Siodmak, Curt 1902- DLB44

Sissman, L. E. 1928-1976...................... DLB5

Sisson, C. H. 1914- DLB27

Sitwell, Edith 1887-1964...................... DLB20

Skelton, Robin 1925- DLB27

Skipsey, Joseph 1832-1903 .... DLB35

Slavitt, David 1935- DLB5, 6

A Slender Thread of Hope: The Kennedy Center Black Theatre Project DLB38

Slick, Sam (see Haliburton, Thomas Chandler)

Sloane, William, Associates DLB46

Small Presses in Great Britain and Ireland, 1960-1985................................. DLB40

Small Presses I: Jargon Society Y84

Smith, Alexander 1830-1867 .... DLB32

Smith, Betty 1896-1972......................... Y82

Smith, Carol Sturm 1938- Y81

Smith, Charles Henry 1826-1903.............. DLB11

Smith, Charlotte 1749-1806 .... DLB39

Smith, Cordwainer 1913-1966.................. DLB8

Smith, Dave 1942- DLB5

Smith, Dodie 1896- DLB10

Smith, E. E. 1890-1965 .... DLB8

Smith, Elihu Hubbard 1771-1798 .... DLB37

Smith, Elizabeth Oakes (Prince) 1806-1893...... DLB1

Smith, George O. 1911-1981 .... DLB8

Smith, H. Allen 1906-1976 .... DLB11, 29

Smith, Harrison, and Robert Haas [publishing house] DLB46

Smith, Iain Crichten 1928- DLB40

Smith, J. Allen 1860-1924 .... DLB47

Smith, John 1580-1631 .... DLB24, 30

Smith, Josiah 1704-1781....................... DLB24

Smith, Ken 1938- DLB40

Smith, Lee 1944- Y83

Smith, Mark 1935- Y82

Smith, Michael 1698-circa 1771................ DLB31

Smith, Red 1905-1982......................... DLB29

Smith, Samuel Harrison 1772-1845............. DLB43

Smith, Samuel Stanhope 1751-1819 .... DLB37

Smith, Seba 1792-1868 ....DLB1, 11

Smith, Stevie 1902-1971 .... DLB20

Smith, Sydney Goodsir 1915-1975.............. DLB27

Smith, William 1727-1803 .... DLB31

Smith, William 1728-1793 .... DLB30

Smith, William Jay 1918- DLB5

Smollett, Tobias 1721-1771.................... DLB39

Snellings, Rolland (see Touré, Askia Muhammad)

Snodgrass, W. D. 1926- DLB5

Snow, C. P. 1905-1980......................... DLB15

Snyder, Gary 1930- DLB5, 16

Solano, Solita 1888-1975....................... DLB4

Solomon, Carl 1928- DLB16

Sontag, Susan 1933- DLB2

Sorrentino, Gilbert 1929- DLB5; Y80

Southerland, Ellease 1943- DLB33

Southern, Terry 1924- DLB2

Southern Writers Between the Wars............ DLB9

Spark, Muriel 1918- DLB15

Sparks, Jared 1789-1866.....................DLB1, 30

Spellman, A. B. 1935- DLB41

Spencer, Elizabeth 1921- DLB6

Spender, Stephen 1909-....................... DLB20

Spicer, Jack 1925-1965 ....DLB5, 16

Spielberg, Peter 1929- Y81

Spinrad, Norman 1940- DLB8

Squibob (see Derby, George Horatio)

Stafford, Jean 1915-1979...................... DLB2

Stafford, William 1914- DLB5

Stage Censorship: "The Rejected Statement" (1911), by Bernard Shaw [excerpts]........ DLB10

Stallings, Laurence 1894-1968...............DLB7, 44

Stallworthy, Jon 1935- DLB40

Stampp, Kenneth M. 1912- DLB17

Stanford, Ann 1916- DLB5

Stanton, Frank L. 1857-1927 .... DLB25

Stapledon, Olaf 1886-1950 .... DLB15

Starkweather, David 1935- DLB7

Steadman, Mark 1930- DLB6

The Stealthy School of Criticism (1871), by Dante Gabriel Rossetti DLB35

Stearns, Harold E. 1891-1943 .... DLB4

Steele, Max 1922- Y80

Steere, Richard circa 1643-1721 .... DLB24

Stegner, Wallace 1909- DLB9

Stein, Gertrude 1874-1946 .... DLB4

Stein, Leo 1872-1947.......................... DLB4

Stein and Day Publishers DLB46

Steinbeck, John 1902-1968 .... DLB7, 9; DS2

Stephens, Alexander H. 1812-1883............DLB47

Stephens, Ann 1813-1886 ....DLB3

Stephens, Charles Asbury 1844?-1931.........DLB42

Stephens, James 1882?-1950..................DLB19

Sterling, James 1701-1763....................DLB24

Stern, Stewart 1922- DLB26

Sterne, Laurence 1713-1768..................DLB39

Stevenson, Anne 1933- DLB40

Stevenson, Robert Louis 1850-1894 ....DLB18

Stewart, Donald Ogden 1894-1980 ......DLB4, 11, 26

Stewart, Dugald 1753-1828....................DLB31

Stewart, George R. 1895-1980..................DLB8

Stewart and Kidd Company DLB46

Stiles, Ezra 1727-1795 ....DLB31

Still, James 1906- DLB9

Stith, William 1707-1755 ....DLB31

Stockton, Frank R. 1834-1902 ....DLB42

Stoddard, Richard Henry 1825-1903...........DLB3

Stoddard, Solomon 1643-1729.................DLB24

Stoker, Bram 1847-1912.......................DLB36

Stokes, Thomas L. 1898-1958 ....DLB29

Stone, Melville 1848-1929 ....DLB25

Stone, Samuel 1602-1663......................DLB24

Stoppard, Tom 1937- DLB13

Storey, Anthony 1928- DLB14

Storey, David 1933- DLB13, 14

Story, Thomas circa 1670-1742................DLB31

Story, William Wetmore 1819-1895.............DLB1

Storytelling: A Contemporary Renaissance Y84

Stoughton, William 1631-1701.................DLB24

Stowe, Harriet Beecher 1811-1896 ....DLB1, 12, 42

Stowe, Leland 1899- DLB29

Strand, Mark 1934- DLB5

Stratemeyer, Edward 1862-1930...............DLB42

Straub, Peter 1943- Y84

Streeter, Edward 1891-1976...................DLB11

Stribling, T. S. 1881-1965 ....DLB9

Strother, David Hunter 1816-1888 ....DLB3

Stuart, Jesse 1906-1984....................DLB9; Y84

Stuart, Lyle [publishing house] DLB46

Stubbs, Harry Clement (see Clement, Hal)

The Study of Poetry (1880), by Matthew
      Arnold DLB35

Sturgeon, Theodore 1918- DLB8

Sturges, Preston 1898-1959....................DLB26

Styron, William 1925- DLB2; Y80

Suckow, Ruth 1892-1960 ....DLB9

Suggs, Simon (see Hooper, Johnson Jones)

Sukenick, Ronald 1932- Y81

Sullivan, C. Gardner 1886-1965 ....DLB26

Sullivan, Frank 1892-1976.....................DLB11

Summers, Hollis 1916- DLB6

Surtees, Robert Smith 1803-1864..............DLB21

Surveys of the Year's Biography
      A Transit of Poets and Others: American
            Biography in 1982 ....Y82
      The Year in Literary Biography Y83
      The Year in Literary Biography Y84

Surveys of the Year's Drama
      The Year in Drama Y82
      The Year in Drama Y83
      The Year in Drama Y84

Surveys of the Year's Fiction
      The Year's Work in Fiction: A Survey Y82
      The Year in Fiction: A Biased View Y83
      The Year in Fiction Y84

Surveys of the Year's Poetry
      The Year's Work in American Poetry........Y82
      The Year in Poetry Y83
      The Year in Poetry Y84

Sutro, Alfred 1863-1933......................DLB10

Swados, Harvey 1920-1972 ....DLB2

Swain, Charles 1801-1874 ....DLB32

Swallow Press...............................DLB46

Swenson, May 1919- DLB5

Swerling, Jo 1897- DLB44

Swift, Jonathan 1667-1745....................DLB39

Swinburne, A. C. 1837-1909...................DLB35

Swinnerton, Frank 1884-1982 ....DLB34

Swisshelm, Jane Grey 1815-1884 ....DLB43

Swope, Herbert Bayard 1882-1958 ....DLB25

Symons, Arthur 1865-1945....................DLB19

Synge, John Millington 1871-1909.........DLB10, 19

T

Taggard, Genevieve 1894-1948 .... DLB45

Taradash, Daniel 1913- DLB44

Tarbell, Ida M. 1857-1944 .... DLB47

Tarkington, Booth 1869-1946 .... DLB9

Tashlin, Frank 1913-1972 .... DLB44

Tate, Allen 1899-1979 .... DLB4, 45

Tate, James 1943- DLB5

Taylor, Bayard 1825-1878 .... DLB3

Taylor, Bert Leston 1866-1921 .... DLB25

Taylor, Charles H. 1846-1921 .... DLB25

Taylor, Edward circa 1642-1729 .... DLB24

Taylor, Henry 1942- DLB5

Taylor, Sir Henry 1800-1886 .... DLB32

Taylor, Peter 1917- Y81

Teasdale, Sara 1884-1933 .... DLB45

The Tea-Table (1725), by Eliza Haywood
       [excerpt] DLB39

Tenn, William 1919- DLB8

Tennant, Emma 1937- DLB14

Tenney, Tabitha Gilman 1762-1837 .... DLB37

Tennyson, Alfred 1809-1892 .... DLB32

Tennyson, Frederick 1807-1898 .... DLB32

Terhune, Albert Payson 1872-1942 .... DLB9

Terry, Megan 1932- DLB7

Terson, Peter 1932- DLB13

Tesich, Steve 1943- Y83

Thacher, James 1754-1844 .... DLB37

Thackeray, William Makepeace 1811-1863 ..... DLB21

The Theatre Guild DLB7

Theroux, Paul 1941- DLB2

Thoma, Richard 1902- DLB4

Thomas, D. M. 1935- DLB40

Thomas, Dylan 1914-1953 .... DLB13, 20

Thomas, Edward 1878-1917 .... DLB19

Thomas, Gwyn 1913-1981 .... DLB15

Thomas, Isaiah 1750-1831 .... DLB43

Thomas, John 1900-1932 .... DLB4

Thomas, Joyce Carol 1938- DLB33

Thomas, Lorenzo 1944- DLB41

Thomas, R. S. 1915- DLB27

Thompson, Dorothy 1893-1961 .... DLB29

Thompson, Francis 1859-1907 .... DLB19

Thompson, John R. 1823-1873 .... DLB3

Thompson, Ruth Plumly 1891-1976 .... DLB22

Thompson, William Tappan 1812-1882 ......DLB3, 11

Thomson, James 1834-1882 .... DLB35

Thomson, Mortimer 1831-1875 .... DLB11

Thoreau, Henry David 1817-1862 .... DLB1

Thorpe, Thomas Bangs 1815-1878 ....DLB3, 11

Thoughts on Poetry and Its Varieties (1833),
       by John Stuart Mill DLB32

Thurber, James 1894-1961 ....DLB4, 11, 22

Thwaite, Anthony 1930- DLB40

Thwaites, Reuben Gold 1853-1913 .... DLB47

Ticknor, George 1791-1871 .... DLB1

Ticknor and Fields (revived) DLB46

Time and Western Man (1927), by Wyndham
       Lewis [excerpts] DLB36

Time-Life Books DLB46

Times Books DLB46

Timothy, Peter circa 1725-1782 .... DLB43

Timrod, Henry 1828-1867 .... DLB3

Tiptree, James, Jr. 1915- DLB8

Titus, Edward William 1870-1952 .... DLB4

Toklas, Alice B. 1877-1967 .... DLB4

Tolkien, J. R. R. 1892-1973 .... DLB15

Tom Jones (1749), by Henry Fielding [excerpt].. DLB39

Tomlinson, Charles 1927- DLB40

Tomlinson, Henry Major 1873-1958 .... DLB36

Tompson, Benjamin 1642-1714 .... DLB24

Tonks, Rosemary 1932- DLB14

Toole, John Kennedy 1937-1969 .... Y81

Toomer, Jean 1894-1967 .... DLB45

Tor Books DLB46

Tough-Guy Literature DLB9

Touré, Askia Muhammad 1938- DLB41

Tower Publications DLB46

Towne, Benjamin circa 1740-1793 .... DLB43

Towne, Robert 1936- DLB44

Tracy, Honor 1913- DLB15

Traven, B. 1882? or 1890?-1969................ DLB9

Travers, Ben 1886-1980......................DLB10

Tremain, Rose 1943- DLB14

Trends in Twentieth-Century
Mass Market Publishing...................DLB46

Trent, William P. 1862-1939 ....DLB47

Trescot, William Henry 1822-1898.............DLB30

Trevor, William 1928- DLB14

Trilling, Lionel 1905-1975.....................DLB28

Tripp, John 1927- DLB40

Trocchi, Alexander 1925- DLB15

Trollope, Anthony 1815-1882 ....DLB21

Trollope, Frances 1779-1863 ....DLB21

Troop, Elizabeth 1931- DLB14

Trotti, Lamar 1898-1952 ....DLB44

Troupe, Quincy Thomas, Jr. 1943- DLB41

Trumbo, Dalton 1905-1976....................DLB26

Trumbull, Benjamin 1735-1820 ....DLB30

Trumbull, John 1750-1831 ....DLB31

Tucker, George 1775-1861 ....DLB3, 30

Tucker, Nathaniel Beverley 1784-1851......... DLB3

Tucker, St. George 1752-1827.................DLB37

Tunis, John R. 1889-1975 ....DLB22

Tuohy, Frank 1925- DLB14

Tupper, Martin F. 1810-1889 ....DLB32

Turbyfill, Mark 1896- DLB45

Turco, Lewis 1934- Y84

Turnbull, Gael 1928- DLB40

Turner, Charles (Tennyson) 1808-1879 ....DLB32

Turner, Frederick 1943- DLB40

Turner, Frederick Jackson 1861-1932.........DLB17

Twain, Mark (see Clemens, Samuel Langhorne)

Tyler, Anne 1941- DLB6; Y82

Tyler, Moses Coit 1835-1900 ....DLB47

Tyler, Royall 1757-1826 ....DLB37

U

Under the Microscope (1872), by A. C.
Swinburne DLB35

Universal Publishing and Distributing
Corporation..............................DLB46

Upchurch, Boyd B. (see Boyd, John)

Updike, John 1932- DLB2, 5; Y80, 82; DS3

Upton, Charles 1948- DLB16

Upward, Allen 1863-1926 ....DLB36

Ustinov, Peter 1921- DLB13

V

Vail, Laurence 1891-1968 .... DLB4

Vajda, Ernest 1887-1954 ....DLB44

Van Anda, Carr 1864-1945.....................DLB25

Vance, Jack 1916?- DLB8

Van Doran, Mark 1894-1972...................DLB45

van Druten, John 1901-1957 ....DLB10

Van Duyn, Mona 1921- DLB5

Van Dyke, Henry 1928- DLB33

Vane, Sutton 1888-1963.......................DLB10

Vanguard Press................................DLB46

van Itallie, Jean-Claude 1936- DLB7

Vann, Robert L. 1879-1940....................DLB29

Van Rensselaer, Mariana Griswold 1851-1934.. DLB47

Van Rensselaer, Mrs. Schuyler (see Van
Rensselaer, Mariana Griswold)

Van Vechten, Carl 1880-1964 ....DLB4, 9

van Vogt, A. E. 1912- DLB8

Varley, John 1947- Y81

Vassa, Gustavus (see Equiano, Olaudah)

Vega, Janine Pommy 1942- DLB16

Veiller, Anthony 1903-1965 ....DLB44

Very, Jones 1813-1880 .... DLB1

Vidal, Gore 1925- DLB6

Viereck, Peter 1916- DLB5

Viewpoint: Politics and Performance, by David
Edgar DLB13

The Viking Press DLB46

Villard, Henry 1835-1900 .... DLB23

Villard, Oswald Garrison 1872-1949........... DLB25

Volland, P. F., Company DLB46

Vonnegut, Kurt 1922- DLB2, 8; Y80; DS3

Vroman, Mary Elizabeth circa 1924-1967....... DLB33

W

Wagoner, David 1926- DLB5

Wain, John 1925- DLB15, 27

Wainwright, Jeffrey 1944- DLB40

Wakoski, Diane 1937- DLB5

Walck, Henry Z. [publishing house] DLB46

Walcott, Derek 1930- Y81

Waldman, Anne 1945- DLB16

Walker and Company DLB46

Walker, Alice 1944- DLB6, 33

Walker, Joseph A. 1935- DLB38

Walker, Ted 1934- DLB40

Wallant, Edward Lewis 1926-1962...........DLB2, 28

Walpole, Horace 1717-1797 .... DLB39

Walpole, Hugh 1884-1941..................... DLB34

Walsh, Ernest 1895-1926 ....DLB4, 45

Wambaugh, Joseph 1937- DLB6; Y83

Ward, Artemus (see Browne, Charles Farrar)

Ward, Douglas Turner 1930- DLB7, 38

Ward, Lynd 1905- DLB22

Ward, Mrs. Humphry 1851-1920.............. DLB18

Ward, Nathaniel circa 1578-1652.............. DLB24

Ware, William 1797-1852..................... DLB1

Warner, Rex 1905- DLB15

Warner, Susan Bogert 1819-1885 ....DLB3, 42

Warner, Sylvia Townsend 1893-1978.......... DLB34

Warner Books DLB46

Warren, John Byrne Leicester (see De Tabley, Lord)

Warren, Lella 1899-1982 .... Y83

Warren, Mercy Otis 1728-1814................ DLB31

Warren, Robert Penn 1905- DLB2; Y80

Washington, George 1732-1799 .... DLB31

Wasson, David Atwood 1823-1887.............. DLB1

Waterhouse, Keith 1929- DLB13

Waterman, Andrew 1940- DLB40

Watkins, Vernon 1906-1967................... DLB20

Watt, W. J., and Company..................... DLB46

Watterson, Henry 1840-1921.................. DLB25

Watts, Alan 1915-1973 .... DLB16

Watts, Franklin [publishing house] DLB46

Waugh, Auberon 1939- DLB14

Waugh, Evelyn 1903-1966.................... DLB15

Weatherly, Tom 1942- DLB41

Webb, James Watson 1802-1884................ DLB43

Webb, Mary 1881-1927....................... DLB34

Webb, Walter Prescott 1888-1963 .... DLB17

Webster, Augusta 1837-1894 .... DLB35

Webster, Noah 1758-1843...........DLB1, 37, 42, 43

Weems, Mason Locke 1759-1825 .... DLB30, 37, 42

Weidman, Jerome 1913- DLB28

Weinbaum, Stanley Grauman 1902-1935........ DLB8

Weiss, John 1818-1879 .... DLB1

Weiss, Theodore 1916- DLB5

Welch, Lew 1926-1971? DLB16

Weldon, Fay 1931- DLB14

Wells, Carolyn 1862-1942 .... DLB11

Wells, Charles Jeremiah circa 1800-1879 .... DLB32

Wells, H. G. 1886-1946....................... DLB34

Wells, Robert 1947- DLB40

Wells-Barnett, Ida B. 1862-1931............... DLB23

Welty, Eudora 1909- DLB2

Wescott, Glenway 1901- DLB4, 9

Wesker, Arnold 1932- DLB13

Wesley, Richard 1945- DLB38

Wessels, A., and Company..................... DLB46

West, Anthony 1914- DLB15

West, Jessamyn 1902-1984..................DLB6; Y84

West, Mae 1892-1980........................ DLB44

West, Nathanael 1903-1940...............DLB4, 9, 28

West, Paul 1930- DLB14

West, Rebecca 1892-1983...................DLB36; Y83

Western Publishing Company DLB46

Wetherell, Elizabeth (see Warner, Susan Bogert)

Whalen, Philip 1923- DLB16

Wharton, Edith 1862-1937 .... DLB4, 9, 12

Wharton, William 1920s?- Y80

What's Really Wrong With Bestseller Lists........ Y84

Wheatley, Phillis circa 1754-1784.............. DLB31

Wheeler, Charles Stearns 1816-1843 .... DLB1

Wheeler, Monroe 1900- DLB4

Wheelock, John Hall 1886-1978............... DLB45

Wheelwright, John circa 1592-1679 .... DLB24

Wheelwright, J. B. 1897-1940 .... DLB45

Whetstone, Colonel Pete (see Noland, C. F. M.)

Whipple, Edwin Percy 1819-1886 .... DLB1

Whitaker, Alexander 1585-1617............... DLB24

Whitcher, Frances Miriam 1814-1852 .... DLB11

White, Andrew 1579-1656..................... DLB24

White, Andrew Dickson 1832-1918............ DLB47

White, E. B. 1899-1985..................... DLB11, 22

White, Edgar B. 1947- DLB38

White, Horace 1834-1916 .... DLB23

White, William Allen 1868-1944..............DLB9, 25

White, William Anthony Parker (see Boucher, Anthony)

White, William Hale (see Rutherford, Mark)

Whitehead, James 1936- Y81

Whiting, John 1917-1963..................... DLB13

Whiting, Samuel 1597-1679 .... DLB24

Whitlock, Brand 1869-1934 .... DLB12

Whitman, Albert, and Company................ DLB46

Whitman, Sarah Helen (Power) 1803-1878 ...... DLB1

Whitman, Walt 1819-1892.................... DLB3

Whitman Publishing Company DLB46

Whittemore, Reed 1919- DLB5

Whittier, John Greenleaf 1807-1892............ DLB1

Whittlesey House........................... DLB46

Wideman, John Edgar 1941- DLB33

Wieners, John 1934- DLB16

Wiggin, Kate Douglas 1856-1923.............. DLB42

Wigglesworth, Michael 1631-1705 .... DLB24

Wilbur, Richard 1921- DLB5

Wild, Peter 1940- DLB5

Wilde, Oscar 1854-1900 .... DLB10, 19, 34

Wilde, Richard Henry 1789-1847................ DLB3

Wilder, Billy 1906- DLB26

Wilder, Laura Ingalls 1867-1957 .... DLB22

Wilder, Thornton 1897-1975............... DLB4, 7, 9

Wiley, Bell Irvin 1906-1980 .... DLB17

Wilhelm, Kate 1928- DLB8

Willard, Nancy 1936- DLB5

Willard, Samuel 1640-1707..................... DLB24

Williams, C. K. 1936- DLB5

Williams, Emlyn 1905- DLB10

Williams, Garth 1912- DLB22

Williams, George Washington 1849-1891....... DLB47

Williams, Heathcote 1941- DLB13

Williams, Hugo 1942- DLB40

Williams, Isaac 1802-1865 .... DLB32

Williams, Joan 1928- DLB6

Williams, John A. 1925- DLB2, 33

Williams, John E. 1922- DLB6

Williams, Jonathan 1929- DLB5

Williams, Raymond 1921- DLB14

Williams, Roger circa 1603-1683................ DLB24

Williams, Samm-Art 1946- DLB38

Williams, Sherley Anne 1944- DLB41

Williams, T. Harry 1909-1979.................. DLB17

Williams, Tennessee 1911-1983....... DLB7; Y83; DS4

Williams, William Appleman 1921- DLB17

Williams, William Carlos 1883-1963 ....DLB4, 16

Williams, Wirt 1921- DLB6

Williamson, Jack 1908- DLB8

Willingham, Calder Baynard, Jr. 1922- DLB2, 44

Willis, Nathaniel Parker 1806-1867............. DLB3

Wilmer, Clive 1945- DLB40

Wilson, A. N. 1950- DLB14

Wilson, Angus 1913- DLB15

Wilson, Augusta Jane Evans 1835-1909 .... DLB42

Wilson, Colin 1931- DLB14

Wilson, Harry Leon 1867-1939................. DLB9

Wilson, John 1588-1667 .... DLB24

Wilson, Lanford 1937- DLB7

Wilson, Margaret 1882-1973.................... DLB9

Wilson, Michael 1914-1978 .... DLB44

Wilson, Woodrow 1856-1924 .... DLB47

Winchell, Walter 1897-1972 .... DLB29

Windham, Donald 1920- DLB6

Winsor, Justin 1831-1897..................... DLB47

Winthrop, John 1588-1649 .... DLB24, 30

Winthrop, John, Jr. 1606-1676 .... DLB24

Wirt, William 1772-1834...................... DLB37

Wise, John 1652-1725 .... DLB24

Wisner, George 1812-1849 .... DLB43

Wister, Owen 1860-1938 .... DLB9

Witherspoon, John 1723-1794................. DLB31

Wodehouse, P. G. 1881-1975 .... DLB34

Woiwode, Larry 1941- DLB6

Wolcott, Roger 1679-1767 .... DLB24

Wolfe, Gene 1931- DLB8

Wolfe, Thomas 1900-1938.................DLB9; DS2

Wollstonecraft, Mary 1759-1797............... DLB39

Wood, Benjamin 1820-1900 .... DLB23

Wood, Charles 1932- DLB13

Wood, Mrs. Henry 1814-1887 .... DLB18

Wood, William ?-? DLB24

Woodbridge, Benjamin 1622-1684 .... DLB24

Woodmason, Charles circa 1720-? DLB31

Woodson, Carter G. 1875-1950................ DLB17

Woodward, C. Vann 1908- DLB17

Woolf, David (see Maddow, Ben)

Woolf, Virginia 1882-1941 .... DLB36

Woollcott, Alexander 1887-1943.............. DLB29

Woolman, John 1720-1772 .... DLB31

Woolner, Thomas 1825-1892................. DLB35

Woolsey, Sarah Chauncy 1835-1905........... DLB42

Woolson, Constance Fenimore 1840-1894 ..... DLB12

Worcester, Joseph Emerson 1784-1865......... DLB1

The Works of the Rev. John Witherspoon (1800-1801)
    [excerpts] DLB31

A World Chronology of Important Science
    Fiction Works (1818-1979) DLB8

World Publishing Company DLB46

Wouk, Herman 1915- Y82

Wright, Charles 1935- Y82

Wright, Charles Stevenson 1932- DLB33

Wright, Harold Bell 1872-1944.................. DLB9

Wright, James 1927-1980...................... DLB5

Wright, Jay 1935- DLB41

Wright, Louis B. 1899-1984 .... DLB17

Wright, Richard 1908-1960...................... DS2

Wright, Sarah Elizabeth 1928- DLB33

Writing for the Theatre, by Harold Pinter DLB13

Wylie, Elinor 1885-1928.....................DLB9, 45

Wylie, Philip 1902-1971 .... DLB9

Y

Yates, Richard 1926- DLB2; Y81

Yeats, William Butler 1865-1939 .... DLB10, 19

Yezierska, Anzia 1885-1970 .... DLB28

Yonge, Charlotte Mary 1823-1901.............. DLB18

Yoseloff, Thomas [publishing house].......... DLB46

Young, Al 1939- DLB33

Young, Stark 1881-1963........................ DLB9

Young, Waldeman 1880-1938 .... DLB26

"You've Never Had It So Good," Gusted by
    "Winds of Change": British Fiction in the
    1950s, 1960s, and After................... DLB14

Z

Zangwill, Israel 1864-1926..................... DLB10

Zebra Books DLB46

Zebrowski, George 1945- DLB8

Zelazny, Roger 1937- DLB8

Zenger, John Peter 1697-1746.............. DLB24, 43

Zimmer, Paul 1934- DLB5

Zindel, Paul 1936- DLB7

Zubly, John Joachim 1724-1781 .... DLB31

Zu-Bolton II, Ahmos 1936- DLB41

Zukofsky, Louis 1904-1978 .... DLB5